日　英

佛　敎　語　辭　典

A　DICTIONARY

OF

JAPANESE　BUDDHIST　TERMS

日 英 佛 教 語 辭 典

A DICTIONARY
OF
JAPANESE BUDDHIST TERMS

*Based on References in
Japanese Literature*

BY
HISAO INAGAKI
Ryukoku University

in
collaboration with

P. G. O'NEILL
School of Oriental and African Studies
University of London

HEIAN

First American Edition 1989

HEIAN INTERNATIONAL, INC.
P.O. BOX 1013
UNION CITY, CALIFORNIA 94587

Library of Congress Catalog Card Number: 88-82776

89 90 91 92 10 9 8 7 6 5 4 3 2 1

Printed in the United States of America

ISBN NO.: 0-89346-311-6

FOREWORD

Throughout Japan's recorded history, Buddhism has permeated her life and thought so deeply that a general knowledge of it is necessary for any understanding of her past or of her present traditions. An adequate appreciation of her writings requires a more precise knowledge, and it is here that the present work will be invaluable to western readers.

By deriving virtually all its main entries from Japanese literary works rich in Buddhist references, it provides in an easily accessible form details of the wide range of Buddhist terms, persons, ceremonies, texts, sects and teachings necessary for any intelligent reading of her literature. With its help, the significance of Buddhist allusions will become clear and this will give the text itself a colour and richness that would otherwise never appear.

The very nature of Buddhism and its role in Japan mean that no reference work in this field can claim to be wholly complete, but the present work is on a far larger scale than was ever envisaged at the outset and there can be few occasions when even the specialist reader will fail to find enlightenment. This dictionary is a most welcome product of the impressive scholarship of its compiler in the fields of language and Buddhist studies generally and, no less, of his dedication to the task he set himself. It is also gratifying to me personally that it was prompted by his experiences as a fellow-teacher in London. My part in the undertaking has throughout been essentially editorial, but it has been a privilege to be associated with a work which is at the same time scholarly and practical, and which so fully meets a need long and keenly felt by westerners interested in any aspect of Japanese life and culture.

This dictionary will provide them with a convenient key to a subject that can be very elusive and confusing, and yet is absolutely basic to an understanding of Japan.

P.G. O'Neill

London, June 1984

PREFACE

It is my great pleasure that part of the result of my work during my tenure at the School of Oriental and African Studies, University of London, has now been published. When I began to make cards for a glossary of Buddhist terms from Japanese classics about ten years ago, I had no intention of making a "dictionary" as in the title. My original design was to compile a glossary, rather than a dictionary, which gave simple English equivalents or short explanations of Buddhist terms occurring in popular Japanese classics, as a practical guide for students of Japanology and Buddhism. Any suggestion of making a dictionary would have appeared to be beyond my ability and outside the scope of one man's work.

When I told my colleague, Professor P.G. O'Neill, about the need for such a glossary and my intention to make one, he showed deep interest and kindly agreed to collaborate with me. Thus we started on the tedious and apparently interminable work. As I made cards from the texts I read, my collaborator checked the English and the general presentation. Although the work was often interrupted for various reasons, in the course of several years the cards grew enormously in number. Their content also changed from mere explanations of the meanings of terms to include fuller accounts of doctrinal implications and historical references, wherever appropriate. Without noticing myself the change of policy, I became more and more deeply involved in the work.

The classics I selected for trial runs from a vast collection of literature were shorter ones, such as *Makura no sōshi, Hōjōki, Tsurezure-gusa, Taketori monogatari, Yamato monogatari* and *Ise monogatari.* I also quickly went through the *Ōkagami.* Still in an early stage, I began to collect terms from the *Shasekishū* but did not finish it until much later because of the great number of highly technical terms. In fact, the *Shasekishū* became the main source from which nearly a quarter of the entries listed have been taken. Further, the variety and nature of the Buddhist terms from the *Shasekishū* have given this work the definitive feature of a "dictionary". Being a Zen monk of extensive learning, well-versed in Kusha, Vinaya, Tendai and Shingon as well as Zen, the author, Mujū Ichien (1226-1312), freely used terms and concepts from a wide area of Buddhist studies in presenting in the ten-fascicle collection of stories a simple and basic teaching of the Buddha, the law of karma. I often found it necessary to make cards for several related concepts in order to explain one term, and this policy soon became a standard one for other texts, too.

Other big works dealt with include the *Kokon chomonjū, Taiheiki* and, partially, *Heike monogatari.* The voluminous *Konjaku monogatari* and the *Nihon ryōiki,* which represent two peaks of the Japanese Buddhist literature, have been excluded from the scope of the present work simply because of lack of time. Among the classics I worked on, both the *Heike monogatari* and the *Taiheiki* with their deceptively nonchalant title of "*monogatari*" (tale) are, in fact, so full of Buddhist terms, sometimes highly impregnated ones, that to deal with them satisfactorily required an unexpectedly long period of time. Considerations of time finally forced me to leave the *Heike monogatari* at the end of the second fascicle.

Throughout the course of the work I made it my basic principle not to omit even simple terms and to give as many compounds and phrases as possible. References to literary sources are given for most of the terms. When such references are absent, the terms concerned are either very common or are additional entries provided in order to explain concepts related to other terms. A small number of entries have been given from the viewpoint of the function of this work as a *dictionary,* e.g. the main Buddhist sects and their founders. For Buddhist scriptures, references to the *Taishō Tripitaka,* both in volume and scripture numbers, are given, if available.

The readings of terms often presented difficult problems. It sometimes happens that one and the same word was pronounced differently in different periods and also in different schools and traditions. I have made simple notes in such cases. Sanskrit originals have been provided wherever they are considered useful.

The basic work of making cards would be still continuing now if I had not left London permanently to return home to Japan three years ago. It was my father's sudden illness in 1980 that made me decide to go back to my old parents who had been without me for many years. Unfortunately, they did not live to see me and my wife on our return home, but our repatriation has offered me a chance to give shape to the work done in London.

My sincere thanks are due to the publishers Nagata Bunshōdo and Heian International, who kindly undertook this costly enterprise without knowing exactly the sales prospect of the publication. In making the indexes I was greatly indebted to Miss Hiroko Yoshimoto, my sister-in-law, for the laborious task of making cards and arranging them for the stroke index; Professor Ryūei Yoshida for preparing the Chinese-Japanese character index; Rev. Takao Nishioka for making the Japanese index; and Rev. Kazuo Nasu for making the Sanskrit and Pali index. At the proof stage a number of colleagues and friends carefully read part or the whole of the proofs and gave me valuable suggestions. Here I mention their names with deep gratitude: Professor Esho Sasaki, Mr. Dennis Hirota, Rev. Yukinori Tokiya, Professor Michio Tokunaga, Professor Zenshō Asaeda, Rev. Meisei Tatsuguchi, Rev. Shōhaku Asada, Dr. and Mrs. Toshikazu Arai, Rev. Hidenori Kiyomoto, Rev. and Mrs. Shōju Akutagawa, and Miss Kyōko Nishizaki. Most of the above-mentioned persons who assisted me in making the indexes also helped me with proof-reading. Lastly, I wish to take this opportunity to thank my wife, Eiko, for helping me in many ways.

In all stages of preparing the work for publication Professor O'Neill has rendered invaluable service. He carefully read the entire proofs at two different stages, gave me additional useful suggestions, advised me about the format, and so forth. Without his enthusiasm and expertise the dictionary would not have achieved the present standard which is the highest I can hope for. A significant great part of any merit this work may have is attributable to Professor O'Neill; for the inadequacies and any mistakes that may have crept in I am solely responsible. As I am well aware of the incompleteness of this publication as a dictionary, I wish to resume the basic card-making work in the near future to produce an enlarged, perhaps more useful, edition.

H. Inagaki

Takatsuki, June, 1984

EXPLANATORY NOTES

[1] JAPANESE

1. In romanizing Japanese, the Hepburn system is used. Note special assimilated sound, '*jji*', which occurs in '*shijji*'.

2. The syllabic nasal '*n*' before a vowel or '*y*' is followed by an apostrophe: e.g. *shin'in, zen'aku, an'yo*.

3. Romanized Japanese sounds are not meant to be accurate reproductions of the readings of terms at the time when they were used in the work in question. In many cases, they have been altered to accommodate general readers, as for example: '*kwa*', '*gwa*', '*ye*' are replaced by '*ka*', '*ga*' and '*e*', respectively.

4. The old forms of characters as found in the standard editions of classical works are used throughout.

5. For proper names and technical terms, characters are usually supplied.

6. An asterisk* indicates that the preceding term or name is a main entry to which cross-reference can be made.

[2] CHINESE

1. In romanizing Chinese, a slightly modified Wade-Giles system is used.

2. '*E*' and '*u*' are used for '*ê*' and '*ŭ*', respectively. Hence, '*lê*', for example, is replaced by '*le*' and '*ssŭ*' by '*ssu*'.

[3] SANSKRIT

1. In transcribing Sanskrit, a popular system as used in U. Wogihara's *Sanskrit-Japanese Dictionary*, ed. N. Tsuji, 1964–67, is adopted.

2. The following words are treated as terms in general use and are therefore given without diacritical marks: 'bodhi' (for Japanese, *bodai*), 'bodhisattva' (*bosatsu*), 'buddha' (*butsu*), 'dharani' (=*dhāranī*; *darani*), 'dharma' (*hō*), 'Hinayana' (=*hīnayāna*; *shōjō*), 'karma' (*gō*), 'Mahayana' (=*mahāyāna*; *daijō*), 'mandala' (=*mandala*; *mandara*), 'mantra' (*shingon*), 'mudra' (=*mudrā*; *in*), 'Nirvana' (=*nirvāna*; *nehan*), 'pratyekabuddha' (*engaku*), 'samsara' (=*samsāra*; *rinne* or *shōji*), 'Sangha' (=*samgha*; *sōgya*), 'shravaka' (=*śrāvaka*; *shōmon*), 'sutra' (=*sūtra*; *kyō*) and 'tathagata' (=*tathāgata*; *nyorai*).

3. Ordinary Sanskrit terms are italicized and usually translated or provided with cross-references to entry-words.

[4] ENGLISH

1. Some frequently used terms are given in English without references: e.g. 'birth and death' (for Japanese *shōji* or *rinne*), 'buddha' (*butsu*), 'buddhahood' (*bukka*), 'Buddhist law' (*hō*), 'Buddhist Way' (*butsudō*), 'enlightenment' (*satori*), 'Pure Land' (*jōdo*), 'Pure Land Buddhism' or 'Pure Land teaching' (*Jōdomon*), 'precept' (*kai*), 'vow' (*gan*).

2. Less common terms are given in English with Japanese equivalents in parentheses: e.g. Matrix-store Realm Mandala (*Taizōkai mandara**).

[5] PROPER NOUNS

1. The names of historical persons are given in the languages of their origin (except for Korean names which are read in Chinese) and followed where appropriate by their Japanese readings in parentheses: e.g. Nāgārjuna (Ryūju*), Ajātaśatru (Ajase*).

2. The names of buddhas and bodhisattvas are given in

Japanese, with main entries indicated as appropriate, and their Sanskrit forms in parentheses, when given: e.g. Shakamuni*, Dainichi* (Mahāvairocana) and Miroku* (Maitreya).

3. The names of non-Japanese countries, places, dynasties, etc., are given in the original languages, followed by their Japanese readings, except for common ones: e.g. Magadha (Makada*), Śrāvastī (Shae*), but T'ang, Sung.

4. The names of heavens, continents, mountains and the like which are conceived in Buddhist cosmology are written in Sanskrit, with their Japanese readings in parentheses.

5. For convenience, the names of mountains have sometimes been translated as such: e.g. Mt. Lu (Rozan).

6. The titles of works, including dharanis ('spells'), are given in Japanese and italicized, and important ones are usually translated. If there is no cross-reference to a main entry, Chinese characters are supplied if applicable: e.g. *Hoke-kyō**, *Kōsan-hannya* 光讚般若.

7. The names of historical Japanese persons are written in the Japanese way with the family name first, with the '*no*' between this and the personal name omitted: e.g. Minamoto Tamenori.

[6] TAISHŌ TRIPITAKA REFERENCES

References to Buddhist scriptures are given by the volumes and text numbers of the *Taishō shinshū daizōkyō* (popularly known as *Taishō Tripitaka* and abbreviated to TT.), ed. J. Takakusu and K. Watanabe, 55 vols., Tokyo, 1924–29. For example, 'TT. 8, No. 251' means 'the *Taishō Tripitaka*, Vol. 8, text number 251'. Very occasionally, references are given to the *Dainihon zokuzōkyō*, published 1905–12, which is abbreviated to Zoku.

[7] ABBREVIATIONS

abbr.＝abbreviation   Ch.＝Chinese
esp.＝especially   fasc.＝fascicle
Ja.＝Japanese   lit.＝literally
n.＝name   Pre.＝Preface
Sk.＝Sanskrit   tr.＝translated

[8] REFERENCES TO THE SUPPLEMENT

A star mark ☆ indicates that reference should be made to the Supplement.

SOURCE REFERENCES WITH ABBREVIATIONS

The Japanese classics from which entry-words originate and their abbreviated titles are as follows. The full titles with their English translations are followed by short descriptions of the works, including the dates of composition and the authorship, and references to the texts as given in the *Nihon koten bungaku taikei*, Iwanami Shoten, Tokyo (abbreviated to NKT.).

Hei.＝*Heike monogatari* 平家物語 (*'Tales of the Heike clan'*); 12 vols.; history of the rise and fall of the Heike clan; written toward the end of the 12th century and traditionally attributed to Shinano Zenji Yukinaga 信濃前司行長; NKT. Vols. 32–33; numerals following the title abbreviation refer to chapters.

Ho.＝*Hōjōki* 方丈記 (*'Writings from a 10-foot square room'*); 1 vol.; by Kamo Chōmei 鴨長明; an account of the vicissitudes of the world as seen in wars, fires, earthquakes, etc., and also a description of the author's state of mind in his retired life; completed in 1212; NKT. Vol. 30.

IH.=*Ichigon hōdan* 一言芳談 ('*One-word fine sermons*'); 2 vols.; a Pure Land Buddhist work compiled in the 14th century; author unknown; NKT. Vol. 83.

Ise.=*Ise monogatari* 伊勢物語 ('*Tales from Ise*'); 1 vol.; some 125 stories centring on Ariwara Narihira 在原業平; written in the middle of the Heian period (784–1192); author unknown; NKT. Vol. 9.

K.=*Kokon chomonjū* 古今著聞集 ('*Collection of well-known stories ancient and modern*'); 20 vols.; some 700 stories divided into 30 sections under the headings of Shinto, Buddhism, etc., with the stories in each section arranged chronologically; compiled in 1254 by Tachibana Narisue 橘成季; NKT. Vol. 84; numerals following the title abbreviation indicate story numbers.

Ma.=*Makura no sōshi* 枕草子 ('*Pillow stories*'); 3 vols.; a collection of some 300 short essays by Sei Shōnagon 清少納言 about her court life, travels, events in daily life, etc.; composed in the late 10th or early 11th century; NKT. Vol. 19; numerals following the title abbreviation indicate essay numbers.

O.=*Ōkagami* 大鏡 ('*A great mirror*'); 8 vols.; a historical account of the period 850–1025, centring on the Fujiwara family; author unknown; compiled in the late Heian period; NKT. Vol. 21; numerals following the title abbreviation indicate volume numbers.

S.=*Shasekishū* 沙石集 ('*Collection of sand and stones*'); 10 vols; stories compiled by Mujū 無住 to explain Buddhist teachings on morality and religious practices; completed in 1283; NKT. Vol. 85; volumes and sections are indicated by roman and Arabic figures, respectively; the fifth and the tenth volumes are each divided into two parts, which are shown as 'Va', 'Vb', 'Xa' and 'Xb'.

Ta.=*Taketori monogatari* 竹取物語 ('*Story of a bamboo cutter*'); 2 vols.; a romantic story of a beautiful lady from Heaven found as a baby in a bamboo stem; written in the Heian period; author unknown; NKT. Vol. 9.

Tai.=*Taiheiki* 太平記 ('*History of the great peace*'); 40 vols.; history of a turbulent period of some 50 years during the 14th century; written in the latter half of the 14th century; some attribute the work to the priest Kojima 小島法師; NKT. Vol. 34.

Tsu.=*Tsurezure-gusa* 徒然草 ('*Gleanings from my leisure hours*'); 2 vols.; a collection of essays in 243 sections by Yoshida Kenkō 吉田兼好, written around 1330–31; NKT. Vol. 30; numerals following the abbreviation indicate sections.

Ya.=*Yamato monogatari* 大和物語 ('*Tales from Yamato*'); 2 vols.; 173 stories with two supplementary ones, mostly romantic stories, compiled in the middle of the 10th century; author unknown; NKT. Vol. 9.

For the source references and abbreviations for the Supplement, see pp. 477–8.

A

Abi 阿鼻 Sk. *avīci*; also *muken* 無間 'incessant'; the lowest part of hell where sinners suffer interminable pain. [S. I–3; Tai. 10, 12, 20.]

~-**goku** --獄 'Avīci hell.' [S. II–6.]

Abidatsuma-kusha-ron 阿毘達磨倶舎論 '*The Discourse on the Repository of Abhidharma Discussions*'; Sk. *Abhidharma-kośabhāṣya*, written by Vasubandhu (Seshin*); 30 fasc., tr. by Hsüan-chuang (Genjō*) [TT. 29, No. 1558]; a comprehensive treatise discussing the doctrines of Hinayana.

Abidatsumazō 阿毘達磨藏 Sk. *abhidharma-piṭaka*, 'collection of *abhidharma* literature'; discourses explaining the Buddha's teaching. One of the three or five divisions of Buddhist scriptures. Cf. *gozō* and *sanzō*.

Abō rasetsu 阿防羅刹 See next entry. [S. III–2.]

Abō rasetsu 阿傍羅刹 'Abō *rākṣasa*'; also 阿坊 and 阿旁羅刹; *abō* is a type of guardian of hell, distinguished by having the head and legs of an ox and human hands. The fact that he is as fearsome as a *rākṣasa* (*rasetsu**) gives rise to the term 'abō rasetsu'.

Abudatsuma 阿浮達磨 Sk. *adbhuta-dharma* 'a miraculous thing'; translated as *mizou-hō** 未曾有法; one of the nine and twelve kinds of scriptures (*kubu-kyō** and *jūnibu-kyō**); an account of miracles performed by the Buddha or other deity.

Agon 阿含 Sk. *āgama*, lit. 'coming'; a traditional doctrine. I. Generally, in India, a traditional teaching; a sacred scripture. II. A Buddhist scripture; the Buddha's teaching. III. Hinayana sutras; see *Agon-gyō**.

~-**gyō** --經 'Āgama sutras'; in the Chinese collection of

scriptures, the division of sutras belonging to Hinayana. There are four groups: (1) *Jō-agon-gyō** 長阿含經,'*Long Āgama Sutras*'; (2) *Chū-agon-gyō** 中阿含經 '*Middle-Length Āgama Sutras*'; (3) *Zōitsu-agon-gyō** 增一阿含經 '*Increasing-by-One Āgama Sutras*'; and (4) *Zō-agon-gyō** 雜阿含經 '*Miscellaneous Āgama Sutras*'.

Ahadana 阿波陀那 Sk. *avadāna*; translated as *hiyu** 譬喻; an exposition of the Dharma through allegories; a parable; one of the nine and twelve kinds of scriptures (*kubu-kyō** and *jūnibu-kyō**).

Ahō rasetsu 阿放羅剎 See *abō rasetsu*. [Tai. 20, 33.]

Ai 愛 'Love, lust.' I. Egoistic desire, e.g. sexual desire and the pursuit of fame; defiled desire. II. Undefiled love; the love of a buddha or bodhisattva for living beings. III. Attachment to one's existence; one of the twelve causations (*jūni-innen**).

Aibetsuriku 愛別離苦 'The pain of separating from those one loves'; one of the eight pains (*hakku**). [S. III–1, 3, 4; Tai. 20.]

Aigyō 愛樂 'Love and enjoyment'; often used for the pleasure of hearing and studying the Buddhist law.

Aii 愛恚 Abbr. of *tonnai** 貪愛 'greed' and *shinni** 瞋恚 'anger'. [S. VII–6.]

Aijaku 愛著 'Love-attachment'; attachment to objects pleasurable to the senses; attachment to a loved one.

Aiken 愛見 I. 'Love and (wrong) views'; passions and wrong views. II. The feeling of attachment. [S. Xb–1.]

Aiku Daiō 阿育大王 'The Great King Aśoka'; see *Aiku Ō*. [S. VIII–22.]

Aiku Ō 阿育王 'King Aśoka'; also Ayuka 阿輸迦 and translated as Muyū 無憂 'Sorrowless'; the third king of the Maurya dynasty in Magadha, Central India, who reigned from 268 to 232 B.C. When he conquered Kaliṅga, he witnessed untold miseries of war, which converted him to Buddhism. He had his messages of the Buddhist law inscribed on stone pillars and rocks throughout his kingdom, and ruled it according to the Buddhist ideal. He convened the third Buddhist convention in the capital, Pāṭaliputra, and invited 1,000 elders to it. He sent emissaries of the Dharma to such countries as Syria, Egypt, and Sri Lanka, and also built many pagodas throughout the country.

Ainen 愛念 'Love, attachment.' [S. VII–2.]

Aitta 阿逸多 Sk. Ajita; another name for Miroku* (Maitreya). [Tai. 15.]

Aizen hōtō 愛善(＝染)寶塔 A tower in which is enshrined a statue of Aizen Myōō*. [Tai. 5, 7.]

Aizen Myōō 愛染明王 Sk. Rāga Vidyārāja; the God of Love. Though having a fierce appearance, he is full of affection. [Tai. 18.]

～ **no hō** ----の法 'The ritual dedicated to Aizen Myōō' to pray for the winning of a person's affection or the suppression of one's enemy. [Tai. 33.]

Ajari 阿闍梨 Sk. *ācārya*; a Buddhist teacher, esp. an eminent monk of the Shingon* or Tendai* sects.

～ **kanjō** ---灌頂 The *abhiṣeka* (*kanjō**) ceremony performed for those who become *ācāryas* (*ajari**); see *denbō kanjō*.

Ajase 阿闍世 Sk. Ajātaśatru; translated as Mijōon 未生怨 'Revengeful before Birth'; the son of King Bimbisāra (Binbashara*) of Magadha (Makada*). At the instigation of Devadatta (Daibadatta*), he usurped the throne and imprisoned his parents. Later, he repented of his evil acts before the Buddha and became his patron. He died 24 years after the Buddha. [S. Xa–2.]

Aji 阿字 Also 𤙉字; the first sound, 'A', in the Sanskrit alphabet. In esoteric Buddhism, the belief is that it embodies the mystic truth, and that one who meditates on it will attain buddhahood. [Hei. 2; Ho. 19; S. II–8, III–1, Va–12, Vb–9.]

～ **honpushō** --本不生 'The letter A (indicating) the originally unproduced (state of things)'; the esoteric principle that all phenomena are originally unproduced. This principle is represented by the first sound of the Sanskrit alphabet, 'A'. [S. Xb–3; Tsu. 144.]

～-**kan** --觀 'Meditation on the letter A'; also *gatsurin-kan** 月輪觀 'meditation on the moon-wheel', *aji-gatsurin-kan* 阿字 月輪觀 'meditation on the letter A in the moon-wheel', etc. In this meditation a practitioner sits in the lotus or half-lotus posture with a painting of the moon in front of him which measures 16 inches in diameter and in which is drawn a lotus with eight petals; on the lotus is drawn a Sanskrit letter A in gold. He keeps meditating on the letter while uttering 'A' as he breathes in and out, until he is able to see the letter in the moon whether he keeps his eyes open or closed. Then he practises meditation on the 'A-moon' in his mind, which is the real substance of the painted 'A-moon'. When this meditation is completed, dualistic views regarding evil passions and enlightenment, the realm of birth and death and Nirvana, etc., are destroyed and buddhahood is attained with the present body. [S. Xb–3.]

Aka 閼伽 Sk. *argha*; also 阿伽 and *akka* 遏伽; holy 'water' to be offered to a buddha, deity or deceased person.

～-**dana** --棚 '(Holy) water shelf'; a shelf for offerings. [Ho.29; Tsu. 11.]

～-**i** --井 'A well' from which water to be offered to a deity at a shrine or to a deceased person at the grave is obtained. [Tai. 29.]

～ **no mizu** --の水 Water to be offered to a buddha or deity. [Hei. 2; Tai. 39.]

Akago nenbutsu あか子念佛 'A baby's *nenbutsu*'; the *nenbutsu** practised with the heart of a baby. [IH.]

Ako 下火 'To light a fire'; lighting firewood to cremate a dead body. [Tai. 30, 33, 40.]

～ **butsuji** --佛事 'A Buddhist ceremony of lighting firewood' to cremate a dead body; this is part of the funeral service in the Zen* sect.

Akuchishiki 惡知識 'An evil friend or teacher'; cf. *zenjishiki*. [S. II–10.]

Akudō 惡道 'Evil path'; an evil realm, such as hell and the realm of animals.

Akuen 惡緣 'An evil condition'; a thing or person that causes one to do an act which is evil or contradicts the Buddhist teaching. [S. I–9, Va–1.]

Akugō 惡業 'Evil karma'; evil acts.

Akushu 惡趣 'Evil realms'; the states of existence, such as hell, the realm of hungry spirits, and the realm of animals, to which evil-doers are destined. [S. Va–1, VII–20, VIII–22; Tai. 39.]

Akusō 惡相 'Evil signs' such as those at the time of death, e.g. hallucinations, mental derangement and ominous bodily symptoms. [Tai. 20.]

Amadō 尼堂 'A convent.'

Ama no hagoromo 天の羽衣 'The feather robe of a heavenly being.' [Tai. 11.]

Amida 阿彌陀 N. of the buddha in the Western Pure Land; Sk. *amita* 'infinite', which stands for *amitābha* 'infinite light' and *amitāyus* 'infinite life'; hence, translated as Muryōkō* 無量光 and Muryōju* 無量壽 respectively; also called Muryōshōjō 無量 清淨 'Immeasurably Pure', Jinjippō-mugekō* 盡十方無礙光 'Light Unhindered in the Ten Directions', etc. The *Muryōju-kyō** presents 12 epithets of this buddha which are associated with the 12 kinds of light he possesses. Amida is one of the most popular buddhas in Mahayana and is mentioned in more than 200 sutras, of which the *Muryōju-kyō* is most important. According to this sutra, Amida was previously a king. When he met a buddha, called Sejizaiō* 世自在王 (Lokeśvararāja), he too wished to become a buddha. He then renounced the world and became a mendicant, called Hōzō* 法藏 (Dharmākara). He made 48 vows and performed various bodhisattva practices to fulfil them. After many aeons of time, his vows were fulfilled, and he became a buddha of infinite light and life. His land in the west, which is also part of the result of his vows and practices, is called Gokuraku* 極樂 (Sukhāvatī), 'Utmost Bliss'. As promised in the 18th vow (see *hongan no mon*), those who have sincere faith in Amida and recite his name (*nenbutsu**) are able to be born in his land after death through his power. Amida is a transcendental buddha, as contrasted to a historical buddha, and is generally regarded as a reward-body buddha (*hōjin** 報身; *sambhogakāya*). The school of Buddhism centring around Amida is known as Pure Land Buddhism (*jōdokyō* 淨土敎 or *jōdomon** 淨土門). It arose in India, grew in China, and attained a fuller development in Japan. Amida is thus the principal buddha worshipped in the Jōdo*, Jōdoshin* and other Pure Land sects. In esoteric Buddhism Amida is one of the five buddhas in the five cardinal directions; cf. *gobutsu* and *gochi nyorai*.

〜 **Butsu** ---佛 I. 'Amida Buddha'; see *Amida*. II. Refers to the *nenbutsu**. [Ho. 36.]

〜 **goma** ---護摩 A *goma** (Sk. *homa*) ritual to pray to Amida for protection from evils and for long life. [K. 59.]

~-**hijiri** - - - 聖 'Amida saint'; an epithet for Kōya*.

~-**kō** - - - 講 'A gathering devoted to Amida'; also *ōjō-kō* 往生講 'a gathering for the attainment of birth in the Pure Land'. This type of gathering became popular among the nobility towards the end of the Heian period (794–1192). According to the *Ōjō-kōshiki** 往生講式 by Yōkan*, who began these gatherings, they took place on the 15th of the month, but popularly, they were held on other days, too. [K. 155.]

~-**kōshiki** - - - 講式 See *Ōjō-kōshiki*. [K. 51.]

~-**kyō** - - - 經 '*The Amida Sutra*'; 1 fasc., tr. by Kumārajīva (Kumarajū*) [TT. 12, No. 366] ; one of the basic canons of Pure Land Buddhism (*Jōdo sanbukyō**). The title of the Sanskrit text is *Sukhāvatīvyūha* '*Glorious Adornment of Sukhāvatī* (the land of happiness)'. The sutra briefly describes pleasurable aspects of Amida's land and mentions that innumerable buddhas of the six directions praise his virtue and testify to the truth of this sutra. It then explains that one who holds fast to his name will be born in his land. [IH.; K. 701; S. VI–13, VII–21].

~ **no daishu** - - - の大呪 Also, *Amida no daizu* or *daiju*; 'the great spell of Amida'. Refers to *Muryōju-nyorai-konpon-darani* 無量壽如來根本陀羅尼, which reveals Amida's inner realization, vows, and merit. The spell used in Japan is the one translated by Amoghavajra (Fukū*), which appears in the *Muryōju-nyorai-kangyō-kuyō-giki* 無量壽如來觀行供養儀軌 [TT. 19, No. 930], and is also called *Jūkanromyō* 十甘露明. This is one of the three spells of Amida, the other two being the one-letter spell (*ichijishu* 一字呪) and the small spell (*shōshu* 小呪). [Ma. (variant text)]

~ **no ennichi** - - - の縁日 'Amida's *ennichi*'; the 15th of the month when Amida is believed to be in closer relation with men. Cf. *ennichi*. [K. 711.]

~ **renga** - - - 連歌 'Amida linked-verse'; a linked verse with each line beginning with the sacred phrase *namu amida butsu** 南無阿彌陀佛; a kind of *myōgō renga** 名號連歌, often composed as an act of transferring merit to a deceased person (*tsuizen** 追善). [S. Vb–7.]

~ **sanzon** --- 三尊 'The Amida triad'; Amida* and his two attendant bodhisattvas, Kannon* and Seishi*.

~**-shiyui-kyō** --- 思惟經 Refers to the *Amidabutsu-daishiyui-kyōsetsu-jobun* 阿彌陀佛大思惟經說序分, which appears in the *Darani-jūkyō* 陀羅尼集經 [TT. 18, No. 901, p. 800 ff.].

~ **wasan** --- 和讚 'A Japanese hymn eulogizing (the merit of) Amida*.' [K. 48.]

Anagonka 阿那含果 Sk. *anāgāmi-phala*; see *fugenka*.

Ana myōga あな冥加 'O God!'; an exclamatory remark. [K. 551.]

Anan 阿難 Abbr. of Ananda 阿難陀; Sk. Ānanda; a cousin and one of the ten great disciples (*jūdai-deshi**) of the Buddha. After he entered the Buddha's order, he constantly attended on the Buddha for more than 20 years and committed all his sermons to memory. He was therefore renowned as 'first and foremost in hearing the sermons' (*tamon daiichi** 多聞第一). After the Buddha's death, Ānanda recited the sermons, which were later compiled as a collection of sutras. [S. III–3, IV–1; Tai. 35.]

Anchin kokka-hō 安鎭國家法 'The ritual for securing the peace and quiet of the state'; an esoteric ritual performed in the imperial palace, in which Fudō* is the principal deity; abbreviated as *kokuchin* 國鎭; one of the four great rituals of the Mountain School of Tendai (*sanmon shika-daihō**). A similar ritual performed at an ordinary house is called *kachin* 家鎭 or *chintaku* 鎭宅.

Anchin kokka no hō 安鎭國家の法 See *anchin kokka-hō*. [Tai. 12.]

Andae 安陀會 Sk. *antar-vāsa*; one of the three robes of a monk; see *sanne*.

Ango 安居 'Peaceful dwelling'; Sk. *vārṣika*; originally the rainy season of three months, from the 16th of the 4th month to the 15th of the 7th month, during which monks stay in their monasteries concentrating on Buddhist studies and the practice of Buddhism. [K. 46; Tai. 39.]

Angya 行脚 'Travelling (for the sake of the Buddhist practice).' [Tai. 20.]

Anja 行者 One who does miscellaneous work in a Zen* temple. [Tai. 39, 40.]

Anjin 安心 'A settled heart'; faith; assurance; firm belief.

Anne 安慧 Sk. Sthiramati; an Indian master of the Yogācāra school (*Yugagyōha**) around the seventh century; one of the ten great masters of the Consciousness-Only doctrine. [S. III–1.]

Annyō 安養 'Peace and sustenance'; another name for Amida's* Pure Land. [S. IV–1; Tai. 6.]

~-kai --界 'The Realm of Peace and Sustenance'; another name for Amida's* Pure Land. [Tai. 18.]

Anokudatchi 阿耨達池 'Lake Anavatapta'; *anavatapta* lit. means 'no heat or fever'. The lake believed to lie in the northern part of the Himalayas and to be the origin of the four main rivers which flow through the Jambu continent (Enbudai*); cf. *Kōsuisen.*

Anokutara-sanmyaku-sanbodai 阿耨多羅三藐三菩提 Sk. *anuttara-samyak-sambodhi*, the highest, perfect enlightenment.

Anrakugyō-hon 安樂行品 'Chapter on Peaceful Practices'; the fourth chapter, and one of the four most important chapters, of the *Hoke-kyō**. The four peaceful practices with body, mouth, mind and vows are explained in this chapter. [S. IV–1.]

Anraku-shū 安樂集 '*Collection of Passages Concerning Birth in the Pure Land*'; 2 fasc., by Tao-ch'o 道綽 (Dōshaku*) [TT. 47, No. 1958]. The work expounds the Pure Land teaching based mainly on the *Kanmuryōju-kyō**. One of the canonical texts of the Jōdoshin* sect.

Anryūtai 安立諦 'Established truth'; reality in the worldly sense which is recognized as existent in the light of relative truth. Opposite of *hianryūtai**; cf. *sezokutai.* [S. IV–1.]

Anshitsu 庵室 A monk's hut.

Anshō no hōtō 暗證之朋黨 'Those with obscure realization'; see *anshō no zenji.* [Tai. 24.]

Anshō no zenji 暗證の禪師 'Meditation master with obscure realization'; a Zen* monk who clings to meditation and lacks any knowledge of Buddhism. [Tsu. 193.]

An'yō(kai) 安養(界) See *Annyō(kai).*

Arakan 阿羅漢 Also *rakan* 羅漢; Sk. *arhat*, which is interpreted as 'killing the enemy (i.e. evil passions)' or 'worthy (of offerings)'; hence, also *setsuzoku* 殺賊 and *ōgu** 應供. I. One of the ten epithets of a buddha; see *jūgō*. II. A Hinayana saint who has completely destroyed his evil passions and attained emancipation from cycles of birth and death; cf. *shika*.

~-ka ---果 Sk. *arhat-phala*, 'the fruit of arhatship', which is to be attained by destroying all evil passions; the last of the four stages of sainthood in Hinayana; cf. *shika*. [Tai. 35.]

Arannya 阿蘭若 Sk. *araṇya*; a forest; a hermitage; a dwelling-place for monks. [K.36.]

Araya 阿賴耶 Sk. *ālaya*; see *arayashiki*. [S. III–1.]

~-shiki ---識 Sk. *ālaya-vijñāna*, 'store-consciousness'; the eighth and the most fundamental of the eight levels of consciousness established in the doctrine of the Hossō* sect. It stores all potential energy for the mental and physical manifestations of one's existence, and supplies the substance to all existences. It also receives impressions from all functions of other consciousnesses and retains them as potential energy for their further manifestations and activities; cf. *hasshiki*.

Arennya 阿練若 More popularly, *arannya** 阿蘭若; Sk. *araṇya*; see *arannya*.

Asakō 朝講 'Morning lecture.' [Ma. 33.]

Asaza 朝座 'Morning gathering'; morning sermon. [Ma. 33.]

Ashida sen 阿私陀仙 'The hermit Asita.' Two different persons of the same name are mentioned in the scriptures: (1) A seer who visited the Buddha when he was born and foretold that he would become a great king or sage. (2) Shakamuni's* teacher in one of his past lives who expounded the *Hoke-kyō** to him.

Ashi sen 阿私仙 'The hermit Asita'; see *Ashida sen*. [K. 52.]

Ashuka Ō 阿輸伽王 See *Aiku Ō*. [S. VIII–22.]

Ashuku 阿閦 Sk. Akṣobhya, lit. 'immovable'; n. of a buddha in the east. In esoteric Buddhism, one of the five buddhas (*gobutsu**) of the Diamond-Realm Mandala (*Kongōkai mandara**); cf. *gochi nyorai*.

Ashura 阿修羅 Sk. *asura*; a type of demi-god; one of the ten kinds of beings living in different states of existence (*jikkai**) and one of the eight supernatural beings who protect Buddhism (*hachibushū**). Originally a Hindu god, Asura became an evil spirit who is constantly engaged in fighting with Indra (Taishaku*). In Buddhism, *asura* are generally considered as evil and fearsome spirits fond of fighting, but some of them are good spirits and protectors of Buddhism.

Asōgi 阿僧祇 Sk. *asaṃkhya* or *asaṃkhyeya* 'incalculable'; a great number. [S. VI–10.]

Azari 阿闍梨 See *ajari*.

B

Bagabon 薄伽梵 Sk. *Bhagavat*; the Honoured One; an epithet of a buddha; cf. *jūgō*. [Tai. 2.]

Bai 唄 Abbr. of *bainoku**; see also *bonbai*.

Bainoku 唄匿 Sk. *bhāṣā*; also *bachoku* 婆陟, *bashi* 婆師; abbreviated as *bai* 唄, and translated as *sanju* 讚頌 and *sandan* 讚嘆; the chanting of hymns.

Baishi 唄師 'A chanting priest'; one who leads the chanting of verses eulogizing the Buddha's virtue, etc.; one of the seven priests taking main parts in a big service; see *shichisō*.

Bakku 抜苦 'Getting rid of pain or suffering.'

Banpō 萬法 See *manbō*.

Banshukke 晩出家 'Renouncing the world (i.e. becoming a priest) in one's later years.' [S. II–1, Xb.–3.]

Bansō 伴僧 'An assistant priest.'

Baramon 婆羅門 Sk. *brāhmaṇa*; the priestly caste in India; a brahmin. [Tai. 37.]

~ **sōjō** ---僧正 'The brahmin *sōjō**'; an Indian monk, named Bodhisena (Bodaisenna* 菩提僊那), who came to Japan in 736 and was well treated by the emperor. He was appointed *sōjō* in 751 and took the leading part in the Buddhist service in celebration of the great new statue of the buddha dedicated at the Tōdaiji,* Nara, in 752. He died in 760 at the age of 57. *Baramon sōjō* was the name by which he was popularly known. [Tai. 24.]

Batō Kannon 馬頭觀音 'Horse-crowned Kannon'; one of the six kinds of Kannon* (*rokkannon**). He is the lord of the realm of animals, and the manifestation of Amida* Buddha in a fierce form. [S. II–4.]

Batsudaiga 拔提河 'The River Hiraṇyavatī'; the river in Kuśi-nagara near which the Buddha passed away; 'Batsudai' is part of 'Shiranabatsudai' 尸賴拏拔提, a transcription of 'Hiraṇyavatī'. [Tai. 18.]

Bekkyō 別教 'The distinct teaching'; the third of the four doctrinal teachings of the Buddha classified in Tendai*; the distinctively Mahayana teaching which shows that although things are dis-tinguishable in their phenomenal aspects, their essence is the same; see *kehō no shikyō*. [S. IV–1, Va–6.]

Benzaiten 辨才天 Strictly, 辯才天; Sk. Sarasvatī; also Benten 辨天; a goddess of music, eloquence, wealth, and wisdom; being originally a deification of a river, her shrines are often built by the sea, rivers, and lakes. [Tai. 18, 27.]

Bessō 別相 I. 'A special feature or characteristic', as contrasted with *tsūsō** 通相 'a common feature or characteristic'. II. One of the six aspects which, according to the Kegon* teaching, each and every existing thing possesses; see *rokusō*.

Betsugan 別願 'The specific vow'; the vow made specifically by a particular bodhisattva; opposed to *tsūgan**.

Betsugedatsukai 別解脱戒 'Individually emancipating precepts'; Sk. *pratimokṣa*; also *betsugedatsu ritsugi* 別解脱律儀. A general term for ordinary precepts laid down for monks, nuns, novices, and laymen. They are prescribed for specific offences, and those who have received precepts are delivered from the evils of their offences; hence, 'individually emancipating'. [Tai. 15.]

Betsuji 別時 Refers to *betsuji nenbutsu**. [IH.; K. 551.]

~ **nenbutsu** --念佛 Recitation of the *nenbutsu** for a fixed period of time.

~ **no nenbutsu** --の念佛 See *betsuji nenbutsu*. [S. IV–7.]

Betsuri no kugen 別離の苦患 'Pain of separation (from one's beloved)'; see *aibetsuriku*, one of the eight pains (*hakku**). [S. III–1.]

Bettō 別當 The title of the head priest of the Kōfukuji* 興福寺 and some other big temples. Rōben* 良辨 (689–773) was the first to hold this title at the Tōdaiji* in 752.

Bibutsuryaku 毘佛略 Sk. *vaipulya* 'extensive'; translated as *hōkō** 方廣; a kind of scripture which expounds principles of truth *in extenso*; one of the nine and twelve kinds of scriptures (*kubu-kyō** and *jūnibu-kyō**).

Biku 比丘 Sk. *bhikṣu*; a Buddhist monk.

Bikuni 比丘尼 Sk. *bhikṣunī*; a Buddhist nun.

Bikusō 比丘僧 Sk. *bhikṣu-saṃgha*; community of monks; a monk. [S. II–8.]

Binayazō 毘奈耶藏 Also *binizō* 毘尼藏, *ritsuzō* 律藏, etc. Sk. *vinaya-piṭaka*, 'collection of precepts'. One of the three or five divisions of the Buddhist scriptures, which contains rules of conduct, disciplinary provisions, etc. Cf. *gozō* and *sanzō*. [S. II–8.]

Binbashara 頻婆娑羅 Sk. Bimbisāra; the fifth king of the Śaiśnāga Dynasty in Magadha (Makada*) and a follower of the Buddha. In his late years he was imprisoned by his son Ajātaśatru (Ajase*) and died in jail. [S. Xa–2.]

Bingara 頻伽羅 Refers to *karyōbinga**. [Tai. 18.]

Bini 毘尼 Sk. *vinaya*; precepts. [S. III–5.]

~ no seimon --の制門 'Prohibiting evil-doings in the precepts.' [S. IV–1.]

~-zō --藏 See *binayazō*.

Binzuru 賓頭盧 Sk. Piṇḍola-bhāradvāja; the Buddha's disciple and one of the 16 arhats (*arakan**). In China and Japan his image is placed in the dining hall of a temple. It is believed in Japan that touching his image cures diseases. [Ta.]

Biran 毘嵐 Sk. *vairambhaka*; also 毘藍, *biranba* 毘藍婆, etc., and translated as *jinmōfū* 迅猛風, *senpū* 旋風, etc.; a very strong wind which blows at a time of cosmic change; cf. *daisansai*. [Tai. 19.]

Biru 毘盧 Abbr. of Birushana*; Vairocana Buddha. [S. I–3, II–5.]

Biruri Ō 毘琉璃王 'King Virūḍhaka'; also Ruri Ō 瑠璃王; also called Akushō Ō 惡生王 'King Evil-Born'; a son of King Prasenajit (Hashinoku Ō*) of Śrāvastī (Shae*). He usurped the throne and killed his father, and also attacked Kapilavastu (Kabira-jō*) and massacred the Śākya (Shaka*) clan.

Birushana 毘盧遮那 Sk. Vairocana, 'illuminating'. I. The principal buddha in the *Kegon-gyō**, considered to be a reward-body (*hōjin**). II. A Dharma-body (*hosshin**) in the Tendai* sect. III. The principal buddha in the Shingon* sect, considered to be a Dharma-body and known as Dainichi* 大日. [S. I–1.]

~ **goshō** ‐‐‐‐五聖 The five buddhas, with Dainichi* in the centre, in the Diamond Realm Mandala (*Kongōkai mandara**). See *gobutsu*. [K. 64.]

Bishamon 毘沙門 Sk. Vaiśravaṇa; also Tamonten* 多聞天, etc; one of the four guardian gods of the four directions (*shitennō**). He protects the northern sphere. [K. 565; O. V; S. Vb–7; Tai. 3, 11, 18, 29.]

~**-dō** ‐‐‐堂 'A Bishamon hall.' [S. Vb–7.]

~ **no hō** ‐‐‐の法 'A ritual dedicated to Bishamon' as a prayer for victory in a war; cf. *shōgun Bishamon hō*. [Tai. 29.]

~ **tennō** ‐‐‐天王 The King Vaiśravaṇa. See *Bishamon*. [K. 53, 54.]

Bishukatsuma 毘首羯磨 Sk. Viśvakarman; n. of a subject of Indra (Taishaku*) who is in charge of architecture and craftsmanship. He is worshipped as a god in India. [Tai. 11, 14.]

Bō 坊 Refers to *sōbō** 僧坊: a temple building where monks live.

Bodai 菩提 Sk. *bodhi*: I. The highest wisdom; enlightenment. II. The repose or salvation of the dead.

~**-daruma** ‐‐達磨 Sk. Bodhidharma; the first patriarch of Zen* in China. Originally, a man from south India, said to be the third son of a king. After studying Buddhism under Prajñātāra (Hannyatara 般若多羅) and receiving from him the transmission of Zen, he propagated Mahayana in India. Later, in 520 according to tradition, he went to China. After his interview with Emperor Wu-ti 武帝 (Butei), he went to Shao-lin-ssu 少林寺 (Shōrinji) on Mt. Sung 嵩山 (Sūzan), where he sat unmoving day and night.

There he took as his disciple Hui-k'e 慧可 (Eka), who thus became the second patriarch. He died in 528 or, according to another tradition, 536, and was posthumously given the title of Yüan-chüeh Ta-shih 圓覺大師 (Engaku Daishi) by Emperor Tai-tsung 代宗 (Daisō) of the T'ang dynasty (618–907).

∼ **dōjō** -- 道場 'The place or seat of enlightenment'; the place where one becomes a buddha.

∼**-ji** -- 寺 'A Bodhi temple'; the temple where prayers are offered for the repose or salvation of one's dead ancestors; a family temple; also *bodaisho** 菩提所 and *kōge-in** 香華院; cf. *uji-dera*. [Tai. 36.]

∼**-ju** -- 樹 'The Bodhi tree'; the tree under which the Buddha attained enlightenment. The Sk. name of the tree is *pippala*, also known as *aśvattha*.

∼**-kō** -- 講 'Bodhi-gathering'. The monthly gathering at the Unrin'in 雲林院, Kyoto, at which the *nenbutsu** was practised and lectures given on sutras for the purpose of attaining birth in Amida's* Pure Land and for the realization of Bodhi. [O.I.]

∼ **no gokui** -- の極位 'The ultimate stage of enlightenment.' [S. Xb–2.]

∼ **no gyō** -- の行 'Practices for attaining enlightenment.' [Tai. 37.]

∼ **no michi** -- のみち 'The path to enlightenment.' [K. 500.]

∼ **no myōka** -- の妙果 'The wondrous fruit of enlightenment.' [S. Xb–2.]

∼ **o inoru** -- を祈る To pray for the repose of the dead; to pray that the dead will be born in Amida's* Pure Land. [Tai. 4.]

∼ **o toburau** -- を弔ふ To pray for the repose of the dead.

∼**-satta** -- 薩埵 Sk. *bodhisattva*; popularly abbreviated to *bosatsu**.

∼**-senna** -- 僊(or 仙)那 Sk. Bodhisena; see *Baramon sōjō*.

∼**-shi** -- 子 N. of a fruit produced in the Himalayas and called '*bo-di-ci*' (or *bo-dhi-rtsi*) in Tibetan, which is used for making rosaries. The term is often mistakenly taken to mean the fruit of a *bodaiju** (Bodhi-tree). [Tai. 35.]

∼**-shin** -- 心 Sk. *bodhi-citta*; 'aspiration for enlightenment'; Bodhi-mind.

～**-shin kisei** --心祈請 'Praying for the (endowment of) Bodhi-mind.' [S. I–8.]

～**-sho** --所 'A Bodhi place'; the same as *bodaiji**.

～ **soku jishin** --卽自心 'Enlightenment is (to know) one's own mind'; the real essence of one's mind is Bodhi. [S. III–1.]

Bōkan 坊官 Also *chōmu* 廳務 and *zaichō* 在廳; an attendant of an ordained member of the imperial family. Though shaven-headed and wearing the monk's robe, he marries, wears a sword and eats meat like an ordinary layman. [Tai. 9, 21.]

Bonbai 梵唄 The chanting of hymns; *bon* 梵 means *bondo* 梵土 (India) and *bai* 唄 is an abbr. of *bainoku**. Also means *nyoraibai**.

Bonbu 凡夫 'An ordinary man,' as opposed to a sage (*shōja* 聖者).

Bondo 梵土 'Brahma's land'; India.

Bonge 凡下 'The ordinary, lower order of people.'

Bongyō 梵行 'Brahma's acts'; morally pure acts. I. In India, the religious practices performed by brahmins. II. Moral practices; practices which accord with the precepts, esp. chastity. III. Generally, in Buddhism, practices prescribed by the Buddha for attaining emancipation.

Bonjō 凡情 'Emotion of an ordinary man'; delusions as conceived by an ordinary man.

Bonkai 犯戒 Also *honkai*; 'breaking of precepts'.

Bonmō 梵網 Refers to the *Bonmō-kyō**. [S. I–9.]

～**-kyō** --經 '*Brahma-net Sutra*'; 2 fasc., translated by Kumāra-jīva (Kumarajū*) [TT. 24, No. 1484]; the sutra presents Maha-yana precepts for bodhisattvas. [S. IV–1, Va–1, VII–25, IX–10, Xb–1.]

～ **no jūjū** --の十重 *Jūjūkai* 十重戒 'the ten major precepts', given in the *Bonmō-kyō**: (1) not to kill or induce others to kill, (2) not to steal or make others steal, (3) not to engage in or make others engage in sexual intercourse, (4) not to lie or make others lie, (5) not to sell or make others sell intoxicating liquors, (6) not to talk of or make others talk of a fault in a bodhisattva, monk, or nun, (7) not to praise oneself and abuse others or make others do so, (8) not to be mean or make others be mean, (9) not to give vent to anger and treat others harshly or make others do so, and (10) not to abuse or make others abuse the three treasures (*sanbō**, i.e. Buddha, Dharma, and Sangha). [S. I–1.]

Bonnō 梵王 'The Brahma King'; the king of the Brahma Heaven (Bonten*); the same as Bontennō* 梵天王. [S. VII–4.]

Bonnō 煩悩 'Afflictions'; Sk. *kleśa*; mental functions which disturb and pollute the mind and body; evil passions.

～-**gō** --業 'A karma created by evil passions.' [S. Vb–8.]

～ **honkū** --本空 'Evil passions are essentially void.' [S. Va–5.]

～-**ma** --魔 'The devil of evil passions'; one of the four devils (*shima**); evil passions are so called because they torment one's mind and body.

～ **mōzō** --妄想 'Evil passions and delusory thoughts.' [S. IV–9.]

～ **no aka** --の垢 'The grime of evil passion.' [Hei. 2.]

～ **no taiga** --の大河 'The great river of evil passions'; an analogy to show that evil passions are boundless and engulf sentient beings. [Tai. 33.]

～-**shō** --性 'The (real) nature of evil passions.' [S. Xa–6.]

～-**shō** --障 'Hindrance of evil passions'; Sk. *kleśa-āvaraṇa*; evil passions which hinder the practice of the Buddhist path and the realization of Nirvana; one of the two kinds of hindrances (*nishō**); cf. *shochishō*.

～ **soku bodai** --即菩提 'Evil passions are themselves enlightenment'; according to the Mahayana principle of non-duality, the real essence of one's passions is the same as enlightenment. [S. Va–5.]

Bonnon 梵音 'Brahma's voice'. I. A buddha or bodhisattva's voice preaching the law. II. A voice chanting a sutra. [Tai. 24.]

Bonryo 凡慮 'An ordinary man's thought.' [Tai. 33.]

Bonsei no gyōgi 犯制の行儀 The procedure to be followed when one is found guilty of breaking precepts. [S. III–5.]

Bonseki 梵席 'Brahma's seat'; a Buddhist meeting. [Tai. 24.]

Bonshin 凡心 'An ordinary (man's) mind'; an unenlightened mind full of delusions and evil passions. [S. VI–16.]

Bonshin 凡身 'The body of an ordinary man.' [S. II–9.]

Bonshō 凡聖 Also *bonjō*; 'ordinary beings and holy men'.

~ **dōgodo** --同居土 'The land where ordinary people and sages live together'; one of the four kinds of lands (*shido** 四土) distinguished in the Tendai* sect.

~ **funi** --不二 'Not discriminating between ordinary beings and sages.' [S. Xb–3.]

Bonsō 凡僧 'An ordinary priest'; a priest of low rank. [K. 520.]

Bonsō 梵僧 'An Indian monk.' [Tai. 24.]

Bonten 梵天 I. 'The Brahma Heaven' in the realm of form (*shikikai**). II. The King of the Brahma Heaven.

~**-nō** --王 'The King of the Brahma Heaven.' [K. 53.]

Bonzei 梵砌 'Brahma's stone steps'; refers to a Buddhist temple. [Tai. 15.]

Bosatsu 菩薩 I. Abbr. of *bodaisatta* 菩提薩埵, Sk. *bodhisattva*; one who makes vows to attain enlightenment (*bodai**) and save suffering beings, and thus sets out on the course of practice (known as *ropparamitsu**) which requires a long period of time to complete. He who has accomplished the bodhisattva practice is a buddha. II. A title of respect given by the emperor to a monk of outstanding virtue. The first such instance in Japan was in 749 when Gyōgi* 行基 (668–749) was given the title of *daibosatsu** by Emperor Shōmu*.

~**-kai** --戒 'The rules of conduct for bodhisattvas.' [S.III–5.]

Bōzu 坊主 Also 房主; 'the head-priest of a temple.'

Buddagaya 佛陀伽耶 Buddhagayā; n. of the place in central India where the Buddha attained enlightenment.

Bugyō 奉行 'Upholding and practising'; upholding the teaching and practising it; also, respectfully practising the method of salvation.

Bukka 佛果 'Fruition of buddhahood'; a buddha's enlightenment attained as the result of the practices of a bodhisattva.

~ **bodai** --菩提 'The fruition of buddhahood and enlightenment.' [Tai. 36.]

Bukkai 佛界 'The buddhas' realm'; one of the ten states of existence (*jikkai**). [S. V–1, Xb–1.]

Bukkaku 佛閣 A general term for Buddhist buildings.

Bukke 佛家 Also *bukka*; 'the Buddha family'. I. Buddhists. II. Monks. III. Bodhisattvas of higher ranks. IV. A buddha land.

Bukken 佛見 'The buddha's sight.'

Bukkyō 佛境 'The sphere of the buddha.' [K. 64.]

Bukkyō 佛經 'A Buddhist sutra.'

Bumo shichō no onden 父母師長の恩田 'The field of (repaying) indebtedness to one's parents, teachers and elders'; one of the three fields of merit; see *onden* and *sanfukuden*. [S. IV–9.]

Bunbetsu 分別 See *funbetsu*.

Bundan 分段 'Part, partition.' I. Difference, distinction. [K. 468.] II. Refers to *bundan shōji**. Cf. *bundanshin* under *nishin*. [Tai. 5.]

∼ **dōgo** --同居 States of existence with limited spans of life in which ordinary people and sages live together. [Tai. 5.]

∼ **shōji** --生死 States of existence in transmigration in which people have limited spans of life.

Bunshin 分身 'Dividing one's body' into many parts; said of the manifestation by a buddha or bodhisattva of many bodies of incarnation. [Tai. 18.]

Bunzai 分齊 'Degree, state, rank.'

Buppō 佛法 'The Buddhist law'; Buddhist teaching.

∼**-metsujin-kyō** --滅盡經 '*The Extinction of the Buddha-Dharma Sutra*'; refers to *Hō-metsujin-kyō**. [Tai. 24.]

∼**-sha** --者 'One (engaged) in the Buddhist law'; one who studies and practises Buddhism; a good and true Buddhist.

∼ **tōzen no reichi** --東漸の靈地 'A holy place on the route of the gradual eastward transmission of the Buddhist law.' [Tai. 18.]

Buritsu kenjō 扶律顯常 See *furitsu kenjō*.

Bussha 佛舍 'A Buddhist temple.' [K. 38.]

Busshari 佛舍利 'The relics of the Buddha'; see *shari*. [K. 51; S. II–1; Tai. 24, 36.]

Busshi 佛子 'The Buddha's son.' I. The Buddha's disciple; a Buddhist. II. A general term for bodhisattvas. III. All living beings, who are regarded by the Buddha as his children.

Busshi 佛師 'A sculptor of Buddhist images.'

Busshin'in 佛心印 'The Buddha-mind seal'; see *shin'in.*

Busshin-ryō 佛神領 'An estate belonging to a temple or shrine.'

Bussho 佛所 I. The place where a buddha is. II. The hall where a statue of a buddha is enshrined. [K. 441.] III. The quarter in a town where Buddhist sculptors live.

Busshō 佛性 'Buddha-nature.'

∼ **jōjū** - -常住 'The eternal presence of the Buddha-nature'. [S. I–6.]

∼ **reikō** - -靈光 'The mystic radiance of the buddha-nature'; the mystic spirituality of the buddha-nature inherent in each living being. [S. VIII–23.]

Busshōbi 佛生日 'The Buddha's birthday,' i.e. the eighth of the fourth month. [Tai. 8.]

Busshu 佛種 'The seed of buddhahood.' [Tai. 29, 30, 39.]

Busso 佛祖 'Buddha-patriarch.' I. Buddha. II. The Buddha and patriarchs.

Butchiken 佛知見 'The wisdom or insight of the Buddha.' [S. III–5, 8, VI–16.]

Butchō 佛頂 'The crown of the Buddha's head'; Sk. *uṣṇīṣa*; also *nikkei** 肉髻; one of the 32 physical characteristics of the Buddha (*sanjūni-sō**).

∼**-ju** - -呪 See *Daibutchō-ju.*

Butchoku 佛勅 'The Buddha's edict.' [S. VI–18.]

Butsu 佛 Abbr. of *butsuda* 佛陀; Sk. *buddha*, 'an enlightened one'. The term specifically refers to Shakamuni* Buddha, the founder of Buddhism, but is also used for other enlightened sages; Mahayana recognizes many buddhas. For the ten epithets for the Buddha, see *jūgō*; for various views of buddha bodies, see *nishin, sanshin, shishin* and *jusshin*. **See also** *hotoke*☆.

Butsuda 佛陀 Sk. *buddha*; see *butsu.*

Butsudan 佛壇 'An altar for worshipping a buddha'; a shrine of a buddha.

Butsuden 佛殿 'A buddha-hall'; a hall where statues of a buddha and bodhisattva(s) are enshrined. [Tai. 24.]

Butsudeshi 佛弟子 'A disciple of the Buddha.'

Butsudō 佛道 I. The Buddhist Way; the path leading to enlightenment. II. The Buddha's enlightenment; Bodhi (*bodai**).

Butsu-e 佛會 'The Buddha's assembly.' [S. Va–2.]

Butsugen 佛眼 I. 'Buddha-eye.' II. Refers to *Butsugenson**.

～ **no hō** --の法 The rite performed for Butsugenson* for the
purpose of stopping calamities. [Tai. 8.]

～**-son** --尊 Sk. Buddhalocanā; also translated as Kokūgen
虚空眼, Butsugen-butsumo 佛眼佛母, etc.; a form of deification
of the Buddha's eye worshipped in esoteric Buddhism.

Butsugu 佛供 'Offerings to the Buddha', such as incense, flowers,
and candles.

Butsui 佛意 'The Buddha's intention.'

Butsuin 佛印 Pronounced *butchin*; 'the Buddha-seal'. I. Abbr.
of *busshin'in** 佛心印. II. The distinctive mark or quality of
the Buddha. III. The manual sign (*inzō** 印相) of a buddha.

Butsuji 佛事 I. The Buddha's altruistic activity. II. Any deed
which complies with the Buddhist Way. III. A Buddhist service,
e.g. for the dead.

～**-mon** --門 'The gate of Buddhist activity'; the aspect of
Buddhism in which verbal teachings are provisionally established.
[S. IV–1, Va–6, Xb–1.]

Butsujō 佛乘 'The buddha-vehicle'; the path leading to buddhahood.

Butsumotsu 佛物 'Offerings made to the Buddha.' [Hei. 3; S. IX–
8; Tai. 20.]

Butsumyō 佛名 'A buddha's name.'

～**-e** --會 The annual ceremony of reciting the names of
buddhas of the past, present, and future at the imperial palace
in order to expunge past sins. It originated from the expiation
ceremony held by Kōbō* Daishi and others at the imperial
palace on the 23rd day of the 12th month, 824. From 853, the
ceremony was held from the 19th to the 21st days of the 12th
month. From the 12th century, the ceremony was held for only

one day or one night, and was finally discontinued from about the Eiwa era (1375–1379). The names of the buddhas which were recited at first numbered 13,000, but from 918 they were reduced to 3,000. Cf. *Gobutsumyō.*

∼ **sange no hō** --懺悔の法 'The rite of repentance through (re-citing) buddhas' names'; refers to *butsumyō-e** 佛名會. [Tai. 35.]

Butsuniku 佛肉 'The Buddha's flesh'; the Buddha's body; here, part of it. [Tai. 8.]

Butsushari 佛舍利 See *busshari.*

Butsuzen butsugo no dōshi 佛前佛後の導師 'The teacher before the Buddha (Miroku*) and after the Buddha (Shakamuni*)'; refers to Jizō*, who saves living beings during the period when there is no buddha in the world. [Tai. 20.]

Butsuzō-kyō 佛藏經 '*The Buddha Repository Sutra*'; 3 or 4 fasc., tr. by Kumārajīva (Kumarajū*) [TT. 15, No. 653]. The sutra emphasizes the importance of remembering Buddha, Dharma, Sangha, etc., and of the observance of precepts, etc. [S.IV–1, VI–17, Xa–6.]

Buttoku 佛德 'The Buddha's virtue.' [S. II–6.]

Byakue 白衣 'White robe'; one who wears white clothes; hence, a layman. [S. III–3.]

Byakuren 白蓮 'A white lotus.'

∼ **no majiwari** --の交 'The White Lotus Association'; see *Byakurensha.* [Tsu. 108.]

∼**-sha** --社 Ch. *Pai-lien-shê*; 'the White Lotus Society', estab-lished with more than 120 members by Hui-yüan 慧遠 (Eon*) on Mt. Lu 廬山 (Rozan) in 402 in order to meditate on Amida* Buddha.

Byakusangai-butchō-ju 白傘蓋佛頂呪 See *Daibutchō-ju.*

Byōdō 平等 'Equality'; non-discrimination; evenness; pervasive-ness.

∼ **ittai** --一體 'Sameness and oneness.'

∼ **muni no chie** --無二の智慧 'The equal and non-dual wisdom'; the wisdom of realizing absolute reality; the undifferentiated wisdom. [S. Xa–5.]

~ **musō no chie** - - 無相の智慧 'The wisdom of equality and non-characteristics'; the wisdom of seeing things in their ultimate reality of non-discrimination and non-characteristics. [S. Va–6.]

~ **no isshin** - - の一心 'The equal One Mind'; the absolute mind-nature which is undifferentiated and pervasive to all beings. [S. III–8.]

~ **no jihi** - - の慈悲 'Impartial compassion.' [S. IX–10.]

~ **no ri** - - の理 'The principle of equality'; the reality-principle that all existences are, in their essential nature, equal and undistinguishable. [S. Vb–9.]

~ **no shinji** - - の心地 'The equal mind-base'; the original mind-nature which is universal and undifferentiated. [S. IV–1.]

~**-shōchi** - - 性智 'The wisdom of (observing the ultimate) equality (of all things)'; Sk. *samatā-jñāna*; one of the four wisdoms (*shichi*****) and the five wisdoms (*gochi*****).

C

Chi 智 'Wisdom'; see *nichi*☆ and *sanchi*☆.

Chiai 癡愛 Short for *guchi* 愚癡 'ignorance and stupidity' and *ton'ai* 貪愛 'greed and attachment'. [S. IV–9, IX–10.]

Chiben 智辨 'Intelligence and eloquence.' [Tai. 24.]

Chibon 智品 'Level of wisdom'; wisdom; intellect. [S. I–3.]

Chige 智解 'Intellectual understanding.'

~ **jōryō** - - 情量 'Intellectual understanding and calculation.' [S. Va–5.]

Chigi 地祇 'An earth deity'; cf. *tenjin chigi*.

Chigi 智顗 Ch. Chih-i (538–97); the third patriarch of the T'ien-t'ai (Tendai*****) sect, who secured its foundation and is regarded as its founder; popularly known as Master T'ien-t'ai 天台大師 (Tendai Daishi*****) or Master Chih-che 智者大師 (Chisha Daishi*****).

Chigo 兒 Also 稚兒; 'a child'. I. A servant-boy in a temple. [Tai. 21.] II. A boy or girl who, dressed in ornamental clothes, participates in a parade on the day of a special Buddhist or Shinto service or festival. [K. 573.]

Chigū 値遇 Pronounced *chigu*; 'rare encounter'; used to describe an encounter with a buddha or the Buddhist teaching.

~ **ketsuen** --結縁 Pronounced *chigu kechien*; to do something as it presents itself and, thereby, provide an opportunity for other people to come to Buddhism. [IH.]

Chigyō 智行 'Wisdom and practice.'

~ **kenbi** --兼備 'Possessed of both wisdom and practice'; possessed of both outstanding wisdom and the merit of correct practices. [Tai. 15.]

Chiken 知見 I. 'Knowing and seeing.' II. Insight and thought.

~ **jōryō** --情量 'Thinking and calculating.' [S. Va–5.]

Chikurin shōja 竹林精舎 Sk. Veṇuvana-vihāra; the first Buddhist monastery built in Magadha, India, for the Buddha. [Hei. 2.]

Chikushōdō 畜生道 'The realm of animals'; one of the ten realms (*jikkai** 十界).

Chimon 智門 'Wisdom-aspect'; one of the two aspects of a buddha's virtue, the other being *himon* 悲門 'compassion-aspect'. [S. I–3.]

Chingo kokka 鎮護國家 'Protecting the state.'

~ **no kyōō** ----の經王 'The king of the sutras which protect the state'; here refers to the *Daihannya-kyō**; cf. *gokoku sanbukyō*. [Tai. 23.]

Chinju 鎮守 '(A shrine of) peace and protection'; a shrine in the precincts of a temple where a non-Buddhist divinity is enshrined to keep devils away.

Chiron 智論 '*Wisdom Discourse*'; refers to *Daichido-ron**. [S. IV–1.]

Chisha Daishi 智者大師 'Master Chih-che'; the title given to Master T'ien-t'ai 天台大師 (Tendai Daishi*) or Chih-i 智顗 (Chigi*) by Emperor Yang-ti 煬帝 (Yōdai) in 591. [S. I–3.]

Chishiki 知識 'Knowledge'; a teacher; cf. *zenjishiki*. [S. I–10; Tai. 24, 27.]

Chishin 智心 'Enlightened mind.' [S. II–4.]

Chishō 智性 'Wisdom-nature'; one's innate wisdom. [S. II–4.]

Chishō 智證 See *Enchin*. [S. Xb–3.]

~ **Daishi** --大師 See *Enchin*. [Tai. 15.]

Chisoku 知足 I. 'Contentment'. II. Refers to Chisokuten*. [S. II–5, 8.]

~**-ten** --天 'Contentment Heaven'; refers to the Tuṣita Heaven (Tosotsuten*). [S. II–5.]

Chizō 智增 'Predominance of wisdom'; said of the spiritual quality of a type of bodhisattva in whom wisdom is predominant and compassion is less obvious; the opposite of *hizō** 悲增. [S. Xa–1.]

Chōbutsu osso 超佛越祖 'Transcending the Buddha and surpassing the master'; a Zen* phrase emphasizing the absolute experience of *satori**. [Tai. 24.]

Chōdatsu 調達 Also Jōdatsu; abbr. of Chōbadatta 調婆達多; also Daibadatta* 提婆達多; Sk. Devadatta; the Buddha's cousin who attempted to kill him and take over the leadership of the Buddhist order. [S. II–6, Va–4, Xa–2, Xb–3; Tai. 24.]

Chōfuku 調伏 See *jōbuku*.

Chōgō 長講 See *jōgō*.

Chōja 長者 I. Sk. *gṛha-pati*; 'a rich, elderly man of virtue'. II. The title of the head priest of the Tōji*, Kyoto.

Chōka 鳥窠 'A bird's nest'; Ch. Niao-k'e; a nick-name for Tao-lin 道林 (Dōrin*). [S. Va–5.]

Chōkō 長講 See *jōgō*.

Chokuganji 敕願寺 'A temple (erected) at an emperor's decree'; also *chokuganjo* 敕願所; a temple erected by the emperor to offer up a particular prayer; cf. *goganji*. [Tai. 24, 40.]

Chokuganjo 敕願所 The same as *chokuganji**.

Chōmon 聽聞 'Listening' to a sermon.

Chōrai 頂禮 Worshipping with one's head touching the ground; the most reverential form of worship.

Chōrō 長老 'Elder.' I. A title of respect for a monk of wisdom and virtue who has been in the priesthood for many years. II.

A title of respect for a Zen* monk, especially the head of a big temple.

Chōshō Ō 頂上王 See 頂生王 next entry. [S. Xa–8.]

Chōshō Ō 頂生王 'Head-born King'; a universal monarch in ancient times, born from an eruption on his father's head. He had conquered all the four continents (*shishū**) but, not content with that, he attempted to conquer Trāyastriṃśa Heaven (Tōriten*) but failed and died. It is said that the king was one of the Buddha's previous incarnations. [S. Xa–8.]

Chōso biku 鳥鼠比丘 'A bat monk'; a derogatory term for a monk who has broken precepts. [S. IV–1.]

Chū-agon-gyō 中阿含經 '*Middle-Length Āgama Sutras*'; Sk. *Madhyama-āgama-sūtra*; one of the four collections of sutras in the Āgama (*agon**) division belonging to Hinayana; 60 fasc., tr. by Saṃghadeva (Sōgyadaiba 僧伽提婆) about the beginning of the fifth century [TT. 1, No. 26]. This collection contains 222 sutras. See *Agon-gyō*.

Chūdai hachiyō-in 中臺八葉院 'The central eight-petal section'; the central part of the Matrix-store Realm Mandala (*Taizōkai mandara**) where nine deities are portrayed—Dainichi* sitting in the centre and eight buddhas and bodhisattvas sitting on the eight petals of a lotus. [Hei. 3.]

Chūdan 中壇 'The central platform' for the fierce spirit Fudō* in the Five-Platform Ritual (*Godan-hō**). [S. I–3.]

Chūdō 中堂 Refers to the Konponchūdō; See *Enryakuji*. [K. 52.]

Chūdō 中道 'The Middle Way'; the principle of non-duality; the principle of reality which lies beyond existence and non-existence, hence, 'middle'. [S. IV–1.]

Chūganha 中觀派 The Mādhyamika school; one of the two Mahayana schools in India, the other being the *Yugagyōha**. This school, founded by Nāgārjuna (Ryūju*), emphasizes the voidness of all existences.

Chūgen 中間 Refers to *chūgen hosshi**. [K. 601.]

∼ hosshi --法師 See *shimo hosshi*. [Hei. 2; K. 228, 549, 604.]

Chūin 中陰 'Intermediate shadow.' I. An intermediate state between death and the next life. Also *chūu** 中有. II. A period of seven weeks after death, during which a dead person stays in this suspended state.

～ no hikazu --の日數 'The *chūin** period of (forty-nine) days.' [Tai. 18.]

Chūki 中機 'A man of medium capability.' [Tai. 24.]

Chūkō 中劫 'A medium *kalpa*.' See *kō*.

Chūrin 稠林 'A dense forest, jungle'; Sk. *gahana*; often used as an analogy for intense evil passions and false views from which it is difficult to free oneself; cf. *shōji no chūrin*.

Chūten 中天 'Central India'; *ten* is an abbr. of *tenjiku* 天竺 'India.' [S. IV–1.]

Chūtō 偸盗 'Stealing'; cf. *gokai*, *hassaikai* and *jikkai*.

Chūu 中有 'An intermediate state'; Sk. *antarā-bhava*; the state of existence between death and a new life; the same as *chūin**. [S. IV–9; Tai. 6.]

～ no shiryō --の資糧 'Provisions during the intermediate state (between death and a new life).' [S. IV–9.]

～ no tabi --の旅 'Travelling in the intermediate state (between death and a new life).' [S. IV–9, VII–11.]

Chūzon 中尊 Also *chūson*; 'the central deity'. [O.V.]

D

Dabi 茶毗 Pali *jhāpeti*; 'cremation.'

Daginiten 吒 (or 咤) 祇尼天 See *Dakiniten*. [Tai. 26, 36.]

～ no hō ----の法 'The rite dedicated to Ḍākinī'; see *Dakiniten*. [Tai. 26.]

Daiba-bon 提婆品 'Chapter on Devadatta'; the 12th chapter of the *Hoke-kyō**. [Tai. 10.]

Daibadatta 提婆達多 Sk. Devadatta; also, simply, Daiba 提婆 and Chōdatsu* 調達; translated as Tenju 天授 'Endowed by Heaven', etc.; a cousin of Shakamuni* and a follower of his teaching, he attempted to take over the leadership of the Buddhist order and even to kill the Buddha. He incited Prince Ajātaśatru (Ajase*) to kill his father, King Bimbisāra (Binbashara*), and usurp the throne. Because of his grave offences, it is said that he fell into hell while still alive. [S. Va–4.]

Daibon 大梵 Refers to Daibonten*. [Tai. 17.]

Daibon-gyō 大品經 Refers to *Makahannya-haramitsu-kyō**. [S. IV–1.]

Daibon-hannya-kyō 大品般若經 Refers to *Makahannya-haramitsu-kyō**.

Daibonnō 大梵王 'King Mahābrahman'; the king who reigns in the Mahābrahman Heaven (Daibonten*). [Tai. 24.]

Daibonten 大梵天 'The Mahābrahman Heaven'; the First Meditation Heaven (*shozenten**) in the Realm of Form (*shikikai**) where King Mahābrahman lives.

Daibontennō-monbutsu-ketsugi-kyō 大梵天王問佛決疑經 '*The Sutra on King Mahābrahman's Questions to the Buddha and Clarification of Doubts*'; the Zen* text containing the story of 'the Buddha's lifting the flower and smiling' (*nenge mishō**); the text is considered to have been compiled in China; abbreviated as *Monbutsu-ketsugi-kyō* 問佛決疑經. [Tai. 24.]

Daibosatsu 大菩薩 'A great bodhisattva (*bosatsu**).' I. A bodhisattva who has attained the stage of non-retrogression (*futai**) and is thus assured of becoming a buddha. II. A title of respect for any bodhisattva. III. A title of respect for a monk of outstanding virtue: e.g. Gyōgi* was given this title by Emperor Shōmu* in 749. IV. Refers to the god Hachiman who was considered to be an incarnation of a great bodhisattva. [K. 173; Tai. 13.]

Daibutchō-darani 大佛頂陀羅尼 See *Daibutchō-ju*. [S. Vb–11.]

Daibutchō-ju 大佛頂呪 Also *Butchō-ju* 佛頂呪 and *Ryōgon-ju* 楞嚴呪. Refers to the *Byakusangai-butchō-ju* 白傘蓋佛頂呪 given in the *Shuryōgon-gyō* 首楞嚴經 [TT. 19, No. 945]. The spell, consisting of 427 phrases, is believed to be effective in driving away evil spirits, curing illnesses, etc. [K. 49.]

Daibutchō nyorai mitsuin shushō ryōgi shobosatsu mangyō shuryōgon-gyō 大佛頂如來密因修證了義諸菩薩萬行首楞嚴經 See *Shuryō-gon-gyō*.

Daichi 大智 'Great wisdom'; the wisdom of knowing absolute reality.

Daichido-ron 大智度論 '*Great Wisdom Discourse*'; a commentary on the *Makahannya-haramitsu-kyō** attributed to Nāgārjuna (Ryūju*); 100 fasc., tr. by Kumārajīva (Kumarajū*) [TT. 25, No. 1509]. [S. IV–1, Xb–1.]

Daichiron 大智論 '*Great Wisdom Discourse*'; refers to the *Daichido-ron** attributed to Nāgārjuna (Ryūju*). [S. IV–1, 9.]

Daidanna 大檀那 'A great donor.' [S. Vb–10.]

Daie 大衣 'A large robe'; Sk. *saṃghāṭī*; the same as *sōgyari**; one of the three kinds of robes (*sanne**). [Tai. 17, 26.]

Daie 大會 'A large assembly'; the same as *daishūe* 大集會, an assembly of many monks and laymen. [Tai. 24, 40.]

Daienkyōchi 大圓鏡智 'The great perfect mirror-wisdom'; Sk. *ādarśa-jñāna*; the wisdom which reflects all phenomenal things as if in a clear mirror; one of the four wisdoms (*shichi**) and the five wisdoms (*gochi**).

Daiga 大我 'Great self'; one's true self is completely free and not subject to any restriction or hindrance, being identical with Nirvana; opposed to *shōga* 小我, 'the small self' bound by false desires and attachment. [S. III–8.]

Daiganriki 大願力 'Great vow-power'; extraordinary power or energy produced by a bodhisattva's vow. [Ta.]

Daigen no hō 大元の法 See *Taigen no hō*.

Daigo 醍醐 I. Sk. *maṇḍa*, lit. 'clarified butter'; the last and most refined of the four milk products; used for the supreme teaching of the Buddha as found, according to the Tendai* sect, in the *Hoke-kyō** and *Nehan-gyō**, or, according to the Shingon* sect, in the esoteric texts. See *gomi*. II. Refers to Daigoji.

~ **no sakura-e** --の櫻會 'Cherry-blossom meeting at the Daigo-ji'; the annual service at the Daigoji in Kyoto in the 3rd month, which was followed by a cherry-viewing party. [K. 198.]

Daigoji no sakura-e 醍醐寺の櫻會   See *Daigo no sakura-e*. [K. 533.]

Daigon 大權   'A great incarnation'; a great divinity who has appeared in this world in human form. [S. I–3, 8; Tai. 6.]

Daihannya 大般若   Refers to the *Daihannya-haramitta-kyō**. [K. 68, 637; Ma. 103; S. I–6, II–10, VII–23; Tai. 5, 6, 38.]

~**-haramitta-kyō** - - -波羅蜜多經   Sk. *Mahāprajñā-pāramitā-sūtra* 'the *Great-Wisdom Sutra*'; 600 fasc., tr. by Hsüan-chuang (Genjō*) in 659 [TT. 5–7, No. 220].

~**-haramitta-shin-gyō** - - -波羅蜜多心經   Refers to *Hannya-shin-gyō**. [O. VI.]

~**-kyō** - - -經   Refers to the *Daihannya-haramitta-kyō**. [Tai. 23.]

~**-kyō shindoku no kuriki** - - -經眞讀の功力   'The efficacy of chanting the whole of the *Daihannya-kyō**'; see *shindoku*. [Tai. 23.]

~ **no dei** - - -の泥   'Gold powder used in copying the *Daihannya-kyō**.' [S. VII–16.]

~ **no midokyō** - - -の御讀經   'Chanting of the *Daihannya-haramitta-kyō**.' [K. 3.]

Daihatsu-nehan-gyō 大般涅槃經   '*The Sutra on the Great Extinction*'; Sk. *Mahāparinirvāṇa-sūtra*; 40 fasc., tr. by Dharmakṣema (Don-mushin 曇無讖) [TT. 12, No. 374]. This is the Mahayana account of the Buddha's passing away. The sutra also explains the eternal presence of the Buddha and the inherence of buddha-nature in every living being.

Daihi 大悲   'Great compassion.'

~ **daijuku** - -代受苦   Bodhisattvas' 'taking upon themselves the sufferings (of sentient beings) out of their great compassion', even subjugating themselves to the torments of hell. [S. I–10.]

~ **honzei** - -本誓   'The original vow arising from great compassion.' [S. II–6.]

~**-ju** - -呪   Also ~*-shu*; 'the spell of great compassion', refers to *Senju-darani**. [Hei. 3.]

~**-kyō** - -經   '*The Great Compassion Sutra*'; 5 fasc., tr. by Narendrayaśas (Narendairiyasha 那連提黎耶舍) and Fa-chih 法智 (Hōchi) in the 6th century [TT. 12, No. 380]. The sutra gives an account of the Buddha's death, his transmission of the Dharma, the merit of making offerings to his relics, etc. [S. VI–18.]

∼ no guzei --の弘誓 'The universal vow of great compassion'; refers to Amida's vow. [Tai. 6.]

∼-riki --力 'Power of the great compassion.' [K. 39.]

Daihōben-butsu-hōon-gyō 大方便佛報恩經 '*The Sutra on the Buddha's Repayment of his Indebtedness (to his Parents) by Great and Skilful Means*'; 7 fasc.; translator unknown [TT. 3, No. 156]; the sutra expounds the Buddha's acts of repaying indebtedness to his parents, e.g. by visiting the Trāyastriṃśa Heaven (Tōriten*) to preach the Dharma for his mother.

Daihōdō-daishū-kyō 大方等大集經 See *Daishū-kyō*.

Daihō hihō 大法祕法 'Great and secret ritual practices.' [Hei. 3; Tai. 8.]

Daihōkō-jūrin-gyō 大方廣十輪經 '*The Great Extensive Sutra on the Ten Wheels*'; 8 fasc.; the translator unknown [TT. 13, No. 410]. This sutra expounds the virtue of Jizō*.

Daiichigi 第一義 Refers to *daiichigitai**. [S. Pref., I–10, Va–12; Tai. 24.]

∼-kū ---空 'The first-principle void'; Sk. *paramārtha-śūnyatā*; one of the 18 kinds of void distinguished in the *Daibon-hannya-kyō**, etc.; void as the first or ultimate principle, i.e. void beyond all relative concepts; cf. *jūhachikū*. [S. IV–9.]

∼-tai ---諦 Sk. *paramārtha-satya* 'the first principle'; the ultimate reality; also *shintai** 眞諦 and *shōgitai** 勝義諦. One of the two aspects of reality, the other being reality in the worldly sense (*sezokutai**).

Daiitoku 大威德 Refers to Daiitoku Myōō*. [Tai. 18.]

∼-ju ---呪 'The spell of great majesty'; refers to the *Shijōkō-daiitoku-shōsai-kichijō-darani-kyō* 熾盛光大威德消災吉祥陀羅尼經; 1 fasc., tr. by Amoghavajra (Fukū*) [TT. 19, No. 963]. This is a sutra expounding the merit of the spell of the Tathagata Shijōkō* 熾盛光 ('Blazing Light').

∼ Myōō ---明王 Sk. Yamāntaka Vidyārāja; one of the five *myōō* deities (*godai-myōō**). He has three faces and six arms, and rides a big white ox. Assuming a fearsome appearance, he subdues deadly snakes and evil dragons. It is believed that, in his original state, he is Amida*. [Tai. 12.]

~ **no hō** ---の法 'A ritual dedicated to Daiitoku Myōō*' to pray for the subjugation of evil dragons, devils and enemies. [Tai. 20]

Daiji 大士 'A great being'; Sk. *mahāsattva*, which is transcribed as *makasatsu** 摩訶薩; the same as *bosatsu** 菩薩, *bodhisattva*.

Daiji 大事 'Important matter.' I. The most important thing one should do, i.e. seeking to attain enlightenment. [Tsu. 59.] II. Refers to *daiji innen* 大事因縁; the most important cause for which the Buddha appeared in the world, i.e. expounding the Dharma to save sentient beings. Cf. *ichidaiji no innen*.

Daiji 大慈 'Great compassion, great mercy.'

~ **daihi** --大悲 'Great compassion and great mercy.'

~ **daihi no honji** --大悲の本地 'The original state of the one of great compassion and mercy'; refers to Kannon*. [Tai. 6.]

~ **daihi no Kanzeon** --大悲の観世音 'Kanzeon of great compassion and mercy'; see *Kannon*. [Tai. 12.]

~ **daihi no satta** --大悲の薩埵 'A bodhisattva of great compassion and mercy'; here refers to Jizō*. [Tai. 20.]

Daijik-kyō 大集經 See *Daishū-kyō*.

Daijinzū 大神通 'Great supernatural power.' [Tai. 24.]

Daijizaiō Bosatsu 大自在王菩薩 'Great Sovereign-King Bodhisattva'; the original deity who was reincarnated as Hachiman, the god of war. [K. 1.]

Daijizaiten 大自在天 'Maheśvara Heaven'; the highest heaven in the Realm of Form (*shikikai**), where the god Maheśvara (*Maheishubara**) lives. It is also used to refer to the sixth heaven in the realm of desire (*yokkai**). [S. II–8.]

Daijō 大定 'Great meditation.' [S. IV–1.]

Daijō 大乗 'The Great Vehicle'; Sk. *mahāyāna*; the teaching which conveys all sentient beings to buddhahood; opposite of *shōjō* 小乗, Hinayana. Also a Mahayana sutra.

~-**hifundari-kyō** --悲分陀利經 See *Hike-kyō*.

~-**honshō-shinjikan-gyō** --本生心地觀經 An 8-fascicle sutra [TT. 3, No. 159]; often abbreviated to *Shinjikan-gyō**.

~-kai --戒 'Mahayana precepts'; the precepts to be observed by bodhisattvas; hence, also, *bosatsukai** 菩薩戒. They include the ten major precepts and the forty-eight minor ones of the *Bonmō-kyō** and the threefold pure precepts (*sanjujōkai**). Cf. *Bonmō no jūjū* and *shōjōkai*. [Tai. 15.]

~-kaidan'in --戒壇院 'The hall of the Mahayana-precept platform'; n. of one of the nine main halls on Mt. Hiei. This is where the Mahayana precepts are given to monks. [Tai. 15.]

~-kishin-ron --起信論 '*The Awakening of Faith in Mahayana*'; a Mahayana discourse attributed to Aśvaghoṣa (Memyō* 馬鳴); there are two Chinese translations, one by Paramārtha (Shindai*) [TT. 32, No. 1666] and the other by Śikṣānanda (Jisshananda 實叉難陀) [TT. 32, No. 1667].

~ kyō --經 'A Mahayana sutra.'

~-rishu-ropparamitta-kyō --理趣六波羅蜜多經 '*The Sutra on the Mahayana Principle of Six Pāramitās*'; 10 fasc., tr. by Prajñā (Hannya 般若) [TT. 8, No. 261]. This sutra expounds the Six Pāramitā practices (*ropparamitsu**).

~ zengon no kuni --善根之國 'A land of Mahayana goodness.' [K. 53.]

Daijuku 代受苦 See *daihi daijuku*. [S. II–9.]

Daikaishu 大海衆 'A great ocean-like multitude.' I. Monks who are indistinguishable from each other just as the sea water is of uniform taste though rivers flowing into it have different tastes; also used to mean many monks. II. The general name for the bodhisattvas in Amida's* Pure Land; see *daikaishu bosatsu*.

~ bosatsu ---菩薩 'A great ocean-like multitude of bodhisattvas'; also *shōjō daikaishu bosatsu* 清淨大海衆菩薩; refers to all the bodhisattvas living in Amida's* Pure Land.

Daikō 大劫 'A large *kalpa*.' See *kō*.

Daikokuten 大黑天 'Mahākāla God'; also Daikokujin 大黑神 and Daiji 大時; usually transcribed as Makakaraten* 摩訶迦羅天. In esoteric Buddhism, he is an incarnation of Dainichi* in the fearsome form of a *yakṣa* (*yasha**) king, and is depicted as having a head and eight arms or three heads and six arms. He is a war god, a god of wealth and happiness, and a cemetery god. As a war god, he is considered in India as an incarnation or retainer of Śiva or his consort, Durgā. He is also sometimes considered as an incarnation of Maheśvara (Daijizaiten*). In Japan he is identified with a Shinto god, Ōkuninushi-no-mikoto 大國主命, who is portrayed as standing astride two sacks of rice and carrying a big bag on his back.

Daikyōkan 大叫喚 'Great shrieking'; refers to *daikyōkan jigoku*, one of the eight scorching hells (*hachinetsu jigoku**). [Tai. 12, 17.]

Daimyōsō 題名僧 'Title priests'; ordinary priests participating in a big service other than the seven priests in the leading roles (*shichisō**). They are so called because they read out the title of the sutra after the *dokushi**. [O. VI.]

Dainehan-gyō 大涅槃經 Abbr. of *Daihatsunehan-gyō**. [S. Va–1.]

Dainenbutsu 大念佛 'Big *nenbutsu*'; reciting the *nenbutsu** in a loud voice. [S. IV–1.]

Dainichi 大日 Sk. Mahāvairocana, 'great illumination'; the central buddha in the Shingon* sect, who is the embodiment of the reality of the universe. [S. I–1, Vb–10, VI–1; Tai. 10, 18.]

~ **Henjō** --遍照 'Mahāvairocana, the Universally Illuminating One.' [Tai. 2, 18.]

~**-kyō** --經 Sk. *Mahāvairocana-sūtra*; the popular title of *Daibirushana-jōbutsu-jinpenkaji-kyō* 大毘盧遮那成佛神變加持經, 7 fasc., tr. by Śubhākarasiṃha (Zenmui*) [TT. 18, No. 848]; one of the three sutras of the Shingon* sect. [Hei. X; S. Va–12.]

~**-kyō-sho** --經疏 '*The Commentary on the Mahāvairocana Sutra*' by Śubhākarasiṃha (Zenmui* 善無畏); 20 fasc. [TT. 39, No. 1796]; this is the record by I-hsing 一行 (Ichigyō*) of Śubhākarasiṃha's lectures on the *Dainichi-kyō** for Emperor Hsüan-tsung 玄宗 (Gensō) (685–762).

~ **no inmon** --の印文 'The inscribed passage by Dainichi.' [S. I–1.]

Dainika 第二果 'The second fruit'; the second of the four stages of spiritual attainment in Hinayana; *ichiraika** 一來果 or *shida-gonka* 斯陀含果; see *shika*. [S. II–1.]

Daira 提羅 Abbr. of *sendaira** 扇提羅 or 旃提羅; Sk. *ṣaṇḍha*; one who has no distinctive sexual organ; a eunuch. [Tai. 24.]

Dairokuten 第六天 'The Sixth Heaven', i.e. of the six heavens in the realm of desire. It is called Takejizaiten* 他化自在天; Sk. *Paranirmitavaśavartin*, meaning 'having power over (enjoyments) magically created by others (in the lower heavens).' The palace of the king of devils is in this heaven; cf. *maō*. [S. I–1; Tai. 16.]

~ **no maō** ---の魔王 'The king of devils in the Sixth Heaven'; see *maō*. [Tai. 12.]

Dairon 大論 '*The Great Discourse*'; refers to the *Daichido-ron** attributed to Nāgārjuna (Ryūju*).

Daisanka 第三果 'The third fruit'; the third of the four stages of spiritual attainment in Hinayana; the same as *fugenka** 不還果 or *anagonka* 阿那含果: see *shika*. [S. Xa–2.]

Daisansai 大三災 'Three great calamities' which occur at the end of the world: (1) *kasai* 火災, seven suns appear in the sky and burn out the world; (2) *suisai* 水災, the whole world is flooded with water; and (3) *fūsai* 風災, everything in the world is blown away by strong winds; cf. *shōsansai*. [Tai. 8.]

Daisei funnu no akugen 大勢忿怒の悪眼 'Vicious eyes showing great strength and fury'; a fearsome look to frighten away enemies. [Tai. 23.]

Daisei funnu no katachi 大勢忿怒の形 'A form showing great strength and fury'; a fearsome incarnation of a divinity to supress adversaries of Buddhism, e.g. Fudō*. [Tai. 12.]

Daiseishi 大勢至 Often abbreviated as Seishi 勢至; Sk. Mahāsthāmaprāpta. One of the two attendant bodhisattvas of Amida*, who stands on his right-hand side and represents wisdom.

Daisen 大千 Abbr. of *daisenkai**. [S. Xb–3.]

~**-kai** --界 'A great thousand worlds'; refers to *sanzen-daisensekai**. [Tai. 23.]

Daisessen 大雪山 'The great snowy mountains'; the Himalayas. [Tai. 12.]

Daisetsu 大刹 A big temple; cf. *setsu* III. [Tai. 24.]

Daishi 大師 'A great master'. I. A title of respect for a buddha or a high priest. II. Refers to Kōbō* Daishi. III. Abbr. of *daishigō**.

~-**gō** --號 'The title "Great Master" '; the title of honour and respect conferred posthumously by an emperor on a priest of great distinction. Saichō* and Ennin* were the first priests given this title in Japan (in 856).

~ **go-nyūjō no muro** --御入定の室 'The cave in which (Kōbō) Daishi dwells in a state of meditation'; this cave is at Oku-no-in 奥の院 on Mt. Kōya; cf. *Kūkai*. [Tai. 39.]

Daishijōkō no hō 大熾盛光の法 'The great blazing-light ritual'; the same as *shijōkō-hō**. [Tai. 36.]

Daishika 第四果 'The fourth fruit'; the last of the four stages of spiritual attainment in Hinayana; it refers to the stage of arhat (*arakan**). Cf. *shika*. [S. II-1.]

Daishi kanjō no kishō 大師勸請の起請 'Invoking (Jie) Daishi' to appear as a witness to the truth of one's words. As to its origin, according to the *Kokon chomonjū*, when Jie Daishi (Ryōgen*) of Mt. Hiei heard of an allegation that he did not abide by the precepts, he wrote an invocation to the Buddha, Dharma, and Sangha requesting them to prove his innocence and made it public. [Tsu. 205.]

~-**mon** -------文 'A written invocation for invoking (Jie) Daishi'; any invocation to a deity is so called because Jie Daishi (Ryōgen*) was the first to draw up such an invocation. [Tai. 17.]

Daishi Tosotsuten 第四兜率天 'Tuṣita Heaven, the fourth (in the realm of desire)'. See *Tosotsuten*. [K. 64.]

Daishō 大小 'Great and small'; refers to *daijō** (Mahayana) and *shōjō** (Hinayana).

Daishō 大聖 'A great sage'; a buddha or a bodhisattva.

~ **seson** --世尊 'The great world-honoured sage'; the Buddha.

~ **Shakuson** --釋尊 'The great sage Shakamuni*.' [Tai. 18.]

Daishō kyōmon 大小教門 'Great and small teaching gates'; Mahayana and Hinayana teachings. [S. III-1.]

Daishu 大衆 'Multitudes of people, a big assemblage'. I. People in the world. II. A general term for the monks of a temple or an assemblage. III. All those who hear the sermon at the meeting.

Daishū-kyō 大集經 '*The Great Collection Sutra*'; 60 fasc., tr. by Dharmakṣema (Donmushin 曇無懺), *et al.* [TT. 13, No. 397]; also *Daijik-kyō*; the full title is *Daihōdō-daishū-kyō* 大方等大集經; Sk. *Mahāsannipāta-sūtra*. In this sutra the Buddha explains to other buddhas and bodhisattvas the Mahayana principles, such as the theory of emptiness (*kū**). The sutra is also strongly characterized by esotericism. [S. II–10, VI–18.]

Daisōjō 大僧正 'A great archbishop'; the highest of the three grades of *sōjō** and thus the highest rank in the Buddhist hierarchy; Gyōgi* was the first to be nominated as *daisōjō* in 745.

Daitō 大塔 'The Great Tower' on Mt. Kōya. [Hei. 2.]

Daitoku 大德 'Great virtue'; a title used of a revered monk.

Daizō-e 大藏會 'A service for the large collection (of Buddhist scriptures)'; the same as *issaikyō-e**.

Daizōkyō 大藏經 'A great collection of sutras'; the entire collection of Buddhist texts. [Tai. 12.]

Dakiniten 荼吉尼天 Also 吒枳尼天 and Daginiten* 吒祇尼天; Sk. Ḍākinī; a kind of *yakṣa* (*yasha**) attending Daikokuten* believed to live on human bezoar (*nin'ō* 人黃) which is said to give some supernatural power to one who eats it. He used to eat a man's bezoar six months before he died, but the remonstrations of Dainichi*, incarnated as Daikokuten*, led him to eat it only after a man had died.

Dan 壇 'Altar'; refers to *gomadan* 護摩壇, an altar for *goma** (Sk. *homa*) ritual. [K. 59; Tai. 12.]

Dan 檀 Sk. *dāna*; donation, charity.

~-haramitsu -波羅蜜 Sk. *dāna-pāramitā*, 'charity *pāramitā*; one of the six *pāramitā* (*haramitsu**) practices; see *ropparamitsu*. [S. Xa–5; Tai. 37.]

Dandokusen 檀特山 Mt. Daṇḍaloka; a mountain in North India where the Buddha, born as a crown prince called Sudāna in one of his former lives, performed the practices of a bodhisattva. In China and Japan it is often regarded mistakenly as the place where the Buddha performed asceticism after renouncing the world.

[S. III–1; Tai. 33.]

Dangi 談義 'Discussion of the principles and meanings'; exposition; lecturing.

Danna 檀那 Also 陀那; Sk. *dāna-pati*. I. A donor; one who makes a donation to the Buddha, a monk, temple, etc. II. One who bears the expense of a Buddhist service, sermon, etc.

~**-dera** --寺 'A gift temple'; originally, a temple which gives the gift of Dharma or to which one makes donations; popularly, a term for one's family temple.

Dannotsu 檀越☆ Sk. *dānapati*; translated as *seshu** 施主; a donor; cf. *danna*.

Dan'otsu 檀越 See *dannotsu*.

Danse 檀施 'Donation, charity'; *dan* is a transcription of Sk. *dāna* 'charity'. [Tai. 33.]

Danshi 彈指 See *tanji*.

Danto 檀度 Perhaps used for 檀徒, a member of a temple who makes donations to support it. [Tai. 17, 18, 36.]

Danwaku 斷惑 'Destruction of delusions'; cf. *waku*. [S. IV–1.]

Darani 陀羅尼 Sk. *dhāraṇī*; a mystic phrase, a spell; translated as *sōji** 總持.

~**-zō** ---藏 Sk. *dhāraṇī-piṭaka*, 'a collection of mystic spells', which includes esoteric texts. One of the five divisions of Buddhist scriptures; cf. *gozō*.

Daruma 達磨 I. Sk. *dharma*; see *hō*. II. Abbr. of Bodaidaruma*. [S. Vb–10; Tai. 24, 26.]

~ **sairai** --西來 'Bodhidharma's coming (to China) from the west (i.e. India)'; cf. *sairai no shūshi*. [S. Vb–10.]

~**-shū** 達磨宗 'The sect founded by Bodhidharma (Bodaidaruma*)'; the Zen* sect. [Tai. 24, 40.]

Deibutsu 泥佛 'A gilt statue of the Buddha.' [S. VII–16, 17.]

Denbō 傳法 'Transmission of the Dharma.'

~ **kanjō** --灌頂 'The Dharma-transmission *abhiṣeka* ceremony'; the secret *abhiṣeka* (*kanjō**) ceremony for conveying Mahāvairocana's Dharma to the pupil before he becomes a master of esoteric Buddhism; also called *fuhō kanjō* 付法灌頂 and *ajari kanjō* 阿闍梨灌頂. [Hei. 2.]

~ **no shi** -- の師 'A master who transmits the Dharma or law.' [S. II–8.]

Dengyō 傳教 See *Saichō*. [S. Xb–3.]

~ **Daishi** -- 大師 See *Saichō*. [Tai. 15, 18, 20.]

Denju 傳授 'Handing down (of the teaching).'

Denpō 傳法 See *denbō*.

Do 度 'Ferrying across (the sea of birth and death)'; salvation; emancipation.

Dō 堂 A temple building.

Dō 道 'Way, path, passage.' I. The path of transmigration leading from one realm to another; see *sandō* and *rokudō*. II. The path leading to enlightenment; see *hasshōdō*. III. The absolute, unhindered path, i.e. Nirvana or Enlightenment.

Dōban 幢幡 'A banner'; a kind of temple banner used as the ensign of a buddha or a bodhisattva; also used as a temple decoration.

Dōbon 道品 'The (thirty-seven) elements of the Way'; see *sanjūshichi dōbon*. [S. II–1.]

Dōbuku 道服 'Clothes for (the pursuit of) the Way'; a kind of simple robe worn by a priest. [Tai. 14.]

Dōdatsu 堂達 See *shichisō*.

Dōdōji 堂童子 'A hall-boy'; one who distributes baskets of lotus petals made of paper or leaves of *shikimi* 樒 (anise trees) at a Buddhist service. [Ma. 116.]

Dōgen 道元 The founder of the Japanese Sōtō sect (1200–1253). Son of a government minister (*naidaijin* 內大臣), Kuga Michichika 久我道親, he lost his mother when young, and entered Mt. Hiei at the age of 13 to become a novice. Later, he went to see Eisai* at the Kenninji 建仁寺 and became his disciple. After Eisai's death, he went to China with Myōzen 明全, Eisai's successor, in 1223. He attained enlightenment under the guidance of Ju-ching 如淨 (Nyojō) of the T'ien-t'ung-ssu 天童寺 (Tendōji). He returned to Japan in 1227, and lived in Kyoto for more than ten years, first in the Kenninji and later in the Kōshōji 興聖寺. In order to avoid association with secular powers, which would hinder the practice of Zen*, he retired deep into the mountains in Echizen

Province (the present Fukui Prefecture) and built a temple called Daibutsuji 大佛寺 (later changed to Eiheiji 永平寺), which became the centre of Sōtō Zen practice. In 1247, he visited Kamakura at the request of Hōjō Tokiyori 北條時賴, who offered to build a temple for him, but he declined the offer and returned to Echizen. His works include *Shōbōgenzō** 正法眼藏, 95 fasc., and *Eihei-shingi* 永平清規. His *Gakudō-yōjin-shū* 學道用心集 written in Kyoto soon after his return from China, is a useful guide to beginners. In 1854, he was posthumously given the name and title of Busshō-dentō Kokushi 佛性傳東國師, and further, in 1879, those of Jōyō Daishi 承陽大師.

Dōgo 同居　'Dwelling together'; refers to *bonshō dōgodo**. [Tai. 5.]

Dōgō 道業　'Practice of the Way'; practice for attaining enlightenment. [S. IV–9, Va–3, VIII–23.]

Dōgyō 同行　'A fellow-practitioner.'

Dōgyō 道行　'The practice of the Way.' I. Buddhist practices. II. The wisdom of enlightenment and practices. [Tai. 25.]

Dōhō 同法　'The same teaching'; the same method of salvation; also, those who practise the same method of salvation.

Dōji 同事　'Sharing a task; doing the same thing together'; one of the four methods employed by bodhisattvas to approach and convert people; see *shishōbō*. [S. VI–6.]

Dōjō 道場☆　A place where the Buddha is worshipped and the Buddhist Way is practised.

Dōjō itchi 動靜一致　'Harmony between activity and stillness'; said of the ideal state of mind in which mental activities are in perfect accord with, or supported by, tranquillity; a state of balance between physical acts and inner tranquillity. [S. IV–1.]

Dōju 堂衆　See *dōshu*.

Dōka 道果　'The fruition of the Buddhist Way'; Nirvana. [S. II–1.]

Dokkaku sen(nin) 獨覺仙(人)　'Self-enlightened hermit'; n. of a hermit who was a previous incarnation of the Buddha; see *Ikkaku sennin* 一角仙人.

Dokko 獨古　See next entry. [S. Xb–3.]

Dokko 獨鈷 (also 獨股)　A single *vajra* (*kongōsho** 金剛杵) used in esoteric Buddhism; also, *tokko, toko*. It is a bar made mainly of iron and copper, with both ends shaped like a spear-head. [Ma. 23.]

Dokku 毒鼓 'A poison-drum'; a drum which, being daubed with poison, can kill anyone who hears its sound. In the *Nehan-gyō**, it is used as a metaphor to show that the teaching explaining the eternal presence of buddha-nature 'kills' evil beings and converts them to Buddhism. [S. II–10.]

Dokkyō 讀經 See *dokyō*.

Dokuku 毒鼓 See *dokku*.

Dokuru shikyō shijū hyakusai 特留此經止住百歲 'I (i.e. the Buddha) will especially keep this sutra for 100 years.' A passage from the *Muryōju-kyō**, where the Buddha states that, after the destruction of Buddhist teachings in the future, he will keep only this sutra in the world for another 100 years. [S. II–8.]

Dokushi 讀師 Also *tokuji*. See *shichisō*.

Dokuson 特尊 (=獨尊) 'The most revered one', i.e. the Buddha. [S. III–1.]

Dokyō 讀經 Commonly, *dokkyō*; 'chanting a sutra'.

Dōnen 道念 'Thought of the Way'; aspiration for the Buddhist Way or enlightenment.

Dōnin 道人 'One who walks the Buddhist Way'; one who has attained enlightenment. [S. III–3, IV–9, Vb–11.]

Donran 曇鸞 Ch. T'an-luan (476–542); the first of the five Pure Land masters (*Jōdo goso** 淨土五祖) and the third of the seven patriarchs in the tradition of the Jōdoshin sect (*shichi-kōsō** 七高僧). He first studied the four-discourse teaching (Shironshū* 四論宗) and became conversant with the philosophy of the void. Later, he sought the Taoist way of longevity and received Taoist scriptures from T'ao Hung-ching 陶弘景 (Tō Kōkei). When he met Bodhiruci (Bodairushi 菩提流支) in Lo-yang and received from him the *Kanmuryōju-kyō**, he burnt the Taoist texts and was converted to Pure Land Buddhism. His *Ōjō-ronchū** is a Pure Land classic providing a basis for the doctrinal systems of Tao-ch'o (Dōshaku*), Shan-tao (Zendō*), Shinran* and others. [S. II–8, Xa–1.]

~ **no chū** --の註 'T'an-luan's commentary' on the *Jōdo-ron** 淨土論 by Vasubandhu. See *Ōjō-ronchū**. [S. II–8.]

Dōrin 道林 Ch. Tao-lin (741–824); the eighth in the lineage of the Niu-t'ou 牛頭 (Gozu) school of Zen*; as he lived in the branches of a pine tree in the precincts of a temple, he was popularly called Master Bird's Nest 鳥窠禪師 (Chōka* Zenji). [S. Va–5.]

Doryō 度量 See *takuryō*.

Dōsen 道宣 Ch. Tao-hsüan (596–667); the founder of the Nan-shan 南山 (Nanzan) school of the Lü (Ritsu*) sect in China. He assisted Hsüan-chuang (Genjō*) in translating volumes of precept texts and biographies of monks. As he lived in earlier days at a temple on Mt. Chung-nan 終南 (Shūnan), he was popularly called Precept Master of Nan-shan 南山律師 (Nanzan Risshi) or Great Master of Nan-shan 南山大師 (Nanzan Daishi*). [Tai. 8.]

Dōsha 堂舍 'A Buddha hall and a monks' residence'; a general term for temple buildings.

Dōsha 道者 'A practitioner of the Buddhist Way.' [Tai. 5.]

Dōshaku 道綽 Ch. Tao-ch'o (562–645); the second of the five Chinese Pure Land masters (*Jōdo goso* 淨土五祖) and the fourth of the seven patriarchs in the tradition of the Jōdoshin* sect (*shichi-kōsō* 七高僧). He entered the priesthood at 14 and became well-versed in the *Nirvana Sutra* (*Nehan-gyō*). At 40, when he visited Hsüan-chung-ssu 玄中寺 (Genchūji) and read an inscription in praise of T'an-luan 曇鸞 (Donran*), he became an aspirant to the Pure Land. He stayed at the temple and practised the *nenbutsu** as many as 70,000 times a day. He lectured on the *Kanmuryōju-kyō** more than 200 times, and propagated the Pure Land teaching extensively. He wrote a 2-fasc. work, *Anraku-shū** 安樂集.

Dōshi 導師 I. A spiritual leader. II. The chief priest who conducts a Buddhist service.

Dōshin 道心 'Aspiration for the Way', i.e. for enlightenment; desire to attain Bodhi; Bodhi-mind.

~**-ja** --者 See *dōshinsha*.

~ **kengo** --堅固 'The firm Bodhi-mind'; unshakable determination to attain enlightenment. [K. 57; Tai. 13, 37.]

~**-sha** --者 'One who has an aspiration for the Way'; one who aspires to enlightenment. [S. Xa–10, Xb–3.]

~ **zuku** --づく 'The aspiration for Bodhi arises.' [O.V.]

Doshō 度生 'Saving living beings.'

Dōshu 堂衆 I. A priest who was formerly a personal attendant of a scholar-priest. [S. III–5.] II. A priest of a lower rank in the Tendai* sect engaged in miscellaneous works at a temple, especially at one of the three main halls on Mt. Hiei. III. In the Jōdoshin* sect, an assistant priest of the head temple who performs services.

Dōshuchi 道種智 See *sanchi*.

Dōsō 堂僧 'A priest (who works as the keeper) of a Buddhist hall.' [S. Xb–2; Tsu. 238.]

Dōtai muen no jihi 同體無緣の慈悲 The compassion originating from the insight of seeing the ultimate identity between oneself and other beings and of realizing the non-substantiality of living beings; cf. *san'en no jihi*. [S. I–3.]

Dōzoku 道俗 Priests and laymen.

~ **nannyo** --男女 'Priests and laymen, both men and women.'

E

E 會 'To gather; to understand.' I. A gathering; a congregation. II. A special service or lecture-meeting, e.g. *Nehan-e*, *Yuima-e* and *Saishō-e*. III. An assembly of practitioners under a specific master. IV. Understanding.

Echū 會中 'In the assembly'; among those in the assembly. [Tai. 24.]

Edo 穢土 'Defiled land'; refers to this world, which is defiled by evil passions, as opposed to *Jōdo** 淨土 'the Pure Land'.

Ehatsu 衣鉢 Also *ehachi* and *ihatsu*; 'a robe and bowl'; Sk. *pātra-cīvara*; abbr. of *sanne ippatsu**. Symbolically, the essence of Buddhism to be transmitted from master to disciple. [S. VI–18, Xa–6; Tai. 26.]

Ehō 依報 'Dependent reward'; the part of the reward on which one's existence depends; the secondary and circumstantial part of the reward which one receives in this life as the result of acts in previous lives, such as house, utensils and surroundings; the term is contrasted with *shōbō** 正報. [S. Va–5.]

Eigō 永劫 See *yōgō*.

Eikan 永觀 See *Yōkan*.

Eisai 榮西 Also Yōsai; the founder of the Japanese Zen* sect (1141–1215). Ordained at 14, he studied and practised the Tendai* teaching. He went to Sung China in 1168 and brought back Tendai scriptures in the same year. In 1187, he travelled to China again, where he received the Rinzai Zen tradition from Hsü-an Huai-ch'ang 虛庵懷敞 (Koan Eshō). After returning home in 1191, he built the Shōfukuji 聖福寺, the first Zen temple in Japan. In the face of bitter attacks from Tendai monks on this newly introduced sect, Eisai approached the Kamakura Shogunate, the government of the time. In 1202, the government built the Kenninji 建仁寺 in Kyoto, and appointed him as the first chief abbot. In order to appease the monks of Mt. Hiei, the temple was made a centre of Tendai and esoteric Buddhism as well as Zen. In 1215, he founded the Jufukuji 壽福寺 in Kamakura, and died in the same year. He introduced the cultivation of tea into Japan, and wrote a book, entitled *Kissa-yōjō-ki* 喫茶養生記 '*A Record of Drinking Tea and Nourishing the Spirit*'. His other works include *Kōzen-gokoku-ron** 興禪護國論 '*Discourse on the Propagation of Zen and the Protection of the State*', which is the first Zen work in Japan. He was given the posthumous title of Senkō Kokushi 千光國師. [S. Xb–3.]

Ekan 懷感 Ch. Huai-kan (7th to 8th centuries); one of the disciples of Shan-tao 善導 (Zendō*) and the author of the *Gungi-ron** 群疑論. At first he studied the Hossō* teaching, and later took refuge in Amida* through the guidance of Shan-tao. He is said to have accomplished the Nenbutsu Samādhi (*nenbutsu-zanmai**).

Eken no mono 壞見の者 'One who rejects the (right) view.' [S. II–10.]

Ekō 廻向 (also 回向) I. To transfer one's merit to another. II. To transfer one's merit to buddhahood in order to attain it. [S. II–7.] III. To transfer the merit of chanting of a sutra, etc., to a dead man so that he may rest in peace and happiness. [K. 680.] IV. To transfer one's merit to the attainment of birth in Amida's* land. V. Refers to *ekōmon**. [Ma. 263.]

~-mon --文 I. A verse expressing the intention of transferring one's merit to other beings so that they too may attain buddhahood. II. A passage glorifying the virtue of a buddha, etc.

waka o ~ 和歌を-- 'To write a *waka* as an offering to the Buddha.' [K. 194.]

Ekō 壞劫 'The *kalpa* of destruction'; one of the four periods of cosmic change. See *shikō*.

Ekō hōtō 慧光法燈 'The light of wisdom and the lamp of the Dharma.' [Tai. 5.]

Ekoku 穢國 'The defiled land'; refers to this world, defiled by evil passions; opposite of *Jōdo**, the Pure Land. [IH.]

Emon 慧文 Ch. Hui-wen; a monk who lived during the Northern and Southern dynasty (420–589). He especially studied the works of Nāgārjuna (Ryūju*) and attained enlightenment. His thought was transmitted to Hui-ssu (Eshi*), thereby opening up the way to the founding of the T'ien-t'ai (Tendai*) sect by the Master T'ien-t'ai (Tendai Daishi*).

Emyō 慧命 'Wisdom-life'; the secret knowledge of Buddhism.

~ o tsugu --をつぐ To inherit the secret knowledge of Buddhism. [S. II–5.]

En 緣 I. Condition; indirect cause. II. An object of perception. III. Tie or relationship with other persons or worldly affairs.

~ naki shujō -なき衆生 'Those beings who have no relationship' with salvation through a buddha or bodhisattva. [S. II–5.]

Enbu 閻浮 Refers to *enbudai**. [Tai. 2.]

~-dai --提 Sk. Jambudvīpa or Jambūdvīpa; in the Buddhist cosmology, the continent situated to the south of Mt. Sumeru (Shumisen*). This is a triangular island inhabited by ordinary human beings. The name derives from *jambu* (mango) because this continent produces a good deal of the fruit. Cf. *shishū*. [Hei. 2; K. 53; S. IV–1.]

~-dangon --檀金 Sk. *jambū-nada-suvarṇa*; the purplish gold said to be obtained from the river running through the mango (*jambu*) forest in the Jambudvīpa (Enbudai*) continent. [Hei. 2.]

Enchin 圓珍 The fifth *zasu** of the Enryakuji* on Mt. Hiei (814–891). He went to China in 853 and returned in 858. He was appointed *bettō** of the Onjōji*, the name of which was then changed to Mii-dera. A great Tendai* scholar, he left works in more than 100 fasc. [Tai. 15.]

Enchō 圓頂 'A round head'; a shaven head. [Tai. 39.]

Endon 圓頓 'The perfect and sudden (teaching)'; refers to the Tendai* teaching because it is regarded as the perfect Mahayana teaching which enables one to attain enlightenment very quickly. [S. Xb–3; Tai. 17.]

~ no gakusha --の學者 'One who studies the perfect and sudden (Tendai teaching).' [S. V–1.]

~ no gegyō --の解行 'Understanding and practice of the perfect and sudden (Tendai teaching).' [S. Va–1.]

~ no kyōbō --の教法 'The doctrine of the perfect and sudden (Tendai teaching).' [S. Va–2.]

~ shikan --止觀 'Perfect and sudden *shikan** meditation'; the practice of meditation which directly aims at realizing the ultimate reality; also *maka shikan* 摩訶止觀; one of the three kinds of *shikan* (*sanshu shikan**). [S. Va–1.]

Engaku 圓覺 'Perfect enlightenment'; refers to the *Engaku-kyō**. [S. IV–1, Vb–10.]

~-kyō --經 '*The Perfect Enlightenment Sutra*'; abbr. of *Daihōkō-engaku-shutara-ryōgi-kyō* 大方廣圓覺修多羅了義經; 1 fasc.; said to have been translated into Chinese by Buddhatāra (Buddatara 佛陀多羅) in 693 [TT. 17, No. 842]. In this sutra the Buddha expounded the principle of perfect enlightenment to 12 bodhisattvas, such as Monju* and Fugen*. [S. I–9,IV–1; Tai. 24.]

~ no jūni no bosatsu --の十二の菩薩 'The 12 bodhisattvas mentioned in the *Engaku-kyō*': Monju* 文殊, Fugen* 普賢, Fugen 普眼, Kongōzō 金剛藏, Miroku* 彌勒, Shōjōe 清淨慧, Itokujizai 威德自在, Bennon 辨音, Jōshogosshō 淨諸業障, Fukaku 普覺, Engaku 圓覺, and Kenzenshu 賢善首. [S. Vb–10.]

Engaku 緣覺 Sk. *pratyekabuddha*; one of the two kinds of Hinayana sages, the other being *shōmon**; also *byakushibutsu* 辟支佛 and *dokkaku* 獨覺. An *engaku* attains emancipation without a teacher's guidance by observing the principle of 12 causations (*jūni-innen**).

Engi 緣起 Sk. *pratītya-samutpāda*; coming into existence by depending on other things; dependent origination. [S. I–3.]

~ **no kesō** --の假相 'Temporary appearances of things which have come into existence through dependent origination.' [S. Xb–1.]

Engyō 圓敎 'The perfect teaching.' I. In Tendai*, the last of the four doctrinal teachings of the Buddha, which represents the ultimate teaching of Mahayana; the teaching of the *Hoke-kyō**, *Nehan-gyō**, etc., which shows that phenomenal things are themselves absolute reality; see *kehō no shikyō*. [S. Va–6.] II. In Kegon*, the last of the five teachings, which expounds the principle of interpenetration between existing things; see *gokyō*.

En'in 緣因 'An assisting cause'; refers to *en'in busshō* 緣因佛性; see *sanshin busshō* and *san'in busshō*. [S. Va–4.]

Enjō 圓成 'Perfect accomplishment'; refers to *enjō jisshō**. [S. III –1.]

~**-jisshō** --實性 Sk. *pariniṣpanna-svabhāva*, 'the nature (of existence) being perfectly accomplished'; said of the highest state of existence conforming to the ultimate reality. Cf. *sanshō*. [S. III–1.]

Enjudō 延壽堂 'A hall for lengthening one's life'; also *nehandō** 涅槃堂, *anrakudō* 安樂堂, etc.; a room for sick monks; also, a crematorium.

Enku 厭苦 'Disgust with the sufferings' of the world.

Enma 閻魔 Also, 炎魔, 琰魔; Sk. Yama; the lord of the realm of the dead.

~**-gū** 炎魔宮 'Yama's palace.' [K. 72.]

~ **hōō no chōtei** 炎魔法皇の廳庭 'The court of Yama, the Lord of the Law.' [K. 557.]

~ **no chō** 焰魔の廳 'Yama's court' where the merits and sins of the dead are judged and sentences are passed on them.   [K. 56.]

~ **Ō** 閻魔王 'King Yama.' [K. 56, 459; S. II-5.]

~ **ōgū** 炎魔王宮 'The palace of King Yama.' [K. 56; S. II-6; Tai. 26.]

~ **ōkai** 炎魔王界 'King Yama's realm.' [S. III-2, VII-7.]

~ **tengu** 炎魔天供 'The ritual for the god Yama' performed to cure illnesses, stop calamities, attain longevity, etc. [S. II-5.]

Enmu 縁務 '(Secular) relations and duties'; secular matters. According to the *Makashikan**, there are four kinds of secular matters which hinder concentration on meditation: (1) *seikatsu* 生活, one's livelihood; (2) *jinji* 人事, personal relationships; (3) *ginō* 伎能, skill in the arts; and (4) *gakumon* 學問, learning. [S. VI-10.]

Ennichi 縁日 Abbr. of *uennichi* 有縁日; the day of close relationship with a particular buddha or deity: e.g. Amida's* *ennichi* is the 15th and Kannon's* the 18th. [K. 711.]

Ennin 圓仁 The third *zasu** of the Enryakuji* on Mt. Hiei (794–864). He became Saichō's* disciple at 15, and went to China in 838, where he studied esoteric Buddhism, the T'ien-t'ai (Tendai*) teaching and Sanskrit. He returned home in 848, and was appointed *zasu* in 854. With his introduction of esoteric Buddhism, the Tendai teaching became largely esoteric. He also built the Monjudō 文殊堂 on Mt. Hiei for the continual practice of the *nenbutsu**. He wrote many works in about 100 fasc., including commentaries on the *Kongōchō-kyō** and *Soshitsuji-kyō**. The record of his travel to China, *Nittō-guhō-junrei-gyōki* 入唐求法巡禮行記, is a useful source of information about T'ang China. He was posthumously given the name and title of Jikaku Daishi 慈覺大師.

En-no-gyōja 役行者 'The ascetic En'; see *En-no-Ozunu.* [K. 36.]

En-no-Ozunu 役小角 The founder of the Shugendō* school. Popularly called En-no-gyōja 役行者, En-no-ubasoku*, etc., he is said to have been born in 634. From the age of 32, he practised esoteric Buddhism on Mt. Katsuragi 葛城 for more than 30 years until he attained miraculous powers. He laid the foundations of esoteric mountain Buddhism by opening up sacred mountains such as Mt. Kinbu 金峰 and Mt. Ōmine 大峰. He was exiled to one of the Izu Islands in 699, and pardoned two years later, but it is not known how he spent the last years of his life.

En-no-ubasoku 役優婆塞 'Upāsaka En'; see *En-no-Ozunu*. [Tai. 26.]

Ennyadatta 演若達多 Sk. Yajñadatta, 'given by a sacrificial rite'; also 延若達多 and Yanyadatta 耶若達多; translated as Shiju 祠授; used as the name of a person born as the result of a prayer to a god; commonly, used as the name of a person in exemplary stories. [S. Xb–2.]

Enō 慧能 Ch. Hui-neng (638–713); the sixth patriarch of the Chinese Ch'an (Zen*) sect. Born in a poor family, he supported his mother and himself by selling fire-wood. One day, when he heard the *Kongō-kyō** being chanted, he aspired to the Buddhist Way. At 24, he went to see Hung-jen 弘忍 (Kōnin), the fifth patriarch, and lived in his monastery for some time. After he received the transmission of the Dharma, he left the monastery. Later his line of transmission, which was characterized by sudden enlighten-ment (*tongo* 頓悟) and thrived in south China, came to be known as the Southern School of Ch'an (Nanshū-zen 南宗禪). This was in contrast to the teaching of gradual enlightenment (*zengo* 漸悟) which was started by another disciple of Hung-jen, Shen-hsiu 神秀 (Jinshū), and was called the Northern School of Ch'an (Hokushū-zen 北宗禪). Hui-neng's line of transmission enjoyed greater popularity, and developed into five schools (*goke** 五家). His sayings were compiled into the *Rokuso-dankyō* 六祖檀經 (*The Sixth Patriarch's Platform Sutra*). He was given posthumous titles, such as Ch'an Master Ta-chien 大鑑禪師 (Daikan Zenji).

En'ō no sen 閻王の宣 'Declaration of King Yama'; cf. *Enma*. [K. 56.]

Enri 厭離 See *onri*.

~ edo --穢土 See *onri edo*.

Enryakuji 延暦寺 The head temple of the Tendai* sect on Mt. Hiei. The origin of the temple dates back to 785, when Saichō* built a hut on Mt. Hiei to study and practise Buddhism. Three years later, it was converted into a temple, called Hieizanji 比叡山寺 (later, changed to Ichijōshikan'in 一乗止觀院; the present Konponchūdō 根本中堂). In 823, by imperial order, the temple was named Enryakuji ('Enryaku' was the name of the era in which Saichō founded the temple). In 824, Gishin 義眞 was appointed its first *zasu**. New buildings were erected by him and his successors, until the total number of buildings exceeded 3,000. At the time of the fifth *zasu*, Enchin*, an internal conflict led him and his followers to leave the mountain and live in the Onjōji* (858). The Enryakuji then came to be known also as *sanmon** 山門 'the mountain school' to distinguish it from the Onjōji, which was called *jimon** 寺門 'the temple school'. Monks of the two temples were often involved in fighting each other, and the number of armed monks increased rapidly. The Enryakuji monks also ran riot in the streets of Kyoto when their demands were not met. In 1571, Oda Nobunaga sent his army to attack them, and burnt down almost all the buildings. The temple was restored later, in the Edo period (1603–1867).

Enshū 圓宗 'The round sect(s)'; the perfect teaching sect(s); ordinarily refers to the Tendai* and Kegon* sects, but here to the former. [Tai. 15, 18.]

~ **kenmitsu** --顯密 'The perfect teaching (which embodies) both the exoteric and esoteric (teachings)'; refers to the Tendai* teaching which embraces both these types. [Tai. 27.]

Entsū 圓通 Also *enzū*; 'perfect penetration.' I. Said of the ultimate essence of existence or the ultimate principle, which completely penetrates all existing things. II. Said of the wisdom of enlightenment, which penetrates to the ultimate essence of existence.

~ **Daiji** --大士 Also Enzū Daishi; 'the Great Being of Perfect Penetration'; another name for Kannon*; 'Perfect Penetration' refers to the wisdom of enlightenment which penetrates to the ultimate essence of existence; 'Daiji' is another name for a bodhisattva. [Tai. 16.]

En'yū 圓融 Pronounced *ennyū*; 'perfect and fused together'; said of the reality-principle established in the Tendai* and Kegon* sects that all existences are in themselves perfect and interfused. [S. Vb–11.]

~ **nenbutsu** --念佛 The *nenbutsu** practised in such a way that the merit of one's practice pervades others and theirs pervades oneself. [K. 53.]

Enza 宴坐 Sitting in meditation. [K. 64.]

Enza 圓座 A cushion made of a coil of plaited straw, etc. [K. 64.]

Enzu 緣ず To take something as an object of perception; to perceive; cf. *en*.

Eon 慧遠 Ch. Hui-yüan. I. Hui-yüan of Mt. Lu 廬山 (334–416); see *Rozan no Eon*. II. Hui-yüan of the Ching-ying-ssu 淨影寺 (523–592); the author of more than 50 works.

Eri 會離 Refers to *onzōeku* 怨憎會苦 'the pain of meeting those one hates' and *aibetsuriku* 愛別離苦 'the pain of separating from those one loves'; two of the eight pains (*hakku**). [S. IV–9.]

Esen 依詮 'Depending on verbal explanation'; refers to *esen danshi**. [S. Xb–2.]

~ **danshi** --談旨 'Explaining the tenet (of the reality-principle) by resorting to verbal explanations'; cf. *haisen danshi*.

Eshajōri 會者定離 'Those who meet must part.' [K. 470; Tai. 20.]

Eshi 慧思 Ch. Hui-ssu (515–577); the second patriarch of the Chinese T'ien-t'ai (Tendai*) sect; also called the Great Master Nan-yüeh 南嶽大師 (Nangaku Daishi) because he lived on Mt. Nan-yüeh.

Eshin 依身 'The body on which one depends'; so described because one's existence depends on it and because one's sense organs lie within it. [IH.]

Eshin 廻心 'To turn one's thought (towards a Buddhist end).' I. Refers to *eshin sange* 廻心懺悔 'to turn one's thought (towards goodness) and repent (one's evil acts)'. II. Refers to *eshō kōdai* 廻小向大 'to turn from Hinayana towards Mahayana'; converting from Hinayana to Mahayana. III. In the Jōdoshin* sect, converting from a self-power (*jiriki**) teaching to the other-power (*tariki**) teaching; giving up an attachment to one's self-power and attaining absolute faith in Amida's* salvation.

Eshin Sōzu 惠心僧都 See *Genshin*. [S. Va–11.]

Eshō 依正 Refers to *ehō** 依報 and *shohō** 正報; respectively, the dependent or secondary result and the primary result of past karma; one's environment and one's mind and body. [S. I–3, IV–1, Va–6, Xb–1.]

Esu 廻す 'To turn (one's thought, etc.) towards (a Buddhist end, etc.)'; cf. *ekō* and *eshin*.

Esu 會す I. To understand. II. To harmonize apparently contradictory statements in the scriptures.

Eta 依他 'Depending on other things'; refers to *etakishō**. [S. III–1.]

~-**kishō** --起性 Sk. *paratantra-svabhāva*, 'the nature (of existence) arising from dependence on other things'; said of the existences arising from causes and conditions. Cf. *sanshō* 三性.

Eza 會座 'Place of assembly, meeting-place, congregation.'

F

Fuchisoku 不知足 'Not knowing contentment.' [S. IV–9, Xa–4.]

Fuchūtō-kai 不偸盗戒 'The precept that one should not steal'; one of the five precepts (*gokai**), the eight precepts (*hassaikai**), and the ten precepts (*jikkai**). [S. III–7.]

Fudankyō 不斷經 'Continuous chanting of a sutra', performed for a fixed period by a number of priests. [Ma. 160.]

Fudan nyohōkyō 不斷如法經 'Continuous (copying of the *Hokekyō*) sutra according to the law' during a fixed period of time, e.g. one, two or three weeks, to pray for the repose of the souls of dead persons, etc.; cf. *nyohōkyō*. [Tai. 11.]

Fudaraku nōke no shu 補墮落能化の主 'The Lord Saviour of Mt. Potalaka'; refers to Kannon*. [Hei. 2.]

Fudarakusen 補陀落山 'Mt. Potalaka'; also 補陀樂山, 補墮落山, etc., and translated as Kōmyōzan 光明山, Kaichōzan 海鳥山, etc. The mountain on the south coast of India, where Kannon* is believed to be dwelling. [S. II–5; Tai. 18.]

Fudō 不動 'Immovable'; Sk. Acalanātha, or simply Acala; the most important and popular *myōō** 明王 (*vidyā-rāja*) or fierce spirit. He is a messenger of Dainichi*, and assumes a frightful

form, holding a sword in his right hand and a rope in his left.
See *godai-myōō*.

~ **goma** --護摩 The ritual of 'offering fire to Fudō'. [K. 52.]

~ **jiku enmei no hō** --慈救延命の法 The ritual dedicated to
Fudō in which the *jikuju** is recited and a prayer is offered to
him to extend one's life-span. [Tai. 33.]

~ **kuyōhō** --供養法 'The ritual of offering (fire *goma**) to Fudō.'
[K. 52.]

~ **Myōō** --明王 'The fierce spirit Fudō.'

~ **no ken** --の剣 The sword held in the right hand of Fudō,
which cuts evil passions and destroys devils. [S. II-7.]

~-**son** --尊 'The revered Fudō.'

~-**son shisha** --尊仕者 A boy-servant sent by the deity Fudō to
serve a Shingon* practitioner. [K. 52.]

Fugen 普賢 N. of a bodhisattva; Sk. Samantabhadra. He represents the intrinsic principle (*ri* 理), meditation (*jō* 定), and
practice (*gyō* 行) of all buddhas, as contrasted with Monju* who
represents wisdom (*chi* 智) and realization (*shō* 證). He is the
right-hand attendant of Shakamuni* Buddha, and is often
portrayed mounted on a white elephant. [S. Vb-10; Tai. 18.]

~ **enmei** --延命 Refers to *Fugen enmei-hō**. [Hei. 3; Tai. 1.]

~ **enmei-hō** --延命法 'The Samantabhadra rite for longevity';
the ritual performed for the Twenty-armed Samantabhadra
(Fugen*) Bodhisattva to pray for a long life; one of the four great
rituals of the Mountain School of Tendai* (*sanmon shika-daihō**).

~ **jūgan** --十願 I. 'The ten vows of Fugen Bodhisattva'. II.
Refers to 'Fugen-gyōgan-bon' 普賢行願品 'Chapter on Fugen's
Practice and Vows' of the *Kegon-gyō**, in which the ten vows
appear. [Ma. 198.]

~ **no jūgan** --の十願 See *Fugen jūgan*. [S. III-1.]

Fugenka 不還果 Sk. *anāgāmi-phala*, 'the fruit of not returning',
attained by destroying subtle evil passions; the third of the four
stages of sainthood in Hinayana. One who has attained this stage
is no longer subject to rebirth in the realm of desire (*shikikai**);
hence, 'not returning'; cf. *shika*.

Fugen shikishin 普現色身 'Manifesting physical forms everywhere.'

[S. I–3.]

Fugyō 不輕 Abbr. of Jōfugyō*; n. of a bodhisattva. [S. II–10.]

~ **Bosatsu** --菩薩 'Fugyō Bodhisattva'; see Jōfugyō. [Tai. 39.]

~ **kyōki no shujō** --輕毀の衆生 Those who despised and harmed Jōfugyō Bodhisattva. [S. II–10.]

Fuhō kanjō 付法灌頂 'The Dharma-transmission *abhiṣeka* ceremony'; see *denbō kanjō*.

Fuhōzō 付法藏 'Transmission of the Dharma-store'; transmission of the Buddhist teaching. [S. IV–1.]

~ **no sanzō** ---の三藏 One who is well-versed in all the three divisions of the Buddhist teaching (*sanzō**) and is entrusted with the transmission of the Dharma. [S. VIII–23.]

~ **no soshi** ---の祖師 'Masters who transmit the Buddhist teaching.' [S. IV–1.]

Fujain-kai 不邪婬戒 'The precept that one should not commit adultery'; one of the five precepts (*gokai**), the eight precepts (*hassaikai**), and the ten precepts (*jikkai**). [S. III–7.]

Fujikan 布字觀 A meditation in which one places Sanskrit letters, such as 'A', on various parts of the body and impresses the body with the significance of these letters. [K. 64.]

Fujōju 不定聚 'Those who are not certain.' I. Those whose destinies are not certain; one of the three kinds of people distinguished according to the three different spiritual capacities; cf. *sanjōju*. II. In the Jōdoshin* sect, those who practise the *nenbutsu** with self-power in compliance with the Twentieth Vow and, consequently, will be born into temporary regions of the Pure Land.; cf. *jajōju* and *shōjōju*.

Fujōkan 不淨觀 'Contemplation on the impurity' of one's body; this is practised to remove one's evil passions and false desires; see *gojōshinkan*. [IH.]

Fujō no ningen 不定の人間 'Uncertain (life of) man'; man's life may end at any time. [Tai. 18.]

Fukaku 不覺 'Unenlightened, ignorant.'

Fukō sekai 浮香世界 A mistake for *Shukō sekai** 衆香世界. [Tai. 39.]

Fukū 不空   The popular name for Fukūkongō 不空金剛 (705–74);
Sk. Amoghavajra; the sixth patriarch of the Chen-yen (Shingon*)
tradition, he was born in north India or, according to other
traditions, Sri Lanka, and, at the age of 14, travelled to Java,
where he met Vajrabodhi (金剛智 Kongōchi) and became his
disciple. He went to China with the master in 720, and assisted
him in the translation of esoteric texts while studying esoteric
Buddhism under him. After the master's death, he went to India
to obtain Sanskrit texts. He returned to China in 746, and engaged
in translating esoteric texts and spreading esoteric Buddhism. He
was well received by the emperors, and was given the title Kuang-
chih San-tsang 廣智三藏 (Kōchi Sanzō) by Emperor Tai-tsung
代宗 (Daisō) in 765. Works he translated number 110. [Tai. 29.]

Fukubun 福分   Accumulated merit which brings about happiness
in the world. [S. I–7.]

Fukuchi 福智   'Merit and wisdom.'

∼ **no nihō** --の二報   'The two rewards of (outstanding) merit
and wisdom.' [Tai. 24.]

Fukuden 福田   'A field of merit'; Sk. *puṇya-kṣetra*. I. Refers to a
buddha or monk, because merit accrues to a person who makes
offerings to him, just as a field yields crops. Cf. *sanfukuden*. II.
Refers to the three treasures (*sanbō**), i.e. Buddha, Dharma and
Sangha.

Fukugō 福業   'Meritorious acts'; acts which produce merit and
happiness. [S. II–10, VI–17.]

Fukūjōju 不空成就   'Non-fruitless accomplishment'; Sk. Amoghasiddhi; n. of a buddha in the north. In esoteric Buddhism, one of
the five buddhas (*gobutsu**) of the Diamond-Realm Mandala
(*Kongōkai mandara**); cf. *gochi nyorai*.

Fukūkensaku Kannon 不空羂索觀音   Also Fukūkenjaku Kannon;
'the Avalokiteśvara of the Unfailing Fishing Line'; Sk. Amogha-
pāśa-avalokiteśvara; one of the six kinds of Kannon (*rokkannon**).
He carries a fishing line with which to bring people safely to the
bank of enlightenment. [O. V.]

Fukūkensaku-kyō 不空羂索經   Also *Fukūkenjaku-kyō*; '*The Unfailing Fishing Line Sutra*'; a short title for *Fukūkensaku-jinpen-
shingon-gyō* 不空羂索神變眞言經; 30 fasc., tr. by Bodhiruci

(Bodairushi 菩提流志) [TT. 20, No. 1092]. This sutra expounds the spells, method of recitation, mandala, merit, etc., of Fukūkensaku Kannon*. [O. V.]

Fukūkensaku nijūshichikan gyō 不空羂索廿七卷經　Also *Fukūkenjaku...*; '*the 27-fascicle Unfailing Fishing Line Sutra*'; refers to the *Fukūkensaku-kyō**. [S. II–8.]

Fukuriki 福力　'Power of merit and wealth.' [S. IX–4.]

Fukusha 福舍　'A house of merit'; may be used to refer to a temple. [S. II–5.]

Fukyō 不輕　See *Fugyō*.

Fumōgo-kai 不妄語戒　'The precept that one should not lie'; one of the five precepts (*gokai**), the eight precepts (*hassaikai**), and the ten precepts (*jikkai**). [S. III–7.]

Fumon-bon 普門品　'Chapter on the Universal Gate'; the twenty-fifth chapter of the *Hoke-kyō**, in which Kannon's* compassionate salvation is fully expounded; also called *Kannon-gyō**. [Tai. 13, 20.]

Funbetsu 分別　'Discrimination.'

~ **ketaku** --計度　'Discrimination and calculation'; thinking with discrimination. [S. IV–1.]

~ **mōryo** --妄慮　'Discrimination and delusory thoughts.' [S. IV–9.]

~ **takuryō** --度量　'Discriminating and calculating'; often used in the sense of delusory thinking. [S. Xb–2.]

Funi ittai 不二一體　'Non-duality and oneness.'

Funnu 忿怒　'Enraged, angered'; cf. *daisei funnu no katachi*.

~ **no akugen** --の惡眼　See *daisei funnu no akugen*. [Tai. 23.]

Fuonju-kai 不飲酒戒　'The precept that one should not drink intoxicants'; one of the five precepts (*gokai**), the eight precepts (*hassaikai**), and the ten precepts (*jikkai**). [S. III–7.]

Furitsu kenjō 扶律顯常　Pronounced *buritsu kenjō*; also *furitsu* (or *buritsu*) *danjō* 扶律談常; 'supporting precepts and expounding the eternal'; said of the teaching of the *Nehan-gyō**, which exhorts people not to break precepts and expounds the eternal presence of buddha-nature. [S. IV–1.]

Furuna 富楼那　Sk. Pūrṇa or Pūrṇa-maitrāyanīputra; one of the ten great disciples of the Buddha, renowned for his eloquence.

~ **no benzetsu** ---の辯説 'The eloquence of Pūrṇa.' [K. 431; Tai. 23, 24, 36.]

~ **Sonja** ---尊者 'The Venerable Pūrṇa or Pūrṇa-maitrāyanī-putra.' [Tai. 39.]

Furyōgi 不了義 'Not revealing the (whole) meaning (of the Buddhist law)'; the opposite of *ryōgi**.

Furyō no mōnen 不了の妄念 'Delusory thoughts which do not realize (reality).' [S. IV–9.]

Furyū monji 不立文字 'Not establishing words'; said of the mind-to-mind transmission of the Zen* spirit beyond the range of words. [S. IV–1.]

~ **no shū** ----の宗 'The sect which does not establish words'; the Zen* sect. [S. IV–1, Vb–10.]

Fusatsu 布薩 Sk. *upavasatha*, Pali *uposatha*; a regular meeting of monks and other members of the order held twice a month, i.e. on the 15th and 30th of the lunar month, at which precepts are read out and any transgressions repented. [S. IV–1, Xb–1.]

Fuse 布施 'Gift,' whether in cash or goods, to a person, esp. a priest; Sk. *dāna*.

Fusemotsu 布施物 'That which is donated (to a priest or temple)'; a donation. [S. VI–16.]

Fusesshō-kai 不殺生戒 'The precept that one should not kill living things'; one of the five precepts (*gokai**), the eight precepts (*hassaikai**), and the ten precepts (*jikkai**). [S. III–7.]

Fushin 普請 Pronounced *fushō*; 'universal request'; originally, in Zen*, having monks undertake labour service at a temple; used for holding a Buddhist service. [Tai. 36.]

Fushō 不生 I. 'Not arising'; said of phenomenal existences which appear to exist but, from the viewpoint of the absolute reality, do not exist. II. 'Not to be born.'

~ **fumetsu** --不滅 'Neither arising nor perishing.' A phrase often used to describe the ultimate reality of things. [S. I–1.]

Fushō 普請 See *fushin*.

Fushō no Amida Butsu...mōshite 不請の阿彌陀佛...申して 'Reciting the *nenbutsu** unwillingly.' For the common Buddhist usage of the term '*fushō*', see *fushō no tomo* below. [Ho. 36.]

Fusho no bosatsu 補處の菩薩 'A bodhisattva who will take up a (buddha's) place (in the next life)'; a bodhisattva of the highest stage, esp. Miroku* (Maitreya). Cf. *isshō fusho*. [S. II–8.]

Fushō no tomo 不請の友 'A friend who helps one without being asked to do so'. Said of bodhisattvas who approach sentient beings as their friends and relieve their suffering.

Futai 不退☆ 'Not falling back'; Sk. *avinivartantya, avaivartika*; unyielding, steadfast; proceeding to the highest enlightenment without falling back to a lower spiritual stage. Cf. *gyōgō futai*. [S. II–8.]

 ∼ **no gyōgaku** --の行學 'Unremitting practice and study'; diligent and indefatigable practice and study. [Tai. 18.]

∼ **no tsutome** --のつとめ 'An uninterrupted service.' [K. 6.]

Fuzō-fugen-gyō 不增不減經 '*The Sutra on* (*the Reality-Principle of*) *Neither Increasing nor Decreasing*'; 1 fasc., tr. by Bodhiruci (Bodairushi 菩提流支) [TT. 16, No. 668]. This sutra explains that sentient beings are possessed of the Tathagata-matrix (*nyoraizō** 如來藏) and will therefore all eventually become buddhas. [S. I–3.]

Fuzoku 付屬 'Commissioning'; the Buddha's entrusting of a task, e.g. of transmitting the Dharma, to a bodhisattva, etc. [S. I–6, III–8; Tai. 18, 24.]

G

Gachirin-kan 月輪觀 See *gatsurin-kan*.

Gai 蓋 I. 'A cover'; a canopy or umbrella; the same as *tengai**. [Tai. 25.] II. 'That which covers (one's mind)'; Sk. *āvaraṇa*; another term for *bonnō** 煩惱 'evil passions'; see *gogai*.

Gaki 餓鬼 Sk. *preta*; 'a hungry spirit'.

~-dō --道 'The realm of hungry spirits'; the second lowest of the ten states of existences (*jikkai**). [Tai. 31.]

Gakki 月忌 The monthly commemoration of a person's death. Cf. *nenki*.

Gakkō 月光☆ 'Moonlight'; Sk. Candraprabha; n. of a bodhisattva; one of the two attendants of Yakushi* Buddha, the other being Nikkō*. [Tai. 3, 9, 18.]

Gakudokuriki 我功德力 'My own merit-power'; one's own power of meritorious practices; one of the three powers. See *sanriki*. [S. II-8.]

Gakuge 學解 'Learning and understanding'; intellectual understanding of the Buddhist teaching. [S. Va-4, Xb-3; Tai. 25.]

Gakuritsu no mono 學律の者 'One who studies precepts' but does not observe them. [S. IV-1.]

Gakuryo 學侶 'A scholarly priest.' [S.I-7; Tai. 17.]

~-gata --方 'Scholar priests'; one of the three groups of priests on Mt. Kōya, the other two being *hijiri-gata** 聖方 (*nenbutsu** practitioners) and *gyōnin-gata** 行人方 (those in charge of miscellaneous duties).

Gakushō 學生 I. In China, a boy who studies non-Buddhist texts at a temple. II. In Japan, a student who has been enrolled at a state or provincial college to become a government official. III. A student who studies Buddhist scriptures at a big temple. IV. A scholar.

Gakushō 學匠 'A student'; a disciple. Opposed to *shishō* 師匠, a master. [Tsu. 124.]

Gaman 我慢 'Self-pride, self-conceit'; one of the seven kinds of pride (*shichiman**). [Tai. 24.]

~-shin --心 'Self-pride.' [Tai. 25.]

Gan 願 'A vow.'

Gan 龕 I. A miniature shrine. II. A coffin; cf. *kigan*.

Ganjin 鑑眞 Ch. Chien-chen (687–763); the Chinese monk who founded the Japanese Ritsu* sect. Ordained at the age of 14, he mainly studied T'ien-t'ai (Tendai*) and Lü (Ritsu) teachings. At the request of a visiting Japanese priest, he attempted to go to Japan. After 11 years, during which he made five unsuccessful attempts and became blind, he finally reached Japan in 754. He lived in the Tōdaiji* and erected a precept-platform (*kaidan**) there. He gave the precepts to more than 400 people, including Emperor Shōmu*. Later he lived in the Tōshōdaiji 唐招提寺, and was given the titles of *daisōjō** and *daikashō-i* 大和尚位 'the rank of great master'.

Ganjo 願書 'A written prayer.' [Tai. 9.]

Ganmon 願文 'A statement or prayer' composed by the organizer of a Buddhist service held in memory of a deceased person. [K. 138; Ma. 84; S. VII–17; Tai. 24; Tsu. 72.]

Hōji no ~ 法事の-- A statement or prayer to be read at a memorial service for a deceased person. [O. I.]

Ganriki 願力 'Power of the vow.'

~ jinen --自然 'The necessary working of (Amida's*) vow-power', which unfailingly saves sentient beings.; cf. *jinen*.

Ganshiki 含識 'One who possesses consciousness'; a sentient being. [K. 58; S. II–8.]

Ganshō saihō 願生西方 'Aspiring to birth (in Amida's* Pure Land) in the west.' [Tai. 18.]

Gantō 雁塔 'The goose tower'; originally, a tower built for the goose (an incarnation of a bodhisattva) which sacrificed itself to teach Hinayana monks; a general term for a Buddhist tower. [Tai. 21.]

Garan 伽藍 Abbr. of *sōgya ranma* 僧伽藍摩 (Sk. *saṃgha-ārāma*), 'a garden for a group of monks'. A Buddhist convent or monastery; a temple.

Gashū 我執 'Attachment to oneself'; ego-attachment; Sk. *ātma-grāha*.; cf. *hosshū*.

Gasō 我相 'The aspect of self'; that which appears as 'self'; attachment to self. [S. IV–1, 9.]

Gasshō 合掌 'Joining of the palms of the hands together' in worship.

Gatsurin-kan 月輪観 Pronounced *gachirin-kan*; 'meditation on the moon-wheel'; also *jōbodaishin-kan* 淨菩提心観; refers to *ajikan**.

Gaya-jō 伽耶城 'Gayā city'; the capital of Magadha (Makada*) in central India at the time of the Buddha. It was to the north of

Buddhagayā (Buddagaya*) where the Buddha attained enlightenment, and near the river Nairañjanā (Nirenzenga*) where he bathed before enlightenment. [Tai. 35.]

Ge 夏 'Summer'; refers to *ge-ango**, a summer retreat. [S. III–5.]

~-ango -安居 A summer retreat for three months starting on the 16th of the 4th month, during which monks are confined in the temple studying and practising meditation. Cf. *ango*.

Gebon 下品 'Lowest grade'; see *kuhon*. [Ma. 97.]

~ geshō --下生 'The lowest grade in the lowest class'; the lowest of the nine categories of aspirants to Amida's* Pure Land (*kuhon**) distinguished in the *Kanmuryōju-kyō**; those who have committed all sorts of evil acts but, on their death, meet good teachers and attain birth in the Pure Land through reciting Amida's name.

Gechū 夏中 The ninety-day period of the summer retreat (*ge-ango**). [S. III–5.]

Gedatsu 解脱 'Liberation, emancipation.'

~ dōsō-e --幢相衣 'The robe of emancipation in the form of a temple banner'; another name for *kesa** (priest's surplice); so called because a *kesa* is worn by one who seeks emancipation (salvation) and its striped pattern looks like that of a temple banner.

~ dōsō no mikoromo --同相の御衣 'The robe showing the universal sign of emancipation'; refers to *kesa** (priest's surplice); the robe of emancipation in the form of a temple banner, since *dō* 同 is used here for 幢; see *gedatsu dōsō-e*. [Tai. 2.]

~ no mon --の門 'The gate of emancipation'; the entrance or path to emancipation. [S. IV–1.]

Gedō 外道 'An outside way'; a non-Buddhist teaching or its followers; cf. *rokushi gedō*.

Gegi 解義 'Understanding of the meaning or principle (of Buddhism).' [S. IV–9.]

Gego 外護 'An outside protector'; a layman who protects and promotes Buddhism; a patron of Buddhism. [S. III–8.]

Gegō 下業 'A low karma'; an inferior and weak act which, though good, brings about little reward. [S. IV-1.]

Gegyō 解行 'Understanding and practice' of the Buddhist teaching.

Gehō jōju no hito 外法成就の人 'A man who has accomplished a non-Buddhist method of practice.' [Tai. 26, 36.]

Geiin 契印 'A manual sign'; Sk. *mudrā*; also *ingei** and *inzō**.

Gejin 外陣 'The outer section' of the Buddha hall of a temple, where the congregation sits; also *gejin* 下陣 'the lower section' because this section is usually lower than the *naijin** 內陣 'the inner section', where a buddha statue is placed and monks chant sutras. [Tai. 34.]

Gekai 下界 'A lower realm'; a lower state of existence.

Geke shujō 下化衆生 'Transforming sentient beings below'; the compassion aspect of the bodhisattva aspiration; cf. *jōgu bodai*. [Tai. 12.]

Geki 下機 'A man of inferior capability.' [Tai. 24.]

Gekū 外空 'External void'; Sk. *bahirdhā-śūnyatā*; the void of things which exist as objects of perception; one of the 18 kinds of void (*jūhachikū**). [S. IV-9.]

Gekuyō 外供養 'Offering external (things)'; see *genkuyō*.

Gekyō 外境 'The external world'; objects of perception.

Gen 驗 I. A miraculous effect. II. Mystical power attained by esoteric practices. III. Prayer or magical performance by a priest of esoteric Buddhism.

~ kurabe - くらべ Testing one's mystical power against that of others. [K. 46; O. III.]

Gengi 玄義 I. 'Essential meaning.' II. Refers to the *Hokkegengi**. [S. III-8.]

Gengō 賢劫 'The Auspicious Kalpa'; n. of the present cosmic period, in which 1,000 buddhas are believed to appear; cf. *jūkō*, *senbutsu* and *shikō*.

Gengu-gyō 賢愚經 See *Gengu-innen-gyō*.

Gengu-innen-gyō 賢愚因緣經 '*The Sutra of Stories about Wise and Stupid People*'; 13 fasc., tr. by Hui-te 慧德 (Etoku), T'an-chüeh 曇覺 (Donkaku), *et al.* [TT. 4, No. 202]. This sutra contains 69 stories of various people explaining how their acts brought about particular effects.

Genja 驗者 Also *genza* and *kenza*; a priest of the Tendai* or the Shingon* sect who performs esoteric practices, especially the type of Buddhist ascetic called *yamabushi**. He prays for recovery from illness, cessation of natural disasters, etc.

Genjō 玄奘 Ch. Hsüan-chuang (600–664); a Chinese monk who went to India via Central Asia and brought back 657 Sanskrit texts. He translated 1,330 fascicles of scriptures into Chinese, including the basic texts of the Hossō* sect. [S. III–1, VI–10, VIII–23; Tai. 38.]

Genjō 賢聖 See *kenshō*.

Genju 賢首 Ch. Hsien-shou; the title given to Fa-ts'ang 法藏 (Hōzō*) by the emperor. [S. IV–9.]

Genkaku 玄覺 Ch. Hsüan-chüeh (d. 713); popularly called Yung-chia 永嘉 (Yōka*), the name of the place where he came from. He received the Ch'an (Zen*) tradition from Hui-neng 慧能 (Enō*), and later propagated it extensively. His *Shōdō-ka* 證道歌 is a well-read Zen classic.

Genke 幻化 I. 'An illusory manifestation' produced by a magician. II. An illusory manifestation produced by a magician (*gen* 幻) and a creation made by the supernatural power of a buddha or bodhisattva (*ke* 化). III. Phenomena produced by one's delusion.

∼ **no jinkyō** --の塵境 'The objective world produced by one's delusion.' See *jinkyō*. [S. III–8.]

∼ **no yo** --の世 'The illusory world'; this world of delusion. [S. III–3.]

Genke 現化 'Manifestation of a transformed body'; an incarnation. [Tai. 20.]

Genkō 減劫 'Decreasing *kalpa*'; a period of cosmic change during which man's life-span decreases from 80,000 to ten years at the rate of one every 100 years. After man's life-span reaches ten, it begins to increase; cf. *zōkō*. [Tai. 18.]

Genkū 源空 See *Hōnen*. [Tai. 24.]

Genkuyō 現供養 'Offering actual things'; offering incense, flowers, lamps, ointment, food, etc., to a deity; also *jihō kuyō*, 事法供養 'offering phenomenal things' and *gekuyō*, 外供養 'offering external things'; the term is used in contrast to *unshin kuyō** 運心供養. [K. 64.]

Genpō 現報 'Maturity (of karma) in the present life'; also *jungenpō* 順現報; one of the three types of karma distinguished according to the different times of their maturity (*sanpō**). [S. VII–5.]

Genrai ekoku 還來穢國 'Returning to the defiled world', i.e. from the Pure Land, to save other living beings. [IH.]

Genryō 現量 'Direct perception'; Sk. *pratyakṣa*; one of the three means of cognition of objects, the other two being *hiryō** and *shōgyōryō**. [S. IV–1, Vb-11.]

~ **mufunbetsu** --無分別 'Direct perception without any discriminative thought.' [S. IV–1, VIII–23.]

Genshin 源信 (942–1017) A Tendai* monk and a great exponent of Pure Land thought; popularly called Eshin Sōzu 惠心僧都 because he lived in the Eshin-in at Yokawa on Mt. Hiei. He lost his father when young, and went up to Mt. Hiei to study Buddhism under Ryōgen*. His *Ōjōyōshū**, which won him great renown not only in Japan but also in China, laid the foundation for Japanese Pure Land teaching. He is thus looked upon as the sixth patriarch in the Jōdoshin* sect. He is also known as the founder of the Eshin school of Tendai.

Genshō 現生 'The present life.'

Genshō 現證 'Manifest evidence'; a proof.

Gentō 現當 'Present and future'; the present and future life.

Gen'yaku 現益 'Benefit in the present life.' [S. II–10.]

Genza 驗者 See *genja*.

Genze 現世 'The present world'; this world or life.

~ **annon** --安穏 'Peace in this world.' [Hei. 2; S. VI–15; Tai. 18.]

Genzen ni 現前に 'In front of oneself; before one's eyes'; said of an object perceived in meditation or with the eyes.

Genzoku 還俗 'Return to secular life.'

Geryō 解了 'Understanding', as of the teaching.

Geshin 解信 'Understanding and belief'; belief in the Buddhist teaching which arises from understanding it. [S. II–1.]

Gesō 外相 'External aspect'; that which is manifest in physical actions. [Tsu. 157.]

Gesu hōshi 下種法師 'A monk of a lower rank'; also, 下手法師, 下衆法師, etc. [S. II–6, IV–1.]

Geten 外典 Also *geden*; 'outer scriptures'; non-Buddhist scriptures; cf. *naiten*. [S. III–1.]

Geyū 外用 'Out-going function; external activity'; activity emanating from within and directed outwards. [S. I–3, IV–1.]

Geza 下座 I. To descend from a raised seat or chair. II. One who sits in a lower position at a Buddhist service.

Giba 耆婆 Sk. Jīvaka; a famous physician in the time of the Buddha. [S. II–6; Tai. 21, 40.]

~ Henjaku ga reiyaku -- 扁鵲が霊藥 'A miraculous medicine administered by Jīvaka or P'ien-ch'üeh.' [Tai. 21.]

Gida-on 祇陀園 '(Prince) Jeta's garden'; also *Giju* 祇樹; see *Giju gikkodoku-on*.

Gien 義淵 Also Giin; a Hossō* master. He was abandoned in infancy but was found and taken to a palace of Emperor Tenchi (reigned 662–671), where he was raised. He entered the priesthood by imperial order and studied Hossō under Chihō 智鳳 of the Gangōji 元興寺, Nara. In 703 he was given the title of *sōjō**, and died in 728. His disciples included Gyōgi* and Rōben*.

Gijō 義淨 Ch. I-ching (635–713). Entering the priesthood when young, he desired to go to India. In 671, he left China and set out for India by sea. After staying there for more than ten years, having visited more than 30 countries on the way, he returned home in 695, bringing back the relics of the Buddha, sutras, etc. Empress Wu 武 conferred on him the title of *san-tsang* 三藏 (*sanzō**) and made him dwell in a temple and translate the texts he had brought from India. He produced translations of 56 texts in 230 fascicles, including *Konkōmyō-saishōō-kyō**. The record of his journey, *Nankai-kiki-den* 南海寄歸傳, 4 fasc., is a useful source of information on the period. [S. Xb–1.]

Giju gikkodoku-on 祇樹給孤獨園 'The Jeta grove, the garden of Anāthapiṇḍada'; Sk. Jetavana-anāthapiṇḍada; the garden offered to the Buddha by Prince Jeta (Gita*), where Sudatta (Shudatsu*) built a monastery known as *Gion shōja**; cf. *Gikkodoku*.

Giki 儀軌 'A manual of rituals' in esoteric Buddhism. [S. II–8.]

Gikkodoku 給孤獨 Sk. Anāthapiṇḍada, 'giver of food to the poor'; refers to Sudatta (Shudatsu*), who built for the Buddha a monastery known as *Gion shōja**; cf. *Giju gikkodoku.*

Gimon 義門 'The aspect of implied meanings'; implications; interpretation of the teaching. [S. I–10, III–8, IV–1, Xb–2.]

Gi-muge 義無礙 See *shimugeben.*

Ginan 疑難 'Doubt, suspicion.'

Gion shōja 祇園精舎 'The Jeta grove monastery'; Sk. Jetavana-vihāra; the monastery built for the Buddha by Sudatta (Shudatsu*); see *Giju gikkodoku-on.* [Hei. 1; OK. V; S. III–3; Tai. 24.]

~ **no Mujō-in** ‐‐‐‐の無常院 'The Impermanence Hall of the Jetavana Monastery', Śrāvastī, India. The Impermanence Hall was in the north-west corner of the monastery, where sick monks were housed while contemplating on the impermanence of all things. [Tsu. 220.]

Giri 義理 I. Reason; the universal principle. II. Use; utility; advantage. III. Meanings or implications that can be discerned and discussed in words (*gi*) and the ultimate principle of reality (*ri*). [S. IV–1.]

Gisei 義勢 'Extended or implied meaning.' [S. II–9.]

Gita 祇多 Sk. Jeta; a prince of Śrāvastī (Shae*) and a son of King Prasenajit (Hashinoku*); cf. *Shudatsu.*

Giya 祇夜 Sk. *geya*; translated as *ōju* 應頌 'a corresponding verse' and *jūju** 重頌 'a verse repeating (an idea already expressed)'; a verse which repeats the essence of an exposition given in prose; one of the nine and twelve kinds of scriptures (*kubu-kyō** and *jūnibu-kyō**).

Gō 業 Sk. *karma*; 'an act'. [S. Va–5.]

~ **innen** ‐因縁 'One's karma and causal relationships.' [S. Va–5.]

~ **ni hikaru** ‐にひかる 'To be drawn by one's karma'; to be affected by the result of one's acts in the past. [S. III–8.]

~ **o mukuu** ‐をむくう 'To reap the reward or retribution of one's acts.' [K. 72.]

~ **o tenzu** -を轉ず 'To turn one's karma'; to change the course of one's karma or improve it. [S. III–8.]

~ **zōjōriki** -増上力 'Power of increasing (evil) karma.' [S. IX–4.]

Gobō 御坊 A polite term used to refer to a monk or temple.

Gobō 御房 A polite term used to refer to a monk. [O. VI; S. I–4.]

Gobu daijōkyō 五部大乘經 'The five Mahayana sutras'; the five sutras considered the most important in the Tendai* sect: (1) *Kegon-gyō** 華嚴經 '*Garland Sutra*'; (2) *Daishū-kyō** 大集經, '*Great Collection Sutra*'; (3) *Daibon-hannya-kyō** 大品般若經, '*Great Prajñāpāramitā Sutra*'; (4) *Hoke-kyō** 法華經, '*Lotus Sutra*'; and (5) *Nehan-gyō** 涅槃經, '*Nirvana Sutra*'. [K. 68.]

Gōbukuhō 降伏法 'A subjugation ritual'; also *jōbukuhō** 調伏法 and *shakubukuhō* 折伏法; an esoteric ritual performed to subdue enemies, devils, etc.

Gōbun 告文 See *gōmon.*

Gobun hosshin 五分法身 'The fivefold (merit) of the Dharma-body'; the five kinds of embodiment of merit attributed to those who have attained enlightenment: (1) *kaishin* 戒身, 'precept-body', free from any offences against the precepts; (2) *jōshin* 定身, 'meditation-body', free from all delusory thoughts and tranquil in heart; (3) *eshin* 慧身, 'wisdom-body', possessed of true insight; (4) *gedatsushin* 解脱身, 'emancipation-body', free from all bonds; and (5) *gedatsu-chiken-shin* 解脱知見身, 'emancipation-knowledge-body', aware of one's attainment of emancipation. [S. III–7.]

Gobu no daijōkyō 五部の大乘經 See *gobu daijōkyō.* [Tai. 13, 36.]

Gobutsu 五佛 'The five buddhas' in esoteric Buddhism. They are Dainichi* (Mahāvairocana) in the centre and four other buddhas in the four directions. The four buddhas in the Diamond Realm Mandala (*Kongōkai mandara**) are: Ashuku* 阿閦 (Akṣobhya) in the east, Hōshō* 寶生 (Ratnasambhava) in the south, Amida* 阿彌陀 (Amitābha) in the west and Fukūjōju* 不空成就 (Amoghasiddhi) in the north. The four buddhas in the Matrix-store Realm Mandala (*Taizōkai mandara**) are: Hōdō 寶幢 (Ratna-ketu) in the east, Kaifukeō 開敷華王 (Saṃkusumitarāja) in the south, Muryōju* 無量壽 (Amitāyus) in the west and Tenkuraion

天鼓雷音 (Divyadundubhimeghanirghoṣa) in the north. [K. 6; S. II–8.]

~ **no shuji** --の種子 'The Sanskrit syllables representing the five buddhas' in esoteric Buddhism. Those of the five buddhas of the Diamond Realm Mandala (*Kongōkai mandara**) are: VAM for Dainichi*, HŪM for Ashuku*, TRĀH for Hōshō*, HRĪH for Amida* and AH for Fukūjōju*. The syllables of the five buddhas of the Matrix-store Realm Mandala (*Taizōkai mandara**) are: ĀH for Dainichi*, A for Hōdō, Ā for Kaifukeō, ĀM for Muryōju* and AH for Tenkuraion. [S. II–8.]

Gobutsumyō 御佛名　See *butsumyō-e*. [Ma. 151, 285; Tsu. 19.]

Gobyō 五瓶　'The five pitchers' used at the ceremony of conferring precepts or special teachings in esoteric traditions (*kanjō**). [Hei. 2.]

~ **no chisui** --の智水　'The water of wisdom in the five pitchers'; the water in the five pitchers symbolizes the Buddha's wisdom to be conferred on the recipient at the *kanjō** ceremony. [Hei. 2.]

Gochi 五智　'The five wisdoms'; in esoteric Buddhism, the five enlightenment-wisdoms: (1) *hokkai-taishōchi** 法界體性智 (*dharma-dhātu-svabhāva-jñāna*), 'the essence of the Dharma-realm (*hokkai**) wisdom', the wisdom of knowing the quintessence of all existences; (2) *daienkyōchi** 大圓鏡智 (*ādarśa-j.*), 'great perfect mirror-wisdom', the wisdom which reflects all phenomenal things as they are, like a clear mirror; (3) *byōdōshōchi** 平等性智 (*samatā-j.*), 'wisdom of (awareness of) the sameness (of all things)', the wisdom of observing the ultimate sameness of everything; (4) *myōkanzatchi** 妙觀察智 (*pratyavekṣaṇā-j.*), 'wisdom of wondrous observation', the wisdom of discerning the distinctive features of all phenomena; and (5) *jōshosachi** 成所作智 (*kṛtya-anuṣthāna-j.*), 'wisdom of accomplishing what is to be done (to benefit sentient beings)', the wisdom of accomplishing metamorphoses. For the five buddhas corresponding to the five wisdoms, see *gochi nyorai*; see also *shichi* 四智 'the four wisdoms' in the Hossō* teaching. [S. I–1, 3.]

~ **no nyorai** --の如來　See *gochi nyorai*. [Tai. 26.]

~ **nyorai** --如來　'The tathagata (*nyorai**) of the five wisdoms'; the five buddhas representing the five wisdoms established in esoteric Buddhism. They are: (1) Dainichi* 大日 (Mahāvairocana) representing *hokkai-taishōchi** 法界體性智; (2) Ashuku* 阿閦 (Akṣobhya) representing *daienkyōchi** 大圓鏡智; (3) Hōshō* 寶生 (Ratnasambhava) representing *byōdōshōchi** 平等性智; (4) Muryōju* 無量壽 (Amitāyus) representing *myōkanzatchi** 妙觀察智; and (5) Fukūjōju* 不空成就 (Amoghasiddhi) representing *jōshosachi** 成所作智. Cf. *gobutsu* and *gochi*.

Godai 五大 'The five great (elements)'; also *godaishu* 五大種 'the five great seeds'; the five elements which constitute things in the world: (1) *chidai* 地大, the earth element; (2) *suidai* 水大, the water element; (3) *kadai* 火大, the fire element; (4) *fūdai* 風大, the wind element; and (5) *kūdai* 空大, the space element. In esoteric Buddhism, the five elements are shown in terms of shapes and colours: (1) the earth element is square and yellow; (2) the water element, circular and white; (3) the fire element, triangular and red; (4) the wind element, crescent and black; and (5) the space element, maṇi-jewel-shaped (see *mani*) and blue. Cf. *gorin*, *rokudai* & *shidai*. [S. Va–12.]

Godai Kokūzō 五大虛空藏 'The five great Kokūzō* Bodhisattvas'; the five transformed manifestations of Kokūzō* Bodhisattva which represent his distinct virtues. [Hei. 3; Tai. 1.]

Godai-myōō 五大明王 'The five great *myōō**'; also *godaison* 五大尊 and *godaison myōō* 五大尊明王: (1) Fudō* 不動 (Acala); (2) Gōzanze 降三世 (Trailokyavijaya); (3) Gundari* 軍荼利 (Kuṇḍalin); (4) Daiitoku* 大威德 (Yamāntaka); and (5) Kongōyasha 金剛夜叉 (Vajrayakṣa). They are presented in the Matrix-store Realm Mandala (*Taizōkai mandara**), and are believed to be incarnations of the five buddhas (*gobutsu**) of the Diamond Realm Mandala (*Kongōkai mandara**).

Godaison 五大尊 'The five great revered ones'; see *godai-myōō*. [Hei. 3; Ma. 278; Tai. 14.]

Godanhō 五壇法 'The five-platform ritual'; a Shingon* ritual often performed at the imperial palace and residences of court nobles to pray for the cessation of calamities, an increase of merit, etc. The ritual consists of the simultaneous performance of services before the platforms of five *myōō** 明王 (Sk. *vidyā-rāja*), such as Fudō*. The ritual was performed at the imperial palace for the first time on the 14th of the 2nd month in the 8th year of Kōhei

康平 (1065).

Godan no hō 五壇の法 See *godanhō*. [Hei. 3; S. I–3; Tai. 1.]

Godō 五道 'The five paths'; also *goshu* 五趣; the five realms, namely, hell and the realms of hungry spirits, animals, men and heavenly beings; cf. *rokudō* and *jikkai*. [S. I–3.]

Godō 悟道 'Enlightenment; attainment of Bodhi (*bodai**).' [S. IV–1.]

Gōdō 業道 'The path of karma'; the same as *gō* 'karma'; any physical, oral or mental act, whether good or evil; as it leads one to a new state of existence, it is called 'the path of karma'.

～ **jinen** -- 自然 'The necessary working of the law of karma'; said of the inevitable reward or retribution of a good or evil act; cf. *jinen*.

Gogai 五蓋 'The five coverings'; the five disorders which cover one's mind and hinder good thoughts; they are: (1) *ton' yoku-gai* 貪欲蓋 (*rāga-āvaraṇa*), greed; (2) *shinni-gai* 瞋恚蓋 (*pratigha-ā.*), anger; (3) *konjin-gai* 惛沈蓋 or *zuimen-gai* 睡眠蓋 (*styāna-ā.*), languor or melancholy; (4) *jōke-gai* 悼悔蓋 (*auddhatya-kaukṛtya-ā.*), restlessness and mortification; and (5) *gi-gai* 疑蓋 (*vicikitsā-ā.*), scepticism.

Goganji 御願寺 'An august prayer (-offering) temple'; a temple erected by an emperor, empress or prince with a particular prayer to be offered up or a vow to be fulfilled. One erected by order of the emperor is also particularly called *chokuganji**. [K. 36.]

Goganjo 御願所 'An august prayer (-offering) place'; the same as *goganji**. [Tai. 21.]

Gōgasha 恆河沙 'Sand-grains of the River Ganges.'

Go-gohyakusai 五五百歳 'Five 500-year periods'; also *go-gohyaku-nen* 五五百年 and *goko-gohyakusai* 五箇五百歳. According to the *Daishū-kyō**, the history of Buddhism after the Buddha's death is divided into five 500-year periods, each characterized by a particular feature: the first by the firm attainment of emancipation (*gedatsu kengo* 解脱堅固); the second by the steadfast practice of meditation (*zenjō kengo* 禪定堅固); the third by the steadfast hearing of the Buddhist teaching (*tamon kengo* 多聞堅固); the fourth by the steady building of many temples (*zōji kengo* 造寺堅固); and the last by the steadfast engagement in doctrinal disputes (*tōjō kengo** 鬪諍堅固). For the theory of gradual degeneration of Buddhism through three periods, see *shōzōmatsu*.

Gogu 互具 'Mutually containing'; see *jikkai gogu*. [S. IV–1.]

Gogyaku 五逆 Abbr. of *gogyakuzai**. [S. IV–1, VI–18, Xa–1; Tai. 2, 13, 20.]

~**-zai** --罪 'The five rebellious sins'; the five deadly sins: killing one's father, killing one's mother, killing an *arhat* (*arakan**), causing the Buddha's body to bleed, and causing disunity in the Buddhist order. Those who have committed any of these five sins will be destined for hell to suffer immeasurable pain for many kalpas (*kō**). Cf. *shijū gogyaku*. [Hei. 1.]

Gohakkō 御八講 See *hakkō*. [K. 79.]

Gohō 後報 'Maturity (of karma) in a life after the next'; also *jungo-hō* 順後報; one of the three types of karma distinguished according to the different times of their maturity (*sanpō**). [S. VII–5.]

Gohō 護法 I. 'Protecting the Buddhist Dharma.' II. Refers to *gohō tendō**. [K. 46; Ma. 23; O. III; Tai. 11.] III. A messenger of a god who protects the Buddhist Dharma. [Tai. 5.]

~ **tendō** --天童 'Heavenly boy who protects the Dharma'; also *gohō dōji* 護法童子. A heavenly boy sent by the divine protectors of the Dharma (such as Taishaku* and Shitennō*) to a follower of Buddhism to protect him. Cf. *gohō* III.

~ **tsukitaru hōshi** --つきたる法師 'A monk attended by a (heavenly boy as) protector of the Dharma.' See *gohō tendō*.

Gohō 護法 Sk. Dharmapāla; one of the ten great exponents of the doctrine of Consciousness-Only in India, born in the middle of the sixth century. He wrote a commentary on the *Thirty Verses on Consciousness-Only* by Vasubandhu (Seshin*), which was later translated into Chinese by Hsüan-chuang (Genjō*); see *Jōyuishiki-ron*.

Gōhō 業報 'A reward or retribution of karma.' [Tai. 11.]

Gohō dōji 護法童子 See *gohō tendō*.

Gohōkō no hi 護法香の火 'Fire of scented wood (into which the deities) protecting the Buddhist Dharma (transform themselves).' [K. 44.]

Gohon 五品 I. 'The five kinds (of meritorious acts)' in the Tendai*
doctrine: (1) 'Zuiki-hon' 隨喜品, rejoicing at hearing the exposition of the *Hoke-kyō** and understanding its teaching; (2)
Dokuju-hon 讀誦品, chanting the sutra; (3) 'Seppō-bon' 説法品,
expounding the sutra to others; (4) 'Kengyō-rokudo-hon' 兼行
六度品, practising the Six Paramitas (*ropparamitsu**) side by side
with the practice of contemplation on the triple truth (*santai**);
and (5) 'Shōgyō-rokudo-hon' 正行六度品, practising perfectly the
Six Paramitas. Those who have accomplished the above meritorious acts are at the level called *kangyō gohon'i**, and their achievement corresponds to the third of the six stages of non-duality
practices (*rokusoku**). II. Refers to *gohon deshi-i**. [S. Va–1.]

~ **deshi-i** - -弟子位 'The stage of disciples performing the five
kinds (of meritorious acts)'; the lowest stage of the Perfect
Teaching (*engyō**) division of Tendai*.

Gohyaku-monron 五百問論 '*A Discourse on Five Hundred Questions*'; abbr. of *Bussetsu-mokuren-mon-kairitsuchū-gohyaku-kyō-
jūji*) 佛説目連問戒律中五百輕重事, 1 fasc.; the translator not
known [TT. 24, No. 1483]. [S.VII–18.]

Gohyaku rakan 五百羅漢 'Five hundred arhats.' I. The five hundred disciples of the Buddha who attained the stage of arhat;
they assembled at the first congregation held soon after the
Buddha's death. [S. II–1.] II. Those arhats said to have assembled at the fourth congregation convened by King Kaniṣka in
the second century.   III. Those arhats popularly worshipped in
China and Japan.

Gōin 業因 'A karma-cause'; a good or evil act as the cause of a
good or evil effect.

Gōja 恆沙 Abbr. of *gōgasha**.

~ **no** - -の As numerous as the sand-grains of the River Ganges.

Goji 五時 'The five periods'; see *gojikyō*. [Hei. 2; Tai. 39.]

~**-kyō** - -教 'Five-period teaching'. Tendai* doctrine classifies
the Buddha's life-time teachings according to the following five
periods: (1) the first three weeks after the Buddha's enlightenment, in which he expounded the *Kegon-gyō**: this is known as
the *Kegon-ji* 華嚴時, 'the Kegon period'; (2) the following 12
years in which he preached Hinayana sutras: the *Rokuon-ji* 鹿苑

時, 'the Rokuon period'; (3) the following eight years in which he expounded various Mahayana sutras, such as the *Yuima-gyō**: the *Hōdō-ji* 方等時, 'the Hōdō period'; (4) the next 22 years in which he expounded the *Hannya-kyō**: the *Hannya-ji* 般若時, 'the Hannya period'; and (5) the last eight years in which he preached the *Hoke-kyō** and the last day of his mission when he expounded the *Nehan-gyō**: the *Hokke-nehan-ji* 法華涅槃時, 'the Hokke and Nehan period'. [O. I.]

Goji darani 五字陀羅尼 'The five-letter dharani'; see *goji Monju-ju*.

Goji-ju 五字呪 'The five-letter spell'; see *goji Monju-ju*.

Goji Monju-ju 五字文殊呪 'The five-letter Mañjuśrī spell'; also *Goji-ju* 五字呪 'five-letter spell' and *Goji-darani* 五字陀羅尼 'five-letter dharani'. The spell consists of the five Sanskrit syllables, A, RA, PA, CA and NA, and is one of Monju's* spells. [K. 64.]

Gojin 五塵 'Five dusts'; the five objects of sensation and perception corresponding to the five sense-organs. They are objects sensed as visual colour or form, sound, odour, taste and touch. They give rise to desires and, thereby, pollute one's mind; hence, 'dust'. Cf. *rokujin*. [S. IV-9, Xa-10.]

Gojisō 護持僧 'A priest who protects'; also 御持僧 and *yoi no sō* 夜居僧; a high priest entrusted with the task of praying at night in the imperial palace for the good health of an emperor. [O. I.]

Gojō-gesa 五條袈裟 'A five-piece surplice'. In India, a monk's wear worn in his own quarters or when he performs miscellaneous jobs. In China and Japan, it is worn over the robe at a Buddhist service.

Gojoku 五濁 Sk. *pañca kaṣāyāḥ*, 'the five defilements or pollutions' which mark the cosmic period in which man's life-span is less than 20,000 years. They are: (1) *kōjoku* 劫濁 (Sk. *kalpa-kaṣāya*), 'defilement of period' because famines, plagues and wars arise during this time; (2) *kenjoku* 見濁 (Sk. *dṛṣṭi-k*.), 'defilement of views' because wrong views arise; (3) *bonnōjoku* 煩惱濁 (Sk. *kleśa-k*.), 'defilement by evil passions' because they become intense; (4) *shujōjoku* 衆生濁 (Sk. *sattva-k*.), 'defilement of sentient beings' because people reject the moral laws and the law of causality, or because they are physically and mentally weak and suffer greatly thereby; (5) *myōjoku* 命濁 (Sk. *āyuṣ-k*.), 'defilement of life' because man's life-span is short. The five defilements become intense when man's life-span decreases to less than 100 years. In Japanese literature the term is popularly used to refer to the defilements and corruptions of the world, which are especially marked in the period of the decadent Dharma (*mappō** 末法). Cf. *jokuakuse*.

∼ **akuse** --惡世 'The evil world with the five defilements.' [Tai. 24.]

∼ **sōō no hōmon** --相應の法門 'The teaching adapted to the period of the five defilements.' [S. Xa–1.]

Gojō no kesa 五帖の袈裟 See *gojō-gesa.* [K. 545.]

Gojōshinkan 五停心觀 'The five meditations for stopping (unwholesome) thoughts'; (1) *fujōkan* 不淨觀, 'meditating on the impurity' of one's body, etc., to remove greed; (2) *jihikan* 慈悲觀, 'compassionate meditation' on all living beings to remove anger and hatred; (3) *innenkan* 因緣觀, 'meditation on the causes and conditions' which give rise to all things, to remove stupidity; (4) *kaifunbetsukan* 界分別觀, 'meditation on element discrimination', that is, on the fact that all things are made up of the six elements (*rokudai**); this removes attachment to self; and (5) *susokukan* 數息觀, 'breathing meditation' to remove distracting thoughts. *Kaifunbetsukan* is sometimes replaced by *kanbutsukan* 觀佛觀, 'meditation on (the physical characteristics of) the Buddha' to remove all evil passions.

Gōjun shujō 恆順衆生 'Always following (the customs and propensities of) sentient beings'; said of the attitude of a bodhisattva when he approaches and saves living beings. [S. II–8.]

∼ **no gan** ----の願 'The vow to follow sentient beings constantly (to save them)'; the ninth of the ten vows of Samantabhadra (Fugen*). Cf. *Fugen jūgan.* [S. III–1.]

Gojū yuishikikan 五重唯識觀 'Fivefold contemplation on consciousness-only'; the method of contemplation used in the Hossō* sect to realize the principle of 'consciousness-only' (*yuishiki**): (1) *kenko zonjitsushiki* 遣虛存實識, delusory existences superimposed on consciousness-based existences are rejected, but existences based on consciousnesses are held to truly exist; (2) *sharan rujunshiki* 捨濫留純識, the spurious (i.e. the objective portion of each consciousness) is rejected, and the genuine consciousness elements (i.e. the subjective portions of each consciousness) are retained; (3) *shōmatsu kihonshiki* 攝末歸本識, the derivative portions of each consciousness (i.e. the objective and seeing portions) are brought back to its original body (i.e. the basis of consciousness which confirms perception); (4) *onretsu kenshōshiki* 隱劣顯勝識 the inferior (i.e. mental attributes which assist the functions of the eight consciousnesses) are rejected, and the superior (i.e. the eight consciousnesses themselves) are retained; and (5) *kensō shōshōshiki* 遣相證性識, the phenomenal aspects of consciousnesses are rejected, and their real nature is realized. The practitioner advances from the lower level of contemplation to a higher one, until he realizes finally the essential nature of existence.

Gōka 業火 'Karma-fire.' I. The fire of evil acts. II. The fire of hell, etc., which burns sinners. [Tai. 15.]

Gōka 業果 Pronounced *gokka*; 'the effect of karma'; the result of an act in a previous life.

～ hōnen no ri --法然の理 'The principle that the effect of karma is inevitable.' [Tai. 35.]

Gokai 五戒 'The five precepts' for laymen and lay-women: (1) *fusesshō* 不殺生, not to kill; (2) *fuchūtō* 不偸盗, not to steal; (3) *fujain* 不邪淫, not to commit adultery; (4) *fumōgo* 不妄語, not to tell lies; and (5) *fuonju* 不飲酒 not to drink intoxicants. [S. I–10, III–8, VI–10, Xa–8; Tai. 26, 35.]

Gokan no hi 五卷の日 'The day of (the lecture on) the fifth fascicle (of the *Hoke-kyō**)'; see *Hoke-kyō no go no kan*.

Goke 五家 'The five houses'; the five Ch'an (Zen*) schools in China, namely, Kuei-yang 潙仰 (Igyō), Ts'ao-tung 曹洞 (Sōtō), Lin-chi 臨濟 (Rinzai), Yün-mên 雲門 (Unmon), and Fa-yen 法眼 (Hōgen).

Goken 五見 'Five (wrong) views': (1) *shinken* 身見, the view that 'self' exists permanently; (2) *henken* 邊見, the view that 'self' continues to exist after death or that it ceases to exist; (3) *jaken* 邪見, the view that rejects causality; (4) *kenjuken* 見取見, attachment to a wrong view; and (5) *kaigonjuken* 戒禁取見, the view that holds some wrong teaching as right for attaining Nirvana or other superior effect.

Goko 五鈷　Abbr. of *gokosho* 五鈷杵; a five-pronged *vajra* (*kongōsho**); a bar with five prongs on each end, used by priests of the highest rank. The five points represent various series of five, especially the five wisdoms (*gochi** 五智).

Goko-gohyakusai 五箇五百歳　See *go-gohyakusai.*

Gokoku sanbukyō 護國三部經　'The three state-protecting sutras': (1) *Hoke-kyō** 法華經; (2) *Konkōmyō-kyō** 金光明經; and (3) *Ninnō-kyō** 仁王經. These sutras have been copied, chanted and expounded with the belief that the merit of these acts would stop calamities in the state and secure peace and security.

Gokon 五根　I. 'The five sense-organs'; eyes, ears, nose, tongue, and the whole body treated as a tactile organ. [S. III–1.] II. 'The five roots' of goodness: (1) *shinkon* 信根, belief in the three treasures (*sanbō**) and the fourfold noble truth (*shishōtai**); (2) *shōjinkon* 精進根 or *gonkon* 勤根, making efforts to practise good; (3) *nenkon* 念根, being mindful of the true law; (4) *jōkon* 定根, concentration; and (5) *ekon* 慧根, investigation of the true nature of things. The five roots of goodness are included in the 37 elements of enlightenment (*sanjūshichi-dōbon**).

Gokosho 五鈷杵　See *goko.*

Gōku 業苦　'Karmic suffering'; suffering which one undergoes as retribution of evil acts done in the past. [S.I–8, III–7.]

Gokui 極位　'The ultimate stage.'

Gokuraku 極樂　'Utmost pleasure'; Sk. *Sukhāvatī*, 'that which possesses ease and comfort'; the name of Amida's* land. [K. 484, 500; Ma. 162; S. I–10, VII–18; Tai. 37.]

～ **jōdo** --淨土　Amida's* 'Pure Land of Utmost Bliss'. [O. V; Tai. 8, 11.]

～ **no son** --之尊　'The Honoured One in the Land of Utmost Bliss'; Amida* of the Western Pure Land. [K. 140.]

～ **sekai** --世界　Amida's* 'World of Utmost Bliss'.

Gokushō 極聖　'The most sacred person,' i.e. Buddha. [S. I–3.]

Gokusotsu 獄率(=卒)　'A demon guardian of hell.'

Gokyō 五敎　'Five teachings.' Kegon* doctrine classifies the Buddha's life-time teachings into the following five groups in an order of increasing depth: (1) *Shōjōkyō* 小乘敎, Hinayana teaching

(2) *Daijō shikyō* 大乘始教, elementary doctrine of Mahayana which refers to Hossō* and Sanron* teachings, (3) *Daijō jūkyō* 大乘終教, the final doctrine of Mahayana, which asserts the existence of buddha-nature in all living beings, (4) *Daijō tongyō* 大乘頓教, the sudden-enlightenment doctrine of Mahayana, as in Zen*, and (5) *Daijō engyō* 大乘圓教, the round (i.e. perfect) doctrine of Mahayana, namely, Kegon teaching. [S. IV–1.]

Gōkyō 業鏡 'Mirror of karma'; see *jōhari no kagami*.

Goma 護摩 Sk. *homa*; a burnt offering; the act of burning firewood, grain, etc., as an offering to a deity in esoteric Buddhism, in order to achieve such objectives as stopping calamities and increasing merit (see *goshuhō**). The actual performance of such a ritual is called *gegoma* 外護摩 (external fire-ceremony) or *jigoma* 事護摩 (phenomenal fire-ceremony). In order to attain enlightenment, the practitioner should simultaneously perform meditation, which is called *naigoma* 內護摩 (internal fire-ceremony) or *rigoma* 理護摩 (noumenal fire-ceremony). The burning of firewood, etc., symbolizes the destruction by wisdom of evil passions and karma.

Gōma no riken 降魔の利劍 'A sharp sword for subduing devils.' [Tai. 17.]

Gomi 五味 'The five tastes'; milk and four milk products obtained at different stages of clarification: (1) *nyū* 乳, milk, (2) *raku* 酪, cream, (3) *shōso** 生蘇 or 生酥, curdled milk, (4) *jukuso** 熟蘇 or 熟酥, butter, and (5) *daigo** 醍醐 (Sk. *maṇḍa*), clarified butter or ghee. Used in the Tendai* sect for the five periods of the teaching of the Buddha.

Gōmon 告文 'A written announcement.' I. A written prayer, petition or invocation to a Buddhist or Shinto deity; the same as *kishōmon**. II. An oracle or divine announcement. [Tai. 27.]

Gon 禁 'Prohibition'; acts prohibited by Buddha.

Gonchi 權智 'The conventional wisdom'; the wisdom of knowing the relative and discriminative aspects of existences; opposed to *jitchi**.

Gonengyō 五念行 'The five mindful practices'; the five practices established by Vasubandhu (Seshin*) for attaining birth in the Pure Land. See *gonenmon* and *gokamon*☆. [S.Xa–1.]

Gonenmon 五念門 'The five practice-gates of mindfulness'; the five practices for attaining birth in the Pure Land presented in Vasubandhu's (Seshin*) *Jōdo-ron**. They are: (1) *raihai* 禮拜, worshipping Amida*; (2) *sandan* 讚嘆, praising his virtue by invoking his name; (3) *sagan* 作願, aspiration for birth in the Pure Land; (4) *kanzatsu* 觀察, contemplation on Amida, the Pure Land and bodhisattvas dwelling there; and (5) *ekō* 廻向, transferring merit to other sentient beings in order to save them from suffering. Cf. *gonengyō* and *gokamon*☆.

Gonge 權化 See *gonke*.

Gongen 權現 'Temporary manifestation'; an incarnation of a buddha or bodhisattva; a Shinto god manifested as such.

~ **Kongō dōji** --金剛童子 'An incarnation in the form of Kongō dōji*.' [Tai. 2.]

~ **no toku** --の德 'The virtue of the incarnate deity.' [Hei. 2.]

Gongo dōdan 言語道斷 'The path of words has been cut'; indescribable. [S. III-8, Vb-10, Xb-3.]

Gongu 欣求 'To aspire and seek'; to aspire to birth in the Pure Land. [IH.]

~ **jōdo** --淨土 'To aspire to birth in the Pure Land.' [Hei. 3; S. VI-10; Tai. 12, 20.]

Gongyō 勤行 'Diligent practice.' I. Effort; practice of the Buddhist Way. II. Popularly, a morning or evening service.

Gonichi hakkō 五日八講 'Eight lectures (on the *Hoke-kyō**) in five days.' [Tai. 39.]

Gonja 權者 'An incarnation'; also *gonge* 權化, *kesha* 化者 and *daigon* 大權; an incarnation of a buddha or bodhisattva. [K. 64; S.I-4, Xb-2; Tai. 15, 36.]

Gonjitsu 權實 'Expediency and truth'; an expedient teaching and the true teaching. [S. II-8, Xb-3; Tai. 24.]

Gonju 勤修 See *gonshu*.

Gonkai 禁戒 Also *kinkai*; 'Buddhist precepts'.

Gonke 權化 'Temporary transformation'; manifestation of the incarnate body of a buddha or a bodhisattva to save living beings; the temporary transformation or manifestation of a thing through supernatural power.

Gonkyō 權教 'Expedient teaching'; the teaching expounded provisionally to those who are not yet ready to understand the true teaching (*jikkyō** 實教). [S. I–8; Tai. 17.]

Gonshu 勤修 'Diligent practice.' [Tai. 5.]

Gonzetsu 言說 'Words and speeches.' I. Verbal explanation; speech. II. Exposition of the Dharma with words; one of the five kinds of exposition of the Dharma by the buddha (*goshu-seppō**).

Goon 五陰 See *goun*.

Goriki 五力 'The five powers' obtained by the practice of the five roots of goodness (*gokon** II): (1) *shinriki* 信力, firm belief in the buddha and Buddhism, which keeps away false teachings; (2) *shōjinriki* 精進力, constant application of great effort, which keeps one's body and mind alert; (3) *nenriki* 念力, mindfulness, which keeps away false thoughts; (4) *jōriki* 定力, deep concentration, which keeps away distracting thoughts; and (5) *eriki* 慧力, deep wisdom, which destroys various delusions. The five powers are included in the 37 elements of enlightenment (*san-jūshichi-dōbon**).

Gōriki 業力 'Power of karma'; the power of good or evil acts which produce good or evil effects. [S. I–7, II–9, VI–15.]

Gorin 五輪 'The five wheels or discs.' I. Another term for *gotai** 五體, the five components of one's body, namely, the head and four limbs. II. In esoteric Buddhism, refers to *godai** 五大, the five elements, namely, earth, water, fire, wind and space. III. The fingers and toes of the Buddha. IV. Abbr. of *gorin sotoba**. [Tai. 26.]

~ **sotoba** --率都婆 'A *stūpa* (*sotoba**) comprising five sections'; a tomb made up of five stone sections of different shapes and sizes, one placed on another; also *gorintō* 五輪塔, *gogedatsurin* 五解脱輪 or simply *gorin** 五輪. The five stones are in order: (1) a square stone at the bottom representing the earth element and inscribed with the Sanskrit letter A; (2) a round stone representing the water element and inscribed VA; (3) a triangular stone representing the fire element and inscribed RA; (4) a crescent stone representing the wind element and inscribed HA; and (5) a mani-jewel-shaped (see *mani*) stone on the top representing the space element and inscribed KHA. These five-stone tombs began to be constructed after the Kamakura period. See *tō*☆.

Goroku 語錄 'A record of (a Zen* master's sermons and) sayings.' [Tai. 26.]

Goryō-e 御靈會 'The soul(-appeasing) ceremony'; a Buddhist service held for the repose of the soul of a dead person who might do harm to people. [Ma. 76; O. V.]

Gosai-e 御齋會 A popular reading, the correct one being *misai-e*; also called *kyūchū gosai-e* 宮中御齋會 'the Gosai-e within the palace'. One of the three annual lecture-meetings held in Nara. It was carried out in the imperial palace for seven days beginning on the 8th of the 1st month, during which vegetarian food (*sai**) was provided and the *Konkōmyō-saishōō-kyō** was expounded for the purpose of securing the peace and well-being of the state. Its origin dates back to 768 (or 766 according to another tradition). [O.V.]

Gose 後世 I. 'The after-life.' II. Birth in Amida's* land after death. [Tsu. 98.] Cf. *nochi no yo*.

~ **bodai** --菩提 'Attainment of enlightenment in the life to come'. [S. I–7, VI–15, 18, VIII–23, Xa–1, 2, Xb–3; Tai. 32.]

~ **bodai no gongyō** --菩提の勤行 The same as ~ *bodai no tsutome*. [S. VII–14.]

~ **bodai no tsutome** --菩提の勤 Meritorious acts conducive to the attainment of enlightenment (or birth in the Pure Land) after death. [S. II–6.]

~**-ja** --者 Also *gosemono*. One who seeks birth in the Pure Land. [IH.; S. VII–21.]

~**-mon** --門 'The (teaching-)gate for the after-life'; the Pure Land teaching; see *Jōdomon*. [IH.]

~**-mono** --者 Also *goseja*. One who seeks birth in the Pure Land. [IH.]

~ **no ada** --のあだ 'Hindrance to birth in the Pure Land.' [IH.]

~ **no akugō** --の惡業 'Retributions for evil acts to be suffered in the after-life.' [Tai. 34.]

~ **no kokoro** --の心 'Aspiration for (happiness in) the after-life.' [IH.; S. II–6.]

~ **no koto** --の事 'Matter concerning the after-life'; a higher spiritual state, especially birth in the land of a buddha. [S. II–6.]

~ **no sawari** --のさはり(障) 'Hindrance to birth in the Pure Land.' [IH.; S. VI–15.]

~ **no seme** --のせめ 'Torment in the after-life.' [O.V.]

~ **no shiryō** --の資粮 'Provisions for the after-life'; merit conducive to the attainment of enlightenment or birth in the Pure Land after death. [IH.]

~ **no tsutome** --のつとめ 'The Buddhist practice performed to secure salvation in the after-life', i.e. to attain birth in Amida's* land in the next life. [IH.; K. 23.]

~ **o negau** --をねがふ 'To seek happiness in the after-life'; especially to aspire to birth in Amida's* Pure Land. [Hei. 1.]

~ **o toburau** --をとぶらう To hold a Buddhist service for the repose of a soul. [K. 138.]

Goshichinichi 後七日 See *goshichinichi mishuhō*.

~ **mishuhō** ---御修法 Also *goshichinichi mishiho*. The annual Shingon* service held at the imperial palace from the 8th to the 14th day of the 1st month, for the purpose of praying for the health of the emperor, the ever-lasting continuity of the imperial lineage, the peace of the state, and for good crops. The term *goshichinichi* 'the latter seven days' was used because various Shinto ceremonies were held during the first week of the New Year. The practice was begun by Kōbō* Daishi in 834, and then became an annual event. It was suspended after the Meiji Restoration, but was revived in 1883 at the Tōji*, Kyoto, and the service has been held there ever since.

Goshiki 五色 'The five (Buddhist) colours', namely, blue, yellow, red, white and black. [Tai. 24.]

Goshin 後身 An incarnation.

Goshin 護身 'Protection of the body' by an esoteric ritual. [K. 601; S. IV–7.]

Goshō 後生 'After-life'; the future life.

~ **bodai** --菩提 'Enlightenment to be attained in the after-life.'

~ **bodai no tsutome** --菩提の勤 'The Buddhist practices for

attaining enlightenment in the after-life.' [S. III–1.]

~ **no itonami** --の營み 'Acts in preparation for the next life'; doing meritorious acts in order to be born into a good realm in the next life. [S. VIII–22.]

~ **no tsumi** --の罪 'Offences in the next life.' [Tai. 29.]

~ **zensho** --善處 'Birth in a good realm in the next life.' [S. VI –15; Tai. 13, 19, 20, 21.]

Gōshō 迎接 A contraction of *raigō injō* 來迎引接, '(Amida's*) coming to welcome and take (an aspirant to his land)'; cf. *raigō*.

~-**e** --會 'A welcoming and taking-in service'; also *mukae-kō* 迎講; a Buddhist service in which a monk plays the role of Amida* Buddha welcoming and taking in an aspirant to the Pure Land.

Gōshō 業障 Also *gosshō*; 'karma-hindrance'; evil karma which hinders progress along the Buddhist Way; cf. *zaishō*. [S. Va–1; Tai. 33.]

Goshōgyō 五正行 'The five right practices (for attaining birth in the Pure Land)'; the five practices set up by Shan-tao 善導 (Zendō*): (1) *dokuju* 讀誦, chanting the sutras; (2) *kanzatsu* 觀察, meditating on Amida* and his land; (3) *raihai* 禮拜, worshipping Amida; (4) *shōmyō* 稱名, reciting the *nenbutsu**; and (5) *sandan kuyō* 讚 嘆供養, praising and making offerings to Amida. The fourth is called *shōjōgō** 正定業 and the rest are called *jogō** 助業.

Goshō kakubetsu 五性各別 'The five mutually distinctive natures' of sentient beings distinguished in the Hossō* sect on the basis of their spiritual capabilities. They are: (1) *bosatsu jōshō* 菩薩定性, the fixed nature of a bodhisattva (*bosatsu**); (2) *engaku jōshō* 緣覺定性, the fixed nature of a pratyekabuddha (*engaku**); (3) *shōmon jōshō* 聲聞定性, the fixed nature of a shravaka (*shōmon**); (4) *sanjō fujōshō* 三乘不定性, the indeterminate nature, i.e. the nature of those capable of becoming any two of the three kinds of sages (*sanjō**) or becoming all three at different stages; and (5) *mushō ujō* 無性有情, beings incapable of becoming any of the three kinds of sages. Of the five kinds, only those of the first and some of the fourth are able to become buddhas. [Tai. 24.]

Goshu 五衆 I. 'The five aggregates'; an older translation for *goun**, five *skandha*. [S. III–8.] II. The five groups of people in the Buddhist order. They are: (1) *biku** 比丘 (*bhikṣu*), monks; (2) *bikuni** 比丘尼 (*bhikṣuṇī*), nuns; (3) *shami** 沙彌 (*śrāmaṇera*), male novices; (4) *shamini** 沙彌尼, (*śrāmaṇerikā*), female novices; and (5) *shikishamana** 式叉摩那 (*śikṣamānā*), female novices who receive pre-ordination training; cf. *shichishu*.

Goshugyō 五種行 'The five kinds of practices'; refers to the practices of the five kinds of practitioners mentioned in the *Hoke-kyō**. See *goshu-hosshi*. [K. 604.]

Goshuhō 五種法 'The five kinds of rituals' established in esoteric Buddhism: (1) *sokusaihō** 息災法, a ritual for stopping calamities; (2) *sōyakuhō** 増益法, one for increasing merit and securing prosperity; (3) *kōchōhō** 鉤召法, one for 'summoning' sentient beings to enable them to attain higher states of existence; (4) *keiaihō** 敬愛法, one for achieving love and respect from others; and (5) *jōbukuhō** 調伏法, one for subduing devils and adversaries.

Goshu-hosshi 五種法師 'The five kinds of priests or practitioners' mentioned in the *Hoke-kyō**: (1) *juji hosshi* 受持法師, one who holds to the *Hoke-kyō*, (2) *dokyō hosshi* 讀經法師, one who reads and chants it, (3) *jukyō hosshi* 誦經法師, one who learns it by heart, (4) *gesetsu hosshi* 解說法師, one who expounds it to others, and (5) *shosha hosshi* 書寫法師, one who copies it.

Goshu-seppō 五種說法 'The five kinds of expositions of the Dharma (by the Buddha)': (1) *gon'on seppō* 言音說法, 'exposition with words'; (2) *zuigi seppō* 隨宜說法, 'exposition in accordance (with the different propensities, needs, etc., of men)'; (3) *hōben seppō* 方便說法, 'presenting the Dharma by employing various expedient means'; (4) *hōmon seppō* 法門說法, 'exposition of the doctrine'; and (5) *daihi seppō* 大悲說法, 'exposition by great compassion' for sentient beings.

Gosō jōshinkan 五相成身觀 'The fivefold meditation for realizing buddhahood'; a mystic method of attaining buddhahood quickly, which comprises the following five meditations: (1) *tsūdatsu bodaishin* 通達菩提心, attainment of the correct knowledge of one's innate Bodhi-mind by meditating on one's mind until one perceives it to be like a full moon; (2) *shū bodaishin* 修菩提心, bringing to perfection the Bodhi-mind by meditating repeatedly on one's mind; (3) *jō kongōshin* 成金剛心, accomplishing the adamantine Bodhi-mind by perceiving in meditation the lotus-flower, *vajra*-pounder (*kongōsho**), etc., of one's favoured buddha; (4) *shō kongōshin* 證金剛心, attainment of the adamantine body through union with one's favoured buddha; (5) *busshin enman* 佛身圓滿, attainment of the buddha's perfect body.

Gosō yuga 五相瑜伽 'The five-aspect practice of spiritual union'; same as *gosō jōshinkan**. [S. II–8.]

Gosui 五衰 'The five marks of decrepitude (in heavenly beings)'; see *tennin no gosui*. [Tai. 17.]

Gotai 五體 'The five body (members)', i.e. the head, arms, and feet.

~ **tōchi** --投地 'Prostrating one's body' in worshipping. [S. II–1.]

Goun 五蘊 'The five aggregates'; also 五陰 *goon*; Sk. *pañca-skandha*; the five constituent elements of all existences: (1) *shiki-un* 色蘊, matter or form; (2) *ju-un* 受蘊, perception; (3) *sō-un* 想蘊, conception (4) *gyō-un* 行蘊, volition; and (5) *shiki-un* 識蘊, consciousness. [Tai. 12.]

Goyō 五葉 'The five petals'; refers to the five Zen* schools in China; see *goke*. [Tai. 24.]

Goyoku 五欲 'The five desires' which arise in connection with the five senses of form, sound, smell, taste, and touch. Also, desire for wealth, sex, food and drink, fame, and sleep. [S. I–9, III–8, IV–9, Va–3, VI–10, VIII–22, Xa–1.]

Goyō no manako 牛羊の眼 'The eye of an ox or sheep'; feeble insight; dull intellect. [S. IV–1.]

Gozan 五山 'The five mountains'; refers to the five principal Zen* temples designated by the government with an order of precedence. At first, about the beginning of the 14th century, the five temples designated as such were only in Kamakura, namely, Kenchōji 建長寺, Engakuji 圓覺寺, Jufukuji 壽福寺, Jōchiji 淨智寺, and Jōmyōji 淨妙寺. Later, in the same century, five more Zen temples in Kyoto were designated as *gozan* temples, namely, Tenryūji 天龍寺, Shōkokuji 相國寺, Kenninji 建仁寺, Tōfukuji 東福寺, and Manjuji 萬壽寺. The order of precedence changed from time to time. [Tai. 26.]

Gōzanze 降三世 Sk. Trailokyavijaya; one of the five great *myōō** 明王 or fierce spirits. He is a messenger of Ashuku* 阿閦; cf.

godai-myōō. [S. I–3.]

Go-Zendō 後善導 Ch. Hou Shan-tao; 'the later (incarnations of or successors to) Shan-tao (Zendō*)'; refers to the two Pure Land masters, Fa-chao 法照 (Hosshō*) and .Shao-k'ang 小康 (Shōkō*), who extensively propagated the Pure Land teaching as taught by Shan-tao.

Gozō 五藏 'Five stores'; the five divisions of Buddhist scriptures. I. The five divisions adopted in the Shingon* sect are given in the *Ropparamitsu-kyō**: (1) *sotaran* 素怛纜 (Sk. *sūtra*), the Buddha's teachings; (2) *binaya* 毘奈耶 (*vinaya*), precepts; (3) *abidatsuma* 阿毘達磨 (*abhidharma*), discourses explaining the Buddha's teachings; (4) *hannyaharamitta* 般若波羅蜜多 (*prajñā-pāramitā*), transcendental wisdom of understanding all existences as void and unsubstantial; and (5) *daranimon* 陀羅尼門 (*dhāraṇī*), mystic spells. II. The five divisions of all Buddhist teachings, given in the *Shaku-makaen-ron**, corresponding to five kinds of beings, viz. men, heavenly beings, shravakas (*shōmon**), pratyekabuddhas (*engaku**), bodhisattvas, and tathagatas (*nyorai**). Some other divisions are mentioned in other texts. [S. II–10.]

Gozu 牛頭 'Ox-head', i.e. an ox-headed demon; a type of guardian of hell, distinguished by having a human body and the head of an ox. [K. 557; S. II–6; Tai. 2, 20, 33.]

~ **sendan** --旃檀 'Ox-head sandalwood'; Sk. *gośīrṣa-candana*; also *shakudan* 赤檀 'red sandalwood'. [Tai. 24.]

Gubu 供奉 Abbr. of *naigubu*; see *naigu*. [O. III.]

Guchi 愚癡 I. Stupidity, ignorance. II. In modern usage, grumbling.

~ **no yakara** --の族 'Stupid persons.' [S. I–3.]

Gujū shaba 久住娑婆 See *kujū shaba no bosatsu*.

Gumonjihō 求聞持法 'A ritual for acquiring good memory'; also called *Kokūzō monjihō** 虚空藏聞持法; a ritual dedicated to Kokūzō* Bodhisattva as a prayer for acquiring good memory.

Gumonji no hō 求聞持の法 See *gumonjihō*. [Tai. 18.]

Gunabatsuma 求那拔摩 Sk. Guṇavarman; a native of Kashmir who went to China in 424 and engaged in lectures on and translations of Buddhist texts. [S. IV–1.]

Gundari 軍荼利 Sk. Kundalin; one of the five *myōō** deities (*godai-myōō**). He has eight arms and a fearsome appearance. It is believed that, in his original state, he is the buddha Hōshō* 寶生.

~ **yasha** ---夜叉 Sk. Kundalin Yakṣa; Gundari *myōō**, sometimes called *yasha** because of his fearsome appearance. [Tai. 12.]

~ **yasha no hō** ---夜叉の法 'The rite dedicated to Kundalin Yakṣa' in order to eliminate various calamities. [Tai. 12.]

Gungi-ron 群疑論 '*Discourse* (*Clearing*) *Many Doubts*'; abbr. of *Shaku-jōdo-gungi-ron* 釋淨土群疑論; 7 fasc., by Huai-kan 懷感 (Ekan*) [TT. 47, No. 1960]. The work explains Pure Land doctrine from the viewpoint of the Hossō* teaching.

Gunjō 群生 'Multitudinous beings'; numerous living beings.

Gunrui 群類 'Multitudinous kinds of beings'; various sentient beings. [S. I–1.]

Guren daiguren 紅蓮大紅蓮 'Crimson Lotus (hell) and Large Crimson Lotus (hell)'; the 7th and 8th of the eight freezing hells (*hachikan jigoku**). Because of extreme cold, the sinner's flesh becomes crimson and is torn into the shape of lotus flowers. [Tai. 17.]

Guse 救世 See *kuse*.

Gūshi 藕絲 'Lotus-root fibres.' [Tai. 23.]

Gusoku 具足 'To contain, comprise, possess.'

Guzei 弘誓☆ 'A great or universal vow' of a bodhisattva.

~ **no fukaki** --のふかき 'Depth of the great vow.' [Hei. 2.]

Guzū 弘通 'To spread (the teaching).'

Gyakuen 逆縁☆ 'An adverse condition'; an act or state which affects adversely one's progress along the Buddhist Way; the opposite of *jun'en**; cf. *jungyaku no nien*. [Tai. 24.]

Gyakushu 逆修 'Performing in advance'; the performance of a Buddhist service for a person before he dies. [S. VI–13, 15, VII–23; Tai. 10, 26.]

Gyakuzai 逆罪 'Rebellious sin'; refers especially to the five deadly sins (*gogyakuzai**). [Tai. 3.]

Gyō 行 I. Those things which arise out of causes and conditions and constantly change; a general term for conditioned things (*ui no hō**); Sk. *saṃskāra*. II. The mental function of 'going' towards external objects; volition; one of the five aggregates (*goun**); Sk. *saṃskāra*. III. An act done with the body, or by speech or thought, with the object of attaining a higher spiritual state. IV. In Pure Land Buddhism, it refers to the *nenbutsu** practice in particular.

Gyōbō 行法 'A method of practice'; a prescribed ritual in esoteric Buddhism; used in the sense of *shuhō** 修法 and *mippō** 密法. [Hei. 2; S. II–5; Tsu. 160.]

Gyōbusshō 行佛性 'Active buddha-nature'; in the Hossō* teaching, certain categories of beings have undefiled 'seeds' (*shūji**) – potentialities of buddha wisdom – which give rise to buddha-hood. This attribute is called *gyōbusshō*; cf. *ribusshō*. [Tai. 24.]

Gyōdō 行道 '(Ceremonial) walking'; chanting a sutra as a file of priests walk round an image of a buddha.

Gyōgan 行願 'Practice and a vow.' I. A vow to do something. II. The practice of a method of salvation with the body and an aspiration or vow in the mind.

Gyōge 行解 'Practice and understanding of the doctrine.' [S. Va–3.]

Gyōgi 行基 Also Gyōki; a Hossō* priest (668–749), a descendant of a Korean king. He studied Buddhism at the Yakushiji* and elsewhere, esp. the Hossō teaching from Gien* 義淵, and travelled about the country building bridges and roads and constructing temples. He was respected by Emperor Shōmu*, who in 741 commissioned him with the task of building the Tōdaiji*. He was given the title of *daisōjō** 大僧正. In 749 he gave the bodhisattva precepts (*bosatsu-kai**) to the emperor, empress and other members of the imperial family, and was then given the title of *daibosatsu** 大菩薩. He was popularly regarded as an incarnation of Monju* (Mañjuśrī). [Tai. 24.]

Gyōgi 行儀 'Manner of performing Buddhist practices.'

Gyōgō 行業 'A Buddhist practice or practices' performed to attain a certain end, e.g. birth in Amida's* land or supernatural power.

~ **futai** --不退 'Carrying out (Buddhist) practices without retreating'; the unyielding and steadfast practice of a method of salvation. [Tai. 12, 32.]

Gyōhaku 澆薄 'Weak and thin'; refers to the period when human virtue is in this state; the same as *masse**; see also *gyōki*. [Tai. 24.]

Gyōhō 行法 See *gyōbō*.

Gyōin 行淫 'To commit an act of adultery.' [S. Va–5.]

Gyōjūzaga 行住坐臥 'Walking, standing, sitting, and lying'; the four modes of acts (*shiigi**) which are meant to embrace all man's activities. [S. Xb–3.]

Gyōki 行基 See *Gyōgi*.

Gyōki 澆季 'A period of weakening (human virtue)'; same as *masse**. [Hei. 1; Tai. 1, 24, 25, 27.]

Gyōmon 行門 'Practice-gate'; the practice aspect of the teaching.

Gyōnin 行人 'A practitioner'; a person who practises the Buddhist teaching.

~-gata --方 'Those who perform (miscellaneous duties at temples)'; one of the three groups of priests on Mt. Kōya, the other two being *hijiri-gata** 聖方 (*nenbutsu** practitioners) and *gakuryo-gata** 學侶方 (scholarly priests). They were in charge of offering incense, lamps, food, etc., to deities, and also of dealing with the secular affairs of a temple.

Gyōsō 行相 'Activity-aspect'.   I. Mental function or activity.   II. Aspect; characteristic.   III. The manner of practice.

Gyōtō 行盗 'To commit an act of robbery.' [S. Va–5.]

Gyōtoku 行德 'The merit of (Buddhist) practices.' [Tai. 27.]

Gyōyoku 樂欲 'To seek and desire'; the desire to pursue agreeable things. [Tsu. 9.]

Gyōzetsu-muge 樂說無礙 See *shimugeben*.

Gyōzō 形像 'The form and image' of a divinity. [S. II–6.]

H

Hachibushu 八部衆 The eight kinds of gods and demi-gods who protect Buddhism: (1) *ten* 天, gods or heavenly beings; (2) *ryū* 龍, dragons; (3) *yasha** 夜叉, yakṣas; (4) *kendatsuba** 乾闥婆, gandharvas; (5) *ashura** 阿修羅, asuras; (6) *karura** 迦樓羅, garuḍas; (7) *kinnara** 緊那羅, kiṃnaras; and (8) *magoraga** 摩睺羅迦, mahoragas.

Hachidai-jigoku 八大地獄 'The eight great hells': (1) *tōkatsu** 等活, 'equally reviving'; (2) *kokujō* 黑繩, 'black rope'; (3) *shugō** 衆合, 'uniting'; (4) *kyōkan* 叫喚, 'shrieking'; (5) *daikyōkan* 大叫喚, 'great shrieking'; (6) *shōnetsu** 焦熱, 'scorching heat'; (7) *daishōnetsu** 大焦熱, 'great scorching heat'; and (8) *muken* 無間, 'without intermission'. [Tai. 7.]

Hachidai-ryūō 八大龍王 'The eight great dragon kings' mentioned in the *Hoke-kyō**: (1) Nanda 難陀, Nanda,☆ (2) Batsunanda 跋難陀, Upananda, (3) Shagara 沙伽羅, Sāgara, (4) Washukitsu 和修吉, Vāsuki, (5) Tokushaka 德叉伽, Takṣaka, (6) Anabadatta 阿那婆達多, Anavatapta, (7) Manashi 摩那斯, Manasvin, and (8) Ubara 優婆羅, Utpalaka. [Tai. 2.]

Hachifū 八風 See *happū*.

Hachiji Monju 八字文殊 'Eight-syllable Mañjuśrī.' I. A kind of Mañjuśrī Bodhisattva whose attributes are represented by eight Sanskrit syllables, i.e. OṂ, ĀḤ, VI, RA, HŪṂ, KHA, CA, and RAḤ. II. Refers to *hachiji Monju hō**. [Hei. 3; Tai. 1.]

～ hō ----法 Also *Monju hachiji hō*; 'the eight-syllable Mañjuśrī rite'; first performed in 850 by Ennin* to pray for the recovery from illness of Emperor Ninmyō 仁明; said to be effective against the effects of natural calamities, esp. eclipses of the sun and moon, harm from ghosts, the disasters of war, etc.

Hachijūshu-kō 八十種好 'The eighty minor marks of physical excellence' of a buddha; also *hachijū-zuikō* 八十随好.

Hachikan hachinetsu 八寒八熱 Also *hakkan hachinetsu*; refers to *hachikan-jigoku** and *hachinetsu-jigoku**. [Tai. 20.]

～ **no nairi** ----の泥梨 'The eight freezing and eight burning hells.' [S. II–5.]

Hachikan-jigoku 八寒地獄 Also *hakkan-jigoku*; 'the eight freezing hells': (1) Abuda 頞部陀 (Arbuda), 'Swelling'; (2) Nirabuda 尼剌部陀 (Nirarbuda), 'Tumour'?; (3) Aseta 頞哳吒 (Aṭaṭa), 'Atata' (a cry); (4) Kakaba 臛臛婆 (Hahava), 'Hahava' (a cry); (5) Kokoba 虎虎婆 (Huhuva), 'Huhuva' (a cry); (6) Upara 嗢鉢羅 (Utpala), 'Blue Lotus'; (7) Hadoma 鉢特摩 or Guren 紅蓮 (Padma), 'Red Lotus'; and (8) Makahadoma 摩訶鉢特摩 or Daiguren 大紅蓮 (Mahāpadma), 'Large Red Lotus'; see *Guren daiguren.*

Hachiman Daibosatsu 八幡大菩薩 'The Great Bodhisattva Hachiman'. Hachiman, the god of archery and war, was originally Emperor Ōjin. He was the first Shinto god to be given the title of *daibosatsu**, and is also regarded as an incarnation of Amida* Buddha. [S. Vb–11; Tai. 9, 10, 18, 29, 39.]

Hachiman no hōmon 八萬の法門 'Eighty thousand Dharma-gates'; all the Buddhist teachings, numbering 80,000. More popularly, the teachings are said to number 84,000. [IH.]

Hachiman-shisen no hikari 八萬四千の光 'Eighty-four thousand rays of light (emitted by the buddha).' [Hei. 2.]

Hachiman-shisen no hōmon 八萬四千の法門 'Eighty-four thousand teaching-gates'; the innumerable teachings of the Buddha are shown by this number. [S. IV–1, VI–14.]

Hachinan 八難 'Eight difficulties'; the eight places or conditions in which one is unable to see a buddha or hear the Dharma: (1) *zai jigoku* 在地獄, being in hell; (2) *zai chikushō* 在畜生, being in the state of an animal; (3) *zai gaki* 在餓鬼, being in the state of a hungry ghost; (4) *zai chōjuten* 在長壽天, being in the heaven of long life; (5) *zai uttan'otsu* 在欝單越, being in Uttarakuru (Hokkuru*), the continent to the north of Mt. Sumeru (Shumisen*) where people always enjoy great happiness; (6) *rōmō on'a* 聾盲瘂, being deaf, blind, and mute; (7) *sechi bensō* 世智辯聰, being knowledgeable about worldly affairs, and eloquent; and (8) *butsuzen butsugo* 佛前佛後, living during the period before or after the Buddha's appearance in the world. [S. IV–9.]

Hachinetsu-jigoku 八熱地獄 'The eight scorching hells'; another name for *hachidai jigoku**.

Hachion 八音 See *hatton*.

Hachiōnichi 八王日 'The eight-king days'; the eight days of the year when celestial and terrestrial gods and *yin* 陰 and *yang* 陽 forces change: namely, (1) *risshun* 立春, the beginning of spring, (2) *shunbun* 春分, the vernal equinox, (3) *rikka* 立夏, the beginning of summer, (4) *geshi* 夏至, the summer solstice, (5) *risshū* 立秋, the beginning of autumn, (6) *shūbun* 秋分, the autumnal equinox, (7) *rittō* 立冬, the beginning of winter, and (8) *tōji* 冬至, the winter solstice.

Hachisu no mi はちす(蓮)の身 'Body on a lotus-blossom (in Amida's* Pure Land)', where one is reborn on a lotus-blossom. [Hei. 1.]

Hachisu no utena 蓮の臺 'The calyx of a lotus blossom,' i.e. in a pond of Amida's* Pure Land. [Tai. 1.]

Hachiyō 八葉 'Eight petals (of a lotus)'; refers to *Chūdai hachiyō-in**. [Hei. 3.]

∼ no chūson --の中尊 'The central deity in the *Chūdai hachiyō-in** section' of the Matrix-store Realm Mandala (*Taizōkai mandara**), i.e. Dainichi* Buddha. [Hei. 3.]

∼ no mine --の峯 'The eight peaks (of Mt. Kōya) in the form of a lotus blossom with eight petals'; they are seen from the Great Tower (Daitō 大塔) on Mt. Kōya; cf. *chūdai hachiyō-in*. [Tai. 22.]

Haisen 癈詮 'To abolish verbal explanation'; refers to *haisen danshi**. [S. III–8, Xb–2.]

∼ danshi --談旨 'To abolish verbal explanation and (thereby) tell of the tenet'; the ultimate reality-principle is only revealed by not resorting to verbal explanations; cf. *esen danshi*. [S. IV–1, Vb–10.]

Haitsudai 波逸提 Pali *pācittiya*; Sk. *pātayantika*; a group of minor offences for a monk or nun; there are 90 offences which fall in this group; an offender is said to fall into hell but, if he repents, the sin is pardoned. [S. III–5.]

Hajun 波旬 Sk. Pāpīyas; the name of the devil king said to dwell in the Paranirmitavaśavartin Heaven (Takejizaiten*). He is intent on preventing Buddhists from attaining their goal. [Hei. 3; Tai. 7, 9.]

Hakai 破戒 'Violation of precepts.'

~ **muzan no biku** --無慚の比丘 'A monk who has violated precepts and has no sense of shame.' [Tai. 12.]

~ **muzan no sō** --無慚之僧 'A priest who has violated precepts and has no sense of shame.' [K. 578.]

Hakkai 八戒 'The eight precepts'; see *hassaikai*. [S. I–10.]

~**sai** --齋 See *hassaikai*.

Hakken 法眷 'A Dharma relation'; a Zen* term used to refer to fellow-practitioners under the same master; also, generally, disciples or Buddhist companions. [Tai. 25, 26.]

Hakkō 八講 Also *hakō*; refers to *hokke hakkō** or *saishō no gohakkō**. [Ma. 31, 32; S. VI–7; Tai. 24.]

Hakku 八苦 'The eight pains': (1) *shōku* 生苦, the pain accompanying one's birth, (2) *rōku* 老苦, the pain of getting old, (3) *byōku* 病苦, the pain of illness, (4) *shiku* 死苦, the pain of death, (5) *aibetsuriku* 愛別離苦, the pain of separating from those one loves, (6) *onzōeku* 怨憎會苦, the pain of meeting those one hates, (7) *gufutokku* 求不得苦, the pain of not getting what one seeks, and (8) *goonjōku* 五陰盛苦, the pain accompanying the growth of one's mind and body. [Tai. 39.]

Hakkudokuchi 八功德池 'Ponds with (water possessing) eight qualities'; refers to ponds in Amida's* Pure Land; cf. *hakkudokusui*. [Tai. 11.]

Hakkudokusui 八功德水 'The water possessing eight qualities'. According to the *Shōsan-jōdo-kyō* 稱讚淨土經, the eight qualities consist of its being: (1) pure, (2) cool, (3) good-tasting, (4) soft, (5) moistening, (6) comforting, (7) thirst-quenching, and (8) nourishing. The water of the ponds of Amida's* land and that of the seven oceans encircling Mt. Sumeru (Shumisen*) are said to possess those qualities. [K. 58; S. II–8.]

Hakō 八講 See *hakkō*.

Hakubaji 白馬寺 Ch. Pai-ma-ssu; 'the White Horse Temple'; the first temple in China built in Lo-yang 洛陽 (Rakuyō) when Kāśya-pamātaṅga (迦葉摩騰 Kashōmatō*) and Chu Fa-lan 竺法蘭 (Jiku Hōran*) came from India in 67 A.D. [Tai. 24.]

Hakuji 薄地 'The slight or inferior level or stage.' I. A bodhisattva stage at which one's false desires and delusions have become 'slight'. II. The lowest of the three levels of ordinary beings, the other two being *naibon* 内凡 'inner ordinary (beings)' and *gebon* 外凡 'outer ordinary (beings)'. In this case, *haku* means 'contemptuous, mean'; it is also interpreted in the sense of *hitsu* 逼 'oppressed (by various sufferings)' or *haku* 博 'extensive (number of people on this level)'.

~ **no bonbu** -- の凡夫 'Ordinary people at the inferior level (of spirituality).' [Tai. 23.]

Hakurochi 白鷺池 'White-heron pond'; the pond said to have been in the Bamboo-grove monastery (Chikurin shōja*). [Hei. 2.]

Handoku 般特 Refers to Shurihandoku*. [S. II–1.]

Hanju-san 般舟讃 '*Hymns on the Hanju (Zanmai)*'; 1 fasc., by Shan-tao (Zendō*) [TT. 47, No. 1981]. This work eulogizes Amida's* Pure Land and explains the method of attaining birth there. The full title is *E-kangyō-tō-myō-hanjuzanmai-gyōdō-ōjō-san* 依観經等明般舟三昧行道往生讃. [S. II–8, IV–1, VI–10.]

Hankaza 半跏坐 'Half-cross-legged sitting'; the half-lotus posture, sitting with the right foot placed on the left knee and the left foot placed under the right knee.

Hannya 般若 I. Sk. *prajñā*; transcendental wisdom; cf. *rokuhi hannya* and *sanhannya*. II. Refers to *Hannya-haramitta-kyō*. See also *shobu no hannya*.

~ **kōdoku no chikara** -- 講讀の力 'The efficacy of chanting the *Hannya-kyō* (i.e. *Daihannya-kyō**).' [Tai. 23.]

~ **no chika** -- の智火 'The wisdom-fire of Prajñā'; the tran-scendental wisdom destroys delusions, hence 'fire'. [S. IV–9.]

~ **no hōmi** -- の法味 'The taste of the Dharma of *hannya*.' [S. VII–23.]

~-**shin-gyō** -- 心經 '*The Essence of Prajñāpāramitā sutra*'; Sk. *Prajñāpāramitā-hṛdaya-sūtra*. A short sutra presenting the gist of the transcendental wisdom of the void (*hannya**). Of the six Chinese translations, the one by Hsüan-chuang 玄奘 (Genjō*)

[TT. 8, No. 251] is the most popular. Cf. *Daihannya-haramitta-shin-gyō* and *Shingyō*.

~**-zō** --藏 'Collection of *Prajñā-pāramitā* sutras' which expound the voidness of all existences. One of the five divisions of the Buddhist teachings given in the *Ropparamitsu-kyō**. See *gozō*. [S. II–8.]

Hansoku Ō 斑足王 Also 班足王; King Kalmāṣapāda ('spotted feet'); a legendary king of Devala (Tenra 天羅) in ancient times. In accordance with the instruction of a wrong teacher, he planned to make a sacrifice of the heads of 1,000 kings. After capturing 999 kings, the 1,000th king, named Fumyō 普明, had a *Ninnō-e** service held for a day, to which 100 priests were invited. The first priest expounded a verse on impermanence. On hearing this, Fumyō and Hansoku attained emancipation. The 1,000 kings were then released and allowed to go home. Hansoku is believed to be a previous incarnation of Aṅglimāla (Ōkutsumara*). [Tai. 23.]

Hansoku Taishi 斑足太子 'Prince Kalmāṣapāda'; see *Hansoku Ō*. [Tai. 36.]

Happū 八風 'The eight winds'; also *happō* 八法, the eight *dharma* or things. The eight elements which 'fan' one's love and hate; hence, they are called 'winds'. They are: (1) *ri* 利, profit, (2) *ai* 哀, sorrow, (3) *ki* 毀, slander, (4) *yo* 譽, fame, (5) *shō* 稱, praise, (6) *ki* 譏, censure, (7) *ku* 苦, pain, and (8) *raku* 樂, pleasure. [S. III –3.]

Harai 波羅夷 See *haraizai*. [S. III–5.]

~**-zai** ---罪 'The *Pārājika* offences'; the four gravest offences for a monk: (1) having sexual intercourse, (2) stealing, (3) homicide, and (4) lying about his spiritual attainment. Committing one of these offences involves permanent expulsion. [S.I–1.]

Haramitsu 波羅蜜 (or 密) Sk. *pāramitā*; translated as *do* 度 'crossing over, salvation' and *tōhigan* 到彼岸 'reaching the other shore (i.e. Nirvana)'; attainment of the state of emancipation; perfection of Buddhist practices. There are six kinds of practice required of a bodhisattva in order to attain enlightenment; these are called *ropparamitsu**.

Harana-koku 波羅奈國 Bārāṇasī; n. of a kingdom and its capital in central India at the time of the Buddha; also known as Kāśī (迦尸國 Kashi-koku); the capital was near present-day Benares. In the city was the Deer Park (鹿野苑 Rokuya-on*), where the Buddha expounded the Dharma for the first time after his enlightenment and converted his five former companions. [Tai. 35, 37.]

Hashinoku 波斯匿　Sk. Prasenajit; see next entry.

~ **Ō** --- 王　'King Prasenajit'; the king of Śrāvastī (Shae*) and a great patron of the Buddha. [Tai. 24, 35.]

Hassai 八災　Refers to *hassaigen* 八災患; the eight disturbances to meditation, i.e. sorrow, joy, pain, pleasure, consideration (*jin* 尋, Sk. *vitarka*), reflection (*shi* 伺, *vicāra*), exhalation and inhalation. After removing these, one attains the fourth meditation of the realm of form (*shikikai**). [Tsu. 238.]

Hassaikai 八齋戒　'The eight precepts of abstinence' according to which a lay Buddhist should abstain from the following on fixed days of the month: (1) killing living beings; (2) stealing; (3) sexual intercourse; (4) telling lies; (5) drinking intoxicants; (6) such acts as wearing bodily decoration, using perfume, singing and dancing, and going to see dances or plays; (7) sleeping in a raised bed; and (8) eating after noon. The first seven are *kai** 戒 and the last is *sai** 齋. Also called *hakkaisai* 八戒齋.

Hasshiki 八識　The eight consciousnesses established in the Hossō* sect: (1) *genshiki* 眼識, visual consciousness, (2) *nishiki* 耳識, auditory consciousness, (3) *bishiki* 鼻識, olfactory consciousness, (4) *zesshiki* 舌識, gustatory consciousness, (5) *shinshiki* 身識, tactile consciousness, (6) *ishiki* 意識, thought-consciousness, the function of which is to discriminate objects, (7) *manashiki* 末那識, *manas*-consciousness, the function of which is to perceive the subjective portion of the eighth consciousness and erroneously regard it as one's ego, thereby creating ego-attachment, and (8) *arayashiki** 阿賴耶識, *ālaya*-consciousness, the foundation consciousness of one's existence, which stores all potential energy for the mental and physical manifestations of one's existence. [S. III–1.]

~ **gojū no myōkyō** -- 五重之明鏡　'A clear mirror of fivefold contemplation with regard to the eight consciousnesses'; *gojū* refers to *gojū yuishikikan** established in the Hossō* sect; see also *hasshiki*. [Tai. 17.]

Hasshōdō 八聖道, 八正道 'The eightfold holy path'; the eight items of practice for attaining Nirvana; Sk. *ārya-aṣṭāṅgika-mārga*: also *hasshi-shōdō* 八支聖道, *hasshō-dōbun* 八聖道分, etc. They are: (1) *shōken* 正見, right views; (2) *shōshiyui* 正思惟, right thoughts; (3) *shōgo* 正語, right speech; (4) *shōgō* 正業, right acts; (5) *shōmyō* 正命, right living; (6) *shōshōjin* 正精進, right effort; (7) *shōnen* 正念, right mindfulness or recollection; and (8) *shōjō* 正定, right meditation.

Hasshū 八宗 'The eight sects'; Kusha*, Jōjitsu, Ritsu*, Hossō*, Sanron*, Kegon*, Tendai* and Shingon*. The first six arose in the Nara period (710–94) and the last two in the Heian period (794–1192). [Tai. 24.]

~-ha --派 'The eight sects'; see *hasshū*. [Tai. 24.]

~ kushū --九宗 'The eight or nine sects.' The nine sects are Kusha*, Jōjitsu, Ritsu*, Hossō*, Sanron*, Tendai*, Kegon* Shingon* and Zen*. Cf. *rokushū* and *jūsanshū*. [Hei. 2.]

Hasshu-bonnonjō 八種梵音聲 See *hatton*.

Hasshu-shōjōon 八種清淨音 See *hatton*.

Hassō 八相 'Eight aspects'; the eight major events in the Buddha's life. There are several traditions, one of which is: (1) *gōtosotsu* 降兜率, descending from the Tuṣita (Tosotsu*) Heaven; (2) *takutai* 託胎, being conceived in the mother's womb; (3) *shusshō* 出生, birth; (4) *shukke* 出家, renunciation of the world; (5) *gōma* 降魔, defeating devils; (6) *jōdō* 成道, enlightenment; (7) *tenpōrin* 轉法輪, preaching the law; and (8) *nyūnehan* 入涅槃, passing into Nirvana.

~ jōdō --成道 'Becoming a buddha by (manifesting) eight aspects.' [Tai. 15, 18, 39.]

~ no kegi --の化儀 'The (Buddha's) method of converting people by (manifesting himself in this world showing) eight aspects.' [S. II–5.]

Hatsumu 撥無 'To reject and negate'; often used in the phrase *inga o hatsumu su**. [S. III–5.]

Hattō 法堂 'A Dharma-hall'; a hall in a Zen* temple where the exposition of the Dharma takes place; this building corresponds to the *kōdō* 講堂 'lecture-hall' in the temples of some other sects. A *hattō* is usually built behind the *butsuden** 佛殿 'buddha-hall'.

[S. Xb–3; Tai. 24.]

Hatton 八音　The eight superior qualities of the Buddha's voice; also called *hasshu-shōjōon* 八種清淨音 and *hasshu-bon'onjō* 八種梵音聲. There are several traditions, but the *Hokkai-shidai* 法界次第 gives the following: (1) *gokukōon* 極好音, the most pleasant voice, (2) *nyūnan'on* 柔軟音, the soft voice, (3) *wachakuon* 和適音, the harmonious voice, (4) *son'eon* 尊慧音, the dignified and wise voice, (5) *funyoon* 不女音, the masculine voice, (6) *fugoon* 不誤音, the unerring voice, (7) *jinnon'on* 深遠音, the deep and far-reaching voice, and (8) *fukatsuon* 不竭音, the inexhaustible voice.　[S. III –1.]

Heizei 平生　'At ordinary times'; opposite of *rinjū** 'at the time of death'.

Henge 反化　See *henge* 變化. [Tai. 24.]

Henge 遍計　'All-pervasive calculation'; refers to *henge shoshūshō**. [S. III–1, Vb–8.]

～-shoshū --所執　Existences produced from 'all-pervasive attachment'; see *henge shoshūshō*.　[S. III–1.]

～-shoshūshō --所執性　Sk. *parikalpita-svabhāva*, 'the nature (of existence) produced from all-pervasive imagination'; said of the existences produced from one's illusory attachment and falsely considered to be real. Cf. *sanshō* 三性.

Henge 變化　'A transformation, incarnation.'

～ no hito --の人　'(A deity) incarnated in human form.'　[S. II –1; Ta.]

～ no mono --のもの(物)　'A transformation, incarnation'; a deity or a spirit transformed into a man, etc.　[Ma. 179; Ta.]

Henja 邊邪　Refers to *henken** 邊見 and *jaken** 邪見; cf. *goken*. [S. Va–1.]

Henjōju 變成就　'Accomplishing a change.'　I. N. of an immoral esoteric rite, advanced by a Shingon* school called Tachikawa-ryū* 立川流, in which a sexual union is considered to represent the unity of the noumenal principle and transcendental wisdom. [S. VI–16.]　II. Refers to *henjō nanshi**.

Henjō nanshi 變成男子　'Transforming (a woman) into a man.' As a woman is said to be incapable of practising the Buddhist path properly and becoming a buddha, a woman who seeks to attain buddhahood must be transformed into a man, and many bodhisattvas make a vow to effect this.

~ **no hō** ----の法 An esoteric rite to change a female embryo into a male one. [Hei. 3; Tai. 1.]

Henken 邊見 'Extreme view'; the view that 'self' will continue to exist after death or that it will cease to exist; one of the five wrong views (*goken**).

Henkū 偏空 'One-sided (view of) emptiness'; a one-sided view that understands the doctrine of emptiness in negative terms only; also *tankū**. [S. III–8.]

~ **no ge** --の解 'Understanding (the doctrine of) emptiness in a wrong, one-sided way'; a relative and biased view of the doctrine of emptiness. [S. III–8.]

Henshō jūninen 遍(=偏)小十二季 'Exclusively (expounding) Hinayana for 12 years'; according to the Tendai* doctrine, the Buddha expounded only Hinayana teachings for the first 12 years after he attained enlightenment. [Tai. 18.]

Henshū 偏執 Also *henjū*; 'biased and attached'; a biased and misguided view; attachment to a wrong view.

~ **gaman** --我慢 'A biased view and self-pride'; attachment to one's own view. [S. IV–1.]

~ **gaman no kokoro** --我慢の心 'A heart imbued with a biased view and self-pride'. [S. I–10.]

~ **gasō** --我相 'Clinging to one's biased view.' [S. IV–1.]

~ **zehi** --是非 'A biased view as to the right and wrong (teachings).' [S. IV–1.]

Hianryūtai 非安立諦 'Non-established truth'; reality in the absolute sense which is beyond words and concepts. Opposite of *anryūtai**; cf. *shintai*. [S. IV–1, Xb–2.]

Hibō 誹謗 Also *hihō*; 'slandering (the Dharma).'

~ **shōbō** --正法 'Slandering the true law'; rejecting the Buddhist teaching. [S. IV–1.]

Hichi no hōben 悲智の方便 The means of salvation which arises out of and is supported by compassion and wisdom. [S. II–7.]

Hiden 悲田 'A field of compassion'; the act of giving things to the poor or needy produces merit, so it is compared to a field or farm; also *bingū fukuden* 貧窮福田; one of the three fields of merit (*sanfukuden**). [S. IV–9, VII–11, 25.]

Higa 彼我 'He and I'; an external object and the subjective self; subject-object discrimination.

Higakushō 非學生 'Non-student'; one who is not a student; a student of Buddhism unworthy of the name. Cf. *gakushō*. [S. Va–6.]

Higan 彼岸 'The other shore.' I. The other shore of the stream of transmigration, i.e. Nirvana. II. Accomplishment of a task. III. Refers to *higan'e**.

~**-e** --會 'The *higan* festival'; the Buddhist services held twice a year, in spring and autumn, for a period of seven days over the equinox.

~**-jo** --所 'The place for performing the *higan** service' at each of the 21 Sannō* shrines. [Tai. 15.]

Higan 悲願 'The compassionate vow' of a buddha or bodhisattva.

Higō 非業 'Not karma'; not arising from some karmic cause in a previous life; often used of an untimely death caused by some accident, calamity, etc. [Tai. 26.]

Hihō 非法 'Unlawful'; against the law; not observing the precepts; an unlawful and heretical view or teaching. [S. Xa–6.]

Hihō 祕法 'An esoteric method (of practice)'; same as *shubō**.

Hiji 非時 'Wrong time'; refers to *hijijiki* 非時食, taking a meal at the wrong time (i.e. after noon) or a meal taken then. [K. 551; Tsu. 60.]

Hijiri 聖 'A holy man, a sage'. I. An epithet for a man of outstanding wisdom and virtue. II. Especially, an epithet for a virtuous priest: e.g. Amida-hijiri* 阿彌陀聖 and Ichi-no-hijiri* 市聖 for Kōya* (903–72). III. An epithet for a monk who lives in a particular place: e.g. Kōya-hijiri* 高野聖. IV. An epithet for a monk who walks about the country; such a monk is called *yugyō-hijiri** 遊行聖. V. Generally, an epithet for a monk without out a priestly rank.

~**-gata** -方 'The sages'; *nenbutsu** practitioners on Mt. Kōya. See *Kōya hijiri*.

Hijō jōbutsu 非情成佛 'Insentient things attaining buddhahood'. Also *sōmoku jōbutsu**.

Hike-kyō 悲華經 '*The Compassion Lotus Sutra*'; 10 fasc., tr. by Dharmakṣema (Donmushin 曇無讖) [TT. 3, No. 157]; there is another translation, 8 fasc., with the title of *Daijō-hifundari-kyō* 大乘悲分陀利經 [TT. 3, No. 158]; the Sanskrit title is *Karuṇā-puṇḍarīka-sūtra*. [S. II–10, VI–18.]

Himitsuju 祕密咒 'A mystic spell.' [Tai. 2.]

Himitsu kanjō 祕密灌頂 'Mystic sprinkling on the head.' I. Generally, a ceremony in which a specific spiritual status is conferred on a disciple by a master in esoteric Buddhism. II. The last of the five stages of conferment of spiritual status, in which one attains the most abstruse wisdom. [K. 52.]

Himitsushu 祕密主 'Lord of Mystery'; refers to Kongōsatta*.

Himon 悲門 'Compassion-aspect'; cf. *chimon*. [S. I–3.]

Hinin bōshi 非人法師 'A non-human priest'; a Buddhist hermit who has renounced the world. [IH.]

Hi no in 火の印 See *kain*.

Hinshi 貧士 'A poor gentleman'; a Buddhist mendicant; the same as *shamon**. [S. Pref.]

Hipparakutsu 畢波羅窟 Sk. *Pippala-guhā*; n. of the cave near Rājagṛha (*Ōshajō**) where the first conference was held soon after the Buddha's death. [S. IV–1.]

Hiryō 比量 'Inference'; Sk. *anumāna*; one of the three means of cognition of objects, the other two being *genryō** and *shōgyōryō**. [S. IV–1.]

Hiryū Daisatta 飛瀧大薩埵 'The Great Bodhisattva Hiryū'; Hiryū Gongen* is believed to be an incarnation of Senju Kannon*. [Hei. 2.]

Hiryū Gongen 飛瀧權現 The Gongen* god dwelling in Nachi 那智, Wakayama Prefecture. [Hei. 2.]

Hisōhihisōjo 非想非非想處 Also Hisōhibisōjo; 'Abode of neither Thought nor Non-Thought'; also Hisōhihisōten 非想非非想天; Sk. Naivasaṃjñā-nāsaṃjñā-āyatana; the fourth and the highest of the four abodes in the realm of non-form (*mushikikai**), where inhabitants are free of ordinary discriminative thoughts and retain only the barest traces of any discriminative thoughts at all; cf. *mushikikai.*

Hisōhihisōten 非想非非想天 Also Hisōhibisōten 'Heaven of neither Thought nor Non-Thought'; see *Hisōhihisōjo.* [Tai. 16.]

Hisōten 非想天 Abbr. of Hisōhihisōten*. [Tai. 21.]

Hitsujō 必定 'Certainly fixed'; the stage of certainty of attaining buddhahood. The term appears in the 'Igyō-bon' 易行品 of Nāgārjuna (Ryūju*), in which it is said that he who thinks of Amida and calls his name enters this stage. The term is used as a synonym of *futai** 不退 and *shōjōju** 正定聚. [S. Xa–1.]

～ **no gō** -- の業 'An act for attaining the stage of certainty (of buddhahood).' [S. Xa–1.]

Hitsuju 筆受 A member of a group of Chinese translators; one in charge of copying down what the chief translator has rendered from Sanskrit. [Tsu. 108.]

Hiyu 譬喩 I. 'An analogy; an allegory.' II. A scriptural parable; Sk. *avadāna*; one of the nine and the twelve kinds of scriptures (*kubu-kyō** and *jūnibu-kyō**), which expounds the Dharma through allegories.

Hizō 祕藏 'A secret treasury'; i.e. a secret teaching. [S. II–8.]

Hizō 悲增 'Predominance of compassion'; said of the spiritual quality of a type of bodhisattva in whom compassion is predominant and wisdom is less obvious; the opposite of *chizō**. [S. Xa–1.]

Hō 法 Sk. *dharma.* I. Law, truth. II. The Buddha's teaching. III. An object of thought. IV. A thing, element.

Hō 報 'Reward, retribution'; the effect of an action.

Hōai 法愛 'Love of the Dharma'; love of the Buddhist law. [S. VI–5.]

Hōben 方便 'A method, means, device' as of saving suffering beings; Sk. *upāya.*

～ **anryūtai** --安立諦 'Provisionally established truth'; truth explained in words. [S. Xb-2.]

～-**bon** --品 'Chapter on Expedient Means'; the second chapter of the *Hoke-kyō**. This chapter explains that the Three-Vehicle teachings (*sanjō**), i.e. the teachings applicable to bodhisattvas, pratyekabuddhas (*engaku**), and shravakas (*shōmon**), are provisional and that the One-Vehicle teaching (*ichijō**) presented in the *Hoke-kyō** is the only real teaching of the Buddha. [K. 42; O. III.]

～ **kyōke** -- 敎化 'Teaching and converting by skilful means.' [S. III–1.]

～ **no gimon** -- の義門 'The principle-gate of expedient means'; the aspect of the teaching having the aim of guiding people; provisional and introductory teaching. [S. IV–1.]

～ **no mon** -- の門 'The gate of expedient means'; an expedient means of guiding people to Buddhism. [Tai. 36.]

～ **riki** -- 力 'Power of expediency'; the power to exercise skilful means to save living beings. [Tai. 24.]

～ **uyodo** -- 有餘土 The land temporarily established (for those who have destroyed major evil passions, thereby attaining emancipation from transmigration in the three realms [*sangai**], but who still) have other (minor delusions to be dealt with); one of the four lands (*shido**) distinguished in the Tendai* sect; also called *hōbendo* 方便土 and *uyodo* 有餘土.

Hōbō 謗法 Also bōhō; 'abuse of the Dharma'; reviling the Buddhist teaching. [S. VI–10.]

Hōdan 法談 'Preaching the Dharma'; expounding the Buddhist teaching. [Tai. 4.]

Hōdo 報土 'Land of recompense'; a buddha's land created by his vows and practices.

Hōdo 寶土 'The treasure land'; refers to Amida's* land. [K. 57.]

Hōdō 法堂 See *hattō*.

Hōdō shōgon 寶堂莊嚴 'Adornment of a treasure-hall'; adorning a temple with decorations. [Tai. 24.]

Hōe 法衣 'The Dharma-robe'; a monk's robe; see *sanne*.

Hōe 法會 'A Buddhist service.'

Hōgai 寶蓋 'A jewelled canopy.' [S. II–8.]

Hōgen 法眼 'Dharma-eye.' I. Wisdom or insight to see the reality of things or the essence of the Buddha's teaching. II. Refers to *hōgen-kashō-i**. [Hei. 3; Tai. 5.]

～**-kashō-i** -- 和尚位 'The rank of Master of the Dharma-eye'; the rank of the priesthood next to *hōin-daikashō-i**.

Hōgen 法驗　See *hōken*.

Hōgi 法義　'The meaning of the Buddhist teaching.'

Hōgō 寶號　'Treasure-name'; the sacred and revered name of a buddha or bodhisattva. [Hei. 2; K. 64; S. II–5.]

Hōhō 方袍　'A square robe'; also *hōbuku* 方服; refers to the three robes of a monk (*sanne** 三衣). [Tai. 39.]

Hōi 法威　'Power of the Dharma.' [Tai. 8, 15, 20, 23.]

Hōin 法印　'The seal of the Dharma.'　I. The basic teaching which distinguishes Buddhism from other teachings; cf. *sanbō-in*.　II. Manual signs used in esoteric Buddhism; cf. *ingei*.　III. Refers to a particular rank of the priesthood, *hōin-daikashō-i**; later a title of honour given to Buddhist sculptors, painters, poets, etc. [Hei. 3; K. 59; S. Vb–2.]　IV. The mark of the ultimate reality or enlightenment. [S. Vb–11.]

~-daikashō-i -- 大和尚位　'The rank of the Dharma-seal great master'; the highest of the three higher ranks of the priesthood, corresponding to the older term *sōjō**; the other two were *hōgen-kashō-i** 法眼和尚位　and *hokkyō-shōnin-i** 法橋上人位　which corresponded to *sōzu** and *risshi**, respectively. These new titles came to be used in 864. [K. 59.]

Hōitsu 放逸　'Unrestrained, indolent, wanton.'

Hōjin 報身　'Reward-body'; Sk. *sambhogakāya*; the body of a buddha received as the result of his meritorious practices; one of the three bodies of a buddha (*sanshin**).

Hōji-san 法事讚　'*Hymns for Services*'; 2 fasc., by Shan-tao 善導 (Zendō*) [TT. 47, No. 1979]. The work contains hymns in praise of Amida* and hymns of repentance which are to be chanted between passages of the *Amida-kyō**. The full title is *Tengyō-gyōdō-gan-ōjōjōdo-hōjisan* 轉經行道願往生淨土法事讚. [Tsu. 227.]

Hōjō 方丈　'Ten feet square.'　I. A 10-foot square room.　II. The room of a head priest.　III. A head priest.

Hōjō 放生　'Releasing living things', such as fish and birds.

~ dai-e -- 大會　'A great life-releasing ceremony.' Cf. *hōjō-e*. [K. 703.]

~-e -- 會　'Life-releasing ceremony', in which fish and birds held in captivity are set free. The ceremony was popularly practised in China and Japan as a positive way of doing good. In Japan it was first held in 720 at Usa 宇佐 Hachiman-gū. Later, since 974, the ceremony was held at Iwashimizu 石清水 Hachiman-gū on the 15th of the 8th month. After being discontinued for about 200 years, the ceremony was revived in 1679. Minamoto Yoritomo 源頼朝 started a *hōjō-e* at Tsurugaoka 鶴岡 Hachiman-gū in 1187. The ceremony consists of chanting a spell and freeing fish into a pond or river, or setting birds free. [K. 230, 499, 703; O. VI; Tai. 24.]

Hōju 寶珠 Also *hōshu*; 'a treasure-gem'; refers to *manishu** 摩尼珠 'a mani gem'.

Hōjū hōi no kotowari 法住法位の理 The principle of reality in which things are perceived in their original states; the phrase '*hōjū hōi*' (lit. 'dharmas dwell in the dharma state') appears in the *Hoke-kyō**. [S. IV–1.]

Hōkai 法界 See *hokkai*.

Hōkai 寶海 'Treasure Sea'; Sk. Samudrareṇu; n. of a minister mentioned in the *Hike-kyō** who later became Shakamuni*; see *Mujōnen*.

Hoke-kyō 法華經 '*The Lotus Sutra*'; abbr. of *Myōhōrenge-kyō**.

 ~-kaidai - - -開題 '*Explanation of the Title of the Lotus Sutra*'; a work by Kūkai*, 5 fasc. [TT. 56, No. 2190].

 ~ no go no kan - - -の五の卷 'The fifth fascicle of the *Hoke-kyō**'; it includes the following chapters: (1) 'Daibadatta-bon' 提婆達多品 (Chapter on Devadatta); (2) 'Kanji-bon' 勸持品 (Chapter on Exertion); (3) 'Anrakugyō-hon' 安樂行品 (Chapter on Peaceful Practice); and (4) 'Jūjiyushutsu-bon' 從地涌出品 (Chapter on the Emergence of Bodhisattvas from Gaps in the Earth). During the four-day period of lectures on the *Hoke-kyō* (*Hokke hakkō**), the fourth day has the special name *gokan no hi* 五卷の日 because the fifth fascicle is expounded in the morning session. This day is considered especially important because of the great importance attached to the 'Daibadatta-bon'. [Tai. 21.]

 ~ tendoku - - -轉讀 'Chanting of the *Hoke-kyō*'; see *tendoku*. [K. 56, 59.]

Hōken 法驗 'The efficacy of the Dharma'; the effect of the performance of a method of practice; cf. *sōji no hōken*. [K. 266, 595, 604; Tai. 12.]

Hōkenrin 法慳悋(=悋) 'Meanness with the Dharma'; being reluctant in teaching others. [K. 495.]

Hōki 法喜 'Joy of (hearing or practising) the Dharma.' [S. IV–1.]

Hōki 法器 'A vessel of the Dharma'; a man capable of receiving the Dharma; often, a man of outstanding capacity for doing this. [S.Va–4, Xa–8.]

Hōki 法機 'Capacity for receiving the Dharma'; often, a man of outstanding capacity for understanding and practising the Dharma. [S. Va–4.]

Hokkai 法界 'Dharma-realm, dharma-essence'; Sk. *dharma-dhātu*. I. The realm or sphere of the ultimate reality. II. The whole universe. III. The objects of the mind in general.

~-gū --宮 Also *Hōkaigū*; 'the Dharma-realm Palace'; the palace of Dainichi* of the Matrix-store Realm Mandala (*Taizōkai mandara**), which is located in the Maheśvara Heaven (Daijizai-ten*). The full name is Kōdai Kongō Hōkaigū 廣大金剛法界宮 'The Great Palace of the Diamond(-like) Dharma-realm'. [S. I–1, II–8.]

~ no sangan --の三觀 'The three levels of contemplation for (realizing the ultimate reality of) the universe' in the Kegon* teaching; see *sangan* II.

~ no shujō --の衆生 'Sentient beings throughout the universe.' [S. Va–4, VII–17.]

~ riki --力 'The power of the Dharma-realm'; the power of buddha-nature which works to enlighten one from within. One of the three powers; see *sanriki*. [S. II–8.]

~-taishōchi --體性智 'The essence of the Dharma-realm wisdom'; Sk. *dharma-dhātu-svabhāva-jñāna*; the wisdom of knowing the quintessence of all existences; in esoteric Buddhism, one of the five wisdoms (*gochi**).

~ tōru --等流 'Homogeneous outflow from the Dharma-realm'; that which comes from the realm of ultimate reality without changing its quality, e.g. the Buddha's teaching and voice. [S. Va–1.]

Hokke 法華(also 法花) Refers to *Hoke-kyō**, the *Lotus Sutra*.

~-dō --堂 Abbr. of *Hokke-zanmai-dō* 法華三昧堂. A hall where the Hokke meditation (*Hokke-zanmai**) is practised. [Tsu. 25.]

~-**gengi** --玄義 '*The Deep Meanings of the Hoke-kyō**'; 20 fasc., by Chih-i 智顗 (Chigi*); the full title is *Myōhōrenge-kyō-gengi* 妙法蓮華經玄義 [TT. 33, No. 1716]. It is a series of lectures on the essential doctrine of the *Hoke-kyō* given by Chih-i in 593 and recorded and edited by his disciple Kuan-ting 灌頂 (Kanchō); one of the three major works of Master T'ien-t'ai (Tendai Daishi*).

~ **hakkō** --八講 Also, simply, *hakkō* 八講; 'eight lectures on (eight fascicles of) the *Hoke-kyō**'; with two lectures in a day, one in the morning and one in the evening, the whole session covers four days; cf. *gokan no hi* and *ikke hakkō*.

~ **ichijō** --一乘 'The One-Vehicle teaching of the *Hoke-kyō**'; cf. *ichijō*. [K. 49.]

~ **nenbutsu ichigu** --念佛一具 '(The teaching of) the *Hoke-kyō** and (that of) the *nenbutsu** are one.' [S. IV–1.]

~ **no gokaidai** --の御開題 See *Hoke-kyō kaidai*. [S. IV–1.]

~ **no jisha** --の持者 'Holder of the *Lotus Sutra*'; one who chants the *Hoke-kyō** and follows its teaching. [K. 56.]

~ **sanbukyō** --三部經 'The triple sutras of Hokke'; the three principal sutras used in the Tendai* and Nichiren* sects. They are: (1) *Muryōgi-kyō* 無量義經, which serves as an introduction to the *Lotus Sutra*; (2) *Hoke-kyō** 法華經, the *Lotus Sutra*, which is the main discourse of the Hokke teaching; and (3) *Fugenkan-gyō* 普賢觀經, which serves as the conclusion of the Hokke teaching; cf. *kaiketsu no nikyō*.

~ **senbō** --懺法 I. 'The Hokke method of annulling sins'; see *hokke-zanmai*. II. An abridged text of the *Hokke-zanmai-sengi* 法華三昧懺儀 by Chih-i 智顗 (Chigi*), based on the *Hoke-kyō** and other Mahayana sutras [TT. 46, No. 1941]. The text was popularized in Japan by Ennin*, and was recited every morning on Mt. Hiei.

~ **tendoku** --轉讀 'Chanting of the *Hoke-kyō**'; see *tendoku*. [K. 56.]

~-**zanmai** --三昧 'The Lotus *Samādhi*'; Sk. *saddharma-puṇḍarīka-samādhi*. One of the four kinds of *Samādhi* (*shishu-zanmai** 四種三昧) practised in the Tendai* sect; also called *hangyō-hanza-zanmai* 半行半坐三昧. A method of meditation, based on the *Hoke-kyō** and the *Kan-fugen-bosatsu-gyōhō-kyō* 觀普賢菩薩行

法經, in which one chants the *Hoke-kyō* while circumambulating the hall and contemplating the principles of the Middle Path (*chūdō** 中道) and of the ultimate reality (*jissō** 實相). The period of the practice is fixed at three weeks. It is also called *Hokke senbō** 法華懺法 (or simply *Hokkesen* 法華懺), 'the Hokke method of annulling sins', because it is practised for that purpose.

~-zanmai-kyō 法花(=華)三昧經 '*Dharma-flower Samādhi Sutra*'; 1 fasc., tr. by Hui-yen 智嚴 (Chigon) [TT. 9, No. 269]; the sutra explains the meditation on the void. [S. IV-1.]

Hokku-kyō 法句經 '*Dharma-phrase Sutra*'; Sk. *Dharmapada*; a collection of verses comprising the basic teaching of Buddhist morality [TT. 4, No. 210.]; the Pali version, *Dhammapada*, is more popularly known. The Chinese translation comprises 758 verses.

Hokkuru 北俱盧 Sk. Uttarakuru; translated as Uttan'otsu 欝單越, etc.; one of the four continents (*shishū**), it lies to the north of Mt. Sumeru (Shumisen*). The continent is square, and its inhabitants enjoy a long life of 1,000 years and all sorts of pleasure. It is superior to the three other continents in respect of the inhabitants' physical qualities, material abundance, etc.

Hokkyō 法橋 'Dharma-bridge'; abbr. of *hokkyō-shōnin-i**. [S. Va–7.]

~-shōnin-i --上人位 'The rank of the Master of the Dharma-bridge'. See *hōin-daikashō-i*.

Hōkō 方廣 'Righteous and extensive'; Sk. *vaipulya* 'extensive'. I. A general term for Mahayana teachings. II. One of the nine and the twelve kinds of scriptures (*kubu-kyō** and *jūnibu-kyō**); a scripture which expounds principles of truth *in extenso*.

Hokukuru 北俱盧 See *Hokkuru*.

Hokurei 北嶺 'The northern mountain'; Mt. Hiei.

Hōkyōin-darani 寶篋印陀羅尼 'The treasure-casket seal dharani'; Sk. *karaṇḍa-mudrā-dhāraṇī*; the spell appears in the *Hōkyōin-darani-kyō* 寶篋印陀羅尼經, 1 fasc. [TT. 19, No. 1022]; one of the three spells chanted daily in the Shingon* and Tendai* sects. The spell, composed of 40 phrases, has great merit; if one invokes it even seven times one's ancestor undergoing torments in hell can be instantly reborn in Amida's* land. The spell is also effective in removing sufferings and healing illnesses. [S. II–8, VII–24, Xb–1; Tsu. 222.]

Hōmei 報命   See *hōmyō*.

Hōmetsu 法滅   'Extinction of the Dharma'; the period after that of the last and decadent law (*mappō**), when the Buddhist teaching will cease to exist.   [S.III–5, IV–2, IX–13; Tai. 21, 24.]

Hō-metsujin-kyō 法滅盡經   '*The Extinction of the Dharma Sutra*'; 1 fasc.; translator not known   [TT. 12, No. 396].

Hōmi 法味   'Taste of the Dharma'; the Dharma which tastes good. The Buddhist law is so called because it delights anyone who receives it.

～ **o sasagu** --を捧ぐ   'To offer up the nectar of the Dharma'; to practise the Buddhist teaching.   [S. I–8.]

Hōmon 法文   'A Dharma text', a passage which expounds the Buddhist Dharma.

～ **no sata** --の沙汰   'Discussion on passages of a sutra.'   [IH.]

Hōmon 法門   'Dharma-gate'; the Buddhist teaching; a doctrine or creed; a sermon.

～ **dangi** --談義   'Discussion of the Buddhist teaching.'   [S. III–8.]

Hōmu 法務   'Dharma-duty.'   I. The duties of a priest, or other work connected with Buddhism.   II. Chief administrator of a big temple. This post was first set up in the Tōji*, and later in the Enryakuji* and Kōfukuji* too.   [K. 65; Tai. 24.]

Hō-muge 法無礙   See *shimugeben*.

Hōmyō 法名   'Dharma name', the Buddhist name given to a person at the time of his initiation. Also called *kaimyō** ('precept name') because it is given by the master when the initiate accepts the Buddhist precepts.

Hōmyō 法命   'Dharma-life'; the flow of the Dharma from master to disciple.

Hōmyō 報命   'Rewarded life-span'; the measure of life allotted to a living being as the result of karmas from his (or its) former lives.   [IH.; S. I–8, etc.]

Honbon 品々   'Chapters' of a sutra.

Honchi 本地 See *honji*.

Hondō 本堂 'The main hall' of a temple where the principal buddha or bodhisattva is enshrined.

Hōnen 法然 The founder of the Jōdo* sect (1133–1212). Born in Kume 久米, Mimasaka Province (the present Okayama Prefecture), he was named Seishimaru 勢至丸. When he was nine, his father, a provincial official, was killed by the opposing faction. In accordance with the father's dying wish, he entered the priesthood under Kankaku 觀覺 of the Bodaiji. At 15, he went to Mt. Hiei, where he studied under Genkō 源光 and Kōen 皇圓 and, later, from Eikū 叡空. From Eikū he received the name Hōnen-bō Genkū 法然房源空. At 24, he left the mountain and visited distinguished scholars in Nara and Kyoto. He later went up Mt. Hiei again to seek the way to salvation. At 43, as he read the whole collection of scriptures over and over again in the Hōonzō 報恩藏 Library, he came across the commentary on the *Kanmuryōju-kyō** by Shan-tao 善導 (Zendō*), in which it is taught that continuous recitation of the *nenbutsu** is the way to salvation. He instantly realized Amida's* saving power and took refuge in him. He left the mountain to live in Kyoto and began to propagate the *nenbutsu* teaching among people of all walks of life. In 1198, at the request of the Lord Chancellor Fujiwara Kanezane 藤原兼實, he composed the *Senjaku-hongan-nenbutsu-shū**, which presents the essentials of the *nenbutsu* teaching. Soon, the popularity of his teaching invited the jealousy of monks of other sects. In 1204, monks of the Enryakuji* on Mt. Hiei urged the *zasu**, Shōshin 性眞, to take action to stop the *nenbutsu* teaching. In 1206, when Hōnen's two disciples were accused of seducing a court-lady, the persecution of the *nenbutsu* began. The two disciples were executed, and Hōnen was exiled to Shikoku. Soon after he was pardoned and allowed to return to Kyoto in 1211, he became ill and died in the following year. Posthumously he was given the names and titles of Ekō Bosatsu 慧光菩薩, Kachō Sonja 華頂尊者, Enkō Daishi 圓光大師, etc. He is also popularly called Ganso Shōnin 元祖上人, Yoshimizu Daishi 吉水大師, Kurodani Shōnin 黑谷上人, etc. His works were compiled into the *Kurodani-shōnin-gotōroku* 黑谷上人語燈錄, 18 fasc., and more than ten biographies of him were written. [S. IV–9.]

~-**bō no shōnin** --房の上人 'The sage, Hōnen-bō'; refers to Hōnen*. [S. IV–9.]

Hongaku 本覺 'The original state of enlightenment', as opposed to *shikaku** 始覺.

~ **fushō no shinchi** --不生の心地 'Awareness of the non-arising (of all things) in the original state of enlightenment.' [S. I–9.]

~ **no miyako** --の都 'The capital of original enlightenment', i.e. the original state of a buddha. [IH.]

~ **no myōshin** --の明心 'The originally enlightened brilliant mind.' [S. Xb–2.]

~ **no shinshin** --の眞心 'One's true mind which is originally enlightened (to reality).' [S. III–8.]

~ **shinnyo** --眞如 'The True Thusness which is the original state of enlightenment.' [Tai. 36.]

Hongan 本願 'The original vow'; Sk. *pūrva-praṇidhāna*. I. The vow of a bodhisattva made at the outset of his religious career. II. Specifically, Amida's* original vow; especially, his 18th vow (see *hongan no mon*). III. The desire or aspiration of a person made in a previous life. IV. The sponsor of a Buddhist service or the initiator of a plan to build a temple, etc. Cf. *shiguzeigan*☆.

~ **no mon** --の文 'The text of the original vow'; refers to Amida's* 18th vow, namely: "If, after I have attained buddha-hood, sentient beings in the ten directions who have sincere minds, serene faith, and a desire to be born in my country, should not be born there even with ten *nenbutsu** recitations, may I not attain perfect enlightenment—excepted are those who have committed the five deadly sins and abused the true law."

~-**riki** --力 'The power of the original vow.' [IH.]

~ **shōnin** --上人 'A noble priest who has made a particular vow.' [S. III–5.]

~ **tariki** --他力 'The other-power of (Amida's) original vow'; the power of the original vow which works upon sentient beings to save them. [IH.]

~ **zenni** --禪尼 'A nun who has made some specific vows.' [K. 36.]

Hōni 法爾 'According to rule'; naturally; spontaneous working of the universal law. [S. Va–12.]

Honji 本地 'The original state' from which an incarnation has been manifested.

~-shin --身 'The original body' of a deity from which his derivative form is manifested. [K. 63.]

~ suijaku --垂跡 'Manifestation from the original state'; incarnations of buddhas and bodhisattvas as Shinto gods.

Honji 本事 'An original matter'; a kind of scripture containing narratives of past lives of the Buddha's disciples; Sk. *itivṛttaka*; one of the nine and the twelve kinds of scriptures (*kubu-kyō** and *jūnibu-kyō**).

Honji honzan 本寺本山 'The head temple' of a sect. [Tsu. 165.]

Honkō shakuge 本高迹下 'High in the original state and low in the state of incarnation'; the majestic state of buddhahood reveals its incarnations in less conspicuous forms; cf. *shakkō honge*. [Tai. 36.]

Honmyōsei 本命星 The star in the Great Bear which corresponds to the time at which one was born; cf. *tenshi honmyō no dōjō*.

Honpushō 本不生 'Originally unproduced'; Sk. *ādy-anutpāda*. The ultimate reality of things is a tranquil state in which nothing comes into existence and nothing disappears; cf. *aji honpushō*. [S. Vb–9.]

~-zai ---際 'The ultimate state of (things) being unproduced'; the ultimate state in which one does not see things as being produced or perishing. [S. II–8.]

Honrai buji 本來無事 'Originally free from worries'; said of the original state of things, which is tranquil and peaceful. [S. Xb–3.]

Honshi 本師 'The original or foremost teacher.' I. Refers to the Buddha Shakamuni*. II. The founder of a sect. III. One's teacher.

Honshin 本心 'The original mind'; one's true mind, which is buddha-nature. [S. III–8.]

Honshō 本生 Also *honjō*; 'an original life'; Sk. *jātaka*; a story of past lives of the Buddha; one of the nine and the twelve kinds of scriptures (*kubu-kyō** and *jūnibu-kyō**).

Honshō 本性 'One's original nature'; i.e. the buddha-nature. [S.

II–4.]

~ **no Kannon** --の觀音 'Kannon* (as the personification) of one's original nature.' [S. II–4.]

~ **no Mida** --の彌陀 'Amida* residing in the essential nature (of a living being).' [S. IV–1.]

Hon'u 本有 Often pronounced *honnu*; 'the original state; that which originally exists.'

~ **fukai** --不改 '(Retaining) the original state and not altering it'; immutability of the original nature. [S. II–8.]

~ **jōjū shūhen hokkai no myōtai** --常住周遍法界の妙體 'The wondrous body which originally and eternally exists and pervades the universe'; said of the quintessence-body of the Buddha. [Tai. 18.]

~ **mandara** --曼荼羅 'The inherently existing mandala'; refers to the Matrix-store Realm Mandala (*Taizōkai mandara**), which represents the reality-principle inherent in phenomenal existences.

~ **no manda** --の萬荼 Same as *hon'u mandara**. [S. II–8.]

~ **no reikō** --の靈光 'The spiritual light which originally exists in a person.' [S. Vb–9.]

Honzei 本誓 'The original vow' of a buddha or bodhisattva; the same as *hongan**. [S. II–4, 5, Xa–8; Tai. 2.]

Honzetsu 本質 'Essential, basic quality', as of the phenomenal world.

Honzon 本尊 I. 'The main revered' figure worshipped at a particular temple or in a particular ritual. II. The figure worshipped by a particular individual. [Tsu. 98.]

Hōō 法王 'King of the Dharma'; refers to a buddha. [S. II–5.]

Hōō 法皇☆ 'Dharma emperor'; a title accorded an emperor who, after his abdication, had his head shaved to enter the priesthood. The first *hōō* was the Emperor Uda (reigned 887–897).

Hōon 法音 'Sound of the Dharma'; the Buddhist teaching. [K. 39; S. II–10, VI–17.]

Hōon-gyō 報恩經 '*Repaying Indebtedness Sutra*'; abbr. of *Dai-hōben-butsu-hōon-gyō**.

Hōraku 法樂 'Enjoyment of the Dharma'; pleasure one can enjoy through the recitation of a sutra, meditation, etc. [S. I–3.]

Hōri 法利 'The merit or benefit of the Buddhist law.'

Hōri 法理 'A Dharma principle'; a doctrinal principle; a principle of reality or truth. [Tai. 24.]

Hōriki 法力 'Power of the Buddhist Dharma.'

Hōrin 法輪 'The wheel of the Dharma'; Sk. *dharma-cakra*; refers to the Buddha's teachings. 'Wheel' has dual meanings: (1) the Buddha's teachings are compared to the Tenrinjōō's* wheel treasure (*rinbō**￼ 輪寶) because they crush all the evils of sentient beings and (2) they are like a wheel in motion because they spread endlessly from one person to another.

~ **o tenzu** --を轉ず 'To turn the wheel of the Dharma'; to expound the Buddhist law.

Hōron 法論 'Discussion about the Buddhist teaching.'

Hōryū 法流 'Dharma-stream'; transmission of the teaching; a school or sect of Buddhism.

Hōse 法施 I. 'Gift of the Dharma', i.e. expounding the Dharma to someone. [S. VI–17.] II. Chanting a sutra or reciting a spell, etc. [S. I–2, 4.]

Hōseki 法席 'A Dharma assembly'; a Buddhist service or meeting. [Tai. 24.]

Hōshi 法師 See *hosshi*.

Hōshinnō 法親王 A prince who has been given the title of *shinnō* after becoming a priest. [Hei. 3.]

Hōshō 寶生 'Treasure-producing'; Sk. Ratnasambhava; n. of a buddha in the south. In esoteric Buddhism, one of the five buddhas (*gobutsu**) of the Diamond Realm Mandala (*Kongōkai mandara**); cf. *gochi nyorai*.

Hōshuhō 寶珠法 Also *kōjubō*; 'rite of the gem'; abbr. of *nyoihō-shu-hō**. [K. 67.]

Hōshuku Daibosatsu 法宿大菩薩 'The Great Bodhisattva Dharma-Lodging'; a title given to Daihiei Myōjin 大比叡明神, a guardian god of Mt. Hiei. [Tai. 18.]

Hosse 法施 See *hōse*.

Hosshi 法師 'Dharma-exponent'; one who is well-versed in Buddhist teachings and expounds them to others; a man of virtue who practises the Buddhist Way; a Buddhist master; or simply, a priest.

~-shi --子 'A son of a Dharma master'; a son who has been initiated into the priesthood. [O. V.]

Hosshin 法身☆ 'Dharma-body'; Sk. *dharmakāya*; the body of the ultimate reality, one of the three bodies of a buddha (*sanshin**), and also of the two, four and ten bodies; cf. *nishin*, *shishin*, *jusshin*, *musō hosshin* and *tōru hosshin*. [S. I–1, 3, II–4, 9, III–7, Xb–3.]

~ jōgō no setsu --常恆の說 'The perpetual exposition of the Dharma by the Dharma-body Buddha (i.e. Dainichi*).' [S. II–8.]

~ jōjū no jumyō --常住の壽命 'The life-span representing the eternally abiding law-body'; said of Amida's* infinite life. [S. IV–1.]

~ musō --無相 'Formlessness of the Dharma-body.' [S. I–3.]

~ no daiga --の大我 'One's great self which is Dharma-body'; one's true nature is completely free and encompasses all existences, being identical with Dharma-body. [S. III–8.]

~ no emyō --の慧命 'The wisdom-life of the Dharma-body'; the life of wisdom in the body of reality. [S. Va–3.]

~ no reishō --の靈性 'The spiritual nature of the Dharma-body'; the mystic and transcendental nature of the Dharma-body. [S. VII–25.]

~ shogu no jikkai --所具の十界 'The ten realms contained in the Dharma-body.' [S. I–3.]

~ wa musō --は無相 'The Dharma-body is formless.' [S. II–9.]

Hosshin 發心 'To awaken aspiration (for Bodhi).'

~ no hito --の人 'A man who has awakened aspiration for Bodhi.' [IH.]

Hosshō 法性 'Dharma-nature'; the quintessence of existing things; the ultimate nature of things.

~ jakunen --寂然 'The Dharma-nature is tranquil.' [S. Va–1.]

~ jōjū --常住 'The eternal presence of the Dharma-nature.' [Tai. 24.]

Hosshō 法照 Ch. Fa-chao (8th century); one of the prominent Chinese Pure Land masters. He first went up Mt. Lu (Rozan 廬山) where he practised the Nenbutsu Samādhi (*nenbutsu zanmai**), and later, in 766, he saw Amida in a vision and learned from him the method of chanting the *nenbutsu** in five cadences (*goe-nenbutsu*): his works include *Goe-hō ji-san* 五會法事讚. His *nen-butsu* method was widely practised and won him the title of Wu-hui Fa-shih 五會法師 (Goe Hosshi). The emperor gave him a posthumous title, Ta-wu He-shan 大悟和尚 (Daigo Kashō). Fa-chao was also called Hou Shan-tao 後善導 (*Go-Zendō**), 'the later (incarnation of or successor to) Shan-tao'.

Hosshū 法執 'Attachment to the Dharma or elements.' I. Attachment to a specific teaching. [S. Xa–10.] II. A feeling of attachment that external objects or their constituent elements really exist; this attachment has to be eliminated in the course of a bodhisattva's practice; Sk. *dharma-grāha*; cf. *gashū*.

Hossō 法相 'Dharma-characteristic, dharma-aspect.' I. Characteristics or qualities of dharma, or elements. II. The essential nature of things; the reality-aspect. III. Doctrine or tenet. IV. Abbr. of Hossōshū*.

~ **Daijō** --大乘 'Hossō (of the) Great Vehicle.' [S. III–1.]

~-**shū** --宗 'The dharma-characteristics sect'; a Mahayana sect founded in China in the T'ang dynasty based on the scriptures asserting that all existences are reducible to the consciousnesses. One of the six sects in the Nara period (710–794); see *rokushu*. Cf. *Jōyuishiki-ron*. [S. Xb–2.]

Hōtō 法燈 'Lamp of the Dharma'; the Buddhist teaching which dispels spiritual darkness like a lamp.

Hotoke 佛 'Buddha'; see *butsu*.

~ **no michi** -の道 'The Buddhist Way'; Buddhist teaching; the way to buddhahood. [K. 146; Tsu. 4.]

Hotsubodaishin 發菩提心 'Awakening the Bodhi Mind'; aspiring to attain enlightenment; see *bodaishin*.

Hotsumu 撥無 See *hatsumu*.

Hotsuro sange 發露懺悔 'To confess and repent' of one's offences and vow not to commit them again. [S. III–2.]

Hottai 法體 'Dharma-body, Dharma-substance.' I. The essential substance of a thing or things. II. The elements constituting existences. III. That which belongs to the Buddha, as opposed to that which belongs to those to be saved by him. IV. An object of belief, e.g. a particular buddha or his name.   V. A respectful word for a priest or lay Buddhist.

Hōyō 法用   The same as 法要; a Buddhist service.   [S. VI–13.]

Hōzō 法藏   'Dharma-store.'   I. 'Store of the Dharma'; all the Buddhist teachings.   II. Sk. Dharmākara; the name of the bodhisattva who later became Amida*.   III. Ch. Fa-ts'ang (643–712); the third patriarch of the Hua-yen (Kegon*) sect. He assisted Śikṣānanda (Jisshananda) in translating the *Kegon-gyō**, and lectured on the text by order of Empress Wu 則天武后 (Sokutenbukō). He was then given the title Hsien-shou 賢首 (Genju*). He wrote many works, including the voluminous commentary in 20 fasc. on the *Kegon-gyō* and is looked upon as the systematizer of the Kegon sect.

~ **biku** --比丘   'Dharmākara *Bhikṣu*'; the bodhisattva who later became Amida*.   [S. IV–1.]

Hōzō 寶藏   'Treasure Store'; Sk. Ratnagarbha; n. of a buddha who was originally the son of a minister in the country called Sandairan* 珊提嵐 (Śaṇḍilya); his story appears in the *Hike-kyō**; see *Mujōnen*.

Hyakkai 百界   '100 realms' conceived in the Tendai* teaching. There are ten states of existence (*jikkai**), from hell up to the buddha realm, and each of them contains all the ten realms as potential existences. There are therefore 100 realms in all. Cf. *sanzen* 三千.

Hyakubuku shōgon 百福莊嚴   'Glorification with 100 merits'; after completing all the necessary practices for becoming a buddha, a bodhisattva performs further meritorious acts to gain the glorious physical perfection of a buddha. He thus performs 100 acts of merit for each of the 32 physical characteristics of excellence. [Tai. 33.]

Hyakugyō ritsugi 百行律儀   'The 100 acts in compliance with the precepts'; all acts in daily life are in compliance with the Buddhist precepts.   [S. Va–3.]

Hyakunichi-kō 百日講   'A 100-day lecture' on the *Hoke-kyō**; see *kō* II.

Hyakunichi no kegyō 百日の加行   'A 100-day preparatory practice'; see *kegyō*.   [S. II–5.]

Hyakunichi sennichi no kō 百日千日の講 'A 100-day lecture-meeting and a 1,000-day lecture-meeting' (*hyakunichi-kō** and *sennichi-kō**, respectively). [O. V.]

Hyakuō chingo no garan 百王鎮護の伽藍 'The temple for the protection of a 100 kings'; another name for the Enryakuji*. [Tai. 14.]

Hyakusō 百僧 'A 100 priests'; refers to a company of 104 priests participating in a big service, including seven main ones (*shichisō**). [O. VI.]

Hyakuyu-kyō 百喩經 '*A 100-parable Sutra*'; abbr. of *Hyakku-hiyu-kyō* 百句譬喩經, 4 fasc., tr. by Guṇavṛddhi (Gunabiji 求那毘地) [TT. 4, No. 209]. [S. III–2, IV–1.]

Hyōbyaku 表白 Also *hyōhaku*; 'pronouncement'; a statement read at a Buddhist service or lecture-meeting; the same as *keibyaku** 啓白.

I

Ichibutsudo 一佛土 'A buddha land'; refers to Amida's* land. [K. 291.]

Ichibutsujō 一佛乘 'The single buddha-vehicle'; the only way to buddhahood; the same as *ichijō** 一乘. [S. Vb–9.]

Ichibutsu jōdo 一佛淨土 'A buddha's pure land'; refers to Amida's* Pure Land. [K. 291.]

Ichidai 一代 '(The Buddha's) lifetime.'

~ **no kyōmon** --の教門 '(The Buddha's) lifetime teaching-gates'; the Buddha's lifetime teachings. [S. III–8.]

~ **(no) sekkyō** --(の)説教 '(The Buddha's) lifetime teachings.' [Tai. 15.]

~ **no shōgyō** --の聖教 '(The Buddha's) lifetime sacred teachings.' [S. III–8.]

～ **no shokyō** --の諸教 '(The Buddha's) lifetime teachings.' [S. IV-9.]

Ichidaiji no innen 一大事の因縁 I. 'The most important cause' for which the Buddha appeared in the world; cf. *daiji*. II. The most important thing to be done in one's life, i.e. deliverance from transmigration and the attainment of enlightenment. [Tsu. 188.]

Ichidai-sanzenkai 一大三千界 'A great 3,000 world'; a trichiliocosm; see *sanzen-daisen-sekai*. [Tai. 12.]

Ichie 一會 'One meeting'; a Buddhist service or meeting. [Tai. 11.]

Ichigo 一期 'One's life-time.'

～ **no daiji** --の大事 'The most important matter or occasion in one's whole life.' [S. IV-8.]

～ **no gyōgō** --の行業 'Acts during one's whole life.' [S. Xa-6.]

Ichigō shokan 一業所感 'The same result brought about by the same act'; said of the same state of life shared by two or more people as the result of the same sort of act done in previous lives. [Hei. 3; Tai. 10, 16, 31.]

Ichigyō 一行 Ch. I-hsing (683–727); popularly, I-hsing A-she-li 一行阿闍梨 (Ichigyō Ajari) or I-hsing Ch'an-shih 一行禪師 (Ichigyō Zenji). He studied Ch'an (Zen*) under P'u-chi 普寂 (Fujaku) and later, precepts, mathematics, astronomy, etc. When Śubhākarasiṃha (Zenmui 善無畏) came to China, he studied esoteric Buddhism under him and helped him to translate the *Dainichi-kyō**. Later, he received initiation (*kanjō**) from Vajrabodhi (Kongōchi 金剛智) and further studied esoteric Buddhism under him. He was given the posthumous title Ta-hui Ch'an-shih 大慧禪師 (Daie Zenji). [S. Xb-2.]

Ichiji kinrin 一字金輪 Also *Ichiji konrin*; 'One-Syllable Golden-Wheel'; a deity produced from the Buddha's head; his spell 'BHRŪṂ' is said to be effective in curing deafness, muteness, etc., and also in securing easy birth. [Hei. 3.]

Ichijiki no aida 一食の間 'The time for a meal'; for a short period of time. [S. II-5.]

Ichiji Monju 一字文殊 'One-letter Mañjuśrī'; also Ikkei Monju 一髻文殊, 'One-tuft Mañjuśrī'; Sk. Ekajaṭa Mañjuśrī; a form of Monju* Bodhisattva dwelling in meditation on the augmentation of merit. The Sanskrit letter representing this deity is ŚRĪ, but, according to another tradition, a combination of four letters: CHA, LA, HA and YA. A ritual dedicated to him is performed for the purpose of increasing one's merit and, particularly, of securing easy birth and curing illnesses. [Tai. 33.]

Ichiji saishō butchō rinnō 一字最勝佛頂輪王 'One-Syllable Supreme Buddha's Head Wheel-King'; see *Kinrin butchō*.

Ichiji sanrai 一字三禮 'Three worshippings for one character'; when copying a sutra, one bows in worship three times each time one writes a character. [Tai. 13, 39.]

Ichijitsu 一實 'One reality.' I. Refers to the ultimate reality; a synonym of *shinnyo** 眞如 'True Thusness'. II. Refers to the One-Vehicle teaching (*ichijō**), as being the only real method of salvation.

~ **endon** ‑‑圓頓 'The one reality(-principle) and perfect (teaching which enables one to attain buddhahood) very quickly'; said of the Tendai* doctrine. [Tai. 1, 24.]

~ **musō** ‑‑無相 'The one reality (-principle) in which there is no mark of distinction.' [Tai. 18.]

~ **no kyōgai** ‑‑の境界 'The realm of one reality'; the realm of the ultimate reality. [S. Xb‑3.]

Ichijō 一定 'Definite, certain.'

~ **no ōjōnin** ‑‑の往生人 'One whose birth (in the Pure Land) is certain.' [S. Xa‑10.]

~ **ōjō** ‑‑往生 'Definite attainment of birth (in the Pure Land).' [S. Xa‑1.]

Ichijō 一乘 I. 'The One Vehicle'; the single path to enlightenment to be taken by all living beings. II. The sutra expounding the One-Vehicle teaching, i.e. the *Hoke-kyō*.* [K. 7; Tai. 34.]

~ **bodai no michi** ‑‑菩提の道 'The One-Vehicle path to enlightenment'; the Mahayana way of attaining enlightenment. [K. 472; S. Xa‑4.]

~ **dokuju** ‑‑讀誦 'Chanting of the One-Vehicle (sutra) (i.e. the *Hoke-kyō**).' [Tai. 18.]

~ **hōben sanjō shinjitsu** ‑‑方便三乘眞實 'The One-Vehicle teaching is provisional, and the Three-Vehicle teaching is real'; an assertion made by the Hossō* sect; cf. *sanjō*. [S. IV–1.]

∼ **Mida Kannon uen no kuni** --彌陀觀音有緣の國 'The country closely related to Amida* and Kannon* of the One-Vehicle teaching.' [S. II–4.]

∼ **no chikara** --の力 'The power of the One-Vehicle teaching' of the *Hoke-kyō**. [K. 681.]

∼ **no hō** --の法 'One-Vehicle Dharma'; the teaching of the *Hoke-kyō** which expounds the method of attaining buddhahood for all sentient beings. [Ma. 97; O. I.]

∼ **no hōmi** --の法味 '(Excellent) taste of the Dharma of the One-Vehicle (teaching)'; a full appreciation of the Tendai* teaching. [Tai. 34.]

∼ **no kyōbō** --の敎法 'The One-Vehicle teaching'; refers to the *Hoke-kyō**. [Tai. 18.]

Ichinen 一念 I. 'One thought(-moment)'; one moment. [Tsu. 92.] II. Exclusive thought; concentration. III. One recitation of the *nenbutsu**. IV. Single-hearted faith in Amida*. [K. 66.]

∼ **fushō** --不生 'Non-arising of one (delusory) thought'; said of the moment of intuitive realization of the ultimate reality in which delusory thought ceases to arise. [S. III–8, IV–1, Va–5, Xb–1, 3.]

∼ **gohyakushō kenen muryōkō** --五百生繫念無量劫 'A thought (of affection will keep the persons concerned together) for 500 lives, and a concentrated thought (will keep them together) for innumerable *kalpa* (*kō**).' [Tai. 11, 37.]

∼ **kegu no kokorozashi** --希求の心ざし 'The one thought of aspiration' for birth into Miroku's* Pure Land. [S. II–8.]

∼ **munen** --無念 'One thought, non-thought'; realization of non-thought by putting an end to delusory thought-activity; cf. *ichinen fushō*. [S. IV–1.]

∼ **no aji** --の阿字 'One thought on the syllable A'; cf. *ajikan*. [S. II–8.]

∼ **no hosshin** --の發心 'Awakening of aspiration (for enlightenment).' [Tai. 13.]

∼ **no nenbutsu** --の念佛 I. One recitation of the *nenbutsu**. II. The single-minded recitation of the *nenbutsu*. [Tsu. 227.]

∼ **sanzen** --三千 '3,000 (existences are contained) in one thought';

an essential doctrine of the Tendai* sect which holds that the whole universe, with its 3,000 modes of existence is contained in a single thought of a practitioner or in each individual thing. For '3,000 existences', see *sanzen* 三千. [S. Vb–9; Tai. 17.]

~ **sōō** - -相應 'Whole-hearted thought which complies (with the ultimate reality or the Buddha's intention).' [S. III–1, IV–1.]

~ **tanen** - -多念 'One *nenbutsu**, many *nenbutsu*'; a point of discussion in the Pure Land school as to whether one *nenbutsu* is sufficient for attaining birth in the Pure Land or whether many *nenbutsu* are required. [K. 66.]

Ichi no chōja 一の長者 The first in rank of the four chief priests of the Tōji*, Kyoto. [K. 65.]

Ichi-no-hijiri 市の聖 'The sage of the streets'; an epithet for Kōya* who walked about Kyoto teaching people to recite the *nenbutsu**.

Ichi-no-shōnin 市上人 'The noble man of the streets'; an epithet for Kōya*; see *Ichi-no-hijiri*.

Ichinyo 一如 'Oneness.' I. Non-discrimination between, and the sameness of, two or more things. II. The essential substance of all existences; a synonym of *shinnyo** 眞如, *hosshō** 法性, *jissō** 實相, etc.

Ichiō 一往 'One going'; a superficial (view), as opposed to *saiō** 再往 'second going', i.e. deeper consideration.

~ **no gimon** - -の義門 A superficial significance or interpretation. [S. II–8.]

Ichiraika 一來果 'The fruit of returning once more'; Sk. *sakṛd-āgāmi-phala*, also *shidagonka** 斯陀含果; the second of the four stages of sainthood in Hinayana. One who has attained this stage is subject to rebirth only once more in each of the human and the heavenly realms before attaining the final emancipation; cf. *shika*.

Ichirai ketsuen 一來結緣 Pronounced *ichirai kechien*; 'to come once and establish a relationship'; visiting a temple or shrine once to establish a relationship with a buddha or bodhisattva. [Tai. 12.]

Ichiri byōdō 一理平等 'Sameness (of all existences in the light) of the (absolute) principle.'   [S. IV–9.]

Ichisendai 一闡提   See *issendai*.

Ichitanji 一彈指   Also *ichidanshi*; 'one snapping of the fingers'; a very short time; see *tanji* II.   [S. Xb–3; Tai. 30.]

Ida 韋陀   I. Sk. *Veda*; also Beida 吠陀, etc.; the religious literature of the Aryan race composed between 1,500 and 1,000 B.C., which has four divisions: *Ṛg-Veda*, *Sāma-V.*, *Yajur-V.*, and *Atharva-V.* II. Sk. Skanda; see *Idaten*.   [S. VI–18.]

Idaike 韋提希   Sk. Vaidehī; the wife of King Bimbisāra (Bimba-shara*) of Magadha (Makada*) in the time of the Buddha. In her late years she was imprisoned by her son Ajātaśatru (Ajase*), together with the king. This tragedy in the royal family is recounted in the *Kanmuryōju-kyō**, where she is said to have taken refuge in Amida* Buddha.   [S. VII–25, Xa–2.]

Idaten 韋駄天   Also 韋陀天; Sk. Skanda; a god of Hindu origin who protects Buddhism, popularly known for his ability to travel at great speed. Being also worshipped as a deity who guards food, his statue is often placed in or near the kitchen of a temple.   [Tai. 8.]

Ien 違緣   'An adverse condition or circumstance.'   [S. VII–25.]

Igi 威儀   'Dignified bearing.'   I. Proper deportment; conduct which conforms to the Buddhist rules.   II. The Buddhist rules of conduct.   III. Conduct in daily life; cf. *shiigi*.

～ **gusoku** --具足   'Having the proper demeanour' of a priest. [Ma. 262.]

～**-shi** --師   See *igisō*.   [Ma. 151.]

～**-sō** --僧   'Priest in charge of protocol'; also *igishi* 威儀師; a priest who gives instructions in the procedure of a service or ceremony.   [O. V.]

Igyō 意巧   'Device'; a skilful means of salvation devised with good intent.   [S. II–6.]

Igyō 意樂   'Intention, desire.'

Ijun 違順   Refers to *ikyō* 違境 and *junkyō* 順境, 'disagreeable and agreeable situations', respectively.   [Tsu. 242.]

～ **no kyō** --の境   'Disagreeable and agreeable objects or situations.'   [S. IV–9.]

Iken 異見 'Heretical view.' [Tai. 24.]

Ikkai sōjō 一階僧正 One who has been specially appointed *sōjō** (archbishop) without following the ordinary promotion system of the priesthood. See *sōgō*. [Hei. 3.]

Ikkaku sennin 一角仙人 'A hermit named One-Horn'; Sk. Ekaśṛṅga; also Dokkaku sen(nin)* 獨覺仙(人); a previous incarnation of the Buddha. A long time ago, he was born of a female deer in the mountains near Bārāṇasī (Harana-koku*). As he grew up, his appearance became that of a man but with a horn on his head. He obtained some supernatural power by practising meditation, but then abused it. When he slipped and fell on a wet road, he became angry with the dragons which caused rain to fall and, with his supernatural power, caught them all and confined them in a cave. Then the king sent him a beautiful woman named Śāntā(?) (Senta 扇多) to seduce him. As he succumbed to the temptation, he lost his supernatural power, and the dragons were set free and rain began to fall again. It is said that the beautiful woman was a previous incarnation of Yaśodharā (Yashudara*), the Buddha's wife. [Tai. 37.]

Ikke hakkō 一家八講 'Eight lectures (on the *Hoke-kyō** sponsored) by a specific clan or family'; cf. *hokke hakkō*. [S. Xa–4.]

Ikkō-senju 一向専修 'Single-hearted and exclusive practice' of the *nenbutsu**. [IH.; K. 63.]

~ ni ----に 'Whole-heartedly and exclusively practising (the *nenbutsu**).'

Ikō 已講 'Having lectured'; a priest who has served as a lecturer at the *Yuima-e**, *Saishō-e**, and *Gosai-e**. Hence, called *san'e ikōshi* 三會已講師, of which *ikō* is an abbreviation. [O. V; S. Va–9; Tai. 24.]

Ikyō 異香 Also *ikō*; 'extraordinary fragrance' like the one coming from the buddha-land; one of the phenomena attending the welcome by the sages at the time of an aspirant's death. [K. 64; S. Xb–3; Tai. 24.]

In 印 'A manual sign'; Sk. *mudrā*; a ritual sign with the fingers in esoteric Buddhism; also *ingei** 印契, *inzō** 印相, and *geiin** 契印. [S. Xb–3; Tai. 18; Tsu. 54.]

In 院 I. Originally, in China, 'a courtyard or hall'; also a public building. Later, from the end of the T'ang dynasty (618–907), a temple or a building in the compounds of a temple. Then, the word 寺院 (*jiin*) came to be used as a general name for a temple. II. In Japan, an ex-emperor's residence and also the ex-emperor himself. The application of the title *in* gradually spread: it came to be used also of a retired empress, prince, regent, or *shōgun* (military ruler); and, in the Tokugawa period (1603–1867), of other feudal lords. The custom which then arose of giving the title *in* posthumously to a *samurai* led to it being added to the Buddhist name (*hōmyō**) of a dead person.

Indō 引導 'To lead and guide someone' to salvation.

Inga 因果 'Cause and effect'; causality.

~ **gōhō no toki** --業報の時 'The time when the effect of the cause and retribution of bad karma' becomes manifest. [Tai. 27.]

~ **no dōri** --の道理 'The principle of causality.' [S. VII–6.]

~ **no kotowari** --の理 'The principle of causality.' [S. I–7.]

~ **o hatsumu su** --を撥無す 'To reject and negate the law of causality.' [S. III–5.]

~ **rekinen** --歴然 'The cause and effect are manifest'; said of the certainty of reward for good karma and retribution for evil karma. [Tai. 9, 30, 33.]

Inge 院家 'The *in** family'; the nobles who entered the priesthood at the same time as an ex-emperor and dwelt in halls in the same temple. They were also called *ingeshu* 院家衆 'members of the *in* family', and were distinguished from ordinary priests. Each ordained ex-emperor (*monzeki**) thus had his *inge* priests residing in the same temple. [Tai. 30.]

Ingei 印契 'A manual sign'; Sk. *mudrā*; also *in**, *geiin** and *inzō**.

Ingō 院號 I. The title of an ordained emperor or noble. II. The title of a head priest or archbishop. III. The title of a deceased person given in addition to his Buddhist name.

Ingyō 因行 'The causal practice'; Buddhist practice at the stage of a bodhisattva; the term is construed as *inni no shugyō* 因位の修行; cf. *inni*. [S. VI–18.]

In'i 因位 See *inni*.

Injaku 姪著 'To be greedily attached to.' [Tai. 18.]

Injin 印信 Also *inshin*; 'testimonials' about the transmission of esoteric teaching which a master confers on his disciple. [S. II–5.]

Inji taiji 婬事對治 'The controlling of sexual desires.' [IH.]

Injō 引接 See *injō* 引攝. [Tai. 18.]

Injō 引攝 Also 引接. 'To take in'; said of the compassion of a buddha or bodhisattva in taking in aspirants. [K. 323; S. Xa–8.]

Inka 印可 'A certification' of spiritual achievement given to a disciple by his master. [Tai. 12.]

Innen 因緣 I. 'A cause and a condition'; a cause and a by-cause. II. Relationship. III. A narrative of happenings in the past which explain a person's present state; one of the nine and the twelve kinds of scriptures (*kubu-kyō** and *jūnibu-kyō**).

~ **kegō** --假合 'The temporary union of causes and conditions'; all existences are viewed as temporary manifestations produced from the combination of certain causes and conditions. [S. III–1.]

~ **keu no hō** --假有の法 'Things of temporary existence produced from (the combination of certain) causes and conditions.' [S. Xa–6.]

~ **shoshō no hō** --所生の法 'Things produced by causes and conditions'; all phenomenal existences are the outcome of combinations of various causes and conditions. [S. IV–1.]

~ **wagō** --和合 'Union of causes and conditions.' [S. IV–1.]

Inni 因位 'Causal stage', i.e. the stage of discipline in which bodhisattvas perform various practices; *in* 因 'cause' means the cause of buddhahood; cf. *kai* 果位. [S. II–4, 8.]

Inorishi 祈師 'A prayer priest'; a priest who prays for the repose of a deceased person, the cessation of calamity, etc.; cf. *kitōsō*. [S. VI–1.]

Inshin 印信 See *injin*.

Inshin 淫心 'A lascivious thought, lust.'

Intoku 陰德 'Hidden virtue or merit'; a meritorious act done secretly or unnoticed. [Tai. 15.]

Inufusegi 犬防ぎ 'Dog barrier'; a lattice separating the inner sanctuary from the outer chamber of a temple. [Ma. 116.]

Inzō 印相 'A manual sign'; Sk. *mudrā*; also *in**, *geiin** and *ingei**.

Iō 醫王 'Medicine King'; refers to Yakushi* Buddha. [Tai. 2, 18.]

~ Sannō --山王 'The Mountain-King of Medicine', namely Yakushi*, who is believed to be the original body of Sannō Gongen, the guardian god of Mt. Hiei; see *Sannō*. [Hei. 1; Tai. 2, 17, 21.]

~ Zenzei --善逝 'Medicine-King Sugata'; refers to Yakushi*; *zenzei** is one of the ten ephithets for a buddha. [Tai. 21.]

Iō igyō no michi 易往易行の道 'The path which is easy to follow and easy to practise'; the Pure Land way (*Jōdomon**). [K. 63.]

Iō munin 易往無人 '(Amida's* Pure Land is) easy to go to but empty of people'; said of the difficulty of attaining birth in the Pure Land through one's own power, though, in fact, anyone who entrusts himself to Amida's power can unfailingly attain birth there. [S. IV–1.]

Ippatsu 一鉢 'A bowl'; a begging bowl. [Tai. 11, 12.]

Ippen 一遍 The founder of the Ji sect (Jishū*), 1239–89; popularly called Yugyō Shōnin 遊行上人 'Wandering Saint'. After he was ordained at 15, he studied chiefly the Tendai* teaching. Later he studied the *nenbutsu** doctrine from a follower of Hōnen, and changed his name to Chishin 智眞. In 1275 he visited the Kumano Gongen 熊野權現, and spent a night at the Hongū 本宮 (Main Shrine). While praying to the deity there (who, in his original state, is Amida* Buddha), he was given a verse of inspiration in which the term *ippen* (one universality) was repeated three times. He then changed his name to Ippen, and resolved to spend his life as a wanderer to spread the practice of *nenbutsu*.

Ishin denshin 以心傳心 'Transmitting (the Dharma) from mind to mind' without depending on spoken words or written scriptures. [S. VI–10.]

Ishi no hachi 石の鉢 'Stone bowl'; the stone bowl donated to the Buddha by the Four Guardian Gods (*shitennō**) after he attained enlightenment. [Ta.]

I Shōgun 威(=韋)將軍 See *Iten Shōgun*. [S. VI–18.]

Issaichi 一切智 See *sanchi*.

Issaichichi 一切智智 'Wisdom of all-knowing wisdoms'; refers to a buddha's wisdom, which is distinguishable from the other all-knowing wisdoms (*issaichi**) of *shravakas* (*shōmon**) and *pratyekabuddhas* (*engaku**); cf. *sanchi.*

Issaichige 一切智解 'An understanding of the all-knowing wisdom'; perhaps used for *issaichichi** 一切智智. [S. Xb–3.]

Issaikyō 一切經 'All the scriptures' of Buddhism.

~-e --- 會 'A service dedicated to the whole collection of Buddhist scriptures'; also called *daizō-e* 大藏會. [K. 247, 275, 280.]

~ kuyō --- 供養 'A service dedicated to the whole collection of Buddhist scriptures'; a service held when a hand-written copy of the complete collection of Buddhist scriptures was donated to a temple. [Ma. 262.]

Issai no shuchi 一切の種智 See *issaishuchi*. [S. II–8.]

Issaishuchi 一切種智 'The wisdom of knowing all kinds (of existences and elements)'; the wisdom of the buddha. One of the three wisdoms; see *sanchi.*

Issendai 一闡提 Sk. *icchantika*; one who has no goodness in his nature and, therefore, no possibility of becoming a buddha. [S. II–1.]

Isshi byōdō no jion 一子平等の慈恩 'Compassionate benevolence (of watching over all sentient beings impartially) as if each was one's only child.' [S. Xa–1.]

Isshiki ikkō muhi chūdō 一色一香無非中道 'Even a (small) form or a (slight) scent never fails to accord with the Middle Way'; the Tendai* doctrine that even a small phenomenal thing accords with the truth of the Middle Way (*chūdō**); the phrase comes from the *Makashikan**. [S. Va–1.]

Isshiki ikkō no hana 一色一香の花 'The flower of colour or scent'; refers to the Tendai* doctrine that even a small phenomenal thing reflects the ultimate reality. [Tai. 17.]

Isshin 一心 'One mind.' I. The ultimate and universal mind; the cosmic mind; the buddha-mind which is non-discriminative and pervades the universe. II. A discriminative thought; the perceptive function of consciousness. III. Single-heartedness; concentration. IV. In Pure Land Buddhism, the practitioner's whole-hearted trust in Amida*. V. In the Jōdoshin* sect, the absolute faith transferred to the aspirant by Amida*, which is itself Amida's heart; it is the cause of birth in the Pure Land.

~ **chōrai** --頂禮 'Worshipping single-heartedly with one's head touching the ground.' [S. II–1.]

~ **furan** --不亂 'Single-mindedly and without distraction'; a single-minded thought of Amida*; the phrase comes from the *Amida-kyō**. [S. Vb–9.]

~ **fushō** --不生 'Non-arising of a (discriminative) thought'; the term comes from the *Shinjin-mei* 信心銘, in which it is said, "When one thought does not arise in the mind, the myriad things are free from faults." [S. Vb–9.]

~ **hokkai** --法界 'The One Mind is the quintessence of all existences'; all existences as they exist are embraced in the universal mind-essence; cf. *hokkai*. [S. IV–1.]

~ **hokkai hiu hikū** --法界非有非空 'The essential mind-nature which is the quintessence of all existences is neither existent nor non-existent.' [S. IV–1.]

~ **jissō no chūdō** --實相の中道 '(The principle of) the Middle Way to be realized in the cognition of the reality of One Mind'; to realize the ultimate reality of One Mind is to realize the Middle Way (*chūdō**). [S. IV–1.]

~-**kongō-hōkai** --金剛寶戒 'The one-mind diamond-treasure precepts'; refers to the Mahayana precepts presented in the *Bonmō-kyō**.

~ **no minamoto** --の源 'The source (or the essential substance) of the one (all-comprehensive) mind'; the essential mind-nature which is identical with True Thusness (*shinnyo** 眞如). [S. I–9.]

~ **no myōri** --の妙理 'The wonderful principle of the One Mind.' [S. IV–1.]

Isshō fubon 一生不犯 'Keeping one's chastity all one's life.' [K. 551.]

Isshō fusho 一生補處 '(A bodhisattva who will) take up a (buddha's) place in the next life'; a bodhisattva of the highest stage who will become a buddha in the next life; Sk. *eka-jāti-pratibaddha*; cf. *fusho no bosatsu*. [Tai. 24.]

Isshō namu no kō 一聲南無の功 'The merit of pronouncing "*Namu*

(I pay homage)..." even once.' [S. II–8.]

Issō 一相 'One aspect'; uniformity. [S. Va–6.]

Iteimokuta 伊帝目多 Also *iteiwattaka* 伊帝曰多伽, *iteiottaka* 伊帝越多伽; Sk. *itivṛttaka*; narratives of past lives of the Buddha's disciples; one of the nine and the twelve kinds of scriptures (*kubu-kyō** and *jūnibu-kyō**).

Iten Shōgun 韋天將軍 'General Wei-t'ien'; also I Shōgun 韋 (or 威) 將軍; an incarnation of a heavenly being who manifested himself for Tao-hsüan 道宣 (Dōsen) and inspired him to write two books. [S. VI–18.]

Itsumaki no hi 五卷の日 See *gokan no hi.*

Ittanjiki 一摶食 Also 一揣食; a ball of rice, etc., offered to a monk.

Ittan no jiki 一摶の食 See *ittanjiki.* [S. II–8.]

J

Jain 邪淫 'Committing adultery'; one of the ten evil acts (*jūaku**); cf. *gokai, hassaikai* and *jikkai* 十戒.

Jajōju 邪定聚 'Those who are wrongly established.' I. Those who are certain to fall into evil realms of transmigration; one of the three kinds of people distinguished according to the three different spiritual capacities; cf. *sanju.* II. In the Jōdoshin* sect, those who follow the self-power (*jiriki**) practices and faith prescribed in the Nineteenth Vow and, consequently, will be born into temporary regions of the Pure Land; cf. *fujōju* and *shōjōju.*

Jakan 邪觀 'Wrong meditation or contemplation'; the opposite of *shōkan** 正觀. [S. VI–10.]

Jaken 邪見 'A wrong view'; a view that rejects causality; one of the five views (*goken**) and ten evil acts (*jūaku**).

Jakkō 寂光 'The tranquil light.'

~-do --土 'The land of the tranquil light'; abbr. of *jō jakkōdo**; the land of a Dharma-body buddha (*hosshin**); one of the four kinds of buddha-lands (*shido**) established in the Tendai* sect. [Tai. 18.]

~ no hondo --の本土 'The original land of tranquil light'; refers to *jō jakkōdo**. [Tai. 34.]

Jakudōju 寂道樹 Abbr. of *jakumetsu dōjō** *no bodaiju* 寂滅道場の 菩提樹, the Bodhi tree at the place where the Buddha attained Nirvana (enlightenment); see *bodaiju*. [Tai. 18, 24.]

Jakujō nehan 寂靜涅槃 'Tranquil Nirvana'; the state of extinction of evil passions. [S. Vb–8, 11.]

Jakumetsu 寂滅 'Tranquil and extinguished'; the tranquil state of the complete extinction of passions and cycles of birth and death; a synonym of *nehan** (Nirvana).

~ dōjō --道場 'The place of enlightenment where (the Buddha) attained Nirvana'; the seat of enlightenment under the Bodhi tree near the River Nairañjanā (Nirenzenga*) in Magadha, India.

~ nehan --涅槃 'Nirvana, the state of tranquility and extinction.' [S. Vb–9.]

Jakunen 寂然 'Calm, tranquil.'

~ jōgen --靜閑 'Tranquil and serene.' [S. Va–12.]

Jakushin 著心 'The feeling of attachment'; the same as *shūjaku-shin** 執著心. [Tai. 35.]

Jakusho 著處 'That which one is attached to'; the object of attachment. [S. IV–9, Xa–1.]

Jakushō 寂照 'Tranquil and illuminating'; said of the ultimate reality and transcendental wisdom. [S. III–1, IV–1.]

Jakusō 著相 Abbr. of *shūjaku no sō* 執著の相; the way one is attached to something; attachment. [S. III–8, VI–17.]

Jaku su 着(=著)す 'To be attached (to).'

Jaman 邪慢 'False pride' or 'pride based on a wrong idea,' e.g. the pride of a man of little virtue thinking that he is virtuous; one of the seven kinds of pride (*shichiman**). [Tai. 18, 25.]

Jamyō 邪命 I. 'Wrong life'; an unlawful way of living; the opposite of *shōmyō** 正命. II. Abbr. of *jamyō-jiki**.

～**-jiki** - -食 'Living by unlawful means'; a way of living for a monk in breach of the precepts prescribed by the Buddha. There are four kinds: (1) *ge-kujiki* 下口食, living by farming or prescribing medicine; (2) *gyō-kujiki* 仰口食, living by making use of one's knowledge of astrology, etc.; (3) *hō-kujiki* 方口食, living by using sweet words and flattery; and (4) *yui-kujiki* 維口食, living by practising divination and sorcery.

～ **seppō** - -説法 'Preaching sermons as an unlawful way of living'; preaching sermons in order to make a living. [S. VI–17, Xa–6.]

Ja Ō 闍王 Refers to Ajase* Ō. [S.VII–25, Xa–2.]

Jari 闍梨 Abbr. of *ajari**. [K. 48.]

Jashū 邪執 'Wrong attachment'; wrong views. [Tai. 24.]

Jataka 闍多伽 Sk. *jātaka*; translated as *honshō** 本生; narratives of past lives of the Buddha; one of the nine and the twelve kinds of scriptures (*kubu-kyō** and *jūnibu-kyō**).

Ji 事 'Matter'; phenomena, as opposed to *ri** 理 'noumena'; cf. *jiri*.

～ **no rokudo** - の六度 'The Six Pāramitās (*ropparamitsu**) actually performed' with one's mind and body, as opposed to those conceptually or meditatively practised in the mind only. [S. III–8.]

Ji 時 I. 'Time.' II. N. of a sect; see *Jishū*.

Jibutsudō 持佛堂 'The hall or room housing the image of a buddha' which is worshipped there.

Jidō 慈童 Abbr. of *Jidōnyo chōjashi**. [S. Xb–3.]

～**-nyo chōjashi** - -女長者子 'The child of a rich man named Jidōnyo'; n. of a previous incarnation of the Buddha, who vowed to take in all suffering beings and, owing to the merit of this vow, later attained birth in the Tuṣita Heaven (Tosotsuten*).

Jie Daishi 慈慧大師 'The Master Jie'; the posthumous title for Ryōgen* of the Tendai* sect. [Tai. 24.]

Jige butsujō 自解佛乘 'Understanding the buddha-vehicle teaching with one's intelligence'; understanding the essentials of the *Hoke-kyō** which teaches the path to buddhahood; originally, one of the ten outstanding virtues of the Master T'ien-t'ai (Tendai Daishi*). [Tai. 24.]

Jigen 示現 'Manifestation' of a visible form or inspiration; said of a divine being manifesting his incarnate body or giving inspiration to a man.

Jigō jitoku 自業自得 'To receive upon oneself (the retribution for) one's own acts.' [S. VIII–23.]

~**-ka** ----果 'To receive upon oneself the retribution for one's own acts.' [K. 72.]

Jigoku 地獄 'Hell'; Sk. *naraka* or *niraya*.

~**-e** --繪 'Hell picture'; a painting of hell on a folding screen. [Ma. 77.]

~ **hen** --變 Abbr. of *jigoku hensō**. [K. 387.]

~ **hensō** --變相 'A pictorial presentation of the various aspects of hell.'

~ **no gō** --の業 'An act which causes one to fall into hell.' [S. Xb–1.]

~ **no gō no kaze** --の業の風 'The (strong) wind in hell caused by one's (evil) karma.' [Ho. 9.]

~ **no kama** --の釜 'A cauldron in hell.' [S. VI–18.]

~ **no kanae** --のかなへ(鼎) 'A cauldron in hell' in which evil-doers are boiled alive. [O. IV.]

~ **no ku** --の苦 'The torments of hell.' [K. 57.]

Jigyō no yōbō 自行の要法 'The essential teaching to be practised for one's own (benefit).' [S. II–8.]

Jihi 慈悲 'Mercy, compassion'; *ji* 慈 (*maitrī*) is usually construed as 'giving pleasure and happiness', and *hi* 悲 (*karuṇā*) as 'removing pain and suffering'; for the three kinds of *jihi*, see *san'en no jihi*.

~ **ninniku no hōe** --忍辱の法衣 'The Dharma-robe (i.e. a monk's robe) signifying compassion and forbearance.' [Tai. 12.]

Jihō aigyō 自法愛樂 'Love of one's own law'; love of the teaching one is following. [S. IV–1.]

Ji-hokkai 事法界 'The realm of phenomena'; see *shihokkai*.

Jihō kuyō 事法供養 'Offering phenomenal things'. See *genkuyō*.

Jijimuge hokkai 事事無礙法界 'The mode of existence in which all phenomenal things are mutually unhindered and interfused'; see *shihokkai*.

Jijison 慈氏尊 See *jishison*.

Jijō goi 自淨其意 'One should purify one's thoughts'; the third line of the verse of admonition of the seven past buddhas (*shichibutsu tsūkaige**). [S. IV–1.]

Jijōkai 地上戒 'Precepts (to be observed by bodhisattvas) of the first stage (*shoji**) and above.' [S. IV–1.]

Jiju hōraku 自受法樂 'Self-enjoyment of the bliss of Dharma'; enjoying by oneself the pleasure which accompanies the realization of truth. [Tai. 12, 13.]

Jijuyūshin 自受用身 'Self-enjoyment body (of the buddha)'; one of the four buddha bodies (*shishin**), which partly corresponds to enjoyment- or reward-body (*hōjin**). The buddha body as the reward for the performance of meritorious practices and the cultivation of wisdom. It is in the state of enjoyment of the ultimate truth and of the bliss arising from it; cf. *tajuyūshin*.

Jikai 持戒 'Observance of precepts.'

~ **shōjō** --清淨 'Pure, i.e. perfect, observance of the precepts.' [S. Va–2.]

Jikaku 慈覺 See *Ennin*. [S. Xb–3.]

~ **Daishi** --大師 See *Ennin*. [Tai. 15.]

Jikan 地觀 'Earth contemplation'; refers to *Jisōkan* 地想觀, one of the 16 contemplations (*jūrokkan**). [S. VI–10.]

Jikan 事觀 'Meditation on the phenomenal aspect of reality', as opposed to *rikan** 理觀; cf. *jiri nikan*.

Jiken 自慳 'Being miserly to oneself.' [S. VII–11.]

Jikishi ninshin 直指人心 'Directly pointing at man's mind' and making him realize the buddha-nature.

~ **kenshō jōbutsu** ----見性成佛 'Directly pointing at man's mind, and seeing one's nature, one becomes a buddha'; part of a well-known verse in Zen* attributed to Bodhidharma (Daruma*). [S. III–1.]

~ **no shōshū** ----の正宗 'The true teaching which directly points at man's mind (and makes him realize the buddha-nature)'; the Zen* teaching. [Tai. 26.]

Jikkai 十戒 'The ten precepts' according to which a Buddhist novice (*shami** or *shamini**) should abstain from killing living creatures; stealing; sexual intercourse; telling lies; intoxicating drinks; bodily decoration and perfume; singing and dancing or going to see dances or plays; sleeping in a big bed; eating at wrong times; and keeping money or jewels. [Hei. 1; O. VI; Tai. 13.]

~ **no uta** --の歌 'Poems on the ten precepts' in the *Shinkokinshū* 新古今集 anthology (1205). [Tai. 21.]

Jikkai 十界 'The ten realms' of living beings: (1) hell (*jigoku** 地獄), (2) the realm of hungry spirits (*gaki** 餓鬼), (3) that of animals (*chikushō* 畜生), (4) that of *asuras* (*ashura** 阿修羅), (5) that of men (*ningen* 人間), (6) that of heavenly beings (*tenjō** 天上), (7) that of shravakas (*shōmon** 聲聞), (8) that of pratyeka-buddhas (*engaku** 緣覺), (9) that of bodhisattvas (*bosatsu** 菩薩), and (10) that of buddhas (*butsu** 佛). [S. I–3.]

~ **gogu** --互具 '(Each of) the ten realms mutually contains (the other nine)'; according to the Tendai* view, each of the ten realms, from hell up to the buddha realm, contains in itself the other nine realms.

Jikkyō 實敎 'The true teaching'; the true Mahayana teaching which directly reveals the Buddha's real intention; the opposite of *gonkyō**. [Tai. 17.]

Jiku Hōran 竺法蘭 'Chu Fa-lan'; a monk from central India. He went to China in 67 A.D. with Kāśyapamātaṅga (Kashōmatō*) and produced translations of the *Shijūni-shōgyō**, etc. [Tai. 24.]

Jiku no ju 慈救の呪 See *jikushu*. [S. II–5, 7.]

Jiku-shingon 慈救眞言 'Spell for saving (beings) through compassion'; see *jikushu*.

Jikushu 慈救呪 'Spell for saving (beings) through compassion'; also *jiku-shingon** 慈救眞言. One of the three spells of the fiery deity Fudō*. [K. 64, 187; S. VII–25.]

Jikyō 持經 'Holding a sutra'. I. Devotion to chanting a sutra. II. The sutra which one uses in daily services. [Tai. 10; Tsu. 98.]

~**-ja** --者 'One who holds a sutra'; one who is devoted to chanting a sutra, especially the *Hoke-kyō**. [K. 56, 59; O. II; S. I–10, Xb–1.]

Jimon 寺門 'The temple school' of the Tendai* sect, i.e. the Onjō-ji* 園城寺. It is opposed to *sanmon** 山門, 'the mountain school'.

Jimotsu 寺物 'Property of a temple'; offerings made to a temple. [Hei. 3.]

Ji-muge 辭無礙 See *shimugeben*.

Jin 塵 'Dust, dirt'; an object of sensation or perception; cf. *gojin* and *rokujin*.

Jinbun Shingyō 神分心經 See *shinbun Shingyō*,

Jinen 自然 'Of itself; natural, spontaneous.' I. The natural state of phenomenal existences. II. The state of things as they really are; the ultimate reality; in this sense, the term is used in the compound *mui jinen** 無爲自然. III. The necessary working of the law of karma; in this sense, see *gōdō jinen* 業道自然. IV. The irresistible working of Amida's* vow-power; in this sense, see *ganriki jinen* 願力自然.

~**-chi** --智 'Natural wisdom'; the Buddha's wisdom in realizing the ultimate reality; the wisdom awakened in oneself and not acquired from outside; also, *jinenhonchi* 自然本智 and, simply, *honchi* 本智. [Tai. 18.]

Jinga no sō 人我の相 See *ninga no sō*.

Jingūji 神宮寺 'A Shinto-shrine temple'; a hall in the premises of a Shinto shrine where a buddha or bodhisattva is enshrined. [S. II–2.]

Jinjin 塵塵 'Each and every object of perception'; cf. *rokujin*. [S. VII–25.]

~ **setsudo** --刹土 'Lands as numerous as specks of dust.' [Tai. 16.]

~ **wakō** --和光 'Being as dust with the dust and obscuring the light'; said of a buddha or bodhisattva's altruism in saving suffering beings by transforming himself into a less conspicuous form in order to mingle with them; the same as *wakō dōjin**. [Tai. 24.]

Jinjippō-mugekō 盡十方無礙光 'Light unhindered in the ten directions'; another name for Amida*. The term appears in the *Jōdo-ron** by Vasubandhu (Seshin*).

Jinkō 沈香 Abbr. of *jinsuikō* 沈水香; Sk. *agaru*; transliterated as 阿伽樓, 惡揭嚧, etc.; n. of an aromatic tree which produces incense of fine quality. As its heart and knots are hard and heavy, it sinks in water; hence, *jinsuikō* 'incense which sinks in water'. [Tai. 24.]

Jinkyō 塵境 'Dust-realm'; objects of the six sense-organs, i.e. form, sound, odour, taste, tactile object, and mental object; the objective world as a whole. Cf. *rokujin*. [S. III–8.]

Jinkyōtsū 神境通 'The transcendental faculty regarding external objects'; the transcendental faculty of transforming oneself or objects at will; the same as *jinsokutsū* 神足通; see *rokutsū*.

Jinmiraizai 盡未來際 'Up to the end of the future; to the end of time.' [Tai. 16.]

Jinpen 神變 'Divine transformation'; the manifestation of a miracle by divine, supernatural power.

Jinriki 神力 'Divine or supernatural power.'

Jinrō 塵勞 'Dust and trouble'; another name for *bonnō* 煩惱, evil passions. 'Dust' here refers to *rokujin** 六塵, objects of the six sense-organs, which cause evil passions to arise in the heart and afflict it. [S. IV–1, Va–1, 3, Vb–9, VII–25, IX–2, Xb–2.]

Jinshin 深信 'Deep belief.'

Jinshu 神呪 'A sacred spell.' [S. II–7.]

Jinzū 神通 'Divine or supernatural faculty'; transcendental faculty or power; Sk. *abhijñā*; cf. *rokutsū*.

~ **no mono** --の物 'One who has attained supernatural power.' [K. 424.]

Jippō 十方 'Ten directions', i.e. the four cardinal points, the four intermediate directions, and upwards and downwards.

~ **butsu** --佛 'Buddhas in the ten directions'; all the buddhas throughout the universe. [S. IV–1.]

~ **no jōdo** --の淨土 'Pure lands in the ten directions.' [K. 323.]

Jippō 實法 'The real things'; truly existing things, as contrasted to temporarily existing things (*kehō**). *Hō** 法 here means 'element' or 'thing'. [S. IV–9.]

Jippō jakkō no miyako 實報寂光の都 Refers to *jippōdo* 實報土 'the land of real recompense' and *jōjakkōdo** 常寂光土 'the land of eternity, tranquility, and light'. See *shido*. [S. II–5.]

Jippō mushōgedo 實報無障礙土 'The land of non-hindrance as the true reward (for the performance of meditation practice)'; one of the four lands (*shido**) distinguished in the Tendai* sect. This land is provided for bodhisattvas of higher stages and reigned over by an enjoyment-body-for-others buddha (*tajuyū-shin**); also called *jippōdo* 實報土 and *kahōdo* 果報土.

Jiri 自利 'Benefitting oneself'; the opposite of *rita** 利他.

Jiri 事理 'Phenomena and noumena'; existing things and the reality principle. [Tsu. 157.]

~ **muge** --無礙 'Non-hindrance between phenomena and the noumenal principle'; the interpenetration of phenomenal things and the reality-principle; one of the four categories of existences established in the Kegon* sect; see *shihokkai*. [S. III–8.]

~ **nikan** --二觀 'The two kinds of meditation on the phenomenal aspect and the noumenal principle'; refers to *jikan** 事觀 and *rikan** 理觀; also, *jissōkan* 實相觀 'meditation on the real aspect' and *yuishikikan* 唯識觀 'meditation on the principle of consciousness-only'.

Jiriki 自力 'One's own power'; refers to the practitioner's own power, as opposed to the power of a buddha, esp. Amida*, which is called *tariki**.

Jiriki sōō 地力相應 'Suitable to one's real power.' [S. Xb–3.]

Jirinkan 字輪觀 'Meditation on the Sanskrit letters'; the esoteric practice of imagining a moon in one's heart and then imagining in it the Sanskrit letters signifying the five elements constituting the world or those representing buddhas and bodhisattvas; this meditation is designed to lead one to attain unity with a buddha or other deity. [IH.]

Jiritsu 持律 'Observance of precepts.'

Jisai 持齋 I. Observance of the precept of not eating after noon. [S. VI–9.] II. Observance of various precepts in general. Cf. *sai*.

Jise 自施 'To make a donation to oneself.' [S. VII–11.]

Jisetsu 自説 I. 'One's own view or theory.' II. 'Self-exposition'; the Buddha's expounding of the Dharma of his own accord; Sk. *udāna*; one of the nine and the twelve kinds of scriptures (*kubu-kyō** and *jūnibu-kyō**), in which the Buddha expounded the Dharma without awaiting questions or requests from his disciples.

Jisetsu 時節 'Time, occasion.'

Jisha 持者 'A holder' of a sutra; one who holds to a sutra and keeps it close to his heart.

Jishi 自恣 Sk. *pravāraṇa*; a ceremony at the end of the rainy retreat (*ango**), at which one confesses any transgression of the rules of conduct committed during the retreat. [S. IV–1.]

Jishin honpushō 自心本不生 'One's own mind is originally unproduced.' [S. III–1.]

Jishin-zanmai 慈心三昧 'Absorption in the state of compassion.' [S. Va–4.]

Jishison 慈氏尊 'The compassionate sage'; refers to Miroku* (Maitreya). He is so called because 'Maitreya' literally means 'benevolent, compassionate.' [K. 64.]

Jishō 自性 'The self-nature'; the intrinsic nature or substance of a thing or person. [S. I–9, Va–5.]

~ **byōdō** --平等 'Equality or sameness of the self-nature'; the quintessence of all things is universally pervasive and without distinction. [S. VII–25.]

~-**e** --會 'The self-nature assemblage'; the mystic assemblage of Dainichi* (who is the law-body as the embodiment of the intrinsic nature of all existences) and his attendants, at which he expounds the *Dainichi-kyō** and the *Kongōchō-kyō**. [S. I–3.]

~ **hosshin** --法身 'Self-nature Dharma-body'; the reality-essence body of a buddha; one of the four bodies of a buddha established in the Shingon* sect. The essential body of a buddha, which is identical with the reality-essence of all existences and embodies the ultimate wisdom (*chihosshin* 智法身) and the ultimate reality-principle (*rihosshin* 理法身). [S. I–3, II–5.]

~ **kūjaku** --空寂 'The essential nature (of all existing things) is void and tranquil.' [S. Xb–1.]

~ **mandara** --曼荼羅 'Mandala in one's self-nature'; perfect merit and wisdom contained in one's true nature.

~ **no butsu** --の佛 'The buddha in one's own nature'; said of the buddha-nature in each individual. [S. Vb–11.]

~ **no manda** --の曼荼 See *jishō mandara*. [S. Xa–5.]

~-**shin** --身 'Self-nature body (of a buddha)'; one of the four buddha bodies (*shishin**); the quintessential body of a buddha, which is identical with the ultimate nature of existence; the same as the Dharma-body (*hosshin**).

~ **shōjō** --清淨 'Purity of one's essential nature.' [S. II–4, 8, IV–1, VII–2.]

(**toku**)~ **shōjō hosshō nyorai** (得)--清淨法性如來 '(Attaining) the realization that one's essential nature is pure and that it is identical with the intrinsic nature of things and with tathagata.' See *hosshō* and *nyorai*. [S. II–4.]

~ **shōjō no ren** --清淨の蓮 'The lotus of the inherent purity (of a living being)'; said of the nature of Amida* in man. [S. IV–1.]

~**-zen** --禪 'Meditation in complete harmony with one's true nature.' [S. IV–1.]

Jishō 自證 I. 'Self-realization'; realization of a spiritual truth through one's own effort. [S. II–8.] II. One's inner realization of truth. [S. Xb–2, 3.]

Jishu 寺主 'Master of a temple'; a priest in charge of the general affairs of a temple; cf. *shoshi*. [Tai. 9.]

Jishu 時衆 Also *jishū*; 'followers of the Ji (sect)'; the original name for the Ji sect. The name Jishū 時宗 came to be used officially in the Tokugawa period (1603–1867). See *Jishū*. [Tai. 20, 38, 39.]

Jishū 時宗 'The Ji (Time) sect'; a form of Pure Land Buddhism founded by Ippen* in 1276. It teaches that one should practise the *nenbutsu** diligently as if every moment is the time of death. Originally, this sect had no temple. The founder and his followers wandered about the country encouraging people to recite the *nenbutsu*. For this reason, this sect was also called Yugyō-ha 遊行派 'School of Wanderers'.

Jisō 寺僧 'Temple priest'; a priest of the Onjōji* 園城寺, Shiga Prefecture. It is opposed to *sanzō** 山僧, a priest of the Enryakuji* on Mt. Hiei.

Jisō 事相 'Phenomenal aspect.' I. Phenomena, as contrasted with *rishō** 理性 'the noumenon'. II. The ritual aspect of esoteric Buddhism, as contrasted with *kyōsō** 教相 'doctrinal aspect'. [S. VI–11.]

Jison 慈尊 'A compassionate saint'; refers to Miroku* (Maitreya); cf. *Miroku jison*. [Tai. 15, 18, 24, 39.]

Jissai 實際 'Reality-end'; the ultimate reality. [S. IV–1, Va–6.]

~ (**no**) **richi** --(の)理地 'The noumenal basis of ultimate reality';

the state of absolute reality. [S. IV–1, Xb–1.]

Jissetsu 十刹　Also *jissatsu*; 'the ten temples' (cf. *setsu*); in imitation of China, the ten Zen* temples next in rank to the five principal ones (*gozan**) were designated by the government of Japan in the 14th century. The order of precedence underwent changes and the number of those temples increased as time went on until it reached nearly 50 at the end of the 15th century and over 60 in the late 16th century. [Tai. 26.]

Jisshin 十身　See *jusshin*.

Jisshō 實證　'Actual realization'; enlightenment which one actually attains. [S. IV–1.]

Jisshu-kuyō 十種供養　See *jusshu-kuyō*.

Jisshu no shōri 十種の勝利　See *jusshu no shōri*.

Jissō 實相　'The real aspect'; the real state of things; the ultimate reality.

Jita 自他　'Oneself and others.'

～ **no funbetsu** --の分別　'Discrimination between oneself and others.' [S. VII–6.]

Jitchi 實智　'The true wisdom'; the wisdom of knowing the ultimate reality; opposed to *gonchi**, the wisdom of knowing the discriminative aspects of existences. [S. III–3, Xa–6.]

Jitsuga jippō no mōjō 實我實法の妄情　'The delusory view that a real self and real things exist.' [S. III–1.]

Jitsu-u 實有　'Real existence.' [Tsu. 129.]

Jizai no myōraku 自在の妙樂　'The exquisite pleasure of freedom'; said of the utmost bliss accompanying the attainment of Nirvana, in which one is free from all restrictions. [S. III–8.]

Jizengon 自善根　'One's own good acts.' [S. II–9.]

Jizengon 慈善根　'Good and meritorious acts done (for other beings) out of compassion.' [S. II–6.]

～ **no chikara** ---の力　'The power of compassionate good acts.' [S. II–9.]

Jizō 地藏　Sk. Kṣitigarbha, 'Earth Repository'; n. of a bodhisattva, who saves suffering beings in the evil realms; especially popular as the saviour of the souls of dead children. [K. 459; Ma. 199; S.

I–10, II–5, VII–17.]

~ **Bosatsu** - -菩薩 Kṣitigarbha Bodhisattva. [S. I–6; Tai. 24.]

~-**dō** - -堂 'Jizō hall'; a hall where Jizō is enshrined. [S. II–6; Tai. 8, 24.]

~-**in** - -院 'The Jizō section' of the Matrix-store Realm Mandala (*Taizōkai mandara**). There are nine deities presented in this section, of whom the central figure is Jizō. [S. IV–1.]

~ **Satta** - -薩埵 'Jizō (Bodhi-)sattva.' [Tai. 18, 20, 24.]

Jō 定 'Meditation, concentration.'

Jō 乘 'A vehicle, carriage, transport'; used in the sense of 'a teaching' or 'method of salvation' which 'carries' people to Nirvana; cf. *ichijō*, *nijō* and *sanjō*.

~ **no kankyū** - の緩急 'Being slow or quick in learning'; see *jōkai shiku*. [S. Xb–1.]

Jō 情 'Affection, feeling, emotion'; human feelings, which are delusory; hence, delusion.

Jō-agon-gyō 長阿含經 '*Long Āgama Sutras*'; Sk. *Dīrgha-āgama-sūtra*; one of the four collections of sutras in the Āgama (*agon**) division belonging to Hinayana; 22 fasc., tr. by Buddhayaśas (Buddayasha 佛陀耶舍) and Chu Fo-nien 竺佛念 (Jiku Butsunen) in the fifth century [TT. 1, No. 1]. This collection contains 30 sutras in four divisions. See *Agon-gyō*.

Jōbon Gokuraku 上品極樂 'The Land of Utmost Bliss for the highest class (of aspirants)'; the part of Amida's* Pure Land where the highest class of aspirants will be born; cf. *kuhon*. [K. 63.]

Jōbon jōshō 上品上生 'The highest birth of the highest class'; see *kuhon*. [K. 53.]

Jōbon Ō 浄飯王 'King Śuddhodana (pure, white rice)'; Shaka-muni's* father. [Tai. 18, 33, 35.]

Jōbuku 調伏 'Taming and subduing'; controlling. [S. I–3, 8,III–8, VI–14.]

~-**hō** - -法 'The rite for subduing (devils and adversaries)'; one of the five kinds of rituals in esoteric Buddhism (*goshuhō**).

~ **no hō** - -の法 See *jōbukuhō*. [Tai. 2.]

Jōdatsu 調達 See *Chōdatsu*.

Jōdo 淨土 'The pure land' of a buddha, especially Amida*.

~ **bodai** --菩提 '(Birth in) the Pure Land and (attainment of) enlightenment.' [S. I–7, VIII–1, Xa–1, 4.]

~ **goso** --五祖 'The five patriarchs of Pure Land Buddhism'; the five Chinese Pure Land masters: (1) T'an-luan 曇鸞 (Donran*) (476–542); (2) Tao-ch'o 道綽 (Dōshaku*) (562–645); (3) Shan-tao 善導 (Zendō*) (613–681); (4) Huai-kan 懷感 (Ekan*) (7th to 8th centuries); and (5) Shao-k'ang 少康 (Shōkō*) (d. 805). Cf. *shichikōsō*.

~-**kyō** --經 *'The Pure Land Sutra.'* I. Refers to the three principal sutras used in Pure Land Buddhism; see *jōdo sanbukyō*. II. Refers particularly to the *Amida-kyō**. [S. Vb–9.]

~-**mon** --門 'The Pure Land gate'; the Pure Land way, as opposed to *shōdōmon**. It is the teaching whereby one attains, by Amida's* power, birth in the Pure Land, where one realizes enlightenment.

~ **no gōin** --の業因 'The karmic cause of (birth in) the Pure Land.' [S. Xa–6.]

~-**ron** --論 *'The Discourse on the Pure Land'*; 1 fasc., written by Vasubandhu (Seshin*) and translated into Chinese by Bodhiruci (Bodairushi 菩提流支) [TT. 26, No. 1524]. The full title is *Muryōjukyō-ubadaisha-ganshōge* 無量壽經優婆提舍願生偈. [S. II–8, Xa–1.]

~ **sanbukyō** --三部經 'The triple Pure Land sutras'; the three canons of Pure Land Buddhism: (1) *Muryōju-kyō** 無量壽經; (2) *Kanmuryōju-kyō** 觀無量壽經; and (3) *Amida-kyō** 阿彌陀經.

~ **shin** --眞 'The Pure Land true (teaching)'; n. of the sect founded by Shinran*; see *Jōdo-shinshū*.

~ **shinshū** --眞宗 'The true Pure Land sect' founded by Shinran* (1173–1262), a disciple of Hōnen*. His doctrinal system centring around absolute trust in Amida's* saving power is presented in the *Kyōgyōshinshō**. The date of foundation is popularly given as 1224, when this work is believed to have been written in a draft stage. There are ten major sub-sects, and the total number of their temples is more than 20,000.

~-**shū** --宗 'Pure Land school.' I. Pure Land Buddhism. II. 'Pure Land sect'; n. of the sect founded by Hōnen* in 1175, when he was converted to Pure Land Buddhism upon reading Shan-tao's (Zendō*) *Sanzen-gi*. Until then Pure Land Buddhism had not been an independent sect. Hōnen's *Senjaku-hongan-nenbutsu-shū** is the fundamental text of the Jōdo sect. In it he teaches that anyone who believes in Amida's* original vow (*hongan**) and recites his name (*nenbutsu**) will be born in the Pure Land. Hōnen chose the following scriptures as the basic canons: *Muryōju-kyō** 無量壽經, *Kanmuryōju-kyō** 觀無量壽經, *Amida-kyō** 阿彌陀經 and Vasubandhu's (Tenjin* or Seshin*) *Jōdo-ron** 淨土論. After the founder's death, the Jōdo sect was divided into four schools: (1) Chinzei 鎮西 founded by Benchō 辨長; (2) Seizan 西山 by Shōkū 證空; (3) Chōrakuji 長樂寺 by Ryūkan 隆寬; and (4) Kuhonji 九品寺 by Chōsai 長西. Apart from those, there were two other branches, one started by Kōsai 幸西 and the other by Shinran* 親鸞. The Jōdo-shū usually refers to the Chinzei and Seizan schools, which are still thriving today, while Shinran's Jōdoshin* sect is treated as a different, independent sect.

Jōdō 上堂 'Entering the hall; upper hall.' I. Entering the monks' hall for a meal. II. Entering the Dharma-hall (*hattō**) to deliver a sermon. III. The upper or higher section of a monks' hall.

Jōe 定慧 'Meditation and wisdom.'

~ myōgō --冥合 'The union and harmonizing of meditation and wisdom.' [S. VI–16.]

Jōfugyō 常不輕 Sk. Sadāparibhūta, lit. 'always not despising'; n. of a bodhisattva mentioned in the *Hoke-kyō**. He revered people, saying they would all attain buddhahood in the future, and he himself later became Shakamuni* Buddha.

Jōgen 淨眼 'Pure Eye'; Sk. Vimalanetra; n. of a son of King Myōshōgon* 妙莊嚴 (Śubhavyūha) mentioned in the *Hoke-kyō** who became a bodhisattva. [S. Xa–2; Tai. 39.]

Jogō 助業 'The auxiliary acts'; the four acts which assist the *nenbutsu** practice in Pure Land Buddhism; they are: (1) chanting the sutras, (2) meditating on Amida* and his land, (3) worshipping Amida, and (4) praising and making offerings to him. Cf. *goshōgyō*. [IH.]

Jōgō 定業 'The fixed karma.' I. The karma or act which will definitely bring about its effect. II. The fixed destiny determined by one's acts in the past. [Hei. 2; S. II–6; Tai. 20, 35, 40.]

Jōgō 長講 Also *chōgō* and *chōkō*; 'a long lecture'; a long series of lectures on a particular sutra; also, a monk who gives such lectures; cf. *jōgō-e.* [Tai. 27.]

~-e --會 'A long series of lecture-meetings'; the first instance was in 807 when Saichō* had seven scholars lecture on the *Hoke-kyō*. After that such meetings were held regularly.

Jōgō 淨業 I. 'Pure (meritorious) acts.' II. Practices required for the attainment of birth in the Pure Land.

Jōgu bodai 上求菩提 'Seeking enlightenment above'; the wisdom aspect of the bodhisattva aspiration; cf. *geke shujō.*

Jōgū Taishi 上宮太子 Another name for Shōtoku Taishi*. [S. Xb –3.]

Jōgyō 淨行 'Pure practice'; the pure and unadulterated Buddhist practice.

~ no kokorozashi --の心ざし 'Aspiration for (the pursuit of the) pure Buddhist practices.' [S. I–9.]

Jōgyōdō 常行堂 'The Constant Practice Hall'; also *Jōgyōzan-maidō* 常行三昧堂, *Hanju-zanmai-in* 般舟三昧院, *Jōgyō-zanmai-in* 常行三昧院, etc.; one of the temple buildings on Mt. Hiei, where one practises the Nenbutsu Samādhi (*nenbutsu-zanmai*). [Tai. 17; Tsu. 238.]

Jōgyō-zanmai 常行三昧 'The constant practice Samādhi'; also called *butsuryū-zanmai* 佛立三昧; one of the four meditative practices in the Tendai* sect. This practice consists in walking around a statue of Amida* Buddha for 90 days while calling his name and thinking of him. See *shishu-zanmai.* [K. 54; Tai. 34.]

Jōhari 淨頗梨 'Pure crystal.'

~ no kagami ---の鏡 'The pure crystal mirror' which hangs in Enma's* court; a sinner is made to stand before it and see in it all the sins he has committed in his life. Also called *gōkyō* 業鏡. [K. 556; S. VII–7 (婆 for 頗).]

Jōhokkai 淨法界 'The pure Dharma-realm'; the realm of reality free from all defilements. Cf. *hokkai.* [S. III–1.]

Jōin 定印 'Meditation-seal'; a manual sign representing medita-tion. [K. 49, 62, 64; S. Xb–3.]

Jōjakkōdo 常寂光土 'The land of eternal, tranquil light'; one of the four lands (*shido**) distinguished in the Tendai* sect; the land of a Dharma-body buddha (*hosshin**) or a self-enjoyment-body buddha (*jijuyūshin**).

Jōji 承仕 See *shōji* II.

Jōjishu 長時修 'The sustained practice (of the *nenbutsu** during one's life)'; one of the four practices in Pure Land Buddhism set forth in the *Ōjō-raisan*; cf. *shishu*.

Jōjō 上乗 'A superior vehicle'; the highest teaching. [Tai. 39.]

Jōjū 常住 'Everlasting'; eternality; immutability. [S. I–1.]

~-motsu --物 See *jōjū sōmotsu*. [S. Xb–1.]

~ musō --無相 'Eternal and having no characteristics.' [S. Vb –11.]

~ no busshō --の佛性 'The everlasting buddha-nature.' [S. III– 7.]

~ no hosshin --の法身 'The eternal Dharma-body.' [S. II–4, III –3.]

~ no myōdō --の妙道 'The eternal wondrous path,' i.e. the Buddhist Way. [S. II–7.]

~ sōmotsu --僧物 Properties or provisions kept at a certain place for the use of monks; see *shishu-sōmotsu*.

Jōjuku 成熟 'Ripening, maturing.'

Jōka 上果 'A superior fruit'; a superior spiritual attainment. [Tai. 17.]

Jōkai 上界 'The upper realm'; the heavenly realm or a buddha land. [K. 468.]

Jōkai 乗戒 '(Learning) the teaching and (observing) the precepts'; *jō*, lit. 'vehicle', is here used in the sense of teaching; see *jōkai shiku*. [S. Va–2; Tai. 24.]

~ shiku --四句 'The four-phrase statement concerning learning and precept(-observance)'; the four phrases distinguish four types of practitioners according to different emphases in the learning of the teaching and observance of the precepts: (1) *jōkyū kaikan** 乗急戒緩, quick in learning but slow in precept-observance; (2) *kaikyū jōkan* 戒急乗緩, quick in precept-observance but slow in learning; (3) *jōkai kukyū* 乗戒倶急, quick in

both learning and precept-observance; and (4) *jōkai kukan* 乘戒
俱緩, slow in both learning and precept-observance. An example
of the *jōkyū kaikan* type is Yuima* (Vimalakīrti), for he attained
deep wisdom through learning. Hinayana practitioners are
generally considered to be more intent on observing the precepts,
so they are of the *kaikyū jōkan* type.

Jōkai 淨戒 'Pure precepts'; perfect observance of the precepts.

~-**haramitsu** - -波羅蜜 'Pure precept-Pāramitā'; perfect observance of the precepts, which is conducive to enlightenment; cf.
ropparamitsu. [S. IV–1.]

Jokan no kō 助觀の功 'Function as an aid to meditation.' [S. IV
–1.]

Jōki 上機 'A man of superior capability.' [Tai. 24.]

Jōkō 成劫 'The *kalpa* of creation or formation'; one of the four
periods of cosmic change; see *shikō.*

Jōkō 定光 Also 錠光; Sk. Dīpaṅkara. I. N. of a buddha in the
past. II. N. of a bodhisattva. [S. I–1.]

Jōkon 上根 'Superior capacity'; a man of superior spiritual
capacity.

Jokuakuse 濁惡世 Refers to *gojoku akuse*; 'the evil world with
five defilements'. See *gojoku.* [Ho. 17.]

Jokuse 濁世 'The defiled world'; the world with the five kinds of
defilement (*gojoku** 五濁); cf. *jokuakuse.*

~ **no dōshi** - -の導師 'Leader of the defiled world.' [S. II–5.]

Jōkyū 乘急 'Quick in learning'; dedicated to learning and cultivating wisdom; see *jōkai shiku.* [S. Va–2.]

~ **kaikan** - -戒緩 'Quick in (learning) the teaching and slow in
(observing) the precepts.' [S. IV–1.]

Jōmon 誠文 'A passage of sincerity and truth.' [K. 36.]

Jōmyō 淨名 'Spotless Fame'; refers to the layman Bodhisattva
Yuima*. [S. II–8.]

~ **koji** - -居士 'Layman Jōmyō (Spotless Fame)'; refers to
Yuima*. [O. V.]

~ **koji no ato** - -居士の跡 'The place where the layman Jōmyō
lived'; refers to the small *hōjō** in which he lived. [Ho. 36.]

~-kyō --經 Another name for *Yuima-gyō**. [S. III–4, Va–6.]

~ no toku --の杜口 'Jōmyō's silence', i.e. with regard to the ultimate truth. [S. IV–1.]

Jōmyō kokudo 淨妙國土 'The pure and wondrous land'; refers to Amida's* Pure Land. [S. IV–1.]

Jōmyō no kuni 淨妙の國 'The pure and wondrous land'; a buddha's land. [S. II–8.]

Jōnen 情念 'A passion-ridden thought'; an ordinary man's thought based on conscious or unconscious evil desires. [S. III–8.]

Jōraku-e 常樂會 'Eternal bliss festival'; the name of the Nirvana festival (*Nehan-e**) held at the Kōfukuji*, Nara. [K. 230.]

Jōriki 定力 'The power of meditation.'

Jōroku 丈六 Abbr. of *ichijō rokushaku* 一丈六尺; '16 feet'. The standard height of a transformed buddha (*keshin** 化身), which is twice the height of an ordinary man. [O. V; Tsu. 25.]

Jōruri Iō no shu 淨瑠璃醫王の主 'The King of Medicine who is lord of the Pure Lapis-lazuli World'; refers to Yakushi* Buddha. [Hei. 2.]

Jōruri sekai 淨瑠璃世界 'The Pure Lapis-lazuli World'; the land of Yakushi* Nyorai in the east. [Tai. 18.]

Jōryō 情量 'Delusory calculation'; deluded thinking. [S. III–8.]

Josai yoraku 除災與樂 'Removing calamities and giving happiness.' [Tai. 34.]

Jōsetsu 淨刹 I. 'A pure realm or country'; the pure land of a buddha, esp. Amida*. [K. 36, 72; S. II–9.] II. A fine temple; see *setsu* II. [Tai. 24.]

Jōsha hissui 盛者必衰 See *shōja hissui*.

Jōshiki 情識 'Delusory perception.' [S. II–4.]

Jōshin 定心 'Concentrated thought'; concentration; opposite of *sanshin** 散心, 'distracted thought'.

Jōshō 上生 'Upper birth.' I. Rebirth in an upper heaven, esp. the Tuṣita Heaven (Tosotsuten*). II. See *kuhon*.

Jōshō 定性 'The fixed nature'; the unalterable nature or essence of a person or a thing. [S. III–1.]

Jōshō 縄床 A plain chair with the cushion and back made of cotton and ropes, often used by Zen* monks. [Tsu. 157.]

Jōshō-kyō 上生經 Refers to the *Miroku-jōshō-kyō**. [S. II–8.]

Jōshosachi 成所作智 'The wisdom of accomplishing what is to be done (to benefit sentient beings)'; Sk. *kṛtya-anuṣṭhāna-jñāna*; the wisdom of accomplishing metamorphoses; one of the four wisdoms (*shichi**) and the five wisdoms (*gochi**).

Jōsō 定相 'The fixed state of things'; the changeless and permanent aspect of things. [S. Xb–2; Tai. 25.]

Jōtai 誠諦 'Sincerity and truth.' [K. 36.]

Jōtō 承當 I. Understanding; accepting; agreeing. [Tai. 26.] II. Taking some task as one's responsibility.

Jōtō 常燈 'Permanent lamp'; a lamp which is kept burning all the time.

～ **ryōsho** --料所 'Permanent-lamp lands'; a manor attached to a temple, the income from which is meant to cover the expenses for keeping the lamps of the temple burning all the time. [Tai. 26.]

Jōya 長夜 'The long night' of spiritual darkness. [S. II–3.]

Jōyuishiki-ron 成唯識論 '*The Discourse on the Theory of Consciousness-Only*'; 10 fasc. [TT. 31, No. 1585]. This is mainly a translation by Hsüan-chuang 玄奘 (Genjō*) of Dharmapāla's (Gohō* 護法) commentary on the *Thirty Verses on Consciousness-Only* by Vasubandhu (Seshin*), but it also includes edited translations of other masters' works on the same verses. This is the foundation text of the Hossō* sect.

Jōza 上座 'Upper seat'; a senior priest of a temple who supervises ceremonies and services. Cf. *shoshi*.

Jōzai Ryōzen 常在靈山 'Always dwelling on Vulture Peak'; according to the *Hoke-kyō**, Shakamuni* Buddha dwells eternally on Ryōzen (i.e. Ryōjusen*, Vulture Peak), expounding the Dharma; see *Ryōjusen*. [S. II–5.]

Jōzasō 上座僧 'A senior priest.' [S. IV–1.]

Jōzengō 定善業 'Meditative good act', i.e. meditation on Amida* and his Pure Land. [K. 63.]

Jōzō 淨藏 'Pure Store'; Sk. Vimalagarbha; n. of a son of King Myōshōgon* 妙莊嚴 (Śubhavyūha) mentioned in the *Hoke-kyō**, who became a bodhisattva. [S. Xa–2; Tai. 39.]

Jōzui-butsugaku no gan 常隨佛學の願 'The vow to follow the Buddha always and to learn from him'; the eighth of the ten vows of Fugen* (Samantabhadra); cf. *Fugen jūgan.* [S. III–1.]

Ju 受 'Receiving, perceiving.' I. The act of receiving in general. II. Perception arising out of contact with external objects; one of the 12 causations (*jūni-innen**) and the five aggregates (*goun**); cf. *sanju* 三受.

Ju (also, *zu*) 頌 'Verse.'

Jūaku 十惡 'The ten evil (acts)'; also *jūfuzengō* 十不善業. They are: (1) *sesshō* 殺生, killing living beings; (2) *chūtō* 偸盗, stealing; (3) *jain* 邪淫, committing adultery; (4) *mōgo* 妄語, telling lies; (5) *akku* 惡口, uttering harsh words; (6) *ryōzetsu* 兩舌, uttering words which cause enmity between two or more persons; (7) *kigo* 綺語, engaging in idle talk; (8) *ton'yoku* 貪欲, greed; (9) *shinni* 瞋恚, anger; and (10) *jaken* 邪見, wrong views. [S. II–8, VI –10, 17, 18, Xa–1, 6, Xb–1; Tai. 18, 20.]

~-gō --業 'The ten evil acts'; the same as *jūaku* above.

Jūdai-deshi 十大弟子 'The ten great disciples' of the Buddha: (1) Śāriputra (Sharihotsu* 舍利弗), renowned for his deep wisdom; (2) Mahāmaudgalyāyana (Daimokukenren 大目犍連 or, simply, Mokuren* 目連), renowned for his supernatural power; (3) Mahākāśyapa (Makakashō* 摩訶迦葉), renowned for his strict observance of the *dhūta* practices (*zudagyō**); (4) Aniruddha (Anaritsu 阿那律), renowned for his divine sight; (5) Subhūti (Shubodai 須菩提), renowned for his deep understanding of the principle of the void (*kū**); (6) Pūrṇa-maitrāyaṇīputra (Furuna 富樓那), renowned for his skill in expounding the teaching; (7) Kātyāyana (Kasennen 迦旃延), renowned for his ability in debate; (8) Upāli (Ubari* 優波離), first and foremost in the knowledge and observance of precepts; (9) Rāhula (Ragora* 羅睺羅), first and foremost in the observance of minute rules of conduct; and (10) Ānanda (Anan* 阿難), renowned as one who heard more sermons by the Buddha than anybody else.

Judō 儒童 Sk. Māṇavaka. I. Strictly, the name of Shakamuni* Buddha in one of his former lives when he was a bodhisattva and made offerings to Dīpaṅkara (Jōkō* Butsu) Buddha. [S. III–7.] II. The name of another particular bodhisattva different from the above. [S. I–1.]

Jūfuzengō 十不善業 'The ten evil acts'; see *jūaku.*

Jugan 咒願 Also *shugan*; 'prayer'. [Tai. 2.]

Jūgō 十號 'The ten epithets' for the Buddha: (1) *nyorai** 如來 (*tathāgata*), 'thus-come'; one who has come from Thusness (*nyo**); (2) *ōgu* 應供 (*arhat*), 'one worthy of alms-giving'; (3) *shōhenchi* 正遍知 (*samyak-sambuddha*), 'fully enlightened'; (4) *myōgyōsoku* 明行足 (*vidyā-caraṇa-sampanna*), 'one having wisdom and practice'; (5) *zenzei** 善逝 (*sugata*), 'well-gone', one who has attained emancipation; (6) *sekenge* 世間解 (*loka-vid*), 'the knower of the world'; (7) *mujōshi* 無上士 (*anuttara*), 'the unsurpassed'; (8) *jōgo-jōbu* 調御丈夫 (*puruṣa-damya-sārathi*), 'the tamer of men'; (9) *tenninshi* 天人師 (*śāstā deva-manuṣyāṇām*), 'the teacher of gods and men'; and (10) *butsu seson* 佛世尊 (*buddha-lokanātha* or *buddha-bhagavat*), 'the enlightened and world-honoured one'.

Jūgodaiji 十五大寺 'The fifteen great temples' of Nara. The seven great temples (*shichidaiji**) and the following eight: Sōfukuji 崇福寺, Shinshintaiji 新眞諦寺, Futaiji 不退寺, Hokkeji 法華寺, Chōshōji 超證寺, Ryūkōji 龍興寺, Shōdaiji 招提寺, and Shūkyōji 宗鏡寺. [O. V.]

Jūhachi-dō 十八道 Refers to *jūhachi-dōhō**. [IH.]

~-hō ---法 'The 18 elements of the Way'; the esoteric practice performed with 18 types of manual signs (*mudrā*).

Jūhachi-hen 十八變 'The 18 transformations'; the 18 miraculous manifestations of which a buddha or bodhisattva is capable. [Tai. 24.]

Jūhachi-ken 十八賢 'The 18 sages'; see *jūhachi-kenjō.* [S. Xa–1.]

~-jō ---聖 'The 18 sages'; the 18 most distinguished members of Eon's* Byakurensha* (The White Lotus Society) who performed meditation on Amida* on Rozan (Mt. Lu). [Tai. 12.]

Jūhachi-kū 十八空 'The 18 kinds of void' distinguished in the *Daibon-hannya-kyō**, etc.: (1) *naikū** 內空 (*adhyātma-śūnyatā*), 'internal void'; (2) *gekū** 外空 (*bahirdhā-ś.*), 'external void'; (3) *naigekū* 內外空 (*adhyātma-bahirdhā-ś.*), 'internal and external void'; (4) *kūkū* 空空 (*śūnyatā-ś.*), 'the void of void'; (5) *daikū* 大空 (*mahā-ś.*), 'great void'; (6) *daiichigikū* 第一義空 (*paramārtha-*

ś.), 'the first principle void'; (7) *uikū* 有爲空 (*saṃskṛta-ś.*), 'the void of conditioned things'; (8) *muikū* 無爲空 (*asaṃskṛta-ś.*), 'the void of unconditioned things'; (9) *hikkyōkū* 畢竟空 (*atyanta-ś.*), 'utmost void'; (10) *mushikū* 無始空 (*anavarāgra-ś.*), 'void without beginning'; (11) *sankū* 散空 (*anavakāra-ś.*), 'dispersion-void'; (12) *shōkū* 性空 (*prakṛti-ś.*), 'void in the essential nature'; (13) *jisōkū* 自相空 (*svalakṣaṇa-ś.*), 'void in the characteristic aspects of things'; (14) *shohōkū* 諸法空 (*sarva-dharma-ś.*), 'the void of all things;' (15) *fukatokukū* 不可得空 (*anupalambha-ś.*), 'unobtainable void'; (16) *muhōkū* 無法空 (*abhāva-ś.*), 'the void of non-existence'; (17) *uhōkū* 有法空 (*svabhāva-ś.*), 'the void of existence'; and (18) *muhō-uhōkū* 無法有法空 (*abhāva-svabhāva-ś.*), 'the void of non-existence and existence'. [S. IV-9.]

Juhō 鷲峰 'Vulture Peak', i.e. Ryōjusen*. [K. 38; Tai. 2.]

Juhō kanjō 受法灌頂 'A *kanjō** ceremony of receiving the Dharma'; an esoteric ceremony of receiving teachings from the master. [K. 44.]

Jūichimen Kannon 十一面觀音 'Eleven-faced Kannon'; Sk. Ekadaśamukha Avalokiteśvara; also Daikōfushō Kannon 大光普照觀音; an incarnation of Kannon that saves beings in the realm of *asura* (*ashura**); one of the six kinds of Kannon (*rokkannon**). It is said that the main face represents the stage of a buddha, and the remaining ten (one on each side of the main one, five on top of it, and three on the highest level) represent the ten stages of a bodhisattva. The figure usually has four arms. [Tai. 18.]

Jūichimen no keshin 十一面の化身 'A transformed body of Jūichimen (Kannon*).' [S. I-10.]

Jūjaku 住着 'Dwelling in and clinging to'; attachment. [S. II-7.]

Juji 受持 'To receive and hold'; to hold fast to the teaching, a buddha's name, a spell, etc.

Jūji 十地 'The ten stages' of a bodhisattva; according to the *Kegon-gyō**, they are (from lower to higher stages): (1) *kangiji* 歡喜地 (*pramuditā bhūmi*), 'the stage of joy'; (2) *rikuji* 離垢地 (*vimalā bhūmi*), 'the stage of freedom from defilement'; (3) *hakkōji* 發光地 (*prabhākarī bhūmi*), 'the stage of emission of the light (of wisdom)'; (4) *enneji* 焰慧地 (*arciṣ-matī bhūmi*), 'the stage of glowing wisdom'; (5) *nanshōji* 難勝地 (*sudurjayā bhūmi*), 'the stage of difficulty in overcoming'; (6) *genzenji* 現前地 (*abhimukhī bhūmi*), 'the stage of the manifestation (of reality)'; (7) *ongyōji* 遠行地 (*dūraṃ-gamā bhūmi*), 'the stage of going far (towards the ultimate reality)'; (8) *fudōji* 不動地 (*acalā bhūmi*), 'the immovable stage'; (9) *zenneji* 善慧地 (*sādhu-matī bhūmi*), 'the stage of wondrous wisdom'; and (10) *hōunji* 法雲地 (*dharma-meghā bhūmi*), 'the stage of Dharma-cloud'. In the 52-stage division of the bodhisattva's career, which is widely accepted among Chinese and Japanese Buddhists, the above ten stages correspond to the 41st to the 50th. The *Hannya-kyō** presents a different version of the ten stages. Cf. *gojūni-i*☆. [Tai. 26.]

Jūji 住持 'Dwelling and holding'; the head priest. [S. Xb–2; Tai. 24.]

Jūjō kanbō 十乗觀法 'The ten-stage meditation method' leading to enlightenment, established in the Tendai* sect: (1) *kanfushigikyō* 觀不思議境, 'meditation on the inconceivable/mysterious realm'; (2) *hotsu shinshō bodaishin* 發眞正菩提心, 'awakening the true Bodhi Mind'; (3) *zengyō anjin shikan* 善巧安心止觀, 'the skilful practice of concentration and meditation (*shikan**) to keep one's thought fixed (on reality)'; (4) *habōhen* 破法遍, 'destroying completely (attachments to) elements', that is, the three kinds of delusion (*sanwaku**), by meditating on the triple truth (*santai**); (5) *shikitsūsoku* 識通塞, 'distinguishing what leads to and what obstructs' the realization of the triple truth, and then taking up the former and discarding the latter; (6) *dōbon jōjaku* 道品調適, 'examining and selecting the items of practice suitable (for the practitioner) from among the thirty-seven which lead to enlightenment (*sanjūshichi dōbon**)'; (7) *taiji jokai* 對治助開, 'eliminating faults (by performing the five meditations) for stopping unwholesome thoughts (*gojōshinkan**) and the Six Paramitas (*ropparamitsu**), thereby providing an aid (to successful meditation on the triple truth)'; (8) *chijii* 知次位 or *chiiji* 知位次, 'being aware of the stage (in which one now dwells)' in one's spiritual advancement, thereby removing any pride which may arise out of a misconception that one has attained a higher stage; (9) *nōannin* 能安忍, 'being able to be calm and patient' in both adverse and favourable circumstances; and (10) *muhōai* 無法愛, 'not being attached to spiritual achievement'. The most gifted achieve enlightenment by performing the first of these practices, but others must do two or more. Those who are least gifted must practise all ten.

Jūjō no yuka 十乗の床 'The floor of the ten vehicles'; refers to *jūjō kanbō**. [Tai. 12.]

Jūju 重頌 'A verse repeating (the idea already expressed)'; Sk. *geya*; one of the nine and the twelve kinds of scriptures (*kubu-kyō** and *jūnibu-kyō**).

Jūjū 十重 Refers to *jūjūkai* 十重戒. See *Bonmō no jūjū*.

~-kai --戒 See *Bonmō no jūjū*.

Jukai 受戒 'Accepting the precepts'; a ceremony in which an initiate accepts the Buddhist precepts. [O. V; S. Xb–3.]

Juki 授記 I. 'Giving a prediction to someone about his future attainment of buddhahood'; Sk. *vyākaraṇa*; also *kibetsu**. [Tai. 18.] II. One of the nine and the twelve kinds of scriptures (*kubu-kyō** and *jūnibu-kyō**), which contains prophecies by the Buddha regarding his disciples' attainment of buddhahood; also *wagara** 和伽羅.

Jukkai 十戒 See *jikkai*.

Jūkō 住劫 'The sustenance kalpa'; one of the four periods of cosmic change, in which the universe maintains its complete system. The present *jūkō* is called *gengō** 賢劫 'auspicious kalpa' because 1,000 buddhas appear in the world in this period. Cf. *senbutsu* and *shikō*.

Jūkon 重昏 'Thick darkness'; deep spiritual darkness. [S. Vb–9.]

Jukuso 熟蘇 'Butter'; one of the five tastes. See *gomi*.

Jukyō 誦經 'Chanting a sutra'; also pronounced *zukyō*.

~-motsu --もつ(物) 'Donation (to a priest or priests) for the chanting of a sutra.' [Hei. 3.]

Jūkyō 終教 'The end or final teaching' of Mahayana; refers to the doctrines of buddha-nature and Tathagata-Matrix (*nyoraizō**) as expounded in the *Nehan-gyō** and *Daijō-kishin-ron**; one of the five teachings classified in Kegon*; see *gokyō*. [S. IV–1.]

Jūman(n)oku-do 十萬億土 'Ten thousand billion lands'; the worlds one must pass through before reaching Amida's* Pure Land; *oku* 億 is not exactly 100 million but is used as the translation of the Sanskrit *koṭi* (*kutei**). [Tai. 9.]

~ **no ten** ----之天 'The heaven which exists ten thousand billion worlds away'; refers to Amida's* Pure Land. [Tai. 9.]

Jumyō-kyō 壽命經 '*The Life-Span Sutra*'; 1 fasc., tr. by Amoghavajra (Fukū*) [TT. 20, No. 1135]; the full title is *Issai-nyorai-kongō-jumyō-darani-kyō* 一切如來金剛壽命陀羅尼經. [Ma. 261.]

Jūnan 柔軟 See *nyūnan*.

Junda 純陀 Sk. Cunda; also 准陀, 淳陀 and Shūna 周那; a smith in Pāvā near Kuśinagara. He offered the Buddha a meal, and in taking it the Buddha was poisoned and died. [S. Va–4, Xb–1.]

Jūnen 十念 'Ten thoughts'; specifically refers to ten *nenbutsu** recitations consisting of the phrase 'Namu Amidabutsu'*; cf. *saigo no jūnen*. [S. II–8, Xa–1; Tai. 6, 11.]

Jun'en 順緣 'A favourable condition'; an act or state which affects favourably one's progress along the Buddhist Way; the opposite of *gyakuen**; cf. *jungyaku no nien*. [Tai. 24.]

Jungen(gō) 順現(業) The sort of act which brings about its effect in the present life. [Hei. 3.]

Jungogō 順後業 The sort of act which brings about its effect in the life after next. [Hei. 3.]

Jungyaku 順逆 'Favourable and adverse (conditions).' [S. III–4.]

~ **no en** --の緣 See *jungyaku no nien*. [Tai. 39.]

~ **no nien** --の二緣 Refers to *jun'en** and *gyakuen**; 'the favourable and adverse conditions,' especially for entering the Buddhist Way; e.g. being born in a Buddhist family is a favourable condition, and abusing Buddhism is an adverse one. Even an adverse condition, however, can become a path for entering Buddhism. [Tai. 3.]

Jūnibu-kyō 十二部經 'The 12 kinds of scriptures' distinguished according to different styles of exposition; also *jūnibun-kyō* 十二分經; they are: (1) *shutara** 修多羅 or *kaikyō** 契經 (*sūtra*), the Buddha's exposition of the Dharma in prose; (2) *giya** 祇夜 or *jūju** 重頌 (*geya*), verses which repeat the ideas already expressed in prose; (3) *kada** 伽陀 or *kokiju** 孤起頌 (*gāthā*), verses containing ideas not expressed in the prose section of a sutra; (4) *nidana** 尼陀那 or *innen** 因緣 (*nidāna*), narratives of happenings

in the past which explain a person's present state; (5) *iteimokuta**
伊帝目多 or *honji** 本事 (*itivṛttaka*), narratives of past lives of the
Buddha's disciples; (6) *jataka** 闍多伽 or *honshō** or *honjō* 本生
(*jātaka*), narratives of past lives of the Buddha; (7) *abudatsuma**
阿浮達磨 or *mizou-hō** 未曾有法 (*adbhuta-dharma*), accounts of
miracles performed by the Buddha or other deity; (8) *ahadana**
阿波陀那 or *hiyu** 譬喩 (*avadāna*), an exposition of the Dharma
through allegories; (9) *ubadaisha** 優婆提舍 or *rongi** 論議
(*upadeśa*), discussions of doctrine, often in question and answer
form; (10) *udana** 優陀那 or *jisetsu** 自說 (*udāna*), an exposition
of the Dharma by the Buddha without awaiting questions or
requests from his disciples; (11) *bibutsuryaku** 毘佛略 or *hōkō**
方廣 (*vaipulya*), an exposition of principles of truth *in extenso*;
and (12) *wagara** 和伽羅 or *juki** 授記 (*vyākaraṇa*), prophecies
by the Buddha regarding his disciples' attainment of buddhahood.
Cf. *kubu-kyō*.

Jūnibun-kyō 十二分經 'The 12 divisions of scriptures'; see *jūnibu-kyō*.

Jūni-innen 十二因縁 'The 12 causations'; the 12 links of cause and
effect which explain the origin of the condition of birth and death
to which living beings are subject. They are: (1) *mumyō** 無明
(*avidyā*), spiritual ignorance; (2) *gyō** 行 (*saṃskāra*), blind
volition; (3) *shiki** 識 (*vijñāna*), consciousness; (4) *myōshiki** 名色
(*nāma-rūpa*), mental functions and the formation of physical
elements; (5) *rokunyū** 六入 (*ṣaḍ-āyatana*), the six sense-organs;
(6) *soku** 觸 (*sparśa*), contact with external objects; (7) *ju** 受
(*vedanā*), sensations; (8) *ai** 愛 (*tṛṣṇā*), desire for pleasure; (9)
*shu** 取 (*upādāna*), grasping what one desires; (10) *u** 有 (*bhava*),
the state of existing; (11) *shō* 生 (*jāti*), birth; and (12) *rōshi* 老死
(*jarā-maraṇa*), old age and death.

Jūni-jinshō 十二神將 Also *jūni-shinshō*; 'the 12 heavenly generals';
the twelve *yakṣa* guardians of the *Yakushi-kyō**: (1) Kubira 宮毘
羅 (Kumbhīra); (2) Bazara 伐折羅 (Vajra); (3) Meikira 迷企羅
(Mekhila); (4) Anchira 安底羅 (Antira); (5) Ajira 頞儞羅 (Anila);
(6) Sanchira 珊底羅 (Saṃthila); (7) Indara 因陀羅 (Indāla); (8)
Haira 波夷羅 (Pāyila); (9) Makora or Magora 摩虎羅 (Mahāla);
(10) Shindara 眞達羅 (Cindāla); (11) Shōdora 招杜羅 (Caundhula)
and (12) Bikara or Bigyara 毘羯羅 (Vikāla). They protect, remove

all the sufferings, and fulfil the wishes of those who call on the name of Yakushi* and make offerings to him.

Jūni no gannō 十二の願王 'The king of the 12 vows'; refers to Yakushi* Buddha; see *Yakushi no jūni no seigan.* [Tai. 18.]

Jūni no kan 十二の觀 'Meditation on the 12 (causations)'; for the 12 causations, see *jūni-innen.* [Tai. 37.]

Jūni-nyū 十二入 See *jūni-sho.*

Jūni-shnshō 十二神將 See *jūni-jinshō.*

Jūni-sho 十二處 'The 12 sense-fields'; the six sense-organs (*rokkon**) and their corresponding objects (*rokkyō**).

Jūni-zenju 十二禪衆 'The 12 meditation priests'; a group of 12 priests on Mt. Hiei engaged in the practice of *Hokke-zanmai** and *Jōgyō-zanmai**. [Hei. 2.]

Jūni-zuda 十二頭陀 'The 12 *dhūta* practices'; the 12 rules of frugal living for Buddhist mendicants. They are: (1) living in the forest or fields; (2) living on alms alone; (3) begging alms from house to house without discriminating between rich and poor; (4) eating food at only one place; (5) eating from only one vessel; (6) not eating after the proper time, i.e. noon; (7) wearing only discarded clothes; (8) wearing only three robes (*sanne**); (9) living in a cemetery; (10) living at the foot of a tree; (11) living in the open air; and (12) sleeping in a sitting posture. [S. VI–10.]

Junji 順次 'The next life.' [K. 51.]

~ **no ōjō** --の往生 See *junji ōjō.* [K. 63.]

~ **no shōsho** --の生所 'The place of birth in the next life.' [S. Va–3.]

~ **ōjō** --往生 'Birth (into Amida's* Pure Land) in the next life.' [K. 53, 56.]

Junrei 巡禮 'Pilgrimage.' [K. 545.]

Junshō(gō) 順生(業) The sort of act which brings about its effect in the next life. [Hei. 3.]

Jūnyoze 十如是 'The ten suchness-aspects'; the ten reality aspects of each and every existence established in the Tendai* sect based on the *Hoke-kyō**: (1) *sō* 相, 'form'; (2) *shō* 性, 'nature or quality'; (3) *tai* 體, 'substance' or thing-in-itself; (4) *riki* 力, 'function'; (5) *sa* 作, 'action or motion'; (6) *in* 因, 'cause'; (7) *en* 緣, 'indirect cause or condition'; (8) *ka* 果, 'effect'; (9) *hō* 報, 'reward or retribution'; and (10) *honmatsu kukyōtō* 本末究竟等, ultimate non-differentiation of the above nine aspects from the viewpoint of the triple truth (*santai**), which pervades all existences.

Juraku 受樂 'To enjoy pleasures.'

Jūraku 十樂 'The ten joys' mentioned in the *Ōjōyōshū** which the *nenbutsu** practitioner attains: (1) being received at death by Amida* and a host of bodhisattvas; (2) the blooming of the lotus he has been born into; (3) taking on excellent physical marks and transcendental powers; (4) experiencing the splendour of the Pure Land; (5) endless pleasure; (6) saving those he has been acquainted with; (7) joining the company of the bodhisattvas; (8) seeing Amida and hearing the teaching from him; (9) making offerings to buddhas; (10) advancing to buddhahood. [IH.]

Jūrasetsu 十羅刹 Refers to *jūrasetsunyo* 十羅刹女, 'the ten female *rākṣasa* demons (*rasetsu**)' mentioned in the *Hoke-kyō** as guardians of Buddhism: Lambā, Vilambā, Kūṭadantī, Puṣpadantī, Makuṭadantī, Keśinī, Acalā, Mālādhārī, Kuntī, and Sarvasattvojohārī. [K. 49, 604.]

Jūriki 十力 'The ten powers'; Sk. *daśa-balāni*; the powers attributed to a buddha, giving perfect knowledge of the following: (1) *sho-hisho-chiriki* 處非處智力, distinguishing right and wrong; (2) *gō-ijuku-chiriki* 業異熟智力, knowing the karmas of all sentient beings of the past, present and future, and their outcome; (3) *jōryo-gedatsu-tōji-tōshi-chiriki* 靜慮解脫等持等至智力, knowing all forms of meditation; (4) *kon-jōge-chiriki* 根上下智力, knowing the superior and inferior capacities of sentient beings; (5) *shuju-shōge-chiriki* 種種勝解智力, knowing what they desire and think; (6) *shuju-kai-chiriki* 種種界智力, knowing their different levels of existence; (7) *henshugyō-chiriki* 徧趣行智力, knowing the results of various methods of practice; (8) *shukujū-zuinen-chiriki* 宿住隨念智力, knowing the transmigratory states of all sentient beings and the courses of karma they follow; (9) *shishō-chiriki* 死生智力, knowing the past lives of all sentient beings and the nirvanic state of non-defilement; and (10) *rojin-chiriki* 漏盡智力, knowing how to destroy all evil passions.

Jūrin-gyō 十輪經 Abbr. of *Daihōkō-jūrin-gyō**. [S. II–5, 10, VI–17, 18, Xa–6.]

Jūrokkan 十六觀 'The 16 contemplations' centring on Amida* and his land as presented in the *Kanmuryōju-kyō**. The first 13 are contemplations, in a state of deep meditation, on various aspects of the Pure Land, including Amida, Kannon* and the practitioner himself. The last three contemplations are, in fact, expositions of various good acts to be done in the ordinary non-meditative state of mind, and in this section nine grades of aspirants to the Pure Land (*kuhon** 九品) are distinguished according to different grades of good acts done. The 13 contemplations are: (1) *nissōkan* 日想觀, on the setting sun; (2) *suisōkan** 水想觀, on water; (3) *hōjikan* 寶地觀, on the earth of the Pure Land; (4) *hōjukan* 寶樹觀, on jewelled trees; (5) *hōchikan* 寶池觀, on treasure-ponds; (6) *hōrōkan* 寶樓觀, on jewelled towers; (7) *kezakan* 華座觀, on the lotus-seat of Amida; (8) *zōsōkan* 像想觀, on the image of Amida; (9) *shinshinkan* 眞身觀, on the real body of Amida; (10) *Kannonkan* 觀音觀, on Kannon Bodhisattva; (11) *Seishikan* 勢至觀, on Seishi* Bodhisattva; (12) *fusōkan* 普想觀, on the practitioner himself as he is born in the Pure Land; (13) *zassōkan* 雜想觀, on various manifestations of Amida and the two bodhisattvas.

Jūroku-daikoku 十六大國 'The 16 great kingdoms' in India at the time of the Buddha; there are two traditions. I. According to the *Jō-agon-gyō**, they were: Aṅga, Magadha, Kāśī, Kośala, Vṛji, Malla, Cedi, Vatsa, Kuru, Pañcāla, Matsya, Śūrasena, Aśvaka, Avanti, Gandhāra, and Kamboja. II. The *Ninnō-kyō** gives the following: Vaiśālī, Kośala, Śrāvastī, Magadha, Vārāṇasī, Kapila-vastu, Kuśinagara, Kauśāmbī, Pañcāla, Pāṭaliputra, Mathurā, Ujjayanī, Puṇḍavardhana, Devāvatī, Kāśī, and Campā. [Tai. 33.]

Jūroku-zenjin 十六善神 'The 16 good deities' who protect the *Daihannya-haramitta-kyō**. [K. 68; Tai. 5.]

Juryō 鷲嶺 'Vulture Peak', i.e. Ryōjusen*. [K. 34.]

Juryō-bon 壽量品 'Chapter on Life-Span'; the 16th chapter of the *Hoke-kyō**; the full title is 'Nyorai-juryō-bon' 如來壽量品. This chapter explains that the Buddha's life-span is immeasurable. [Tai. 20.]

Jūsainichi 十齋日 'The ten precept-observing days' each month kept in memory of ten buddhas or bodhisattvas: (1) 1st, for Jōkō* Buddha, (2) 8th, for Yakushi* Buddha, (3) 14th, for Fugen*

Bodhisattva, (4) 15th, for Amida* Buddha, (5) 18th, for Kannon* Bodhisattva, (6) 23rd, for Seishi* Bodhisattva, (7) 24th, for Jizō* Bodhisattva, (8) 28th, for Birushana* Buddha, (9) 29th, for Yakuō* Bodhisattva, and (10) 30th, for Shakamuni* Buddha. On those days lay Buddhists observe the eight precepts (*hassai-kai**); cf. *sai* and *sainichi*. [K. 51.]

Jūsan-shū 十三宗 'The 13 (Buddhist) sects' in Japan: Kegon*, Tendai*, Shingon*, Hossō*, Ritsu*, Jōdo*, Rinzai, Sōto, Ōbaku, Jōdoshin*, Nichiren*, Yūzū-nenbutsu* and Ji*; see also *Zenshū*.

Jūshō kagoku 重障過極 'Extremely heavy hindrance (of sin).' [Tai. 20.]

Juso 呪咀 'A spell or curse.'

Jūsō 住僧 'A resident priest' of a temple. [K. 291.]

Jusshin 十身 Also *jūshin* and *jisshin*; 'the ten bodies' of the Buddha. Two kinds of ten bodies are presented in the *Kegon-gyō**. I. *Gekyō no jusshin* 解境の十身, the ten bodies perceived as parts of the cosmic buddha, Vairocana (Birushana*): (1) *shujōshin* 衆生身, sentient beings of the six realms of transmigration (*rokudō**); (2) *kokudoshin* 國土身, the worlds where they live; (3) *gōhōshin* 業報身, karmas which produce various states of transmigration; (4) *shōmonshin* 聲聞身, shravakas (*shōmon**); (5) *dokkakushin* 獨覺身, pratyekabuddhas (*engaku**); (6) *bosatsushin* 菩薩身, bodhisattvas; (7) *nyoraishin* 如來身, tathagatas (*nyorai**) or buddhas; (8) *chishin* 智身, the wisdom to know reality; (9) *hosshin* 法身, the Dharma or law; and (10) *kokūshin* 虛空身, an empty space which here represents the ultimate substance containing all existing things. II. *Gyōkyō no jusshin* 行境の十身, the ten bodies to be attained by performing meritorious practices: (1) *bodaishin* 菩提身, 'enlightenment body', the manifestation of a buddha body attaining enlightenment; (2) *ganshin* 願身, 'vow body', aspiring to be born in the Tuṣita Heaven (Tosotsuten*); (3) *keshin* 化身, 'transformed body', being born in the king's palace; (4) *jūjishin* 住持身, 'retaining body', retaining the relics in this world after death; (5) *sōgō-shōgonshin* 相好莊嚴身, 'body adorned with excellent physical characteristics'; (6) *seirikishin* 勢力身, 'body of strength,' a body with the power to suppress evils and protect beings; (7) *nyoishin* 如意身, 'body (manifested) at will' for bodhisattvas; (8) *fukutokushin* 福德身, 'body of merit and virtue', a body dwelling in meditation which is the cause of all kinds of merit and virtue; (9) *chishin* 智身, 'wisdom body', a body possessing the four kinds of wisdom (*shichi**); and (10) *hosshin** 法身, 'law-body', a quintessential buddha body.

Jusshu-kuyō 十種供養 'The ten kinds of offerings (to a buddha)' mentioned in the *Hoke-kyō**: (1) *ke* 華, flowers; (2) *kō* 香, incense; (3) *yōraku** 瓔珞, ornaments; (4) *makkō* 抹香, powdered incense; (5) *zukō* 塗香, unguent; (6) *shōkō* 燒香, burning of incense; (7) *sōgai* dōban** 繪蓋幢幡, canopies and banners; (8) *ebuku** 衣服, clothes; (9) *gigaku* 伎樂, dancing and music; and (10) *gasshō* 合掌, joining one's hands in worship. [Tai. 39.]

Jusshu no shōri 十種の勝利 'The ten superior benefits' which aspirants to Amida's* Pure Land receive in their present life. They are, according to Tz'u-yün 慈雲 (Jiun, 963–1032) as quoted in the *Rakuhō-monrui* 樂邦文類: (1) all gods, heavenly generals and their subjects protect them; (2) all bodhisattvas, including the 25 great bodhisattvas (*nijūgo-bosatsu**), protect them; (3) all buddhas protect them, and Amida bathes them in his light; (4) evil spirits, *yakṣa*, *rākṣasas*, poisonous snakes and insects cannot harm them; (5) they do not suffer from fire, floods, drowning, harm by swords, imprisonment, torture by handcuffs, etc., and do not meet untimely deaths; (6) their evil karma is cancelled, including that which would otherwise bring them retribution by taking their lives; (7) they can see in a dream a glorious image of Amida; (8) their hearts are always full of joy, and their minds and bodies full of vitality; (9) they are respected and even worshipped by people of the world; and (10) at the time of death, they have no fear, but dwell in the right state of mind and are full of joy; they see Amida and a host of sages come to welcome them holding golden lotus-seats, and they will be born in the Pure Land. [Tai. 18.]

Jūzen 十善 'The ten good (acts)'; also *jūzengō** 十善業, *jūzendō** 十善道, *jūzengōdō** 十善業道 and *jūzenkai** 十善戒. They are: (1) *fusesshō* 不殺生, not killing living beings; (2) *fuchūtō* 不偸盗, not stealing; (3) *fujain* 不邪婬, not committing adultery; (4) *fumōgo* 不妄語, not telling lies; (5) *fuakku* 不惡口, not uttering harsh words; (6) *furyōzetsu* 不兩舌, not uttering words which cause enmity between two or more persons; (7) *fukigo* 不綺語,

not engaging in idle talk; (8) *futon'yoku* 不貪欲, not being greedy; (9) *fushinni* 不瞋恚, not being angry; and (10) *fujaken* 不邪見, not having wrong views.

~-**dō** --道 'The path of the ten good (acts)'; see *jūzen*.

~-**gō** --業 'The ten good acts'; see *jūzen*.

~-**gōdō** --業道 'The path of the ten good acts'; see *jūzen*.

~-**kai** --戒 'The ten good precepts'; the ten good acts; see *jūzen*.

~ **manjō no kurai** --萬乘の位 'The throne (which is the reward) of the ten good acts and (has) 10,000 chariots (under its command).' [S. Xa–4.]

~ **no kaikō** --の戒功 'The merit accruing from observance of the ten good acts.' [Hei. 1.]

~ **no kairiki** --の戒力 'The (karmic) power produced from observance of the ten good acts.' [Tai. 34.]

~ **no kimi** --の君 'The emperor with the virtue of the ten good acts'; it is believed that the throne is the reward of the ten good acts performed in a previous life. [Tai. 3.]

~ **no kuni** --の國 'The country (reigned over by a king or emperor with the virtue) of the ten good acts.' [Tai. 33.]

~ **no ōi** --の王位 'The throne (which is the reward) of the ten good acts.' [K. 472.]

~ **no ten'i** --の天位 'The throne (which is the reward) of the ten good acts.' [Tai. 21.]

~ **no tenshi** --の天子 The same as *jūzen no kimi**. [Tai. 3, 17.]

~ **no yokun** --の餘薫 'A lingering fragrance from the ten good acts'; the glorious reward of the ten good acts, i.e. the throne. [S. Vb–9.]

Jūzen 十禪 Used for *jūzen* 十善. [Hei. 3.]

Jūzenji 十禪師 Refers to Jūzenji Gongen 十禪師權現, one of the 21 Sannō* shrines, where an incarnation of Jizō* Bodhisattva is enshrined. [Tai. 18.]

Juzu 數珠 'A rosary'; also pronounced *zuzu*.

K

Kabi 加被 Also 加備; 'to add and make someone receive'; the same as *kago** 加護 and *kayū* 加祐; said of the endowment of power and benefit to living beings by a buddha or a bodhisattva. [Tai. 17.]

Kabirae 迦毘羅衞 Sk. Kapilavastu; see *Kabirajō*. [S. Vb–10.]

Kabirajō 迦毘羅城 Sk. Kapilavastu; also Kabirae 迦毘羅衞; n. of the kingdom and also the capital of the Śākya (Shaka*) clan in central India, which produced Shakamuni*.

Kabutsu 果佛 'Buddha at (the stage of) effect'; buddhahood attained as the result of practices by a bodhisattva; cf. *inni*.

Kada 伽陀 Sk. *gāthā*; also 伽他; translated as *ku* 句 'phrase', *fūju* 諷頌 'verse', *kokiju* 孤起頌 'independent verse'; specifically a verse expounding the Dharma or praising the Buddha; a verse containing ideas not expressed in the prose section of a sutra; one of the nine and the twelve kinds of scriptures (*kubu-kyō** and *jūnibu-kyō**). [Tai. 24.]

Kadai 遐代 'Later generations.'

Kago 加護 'Protection' by a buddha, bodhisattva or other deity.

Kagu 加供 'Making offerings' at a Buddhist service. [O. V.]

Kagyō 加行 See *kegyō*.

Kahō 果報 'Effect, reward or retribution' of some acts done.

Kai 戒 'A Buddhist precept'; Sk. *śīla*.

~**-dan** -壇 'Precept dais'; a platform used in the *jukai** ceremony. [Hei. 3; O. V; S. III–5, VI–9, 18, Xb–3; Tai. 15.]

~**-gi** -儀 'The proper rite for conferment of the precepts.' [S. III–8.]

~**-gyō** -行 'Precepts and practice'; the rules of conduct prescribed by the Buddha; also, observance of the precepts received; practice in compliance with the precepts; cf. *kai no shika*. [S. I–8, Xa–6; Tai. 24.]

～**-hō** -法 'The law of precepts'; the law of the Buddha regarding rules of conduct; cf. *kai no shika*.

～**-jōe** -定慧 '(Observance of) precepts, meditation and wisdom'; they are called the three learnings (*sangaku**). [Tai. 18.]

～**-jō shiku** -乗四句 'The four-phrase statement concerning precept(-observance) and learning'; see *jōkai shiku*.

～**-kan** -緩 'Slow in (observing) precepts'; see *jōkai shiku*. [S. Va–2.]

～**-kyū** -急 'Quick in (observing) precepts'; diligent observance of the precepts; see *jōkai shiku*. [S. Va–2.]

～**-mon** -門 'The precept gate'; refers to the Ritsu*. [S. Xb–3.]

～**-myō** -名 'Precept name'; the Buddhist name given when the precepts are accepted. See *hōmyō*.

～ **no shi** -の師 See *kaishi*. [Tai. 11.]

～ **no shika** -の四科 The four divisions of precepts: (1) *kaihō* 戒法, the law of the Buddha regarding rules of conduct; (2) *kaitai* 戒體, 'the substance (for the observance) of precepts', a kind of mental and physical force produced in one's body when one receives precepts, which binds one to abide by them; (3) *kaigyō* 戒行, observance of the precepts received; and (4) *kaisō** 戒相, precepts in their various forms, such as the five precepts (*gokai**) and the 250 precepts for monks.

～**-riki** -力 'Precept power'; the power produced by the observance of the precepts. [O. III.]

～**-shi** -師 'A teacher of the precepts'; one who confers the precepts.

～**-sō** -相 'Precepts in their various forms'; precepts as they should be observed in the heart and with the body, such as the five precepts (*gokai**) and the 250 precepts for the monk; one of the four matters for discussion regarding precepts; cf. *kai no shika* above. [S. III–5, IV–1.]

～**-tai** -體 'The substance of precepts'; a kind of mental and physical force produced in one's body when one receives precepts, which binds one to abide by them; cf. *kai no shika*.

∼-toku -德 'Merit from observing the precepts.' [K. 38.]

∼-wajō -和尚 'Precept master'; the chief of the three masters who preside at the ceremony of accepting the precepts. The other two are *katsumashi** and *kyōjushi**, but the *kai-wajō* performs the ceremony of conferment itself. [O. V, VI.]

Kai 果位 'The stage of fruit or effect'; the stage of fulfilment of bodhisattva practices; the stage of buddhahood; cf. *inni*. [S. IV –1.]

Kaibyaku no hi 開白の日 'The day of the opening statement (of a service)'; the opening day of a Buddhist service or lecture-meeting. [K. 331.]

Kaie 開會 'Opening up and merging'; according to the *Hoke-kyō**, the Buddha first expounded various provisional teachings and then in that sutra, merged them into the One Vehicle teaching (*ichijō**). [S. IV–1.]

Kaigen 戒賢 Sk. Śīlabhadra; an Indian master of the Yogācāra school (*Yugagyōha**) around the 7th century. [S. III–1, VIII–23.]

Kaigen 開眼 I. 'Opening the (spiritual) eyes'; attaining enlightenment. II. Invoking the spirit of a deity in order to inaugurate a painting or statue of him; also, a service held for that purpose.

Kaigyō 開曉 See *kaikyō*.

Kaiken 開顯 Abbr. of *kaigon kenjitsu* 開權顯實, 'opening the expedient teachings and revealing the true one'; refers to the Tendai* interpretation of the *Hoke-kyō**, according to which the Buddha showed in it that the various teachings he had expounded before were expedient ones and that the *Hoke-kyō* was the true teaching. [Tai. 18.]

Kaiketsu no nikyō 開結の二經 'The opening and concluding sutras'; refers to the *Muryōgi-kyō* 無量義經, which serves as an introduction to the *Hoke-kyō** and the *Fugenkan-gyō* 普賢觀經, which presents the method of meditation on Fugen* Bodhisattva's practice by way of showing the practical conclusion of what has been said in the *Hoke-kyō*. These two and the *Hoke-kyō* form a set of three sutras (*Hokke sanbukyō**). [Tai. 11.]

Kaikyō 開曉 Also *kaigyō*; 'to open and illumine'; to enlighten.

[S. III–1.]

Kaikyō 契經 'The (truth) securing thread'; Sk. *sūtra*; see *kyō* and *shutara*; one of the nine and the twelve kinds of scriptures (*kubu-kyō** and *jūnibu-kyō**).

Kain 火印 'The fire *mudrā*'; a manual sign in the form of a triangle which represents fire. [K. 596; Tai. 12.]

Kaisan 開山 'The founder of a temple or sect.'

Kaji 加持 I. Buddha's power transferred to sentient beings. II. The transference of Buddha's power and the response to it by sentient beings. III. A prayer. IV. To perform a mystic prayer to save living beings through the Buddha's power.

~ **kōzui** --香水 I. The esoteric ritual of investing perfume with magical power. II. The ceremony of sprinkling such perfume on the emperor's body on the 14th of the 1st month. [Tsu. 238.]

~ **no jōbutsu** --の成佛 See *sanshu no sokushin jōbutsu.*

~**-riki** --力 'The power of correspondence between (the Buddha's) power and (man's) receptivity.'

~ **su** --す 'To invest with magical power.'

Kajō 嘉祥 Ch. Chia-hsiang; see next entry. [S. Xb–2.]

~ **Daishi** --大師 'Great Master Chia-hsiang'; the popular name for Chi-ts'ang 吉藏 (Kichizō*). [S. VI–10.]

Kakai no ju 火界の呪 Also *kakai shingon* 火界眞言; 'spell of the fire-element'; one of Fudō's* spells. [S.II–5, VII–24.]

Kakai shingon 火界眞言 'Spell of the fire-element'; see *kakai no ju.*

Kakochō 過去帳 A book for recording the names of the deceased and their dates of death. [Hei. 1; Tai. 26.]

Kako shichibutsu 過去七佛 'The past seven buddhas' who appeared in this world: (1) Bibashi 毘婆尸 (Vipaśyin); (2) Shiki 尸棄 (Śikhin); (3) Bishabu 毘舍浮 (Viśvabhū); (4) Kuruson 拘留孫 (Krakucchanda); (5) Kunagonmuni 拘那含牟尼 (Kanakamuni); (6) Kashō* 迦葉 (Kāśyapa); and (7) Shakamuni* 釋迦牟尼 (Śākyamuni). [K. 164.]

Kakudō 覺道 'Realization of the Way'; enlightenment. [Hei. 2.]

~ **no hana** --の花 'The flower of enlightenment.' [Hei. 2.]

Kakugo no renge 覺悟の蓮花 'The lotus of enlightenment.' [S. II –4.]

Kakurin 鶴林 'Crane forest'; another name for the twin-*śāla* trees (*sarasōju**) under which the Buddha passed into Nirvana. It is said that when this happened, the trees all bloomed at once, and the whole forest became white as if cranes had flocked there. [K. 34.]

Kakuryō 覺了 'Realization, awareness, enlightenment.'

Kakusha 覺者 'An enlightened man'; a buddha.

Kanbō 觀法 I. Contemplation on an objective thing or a reality-principle. II. A method of contemplation.

Kanbotsu 勘發 Also *kanpotsu*; 'reprimand, censure'. [K. 57.]

Kanbutsu 灌佛 'Sprinkling (an image of) the Buddha'; sprinkling hydrangea tea (*amacha* 甘茶) on an image of the infant Buddha to celebrate his birthday on the 8th day of the 4th month; this originates from the legend that when Buddha was born dragons poured perfumed water on his body. [Tai. 24; Tsu. 19.]

~ **no mizu** --の水 The water sprinkled over small statues of the Buddha on the anniversary of his birthday. [Tai. 8.]

Kanbutsu-zanmai-kyō 觀佛三昧經 '*Meditation on the Buddha Sutra*'; the full title is *Kanbutsu-zanmaikai-kyō* 觀佛三昧海經; 10 fasc., tr. by Buddhabhadra (Buddabatsudara 佛陀跋陀羅) between 368 and 421 [TT. 15, No. 643]. The sutra expounds the merit of the practice of meditating on buddhas.

Kanchi 觀智 'Wisdom of insight'; meditative observation.

Kanchō 貫頂 The head priest, archbishop; same as *kanshu** and *kansu**. [Tai. 8, 21, 24, 39.]

Kangaku-e 勸學會 'Learning-encouragement meeting'; the meeting held twice yearly, in the third and ninth months, on Mt. Hiei with the participation of 20 Tendai* priests and 20 students of the academy of literature; after the priests lectured on the *Hoke-kyō**, the students wrote poems on the subject of a phrase from it. It first began under the auspices of Yoshishige Yasutane 慶滋保胤 and others in 964. [K. 140.]

Kange 觀解 'Meditation and understanding'; meditative intro-spection. [S. III–1.]

Kangyō 觀行 'A meditative practice.'

~ **gohon** --五品 See *kangyō gohon'i*. [Tai. 17.]

~ **gohon'i** --五品位 'The stage of the five kinds (of meritorious acts) of meditation and other practices'; also *gohon deshii* 五品弟子位 and, simply, *gohon'i* 五品位; the lowest of the eight stages among followers of the Perfect Teaching (*engyō**) established in the Tendai* sect; see *gohon*.

Kangyō 觀經 '*The Meditation Sutra*'; abbr. of *Kanmuryōju-kyō**. [IH.; K. 36; S. I–10, IV–1, Va–4, Xa–1.]

Kanjin 勸進 'Urging' people to do a meritorious act, e.g. to make donations for a good cause.

~-**chō** --帳 I. A list of the names of persons who have been led to a specific teaching of Buddhism. [K. 53.] II. A list of the names of donors who have supported the promoter's cause.

~ **no hijiri** --の聖 The same as *kanjin no shōnin**. [S. Vb–11.]

~ **no shōnin** --の聖人 A virtuous priest who urges people to make donations (for building a temple, etc.). [S. Vb–10.]

Kanjin 觀心 'Meditation on one's mind'; introspection into one's mind-essence, as opposed to *kyōsō** 教相, the theoretical study of the Buddhist teaching. [S. II–8, III–4, 8, Xb–3.]

~ **kufū** --工夫 'Meditation on one's mind and endeavours (to attain enlightenment).' [S. Xb–3.]

~ **no hōmon** --の法門 The aspect of the teaching which deals with meditation on the essence of one's mind. [S. IV–1.]

Kanjizaiō 觀自在王 'The king who can observe freely'; n. of a buddha; in esoteric Buddhism, the real name for Amida*. [S. IV–1.]

Kanjo 灌頂 'Sprinkling (water) on the head'; Sk. *abhiṣecana* or *abhiṣeka*. A ceremony in esoteric Buddhism for conferring the precepts, a certain mystic teaching, etc., on a person.

~ **daihōōji** --大法王子 'A great Dharma-prince who has received *kanjō*.' [Tai. 18.]

~-**ji** --地 Sk. *abhiṣeka-bhūmi*, 'the stage of sprinkling (water) on the head'; the highest stage of bodhisattvahood. [K. 64.]

Kanjō 勸請 'Summoning up' a Buddhist or Shinto deity. Cf. *Daishi kanjō no kishō*.

Kanju 卷數 Also *kanzu*; 'the number of scrolls'; a list of the dharanis or sutras chanted for prayer; it also gives the number of times they are chanted. [Tai. 3, 29.]

Kanju 貫主 See *kansu*.

Kanka 感果 'Effecting a result'; a desired effect brought about by a certain practice. [K. 53.]

Kankin 看經 'Seeing a sutra'; reading a sutra; later, used with the sense of chanting a sutra. [Tai. 17.]

Kanmuryōju-kyō 觀無量壽經 '*The Meditation on the Buddha of Infinite Life Sutra*'; 1 fasc., translated into Chinese by Kālayaśas (Kyōryōyasha 畺良耶舍) in the period 424–442 [TT. 12, No. 365]; one of the three canons of Pure Land schools. The sutra presents 16 contemplations centring on Amida* and his land; see *jūrokkan*.

Kannen 觀念 'Meditative thought.' I. Meditation; contemplation. II. Particularly, contemplation on Amida's* Pure Land. III. In the 16 contemplations on the Pure Land (*jūrokkan**), especially refers to the first, i.e. contemplation on the setting sun. [Ho. 30; K. 50.]

~ **jōza no tsutome** --定坐の勤 'The practice of constantly sitting in meditation.' [Tai. 12.]

Kannō 感應 'Receptiveness and responsiveness'. *Kan* is man's capability of receiving the Buddha's saving power, and *ō* is the Buddha's saving activity; the Buddha's responsive activity in conjunction with man's receptivity.

~ **dōkō** --道交 'Correspondence between the Buddha's power and man's receptivity.' [S. VI–1.]

Kannon 觀音 'One who Observes the Sound (of the World)'; Sk. Avalokiteśvara; abbr. of Kanzeon 觀世音; also Kanjizai 觀自在, Kanzejizai 觀世自在, Kōseon 光世音, etc. Being one of the two bodhisattvas attending Amida,* he has an image of Amida in his crown. He is capable of manifesting 33 forms of incarnation to save people in different states of existence. His original abode is known as Potalaka. In China and Japan, Kannon is popularly worshipped as a female deity. For the different kinds of Kannon, see *rokkannon* and *sanjūsan Kannon*☆.

~**-gyō** --經 '*The Kannon Sutra*'; a popular name for 'Kanzeon

Bosatsu Fumon-bon' 觀世音菩薩普門品 'Chapter on the Universal Gate of the Bodhisattva Avalokiteśvara' in the *Hoke-kyō**; also called 'Fumon-bon' 普門品 'Chapter on the Universal Gate'. [K. 70, 682; S. II-4; Tai. 3, 13.]

~-in --院 'The Kannon section' of the Matrix-store Realm Mandala (*Taizōkai mandara**). There are 21 main deities presented in this section, of whom the central figure is Kannon. [S. IV-1.]

~ no ennichi --の緣日 'Kannon's *ennichi**'; the 18th of the month when Kannon is believed to be in a closer relationship with man. [K. 711.]

Kanro 甘露 Sk. *amṛta*; 'nectar'. [K. 58.]

Kanshō 觀照 'Illuminating (reality)'; having the wisdom to understand things as they are.

~ hannya --般若 Also ~ *bannya*; 'illuminating wisdom'; the transcendental wisdom of realizing reality or absolute truth; one of the three aspects of *hannya* (*sanhannya**). [S. IV-1.]

Kanshōjin 勸請神 'A Shinto god who has been summoned.' [S. I-3.]

Kanshu 貫主 See *kansu*.

Kanshu 貫首 The head priest, archbishop; also *kansu** and *kanchō** [Tai. 2, 32.]

Kansō 官僧 'An officially appointed priest.' I. An officially ordained priest who has received a state certificate. II. A priest who has been appointed to a priestly rank, such as *sōjō** or *sōzu**. [Tai. 12, 16.]

Kansu 貫主 The head priest, archbishop; same as *kanshu** and *kanchō**.

Kantoku 感得 'To obtain by inspiration'; to receive a message or vision by inspiration or obtain something by supernatural means.

Kanzeon 觀世音 'One who Observes the Sound of the World'; Sk. Avalokiteśvara; a fuller form of the name Kannon*. [Tai. 11.]

Karadasen 伽羅陀山 See *Kyaradasen*.

Karitei 訶利帝 Sk. Hāritī; also 訶利底, 訶哩帝, etc., and translated as Shōshiki 靑色, Shōe 靑衣, etc.; more popularly known by

such names as Kishimo 鬼子母, Aishimo 愛子母 and Kudokuten*
功德天. She was a *yakṣa* (*yasha**) living in the outskirts of Rājagṛha (Ōshajō*). Married to a *yakṣa* named Pañcika (Hanshika
半支迦), she bore 500 children. Because of the wicked vow she
had made in her previous life, she went to the town, and there
caught infants and ate them. In order to stop this evil practice,
the Buddha snatched one of her children and hid it. Finding that
a child was missing, she frantically looked everywhere. Then the
Buddha admonished her, pointing out that the suffering of the
parents whose children she had eaten was far greater than hers.
Repenting of her evil act, she was converted to Buddhism and
vowed that she would protect monasteries. In India she is worshipped as a god of easy delivery. She is one of the deities of the
Matrix-store Realm Mandala (*Taizōkai mandara**). [Tai. 1.]

~-mo ---母 See *Kariitei*. [Tai. 1.]

Karura 迦樓羅 Also 伽樓羅 Sk. *garuḍa*; translated as *konjichō**
金翅鳥, etc.; originally, a mythological bird said to eat dragons;
one of the eight kinds of supernatural beings who protect Buddhism (*hachi-bushu**). In esoteric Buddhism, *garuḍa* is believed to
be an incarnation of a deity who saves people.

~-en ---炎 'A garuḍa's flame'; *garuḍa* (*karura**) are believed to
emit flames from their mouths. [Tai. 18.]

Karyōbin 伽陵頻 Refers to *karyōbinga**. [K. 251.]

~-ga ---伽 Sk. *kalaviṅka*; a bird with a sweet song said to be
found in the Himalayas.

~ no koe ---の聲 'The song of a *kalaviṅka*'; see *karyōbinga*.
[K. 251.]

Kasha 火車 'A fiery cart' which carries sinners to hell. [S. II–6.]

Kashō 和尙 The title used for a Buddhist master in the Tendai*
sect; pronounced *oshō** in the Zen* sect, and *wajō* in the Hossō*,
Ritsu*, and Shingon* sects.

Kashō 迦葉 Sk. Kāśyapa. I. The sixth of the seven buddhas in
the past (*kako shichibutsu**). [K. 36.] II. Refers to Makakashō*.
[S. Vb–10.] III. N. of a bodhisattva. [S. I–1.]

~ Butsu --佛 'Buddha Kāśyapa'; the sixth of the seven buddhas
in the past (*kako shichibutsu**). [S. Xb–1; Tai. 18.]

Kashō Daishi 嘉祥大師 See *Kajō Daishi*.

Kashōmatō 迦葉摩騰 Sk. Kāśyapamātaṅga; often abbreviated as Matō; a monk from central India, well-versed in Mahayana and Hinayana teachings. He went to China in 67 A.D. with Chu Fa-lan 竺法蘭 (Jiku Hōran*) and produced translations of the *Shijūni-shōgyō**, etc.

Kasshiki 喝食 'Announcing meal.' I. In Zen*, announcing the menu and supervising at table. II. Refers to *kasshiki anja**. [Tai. 26.]

~ anja --行者 A novice at a Zen* temple who announces the menu and supervises at table when monks are having a meal; abbreviated as *kasshiki**.

Kataku 火宅 'A house on fire'; metaphorically, the three realms (*sangai**) of transmigration, where there are constant fears and pains as in a burning house. The metaphor comes from the *Hoke-kyō**. [S. III–1.]

Katoku 果徳 'Merit (at the stage) of fulfilment'; merit acquired as the result of the practices of a bodhisattva; a buddha's perfect merit.

Katsuai 割愛 'To sever ties of love and affection'; to leave loved ones. [S. IX–2.]

Katsugō 渇仰 'To feel fervently' about a buddha, one's master or his teaching, like a thirsty man seeking water.

Katsumashi 羯磨師 Sk. *karma-ācārya*. Also *katsuma-ajari* 羯磨阿闍梨. One of the three masters of precepts who preside at the ceremony of accepting the precepts. He recites the text of the precepts. Cf. *kai-wajō*, *kyōjushi*.

Kebosatsu 化菩薩 'A transformed bodhisattva.' [K. 63.]

Kebutsu 化佛 'A transformed buddha.'

Kedai 懈怠 Also *ketai*; 'idleness, indolence.'

Kedō rishō 化導利生 'Transforming, guiding and benefitting living beings.' [Tai. 26.]

Keen 化縁 'The conditions for converting people'; the conditions which cause the appearance of a buddha or bodhisattva in the world to convert people. [S. II–5.]

Keen-hōkai ichinen-hōkai 繋縁法界一念法界 'To meditate on the

Dharma-realm and concentrate one's thought on it'; the phrase originally appears in the *Makashikan** 摩訶止観. [S. III –1.]

Kegi 化儀 'The manner or method of teaching.' [S. II–8, 9, IV–1; Tai. 16.]

~ **no shikyō** --の四教 'The four methods of teaching' of the Buddha classified in Tendai* doctrine: (1) *tongyō* 頓教, 'abrupt teaching', the teaching which enlightens one very quickly; this refers to the *Kegon-gyō**; (2) *zengyō* 漸教, 'gradual teaching', the teaching which gradually trains and enlightens pupils; this refers to the Hinayana and other Mahayana teachings; (3) *himitsukyō* 祕密教, 'secret teaching', the teaching whereby the pupils attain different understandings without their knowledge; and (4) *fujō-kyō* 不定教, 'indeterminate teaching', the teaching whereby the pupils attain different understandings while being fully aware of this. Cf. *goji* and *kehō no shikyō*.

Kegon 華(or 花)嚴 'Garland'. I. *Kegon Sutra*; see *Kegon-gyō*. II. Kegon sect; see *Kegonshū*.

~**-e** --會 'The Kegon ceremony' held annually at the Tōdaiji* on the 14th of the 3rd month, at which lectures on the *Kegon-gyō** are given. [Tai. 24.]

~ **gojūsan no chishiki** --五十三の知識 'The 53 teachers mentioned in the *Kegon-gyō**'; see *Kegon no chishiki*. [S. Vb–10.]

~**-gyō** --經 '*The Garland Sutra*'; Sk. *Avataṃsaka-sūtra*; the Mahayana sutra said to have been delivered during the first three weeks after the Buddha's enlightenment. There are three main Chinese translations: (1) 60 fasc., by Buddhabhadra (Kakuken 覺賢) in 418–421 [TT. 9, No. 278]; (2) 80 fasc., by Śikṣānanda (Jisshananda 實叉難陀) in 695–699 [TT. 10, No. 279]; and (3) 40 fasc., by Prajñā (Hannya 般若) in 759–762 [TT. 10, No. 293]. [K. 64.]

~ **no chishiki** --の知識 'Teachers mentioned in the *Kegon-gyō**': the 53 teachers, mentioned in the chapter 'Nyūhokkai' 入法界 of the *Kegon-gyō*, who guided a youth, called Zenzai 善財, in the Buddhist Way. [S. IV–1.]

~**-shū** --宗 'The Kegon (Ch. Hua-yen) sect'; a Mahayana sect founded in China in the Sui-T'ang period based on the *Kegon-gyō**. This sect classifies the Buddha's lifetime teachings into five groups (*gokyō**) and places the Kegon teaching in the highest group. Kegon views the universe as a perfect unity with all existences in it penetrating each other and fusing together (*rokusō en'yū**). The foundation of this sect was laid by Tu-shun 杜順 (Tojun*) and Chih-yen 智儼 (Chigon), and the doctrine was systematized by Fa-tsang 法藏 (Hōzō*). Kegon texts were first brought to Japan from China by Tao-hsüan 道璿 (Dōsen) in 736, followed by Shen-hsiang 審祥 (Shinjō) of Korea, who gave the first lecture on the *Kegon-gyō* in Nara in 740. Shinjō is thus looked up to as the founder of the Japanese Kegon sect. The second patriarch, Rōben* 良辨, became the first head monk (*bettō**) of the Tōdaiji* and contributed a great deal to the popularization of the teaching. Cf. *Birushana Butsu*, *rokushū* and *jūsanshū*.

Kegyō 加行   A preparatory 'practice' to be performed with an 'added' effort, or 'a practice additional' to the main one. The practice performed for seven or up to 100 days prior to the ceremony of conferring precepts in esoteric Buddhism. [S. II–5.]

Kehō 假法   'A temporary thing'; the opposite of *jippō**.

Kehō no shikyō 化法の四教   'The four doctrinal teachings' of the Buddha classified in Tendai* doctrine: (1) *zōkyō* 藏教, 'Piṭaka teaching', the Hinayana teaching; the lowest of the four; (2) *tsugyō* 通教, 'common teaching', the teaching applied to Hinayanists and Mahayanists as well; (3) *bekkyō* 別教, 'distinct teaching', the specifically Mahayana teachings; and (4) *engyō* 圓教, 'round teaching', the ultimate and perfect teaching, such as that contained in the *Kegon-gyō**, *Hoke-kyō** and *Nehan-gyō**. Cf. *goji* and *kegi no shikyō*.

Kei 磬   I. A slab of hard stone cut in the form of a shallow inverted V, and hung from a wooden frame; originally a kind of Chinese musical instrument. It is used in Buddhist services. [K. 153.] II. Today, popularly, a bowl-shaped copper gong placed on a cushion and used in Buddhist services.

Keiaihō 敬愛法   'The rite for achieving love and respect (from others)'; one of the five kinds of rituals in esoteric Buddhism (*goshuhō**). [It aims at ultimately leading sentient beings to enlightenment; cf. *kyōai no hihō*.

Keibyaku 啓白 'The announcement' of the purpose of a rite or service to a buddha, etc.; the same as *hyōbyaku** 表白.

～ no kane --の鐘 The bell struck when an announcement is made at a service. [Tai. 23.]

Keikei 荊溪 Ch. Ching-hsi (711–782); refers to Tannen*. [S. IV–1, Xb–3.]

Keiko 稽古 'Studying the past'; practising the traditional Buddhist Way. [Tai. 17.]

Kekkai 結界 'Binding, i.e. enclosing, an area'; Sk. *sīmā-bandha*; setting up a boundary for the performance of a ritual or ceremony, or for the construction of a temple, etc.

～-ji --地 A sacred area restricted to practitioners or other particular persons, e.g. Mt. Kōya and Mt. Hiei where women were not allowed (*nyonin kekkai* 女人結界).

～ no chi --の地 See *kekkaiji*. [Tai. 18.]

Kemō 希望 'Seeking, desiring'; seeking fame or profit. [S. VI–13.]

Kemyōji 假名字 'A provisional name or word'; from the Mahayana viewpoint of non-substantiality, all things merely exist nominally. The Buddhist Dharma, too, is presented through provisionally established words. [S. Xb–2.]

Ken 慳 'Mean, miserly.'

Kenbutsu 見佛 'Seeing a buddha'; usually, visualizing a transcendental buddha, like Amida*.

～ ichijō no en --一乘の縁 'An act relating one to the One-Vehicle teaching whereby one sees a buddha.' [K. 500.]

Kenchaku 揀擇 'To choose, eliminate.' [S. IV–1.]

Kenchi 揵稚 Also 犍稚, 犍槌, etc.; Sk. *ghaṇṭā*; 'a bell'. [S. IV–1.]

Kendatsuba 乾闥婆 Sk. *gandharva*; also 犍闥婆, 健闥婆, etc.; translated as *kōjin* 香神 'god of incense', *jinkō* 尋香 'seeking incense', *jikikō* 食香 'living on incense or odours', etc. I. A heavenly musician and an attendant of Indra (Taishaku*), who lives on the smell of food and protects Buddhism; one of the eight kinds of supernatural beings who protect Buddhism (*hachibushu**). II. A strolling actor from Central Asia who plays music and is able to create illusory towers in the sky. III. The five constituent elements (*goun** 五蘊) of a dead person during the period of intermediate existence (*chūu** 中有); he is said to live on the smell of food. IV. A general term for magicians.

∼**-jō** --- 城 'The *gandharva*'s castle'; translated as *shinkirō* 蜃氣樓 'sea-serpent towers' and *jinkōrō* 尋香樓 'scent-seeking towers'; originally, illusory towers created by strolling actors from Central Asia; the term is used in the sense of a mirage, and often analogously to show the non-substantiality of things. [Tai. 39.]

Kendō 見道 Sk. *darśana-mārga*, 'the path of insight'; the stage of spiritual progress in which one awakens for the first time the undefiled wisdom with which one penetrates the principle of reality. In Mahayana, it corresponds to the first *bhūmi* (*shoji**). [S. III–1.]

Kendō muni 顯道無二 The same as 見道無二. Realization of the principle of non-duality at the stage of the 'Path of Insight' (*kendō**). [S. IV–1.]

Kendon 慳貪 'Meanness and greed.'

Kenen 係念 'To fix one's thought (on something)'; to concentrate one's thought on Amida's* land. [S. I–10.]

Kenen 繫念 'Securing one's thought (to something)', e.g. to Amida's* Pure Land; see under *ichinen*. [Tai. 11, 38.]

Kenge 見解 'Viewing and understanding.'

Kengō 賢劫 See *Gengō*.

Kengu-innen-gyō 賢愚因緣經 See *Gengu-innen-gyō*.

Kengyō 健行 See *shuryōgon*.

Kengyō 顯敎 'The exoteric teaching', as opposed to *mikkyō** 密敎, the esoteric teaching; a general term for all the Buddhist teachings, both Hinayana and Mahayana, other than *mikkyō*.

Kenin 化人 '(A Buddhist sage) incarnated as a human being.' [K. 36.]

Ken'in 劍印 'The manual sign in the form of a sword in its sheath.' [K. 52.]

Kenjū 顯宗 'Exoteric sect(s).' [Tai. 2.]

Kenkyō 見境 'Seeing and its object'; subjective perception and the objects perceived. [S. Xb–1.]

Kenmitsu 顯密　*Kengyō** 顯教 and *mikkyō** 密教, the exoteric and esoteric teaching, respectively; a classification of the Buddhist teachings used in esoteric Buddhism.

～ **chihō** --知法　'Knowing the teaching of both exoteric and esoteric Buddhism.'　[K. 187, 198.]

～ **guzū** --弘通　'Propagation of the exoteric and esoteric teachings.'　[Tai. 24.]

～**-kai no sangaku** --戒の三學　'The three learnings of the exoteric teaching, esoteric teaching and precepts.'　[Tai. 18.]

～ **zenkyō** --禪教　'The exoteric and esoteric teachings, (together with the schools based on) meditative practices and (those depending on) scriptural studies'; the two pairs of classification for all Buddhist teachings.　[S. III–8, Va–5.]

Kenmon kakuchi 見聞覺知　'Seeing, hearing, perceiving and conceiving in the mind'; all sorts of physical and mental experiences.　[S. Vb–7.]

Kenrō chijin 堅牢地神　See *kenrō jijin*.

Kenrō jigi 堅牢地祇　See next entry.

Kenrō jijin 堅牢地神☆ 'The god of firm earth'; also *kenrō jigi*.　[Hei. 2; Tai. 27, 32, 34.]

Kensaku 羂索　Also *kenjaku*; Sk. *pāśa*; a kind of rope originally used as a weapon or for hunting; in esoteric Buddhism it symbolizes one of the means by which buddhas and bodhisattvas take in and tame evil beings and also suppress the four kinds of devils (*shima**).

Kensei shishi 堅誓師子　'A lion called Kensei.' According to the *Hōon-gyō**, there lived in a mountain a powerful golden-coated lion named Kensei ('Firm Vow'). It loved to hear the sutras chanted by a mendicant who lived in the mountain. A hunter, seeing the lion and wishing to kill it in order to present its golden skin to the king, shaved his head, put on a monk's robe and sat in the branches of a tree. Thinking that he was a real monk, the lion came close to him, whereupon the hunter shot a poisoned arrow at it. As the lion roared angrily and was about to attack him, this thought occurred to it: "He is a monk wearing a proper robe, which is the symbol of all buddhas and saints. I must restrain any evil thought about him." Thus the lion ended his life. It is said that the lion was a previous incarnation of the Buddha and the hunter, one of Devadatta (Daibadatta*). [S. VI –18.]

Kenshō 賢聖 'Wise men and sages'; also *genjō*.

Kenshō godō 見性悟道 'Seeing one's true nature and realizing the Buddhist Way.' [S. III–1.]

Kenshō jōbutsu 見性成佛 'Seeing one's nature and becoming a buddha.' [S. III–1.]

Kensō 健相 See *shuryōgon*.

Kentoku no jōbutsu 顯德の成佛 See *sanshu no sokushin jōbutsu*.

Kenza 驗者 See *genja*.

Keraku 快樂 'Pleasure and happiness.'

~ **futai no jōdo** --不退の淨土 'The Pure Land where there is unabating pleasure.' [S. Xa–7.]

Kerakuten 化樂天 'Creating Enjoyment Heaven'; Sk. Nirmāṇa-rati; the fifth of the six heavens in the realm of desire (*yokkai**), where inhabitants enjoy magical creations of their own.

Keron 戲論 Sk. *prapañca*; 'useless argument'. [S. Pref., VI–10.]

Kesa 袈裟 The Buddhist surplice or sash; Sk. *kaṣāya* or *kāṣāya*.

Keshiki 假色 'Temporary form'; a kind of matter produced in the body at the time of receiving precepts; it belongs to matter-element though shapeless and intangible; the same as *muhyō shiki**. [S. IV–1.]

Keshin 化身 'A transformed body' of a buddha or bodhisattva; Sk. *nirmāṇa-kāya*; one of the three bodies of a buddha (*sanshin**).

Keshō 化生 'To be born transformed.' [K. 1.]

Keshu 化主 'The lord who transforms (people by teaching)'; the lord teacher, i.e. the Buddha. [Tai. 18.]

Kesō 假相 'Temporary appearance.' [S. III–1, Va–6, Xb–1.]

Kesshū 結衆 'A group of people gathered' to perform a specific Buddhist practice, e.g. *nenbutsu**. [K. 53.]

Kesu 化す 'To transform, convert, teach.'

Ketai 假諦 'The truth of temporariness'; the aspect of reality that all existences are temporary, being produced by causes and conditions; an aspect of the triple truth (*santai**). [S. VA–6.]

Ketai 懈怠 See *kedai*.

Ketaku 計度 'Calculating, weighing'; discriminative thought. [S. III–1.]

~ **funbetsu** --分別 'Calculating and discriminating'; delusory discrimination. [S. III–8.]

Ketsuen 結緣 Pronounced *kechien*; 'establishing a relationship' with living beings, with a view to leading them to deliverance; also, establishing a relationship with Buddhism.

~-**kyō** --經 The copying of a sutra by a group of people to establish relations with Buddhism; the most popular sutra used was the *Hoke-kyō**. [K. 69.]

~ **su** --す 'To establish a relationship (with Buddhism)'; to make a donation in order to establish such a relationship. [K. 423.]

Ketsugan 結願 Pronounced *kechigan*; 'concluding vow or prayer'; the last day of a session of Buddhist services held for a fixed period.

Ketsujō no gō 決定の業 Refers to *ketsujō ōjō no gō* 決定往生の業 'the karma or act which definitely produces birth (in Amida's* land).' [S. VI–15.]

Ketsujō ōjō 決定往生 'Unfailing attainment of birth' in Amida's* land. [IH.; S. I–10, VI–6.]

Ketsujū 結集 Sk. *saṃgīti*; 'compiling' the Buddhist teaching; also a meeting held for that purpose. [S.III–3, IV–1.]

Ketsumyaku 血脈 Pronounced *kechimyaku*; 'a blood vessel'; transmission of a certain teaching from a master to his disciple; also the lineage of transmission of the teaching. [Tai. 24.]

Ketsuryō 決了 'Discerning and clarifying' the tenet or meaning.

Keu 希有 'Rare, marvellous.'

Kezō 花藏 Refers to *Rengezō sekai**. [S. II–8.]

Kezoku 化屬 'Transformation of dependents'; family relations whom one should transform by converting them. [Tai. 16.]

~ **kechien** --結緣 Perhaps used for 化俗結緣, [Tai. 16, 36.]

Kezoku kechien 化俗結緣 'Transforming the people of the world and making them establish a relationship (with a buddha or bodhisattva).' [Tai. 12.]

Kezō sekai 華藏世界 Abbr. of *Rengezō sekai**. [Tai. 24.]

Ki 記 'Prediction'; see *juki* and *kibetsu*. [S. III–1.]

Ki 機 'Potentiality' of receiving the teaching; one who is capable of receiving the Dharma; one who is fit to be converted by a buddha or bodhisattva. A general term for man, as opposed to the Dharma or a buddha or bodhisattva.

Kibetsu 記別 'A prediction' given to a disciple by the Buddha about his attaining of buddhahood in the future; also *juki**.

Kibetsu 莂別 The same as *kibetsu* above. [Tai. 1.]

Kibuku 歸伏 'Taking refuge in and submitting oneself' to the Buddhist law or a Buddhist saint.

Kichijō 吉祥 'Good fortune.'

~**-ten** --天 Sk. Śrīmahādevī; a goddess of fortune and beauty; also Kudokuten*.

~ **tennyo** --天女 The same as Kichijōten*. [Tai. 18.]

Kichiku 鬼畜 Abbr. of *gaki** 餓鬼 'hungry ghosts' and *chikushō** 畜生 'animals'. [S. VII–7.]

Kichizō 吉藏 Ch. Chi-tsang (549–623); a San-lun (Sanron*) master, whose parents came from Parthia (Ansoku 安息). He became a novice under Tao-lang 道朗 (Dōrō) at the age of seven, and as he grew up, he became renowned for his extensive learning, especially about the Mādhyamika School (Chūganha*). He lectured on Mādhyamika literature and wrote commentaries on them, thus consolidating the foundation of the San-lun sect. As he lived for some time at the Chia-hsiang-ssu 嘉祥寺 (Kajōji), he was popularly called 'Great Master Chia-hsiang' 嘉祥大師 (Kajō Daishi*). His *Sanron-gengi* 三論玄義 (*Essentials of the Three Discourses*), 1 fasc., is a useful compendium of the San-lun doctrine.

Kidō 鬼道 Refers to *gakidō** 餓鬼道 'the realm of hungry spirits'. [K. 459.]

Kidoku 奇特 I. 'Wonderful, marvellous, extraordinary.' II. A wonderful thing. [Tsu. 73.]

Kie 歸依 'Taking refuge in'; to believe in, worship, or respect the Buddhist law or a Buddhist saint.

Kigan 起龕 'To lift a coffin' before moving it to the cemetery. [Tai. 33, 40.]

~ **butsuji** --佛事 'A Buddhist ceremony of lifting a coffin' before moving it to the cemetery; this is part of the funeral service in the Zen* sect.

Kigo 綺語 'Fine phrases'; idle talk; immoral utterance; one of the ten evil acts (*jūaku**).

Kihō 機法 'One who receives or practises the teaching and the teaching practised'; a practitioner and the Dharma or the teaching provided to him. [S. III–8.]

Kijikoku 龜茲國 Kuccha; an ancient country in central Asia. [S. IV–2.]

Kijō 機情 'Man's emotion or feeling.' I. A man's feelings or state of mind in general. II. A man's false desires or attached views.

Kikai 器界 'Vessel-realm'; the physical environment of one's existence. [S. III–1.]

Kikan 機感 'Man's response' to a buddha or a bodhisattva's salvation. [S. II–8; Tai. 9.]

~ **sōō** --相應 'Man's response in agreement (with a buddha or a bodhisattva's saving activity).' [S. II–5.]

Kikkodoku 給孤獨 See *Gikkodoku*.

~-**on** ---園 See *Giju gikkodoku-on*. [Hei. 2.]

Kikon 機根 'Propensity or capacity of a man.'

Kin 金 I. Gold; one of the seven treasures (*shippō**). II. Used for 磬 (*kin* or *kei**).

Kin 禁 See *gon*.

Kin 磬 See *kei*.

Kinen 祈念 'Prayer.'

Kingen 金言 'Golden words,' i.e. the words of the Buddha.

Kinhi-ron 金錍論 See *Konpei-ron*.

Kinichi 忌日 'A memorial day (for a dead person)' whether in a week, month or year; cf. *nanuka nanuka no kinichi*.

Kinkai 禁戒 See *gonkai*.

Kinnara 緊那羅 Sk. *kinnara*; translated as *ninpinin* 人非人 'human but not human', *kajin* 歌神 'god of music', etc.; a god of music and one of the eight kinds of supernatural beings who protect Buddhism. His appearance resembles man's, but it is difficult to tell whether he is a god, man, or animal. Cf. *hachibushu**.

Ki (no) midokyō 季(の)御讀經 'Seasonal chanting of the sutra'; a service of chanting the *Daihannya-kyō** for three or four days at the imperial palace, performed twice a year, in the second and eighth months; often simply, *midokyō**. [Ma. 151, 278; O. II; Tai. 24.]

Kinrin butchō 金輪佛頂 'The golden-wheel Buddha's head'; n. of a deity produced from the Buddha's head; also called *Ichiji saishō butchō rinnō* 一字最勝佛頂輪王, *Saishō kinrin butchō* 最勝金輪佛頂 and *Tenrinnō butchō* 轉輪王佛頂; cf. *Ichiji kinrin* and *Konrin no hō*.

Kishin 起信 Refers to *Daijō-kishin-ron**. [S. Vb–9.]

Kishin 寄進 'Donation,' especially to a temple.

Kishō 祈請 'Prayer, supplication.'

Kishō 起請 'Invocation, prayer.' I. Summoning up a Buddhist or Shinto deity as a witness to the truth of one's words; cf. *Daishi kanjō no kishō*. [Tsu. 205.] II. Refers to *kishōmon**. [S. Vb–1; Tai. 39.]

~-mon --文 'A written invocation' to a Buddhist or Shinto deity requesting him to act as a witness to the truth of one's words.

Kisō 貴僧 'A virtuous priest.' [Tai. 23.]

Kitōjo 祈禱所 'A prayer(-offering) place.' [Tai. 24, 32.]

Kitōsō 祈禱僧 'Prayer priest'; a priest whose duty is to pray to a deity for the cessation of calamity, the health and longevity of a person, etc. Cf. *oinori no shi*.

Kiu 祈雨 'Praying for rain.' [K. 171, 250.]

Kiyomizu mōde 清水まうで 'Visit to the Kiyomizu-dera.' [K. 568.]

Kizui 奇瑞 'An auspicious sign or phenomenon which is rarely seen.' [K. 64.]

Kō 功 I. 'Effort' in Buddhist practices. II. 'Merit'; the same as *kudoku**; cf. *ku*.

Kō 劫 Sk. *kalpa*; also 劫波, 劫簸, etc.; an immeasurably long period of time; aeons. Its length is metaphorically explained, for instance, as the period required for one to empty a city full of poppy seeds by taking away one seed every three years. There are three kinds of *kalpa*: (1) *shōkō* 小劫, a small *kalpa*; the length of time equivalent to the period during which man's average life-span, which is 10 at the worst time of the period of five defilements (*gojoku** 五濁), increases by one in 100 years until it reaches 84,000 (or equivalent to the period during which man's life-span decreases from 84,000 to 10 at the same rate); (2) *chūkō* 中劫, a medium *kalpa*, which is equivalent to the period of one cycle of increase and decrease of man's life-span as mentioned above; (3) *daikō* 大劫, a large *kalpa*, which is equivalent to 20 medium *kalpas*.

Kō 香 I. Odour; cf. *rokkyō*. II. Incense.

～ **no kesa** --の袈裟 See *kōzome*. [Tai. 11.]

Kō 講 I. A lecture. II. A lecture-meeting at which a Buddhist text is lectured on and its teaching discussed, e.g. *hyakunichi-kō** 百日講. III. A meeting for performing a particular kind of practice, e.g. *nenbutsu-kō* 念佛講 and *ōjō-kō** 往生講. IV. A savings association with an objective of making a group tour to visit a temple or shrine or making a donation to it, e.g. *Ise-kō* 伊勢講. V. A savings association of a secular nature, e.g. *tanomoshi-kō* 賴母子講, a mutually financing association.

Kōan 公案 Originally, in China, a government decree; in Zen*, it is an account of a master's actions or statements, including questions and answers, and is used as an object of meditation for the attainment of enlightenment. *Kōan* began to be used in the T'ang dynasty (618–907), and the Sung dynasty (960–1126) saw the height of their popularity. The number of *kōan* composed in China is said to be 1,700 in all.

Kōban 香盤 'An incense-burner stand.' [S. VII–17.]

Kōbō 弘法 See *Kūkai*. [S. Xb–3.]

Kobōshi 小法師 'A young priest.' [S. Xa–9.]

Kōchōhō 鉤召法 'The ritual for summoning people'; one of the five kinds of rituals established in esoteric Buddhism. It aims at moving living beings of a lower realm to a higher one and also at enlightening their spiritual darkness.

Kōdai kongō hōkaigū 廣大金剛法界宮 'The great palace of the diamond(-like) Dharma-essence.' See *hokkaigū*.

Kōen 講莚 'A lecture meeting.' [Tai. 21.]

Kōfukuji 興福寺 The head temple of the Hossō* sect and one of the seven big temples in Nara (*Nanto no shichidaiji**). Originally, it was called Yamashina-dera 山階寺, built in 669 by Fujiwara Kamatari 藤原鎌足, and was located in Yamashiro Province. In 678 it was moved to Yamato, and in 710, to its present site. It flourished as the tutelary temple of the Fujiwara clan. In the medieval period it was inhabited by armed monks, who often ran riot in the area. After the Meiji Restoration in 1868, the temple was affiliated to the Shingon* sect but later became a Hossō temple again.

Kōge 香花 'Incense and flowers.'

Kōge-in 香華院 'A temple for incense and flowers (to be offered to the souls of one's ancestors)'; a family temple; popularly, *bodaiji** 菩提寺 or *danna-dera** 檀那寺.

Kōgō 曠劫 'Innumerable *kalpas* (*kō**)'; for a very long time. Cf. *tashō kōgō*. [Hei. 1; Tai. 13.]

Kogon 虚言 See *kyogon*.

Kōgyō 講行 'Lecture and practice'; lectures on the Buddhist teachings and the practice of methods of salvation. [S. I–8.]

Kōgyō 講經 Also *kōkyō*; 'lecturing on a sutra'.

Kōi 綱位 'A priestly rank'; refers to *sōgō** *no kurai* 僧綱の位. [S. Vb–2.]

Koji 居士 'A lay believer.'

Koji 擧似 'To mention, relate, tell.'

Kōji 講師 See *kōshi*.

Kojiki 乞食 See *kotsujiki*.

Kōjin 劫盡 'The perishing of the *kalpa*'; the last of the four periods of cosmic change, in which the whole world gradually perishes; cf. *ekō* and *shikō*. [S. I–3.]

Koju shinse no tsumi 虚受信施の罪 'The offence of receiving donations from a devotee deceitfully.' [S. Xb–1.]

Kōka 劫火 '*Kalpa*-fire'; the big fire believed to break out at the end of the world during the period of disintegration (*ekō** 壞劫);

one of the three great calamities (*daisansai**); it is also called *kasai* 火災 (fire calamities); *kō* here means a period of cosmic change. See *shikō*. [Tai. 8, 12.]

Kokai 己界 'One's own world or realm'; refers to one's own body. [S. Va–1.]

Koke 虚假 'False and temporary.'

Kōken 効験 'The efficacy' of a ritual performance; cf. *sanmon no kōken*. [Tai. 12.]

Kōkenju 好堅樹 A kind of tree, said to grow under the soil for a hundred years and then above the ground to full size in a day, measuring 1,000 feet in height. [Tai. 18.]

Kōkigyō-kyō 興起行經 '*The Sutra of Happenings* (*in the Buddha's Previous Lives*)'; 2 fasc., tr. by K'ang Meng-hsiang 康孟詳 (Kōmōshō) in the late second century [TT.4, No. 197]. The sutra gives accounts of happenings in the Buddha's previous lives in relation to the ten traditional incidents in his lifetime.

Kokiju 孤起頌 'An independent verse'; Sk. *gāthā*; a verse containing ideas not expressed in the prose section of a sutra; one of the nine and the twelve kinds of scriptures (*kubu-kyō** and *jūnibu-kyō**).

Kōkitoku Bosatsu 高貴德菩薩 'Noble Virtue Bodhisattva'; refers to Kōmyō-henjō-kōkitoku-ō Bosatsu 光明遍照高貴德王菩薩 (Light-illuminating King of Noble Virtue Bodhisattva). One of the bodhisattvas to whom the Buddha expounded the *Nehan-gyō**. [K. 5.]

Kokka goji no tōryō 國家護持の棟梁 'The head priest of the state-protecting (temple)', namely, the Enryakuji* on Mt. Hiei. [Tai. 27.]

Kokoro o osamu 心を修む 'To control one's mind.' [Ho. 36.]

Kokuanten 黑闇天 Sk. Kālarātṛ ('Dark Night'); a goddess of calamity and ugliness; also Kokuannyo 黑闇女, Kokuyashin 黑夜神, etc.; sister of Kichijōten*. [S. IV–1, VII–25.]

Kokubunji 國分寺 'Provincial temples' which began to be constructed in 741 by the order of Emperor Shōmu*. It was decreed that each province should have a temple for monks and another for nuns. The former were called Kokubunji, Kokubunsōji 國分僧寺 or, more properly, 'Konkōmyō Shitennō gokoku no tera'

金光明四天王護國之寺 'state-protecting temples through the power of the Four Guardian Kings (Shitennō*) in the spirit of the *Konkōmyō-kyō**'. In each provincial temple sutras were chanted and prayers were offered up for the peace of the state and good harvests. In 749, the Tōdaiji* was made the headquarters of all provincial temples for monks, and the Hokke-ji 法華寺 that of the temples for nuns. At first, monks of the Sanron*, Hossō* and Kegon* sects lived in the provincial temples, but later monks of the Tendai*, Shingon*, Jōdo* and Zen* sects also dwelt there. [Tai. 21.]

Kokubunniji 國分尼寺 'A provincial temple for nuns'; a state temple built in each province by a decree of Emperor Shōmu* in 741. The official name was 'Hokke-metsuzai no tera' 法華滅罪之寺 'a temple for eliminating sins by (the merit of) the *Hoke-kyō**'. Ten nuns were stationed in each temple, and regular services were held to eliminate the hindrances to enlightenment possessed by women and secure peace and happiness for them in this life and the next. The Hokkeji, Nara, was later made the head temple of all kokubunniji.

Kokuchin 國鎮 Abbr. of *anchin kokka-hō**.

Kokue no mi 黒衣の身 'A body in a black robe'; a monk. [Tai. 11.]

Kokushi 國師 'A state master.' I. A title given to a monk of outstanding virtue by the head of the state; a monk who received this title was looked on as the spiritual guide of the king or emperor and of the state. In China, Fa-ch'ang 法常 (Hōjō) was the first to receive this title in 550. The title was often conferred posthumously. In Japan, Ben'en (or Bennen) 辨圓 (1202–80) was the first to receive this title (Shōichi Kokushi 聖一國師) posthumously in 1312. The first monk given this title during his lifetime was Musō*. II. A priestly official sent by the central government to a provincial office to superintend monks and nuns. He also lectured on Buddhist texts. This system was introduced in 702, but the name of the official was changed to *kōshi* 講師 in 795.

Kokūzō 虚空藏 'Sky-Repository'; Sk. Ākāśagarbha or Gagana-gañja; n. of a bodhisattva whose wisdom and merit are as vast as the sky. He is the central figure in the Kokūzō-in 虚空藏院

division of the Matrix-store Realm Mandala (*Taizōkai Mandara**); he sits on a lotus-seat, wearing a crown which symbolizes the five wisdoms (*gochi**) and holding a sword symbolizing wisdom in the right hand, and a *cintā-maṇi* (*nyoihōshu**) in the left hand. [Tai. 18.]

~ **monjihō** --- 聞持法 'A ritual (dedicated) to Kokūzō (Bodhisattva) for (acquiring good) memory'; also called *gumonjihō**.

Kōmatsu 劫末 'The end of the *kalpa*'; the end of the cosmic period when the world begins to perish. See *ekō* and *shikō*. [S. II -8, IX-4.]

Komō 虚妄 'Unreal and delusory.'

Kōmon 講問 Refers to *kōshi** 講師 and *monja** 問者. [Tai. 36.]

Komorisō 籠僧 'A priest who confines himself' in a room of mourning for 49 days after a death, during which time he chants sutras. [K. 557; Tai. 39.]

Kōmyō henjō 光明遍照☆ '(Amida's*) light shining all over'. A phrase from the *Kanmuryōju-kyō**. [K. 63.]

Kōmyō shingon 光明眞言 'Light-*mantra*'; refers to the *Fukūdaikanjōkō-shingon* 不空大灌頂光眞言. One who hears this spell will have his sin destroyed. Also sand invested with the magical power of this spell, if sprinkled on the body of a dead person, is capable of removing all his evil karma and enables him to attain deliverance. [K. 64; S. II-5, 8; Tsu. 222.]

Kon 金 Refers to *Kongōkai mandara**. [S. I-1.]

Konbei-ron 金錍論 A popular name for *Kongōhei**. [S. Xb-3.]

Kongō 金剛 Sk. *vajra*. I. A very hard material, which is identified with diamond or the essential substance of gold; often used as an analogy for something hard and indestructible. II. Abbr. of *kongōsho**. III. Abbr. of Kongōjin* or Kongōrikishi*.

~**-chō-kyō** --頂經 '*The Diamond-Peak Sutra*'; 3 fasc.; Sk. *Vajraśekhara-sūtra*; there are three Chinese translations, of which the one by Amoghavajra (Fukū*) is popularly used [TT. 18, No. 865]; the full title is *Kongōchō-issai-nyorai-shinjitsu-shōdaijō-genshō-daikyōō-kyō* 金剛頂一切如來眞實攝大乘現證大教王經, one of the three sutras of the Shingon* sect. [Hei. 2; S. IV-1.]

~**-dōji** --童子 Sk. Kaṇi-krodha also Vajra-kumāra; a deity in the form of a furious-looking boy depicted in the Matrix-store

Realm Mandala (*Taizōkai mandara**); he is the attendant of Kongōsō 金剛鏁 Bodhisattva, but is said to be an incarnation of Amida*.   [Hei. 2, 3; Tai. 2, 5.]

~**-dōji-hō** --童子法   'The ritual dedicated to Kongōdōji' to pray for the stopping of calamities, the subduing of evil spirits, etc. [Hei. 3; Tai. 1.]

~**-dōji no hō** --童子の法   See *Kongōdōji-hō*.   [Hei. 3; Tai. 1.]

~**-hannya** --般若   Refers to *Kongō-hannya-haramitsu-kyō* 金剛般若波羅蜜經, 1 fasc., tr. into Chinese by Kumārajīva (Kumarajū*) [TT. 8, No. 235]. There are five other Chinese translations. Popularly known as the *Diamond Sūtra* (*Kongō-kyō**).   [K. 3; Ma. 198.]

~**-hei** --錍   '*Diamond Essence*'; 1 fasc., by Chan-jan 湛然 (Tannen*) [TT. 46, No. 1932]; the work explains from the viewpoint of the absolute reality that even insentient existences can realize buddhahood.

~**-hōkai** --寶戒   'Diamond-treasure precepts'; refers to the Mahayana precepts presented in the *Bonmō-kyō**; also called *isshin-kongō-hōkai*.   [S. IV-1.]

~ **hokkaigū** --法界宮   See *Hokkaigū*.

~ **ichijō** --一乘   'The One-Vehicle Diamond teaching'; another name for the Shingon* teaching, which is indestructible like a diamond and is the path to enlightenment; cf. *ichijō*.

~**-jin** --神   Sk. Vajrapāṇi, 'Diamond-hand'; also translated as Kongōshu* 金剛手, Shūkongō 執金剛, Jikongōshu 持金剛手 and Kongōrikishi 金剛力士; a type of divinity who protects Buddhism, he holds a hammer with which to crush its enemies. A pair of Kongō gods, Misshaku Kongō* and Naraen Kongō*, are often placed at the entrance of a temple and called *niō**.

~**-kai** --界   'The Diamond Realm'; refers to *Kongōkai mandara**. [Tai. 12, 18.]

~**-kai mandara** --界曼荼(or 陀羅)   'The Diamond Realm Mandala'; Sk. *vajra-dhātu maṇḍala*; one of the two main mandala used in esoteric Buddhism, the other being *Taizōkai mandara**. There are nine assemblies of deities depicted in it, the total number of them being 1,461. See *kue mandara* and *ryōbu mandara*.

~**-kai no sanjūshichi-son** --界の三十七尊   'The 37 divinities of the Diamond Realm Mandala.' [S. II-8.]

~ **kaji** --加持 '(The Buddha's) empowerment as indestructible (as a diamond).' [S. Xb-3.]

~ **kue no mandara** --九會の曼陀羅 'The mandala of the nine Diamond Realm assemblies'; see *kue mandara.* [Tai. 21.]

~**-kyō** --經 '*The Diamond Sūtra*'; see *Kongō-hannya.* [S.III-1, Xa-2; Tai. 35.]

~ **no sho** --の杵 See *kongōsho.* [Tai. 18.]

~**-rikishi** --力士 '*Vajra* wrestler'; another name for Kongōjin*; see also *niō*.* [Tai. 24, 26.]

~**-satta** --薩埵 Sk. Vajrasattva, 'Diamond-being'; also called Kongōshu* 金剛手 'Diamond-hand', Himitsushu* 祕密主 'Lord of Mystery', etc. The second of the eight patriarchs of Shingon* tradition to whom Dainichi* transmitted the esoteric teaching. [S. II-8.]

~ **sho** --杵 'A diamond-pounder'; Sk. *vajra*; a ritual object in esoteric Buddhism, made mainly of iron and copper. There are three kinds: a bar with a single prong on each end (*dokko** 獨鈷), one with three prongs (*sanko** 三鈷), and one with five prongs (*goko** 五鈷).

~**-shu** --手 Sk. Vajrapāṇi, 'Diamond-hand'; another name for *Kongōsatta*.*

~**-zaō** --藏王 See *Zaō Gongen.* [Tai. 26, 35.]

~**-zaō Bosatsu** --藏王菩薩 See *Zaō Gongen.* [K. 42.]

~**-zaō Gongen** --藏王權現 See *Zaō Gongen.* [Tai. 29.]

Konjichō 金翅鳥 'A gold-wing bird'; Sk. *garuḍa*; also *myōjichō* 妙翅鳥; see *karura.* [S. VI-18; Tai. 24, 35.]

Konjō 今生 'This life,' as opposed to the previous life (*zenshō** 前生) or future life (*goshō** 後生).

Konjō 根性 'Propensity, nature.'

Konkōmyō-kyō 金光明經 '*The Golden Splendour Sutra*'; Sk. *Suvarṇa-prabhāsa(-uttama)-sūtra*; one of the three state-protecting sutras in Japan. The merit of this sutra is that wherever it is worshipped, the four Guardian Gods (Shitennō*) protect the state and benefit the people; cf. *Saishō-e.* There are three Chinese translations: (1) *Konkōmyō-kyō* 金光明經, 4. fasc., tr. by Dharmakṣema (Donmushin 曇無讖) [TT. 16, No. 663]; (2) *Gōbu-konkōmyō-kyō* 合部金光明經, 8 fasc., tr. by Pao-kui 寶貴 (Hōki) *et al.* [TT. 16, No. 664]; and (3) *Konkōmyō-saishōō-kyō* 金光明最勝王經, 10 fasc., tr. by I-ching 義淨 (Gijō*) [TT. 16, No. 665].

Konkōmyō-saishōō-kyō 金光明最勝王經 See *Konkōmyō-kyō*.

Konku 金口 'The golden mouth'; refers to the Buddha's mouth, because his body is of a golden colour and also his mouth and tongue are as indestructible as a diamond (*kongō**).

~ no sōjō --の相承 See *konku sōjō*. [Tai. 24.]

~ sōjō --相承 'Transmission (of the teaching originating) from the Golden Mouth'; one of the two kinds of transmission of the teaching distinguished in the Tendai* sect. This is said of the transmission of it from master to disciple, originating from the Buddha and ending in the 24th Indian patriarch, Siṃha (Shishi*). The 24 patriarchs in India are called *saiten nijūshiso* 西天二十四祖 'the 24 patriarchs of the Western Heaven (i.e. India)'. Cf. *konshi sōjō.*

Konku 金鼓 'A metal drum'; also *waniguchi* 鰐口 'crocodile's mouth'; a metal plate hung above the entrance to the main hall of a temple or shrine, where worshippers can sound it by means of a bundle of ropes attached to it. [Ma. 116.]

Konpei-ron 金錍論 See *Konbei-ron*.

Konrin 金輪 'Golden-wheel or disc.' I. The gold layer; one of three layers under the ground (*sanrin**); the gold layer is reached 80,000 *yojana* (*yujun**) below sea-level and is 300,020,000 *yojana* thick. II. Refers to *konrin-ō**. [K. 38; Tai. 12.]

~ butchō --佛頂 See *Shijōkō* I.

~ no hō --の法 The ritual performed in front of a deity called Kinrin butchō* to pray for an end to natural calamities, for easy birth, etc. [Tai. 8.]

~-ō --王 'The golden-wheel king', the king of the four continents. See *tenrinjōō*.

~-zai --際 '(To the depth of) the gold layer.' [Tai. 21, 31, 35, 38.]

Konse 今世 'This life'; the opposite of *gose** 後世 or *raise** 來世.

~ **gose nōindō no on-chikai** --後世能引導の御誓 'The vow (of Jizō*) to guide and teach (living beings) in the present life and the life hereafter.' [Tai. 20.]

Konshi sōjō 今師相承 'Transmission (of the teaching) to the present master'; one of the two kinds of transmission of the teaching distinguished in the Tendai* sect. The reference to 'the present master' is to the founder of the sect, the Master T'ient'ai (Tendai Daishi*). He is thus at the end of the transmission, his predecessors being Hui-ssu 慧思 (Eshi*), Hui-wen 慧文 (Emon*) and Nāgārjuna (Ryūju*). Cf. *konku sōjō*.

Kōsen 香山 'The fragrant mountain'; abbr. of Kōsuisen*.

Kosetsu 虚(=虚)說 'Empty, i.e. false, teaching.' [Tai. 17.]

Kōshi 講師 'A lecturer.' I. One who lectures on a sutra at such ceremonies as the *Hokke-e* and *Saishō-e**. [Tai. 36.] II. Formerly, *kokushi** 國師, a priestly official sent by the central government to a provincial office to superintend monks and nuns; the name of the official was changed to *kōshi* in 795. III. N. of a rank in the scholarly hierarchy in the Jōdo* sect and the Ōtani-ha school of the Jōdoshin* sect.

Koshin no busshō 己心の佛性 'Buddha-nature in one's own mind.' [S. Xa–5.]

Kōshō 公請 Correctly, *kushō*; 'the court's invitation'; the imperial court's invitation to participate in a Buddhist discussion at the imperial palace (*rongi**). [S. Va–9, Xb–2, 3.]

Kōshō 迎攝 See *gōshō* 迎接.

Kōshōhō 鉤召法 See *kōchōhō*.

Kōshō nenbutsu 高聲念佛 'Reciting the *nenbutsu** in a loud voice.' [K. 63, 423.]

Kōso Daishi 高祖大師 'A great patriarchal master.' I. In the Tendai* sect, it refers to Dengyō Daishi*. [Tai. 1.] II. In the Shingon* sect, it refers to Kōbō Daishi*. [S. II–8.]

Kōsuisen 香醉山 'The fragrance-intoxicating mountain'; Sk. Gandha-mādana; n. of the mountain situated in the northernmost part of the continent of Jambudvīpa (Enbudai*). It is filled with a scent which intoxicates all who go there. Between it and the Himalayas (Daisessen*) to the south of it lies Lake Anavatapta

(Anokudatchi*).

Kotoku 古德 'Virtuous men of old times.'

Kōtokuji 講讀師 'A priest who lectures' on a sutra at a Buddhist ceremony. [K. 97.]

Kotsugai 乞匃 'A beggar.'

Kotsujiki 乞食 'Begging for alms.' [IH.; O. II.]

~ **hosshi** --法師 'An alms-begging monk.' [S. Xb–3.]

~ **zuda** --頭陀 'Begging food in conformity to the *zuda** way of life.' [S. Xb–3.]

Kōya 空也 Also Kūya; a Tendai* monk (903–72); born in Kyoto and said to be a son of Emperor Daigo or a grandson of Emperor Ninmei. He entered the priesthood at an early age, and wandered about the country, building bridges, digging wells, etc., while urging people to recite Amida's* name. In 938 he returned to Kyoto and urged people to take refuge in Amida. He was therefore called Ichi-no-hijiri* 市聖, Ichi-no-shōnin* 市上人 and Amida-hijiri* 阿彌陀聖. He went up to Mt. Hiei, where he received precepts from Enshō 延昌 and changed his name to Kōshō 光勝. When an epidemic spread in Kyoto in 951, he carved a large statue of Jūichimen Kannon* and carried it about the city. After the epidemic stopped, he built the Saikōji 西光寺 and enshrined the statue in it.

Kōya Daishi 高野大師 'The great master of Mt. Kōya'; refers to Kūkai*. [S. Vb–11, VI–18.]

Kōya-hijiri 高野聖 'Sages on Mt. Kōya'; *nenbutsu** practitioners on Mt. Kōya. Also called *hijiri-gata**, as distinguished from *gakuryo-gata** and *gyōnin-gata**. [S. I–3.]

Kōya no Daishi 高野の大師 'The great master of Mt. Kōya'; refers to Kūkai*. [S. VI–10; Tsu. 173.]

Kōyō 孝養 See *kyōyō*.

Kōza 高座 'A raised seat' for the leader of a service or the lecturer at a lecture-meeting.

Kōzen-gokoku-ron 興禪護國論 '*The Discourse on the Propagation of Zen and the Protection of the State*'; 3 fasc., by Eisai* [TT. 80, No. 2543]; the first Zen* work in Japan. The author justifies the authenticity of Zen in the face of mounting criticism of it by the older sects. The work is regarded as Eisai's declaration of the establishment of the Zen sect he had brought from China. [S. Xb–3.]

Kōzō 香象 'A scent-elephant'; Sk. *gandha-hastin*; an elephant in rut and, hence, giving off an attractive scent and possessing extraordinary power. [Tai. 14, 24.]

Kōzome 香染 'Dyed with essence of cloves'; hence, yellowish brown; the original colour of the robes of Buddhist monks. *Kō* 香 ('fragrance, incense') is used because in India robes were dyed with the essence of a kind of sandal-wood, called *kaṇṭa* or *kaṇṭala*. [Tai. 27.]

∼ **no hōbuku** --の法服 A robe of a Buddhist monk. [Tai. 24.]

Ku 功 'Merit; accumulation of merit'; cf. *kō* 功 and *kudoku*.

Ku 供 'Offering'; see *kuyō*. [Tai. 24.]

Kū 空 'Void, emptiness'; Sk. *śūnya*, *śūnyatā*; the opposite of *u** 有 'existence'. Generally speaking, Hinayana teaches that 'self' is a delusory fabrication and so should be negated, but Mahayana shows that not only 'self' but also other existing things are originally void. The theory of universal emptiness is fully explained in the Prajñāpāramitā literature (*Hannya-kyō**); cf. *jūhachikū*.

∼ **ke chū no santai** -假中の三諦 'The triple truths of voidness, temporariness and the middle path'; the central teaching of the Tendai* sect; see *santai*. [S. IV–1.]

∼-**ken** -見 'Voidness view'; the view attached to the voidness or non-substantiality of all existences. [S. IV–1.]

∼ **musō** -無相 'Void and formless'; together with *mugan* 無願, they form a threefold contemplation on reality (*sanzanmai* 三三昧). [S. Vb–8.]

∼ **musō no hōmon** -無相の法門 'The teaching of voidness and formlessness (of all existences).' [S. II–8.]

∼ **soku ze shiki** -即是色 'Emptiness-is-itself form'; a phrase from the *Hannyashin-gyō**; non-substantiality is itself material form; cf. *shiki soku ze kū*. [S. IV–1.]

∼-**u no hōron** -有の法論 'The doctrinal argument concerning void and existence'; the argument between the Hossō* and the Sanron* monks as to whether things are void or positively exist.

[Tai. 24.]

Kubira Daishō 宮毘羅大將 'The General Kumbhīra'; one of the 12 *yakṣa* guardians of the *Yakushi-kyō**; cf. *jūni-shinshō*. [O. II; Tai. 12.]

Kubon 九品 See *kuhon*.

Kubu-kyō 九部經 'The nine kinds of scriptures.' I. The following nine out of the 12 kinds of scriptures (*jūnibu-kyō**) are specifically called the *kubu-kyō*: (1) *shutara** 修多羅 (*sūtra*); (2) *giya** 祇夜 (*geya*); (3) *kada** 伽陀 (*gāthā*); (4) *iteimokuta** 伊帝目多 (*iti-vṛttaka*); (5) *jataka** 闍多伽 (*jātaka*); (6) *abudatsuma** 阿浮達磨 (*adbhuta-dharma*); (7) *udana** 優陀那 (*udāna*); (8) *bibutsuryaku* 毘佛略 (*vaipulya*); and (9) *wagara* 和伽羅 (*vyākaraṇa*). II. In Hinayana, the following nine kinds of scriptures are distinguished: (1) *shutara*; (2) *giya*; (3) *kada*; (4) *nidana** 尼陀那 (*nidāna*); (5) *iteimokuta*; (6) *jataka*; (7) *abudatsuma*; (8) *ahadana** 阿波陀那 (*avadāna*); and (9) *ubadaisha** 優婆提舍 (*upadeśa*).

Kubun-kyō 九分經 'The nine divisions of scriptures'; see *kubu-kyō*.

Kubusō 供奉僧 Also *gubusō*. See *kusō*.

Kubutsu 供佛 'Offerings to the Buddha.' [Hei. 2; Tai. 20, 25, 26.]

Kuden 口傳 'Oral transmission'; orally transmitted secret teaching.

Kūden rōkaku 宮殿樓閣 'Palaces and towers'; originally those of the Western Pure Land. [Ho. 34.]

Kudoku 功德☆ 'Merit, virtue.'

~-ten --天 I. Goddess of merit; Sk. Śrīmahādevī; more popularly known as Kichijōten*. [S. IV–1, VII–25.] II. Another name for Karitei*.

Kudon 瞿曇 Sk. Gautama; also, Kushō 舊稱, Kutan 俱譚; the Buddha's family name. [Tai. 24.]

Kue mandara 九會曼荼羅 'The nine-assembly mandala'; another name for the Diamond Realm Mandala (*Kongōkai mandara**), which consists of nine assemblies of deities numbering 1,461 in all. The nine assemblies are: (1) *Jōshin-e* 成身會; (2) *Katsuma-e* 羯磨會; (3) *Sanmaya-e* 三昧耶會; (4) *Daikuyō-e* 大供養會; (5) *Shiin-e* 四印會; (6) *Ichiin-e* 一印會; (7) *Rishu-e* 理趣會; (8) *Gōzanze katsuma-e* 降三世羯磨會; and (9) *Gōzanze sanmaya-e* 降三世三昧耶會.

Kufū 工夫 'Device, contrivance, means'; the making of an effort to attain *satori**. [S. IV–1.]

Kūgan 空観 'Contemplation on the void'; meditation in which one seeks to realize the essential voidness of all existences. [IH.]

Kuge 供花 'Offering of flowers.'

Kūge 空花(or 華) 'Flowers in the sky'; flowers seen in the sky by those who have eye trouble; often used metaphorically as objects which, though devoid of substance, appear to exist to those who have delusions. [S. VII–25; Tai. 23.]

~ **no shōji** --の生死 '(Cycles of) birth and death which are like (delusory) flowers seen in the sky.' [S. VII–25.]

Kugen 苦患 'Pain, suffering.'

Kugō 口業 'The act of speech.'

~ **o osametsubeshi** --ををさめつべし 'To be able to control one's speech'; to be able to guard one's speech against the four evils of lying, harsh words, slander, and idle talk. [Ho. 30.]

Kugō 舊業 'An old karma'; an act done in a former life. [S.VII –9; Tai. 18.]

Kūgō 空劫 'The *kalpa* (*kō**) of annihilation'; one of the four periods of cosmic change. See *shikō.*

Kugu 供具 'Utensils for making offerings'; also offerings made to the Buddha or other deities. [Tai. 36.]

Kugyō 恭敬 'Respect, worship, reverence.'

~**-shu** --修 'The practice of worship (of Amida* and bodhisattvas)'; one of the four practices in Pure Land Buddhism set forth in the *Ōjō-raisan**; cf. *shishu.*

Kuhō 苦報 'Painful retribution.'

Kuhon 九品 Also *kubon*; 'the nine grades' of aspirants to Amida's* Pure Land, expounded in the *Kanmuryōju-kyō**. There are three classes: (1) *jōbon* 上品, 'highest class'; (2) *chūbon* 中品, 'middle class'; and (3) *gebon* 下品, 'lowest class'. Each class is divided into three grades: (1) *jōshō* 上生, 'highest birth'; (2) *chūshō* 中生, 'middle birth'; and (3) *geshō* 下生, 'lowest birth'. Amida's land, in which they will be born, is divided into nine grades, corresponding to the nine grades of aspirants.

~ **Annyōkai** --安養界 '(Amida's*) Land of Peace and Sustenance with the nine levels (of accommodation for the nine grades of aspirants).' [Tai. 18.]

~ **Annyō no onaji utena** --安養の同じ臺 'Similar lotus-seats at the nine levels in the Land of Peace and Sustenance.' [Tai. 6.]

~ **Jōdo** --浄土 'The Pure Land with the nine-grade distinction.' [Tai. 32.]

~ **no Jōsetsu** --の淨刹 'The Pure Land with the nine-grade distinction.' [Tai. 18, 37.]

~ **no kyōshu** --の教主 'The Teaching Lord of the Nine Grades' of the Pure Land, which is divided up according to the nine grades of aspirant; namely, Amida* Buddha. [K. 36.]

~ **no nenbutsu** --の念佛 'Recitation of the *nenbutsu** in nine different tones.' [Tsu. 115.]

~ **ōjō** --往生 'The nine grades of birth' in Amida's* Pure Land. [Hei. 3.]

~ **rendai** --蓮臺 'The nine grades of lotus-seat' for the nine grades of aspirants to Amida's* Pure Land. The aspirants are offered lotus-seats of different qualities at their death, and are taken to the Pure Land. The lotus plants bloom quickly or slowly according to the sum of the aspirants' merits. [Ma. 97; Tai. 18.]

Kūjaku 空寂 'Void and tranquil'; emptiness and tranquillity; commonly said of the Hinayana type of Nirvana.

Kujaku-kyō 孔雀經 Also, *Kuza-kyō*; '*The Peacock Sutra*'. Also *Kujaku-myōō-gyō* 孔雀明王經; the full title is *Butsumo-daikujaku-myōō-gyō* 佛母大孔雀明王經, 3 fasc., tr. into Chinese by Amoghavajra (Fukū*) [TT. 19, No. 982]; a sutra expounding the efficacy and merit of the Great Peacock Dharani (*Daikujaku-ju* 大孔雀呪). This sutra teaches that those who recite this dharani will be able to escape calamities and attain immeasurable merit. The ritual based on this sutra was popularly practised in Japan. Cf. *Kujaku-myōō-gyō no hō*. [Ma. 278.]

~ **(no) hō** ---(の)法 See *Kujaku-myōō-gyō no hō*. [Hei. 3; K. 44.]

~ **no midokyō mishuhō** ---の御讀經御修法 'Chanting of the *Peacock Sutra* and the esoteric ritual' based on it. [Ma. 278.]

Kujaku Myōō 孔雀明王 Sk. Mahāmāyūrī Vidyārājñī; the Great-

Peacock Fierce Spirit. The bodhisattva who made a vow to remove all the hindrances and calamities afflicting living beings, just as a peacock eats even poisonous herbs and worms but turns their poison into nectar. [K. 36.]

～-gyō ----經 '*The Peacock Vidyārāja Sutra*'; abbr. of *Butsumo-daikujaku-myōō-kyō* 佛母大孔雀明王經; see *Kujaku-kyō*.

～-gyō no hō ----經の法 Also *Kujaku-kyō-hō* 孔雀經法. An esoteric ritual performed for the peace and security of the state, cessation of natural disasters, etc., in accordance with the *Kujaku-kyō** and other texts. Frequently performed to pray for rainfall in time of drought.

～-hō ----法 See *Kujaku-myōō-gyō no hō*. [K. 36.]

Kujō no kesa 九條の袈裟 'A robe made of nine strips of cloth.' [K. 63.]

Kujō no shakujō 九條の錫杖 'Nine-stanza *shakujō* (verses)'; the verses consisting of nine stanzas to be chanted while sounding a *shakujō**. [Ma. 263.]

Kujū shaba no bosatsu 久住娑婆の菩薩 'A bodhisattva who dwells in this *Sahā* world (*Shaba**) for a long time.' [S. II–4.]

Kukai 九界 'The nine realms or worlds'; the first nine of the ten states of existence (*jikkai**), i.e. from hell up to the realm of bodhisattvas. [S. I–3; Tai. 16.]

Kukai 苦海 'The sea of suffering', i.e. the world of transmigration. [S. Pref.]

Kūkai 空海 The founder of the Japanese Shingon* sect (774–835); born in Sanuki Province, he studied in Nara and Kyoto. He became a novice at 20, and received ordination at the Tōdaiji* at 22. In 804 he went to China and met Hui-kuo 惠果 (Keika) of the Ch'ing-lung-ssu 青龍寺 (Seiryūji) in Chang-an 長安 (Chōan) from whom he received the 'Dharma-transmission *abhiṣeka*' (*denbō kanjō**) of esoteric Buddhism. He further studied the Hua-yen (Kegon*) and Prajñā-pāramitā (Hannya*) teachings and Sanskrit under other masters. After returning to Japan in 806, he lived in the Jingoji 神護寺 in the north-west of Kyoto and later became the chief abbot of the Tōdaiji. In 816 he opened Mt. Kōya, where he built the Kongōbuji 金剛峯寺 which became the centre of study and practice of esoteric Buddhism. Seven years later, he was given the Tōji* in Kyoto, which became another centre of esoteric Buddhism. In 824, he effectively prayed for rain, and was given the title of *shōsōzu* and later, in 827, that of *daisōzu* (see *sōgō*). He passed away in meditation on Mt. Kōya. He wrote many works, including *Sokushin-jōbutsu-gi* 即身成佛義 'The Principle of Becoming a Buddha with One's Present Body' and *Jūjūshin-ron* 十住心論 'The Discourse on the Ten Stages of Mind'. He was also renowned for calligraphy and sculpture. He was posthumously given the title of *daisōjō** and later, in 921, the name and title of Kōbō Daishi 弘法大師.

Kūkan 空觀 See *kūgan*.

Kuketsu 口決(=訣) 'Oral transmission' of some secret teaching. [Tai. 17.]

　yuiju ichinin no ～ 唯受一人の-- 'The oral transmission of the teaching received by only one person.' [Tai. 24.]

Kukyō 究竟 I. 'Ultimate.' II. Refers to *kukyōsoku**. [Tsu. 217.]

～-soku --即 'The ultimate realization of identity (with Buddha)'; the last of the six stages of identity (*rokusoku** 六即) in Tendai* doctrine; refers to the stage of Buddha's own enlightenment.

Kumai 供米 'Rice offered' to a temple or deity. [K. 395, 520; S. VIII–23.]

Kumaraen 鳩摩羅炎 Sk. Kumārāyaṇa; an Indian, he was at first a minister, but renounced the world and went to Kuccha, where he was warmly received by the king. He married the king's sister, Jīvā; their son was Kumārajīva (Kumarajū*). [S. IV–2.]

Kumarajū 鳩摩羅什 Also 究摩羅什, 鳩摩羅時婆, and 鳩摩羅耆婆; Sk. Kumārajīva (344–413); often abbreviated as Rajū 羅什; translated as Dōju 童壽 'Boy's Life'. His father was an Indian named Kumārāyaṇa (Kumaraen*), and his mother, Jīvā, was a sister of a king of Kuccha. Kumārajīva entered the priesthood at seven and studied both Mahayana and Hinayana in northwest India and elsewhere. He then returned to Kuccha and spread Mahayana. When Fu Chien 苻堅 (Fuken) (338–85) conquered Kuccha, Kumārajīva was invited to China. He went to Chang-an 長安 (Chōan) in 401 and was treated as a state master. For the rest of his life, he translated Buddhist texts, amounting to 35 sutras and discourses in more than 300 fascicles, including

Makahannya-haramitsu-kyō*, *Hoke-kyō**, *Amida-kyō** and *Dai-chido-ron**. He also lectured on the Mādhyamika (Chūganha*) texts and laid the foundation of the San-lun (Sanron*) sect. It is said that he had 3,000 disciples, of whom the following four are especially famous: Tao-sheng 道生 (Dōshō), Seng-chao 僧肇 (Sōjō), Tao-jung 道融 (Dōyū) and Seng-jui 僧叡 (Sōei).

Kūmon 空門 'The teaching of the void.' [S. I–9, IV–1.]

Kumotsu 供物 'An offering.' [K. 71.]

Kūmuhenjo 空無邊處 'Abode of Limitless Space'; Sk. Ākāśa-ānan-tya-āyatana; the lowest of the four abodes in the realm of non-form (*mushikikai**), where inhabitants have no physical bodies and only enjoy boundless space; cf. *mushikikai*.

Kunjū 熏習 Also 薰習; 'repeatedly impregnating with a scent'; said of the impression one's acts leave on one's mind.

Kunō 功能 'Efficacy'; also *kūnō*.

Kunshū 薰修 'Perfuming and practising'; impressing the merit of practices or good acts on one's mind; hence, practising con-tinuously; cf. *kunjū*. [S. II–7, 10, IV–1, VII–25.]

Kuon jitsujō 久遠實成 'The true attainment (of enlightenment) in the remotest past'; commonly said of Shakamuni's* original buddhahood. [Tai. 18.]

~ no kobutsu ----の古佛 'An old buddha who truly attained (enlightenment) in the remotest past.' [Tai. 18.]

Kuri 庫裏 (or 裡) Also *kuin* 庫院, *jikizu* 食厨, etc. I. A building in a temple used for the preparation of food to be offered to the Buddha or served to monks. II. Nowadays, the part of a temple building where the family of the resident priest lives.

Kurin 九輪 'The nine rings'; a column of nine metal rings on the top of a tower; also *kūrin* 空輪 'sky rings' because it rises high in the sky, but, properly, *sōrin* 相輪, *rinsō* 輪相, *kondō* 金幢, etc. [Tai. 21, 26.]

Kuryō 供料 'Provisions to be offered (to the Buddha, the Dharma, a temple, a monk, etc.).'

Kusa 倶舍 See *Kusha*.

Kuse 救世 'World-saving'; also *kuze*, *guse*; a general title for a buddha or bodhisattva.

~ Bosatsu --菩薩 'World-saving Bodhisattva'. An epithet for Kannon*. [K. 35.]

~ Kannon --觀音 'Kannon*, the saviour of the world.' [S. II–4.]

~ Kanzeon --觀世音 'Kannon*, the saviour of the world.' [K. 35; S. Vb–10.]

~ no chikai --の誓 'Vow to save the world'; Kannon's* vow to save living beings. [K. 469.]

Kusha 倶舍 I. Refers to the *Abidaruma-kusha-ron**. [Ma. 116.] II. The Kusha sect founded on the teaching of the *Abidaruma-kusha-ron*.

~ gakushō --學生 'A student of the Kusha* doctrine.' [S. Va–5.]

Kushōjin 倶生神 'The gods born simultaneously with one's own birth'; the two spirits which come into existence when one is born and dwell on one's shoulders all the time. The one on the left shoulder is a male spirit, called *dōmyō* 同名, and records one's good acts; and the one on the right shoulder is a female spirit, called *dōshō* 同生, and records one's evil acts. When one dies, they report on the person's moral acts to Yama (Enma*), the king of the dead. [Tai. 26.]

Kūshū 空宗 'Emptiness sect'; refers to the Sanron* sect which does not recognize any form of existence; opposite of *ushū**. [S. IV–1.]

Kushu rengyō 久修練行 'Practising diligently for a long time.' [Tai. 37.]

Kusō 供僧 Also *gusō*; abbr. of *kubusō* 供奉僧; a priest who makes (daily) offerings to the principal deity of a temple. [K. 520; O. II; S. VI–11.]

Kutei 倶胝 Sk. *koṭi*; translated as 億 ; a great number.

Kūya 空也 See *Kōya*.

Kuyō 供養 I. 'Offering and sustaining'; Sk. *pūjā*; also *kuse* 供施, *kukyū* 供給 and *ku* 供; an offering of food, drink, clothes or the like to a buddha, monk, teacher, dead person, etc. See *jusshu kuyō*. II. A special commemorative service held to mark such things as the construction of a temple or statue or the completion of copying a sutra or sutras.

~ no ganmon --の願文 'A prayer sheet composed for the repose of a deceased person.' [S. Vb–9.]

Kuza-kyō 孔雀經 See *Kujaku-kyō*.

Kyakushō sokumō 隔生則忘 'When life is renewed one forgets (what has happened in the present life).' [Tai. 11.]

Kyaradasen 伽羅陀山 Also 佉羅陀山, etc. 'Mt. Kharādīya'; one of the seven golden mountains surrounding Mt. Sumeru (Shumisen*), where the Buddha is said to have delivered sutras on Jizō*; hence, this mountain is believed to be Jizō's Pure Land. [S. II –5.]

Kyō 經 Sk. *sūtra*; a Buddhist scripture; see *shutara*. *Kyō*, lit. 'warp', is construed as the thread which pierces reality principles and holds them together.

~ **o hirugaesu** -を飜す 'To chant a sutra.' [Tai. 8.]

Kyōai no hihō 敬愛の祕法 'The esoteric rite for achieving love and respect (from others)'; see *keiaihō*. [S. VII–19.]

Kyōbō 教法 'Teaching and Dharma'; teaching.

Kyōden 敬田 'A field of respect'; the act of respecting the Buddha, Dharma, and Sangha produces merit, so it is compared to a field or farm; one of the three fields of merit (*sanfukuden**). [S. IV–9.]

Kyōen 境縁 'External objects'; objects perceived as existing outside one's mind. [S. III–8.]

Kyōgai 境界 I. 'The objective world'; circumstance. II. One's 'sphere' of action or perception. III. That which is within one's capacity.

Kyōgō 輕業 'A light karma'; an act which does not count much; an act of little consequence. [S. VII–22.]

Kyogon 虛言 Also *kogon*; 'a lie.'

Kyōgon rijitsu 教權理實 'Doctrinal expositions are provisional and the noumenal principle is real.' [S. Xb–2.]

Kyōgyō 教行 'Teaching and practice.' [S. Xa–1.]

~**-shinshō** --信證 '*Teaching, Practice, Faith and Enlightenment*'; the abridged title of a work by Shinran* (1173–1262), 6 fasc., which laid the foundation of the Jōdoshin* sect; the full title is *Ken-jōdo-shinjitsu-kyōgyōshō-monrui* 顯淨土眞實教行證文類 [TT. 83, No. 2646].

Kyōhan 教判 '(Critical) classification of teachings.'

Kyōin 教院   Also *kyōji* 教寺; a temple where Buddhist doctrines are studied; opposed to *zen'in** 禪院. [S. III–4.]

Kyōji 教寺 See *kyōin*.

Kyōjushi 教授師   Also *kyōju-ajari* 教授阿闍梨. One of the three masters of precepts who preside at the ceremony of accepting the precepts. He gives instructions to the initiate during the ceremony. Cf. *kai-wajō* and *katsumashi*.

Kyōkaku 驚覺   Also *kyōgaku* and *gyōkaku*; 'awakening' the mind and making it attentive. [K. 53.]

Kyōkan 叫喚 'Shrieking'; Sk. *raurava*; n. of one of the eight great hells (*hachidai jigoku**), where sinners are boiled in a big cauldron or thrown into an iron room with a fierce fire raging, and therefore 'shriek' with pain. [Tai. 12, 17, 27.]

Kyōkan 經卷 'Sutra scrolls.'

Kyōki 教起 'Emergence of a teaching'; origination of a teaching. [K. 36.]

Kyokuroku 曲彔 A kind of tall chair for a priest used at a Buddhist service. [Tai. 10, 27, 33.]

Kyō-kuyō 經供養 A Buddhist service held to celebrate the completion of the copying of a sutra. [Ma. 31.]

Kyōmon 教文 'Passages of a Buddhist scripture.' [S. III–4.]

Kyōmon 教門 'Teaching-gate'.   I. Teaching.   II. A school of Buddhism based on written scriptures; the opposite of *zenmon**. [S. IV–1, IX–13.]

Kyōron 經論 'A sutra and a discourse.'

Kyosetsu 虛說 See *kosetsu*.

Kyōshu 教主 'Teacher; Lord Teacher'; the Buddha.

Kyōsō 教相 'The doctrinal aspect.'   I. The theoretical study of the Buddhist teaching, as opposed to *kanjin** 觀心, the practice of meditation. [Tai. 42.]   II. The doctrinal aspect of esoteric Buddhism, as opposed to *jisō** 事相 'the ritual aspect'.

Kyōyō 孝養 'Filial piety and making offerings (to one's parents)'; performing one's filial duty to parents while they are alive and holding memorial services for them after their death.

~ **bumo** -- 父母 'Devotion to one's parents'; a phrase from the *Kanmuryōju-kyō*. [K. 313.]

~ **no ganmon** -- の願文 'A prayer sheet composed for the repose of one's parents.' [S. Vb–9.]

~ **no sotoba** -- の率都婆 'A *sotoba** tablet as a prayer for the repose of one's dead parents.' [S. Vb–4.]

Kyōzō 經藏 I. 'Collection of sutras'; one of the three (or five) divisions of the Buddhist scriptures, which contains the Buddha's teachings. Also *sotaranzō** and *shutarazō**. II. A repository of Buddhist scriptures.

Kyūchū gosai-e 宮中御齋會 See *gosai-e*.

M

Ma 魔 Sk. *māra*, 'a devil'.

~ **ōjō** -往生 'Rebirth in the realm of devils.' [S. Xa–10.]

Madō 魔道 'The path (or realm) of devils.' [Hei. 3; S. I–6, 7, Xb–1.]

Maen 魔緣 'Devils' conditions'; the devils' work of hindering the good. [Hei. 1; IH.; S. Va–4.]

dai-~ to naru 大--と成る 'To become a great adversary.' [Tai. 15.]

Magō 魔業 'A devil's act'; a devilish act; an act which leads one away from Buddhism. [S. Va–12, Xb–1.]

Magoraga 摩睺羅迦 Sk. *mahoraga*; a type of supernatural being said to have the body of a man and the head of a snake; a god of music; one of the eight kinds of supernatural beings who protect Buddhism (*hachibushu**).

Makada 摩羯陀 Also 摩竭陀, 摩訶陀, etc.; Sk. Magadha; an ancient kingdom in central India. [S. Xb–3; Tai. 24, 35.]

Makaen-ron 摩訶衍論 '*The Discourse on Mahayana*'; another

name for the *Daijō-kishin-ron**.

Makahannya-haramitsu-kyō 摩訶般若波羅蜜經　Sk. *Mahā-prajñā-pāramitā-sūtra*; a source material for the teaching on the void; 27 fasc., tr. by Kumārajīva (Kumarajū*) [TT. 8, No. 233]; often abbreviated as *Daibon-gyō** 大品經 or *Daibon-hannya-kyō** 大品般若經.

Makai 魔界　'The realm of devils.'

Makakaraten 摩訶迦羅天　'Mahākāla God'; see *Daikokuten*. [Tai. 24.]

Makakashō 摩訶迦葉　Sk. Mahākāśyapa; the foremost of the Buddha's disciples. After the Buddha's death he became the head of the order. See *jūdai-deshi*. [K. 46; Tai. 24.]

Makasatsu 摩訶薩　Sk. *mahāsattva*, 'a great being'; translated as *daiji* 大士 'a great man', *daiujō* 大有情 'a great sentient being', *daishin* 大心 '(a man of) great mind', etc.; one with great compassion and energy who seeks to save all living beings; a bodhisattva (*bosatsu**).

Makashikan 摩訶止觀　'*Discourse on Mahayana Meditation and Contemplation*'; 20 fasc., by Chih-i 智顗 (Chigi*) [TT. 46, No. 1911]; the full title is *Tendai-makashikan* 天台摩訶止觀. It is a series of lectures on the Tendai* method of meditation given by Chih-i in 594 and recorded and edited by his disciple Kuan-ting 灌頂 (Kanchō). [S. I–3, VI–10; Tsu. 75.]

Makatsugyo 摩羯 (or 竭) 魚　Sk. *makara*; also *magara* 摩伽羅 or *makara* 摩迦羅, and translated as *geigyo* 鯨魚, etc.; a mythological fish measuring 300 to 700 *yojana* (*yujun**), which is believed to live in the sea and to have a mouth big enough to swallow a boat. [Tai. 35]

Makeishubara 摩醯伊濕伐羅　Sk. Maheśvara; also 莫醯伊濕伐羅, 摩醯濕伐羅 and Makeishura 摩醯首羅; translated as Daijizai 大自在; one of the highest Hindu gods who lives in the Daijizaiten*, the highest heaven in the realm of form (*shikikai**). He is identified with Śiva, has three eyes and eight arms, and rides a white ox.

Makeishura 摩醯首羅　See *Makeishubara*. [Tai. 23.]

Makeishura Ō 摩醯脩羅王　'King Maheśvara'; see *Makeishubara*. [Tai. 34.]

Mamin 魔民 'A devil; a devil's subjects.' [S. Xb–1.]

Mamō 魔網 'The devil's net'; said of devils' acts of trapping people and thwarting them in their pursuit of the Buddhist Way. [S. Xb–3.]

Manbō 萬法 'Ten thousand things'; myriads of elements; all existing things.

~ **o tenzu** --を轉ず 'To turn myriads of things'; to have control over all existences. [S. III–8.]

~ **yuishiki** --唯識 'All things are nothing but the consciousness'; according to the Hossō* doctrine, all phenomenal existences are transformations of and the manifestations from the basic consciousness, *Ālaya* (*arayashiki**); cf. *yuishiki*. [S. III–1.]

Manda 曼荼 I. Sk. *maṇḍa*; essence; cf. *bodai dōjō*. II. Abbr. of *mandara**. III. Abbr. of *mandarake**.

~**-ra** --羅 Sk. *maṇḍala*; translated as *dan* 壇, *rinnen gusoku* 輪圓具足, etc.; originally, a square or circular mound where Buddhist deities were placed for the performance of rituals; popularly, a pictorial representation of deities. Four kinds of mandala are distinguished; see *shishu mandara*, *jishō mandara* and *ryōbu mandara*.

Mandarake 曼陀羅華 Sk. *māndāra* or *māndārava*; also *mandaroku* 曼陀勒, *mandarabon* 曼陀羅梵, etc., and translated as *tenmyō* 天妙, *etsui* 悅意, etc.; a kind of heavenly flower, beautiful to look at and pleasing to the mind of one who sees it.

Man'e 縵衣 Also *manjō* 縵條; Sk. *paṭa*; a robe without proper stripes; originally worn by a novice, but allowed to be worn by a monk when a proper robe is not available. [S. VI–17.]

Man'en 萬緣 'A myriad relations'; all secular relationships; all external things. [S. Vb–9.]

~ **o sutsu** --をすつ 'To abandon all secular engagements.' [S. IV–1.]

~ **o yamu** --をやむ 'To stop all secular connections.' [S. IV–1.]

Mangyō 萬行 'A myriad Buddhist practices.' [S. Pref., IV–1.]

~ **manzen** --萬善 'A myriad practices and good acts'; in Pure Land Buddhism, various meritorious acts other than *nenbutsu** (the recitation of Amida's* name). [S. I–10.]

Mani 摩尼 Sk. *maṇi*; a precious gem of a globular shape with a short pointed top; said to be efficacious in removing misfortune and calamity, cleansing dirty water, etc.

〜**-shu** - -珠 'Maṇi gem.' [Tai. 26.]

Manki 萬機 'Tens of thousands of living beings'; see *ki* 機. [S. II–5.]

Manyo 魔女 'A female devil.' [S. Xb–1.]

Maō 魔王 'The king of devils', said to live in the Sixth Heaven of the realm of desire (*Dairokuten**). [S. I–1, Xa–5, Xb–1.]

Mappō 末法 I. 'The last Dharma; decadent Dharma.' II. Refers to *mappōji**. [Tai. 21, 32.]

〜**-ji** - -時 'The period of the last and decadent Dharma'; one of the three periods after the Buddha's death. See *shōzōmatsu*.

〜 **mannen** - -萬年 'The period of the last Dharma lasting 10,000 years.' [S. II–8.]

Marishiten 摩利支天 Goddess Marīci (lit. mirage); she always precedes the sun and is invisible; possessed of supernatural power, she can remove the sufferings of those who remember her. Her spell, by which a person is made invisible, is used in esoteric Buddhism. [Tai. 5.]

Mashō 魔障 'Devil's hindrance' in the attainment of salvation. [S. II–7, IV–5; Tai. 12, 16.]

〜 **gōbuku** - -降伏 'Subduing or removing the hindrance of devils.' [Tai. 8, 26.]

Masse 末世 'The latter days'; the period of *mappō** 末法; the same as *matsudai**.

〜 **gyōri** - -澆漓 'The latter ages when (human virtue) weakens.' [Tai. 8.]

〜 **jokuran no jibun** - -濁亂の時分 'The latter-day period, a time of defilement and confusion.' [Tai. 27.]

jokuaku no 〜 濁惡の- - 'The latter-day period of defilement and evils.' [Tai. 33.]

Matō 摩騰 Refers to Kashōmatō*. [Tai. 24.]

Matsudai 末代 Also *masse** 末世; 'the latter days'; the period of *mappō** 末法, in which Buddha's teaching declines.

〜 **jaaku no toki** - -邪惡の時 'The latter-day period, a time of wrong-doing and evils.' [Tai. 27.]

~ **no zoku** -- の俗 'The latter-day period when (Buddhism) is secularized.' [Hei. 2.]

Matsugaku 末學 'Students in later periods.' [S. I–10.]

Matsuji 末寺 'A subsidiary temple' under the jurisdiction of the head temple.

Maya 摩耶   Sk. Māyā; originally, n. of the Buddha's mother; in Japan, n. of a mountain in Kobe where there is a temple dedicated to her. [Tai. 7, 8.]

Meido 冥土, 冥途   Also *myōdo*; 'path of obscurity'; the world of the dead ruled by Yama (Enma*); cf. *myōdō* and *myōkai*.

~ **no onmichi-shirube** 冥途の御道しるべ 'Guide to the world of the dead.' [Tai. 10.]

~ **no ryōyū** -- の良友 'A good friend on the road to the world of the dead.' [S. IV–9.]

~ **no shiryō** -- の資糧 'Provisions for (the journey to) the world of the dead.' [S. VIII–22.]

~ **no tabi** -- の旅 'Travelling to the world of the dead.' [S. Xa–6; Tai. 33.]

Meigo 迷悟 'Delusion and enlightenment.'

~ **taiichi** -- 體一 'Delusions and enlightenment are of one substance'; from the viewpoint of absolute reality, delusions and enlightenment are one and the same. [S. Xa–6.]

Meijō 迷情 'Delusory feelings'; delusion. [S. I–3.]

Meikai 冥界   See *myōkai*.

Memyō 馬鳴   Sk. Aśvaghoṣa; an Indian monk and a great exponent of Mahayana Buddhism, who flourished in the 1st century A.D. He wrote of the Buddha's life in verse (*Buddha-carita*) and other works, and also composed Mahayana discourses. [Tai. 12.]

Metsu o toru 滅をとる 'To die.' [K. 64.]

Metsuzai shōzen 滅罪生善 'Extinguishing sins and producing goodness.' [O. III; S. Xb–2; Tai. 11.]

Mezu 馬頭 'Horse head'; i.e. a horse-headed demon; a type of guardian of hell, distinguished by having a human body and the head of a horse. [K. 557; S. II–6; Tai. 2.]

Mida 彌陀   Abbr. of Amida*.

~ **Butsu** - - 佛 'Amida Buddha.'

~ **no hikari** - - の光 'The light of Amida (Buddha).' [K. 71.]

~ **no hongan** - - の本願 'Amida's original vow.' [Hei. 1; K. 469; S. VI–10.]

~ **no hosshin** - - の法身 'Amida's Dharma-body.' [S. Xb–3.]

~ **no mikuni** - - の御國 'Amida's country.' [K. 469.]

~ **no sanzon** - - の三尊 'Amida trio'; Amida and his two attendant bodhisattvas, i.e. Kannon* and Seishi*. [Hei. 2.]

~-**san** - - 讃 'A hymn eulogizing Amida.' [K. 48.]

Midō 御堂 'A Buddhist hall'; a Buddhist family chapel. [Tsu. 105, 134.]

Midokyō 御讀經 I. Chanting of a sutra. II. Refers to *ki no midokyō**.

Mieidō 御影堂 A hall where a portrait of a noble priest who founded the temple or sect is enshrined. [Tai. 11.]

Mijinju 微塵數 'The number of the minutest particles (in the world)'; innumerable, countless. [K. 53.]

Mikkyō 密教 'The esoteric teaching', as opposed to *kengyō** 顯教, the exoteric teaching; the mystic teachings said to have been directly revealed by the Dharma-body Buddha, Dainichi* 大日 (Mahāvairocana); they arose in India later than Hinayana and Mahayana and were systematized in Japan by Kūkai* as the Shingon* sect.

Mippō 密法 'An esoteric method (of practice)'; same as *shubō** 修法.

Mirai yōgō 未來永劫 'An eternal *kalpa* in the future'; see *kō*. [Tai. 33.]

Miroku 彌勒 Sk. Maitreya, 'Benevolent'. The bodhisattva who will appear in this world to become the next buddha after 5,670,000,000 years when he ends his life in the Tuṣita Heaven (Tosotsuten*). [O. V; S. I–3, IV–1, Vb–10, VI–10; Tai. 15.]

~ **Butsu** - - 佛 'Maitreya Buddha.' [S. VI–18.]

~ **geshō** - - 下生 'Maitreya's coming down' to the human world to become a buddha from the Tuṣita Heaven. [K. 48.]

~ **jison** - - 慈尊 'Maitreya, the Compassionate One.' [S. II–8.]

~-jōshō-kyō -- 上生經   The popular title of the *Kan-miroku-bosatsu-jōshō-tosotsuten-gyō* 觀彌勒菩薩上生兜率天經, 1 fasc., tr. into Chinese by Chü-ch'ü-ching-sheng 沮渠京聲 (Sokokyō-shō) in the 5th century [TT. 14, No. 452]. The sutra mentions Miroku's ascent to the Tuṣita Heaven (Tosotsuten*) 12 years later and also praises his distinguished merit.

~ no gyōja -- の行者   One who practises the method of attaining rebirth in the Tuṣita Heaven where he sees Miroku and practises the Buddhist Way under his guidance. [S. II–8.]

~ no jōdo -- の浄土   'Maitreya's pure land,' which is the inner palace of the Tuṣita Heaven. [S. II–8.]

~ ryūju -- 龍樹   'The dragon (-flower) tree of Maitreya'; Miroku will become a buddha under a dragon-flower tree (*ryūgeju*) and deliver sermons to three assemblies; cf. *ryūge-e*. [Tai. 18.]

~ san'e -- 三會   'The three assemblages (or sermons) of Maitreya' which he will hold under the dragon-flower tree when he becomes a buddha. [K. 40.]

~ shusse -- 出世   'Maitreya's appearance in the world.' [S. II–5.]

Misai-e 御齋會   See *gosai-e*.

Mishiho 御修法   Also pronounced *mishuhō* and *mizuhō*; an esoteric practice or rite; in the Shingon* sect, it refers to *goshichinichi mishiho**. [Hei. 3; Ma. 278; O. V; Tai. 12, 15, 24.]

Mishuhō 御修法   See *mishiho*.

Misshaku Kongō 密迹金剛   A Kongō god (*kongōjin**) who protects Buddhism. As one of the pair of Kongō gods often found at the entrance to a temple, he is placed on the left-hand side; cf. *niō*.

Misshū 密宗   'The esoteric school'; refers to the Shingon* sect. [Hei. 3; S. I–4, II–5, Xb–3.]

Mitake 御嶽   Refers to Mt. Kinpu 金峰山, Yamato, the sacred place for mountain Buddhism. [Ma. 115.]

~ sōji -- 精進   A period of self-purification practised for a thousand days prior to a visit to Mt. Kinpu 金峰山. During this period one gets up early in the morning, abstains from eating meat, etc., calls Miroku's* name, and worships him. This is because Miroku is considered to be one of the original bodies of Zaō Gongen*, the deity enshrined at the Kinpusenji. [Ma. 115.]

Mitsugō 密號 'Mystic name'; the esoteric name of a buddha or bodhisattva, e.g. Henjōkongō 遍照金剛 for Dainichi*.

Mitsugon 密嚴 Refers to Mitsugonkoku*. [S. II–8.]

∼-koku --國 'The Land of Mystic Glorification'; n. of Dainichi's* land. [S. I–1.]

Mitsugyō 密行 'A secret practice'; used in the sense of observing precepts very strictly.

∼ daiichi --第一 'The foremost one in the observance of the precepts'; Rāhula (Ragora*), the Buddha's son who became his disciple, was renowned as such.

Mitsuin 密印 'A mystic seal or sign.' I. Refers to a manual sign (*ingei** 印契, *mudrā*) which symbolizes the mystic intention of a buddha or bodhisattva. II. In Zen*, the mystic seal of the buddha-mind; the absolute mind-essence; see *shin'in*. [S. Vb–10.]

Miya no Gobutsumyō 宮の御佛名 The service of reciting 'buddhas' names at the imperial palace'. [Ma. 285.]

Miyo 三世 See *sanze*.

Mizou-hō 未曾有法 'An unprecedented matter'; Sk. *adbhutadharma*; one of the nine and the twelve kinds of scriptures (*kubu-kyō** and *jūnibu-kyō**), which gives an account of miracles performed by the Buddha or other deity.

Mizuhō 御修法 See *mishiho*.

Mizukyō 御誦經 'Chanting a sutra.' [Ma. 21.]

Mizu no in 水の印 'The water *mudrā*'; a manual sign representing water. [Tai. 12.]

Mōen 妄緣 'Delusory objects'; objects as they appear to exist owing to one's innate delusion. [S. Vb–11.]

Mōfunbetsu 妄分別 'False discrimination'; said of the innate mental act of discriminating things in relative terms. [S. III–1, IV–1.]

Mōgo 妄語 'Telling lies'; cf. *gokai*, *hassaikai* and *jikkai*.

Mōgō 妄業 'Delusory karma'; physical, oral, and mental acts which are contradictory to the truth and bring further suffering and delusion. [S. I–1, III–7, 8, Va–1, 5, VI–16, Xa–6, 9.]

Mōjin 妄心 'Deluded mind.'

Mōjō 妄情 'False desire or emotion'; delusory passion.

Mōka tettō 猛火鐵湯 'Fierce fire and molten iron' in hell, with which sinners are roasted and burned. [Tai. 7.]

Mokuren 目連 Sk. Maudgalyāyana; also Mokkenren 目犍連 or Makamokkenren 摩訶目犍連 (Mahāmaudgalyāyana); one of the ten great disciples of the Buddha (*jūdai-deshi**); well known for his supernatural power (*jinzū**). Born as a brahmin's son, he became a disciple of Sañjaya-velaṭṭhiputta, one of the six non-Buddhist teachers (*rokushi gedō**), and was later converted to Buddhism through the exhortation of his friend Śāriputra (Shari-hotsu*). His offerings to a company of monks to save his dead mother from torment in the realm of hungry ghosts (*gaki**) is said to be the origin of the *bon* festival (*urabon**).

～ **sonja** --尊者 'The Venerable Maudgalyāyana'; see *Mokuren*. [Tai. 35.]

Mōkyō 妄境 'An illusory external object.' From the viewpoint of the consciousness-only doctrine (*yuishiki** 唯識), nothing exists outside one's consciousness; to perceive an external object is thus an illusion. [S. I–9, Vb–8, VIII–21.]

Monbō 聞法 Also *monpō*; 'hearing the Dharma'; heeding the Buddhist teaching.

Monbutsu-ketsugi-kyō 問佛決疑經 See *Daibontennō-monbutsu-ketsugi-kyō*.

Mōnen 妄念 'An illusory thought'; a wanton thought; an illusion.

Monja 問者 'A questioner'; one who asks questions at a ceremonial discussion-meeting (*rongi** 論議) held in the imperial palace or a temple on the emperor's order. [Tai. 36.]

Monji no hosshi 文字の法師 A priest who merely studies and follows the literal meaning of the scriptures, without achieving any deep understanding. [Tsu. 193.]

Monju 文殊 Sk. Mañjuśrī; a bodhisattva who represents the wisdom (*chi* 智) and realization (*shō* 證) of all buddhas, as contrasted with Fugen* who represents the intrinsic principle, meditation, and practice. He is the left-hand attendant of Shakamuni* Buddha, and is often portrayed mounted on a lion. [S. Vb–7, 10; Tai. 18, 38.]

～**-e** --會 'The Monju festival'; the annual festival to worship

Monju* on the 8th of the 7th month at various temples, especially at the Tōdaiji* and Saidaiji in Nara. [Tai. 24.]

~ **hachiji hō** --八字法 See *hachiji Monju hō.*

~ **no chie** --の智慧 'The wisdom of Monju.' [Tai. 36.]

Monoimi 物忌 Confinement to one's house on unlucky days or when some evil spirit is believed to be around.

Monshishu 聞思修 'Hearing, thinking about and practising' the Buddhist teaching. [S. Xb–3.]

Monshō 文證 'Written evidence'; scriptural evidence.

Monshu 門主 I. The chief abbot of the Honpa Honganji of the Jōdoshin* sect. II. Used for 門首, the head priest of a temple.

Monto 門徒 'Followers of the (teaching-)gate.' I. Those who come to an assembly. II. Disciples and followers of a teacher. III. Members of a temple, esp. of the Jōdoshin* sect, who make donations to support it. IV. Abbr. of Monto-shū 門徒宗, another name for the Jōdoshin sect; also its followers.

Monzeki 門跡 'The trace of the (teaching-)gate.' I. A temple founded or inhabited by an ordained ex-emperor, prince or princess; also such a member of the imperial family; usually, the honorific *go* is prefixed. The first instance of the use of *go-monzeki* 御門跡 was when ex-Emperor Uda, ordained at the Ninnaji 仁和寺 in 899, went to live there in 904. II. Later, this appellation was applied to nobles. To distinguish them from princes, the latter were called *miya-monzeki* 宮門跡 'imperial *monzeki*', and the nobles or the temples where they lived were called *sekke-monzeki* 攝家門跡 'regent-family *monzeki*' or *jun-monzeki* 準門跡 'sub-*monzeki*'. III. In Tendai* there are nine *monzeki* temples (see *sanmonzeki*), and in Shingon*, six. Also, Jōdo* has one, and Jōdoshin* five.

Mōshū 妄執 'Delusory attachment.'

Motsujimi 沒滋味 'Tastelessness'; that which has no taste; also that which is not easy to crunch; often said of Zen* practice. [Tai. 24.]

Mōzō 妄想 'An illusory thought.'

~**-kyō** --境 'The world created by illusion.' [S. IV–1.]

Mubutsu no dōshi 無佛の導師 'A guide or a teacher (during the period) when no buddha lives (in the world)'. [S. I–6, II–5.]

Mubutsu sekai 無佛世界 'A world where there is no buddha.' [Tai. 18.]

Mudōshin 無道心 'Having no aspiration for Bodhi.' [IH.; S. I–3.]

Muen 無縁 I. 'Unrelated' to a buddha, etc. II. 'Objectless'; absence of an object to be perceived.

～ **no chi** -–の智 'The wisdom of not being cognizant of objects'; objectless wisdom; the wisdom of knowing absolute reality. [S. IV–1.]

～ **no daihi** -–の大悲 'The objectless great compassion'; see *muen no jihi*. [S. Vb–10.]

～ **no gunrui** -–の群類 'The multitudinous beings who are (apparently) unrelated (to a buddha or bodhisattva).' [Hei. 2.]

～ **no jihi** -–の慈悲 'Objectless compassion'; one of the three kinds of compassion (*san'en no jihi*); the compassion of a buddha or bodhisattva of a higher rank which, based on the realization of the void, arises without perceiving any object; cf. *dōtai muen no jihi*.

～ **no shujō** -–の衆生 'The sentient beings who have no relationship' with a particular buddha or bodhisattva; hence, helpless beings who have no way of salvation. [S. III–1.]

Mufunbetsu 無分別 'Non-discrimination.'

Muga 無我 'Non-self'; egolessness. That there is no permanent self in a living being is a basic teaching of the Buddha.

Muge 無礙 'Without hindrance; non-obstruction.'

～ **no ken** -–の見 'A view of non-hindrance'; a wrong view that one can do anything without incurring a painful result. [S. III–5, 8.]

Mugen koke 夢幻虚假 'False and temporary like a dream or illusion.' [S. Vb–11.]

Mugi 無義 'Without meaning or principle'; meaningless; purposeless; opposite of *ugi**. [S. III–8, Xb–3.]

Mugi 無愧 'Not repentant' of evils committed.

Mugon dōjō 無言道場 A hall where one keeps the precept of not talking while controlling one's mind. [S. IV–1.]

Mugū 無窮 'Interminable, endless.'

~ **no shōji** --の生死 'Interminable cycles of birth and death.'
[S. III–7, Vb–11.]

Muhen sekai 無邊世界 'The infinite universe.' [O. V.]

Muhōtō 無縫塔 'A tower without a joint'; a tower made of a single
stone in the shape of an egg; often used as the tomb of a Zen*
monk; popularly, *rantō** 卵塔.

Muhyōshiki 無表色 'Unmanifested form'; see *keshiki*.

Mui 無畏 'Fearlessness'; for a buddha or bodhisattva's fearlessness in expounding the Dharma, see *shimushoi*. [Tai. 24.]

Mui 無意 'No intention'; without intention. [S. Vb–10.]

Mui 無爲 'Inactive, uncreated'; Sk. *asaṃskṛta*; the realm of
inactivity or eternity; the noumenal world; the opposite of *ui**
有爲. [S. III–1.]

~ **jinen** --自然 'As-it-is-ness of the absolute reality'; the state of
things as they really are, which is beyond all change; cf. *jinen*.

~ **jōjū** --常住 'Uncreated and eternal'; said of the ultimate
reality or the final enlightenment. [S. I–1.]

Mujaku 無著 Sk. Asaṅga; a native of Gandhāra in north India
in the fourth century A.D. and a great exponent of the Yogācāra
School (Yugagyōha*). Born as a brahmin's son, he first followed
Hinayana but was later converted to Mahayana. He composed
discourses on the Yogācāra philosophy and practice, including
Shō-daijō-ron 攝大乘論; in Tibetan tradition, the *Yugashiji-ron**
瑜伽師地論 is also ascribed to him. It is traditionally believed
that he often visited Tuṣita Heaven (Tosotsuten*) to receive the
teaching from Miroku* (Maitreya). His younger brother Seshin*
(Vasubandhu) further developed the Yogācāra doctrine.

Mujin 無盡 'Inexhaustible.'

~ **no myōyū** --の妙用 'The inexhaustible wonderful activity or
function.' [S. III–7.]

~**-zō** --藏 'An inexhaustible store of (merit).' [Tai. 24.]

Mujishō 無自性 'Non-self-nature'; the absence of fixed nature in
a thing; non-substantiality. [S. IV–1.]

Mujō 無常 'Impermanence'; Sk. *anitya*; that all things are impermanent is one of the basic principles of Buddhism.

~ **jinsoku** - -迅速 'The swiftness of transitoriness'; impermanence takes life very quickly, and death may come to anybody at any time. [Tai. 23.]

~ **no jinsoku** - -の迅速 See *mujō jinsoku*. [S. Xb–3.]

~ **no sekki** - -の殺鬼 'The murderous demon of impermanence'; impermanence which takes man's life like a demon. [S. III–1, Xa –2; Tai. 18.]

~ **no tora** - -の虎 'The tiger of impermanence'; an analogy to show that impermanence takes one's life. [Tai. 27, 33.]

~ **tenpen** - -轉變 'Being transient and changing.' [S. Vb–9.]

~ **tenpen no yo** - -轉變の世 'Impermanent and changing world.' [S. VIII–21.]

Mujō bodai 無上菩提 'The highest Bodhi or enlightenment.' [K. 46.]

Mujōdō 無上道 'The highest path', i.e. the Buddhist Way or the Buddha's enlightenment. [K. 52; S. III–1.]

Mujōnen 無諍念 'No Thought of Argument'; Sk. Araṇemin; n. of a king in the country called Sandairan* 珊提嵐 (Śaṇḍilya). According to the *Hike-kyō**, he had a minister named Hōkai* 寶海 (Samudrareṇu), whose son renounced the world and became a buddha named Hōzō* 寶藏 (Ratnagarbha). The king and his 1,000 children then aspired to enlightenment under his guidance. The king later became Amida*, and his children became Kannon*, Seishi* and other bodhisattvas and buddhas.

Mujū no shintai 無住の心體 'The mind-essence free of any thought of attachment'; the mind as it is, which does not take anything as its object. [S. IV–1.]

Mukae-kō 迎講 'A welcoming ceremony'; also *gōshō-e** 迎接會; a ceremony, said to have been originated by Genshin*, in which someone plays the part of Amida* coming down to welcome an aspirant to his land; cf. *raigō*. [S. VI–8, Xa–9.]

Muken 無間 'Without interruption, incessant.'

~-**goku** - -獄 Refers to *muken-jigoku**. [Tai. 19.]

~-**jigoku** - -地獄 'The hell of interminable pain'; Avīci Hell (*abi-jigoku* 阿鼻地獄); see *abi*. [Tai. 35.]

~ **no gō** --の業 Karma or acts which cause one to fall into the hell of interminable pain (*muken-jigoku**). [S. II–9, IV–1, VI–10; Tai. 33.]

~**-shu** --修 'The uninterrupted practice (of the *nenbutsu**)'; one of the four practices in Pure Land Buddhism set forth in the *Ōjō-raisan**; cf. *shishu* 四修.

Muku 無垢 'Not defiled'; free from the defilements of evil passions.

~ **munō no hōdo** --無惱の寶土 'The undefiled and suffering-free Treasure Land'; refers to Amida's* Pure Land. [K. 57.]

~ **no jōdō** --の成道 'Attainment of buddhahood in (the world called) Non-Defilement'; said of the dragon girl mentioned in the *Hoke-kyō** who instantly became a buddha in the world called Non-Defilement. [S. III–8.]

~ **sanmai** --三昧 'An undefiled *samādhi*'; a general term for the meditation of a buddha or bodhisattva which is free of defilement by evil passions. [Tai. 18.]

Mukudoku no wa 無功德の話 'The episode of no-merit.' When Emperor Wu-ti 武帝 (Butei) (464–549) of the Liang 梁 dynasty (502–556) asked Bodhidharma (Daruma*) how much merit he had acquired by building temples, Bodhidharma replied, 'No merit'. [Tai. 24.]

Mukui 報 'Result' of some acts in the past; often, retribution for the evil acts in one's previous life.

Mumon 無門 'No gate; without a gate'; also, the gate of nothingness. [S. Vb–10.]

Mumyō 無明 Sk. *avidyā*; 'darkness (of mind)'; ignorance.

~ **jōya** --長夜 'The long night of (spiritual) darkness.' [Tai. 15.]

~ **no neburi** --の眠 'The sleep of spiritual ignorance.' [S. III–1.]

~ **no sake no yoi** --の酒の醉 'Being drunk with the wine of (spiritual) ignorance'; being infatuated with one's own spiritual ignorance. [Tai. 29.]

~ **no umi** --の海 'The sea of ignorance'; the realm of spiritual darkness. [S. IV–1.]

Munen 無念 'Without thought'; absence of discriminative thought, as opposed to *unen**. [S. II–1, III–8, IV–1, Xb–3.]

~ **no shugyō** --の修行 'A practice performed without discriminative thought (or evil desires).' [S. III-8.]

Munetsuchi 無熱池 'Lake of no heat'; also Munetsunōchi 無熱悩池, 'lake of no fever or suffering'; another n. for Anokudatchi*. [Tai. 11, 12, 21, 35.]

Muni 牟尼 Sk. *muni*, 'a sage or saint'; used as an abbr. of Shakamuni*; the Buddha Śākyamuni. [Tai. 18.]

~ **no yuikyō** --の遺教 'The teaching left behind by Shakamuni.' [Tai. 18.]

Muro 無漏 Sk. *anāsrava*, 'undefiled'; pure; the opposite of *uro**.

~**-chi** --智 'Undefiled wisdom'; Sk. *anāsrava-jñāna*; the wisdom of a buddha or other Buddhist sages, which is free from delusions and evil passions.

~ **mushō no kuni** --無生の國 'The undefiled and unproduced land'; a buddha's land which is free of defilements and in perfect harmony with the ultimate reality-principle of non-substantiality. Cf. *mushō*. [S. III-1.]

~ **no jōsetsu** --の淨刹 'The pure realm free of defilements'; refers to a buddha's land. [S. III-1.]

Muryōchi 無了知 'Non-cognition.' [S. IV-1.]

Muryōju 無量壽 'Immeasurable Life'; Sk. Amitāyus; another name for Amida*. In esoteric Buddhism, one of the five buddhas (*gobutsu**) of the Diamond Realm Mandala (*Kongōkai mandara**); cf. *gochi nyorai*. [S. IV-1.]

~**-in** ---院 'The Infinite Life Hall'; another name for the Amida-dō 阿彌陀堂, 'Amida Hall', in the Hōjōji 法成寺, Kyoto. [Tsu. 25.]

~**-kyō** ---經 '*The Buddha of Infinite Life Sutra*'; 2 fasc.; translation is ascribed to Saṃghavarman (Kōsōgai 康僧鎧) [TT. 12, No. 360]. The basic canon of Pure Land Buddhism, which explains how Amida* attained buddhahood and how he saves sentient beings; it also gives a detailed description of his physical glory and his land. The title of the Sanskrit text is *Sukhāvatīvyūha* '*Glorious Adornment of Sukhāvatī* (the land of happiness)'; there are four other Chinese translations.

~**-kyō-ubadaisha-ganshōge** ---經優婆提舍願生偈   See *Jōdo-ron*.

Muryōkō 無量光 'Immeasurable Light'; Sk. Amitābha; another name for Amida*.

Muryōkō 無量劫 'Innumerable *kalpa* (or aeons).' See *kō* 劫. [K. 1.]

Musaichi 無際智 'Boundless wisdom.' [S. I–3.]

Mushi 無師 'Without a teacher.'

~ **jigo** --自悟 'Attaining enlightenment by oneself, without (the guidance of) a teacher.' [S. Xb–2.]

~ **no chi** --の智 'The wisdom attained without a teacher's guidance.' [S. Vb–9.]

Mushikikai 無色界 'The realm of non-form'; Sk. *ārūpya-dhātu*; the highest of the three realms (*sangai**), where there is no material element. There are four heavens or abodes in it: (1) Kūmuhenjo* 空無邊處 (Ākāśa-ānantya-āyatana), 'Abode of Limitless Space'; (2) Shikimuhenjo* 識無邊處 (Vijñāna-ānantya-āyatana), 'Abode of Limitless Consciousness'; (3) Mushousho* 無所有處 (Ākiñcanya-āyatana), 'Abode of Nothingness'; and (4) Hisōhihisōjo* 非想非非想處 (Naivasaṃjñā-nāsaṃjñā-āyatana), 'Abode of neither Thought nor Non-Thought'.

Mushi no rinne 無始の輪廻 'Transmigration which has no beginning.' [S. II–7, IV–9.]

Mushō 無生 'Non-arising'; from the viewpoint of the ultimate reality, nothing comes into existence and nothing perishes. [S. I–8.]

~**-bōnin** --法忍 Sk. *anutpattika-dharma-kṣānti*, 'endurance (i.e. clear cognition) regarding the unproduced nature of all existences'; a higher spiritual state in which one recognizes the immutable reality of all existences.

~**-nin** --忍 Abbr. of *mushōbōnin**. [S. III–1, Xa–1.]

~ **no hito** --の人 'A man of non-arising'; a man who has realized the principle of the non-arising of all existences. [S. Xb–1.]

Mushotoku 無所得 'Non-acquisition'; non-grasping; not clinging to or being attached to what one has obtained or perceived; opposed to *ushotoku**.

Mushousho 無所有處 'The Abode of Nothingness'; Sk. Ākiñca-nya-āyatana; the third of the four abodes in the realm of non-form (*mushikikai**), where inhabitants are not attached to either limitless space or their own consciousness.

Musō 無相 'Formlessness; non-characteristic.'

~ **bodai** --菩提 'Formless Bodhi'; Bodhi or enlightenment itself has no specific form; it is beyond all phenomena and characteristics. [S. III–1.]

~ **hōmon** --法門 'The teaching of formlessness'; the teaching expounding the formless essence of all existences. [S. VII–25.]

~ **hosshin** --法身 'The formless Dharma-body'; the universal transcendental body of the buddha with no specific form. See *hosshin*. [S. I–3.]

~ **jōjū no hosshin** --常住の法身 'The formless and eternal Dharma-body.' [S. II–4.]

~ **munen** --無念 'Without any object of perception and without thought.' [S. II–6.]

~ **munen no kanchi** --無念の觀智 'The wisdom of insight which perceives no object and contemplates nothing.' [S. II–4.]

~ **no bodai** --の菩提 See *musō bodai*. [S. IV–1.]

~ **no hōmon** --の法門 See *musō hōmon*. [S. Xb–1.]

~ **no hosshin** --の法身 See *musō hosshin*. [S. II–4.]

~ **no jitsuri** --の實理 'The reality-principle which takes no phenomenal form.' [S. Vb–9.]

~ **no kyō** --の境 'Objects which have no forms or characteristics.' [S. IV–1.]

~ **no myōtai** --の妙體 'The wondrous body with no form'; the body of the ultimate reality; the Dharma-body (*hosshin**). [S. III–8.]

~ **no ri** --の理 'The principle of the characterless quality.' [S. VI–17.]

~ **no shingon** --の眞言 'The formless spell'; the spell beyond verbal expression. [S. IV–1.]

~ **no shitchi** --の悉地 'A mystic spiritual attainment having no perceptible form,' such as the final enlightenment; as opposed to *usō no shitchi**. See also *shitchi*.

shohō no ~ **naru ri** 諸法の--なる理 'The principle that all

existing things are void and substanceless' and have no definable characteristics; the view of the Sanron* teaching. [Tai. 24.]

Musō 夢想 'An inspiration or oracle received in a dream.' [Tai. 3.]

Musō 夢窓 A Rinzai monk; his other name was Soseki 疎石; 1275–1351. After he was ordained at the age of nine, he extensively studied both exoteric and esoteric teachings. Later, he studied Zen* and finally received certification of his enlightenment experience. At the request of Emperor Godaigo, he dwelt at the Nanzenji, Kyoto. Later, he became the first patriarch of the Tenryūji, Kyoto, and also founded temples, such as the Shinnyo-ji and Saihōji. Emperor Kōmyō gave him the title of *kokushi** and called him Musō Shōgaku Shinshū Kokushi 夢窓正覺心宗 國師, 'the state master Musō of the Enlightened Heart school'. His works include the *Muchū-mondō-shū* 夢中問答集. [Tai. 24.]

Musōten 無想天 'Non-Thought Heaven'; Sk. Āsaṃjñika; one of the heavens in the realm of form (*shikikai**), where those who have accomplished the non-thought meditation (*musōjō* 無想定) are to be born. As all thoughts are extinguished, non-Buddhist practitioners of meditation often take this state of existence as Nirvana.

Mutsu no chimata 六の街 'Six streets'; refers to the six realms of existence (*rokudō**). [Tai. 6.]

Muyoshu 無餘修 'The exclusive practice (of the *nenbutsu**)'; one of the four practices in Pure Land Buddhism set forth in the *Ōjō-raisan**; cf. *shishu* 四修.

Muzan mugi 無慚無愧 'Unrepentant and unashamed (of some evil act done).' [Tai. 37.]

Myō 明 Abbr. of *myōshu** 明呪. [Tai. 18.]

Myō 冥 'Dark, darkness.' I. Spiritual darkness; ignorance. II. A dark state of existence; esp. the three lower realms (*sanmaku-dō**). III. An unseen divinity, such as a buddha or a god. IV. Agreeing or complying with, as in the compound *myōgō* 冥合 'perfect compliance or harmony'.

~ **no yaku** -の益 'Benefits afforded by unseen (beings, i.e. buddhas, bodhisattvas or gods).' [S. I–7.]

Myōden 妙典　See *myōten*.

Myōdo 冥土　See *meido*.

Myōdō 冥道　'Dark path.'　I. The world of the dead ruled by Yama (Enma*); also *myōkai** 冥界 and *meido** 冥土.　II. The world of deities unseen by men. [O. VI.]　III. Deities of the world of Yama; more generally, deities unseen by men. [K. 53; S. III–2; Tai. 39.]

Myōga 冥加　'The invisible protection and power' of a buddha, bodhisattva or other deity. [Tsu. 238.]

Myōga 冥伽　See 冥加. [S. VII–1.]

Myōge 妙解　'Excellent understanding.'

Myōgo 冥護　'Divine protection.' [K. 42.]

Myōgō 名號　'Name' of a buddha or deity.

~ renga --連歌　'A linked verse (beginning) with a sacred name'; a kind of religious linked verse, with each line containing the sacred name of a buddha or a bodhisattva, e.g. *namu amida butsu** 南無阿彌陀佛 and *namu kanzeon bosatsu** 南無觀世音菩薩. Such a verse was often composed as a *tsuizen** 追善 for a deceased person. Cf. *Amida renga*.

Myōgyō 妙行　'A wondrous practice.'

Myōhō 妙法　'The wondrous Dharma.'　I. The wondrous teaching of the Buddha.　II. Refers to the *Hoke-kyō**.

~-renge-kyō --蓮華經　*'The Sutra of the Lotus of the Wonderful Dharma'*; 7 fasc., tr. by Kumārajīva (Kumarajū*) in 406 [TT. 9, No. 262]; Sk. *Saddharma-puṇḍarīka-sūtra*; one of the most popular Mahayana sutras in China and Japan; the basis on which the Tendai* and Nichiren* sects were established. Often abbreviated to *Hoke-kyō**.

Myōjo 冥助　'Unseen help'; a help by unseen divinities. [S. Xa–8.]

Myōjō 妙定　'Excellent meditation.'

Myōju 明呪　See *myōshu*.

Myōkai 冥界　'The world of darkness'; the world of the dead ruled by Yama (Enma*); also pronounced *meikai*; cf. *myōdo* and *myōdō*.

Myōkan 冥官　'Officials of the world of darkness'; officials of the court of Yama (Enma*); cf. *Enna no chō* and *godō no* ∼. [K. 56, 72, 458; S. III–2; Tai. 26.]

Myōkan 冥鑒 '(A deity's) unseen watchfulness'; the same as *myōken** 冥見. [Tai. 27.]

Myōkanzatchi 妙觀察智 'The wisdom of wondrous observation'; Sk. *pratyavekṣaṇā-jñāna*; the wisdom of discerning the distinctive features of all phenomena; one of the four wisdoms (*shichi**) and the five wisdoms (*gochi**).

Myōken 名見 Short for *myōmon** 名聞 'fame' and *kenge** 見解 'viewing and understanding'. [S. IV–9.]

Myōken 妙見 'Wondrous seeing'; Sk. Sudṛṣṭi; the deification in female form of the Great Bear (*hokuto shichisei* 北斗七星). As the Great Bear is considered to be the most excellent of all constellations, she is also known as Sonjōō* 尊星王 'August Star Ruler'. The ritual dedicated to her is called *sonjōō no hō**.

Myōken 冥見 '(A deity's) unseen watchfulness.' [Tai. 21.]

Myōken 冥顯 'Unseen and manifested'; probably, unseen deities and their incarnations. [Tai. 24.]

Myōken 冥譴 'Unseen punishment'; punishment by a deity. [Tai. 17.]

Myōmoku 名目 I. 'Names and items' of doctrinal matters. [S. VI –17.] II. A collection of names and items of doctrinal matters of a particular sect, e.g. *Shichijūgohō-myōmoku* 七十五法名目 and *Shinshū-myōmoku* 眞宗名目.

Myōmoku 冥目 'Closing one's eyes', i.e. death. [S. II–5.]

Myōmon 名聞 'Fame, reputation.'

∼ **riyō** --利養 '(Seeking) fame and profit.'

Myōō 明王 Sk. *vidyā-rāja*; divinities who protect Buddhism, Buddhists and other people from harm; they often assume fierce appearances. See *godai-myōō*.

∼ **no baku** --の縛 Putting a spell on a man or spirit by the power of a *myōō* so that the man cannot move or the spirit is shown in its original form. [Hei. 3; Tai. 5.]

Myōō 冥應 'Unseen working'; said of the beneficial activity of unseen divine beings. [Tai. 5, 18, 20.]

Myōongakuten 妙音樂天　'God of Sweet Music'; another n. for Benzaiten*.

Myōonten 妙音天　'God of Sweet Sound'; abbr. of Myōongaku-ten*.　[K. 291.]

Myōraku 妙樂　See *Tannen*.　[Tai. 24.]

Myōri 名利　'Fame and wealth.'

～ **no kizuna** --の絆　'The bondage of fame and wealth.' [Tai. 12.]

Myōshiki 名色　'Name and form'; Sk. *nāma-rūpa*; one of the twelve causations (*jūni-innen**). *Myō* here refers to mental elements, such as perception and conception, and *shiki* to material elements; together they constitute the psycho-physiological elements of a human being; cf. *goun*.

Myōshōgon Ō 妙莊嚴王　'Wondrous Adorned King'; Sk. Śubha-vyūha; n. of a king mentioned in the *Hoke-kyō**, who aspired to enlightenment and became a bodhisattva named Ketoku 華德 (Padmaśrī). [Tai. 39.]

Myōshu 明呪　Sk. *vidyā*, 'a spell'.

Myōshu 冥衆　Also *myōju*; 'Unseen beings'; deities. [S. VI–18.]

Myōtai 妙體　'The mystic substance.' [S. I–3.]

Myōten 妙典　'The wondrous text'; here refers to the *Hoke-kyō**. [Tai. 11.]

Myōu 妙有　'Wondrous existence'; said of existence beyond or compatible with non-existence; cf. *shinkū*.

Myōun Nyorai 妙雲如來　'Wondrous Cloud Tathagata'; also Myōunsō Butsu 妙雲相佛 and Myōun-jizaiō Nyorai 妙雲自在王如來; the original state of a buddha from which Nāgārjuna (Ryūju*) appeared in this world. [Tai. 24.]

Myōyū 妙用　'Mystic and wondrous function or activity.' [S. I–3, Va–1.]

Myōzu 冥途　See *meido*.

N

Nachi sennichi no gyōja 那智千日の行者 'An ascetic who has finished the practice of (standing naked every day for) 1,000 days' under the Nachi Falls by the Nachi Shrine, Wakayama Prefecture. [K. 28.]

Nademono 撫物 'A stroking thing'; a paper doll or garment used in purification rites to stroke the subject and thus to transfer to it his defilement or sins. [Tai. 6.]

Naiga 内我 'Internal self'; an ego which is falsely recognized and clung to. [S. IV–9.]

Naige hachikai 内外八海 'The eight inner and outer seas'; according to Buddhist cosmology, there are eight seas, or rather belts of water, surrounding Mt. Sumeru (Shumisen*) and lying between mountain-ranges. [Tai. 37.]

Naigu 内供 Also 内宮; 'serving at the inner palace'; abbr. of *naigubu* 内供奉; also *gubu* 供奉; a priest who serves in the Buddhist hall of the imperial palace. Cf. *ushiki*. [Ma. 170.]

Naigubu 内供奉 See *naigu*.

Naiin 内院 'Inner palace'; refers to the inner palace of the Tuṣita Heaven (Tosotsuten*) where Miroku* lives.

~ **no jōshō** --の上生 'Rebirth in the inner palace' of the Tuṣita Heaven. [S. II–8.]

~ **no ōjō** --の往生 'Rebirth in the inner palace' of the Tuṣita Heaven. [S. II–8.]

Naijin 内陣 'The inner sanctum' of a temple; cf. *gejin*.

Naikai gekai 内海外海 'The inner seas and an outer sea'; the seven inner seas and the outer sea which surround Mt. Sumeru (Shumisen*); cf. *shikai*. [Tai. 10, 12.]

Naikan reinen 內鑑冷然 'Inner contemplation is cool'; said of the deep meditation of a buddha or bodhisattva in which reality is perceived in the mind as it is. [S. IV–1.]

Naikū 內空 'Internal void'; Sk. *adhyātma-śūnyatā*; the void of ego; one of the eighteen kinds of void (*jūhachikū**). [S. IV–9.]

Nairi 泥梨 Sk. *niraya*; hell. [S. II–5, VI–10; Tai. 11.]

Naishō 內證 'Inner realization'; realization of the truth, enlightenment.

Naiten 內典 Also *naiden*; 'inner scriptures'; Buddhist scriptures; cf. *geten*. [S. III–1; Tai. 35.]

Namu 南無 Also *namo*; Sk. *namas*; 'adoration to, homage to'; hence, 'I take refuge in'.

~ **Amidabutsu** --阿彌陀佛 'Taking refuge in Amida* Buddha'; recitation of this is popularly practised as the *nenbutsu** in Pure Land Buddhism. [K. 550; S. II–3.]

~ **Budda** (=**Butsuda**) --佛陀 'Homage to the Buddha.' [S. II–9.]

~ **Budda sanbō** --佛陀三寶 'Homage to the Buddha and the Three Treasures.' [S. Xb–3.]

~ **Butsu** --佛 'Homage to the Buddha.' [K. 35.]

~ **Daihi Kannon** --大悲觀音 'Homage to Kannon of the Great Compassion'; an incantation as a prayer to Kannon* for help and protection. [S. Xa–1.]

~ **Kanzeon Bosatsu** --觀世音菩薩 'Homage to Kannon Bodhisattva'; an invocation to Kannon*.

~ **Miroku Bosatsu** --彌勒菩薩 'Homage to Maitreya Bodhisattva.' [K. 64.]

~ **sanze no shobutsu** --三世の諸佛 'Homage to all buddhas of the three periods (i.e. past, present and future).' [S. IX–13.]

~ **wakō zenjin** --和光善神 'Homage to good deities who are incarnations (of buddhas and bodhisattvas).' [S. Xb–3.]

Nanbu 南浮 Abbr. of Nan'enbudai*. [S. II–7, III–3, Va–3.]

Nan'enbudai 南閻浮提 'The southern (continent), Jambūdvīpa'; also Nan'enbushū 南閻浮州, Nansenbushū 南贍部州 and, simply, Enbudai*; one of the four continents (*shishū**); the triangular continent lying in the ocean to the south of Mt. Sumeru (Shumisen*). [S. VIII–22; Tai. 18.]

Nangaku 南嶽 See *Eshi*. [Tai. 24.]

~ **Daishi** --大師 'The Great Master Nan-yüeh'; a popular name for Eshi*. [S. Va–1, VI–10.]

Nange nannyū no mon 難解難入の門 'The (teaching-)gate difficult to understand and difficult to enter'; refers to the path of sages (*shōdōmon**). [K. 63.]

Nango 軟語 'Soft (and tender) words.' [S. Pref., Va–12.]

Nangyō kugyō 難行苦行 'Difficult and painful practices'; ascetic practices. [K. 57.]

Nani-amidabutsu 何阿彌陀佛 'So-and-so Amidabutsu'; a Buddhist name consisting of a character affixed to Amidabutsu. The practice of using such a Buddhist name became popular at the beginning of the Kamakura period (1192–1333) when Chōgen 重源 of the Tōdaiji* called himself 'Namu-amidabutsu'* and gave his disciples such names as 'Kū-amidabutsu' and 'Hō-amidabutsu'. [Tsu. 89.]

Nankyō no hōshi 南京の法師 'Priests of the Southern Capital (i.e. Nara).' [O. V.]

Nansenbushū 南瞻部州 'The Jambū continent in the south'; also Nan'enbushū 南閻浮州, Nan'enbudai* 南閻浮提 and, simply, Enbudai*. [Tai. 12, 18.]

Nanshū 南州 'The southern continent'; refers to Nan'enbudai*, one of the four continents (*shishū**).

Nanto 南都 'The southern capital'; Nara.

~ **hokurei** --北嶺 'The southern capital and the northern mountain'; Nara and Mt. Hiei; temples in Nara and the Enryakuji* on Mt. Hiei. [Tai. 1.]

~ **no shichidaiji** --の七大寺 'The seven big temples in the Southern Capital.' They are: Tōdaiji* 東大寺, Saidaiji 西大寺, Hōryūji 法隆寺, Yakushiji* 藥師寺, Daianji 大安寺, Gangōji 元興寺, and Kōfukuji* 興福寺. [Hei. 2.]

Nanuka nanuka no kinichi 七七の忌日 'Weekly memorial days (for a dead person)'; weekly memorial services are observed for the *chūin** period of seven weeks. [Tai. 20.]

Nanzan Daishi 南山大師 'The Great Master of Nan-shan'; refers to Dōsen*; this title derives from the place where he lived, i.e. Mt. Chung-nan 終南 (Shūnan). [S. IV–9, VI–18, Xb–1.]

Naraen 那羅延 Sk. Nārāyaṇa; see *Naraen Kongō*. [Tai. 18.]

~ **Kongō** ---金剛 'Nārāyaṇa Kongō god'; a divinity who is extremely strong and protects Buddhism. As one of the pair of Kongō gods often found at the entrance to a temple, he is placed on the right-hand side; cf. *kongōjin* and *niō*.

Nara hōshi 奈良法師 'Monks in Nara'; refers to the monks of the Kōfukuji*, Nara, who, like the monks of Mt. Hiei, often made unreasonable demands on the court and went on the rampage if they were not granted. [S. IX–4.]

Naraka 奈落伽 Also 捺落迦, 那羅柯; Sk. *naraka*; 'hell'; often abbreviated as *naraku* 奈落. [Tai. 18.]

Naraku 奈落 Sk. *naraka*; hell.

Nari hachiman no soko 奈利八萬の底 '(To) the bottom of hell which is 80,000 (*yojana* or *yujun** wide).' [Tai. 11.]

Nehan 涅槃 Sk. *nirvāṇa*. I. The final goal of Buddhist aspiration and practice, where evil passions are extinguished and the highest wisdom attained. II. Refers to *Nehan-gyō**.

~**-dō** --堂 'A Nirvana hall'; also *enjudō** 延壽堂, *anrakudō* 安樂堂, etc.; a room for sick monks; also, a crematorium.

~**-dōri no zen** --堂裏の禪 'Zen* meditation in a Nirvana hall'; practising Zen meditation as diligently as if death is imminent; see *nehandō*. [S. Xb–3.]

~**-e** --會 'Nirvana festival'; the festival held on the 15th of the second month in commemoration of the death of the Buddha. [K. 71; Tsu. 220.]

~**-gyō** --經 'The *Nirvana Sutra*'; abbr. of *Daihatsu-nehan-gyō**. [S. II–9.]

~ **no miyako** --の都 'The capital of Nirvana.' [S. Pref.]

Nen 念 I. To recall, remember. II. To think intently, fix one's thought. III. Thought. IV. A thought-moment; a moment.

Nenbutsu 念佛 'Thought of the Buddha.' I. Meditation on the Buddha. II. Recitation of Amida's* name, i.e. to say '*Namu Amidabutsu**' 南無阿彌陀佛, which means 'Homage to Amida Buddha'. III. Refers to Nenbutsu-shū* 念佛宗, the Nenbutsu sects, i.e. the Pure Land sects, such as Jōdo-shū,* Jōdoshin-shū* and Yūzū-nenbutsu-shū*; it particularly refers to the Jōdo sect.

~-chō --帳 The register listing the names of persons who joined the group to practise the *Yūzū Nenbutsu*. [K. 53.]

~ kechien no shu --結縁の衆 'People associated with the *nenbutsu*'; those who practise the *nenbutsu*. [K. 53.]

~-mon --門 'The *nenbutsu* gate'; the *nenbutsu* teaching. [S. I–10, II–8.]

~ no ekō --の廻向 The passage chanted after the recitation of the *nenbutsu**. It is from the *Kan-muryōju-kyō** and reads: 光明遍照十方世界念佛衆生攝取不捨 'Amida's* light shines universally over the worlds of the ten directions, embracing and not forsaking the beings who practise the *nenbutsu*'. [Ma. 263.]

~ no gyōja --の行者 'The *nenbutsu* practitioner'; a follower of Pure Land teaching, who practises the *nenbutsu*. [S. IV–1.]

~ no kō --の功 'The merit of the *nenbutsu* practice.' [Hei. 3; K. 423.]

~ ōjō --往生 'Birth (in Amida's* Pure Land) through the practice of the *nenbutsu*.' [IH.; K. 63.]

~-sha --者 'A *nenbutsu* practitioner.' [K. 550; S. I–10, VIII–10.]

~-shu --衆 'A *nenbutsu* practitioner'; probably, a follower of the Ji* sect. [Tai. 29.]

~-shū --宗 'The Nenbutsu sects'; Pure Land sects, such as Jōdo* and Jōdoshin*, founded on the teaching of the *nenbutsu* and birth in Amida's* land through it. [IH.; S. I–10, VI–10.]

~ shuzen no kō --衆善の功 'The merit of practising the *nenbutsn* and other good acts.' [S. II–5.]

~-zanmai --三昧 'The *nenbutsu samādhi*'; the concentrated practice of reciting the *nenbutsu* whereby the aspirant attains unity with Amida* Buddha. [K. 47, 49; Tai. 22.]

Nenge mishō 拈華微笑 'Lifting the flower and smiling.' Once, when the Buddha was with a congregation on the Vulture Peak (*Ryōjusen**), he lifted a bouquet of flowers offered to him by a god. Nobody understood the meaning except Mahākāśyapa (*Makakashō**), who indicated his understanding by smiling. The Buddha then proclaimed that he would transmit to him the essence of Buddhism. This is the origin of **Zen*** Buddhism. [S. IV–1.]

Nenge shunmoku 拈華瞬目 'Lifting the flower and winking'; see *nenge mishō*. [Tai. 24.]

Nenju 念珠 Also *nenzu*; 'thought beads'; a rosary; so called because one thinks of a buddha, esp. Amida*, and calls his name as one tells the beads; the same as *juzu**. [Tai. 24.]

Nenju 念誦 'To think and recite'; to think intently of a buddha, etc., and recite a sutra, spell, or a buddha's name. [S. I–4, etc.]

Nenki 年忌☆ 'The anniversary of one's death.'

Nenkō 拈香 'To pick out incense'; to offer incense; the same as *shōkō** 燒香.

Nennen 念念 'Every thought-moment.' I. Every moment. II. Every thought; continuous thought, e.g. of Amida*.

Nenryo 念慮 '(Delusory) thought and consideration.' [S. Vb–9.]

Nentō 燃燈 Sk. Dīpaṅkara, 'light-causer'; n. of a buddha of the past. [S. III–1.]

Nenzu 念珠 See *nenju*.

∼-hiki --引 Also 念珠挽; 'one who makes rosaries.' [K. 428.]

Nibusshō 二佛性 'The two kinds of buddha-nature' established in the Hossō* sect, namely, *ribusshō** 理佛性 and *gyōbusshō** 行佛性.

Nibutsu chūgen no daidōshi 二佛中間の大導師 'A great teacher (who appears in the world) between the two buddhas (i.e. the Buddha Shakamuni* and the future Buddha Miroku*)'; refers to Jizō*. [Tai. 18.]

Nichiren 日蓮 The founder of the Nichiren sect (1222–1282). Born in an obscure fishing village in Awa Province (the present Chiba Prefecture), he entered the priesthood at 12. He received proper ordination at 18 and was named Renchō 蓮長. After studying various Buddhist teachings which were practised at the time, he came to the conclusion that they were not the right teachings for salvation in the period of the last Dharma (*mappō**) and that recitation of the title of the *Hoke-kyō**, '*Namu Myōhō-renge-kyō*' (lit. 'Homage to the *Sutra of the Lotus of the Wonderful Dharma*'), was the only effective method of salvation. In 1253, he returned to his home town and began to preach the teaching. It was then that he changed his name to Nichiren. In 1260, he wrote the *Risshō-ankoku-ron* 立正安國論 '*Establishing the Right (Teaching) and Securing the Peace of the State*' and presented it to the then *shikken* (執權, Regent and first minister of the Shōgun of Kamakura), Hōjō Tokiyori 北條時賴. Angered by Nichiren's radical views and criticism of the Kamakura government, Tokiyori exiled him to Izu Peninsula. After he was pardoned in 1263, he returned to Kamakura and resumed his attack on the government and on other sects, which nearly brought him to execution in 1271. He was eventually exiled to Sado Island, where he spent 11 years. After this exile, he settled on Mt. Minobu 身延 in Kai Province (Yamanashi Prefecture), and spent the rest of his life there writing and teaching his disciples, until his illness forced him to leave the mountain. He died in Ikegami 池上 in Musashi Province (Tokyo). He was given the posthumous name and title, Risshō Daishi 立正大師, by Emperor Taishō. His works amounted to more than 400, and his teaching was spread by the 'six elders' (*rokurōsō* 六老僧) and other disciples.

Nidana 尼陀那   Sk. *nidāna*; translated as *innen** 因緣 'happenings in the past' and *engi* 緣起 'a story showing the origin of something'; narratives of happenings in the past which explain the present state of a person or thing; one of the nine and the twelve kinds of scriptures (*kubu-kyō** and *jūnibu-kyō**).

Niga byakudō 二河白道   'Two rivers and a white path'; a parable which appears in the *Sanzen-gi**, by Shan-tao (Zendō*), and illustrates how an aspirant to the Pure Land awakens to a faith in Amida* and attains birth in his land, as follows: a man is travelling to the west. In the wilderness he is pursued by bandits and fierce animals and comes to a place where two rivers meet: one is a river of fire which flows to the south and the other, a river of water which flows to the north. These two rivers are 100 paces wide but endlessly long. Where they meet, there is a narrow white path about five inches wide, leading to the west bank. As fire is raging on one side and water is splashing on the path from the other, he hesitates to take the path, but since death otherwise appears inevitable, he thinks of doing so. Just then he hears a voice from the eastern bank, urging him to go forward across the path, and another voice from the western bank, urging him on. Encouraged by these voices, he proceeds determinedly along the path and soon reaches the western bank, where he enjoys all pleasures. The river of fire represents anger, and that of water, greed. The white path symbolizes the slim possibility of awakening faith in a mind full of evil passions. The voice from the eastern bank is the teaching of Shakamuni*, and that from the western bank, the summons of Amida. The western bank represents the Pure Land. [Tai. 38.]

Nihonkoku-genpō-zenmaku-ryōiki 日本國現報善惡靈異記 'Miraculous stories told in Japan concerning the retributions for good and evil acts in the present life', 3fasc., compiled by Kyōkai 景戒, early 9th century; also known as *Nihon-ryōiki*.

Nijō 二乘 'The two vehicles.' I. The two kinds of teaching applicable to shravakas (*shōmon**) and pratyekabuddhas (*engaku**). II. The two kinds of Buddhist practitioners mentioned in (I).

Nijūgo-bosatsu 二十五菩薩 'The 25 bodhisattvas' mentioned in the *Jūōjō-kyō* 十往生經, who protect aspirants to Amida's* Pure Land: Kanzeon* 觀世音, Daiseishi* 大勢至, Yakuō* 藥王, Yakujō 藥上, Fugen* 普賢, Hōjizaiō 法自在王, Shishiku 師子吼, Darani 陀羅尼, Kokūzō* 虛空藏, Tokuzō 德藏, Hōzō 寶藏, Konzō 金藏, Kongōzō 金剛藏, Kōmyōō 光明王, Sankaie 山海慧, Kegon'ō 華嚴王, Shuboō 衆寶王, Gakkōō 月光王, Nisshōō 日照王, Sanmaiō 三昧王, Jōjizaiō 定自在王, Daijizaiō 大自在王, Byakuzōō 白象王, Daiitokuō 大威德王, and Muhenshin 無邊身. The passage of the sutra concerned appears in Shan-tao's 善導 (Zendō*) *Kannenbōmon* 觀念法門 and is quoted in Genshin's *Ōjōyōshū**. This contributed to the popularity of the 25 bodhisattvas in Japan. It has been widely believed that they come to welcome aspirants to the Pure Land when they die.

Nijūgo no enzū 二十五の圓通 'The 25 methods of attaining perfect penetration' presented in the *Shuryōgon-gyō**. They pertain to specific sense-organs, objects of perceptions, consciousnesses and elements, and are the actual methods whereby particular bodhisattvas and shravakas (*shōmon**) attained perfect penetration into reality (*enzū**). [S. Vb–10.]

Nijūgo-u 二十五有 'The 25 states of existence' to which unenlightened sentient beings are subject. They are: hell; the realms of hungry spirits, animals and *asuras* (*ashura**); the four continents (*shishū**) inhabited by human beings; the Heaven of the Four Guardian Kings (Shiōten*); Tōriten*; Yamaten*; Tosotsuten*; Kerakuten*; Takejizaiten*; Shozenten*; Daibonten*; Nizenten*; Sanzenten*; Shizenten*; Musōten*; Anagonten*; Kūmuhenjo*; Shikimuhenjo*; Mushousho*; and Hisōhihisōjo*. The first 14, from hell to Takejizaiten, belong to the realm of desire (*yokkai**), the next seven, to the realm of form (*shikikai**), and the last four, to the realm of non-form (*mushikikai**); cf. *nijūku-u*.

Nijūhachibu-shu 二十八部衆 'The 28 attendant deities' of Senju Kannon*; it is believed that they protect those who recite his dharani, i.e. *Senju darani**. [Tai. 16, 36.]

Nijūku-u 二十九有 'The 29 states of existence' where unenlightened sentient beings transmigrate. They are the 25 states of existence (*nijūgo-u**), with Anagonten* further divided into five realms.

Nikkei 肉髻 'Fleshy protuberance'; the protuberance on the head of the Buddha; Sk. *uṣṇīṣa*; also *butchō** 佛頂; one of the 32 physical characteristics of the Buddha.

Nikkō 日光 'The sunlight'; n. of a bodhisattva; Sk. Sūryaprabha; one of the two attendants of Yakushi* Buddha, the other being Gakkō*. [Tai. 3, 9, 18.]

Nikon 耳根 'Ear-organ'; the ear.

~ **tokudō no bosatsu** --得道の菩薩 'A bodhisattva who has attained enlightenment by his (sharp) ears.' [S. II–4.]

Ninbō 人法 I. 'Persons and things' in general; the ego and things or elements; here *hō** (Sk. *dharma*) means things in general. II. Living beings and the Buddha's teaching or Buddhist principle; here *hō* means truth or the Buddha's teaching. III. Rules of human conduct; human affairs; secular matters.

Ninchū tenjō 人中天上 'Among human beings or in the heavenly realm above.' [K. 72.]

Ninden 人天 'Human and heavenly beings.'

~ **no shi** --の師 'A teacher of human and heavenly beings'; cf. *tenninshi* 天人師 under *jūgō*. [S. VI–16·]

Ninga 人我 'Selfhood, ego.'

～ **muri** - - 無理 'The principle of egolessness'; the Buddhist principle that there is no permanent self in a living being. [Tai. 24.]

～ **musō** - - 無相 'Formlessness of ego'; ego is a temporary existence devoid of solid substance or permanent entity. [Tai. 24.]

～ **no sō** - - の相 I. The view that an eternally abiding ego exists in oneself. II. Attachment to one's self. [Tsu. 107.]

Ninjin 人身 'Human body'; human existence.

Ninku 人工 'A labourer'; the same as *ninpu* 人夫; a workman at a Zen* temple. [Tai. 39, 40.]

Ninniku 忍辱 'Forbearance, patience.'

～**-e** - - 衣 See *ninniku no koromo*.

～ **no koromo** - - の衣 'A robe of patience'; as the virtue of patience protects one from all kinds of harm, it is compared to a robe; later, this term (also *ninniku-e* 忍辱衣) became a general name for the Buddhist robes. [Tai. 8, 17.]

Ninnō-e 仁王會 'The Benevolent Kings ceremony'; the ceremony based on the *Ninnō-kyō**, in which 100 seats are provided for 100 priests who are invited to lecture on the sutra. The ceremony is believed to be effective in stopping calamities which are befalling the state. The first instance of the ceremony in Japan was in 660, when Empress Saimei had it performed in the court. Later, in 693, Empress Jitō made the *Ninnō-e* one of the annual ceremonies. [Tai. 24.]

Ninnō-gokoku-hannya-haramitta-kyō 仁王護國般若波羅蜜多經 '*The State-protecting Prajñāpāramitā Sutra*'; see *Ninnō-kyō*.

Ninnō-hannya 仁王般若 Also ～*-bannya*; see *Ninnō-kyō*.

Ninnō-kō 仁王講 'The Ninnō lecture-meeting'; a meeting for listening to a lecture on the *Ninnō-kyō**. [K. 33.]

Ninnō-kyō 仁王經 '*The Benevolent Kings Sutra*'; there are two Chinese versions: (1) *Bussetsu-ninnō-hannya-haramitsu-kyō* 佛說仁王般若波羅蜜經, 2 fasc., tr. by Kumārajīva (Kumarajū*) [TT. 8, No. 245] and (2) *Ninnō-gokoku-hannya-haramitta-kyō* 仁王護國般若波羅蜜多經, 2 fasc., tr. by Amoghavajra (Fukū*) [TT. 8, No. 246]. The sutra was preached by the Buddha to the kings of the

16 kingdoms. It states in it that there will be no calamities in the state if the sutra is chanted and expounded. One of the three state-protecting sutras (*gokoku sanbukyō**). The *Ninnō-e** ceremony based on the sutra dates from 660.

Ninshi 人師 I. 'A human teacher'; an ordinary man who teaches others Buddhism. [S. I–10.] II. 'A teacher of men'; a virtuous teacher. [S. Va–2.]

Ninshin 人身 See *ninjin*.

Nin'un 任運 'Naturalness, spontaneity.'

～-ni --に 'Naturally, spontaneously.'

Niō 二王 See *niō* 仁王. [Tai. 9.]

Niō 仁王 Also 二王, 'two kings'; a pair of Kongō gods (*kongō jin**) who protect Buddhism. They are popularly identified as Misshaku* and Naraen*, and their statues are often found at the entrance to a temple.

Nirenzenga 尼連禪河 'River Nairañjanā'; the river which flows near Buddhagayā. The Buddha bathed there after ascetic practices and then proceeded to the Bodhi-tree (*bodaiju**), under which he attained enlightenment.

Niriki 二力 'Two powers'; *jiriki** 自力 (one's own power) and *tariki** 他力 (other-power). [S. II–8.]

Nisai 二際 'The two realms'; the realms of transmigration and the realm of Nirvana.

Nise 二世 'The two worlds'; this world and the next.

～ **no riyaku** --の利益 'The benefit in the two worlds'; i.e. in this world and in the world after death. [S. II–3, 7.]

Nishidan 尼師壇 Sk. *niṣīdana*; also *nishidanna* 尼師壇那; a rug or mat for sitting or lying on. [Tai. 24.]

Nishin 二身 'The two (kinds of buddha) bodies.' I. *Hosshin** 法身 'Dharma-body' and *shōjin** 生身 'live body'; the quintessence-body and accommodative body. Synonyms of these two terms are respectively: *jōshin* 常身 'immutable body' and *mujōshin* 無常身 'transient body'; *musōgōshin* 無相好身 'body without physical characteristics of excellence' and *sōgōshin* 相好身 'body with physical characteristics of excellence'; *hosshin* 法身 'Dharma-body' and *shikishin** 色身 'material body'; *hosshōshin* 法性身

'Dharma-nature body' and *bumoshōjin* 父母生身 'body born from parents'; *hosshō-hosshin* 法性法身 'Dharma-nature Dharma-body' and *zuisekenshin* 隨世間身 'homogeneous body' (lit. 'body conforming to the people of the world').   II. The two aspects of the Buddha Shakamuni*: his physical body (*shōjin* 生身) and his meritorious qualities (*hosshin* 法身) (see *gobun hosshin* 五分法身). III. *Hosshō-hosshin* 法性法身 'Dharma-nature Dharma-body' and *hōben-hosshin* 方便法身 'Expediency Dharma-body'. In the three-body classification (*sanshin** 三身), the former corresponds to *hosshin* 法身 and the latter to *hōjin** 報身 and *ōjin** 應身 or *keshin** 化身. IV. According to T'an-luan 曇鸞 (Donran*), *jissōshin* 實相身 'reality body' and *imotsushin* 爲物身 'body for the benefit of sentient beings'. The latter corresponds to *hōben-hosshin* 方便法身 above.   V. *Bundanshin* 分段身, the body of an ordinary being which undergoes cycles of birth and death, and *hen'yakushin* 變易身, the body of an enlightened sage who can create his body at will in the realm of transmigration.

Nishō 二障 'The two hindrances'; *bonnōshō** 煩惱障, evil passions which hinder the realization of Nirvana, and *shochishō** 所知障, a hindrance to the correct knowledge of objects and to the realization of enlightenment.

Nishu no sō 二取の相 'The appearance of twofold grasping'; the appearance or manifestation of 'the grasping' and 'the grasped', i.e. the subjective perceiving function of one's consciousness and the objects perceived. Cf. *nōshu shoshu*. [S. III–1.]

Nishu-sōmotsu 二種僧物 'The two kinds of things belonging to monks': (1) *genzensō-motsu* 現前僧物, things belonging to the monks of a specific temple, e.g. clothes and food donated to the monks by adherents of the temple; and (2) *shihōsō-motsu* 四方僧物, things to be used by monks from any temple, e.g. temple living-quarters for monks and provisions.

Nisshitsu 入室 'To enter the room'; to become a disciple.

Nitai 二諦 'The twofold truth or reality'; absolute truth and conventional truth; see *shinzoku* I. [S. Va–6, Xb–2.]

Niten no ka 二轉の果 'The result of the twofold turning'; refers to buddhahood which has two aspects, Nirvana and enlightenment (Bodhi or *bodai**). Nirvana is the result of destroying evil passions (*bonnōshō**), and enlightenment the result of removing hindrances to the correct knowledge of objects (*shochishō**); cf. *tenne*.

Nizenten 二禪天 'The Second Meditation Heaven'; one of the heavens in the realm of form (*shikikai**).

Nochi no yo 後の世 I. 'The after-life.' [Tsu. 4, 175.] II. Birth in Amida's* land after death. [Tsu. 58.] Cf. *gose*.

Nōen shoen 能緣所緣 'Objectifying and the objectified'; the subjective perceiving function of consciousness and the object perceived. *En* 'condition' here means 'to have something as an object'; hence, 'objectify' or 'perceive'. [S. III–1.]

Nōjo 能所 'Active and passive (elements)'; subject and object.

Nōke 能化 'One who is able to convert and teach'; a teacher'; the opposite of *shoke* 所化 'one who is converted, a pupil'; cf. *rokudō nōke no Jizō Satta*. [S. I–3, II–4, 5; Tai. 20.]

Nōnen shonen 能念所念 'Thinking and that which is thought; remembering and the object remembered. [S. Xb–3.]

Nōshu shoshu 能取所取 'The grasping and the grasped'; the perceptive function of consciousness and the objects perceived. [S. III–1.]

Nyo 如 'Thusness'; the state of things as they are; the ultimate reality; one of the synonyms of *shinnyo** and *hosshō**. [S. IV–1.]

Nyohō 如法 'In accordance with the law' or the prescribed method.

~-kyō --經 '(Copying of) a sutra according to the law'; said exclusively of copying the *Hoke-kyō**. In Tendai* a special service is held after the copying is completed. [K. 5, 600, 698; S. Xb–2.]

~-kyō-zuka --經塚 'A mound containing a copy of the *Hoke-kyō**.' [Tai. 31.]

~-ni --に 'In accordance with the law or the prescribed rite or method.' [O. II; S. II–7.]

~ no biku --の比丘 The same as *nyohō no sō**. [S. IV–1, VI–18.]

~ no dōshin --の道心 'Aspiration to enlightenment in accordance with the law.' [S. Xb–3.]

~ no ehatsu --の衣鉢 'Robes and a bowl, as prescribed by the law.' [S. VI–18.]

~ no jiritsu --の持律 'The observance of precepts (as strictly) as prescribed.' [S. IV–1.]

~ **no kesa** --の袈裟 'A prescribed robe'; the authentic Buddhist robe. [S. VI–18.]

~ **no sō** --の僧 'A monk (who practises) in accordance with the law.' [S. III–3, VI–9.]

~ **nyosetsu no gongyō** --如說の勤行 'The service performed in compliance with the law and the prescribed rules.' [Tai. 11.]

~ **shugyō no shōnin** --修行の上人 'A revered priest who practises in accordance with the law.' [S. II–8.]

~ **shukke no en** --出家の縁 'An indirect cause for entering the priesthood in compliance with the authentic Buddhist teaching.' [S. II–10.]

Nyoi 如意 I. According to one's wishes; at will. II. A kind of sceptre held in the hand of a monk when he gives a sermon or lecture or officiates at a service. [Tai. 24.] III. Refers to *nyoihōshu**.

Nyoihōshu 如意寶珠 Also *nyoihōju*; Sk. *cintā-maṇi* or simply *maṇi*; a wish-fulfilling gem. Cf. *mani*. [K. 52.]

~**-hō** ----法 'Rite of the wish-fulfilling gem'; also, simply, *hōshuhō** 寶珠法. An esoteric ritual performed with the wish-fulfilling gem, which represents the Buddha's relics, as the main object of worship.

Nyōin 女院 Also *nyoin*; a respectful title given to an empress dowager or grand empress dowager who has shaved her head and taken the title of *mon'in* 門院. [Tsu. 156.]

Nyoirin 如意輪 Refers to Nyoirin Kannon*. [Ma. 199; Tai. 11, 18, 24.]

~ **Kannon** ---觀音 'Kannon (fulfilling people's wishes) with a wish-fulfilling gem (*nyoihōshu** 如意寶珠) and a wheel (*hōrin* 寶輪)'; one of the six kinds of Kannon (*rokkannon**). [S. II–8.]

~ **no henge** ---の反化 'A transformation of Nyoirin Kannon*.' [Tai. 24.]

Nyojitsu no gyō 如實の行 'The practice which complies with the Dharma and reality.' [S. III–3.]

Nyonin kekkai 女人結界 See *kekkai*.

Nyonyo 如如 I. 'Suchness, thusness'; one of the synonyms of *shinnyo** 眞如 and *hosshō** 法性. II. 'Being in the state of thusness or suchness'; being as it is. [S. Va–6.]

~ **no butsu** --の佛 'Buddha in the suchness state of things'; the same as *hosshin** 法身. [S. Vb–11.]

Nyorai 如來 Sk. *tathāgata*, 'thus-come'; popularly construed as 'one who has come from thusness'; an epithet for a buddha.

~**-bai** --唄 'Verses (intoned in praise) of the Tathagata'; the two 4-line hymns praising the virtue of the Buddha, which come from the *Shōman-gyō**. It is chanted at the beginning of a service. [Tai. 11.]

~ **jōjū muu hen'yaku** --常住無有變易 'The Tathagata eternally resides and is not subject to change'; the phrase comes from the *Nehan-gyō**. [Tai. 18.]

~ **kajiriki** --加持力 'The power endowed (to the practitioner) by the Tathagata'; one of the three powers; see *sanriki*. [S. II–8.]

~**-zō** --藏 Sk. *tathāgata-garbha*; 'Tathagata-matrix'; the buddhahood in a living being. [S. I–3, IV–1.]

Nyosetsu no gyō 如說の行 'Practices as prescribed.' [S. III–4.]

Nyosetsu (no) shugyō 如說(の)修行 'Practices as prescribed.' [S. IV –1, Xa–8, Xb–3.]

Nyū 入 Refers to *jūni-sho**. [S. V–1.]

Nyūdō 入道 Lit. 'entering the Way'; one who has shaved his head and entered the Buddhist Way; he wears a Buddhist robe but continues to live in his own home.

Nyūjō 入定 'Entering into *samādhi* or meditation.'

~ **no goten** --の御殿 'The hall or sanctuary where (Kūkai*) entered into meditation.' [IH.]

Nyūjū genmon 入重玄門 'Entering again the mysterious gate'; refers to the highest stage of a bodhisattva, known as *tōgaku** 等覺, because he then repeats all the practices he has performed in his lower stages before proceeding to the stage of a buddha. [Hei. 2.]

~ **no daiji** ----の大士 'A great being (i.e. bodhisattva), who enters again the mysterious gate'; a bodhisattva of the highest stage. [Hei. 2.]

Nyūkan 入觀 Pronounced *nikkan*; 'entering into meditation'. [K. 64.]

Nyūmetsu 入滅 'Passing into Nirvana'; the passing away of a buddha or revered priest.

~ **no gi** --の儀 'The manner of dying'; the posture to be assumed at the time of death. [K. 64.]

Nyūnan 柔軟 'Soft'; tender, kind-hearted.

Nyūnango 柔軟語 'Soft, tender words.' [K. 721.]

Nyūwa 柔和 'Gentle and kind-hearted.' [Tai. 18.]

~ **ninniku** --忍辱 'Gentle and patient.' [Tai. 12, 26.]

O

Oai no kokoro 惡愛の心 'Disliking and liking.' [S. IV–9.]

Obutsumyō 御佛名 See *onbutsumyō*.

Ōge 應化 See *ōke*.

Ōgen 應現 'A corresponding manifestation (of an incarnation)'; that is, one which corresponds to the needs of living beings.

Ōgon 誑言 'Lies.' [S. II–6.]

Ōgu 應供 'Worthy of an offering'; Sk. *arhat*; see *arakan*.

Oinori no shi 御祈の師 See *kitōsō*. [O. II.]

Ōjin 應身 'Corresponding body'; Sk. *nirmāṇakāya*; a body of a buddha manifested to correspond to the different needs and capacities of living beings. Cf. *sanshin*, *shishin* and *shinshin*. [S. II–4, Va–12, Xb–3.]

Ōjō 往生 'Birth' in a buddha or bodhisattva's land, especially Amida's* Pure Land.

~ **Anraku** --安樂 'Birth in (the Land of) Peace and Bliss'; see *Anraku*. [Tai. 18.]

~ **Gokuraku** --極樂 'Birth in the Land of Utmost Bliss (of

Amida* Buddha)'; see *Gokuraku*. [IH.; Ma. 63; Tai. 11.]

~ **Jōdo** --浄土 'Birth in the Pure Land'; see *jōdo*. [S. Xa–1.]

~**-jūin** --十因 '*The Ten Reasons for Birth*', 1 fasc., by Yōkan* 永觀 of the Zenrinji 禪林寺, Kyoto [TT. 84, No. 2683]. The work explains, by giving ten reasons, that the *nenbutsu** is sufficient cause for birth in Amida's* Pure Land.

~**-kō** --講 'A prayer-meeting for birth'; a meeting for practising the *nenbutsu** in order to attain birth in Amida's* Pure Land. [S. IV–7.]

~**-kōshiki** --講式 '*The Order of Service for Birth*'; 1 fasc., by Yōkan* 永觀; also *Amida-kōshiki** 阿彌陀講式 '*The Order of Service in Praise of Amida*'. This work explains the order of service devoted to Amida* which was held on the 15th of the month; cf. *Amida-kō*.

~**-nin** --人 'One who has been born' in Amida's* Pure Land. [O. VI.]

~ **no daiji** --の大事 'The important matter of (how to attain) birth (in Amida's* Pure Land).' [S. IV–8.]

~ **no gegyō** --の解行 'The understanding of and practice for attaining birth in the Pure Land. [IH.]

~ **no go** --の期 'Time to go to the Pure Land.' [K. 212.]

~ **no gō** --の業 'The act which serves as the cause for birth (in Amida's* land).' [IH.; K. 56.]

~ **no gōin** --之業因 'The act which serves as the cause for birth (in Amida's* land).' [K. 53.]

~ **no sokai** --の素懷 'Long-cherished desire for birth (in Amida's* land).' [Hei. 1; K. 53, 197.]

~ **no zuisō** --の瑞相 'Extraordinary, auspicious phenomena attending one's birth' in Amida's* land, such as a purple cloud hanging low at the time of death. [K. 63.]

~**-raisan** --禮讚 Abb. of *Ōjō-raisan-ge**.

~**-raisan-ge** --禮讚偈 '*Hymns of Praise Concerning Birth*'; 1 fasc., by Shan-tao 善導 (Zendo*) [TT. 47, No. 1980]; the complete title of it is *Kan-issaishujō-ganshō-saihō-gokuraku-sekai-amidabukkoku-rokujiraisan-ge* 勸一切衆生願生西方極樂世界阿彌陀佛國六時禮讚偈; also popularly called *Ōjō-raisan* 往生禮讚, *Rokuji-raisan**

六時禮讚 or, simply, *Raisan** 禮讚. This is a collection of passages and hymns with comments from Pure Land sutras and discourses, arranged so as to be used for chanting at six different times in a day. The preface urges people to seek refuge in Amida* and to practise the prescribed method to attain birth in his land.

~-**ronchū** --論註 '*Commentary on the Discourse on Birth*'; a 2-fasc. commentary by T'an-luan (Donran*) on Vasubandhu's (Seshin*) *Discourse on the Pure Land* (*Jōdo-ron**); also called *Jōdo-ronchū* 淨土論註 and simply *Ronchū* 論註 [TT. 40, No. 1819]. This work provides a philosophical basis for the Pure Land teaching, and has had a great influence on the development of Pure Land Buddhism in China and Japan.

~-**yōshū** --要集 '*The Essential Collection Concerning Birth* (*in Amida's Pure Land*)'; a work by Genshin*; 3 fasc. [TT. 84, No. 2682]. [Ho. 29; IH.; S. IV–9, Xa–1, Xb–3.]

Ōke 應化 Also *ōge*; 'responding and transformed'; refers to *ōjin** and *keshin**; accommodative and transformation bodies of a buddha; generally, incarnation of a deity.

~ **no reichi** --の靈地 'A sacred place connected with an incarnation of a deity.' [Tai. 8.]

~ **no shin** --の身 'The corresponding and transformed bodies' of a buddha or bodhisattva; an incarnation; see *ōjin* and *keshin*. [S. II–4; Tai. 12.]

~ **rishō** --利生 'Benefitting living beings by (manifesting) corresponding and transformed bodies.' [Tai. 16.]

~ **rishō no mon** --利生之門 'The gate of benefitting living beings by (manifesting) corresponding and transformed bodies.' [Tai. 18.]

Okkō 億劫 'Myriads of *kalpa*'; myriads of aeons. [S. I–6.]

Okuji fumō no oshie 憶持不忘の教 'The teaching which one remembers and cannot forget (in all future lives).' [S. II–8.]

Oku no in 奧院 'An inner hall or sanctuary' situated in a remote part of the precincts of a temple.

Ōkutsuma 央掘摩 See next entry.

Ōkutsumara 央掘摩羅 Sk. Aṅgulimāla; also Ōkutsuma 央掘摩, Ōkutsu 央掘, etc., and translated as Shiman* 指鬘 'Finger-wreath'. He at first followed a wrong teaching and vowed that he would kill 1,000 people and make a wreath with their fingers. When he attempted to kill his own mother to make the 1,000th person, the Buddha stopped this and converted him to Buddhism. He then practised the Way diligently and finally attained the highest sagehood (*arakanka**). For his previous life, see *Hansoku Ō*.

Ōmine sūdo no sendatsu 大峰數度の先達 Pronounced ...*sendachi*; 'a leader who has performed ascetic practices on Mt. Ōmine (Wakayama Prefecture) several times.' [K. 28.]

On'ai 恩愛 See *onnai*.

Onbutsumyō 御佛名 'Buddhas' names'; refers to *butsumyō-e**. [Ma. 77, 94, 151, 285; Tai. 19, 24.]

Onden 恩田 'A field of (repaying) indebtedness'; the act of repaying indebtedness to one's parents, teachers, etc., produces merit, so it is compared to a field or farm; also called *hōon fukuden* 報恩福田; one of the three fields of merit (*sanfukuden**). [S. IV–9, VII–11, 25.]

Ondoku 恩德 'The virtue of providing benefit' to people; beneficence; benevolent provision.

Ongyō no in 隱形の印 'The mudra (manual sign) by which one is made invisible.' [S. VII–20.]

Ongyō no ju 隱形の呪 'The spell by which one is made invisible.' [Tai. 5.]

Onjo 恩所 'Benefactors', esp. parents. [S. III–1, VII–7, IX–10.]

Onjōji 園城寺 The head temple of the Jimon* School of the Tendai* sect, located in Ōtsu, Ōmi Province; also called Miidera 三井寺 or 御井寺. The name Jimon ('Temple School') is used for the temple in contrast to the Enryakuji* on Mt. Hiei which is called Sanmon* 山門 ('Mountain School'). The temple was first built in 674 by Prince Ōtomo and revived by Enchin* in 858, when it was made a branch temple of the Enryakuji. After that, conflicts between the two temples ensued, and the temple was burnt down several times by monks of the Enryakuji.

Onkiba 御牙 '(Revered) tooth'; the Buddha's teeth. [Tai. 8.]

Onma 陰魔 Also *goonma* 五陰魔 and *gounma* 五蘊魔; the devil of the five constituent elements of one's existence (*goun**), which are so called because they produce various types of pain; one of the four devils (*shima**).

Onmonoimi 御物忌 See *monoimi*. [K. 295.]

Onnai 恩愛 'Affection' for one's parents, child, wife, etc. [Ho. 25; K. 314; Tsu. 142.]

Onnyū 陰入 Refers to *goun** and *jūni-sho**. [S. Va–1.]

Onri 厭離 Also *enri*; 'to detest and leave'; abbr. of *onri edo**. [IH.]

~ **edo** --穢土 'To dislike and (seek to) leave this defiled world.' [K. 470; S. VI–10; Tai. 12, 20.]

Onryō 怨霊 'A revengeful spirit.'

Onteki jōbuku no hō 怨敵調伏の法 'The ritual for subduing loathsome enemies.' [Tai. 20.]

Ōsa 應作 'A corresponding action'; that is, one which corresponds to the needs of living beings; said of a deity's manifestation of an incarnation and his altruistic activity; the same as *ōgen**. [Tai. 18.]

Ōshajō 王舎城 Sk. Rājagṛha; n. of a town in Central India, which was the capital of Magadha.

Oshō 和尙 Sk. *upādhyāya*; originally, the title of a precept-master; later, a title of respect for a virtuous monk. It is pronounced '*oshō*' in the Zen* and Jōdo* sects, '*wajō*' in the Hossō*, Shingon* and Ritsu* sects, and '*kashō*' in the Tendai* sect.

Ōyū 應用 'Functions or activities displayed in correspondence' to the needs of living beings. [S. I–3, II–4, IV–1.]

Ō-zammai 王三昧 'King Samādhi'; the greatest and supreme *samādhi* (concentration) (*sanmai**). [S. IV–1.]

R

Ragora 羅睺羅 Sk. Rāhula, 'obstruction, eclipse'; also Raun

羅云; translated as Fushō 覆障 'covering and hindering', Shōgatsu 障月 'obscuring the moon', etc.; n. of the Buddha's son and one of his ten great disciples (*jūdai-deshi**). After the Buddha's enlightenment, he joined the Buddhist order and was ordained at the age of 20. He strictly observed the precepts and diligently practised the Way, becoming well known as 'the foremost in the observance of the precepts' (*mitsugyō daiichi** 密行第一).

Rahotsu 螺髮 'Curly hair.' [S. II–8.]

Raiban 禮盤 A raised seat before the altar where a priest worships and chants sutras. [K. 468; Ma. 116; S. II–8, VI–4, 8, 13.]

Raigō 來迎 Also *raikō*. 'Welcoming'; the welcoming of an aspirant into the Pure Land by Amida* and/or his attendant bodhisattvas. [Hei. 1; K. 62, 469; S. I–10, IV–1, Xa–1.]

~-in --印 The manual sign Amida* makes when he comes to an aspirant to take him to the Pure Land.

~ no in --の印 See *raigō-in*. [K. 62.]

~ no utena --の臺 'The calyx (of a lotus blossom) sent for welcoming' an aspirant to take him to Amida's* Pure Land. [S. IV–1.]

Raikō 來迎 See *raigō*.

Raisan 禮讚 I. 'Worship and praise' of a buddha; a hymn of praise for a buddha. II. Refers to Shan-tao's *Ōjō-raisan-ge**. [S. VI–10.]

Raise 來世 'The life to come; the after-life.'

Rajū 羅什 Abbr. of Kumarajū*.

Rakan 羅漢 Sk. *arhat*; a Hinayana sage who has attained liberation from the cycle of rebirth; cf. *shika*. [S. I–7, IV–1, Xb–3.]

~-ka --果 'The fruit of the Arhat state'; same as *arakanka**; cf. *shika*. [S. II–1, 10.]

Rakei 螺髻 'A conch-like tuft of hair', as seen on the head of the Brahma King (Bontennō*) or brahmin practitioners. [S. VII–25.]

~ Bonnō --梵王 'The Brahma King with a conch-like tuft of hair.' [S. VII–25.]

Rakusha 落謝 'To fall and fade'; used to describe existing things disappearing into the past. [S. Va–5.]

Ranji 覽字 'The (Sanskrit) syllable RAṂ'; symbolizes the fire of wisdom (*eka* 慧火). [S. VII–24.]

Rannya 蘭若 Abbr. of *arannya**. [K. 36.]

Rantō 卵塔 'An egg-shaped tower'; also *muhōtō** 無縫塔; an egg-shaped stone tower often used as the tomb of a Zen* monk. [Tai. 33.]

Rasetsu 羅刹 Sk. *rākṣasa*; originally, a kind of demon possessing supernatural power and said to bewitch and eat men. Later, some of them became guardians of Buddhism. See *jū-rasetsu*.

~-koku --國 'The land of *rākṣasa*.' [Tai. 20.]

Reichi 靈知 'Mysterious perceptive faculty.'

Reichi 靈智 'Mysterious wisdom'; transcendental wisdom. [S. IV–1.]

Reigen 靈驗 'Mystic efficacy; miraculous virtue.' [S. I–6.]

Reiji 例時 Short for *reiji sahō* 例事作法 'service at the fixed time'; chanting the *Amida-kyō** and reciting the cadenced *nenbutsu** at the fixed time at dusk. This practice originated at the Jōgyōdō*, a hall on Mt. Hiei. [K. 56.]

~ sahō --作法 'Service at the fixed time.'

~ senbō --懺法 'The fixed time (service) and the (Hokke) method of annulling sins'; chanting the *Amida-kyō** at the evening service and chanting the *Hokke-zanmai-sengi* at the morning service; cf. *hokke senbō*. [S. VIII–11.]

Reikan 靈鑑 'Divine overseeing'; overseeing and protecting by a buddha, bodhisattva or god. [Tai. 6, 8.]

Reiki 靈龜 A kind of tortoise; also 'an immortal tortoise'.

~ o o hiku --尾をひく 'A tortoise leaves its trail behind.' After having laid eggs, a tortoise goes away but its tail leaves a trail, so that one can find where the eggs are; an analogy to show that an effort to keep something secret results in betraying it. [S. Vb–10.]

Rei no in 鈴の印 'A mudra (manual sign) in the form of a bell.' [S. II–8.]

Reishō 靈性 'The spiritual nature; mystic nature'; cf. *hosshin no reishō*.

Rekien 歷緣 See *ryakuen taikyō*.

Rekki 劣機 'A man of inferior capacity.' [S. I–3, IV–1.]

~ ōnyū no yōro --應入の要路 'The important road which even men of inferior capacity can enter.' [S. Xa–1.]

Rendai 蓮臺 'A lotus-seat' in Amida's* Pure Land. [IH.; O. VI.]

Renge 蓮華 'A lotus flower.'

Rengezō sekai 蓮華藏世界 'The lotus-repository world'; the land of a reward-body (*hōjin** 報身) buddha: e.g. Shakamuni's* land as expounded in the *Kegon-gyō**, and Amida's* land as set out in the *Kanmuryōju-kyō**.

Rengyō 練行 'Sustained effort in a Buddhist practice.' [K. 36.]

Rennya 練若 Abbr. of *arennya**. [Tai. 24.]

Renshi 連枝 'An off-shoot'; originally, the emperor's brother, but from the Heian period (794–1192), used for the regent's brother, too. Since the Muromachi period (1333–1603) the term is specially used for a relative of the chief abbot of the Honganji, Kyoto.

Ri 理 'Principle'; noumenon; the ultimate principle of the universe as opposed to *ji** 事 'phenomena'.

Ribusshō 理佛性 'Buddha-nature as the noumenal principle'; in the Hossō* teaching, buddha-nature is inherent in all living beings as the ultimate reality-principle; cf. *gyōbusshō**. [Tai. 24.]

Richi 理智 'The noumenal principle and transcendental wisdom'; the ultimate reality-principle and the wisdom illuminating it.

~ funi --不二 'Non-duality of the ultimate principle and the transcendental wisdom.' [S. II–8.]

Rigu no jōbutsu 理具の成佛 See *sanshu no sokushin jōbutsu*.

Ri-hokkai 理法界 'The realm of the noumenal principle'; see *shihokkai*.

Rikan 理觀 'Meditation on the noumenal principle', as opposed to *jikan** 事觀; cf. *jiri nikan*. [S. Xb–3.]

Rikon 利根 'Sharp sense-organ'; superior capacity.

Rimon 利門 'The gateway to benefit'; a way of benefitting oneself. [Tai. 24.]

Rimotsu 利物 'Benefitting living beings.'

~ no suijaku --の垂迹 'An incarnation to benefit living beings.' [Tai. 39.]

Rinbō 輪寶 'The wheel treasure'; one of the seven treasures of the Tenrinjōō* (Cakravartin), which precedes the kings, wherever they go, and destroys enemies and levels the ground. Four kinds of wheels are distinguished corresponding to the four kinds of kings: a golden wheel for the Golden Wheel King, a silver for the Silver Wheel King, a copper for the Copper Wheel King, and an iron for the Iron Wheel King. [Tai. 22.]

Ringe 林下 'In the forest'; a Zen* seminary, so called because it is often built in a forest. [S. Pref.]

Rinjū 臨終 'At the time of death.'

~ **no akusō** --の惡相 'Evil signs at the time of death', which portend imminent tortures in hell; cf. *akusō*. [Tai. 20.]

~ **no gyōgi** --の行儀 'The manner of dying'; dying in the prescribed manner. [S. Xb–3.]

~ **no sahō** --の作法 'The death-bed rite'; dying in the prescribed manner. [S. IV–5, 8, Xb–3.]

~ **shōnen** --正念 'Right thoughts on one's deathbed'; thinking of Amida* Buddha when dying, and thus ensuring the aspirant's birth in the Pure Land. [K. 194; S. II–7, Xa–9.]

Rinkan 輪觀 Refers to *jirinkan**. [IH.]

Rinne 輪廻 'Transmigration'; cycle of births and deaths.

~ **no kuka** --の苦果 'The painful retribution of undergoing transmigration.' [S. III–7.]

Rinnō 輪王 'The Wheel King'; refers to Tenrinjōō*. [S. III–1.]

Rin'ō 輪王 See *rinnō*.

Rinzō 輪藏 'A revolving sutra-repository.' [Tai. 8, 21, 24.]

Rishō 利生 'Benefitting sentient beings.'

~ **hōben** --方便 'An expediency or skilful means to benefit living beings.' [K. 70; S. Xb–3; Tai. 12, 26, 29.]

Rishō 理性 'The noumenal principle'; the noumenon as contrasted with *jisō** 事相 'the phenomenal aspect'.

Risoku 理即 'One's identity (with buddha) as part of the principle of reality'; the stage at which an ordinary person is ignorant of his identity with buddha; the first of the six stages of identity (*rokusoku** 六即) in Tendai* doctrine. [Tsu. 217.]

Risshi 律師 I. 'A precept master'; Sk. *vinaya-dhara*; a Buddhist master who is well-versed in the precepts and/or recites them. II. The third grade in the Buddhist hierarchy, below *sōjō** and *sōzu**; cf. *sōgō*.

Risshū 律宗 'The Ritsu* sect'; one of the six sects which arose in the Nara period (710–794) (*rokushū**) and one of the 13 sects (*jūsanshū**). This sect is based on the Mahayana precepts and teaches that observance of the threefold bodhisattva precepts (*sanjujōkai**) is the cause of enlightenment. The Ritsu tradition was first brought from China to Japan in 754 by Chien-chen 鑑眞 (Ganjin*), who lived in the Tōdaiji* and there erected a precept-platform (*kaidan**). He also founded the Tōshōdaiji 唐招提寺 and made it a centre for study of the precepts. With the erection of two more precept-platforms elsewhere in Japan, the Ritsu sect enjoyed prosperity for some time. Owing to the degeneration of moral standards of monks and nuns, it declined during the Heian period (794–1192), but the Kamakura period (1192–1333) saw some revival movements in Kyoto and Nara. Today there are two schools: (1) the Ritsu sect proper whose head temple is the Tōshōdaiji and (2) the Shingon-ritsu 眞言律 sect which has its headquarters in the Saidaiji 西大寺.

Rissō 律僧 I. 'A priest of the Ritsu* sect.' II. 'A priest who observes precepts.'

Rita 利他 'Benefitting others'; the opposite of *jiri** 自利. [S. VI–17, Xb–2, 3.]

Ritsu 律 I. Precepts; Sk. *vinaya*; rules of conduct for monks and nuns. II. Refers to the Ritsu sect (Risshū*).

Ritsugi 律儀 I. 'Codes of conduct, precepts.' [S. IV–1; Tai. 12.] II. Refers to the Ritsu* sect. [S. Xb–3.]

Ritsuin 律院 'A Ritsu* temple'; also *ritsuji* 律寺; a temple where Ritsu monks lived and studied precepts. [Tai. 32, 38.]

Ritsukai no mon 律戒の門 Pronounced *rikkai no mon*; 'the gate of precepts'; Buddhist precepts. [S. III–1.]

Ritsuzō 律藏 See *binayazō*.

Riyaku 利益 'Benefit.'

Riyō 利養 'Feeding oneself with profit'; profit-making.

Ro 漏 'Outflows, defilements'; Sk. *āsrava*; another term for *bonnō** 煩悩 'evil passions'; see *muro* and *uro*.

Rōben 良辨 Also 朗辨; the second patriarch of the Japanese Kegon* sect (689–773). It is said that in his infancy he was carried away by an eagle to the Kasuga Shrine, Nara, where he was found by Gien* 義淵. He grew up and learned the Hossō* teaching from Gien. In 733, he was appointed by Emperor Shōmu* as head priest of the newly built Kinshōji 金鐘寺, Nara. Later, when the Tōdaiji* was built, he was appointed *bettō** there (see *shishō* 四聖 III). Later he was given the title of *sōjō** 僧正.

Rodan 爐壇 'A platform with a fire-place' for the purpose of performing a *goma** rite. [Tai. 12, 15.]

Rōkaku 樓閣 'A tower.' See *kūden rōkaku*.

Rokkakudō 六角堂 'A hexagonal hall'; the popular name for the Chōhōji 頂法寺, a Tendai* temple in Kyoto; originally, a small hexagonal hall built by Prince Shōtoku*, in which a statue of Nyoirin Kannon* was enshrined. It became Emperor Saga's prayer temple (*chokuganji**) in 822, and was visited by Emperor Kazan in 995. Shinran* attempted a 100-day confinement in the temple in 1201, and received inspiration from Kuse Kannon* on the 95th day, which led him to take the Pure Land teaching. The hall was destroyed by fire several times, and the present building was constructed in 1877. [S. VI–8.]

Rokkannon 六觀音 The six kinds of Kannon* who save living beings in the six realms of transmigration (*rokudō**). There are two traditions. (I) 1. Daihi 大悲, 'Great Compassion', 2. Daiji 大慈, 'Great Mercy', 3. Shishimui 師子無畏, 'Fearless Lion', 4. Daikō-fushō 大光普照, 'Universal Illumination of Great Light', 5. Tennin-jōbu 天人丈夫, 'Hero among Gods and Men', and 6. Daibon-jinnon 大梵深音, 'Great Sacred, Deep Voice'. (II) 1. Shōkannon* 聖觀音 (Sk. Ārya-avalokiteśvara), 2. Senju* 千手 (Sahasra-bhuja-sahasra-netra), 3. Batō* 馬頭 (Hayagrīva), 4. Jūichimen* 十一面 (Ekadaśa-mukha), 5. Fukūkensaku* 不空 羂索 (Amoghapāśa) or Jundei 准提 (Cundī), and 6. Nyoirin* 如意輪 (Cintāmaṇi-cakra). [Hei. 3.]

Rokkon 六根 I. 'The six sense-organs'; (1) *gen* 眼 (*cakṣus*), eyes; (2) *ni* 耳 (*śrotra*), ears; (3) *bi* 鼻 (*ghrāṇa*), nose; (4) *zetsu* 舌 (*jihvā*), tongue; (5) *shin* 身 (*kāya*), the tactile body; and (6) *i* 意 (*manas*), mind; cf. *rokkyō*. II. Refers to *rokkon shōjō-i**. [S. Va–1.]

~-jō - - 淨 Abbr. of *rokkon shōjō**. [S. Va–3; Tsu. 69.]

~ shōjō - - 清淨 'Purification of the six sense-organs.' It is said in the *Hoke-kyō** that one who reads, recites, expounds, or copies that sutra will obtain 800 merits in the eye, 1,200 merits in the ears, 800 merits in the nose, 1,200 merits in the tongue, 800 merits in the body, and 1,200 merits in the mind. One's six sense-organs are thus purified and adorned with these merits. Sometimes abbreviated to *rokkonjō*. [Tai. 8.]

~ shōjō-i - - 清淨位 'The stage of purification of the six sense-organs'; the second lowest stage of the Perfect Teaching (*engyō**) division of Tendai*; a bodhisattva of this stage attains purification of his six sense-organs.

~ zaishō - - 罪障 '(Having) the hindrance of sins committed with one's six sense-organs.' [Tai. 18.]

Rokkyō 六境 'The six objects of perception or cognition'; objects of the six sense-organs (*rokkon**): (1) *shiki* 色 (*rūpa*), colour and shape; (2) *shō* 聲 (*śabda*), sound; (3) *kō* 香 (*gandha*), odour; (4) *mi* 味 (*rasa*), taste; (5) *soku* 觸 (*spraṣṭavya*), tangible objects; and (6) *hō* 法 (*dharma*), objects of the mind.

Rokuchiku 六畜 'The six domestic animals.' They are horses, cows, sheep, dogs, pigs and cocks. [S. VII–25.]

Rokudai 六大 'The six great (elements)'; the six elements constituting all existences: (1) *chidai* 地大, the earth element; (2) *suidai* 水大, the water element; (3) *kadai* 火大, the fire element; (4) *fūdai* 風大, the wind element; (5) *kūdai* 空大, the space element; and (6) *shikidai* 識大, the consciousness element; cf. *shidaishu*. In Shingon*, these elements are considered as the ultimate substance of all existences, including the cosmic buddha, Dainichi*; cf. *rokudai muge*.

~ muge - - 無礙 'Interpenetration of the six great elements'; in Shingon*, the six constituent elements of a person interchange with those of Dainichi* (Mahāvairocana) Buddha and so he is, in essence, identical with Dainichi. Also, in Shingon, the six elements interchange with each other, and their essence is immutable and all-pervasive. [Tai. 39.]

Rokudo 六度 'The Six Pāramitās'; see *ropparamitsu*. [S. I–3, III–8, IV–1, Xb–1.]

Rokudō 六道 'The six paths'; the six lower states of existence, i.e. hell, and the realms of hungry spirits, animals, *asuras*, men, and heavenly beings; cf. *jikkai* 十界. [IH.; K. 46; S. I–6, III–1, VI–10; Tai. 23, 26, 35.]

～ **nōke no Jizō Satta** ‑‑能化の地藏薩埵 'Jizō* Bodhisattva, teacher of the six realms.' [Tai. 20.]

～ **no sō no satadokoro** ‑‑の惣の沙汰所 'The grand judicial court for the six realms'; said of the court of Yama (Enma*). [S. VII–7.]

～ **sannu no chiri** ‑‑三有の塵 'The dust of the six realms and the three existences'; the delusory and defiled states of existence; cf. *sannu*. [Hei. 2.]

Rokuhachi no ganshu 六八の願主 'He who made 48 vows'; refers to Amida* Buddha. [S. II–5.]

Rokuhei 六蔽 'Six coverings'; six evil acts or mental tendencies which 'cover' pure acts: (1) *kendon* 慳貪, meanness, (2) *hakai* 破戒 or *bonkai* 犯戒, breaking of precepts, (3) *shinni* 瞋恚, anger, (4) *kedai* 懈怠, indolence, (5) *sanran* 散亂, distraction, and (6) *guchi* 愚痴, ignorance. [S. IV–1, Xa–5.]

Rokuhi hannya 六譬般若 'The six similes of *hannya*'; in the *Kongō-kyō**, *hannya** (transcendental wisdom) is likened to six things: *mu* 夢 'a dream,' *gen* 幻 'an illusion', *hō* 泡 'a bubble', *yō* 影 'a shadow', *ro* 露 'a dew-drop' and *den* 電 'lightning'. [Tai. 27.]

Rokuhōkai 六法戒 See *roppōkai*.

Rokuji 六時 'The six periods in a day', i.e. three in the daytime and three at night, at which one performs special rites.

～ **raisan** ‑‑禮讚 I. 'Worshipping and praising at six times (in a day).'; services held six times a day in which sutras are chanted and the Buddha's name is recited. [Tai. 12.] II. The hymns in praise of Amida* to be chanted at six different times in one day; they were originally included in the *Ōjō-raisan** of Shan-tao 善導 (Zendō*). [IH.; Tsu. 227.]

～ **shōmyō** ‑‑稱名 'Recitation of the *nenbutsu** at six times' during the day. [K. 63.]

Rokuji-karin 六字訶臨 (or ‑‑加輪) Correctly, 六字河臨, 'the six-syllable (ritual) in a river'. [Tai. 1.]

~-hō ----法 The ritual performed in a river and based on the six syllables representing the six kinds of Kannon (*rokkannon**); it is performed to suppress enemies and remove evil spells.

Rokujin 六塵 'Six dusts (or dirts)'; the six objects of sensation and perception corresponding to the six sense-organs (*rokkon**). They are visual colour and form, sound, odour, taste, tactile object, and mental object. They give rise to desires and, thereby, pollute one's mind; hence, 'dust, dirt'; the same as *rokkyō**; cf. *gojin*. [S. IV–1, Va–1, 12, Vb–8, VIII–23, Xb–2; Tsu. 9.]

~ no genkyō --の幻境 'The illusory world of the six objects of sensation and perception'; the illusory external world. [S. Vb–11.]

Rokuji no myōgō 六字の名號 'The six-character name' of Amida* Buddha, i.e. 'Namu Amidabutsu'* 南無阿彌陀佛. [S. II–8, IV–1.]

Rokujinzū 六神通 'The six transcendental faculties'; see *rokutsū*.

Rokukannon 六觀音 See *rokkanon*.

Rokunyū 六入 'The six enterings.' I. The six sense-organs (*rokkon**); they form one of the twelve causations (*jūni-innen**). II. Objects of the six sense-organs (*rokkyō** or *rokujin**).

Rokusainichi 六齋日 'The six precept-observing days', i.e. 8th, 14th, 15th, 23rd, 29th and 30th every month. It is believed that on those days the Four Guardian Kings (Shitennō*) examine people's acts, or that evil spirits seek opportunities to capture people's minds. People therefore abstain from breaking the precepts, including that of not eating after midday (hence, *sai** 'abstinence'); cf. *sainichi*.

Rokushi gedō 六師外道 'The six teachers outside the (Buddha's) path'; the six religious leaders in central India at the time of the Buddha; also *gedō rokushi* 外道六師. Like the Buddha himself, they were critical of the orthodox Hindu teachings, and travelled about expounding their own religious-philosophical views. They were called '*śramaṇa*' (*shamon** 沙門) and were individually: (1) Pūraṇa-kassapa, who rejected morality and denied retributions for evil acts and rewards for good ones; (2) Makkali-gosāla, known as Ājīvika (*Jamyō gedō* 邪命外道), who held a fatalistic view; (3) Sañjaya-velaṭṭhiputta, a sceptic; (4) Ajita-kesakambala, a materialist and hedonist; (5) Pakuda-kaccāyana, who rejected the law of causality and believed in the independent functions of the seven constituent elements of the universe; and (6) Niganṭhanātaputta, the founder of Jainism, who taught that emancipation of the soul could be attained by asceticism. [Tai. 24.]

Rokushiki 六識 'The six consciousnesses' corresponding to the six sense-organs (*rokkon** 六根) and their objects (*rokkyō** 六境). They are: (1) *genshiki* 眼識, visual consciousness; (2) *nishiki* 耳識, auditory consciousness; (3) *bishiki* 鼻識, olfactory consciousness; (4) *zesshiki* 舌識, gustatory consciousness; (5) *shinshiki* 身識, tactile consciousness; and (6) *ishiki* 意識, nonsensuous consciousness. The six consciousnesses are established in both Mahayana and Hinayana, though interpreted differently. Cf. *hasshiki* and *shiki*.

Rokushu 六趣 'The six destinations or realms'; same as *rokudō**. [S. II–5, 8, III–1, 7; Tai. 5.]

Rokushū 六宗 'The six sects' which arose in the Nara period (710–94): Kusha*, Jōjitsu,*Ritsu*, Hossō*, Sanron* and Kegon*; cf. *hasshū*, *kushū* and *jūsanshū*. [Tai. 24.]

~ **no chōja** --の長者 'The senior of the six sects'; said of the Hossō* sect. [Tai. 24.]

Rokusō 六相 'The six features or aspects' which, according to the Kegon* teaching, each and every existing thing possesses. They are: (1) *sōsō* 總相, totality aspect, or the aspect of comprising various functions; (2) *bessō* 別相, the particularity aspect, or the aspect of retaining a particular function; (3) *dōsō* 同相, the generality aspect, or the aspect of possessing a function common to others; (4) *isō* 異相, the distinctiveness aspect, or the aspect of possessing a distinctive feature; (5) *jōsō* 成相, the formation aspect, or the aspect of constructing something with other elements; and (6) *esō* 壞相, the destruction aspect, or the aspect of retaining specific characteristics.

~ **en'yū** --圓融 Pronounced ~*ennyū*; 'perfect fusion of the six features'. According to the Kegon* teaching, the six features or aspects of existing things, which appear to ordinary people to be separate from each other, are, in the eye of an enlightened sage, perfectly integrated in each existence.

Rokusoku 六即 'The six (stages of) non-duality (practices)' established in the Tendai* sect: (1) *risoku* 理即, the stage at which one is not yet aware of the buddha-nature; (2) *myōjisoku* 名字即, the stage at which one now understands that one has the buddha-nature; (3) *kangyōsoku* 觀行即, the stage at which one practises the Tendai meditation and the Six Pāramitās (*ropparamitsu**); (4) *sōjisoku* 相似即, the stage at which one has attained superior wisdom similar to the true wisdom of the Buddha; (5) *bunshinsoku* 分眞即, the stage at which one partially awakens to true wisdom and thus begins to realize the buddha-nature; and (6) *kukyōsoku* 究竟即, the final stage of enlightenment at which one completely realizes the buddha-nature.

Rokuten 六天 'The six heavens' of the realm of desire (*yokkai**): (1) Shiōten* 四王天; (2) Tōriten* 忉利天; (3) Yamaten 夜摩天; (4) Tosotsuten* 兜率天; (5) Kerakuten* 化樂天; and (6) Takejizaiten* 他化自在天.

Rokutsū 六通 Also *rokujinzū* 六神通; Sk. *ṣaḍ abhijñāḥ*; the six transcendental faculties of a buddha, bodhisattva, or arhat: (1) *jinsokutsū* 神足通, the ability to go anywhere at will and to transform oneself or objects at will; (2) *tengentsū* 天眼通, 'the heavenly eyes' capable of seeing anything at any distance; (3) *tennitsū* 天耳通, 'the heavenly ears' capable of hearing any sound at any distance; (4) *tashintsū* 他心通, the ability to know others' thoughts; (5) *shukumyōtsū* 宿命通, the ability to know the former lives of oneself and others; (6) *rojintsū* 漏盡通, the ability to destroy all evil passions. Cf. *sanmyō*. [S. III–1.]

Rokuya-on 鹿野苑 'Deer Park'; Sk. Mṛgadāva; a park in Bārāṇasī (near present-day Benares) where the Buddha preached his first sermon after enlightenment and converted his five former companions. [S. Va–4.]

Rokuyoku 六欲 'The six desires': (1) *shikiyoku* 色欲, attachment to beautiful colours or sexual desires; (2) *gyōmyōyoku* 形貌欲, love for attractive persons; (3) *igi shitaiyoku* 威儀姿態欲, love for those whose manner of walking, etc., is attractive; (4) *gongo onjōyoku* 言語音聲欲, love for those whose manner of speech is attractive; (5) *saikatsuyoku* 細滑欲, love for those whose skin is smooth and fine; and (6) *ninsōyoku* 人相欲, love for beautiful people. [S. VIII–22, Xa–10.]

Rondan 論談 'Discussion' of Buddhist doctrines.

~ **ketchaku** --決擇 'Discussing (doctrinal matters) and deter-
mining (what is right and what is wrong).' [S. Va–10, Xb–3.]

Rongi 論議 'Discussion'; also 論義. I. A discussion of the
doctrine of a particular sutra, often in a formal way in which
one person presents questions and another answers them. II. A
formal discussion oftenheld during a big service; the one held at
the imperial palace during the *Gosai-e** lecture-meeting is called
uchi-rongi*; such a discussion was also held at the *Yuima-e** and
Hokke-e. [Tai. 34.]   III. A kind of Buddhist scripture which
consists of discussions of doctrine, often in question and answer
form; the same as *ubadaisha**; one of the nine and the twelve
kinds of scriptures (*kubu-kyō** and *jūnibu-kyō**).

Ronzō 論藏 See *taihōzō*. [S. II–10.]

Ropparamitsu 六波羅蜜 'The Six Pāramitās'; the six kinds of
practice by which a bodhisattva attains buddhahood: (1) *fuse
haramitsu* 布施波羅蜜 (*dāna-pāramitā*), charity; (2) *jikai* 持戒 h.
(*śīla-p.*), observing precepts; (3) *ninniku* 忍辱 h. (*kṣānti-p.*),
perseverance; (4) *shōjin* 精進 h. (*vīrya-p.*), energy; (5) *zenjō* 禪定
h. (*dhyāna-p.*), meditation; and (6) *chie* 智慧 h. (*prajñā-p.*), wisdom.
Cf. *haramitsu*. [S. Xa–5; Tai. 37.]

~**-kyō** ----經 '*Six Pāramitās Sutra*'; abbr. of *Daijō-rishu-
ropparamitta-kyō**. [S. II–8.]

Roppōkai 六法戒 'The six dharma-precepts'; the six precepts to
be observed by female novices (*shikishamana**): (1) not touching
men with wanton thoughts; (2) not stealing; (3) not killing; (4)
not telling lies; (5) not eating after midday; and (6) not drinking.

Rōshō fujō 老少不定 'Uncertainty of life, for both young and old.'
[Hei. 1; S. III–3, Va–11.]

Rōshō sadame nashi 老少定めなし 'There is no fixed order for
the old and the young (in respect of the time of death)'; the old do
not necessarily die before the young; the young as well as the
old may die any minute. [S. III–1.]

Rozan no Eon 盧山の慧遠 'Hui-yüan of Mt. Lu' (334–416); a
Chinese monk who established the Byakurensha* 白蓮社 (the
White Lotus Society) on Mt. Lu for the performance of medi-
tation on Amida*. [S. Xa–1; Tai. 12.]

Rufu 流布 'To spread, diffuse.'

Ruri 瑠璃 I. Sk. *vaiḍūrya*; also 琉璃 and *biruri* 毘瑠璃; a blue precious stone, commonly identified with lapis lazuli; one of the seven treasures (*shippō**). II. N. of a king in India; see *Biruri Ō*.

~ **Ō** --王 'King Virūḍhaka'; see *Biruri Ō*.

~ **Taishi** --太子 'Prince Virūḍhaka'; see *Biruri Ō*. [Tai. 35.]

Rushana Butsu 盧舎那佛 Also 盧遮那佛, abbr. of Birushana* Butsu. I. The principal Buddha in the Kegon* sect; the Lord Buddha in the Lotus-Repository World (*Rengezō sekai**), as depicted as the great Buddha image of Nara. II. In the Tendai* sect, Rushana is regarded as a reward- or enjoyment-body (*hōjin**) and is distinguished from Birushana* who is a Dharma-body (*hosshin**) and also from Shakamuni* who is an accommodative or corresponding body (*ōjin**). [Tai. 2.]

Rushi Butsu 樓至佛 'Ruci Buddha'; also 盧至佛, Rusha Butsu 盧遮佛, etc., and translated as Aigyō Butsu 愛樂佛 and Taikoku Butsu 啼哭佛; the last of the 1,000 buddhas who appear in the present cosmic period called *gengō** 'auspicious kalpa'. [S. VI –18.]

Ruten 流轉 'Drifting' in various states of existence; transmigrating.

~ **no gō** --の業 'The karma which causes one to transmigrate.' [S. IV–1.]

~ **no gōin** --の業因 'The karmic cause of transmigration.' [S. III –7.]

~ **no innen** --の因縁 'Causes of and conditions for transmigration.' [S. VIII–23.]

~ **sangai** --三界 'Drifting (i.e. transmigrating) in the three realms (*sangai**).'

~ **shōji** --生死 'Drifting (i.e. transmigrating) in the realms of birth and death.' [S. III–1, VI–10, VIII–1, Xa–2, 5, 9, Xb–3.]

Ryakuen taikyō 歷縁對境 'To pass through conditions and confront objects of the senses'; acts in daily life. [IH.]

Ryōbu 兩部 Refers to *ryōbu mandara**. [S. I–1.]

~ **mandara** --曼荼羅 'The two mandalas'; the Diamond Realm Mandala (*Kongōkai mandara**) and the Matrix-store Realm Mandala (*Taizōkai mandara**). They are the most important mandalas in esoteric Buddhism, each giving different pictorial or symbolic presentations of buddhas, bodhisattvas, and deities. They represent respectively the wisdom aspect (*chi* 智) and the reality-principle aspect (*ri* 理) of the Buddha Dainichi*.

~ **no Dainichi** --の大日 'Mahāvairocana Buddha (as he manifests himself) in the two mandalas'. In the Diamond Realm Mandala he is portrayed as representing the wisdom aspect of Dharma-body (*hosshin**), while in the Matrix-store Mandala he represents the reality-principle aspect of Dharma-body. [S. I–1, II–8.]

Ryōchi 了知 'Cognition; knowledge.'

Ryōga 楞伽 Refers to *Ryōga-kyō**.

~**-kyō** --經 Sk. *Laṅkāvatāra-sūtra*; '*Sutra on* (*the Buddha's*) *Entering* (*the Country of*) *Laṅkā*'. The sutra propounds various Mahayana theories, such as 'eight consciousnesses' (*hasshiki**) and 'Tathagata-matrix' (*nyoraizō**), and is used by the Hossō* and Zen* sects as a text presenting their basic teachings. There are three Chinese translations: (1) *Ryōga-abatsudarahō-kyō* 楞伽阿跋陀羅寶經, 4 fasc., tr. by Guṇabhadra (Gunabatsudara 求那跋陀羅) [TT. 16, No. 670]; (2) *Nyūryōga-kyō* 入楞伽經, 10 fasc., tr. by Bodhiruci (Bodairushi 菩提流支) [TT. 16, No. 671]; and (3) *Daijō-nyūryōga-kyō* 大乘入楞伽經, 7 fasc., tr. by Śikṣānanda (Jisshananda 實叉難陀) [TT. 16, No.672.].

Ryōge 領解 'Receiving and understanding (the teaching).'

Ryōgen 良源 A Tendai* monk (912–85) and the teacher of Genshin*. He began his Buddhist studies on Mt. Hiei at the age of 12, and became conversant with both esoteric and exoteric teachings. In 937, he engaged in doctrinal disputes with Gishō 義昭 of the Gangōji at the *Yuima-e** and defeated him; he thus gained his reputation. He became a Tendai *zasu** in 966, and a *daisōjō** in 981. He was given a posthumous title, Jie Daishi 慈慧大師, in 987. His works include *Gokuraku-jōdo-kuhon-ōjō-gi* 極樂淨土九品往生義.

Ryōgi 了義 'Revealing the (whole) meaning (of the Buddhist law)'; the opposite of *furyōgi**.

Ryōgō 兩業 'The two practices'; *shanagō* and *shikangō*; see *shana shikan*.

Ryōgon 楞嚴 Refers to *Shuryōgon-gyō**. [S. Vb–10, Xb–1.]

~-gyō --經 Refers to *Shuryōgon-gyō**. [S. Xb–2.]

~-ju --呪 See *Daibutchō-ju*.

Ryōhō kujū 令法久住 'Enabling the Dharma to remain for a long time (in the world).' [S. Xb–3.]

Ryōiki 靈異記 Abbr. of *Nihonkoku genpō zenmaku ryōiki**. [K. 484.]

Ryōjusen 靈鷲山 Sk. Grdhrakūṭa, 'Vulture Peak'; the mountain in Magadha, India, where the Buddha expounded many sutras. [Tai. 13.]

Ryōkai 兩界 'The two realms', i.e. the two mandalas, Kongōkai and Taizōkai. See *ryōbu mandara*. [Hei. 3.]

~ mandara --曼荼羅 'Mandalas of the two realms'; the same as *ryōbu mandara**. [K. 63.]

~ no mandara --の曼荼羅 See *ryōbu mandara*. [Tai. 39.]

~ no suijaku --の垂跡 'Incarnations (of Dainichi*) in the two-realm mandalas.' [Hei. 3.]

Ryōkongō 兩金剛 'The two Kongō gods', Misshaku Kongō* and Naraen Kongō*; cf. *kongōjin*. [Tai. 9.]

Ryōnin 良忍 The founder of the Yūzū-nenbutsu sect (1073–1132); see *Yūzū-nenbutsu-shū*. [K. 53.]

Ryōzen 靈山 'Holy Mountain', i.e. Ryōjusen*. [Ma. 197; S. IV–1, Vb–10.]

Ryōzetsu 兩舌 Uttering words which cause enmity between two or more persons; also *rikengo* 離間語; one of the ten evil acts (*jūaku**).

Ryū 龍 'A dragon'; Sk. *nāga*; one of the eight kinds of gods and demi-gods who protect Buddhism (*hachibushu**); a kind of snake-like creature believed to have supernatural power to form clouds and cause rain to fall at will, but to be vulnerable to attack by *garuḍa* (*karura** or *konjichō**) who eat them. Some live on the earth, some in the water and some others in the sky; and some have two heads, and others many heads. Of the dragons which protect Buddhism, eight dragon kings (*hachidai-ryūō**) are often mentioned in Buddhist texts. For the three kinds of torment which dragons are believed to undergo, see *sannetsu*.

Ryūgan 立願 'To make a vow.' [Tai. 18.]

Ryūge-e 龍華會 'The dragon-flower assemblies'; the three assemblies under the dragon-flower tree at which the future buddha Miroku* (Maitreya) will convert people. [S. II–8.]

Ryūge geshō san'e no akatsuki 龍華下生三會の曉 'At the dawn of the three assemblies under the dragon-flower tree when (Miroku*, or Maitreya) descends to this world (from heaven)'; at the time when Miroku delivers sermons after becoming a buddha under the dragon-flower tree. [Tai. 12.]

Ryūgi 竪義 '(One who) establishes a principle'; also *rissha* 竪者 or 立者; at a discussion meeting (*rongi**), one who answers questions by establishing a doctrinal principle. [Tai. 34.]

Ryūgū 龍宮 'The dragon palace.' [K. 52; S. III–3, VI–18.]

~**-jō** --城 'The dragon palace.' [Hei. 2; Tai. 15,18.]

Ryūjin 龍神 'Dragon-god'; a snake-like demi-god said to be possessed of supernatural power, e.g. of bringing rain. [Hei. 2; K. 60; S. Va–1; Tai. 12, 13.]

~ **hachibu** --八部 'The eight kinds of gods and demi-gods, such as dragons', who protect Buddhism; see *hachibushu*. [Tai. 10.]

Ryūju 龍樹 Sk. Nāgārjuna; the greatest exponent of Mahayana Buddhism around the 2nd or 3rd century, regarded as the second buddha and the founder of eight Mahayana sects; celebrated especially as the founder of the Mādhyamika (*Chūganha**) school. [S. IV–1, VI–10, VII–25.]

Ryūmyō 龍猛 Traditionally identified with Ryūju* (Nāgārjuna). This name is used in Shingon* for the third patriarch in the lineage of its transmission. [S. Xb–2.]

Ryūnyo 龍女 'A female dragon', esp. the one mentioned in the *Hoke-kyō**, which describes how an eight-year old female dragon attained buddhahood very quickly. [S. III–8.]

Ryūō 龍王 'A dragon king'; see *hachidai-ryūō*.

Ryūzō 立像 'A standing statue' of a buddha or other deity.

S

Saba さば(生飯) Also pronounced *sanban*. A small quantity of rice, etc., taken from a meal to offer to the spirits. [Ma. 240.]

Sabetsu 差別 See *shabetsu*.

Sagan 鎖龕 'To close a coffin'; to put a lid on a coffin. [Tai. 33, 40.]

～ butsuji --佛事 'A Buddhist ceremony of closing a coffin'; this is part of the funeral service in the Zen* sect.

Sagō 作業 'Act' in the religious sense; a practice leading to enlightenment.

Sai 齋 I. Observance of precepts on fixed days; cf. *hassaikai*. II. Purification of one's physical and mental acts. III. A meal taken before noon. IV. A meal served in a Buddhist service; cf. *toki*.

Saibuku 摧伏 See *zaibuku*.

Saichō 最澄 The founder of the Japanese Tendai* sect (767–822); born in Ōmi Province, he became a novice at 12 and received ordination at 14. In 785, he built a hut on Mt. Hiei, where he chanted the *Hoke-kyō** and other sutras and also studied Chinese T'ien-t'ai (Tendai) scriptures in particular. Three years later, he converted the hut into a temple, which he called Hieizanji 比叡山寺 (later, Ichijō-shikan-in 一乗止觀院). In 794 he held a big service there, which was attended by Emperor Kanmu and eminent monks of temples in Nara. In 804, by imperial order he went to China and received the T'ien-t'ai teaching from Tao-sui 道邃 (Dōsui) and Hsing-man 行満 (Gyōman). He also received the transmission of the Niu-t'ou Ch'an 牛頭禪 (Gozuzen) from Hsiao-jan 翛然 (Shōnen) and esoteric initiation from Hsün-hsiao 順曉 (Jungyō). After he returned home in the following year, he began to propagate the Tendai teaching. In 813 he was appointed Emperor Saga's *gojisō** ('the priest who protects'). In 822 he asked the imperial court for permission to erect a Mahayana ordination platform on Mt. Hiei, but owing to objections by older schools, the permission was not given until seven days after his death. In 866 he was posthumously given the title of *hōin-daikashō-i** and the name and title of Dengyō Daishi*. He was also called Eizan Daishi 叡山大師, Konpon Daishi 根本大師 and Sange Daishi 山家大師. He wrote some 160 works, including *Shugo-kokkai-shō* 守護國界章 '*Discourse on the Protection of the State*', *Hokke-shūku* 法華秀句 '*Wondrous Passages of the Lotus Sutra*' and *Kenkai-ron* 顯戒論 '*Discourse Revealing the (Mahayana) Precepts*'. The *Mappō-tōmyō-ki* 末法燈明記 '*The Lamp in the Period of the Last Law*' is also ascribed to him.

Saido 濟度 'Saving and ferrying across (the sea of transmigration)'; salvation; emancipation.

～ **kukai** --苦海 'To ferry (living beings) across the sea of suffering'; to deliver beings from transmigration. [Hei. 2.]

～ **rishō** --利生 'Saving and benefitting sentient beings.' [Tai. 3, 24, 26.]

Saigatsu 齋月 The 1st, 5th, and 9th months, when one observes the precept of not eating after midday and restrains oneself from evil acts.

Saigokeshū 西牛貨洲 'The western continent where cows are used for money'; one of the four continents (*shishū**); see *Saikudani*.

Saigo no ichinen 最後の一念 'The last thought (at the time of death).' [Tai. 21.]

Saigo no jūnen 最後の十念 'The last ten thoughts'; the ten *nen-butsu** recitations on one's death-bed which, according to the *Kanmuryōju-kyō**, will enable the aspirant to be born in Amida's* Pure Land. [S. VII–8, Xa–10; Tai. 6, 11, 39.]

Saigo no nen 最後の念 'Thinking of the end of one's life'; thinking that one is faced with death; used to describe the seriousness of one's Buddhist practice. [S. Xb–3.]

Saihō jōdo 西方淨土 'The Western Pure Land' of Amida* Buddha. [Hei. 1.]

Saijitsu 齋日 See *sainichi*.

Saikai 齋戒　I. Restraint in one's actions, thereby purifying one's mind and body.　II. The eight precepts for lay men and women; see *hassaikai*. [S. II-9, Xa-2.]

Saikudani 西瞿陀尼　Sk. Aparagodānīya; also Saikuyani 西瞿耶尼 and translated as Saigokeshū* 西牛貨洲; one of the four continents (*shishū**), which lies to the west of Mt. Sumeru (Shumisen*). The continent is round, cows are used as currency, and the inhabitants enjoy a life of 500 years.

Saikuyani 西瞿耶尼　See *Saikudani*.

Saimandara 西曼陀羅　'The western Mandala'; refers to the *Kongōkai Mandara**; one of the two most important mandalas used in esoteric Buddhism which is hung on the western side of a hall. Cf. *tōmandara*. [Hei. 3.]

Sainichi 齋日　Certain days or months when lay Buddhists observe the precepts and abstain from doing evil acts. There are various kinds including: (1) *rokusainichi** 六齋日, 8th, 14th, 15th, 23rd, 29th and 30th every month; (2) *jūsainichi** 十齋日, 1st, 8th, 14th, 15th, 18th, 23rd, 24th, 28th, 29th and 30th; (3) *hachiōnichi** 八王日, the eight days when seasonal changes occur. [Tai. 8.]

Saiō 再往　'Second going'; a closer investigation; deeper meaning revealed by a closer investigation; as opposed to *ichiō**.

Sairai no shūshi 西來之宗旨　'The teaching of one who came from the west (i.e. Bodaidaruma*, or Bodhidharma)'; the Zen* teaching. [Tai. 24.]

Saishō 災障　'Calamities and obstructions.' [S. II-8.]

Saishō 最勝　I. 'Supreme.'　II. Refers to *Konkōmyō-saishōō-kyō**.

～-e --會　Also called *Yakushiji saishō-e* 藥師寺最勝會. One of the three annual lecture-meetings held in Nara. It was a lecture on the *Konkōmyō-saishōō-kyō** held at the Yakushiji* for seven days beginning on the 7th of the 3rd month for the purpose of securing the peace and well-being of the state and praying for the long life of the emperor. It was first held in 830 (or 829 or 768 according to other sources). [O. V.]

～ kinrin butchō --金輪佛頂　'Supreme golden-wheel buddha's head'; see *Kinrin butchō*.

～-kō --講　The annual lecture on the *Konkōmyō-saishōō-kyō**

金光明最勝王經 'Sutra of Golden Splendour' given at the imperial palace on five consecutive days in the fifth month. It began in 1002 or 1010. [K. 60, 331; Tai. 24, 36, 40; Tsu. 22, 48.]

~ **no gohakkō** --の御八講 'The eight lectures on the *Konkōmyō-saishōō-kyō**'; the annual five days of lectures on the sutra. As the sutra has ten fascicles, there are altogether ten lectures, but this lecture-meeting is sometimes called 'the eight-lecture meeting' on the analogy of the eight lectures on the *Hoke-kyō** (*hokke hakkō**).

Saiten 西天 'The western heaven', i.e. India.

Saitō 柴燈 (also 齋燈) A ritual bonfire made at a shrine. [S. II–10.]

Saku 索 Refers to *kensaku**. [K. 52.]

Sakura-e 櫻會 'Cherry-blossom meeting'; see *Daigo no sakura-e*.

Samaya 三昧耶 See *sanmaya*.

Samurai-bōshi 侍法師 'Warrior priest'; a priest in charge of security and miscellaneous jobs in a temple. [K. 396; Tai. 21.]

San'aku 三惡 See *sanmaku*.

San'asōgikō 三阿僧祇劫 'Three immeasurable *kalpas*'; the same as *sandai-asōgikō**.

Sanban 生飯 See *saba*.

Sanbō 三寶 'The three treasures' in Buddhism: (1) *butsu* 佛, the Buddha; (2) *hō* 法, the Dharma or law; and (3) *sō* 僧, the Sangha or the Buddhist priesthood.

~**-e** --繪 Refers to *Sanbō-ekotoba*. [O. III.]

~**-ekotoba** --繪詞 Scrolls of 'paintings and explanations of the three treasures', 3 scrolls, composed by Minamoto Tamenori 源爲憲 (d. 1011). They contain the Buddha's biography, an outline of Buddhist biographies of famous priests and nuns, the origins of important services, etc.

~ **no jūji** --の住持 'Upholding of the three treasures.' [Tai. 24.]

Sanbōin 三法印 'The three marks of the Dharma'; the three characteristic features of the Buddhist teaching as distinguished from other teachings: (1) *shogyō mujō** 諸行無常, 'all things are transient'; (2) *shohō muga* 諸法無我, 'all things are selfless', i.e. unsubstantial; and (3) *nehan jakujō* 涅槃寂靜 'Nirvana is the state of tranquility.'

Sanbon jōju 三品成就 'The three grades of perfection'; the same as *sanbon shijji**. [Tai. 18.]

Sanbon shitchi 三品悉地 Also *sanpon shitchi* and *sanpon shijji*; 'the three grades of *siddhi* (perfection)' to be attained through accomplishment of the Three Mystic Practices (*sanmitsu**): (1) *jōbon shitchi* 上品悉地, 'upper grade of perfection', which means birth in Dainichi's* land (Mitsugonkoku*); (2) *chūbon shitchi* 中品悉地, 'middle grade of perfection', which means birth in one of the pure lands of other buddhas, including that of Amida*; and (3) *gebon shitchi* 下品悉地, 'lower grade of perfection', which means birth in a heavenly palace or an *asura*'s palace.

Sanbu-daihō 三部大法 'The great three-part practice'; the three secret ritual practices in Tendai* esotericism pertaining to the Kongōkai*, Taizōkai* and Soshitsujihō*. [K. 52.]

Sanbutsu 讃佛 'Praise of the Buddha.'

~-jō --乘 'Praising the Buddha-Vehicle'; praising the Buddha's teaching. [S. Xb–3.]

Sanchi 三智 'The three wisdoms.' According to the *Daichido-ron** 大智度論, they are: (1) *issaichi* 一切智, the wisdom of knowing the general aspect of all existences (i.e. voidness); the wisdom of Hinayana sages; (2) *dōshuchi* 道種智, the wisdom of knowing the discriminative aspects of all existences; the wisdom of the bodhisattva; (3) *issaishuchi* 一切種智, the wisdom of knowing all kinds of existences and elements, whether in their general or discriminative aspects; the wisdom of the buddha.

Sandai 三諦 See *santai*.

Sandai-asōgikō 三大阿僧祇劫 'Three great innumerable *kalpas*'; 阿僧祇, Sk. *asaṃkhya*, meaning 'countless', is the unit for a high number. It takes three innumerable *kalpas* for a bodhisattva to complete the practices necessary to become a buddha. 'Great *kalpas* (aeons)' are here referred to in contrast to medium and small *kalpas* (cf. *kō* 劫).

Sandairan 珊提嵐 Sk. Śaṇḍilya; n. of a country in ancient times which appears in the *Hike-kyō**. Its king, named Mujōnen* 無諍念 (Araṇemin), later became Amida*. [Tai. 39.]

Sandai-sōgi 三大僧祇 Abbr. of *sandai-asōgikō**. [S. II–8.]

Sandō 三道 'The three passages'; the three elements of transmigration: (1) *bonnōdō* 煩悩道 or *wakudō* 惑道, evil passions or delusions; (2) *gōdō* 業道, good or evil acts; and (3) *kudō* 苦道, suffering. Each of them functions as the cause of the next. Thus evil passions are the cause of good (i.e. imperfect and defiled good) and evil acts; they in turn act as the cause of suffering; and suffering is then the cause of delusions and evil passions.

Sandoku 三毒 'The three poisons'; the three major evil passions: (1) *ton'yoku* 貪欲 greed; (2) *shinni* 瞋恚, anger; and (3) *guchi* 愚痴, stupidity. [S. III–3, 8, IV–9, VI–10, VIII–8, Xa–1; Tai. 12, 23.]

~ no daija --の大蛇 'The big snake of the three poisons'; an analogy to show that greed, anger and stupidity swallow up sentient beings. [Tai. 33.]

San'e 三衣 See *sanne*.

~ ippatsu --一鉢 See *sanne ippatsu*.

San'e 三會 I. 'The three (annual) lecture-meetings' in Nara, i.e. the *Gosai-e**, *Saishō-e**, and *Yuima-e**; cf. *sandai'e*☆. [O. V.] II. 'The three assemblies' at which the future buddha Miroku* (Maitreya) will expound the teaching; cf. *Ryūge-e*. [Tai. 22, 39.]

San'en no jihi 三緣の慈悲 'Compassion which arises from three kinds of *en** (objects)'; (1) *shujōen no jihi* 衆生緣の慈悲, compassion arising from the perception of sentient beings; this is awakened in the minds of ordinary men or followers of Hinayana, and is called 'small compassion' (*shōhi* 小悲); (2) *hōen no jihi* 法緣の慈悲, compassion arising from the observation of the component elements of sentient beings; this is awakened in the minds of arhats (*arakan**) or bodhisattvas below the First Stage (*shoji**), and is called 'medium compassion' (*chūhi* 中悲); and (3) *muen no jihi** 無緣の慈悲, compassion arising from realization of the void; this is awakened in the minds of bodhisattvas of the First Stage or above, and is called 'great compassion' (*daihi** 大悲). Buddhas have all the three kinds of compassion, but they arise spontaneously and are not dependent on the discriminative perception of sentient beings or elements.

Sanfukuden 三福田 'The three fields of merit'; the three kinds of acts which produce merit: (1) *hiden** 悲田 or *bingū fukuden* 貧窮 福田, giving things to the poor; (2) *kyōden** 敬田 or *kudoku* *fukuden* 功德福田, respecting the three treasures (*sanbō**); and (3) *onden** 恩田 or *hōon fukuden* 報恩福田, repaying indebtedness to one's parents, teachers, etc.

Sangai 三界 'The three realms' of the world of transmigration: (1) the realm of desire (*yokkai* 欲界, Sk. *kāma-dhātu*), which comprises hell, the states of existence of hungry spirits, animals, fighting spirits, and men, and part of heaven; beings of this realm have, among other things, sexual desire and other appetites; (2) the realm of form (*shikikai* 色界, *rūpa-dhātu*), which comprises part of heaven, where beings have neither sexual desire nor other appetites and there are only fine types of matter; (3) the realm of non-form (*mushikikai* 無色界, *ārūpya-dhātu*), which comprises part of heaven, where no material element exists and beings enjoy only meditative states.

〜 **(no) kataku** --(の)火宅 'The three realms (of transmigration) which are like a house on fire'; see *kataku*. [S. IV–9; Tai. 37.]

〜 **muan no kataku** --無安の火宅 'The three realms are like a house on fire where there is no peace.' [S. VII–25.]

〜 **no dokuson** --の特尊 'The most revered one in the three realms', i.e. the Buddha. [S. III–1.]

〜 **no jibu** --の慈父 'The compassionate father of the three realms.' [Tai. 18.]

〜 **no kukai** --の苦海 'The painful ocean of the three realms.' [Tai. 18.]

〜 **no kurin** --の苦輪 'The wheel of suffering in the three realms'; endless cycles of suffering in the three realms. [Tai. 40.]

〜 **no rinne** --の輪廻 'Transmigration in the three realms.' [S. I–9.]

〜 **(no) ruten** --(の)流轉 'Floundering in the three realms'; transmigrating in the three realms. [S. Vb–11; Tai. 35.]

〜 **wa tada kokoro hitotsu nari** --はただ心一つなり 'The three realms are nothing but a single mind.' [Ho. 34.]

〜 **yuiisshin** --唯一心 'The three realms are nothing but a single mind'; the phrase comes from the *Kegon-gyō**. [S. III–1, Vb–9, VII–25.]

Sangaku 三學 'The three learnings'; the three ways of learning:

(1) *kai* 戒, (observance of) precepts; (2) *jō* 定, meditation; and (3) *e* 慧, wisdom (cultivated by studying the Buddhist teaching). [S. II–10, III–8, IV–1, VI–9; Tai. 18.]

Sangan 三觀 'The threefold contemplation.' I. Contemplation on the triple truth (*santai**) in Tendai* teaching: (1) *kūgan* 空觀, contemplation on the void of all existences; (2) *kekan* 假觀, contemplation on the temporariness of all existences; and (3) *chūgan* 中觀, contemplation on the truth of the middle. [Tai. 17.] II. The three levels of contemplation for realizing the ultimate reality of the universe in Kegon* teaching: (1) *shinkūkan* 眞空觀, contemplation on absolute void; (2) *rijimugekan* 理事無礙觀, contemplation on the aspect of interfusion between the noumenal principle and all phenomenal things; and (3) *shūhengan'yōkan* 周徧含容觀, contemplation on the ultimate reality in which all existences interpenetrate and are inclusive of each other.

Sange 懺悔 ☆ 'To repent of one's sins.'

Sangō 三業 'The three kinds of acts'; bodily, verbal and mental acts.

〜 **sōō** --相應 'Harmony between three kinds of acts (i.e. physical, verbal and mental)' in performing practices for attaining birth in the Pure Land. [S. Xa–1.]

Sangō 三綱 See *shoshi*.

Sangō 鑽仰 'To praise and look up to (a buddha, etc.).' [Tai. 17.]

Sangoku denrai 三國傳來 'Transmitted across the three countries'; said of the transmission of Buddhism to Japan from India through China. [Tai. 13.]

Sangoku no buppō 三國の佛法 'Buddhism in three countries,' i.e. India, China and Japan. [Hei. 2.]

Sangoku sōden 三國相傳 The same as *sangoku denrai**. [S. Xa–1.]

Sanhannya 三般若 'The three (aspects of) transcendental wisdom': (1) *jissō hannya* 實相般若, true reality which constitutes the basis of transcendental wisdom; (2) *kanshō hannya* 觀照般若, transcendental wisdom of realizing reality; and (3) *monji hannya* 文字般若, exposition in words of the transcendental wisdom, i.e. various *Hannya-kyō** texts. See *hannya*.

San'in busshō 三因佛性 'The three causes of buddhahood'; according to the *Nehan-gyō**, they are: (1) *shōin busshō* 正因佛性, the buddha-nature or True Thusness which is the proper cause of Dharma-body (*hosshin** 法身); (2) *ryōin busshō* 了因佛性, the wisdom of 'discerning' (*ryō* 了) the reality-principle which accomplishes the transcendental wisdom (*hannya** 般若); and (3) *en'in busshō* 緣因佛性, various meritorious acts which assist (*en* 緣) in the development of buddha-nature and enable one to achieve emancipation (*gedatsu** 解脫). Cf. *sanshin busshō.*

Sanjigō 三時業 'The three times of karma (maturing and bringing about its effect).' The three different periods are distinguished as the times when a good or bad karma done in the present life matures. They are: (1) *jungenju-gō* 順現受業 or *jungen-gō* 順現業, reward or retribution of karma in the present life; (2) *junjiju-gō* 順次受業 or *junji-gō* 順次業, reward or retribution of karma in the next life; and (3) *jungoju-gō* 順後受業 or *jungo-gō* 順後業, reward or retribution of karma in a life after the next. Cf. *sanpō.*

Sanji no gyōhō 三時の行法 'Prescribed methods of practice to be performed at three times in the day (i.e. morning, midday, and evening).' [K. 46.]

Sanjō 三乘 'The three vehicles.' I. The three kinds of teaching applicable to bodhisattvas, pratyekabuddhas (*engaku**), and shravakas (*shōmon**). II. The three kinds of Buddhist practitioner mentioned in (I). [S. II-5.]

Sanjō 散杖 Also *shasuijō* 灑水杖. 'A stick for spraying' scented water on the platform in Shingon* ritual. [S. I-6.]

Sanju 三受 'The three kinds of sensation': (1) *kuju* 苦受, the sensation of pain; (2) *rakuju* 樂受, of pleasure; and (3) *shaju* 捨受, of indifference, or *fuku-furaku-ju* 不苦不樂受, of neither pain nor pleasure.

Sanju 三聚 'The three groups of people.' I. In general Buddhism, the three kinds of people distinguished in accordance with the three different courses of spiritual progress: (1) *shōjōju** 正定聚, those who are certain to attain Nirvana; (2) *jajōju** 邪定聚, those who are certain to fall into evil realms of transmigration; and (3) *fujōju** 不定聚, those whose destinies are not certain. II. In the Jōdoshin* sect, the three kinds of aspirants to the Pure Land: (1) *shōjōju**, those who have attained faith in the other-power (*tariki**) in compliance with the Eighteenth Vow and are certain to be born into the real Pure Land; (2) *jajōju**, those who follow the self-power (*jiriki**) practices and faith prescribed in the Nineteenth Vow and, consequently, will be born into temporary regions of the Pure Land; and (3) *fujōju**, those who practise the *nenbutsu** with self-power in compliance with the Twentieth Vow and, consequently, will be born into temporary regions of the Pure Land.

Sanjujōkai 三聚淨戒 'The threefold pure precepts' to be observed by bodhisattvas: (1) *shōritsugikai* 攝律儀戒, the precept of avoiding all evil acts; (2) *shōzenpōkai* 攝善法戒, the precept of doing all good acts; and (3) *shōshujōkai* 攝衆生戒, the precept of embracing and benefitting sentient beings; cf. *daijōkai*.

Sanjūni-sō 三十二相 'The 32 marks' of physical excellence of a buddha or a cakravartin (*tenrinjōō**); cf. *hachijūshu-kō*.

Sanjūsanten 三十三天 'The heaven of the thirty-three (gods)'; another name for the Trāyastriṃśa Heaven (Tōriten*). [S.IX–13; Tai. 23, 31.]

Sanjūshichi-dōbon 三十七道品 'The 37 elements of enlightenment'; the 37 kinds of practices for attaining Nirvana; also *sanjūshichi-bodaibunpō* 三十七菩提分法. They are: *shinenjo** 四念處, *shishōgon** 四正勤, *shinyoisoku** 四如意足, *gokon** 五根, *goriki** 五力, *shichikakushi** 七覺支, and *hasshōdō** 八聖道.

Sanjūshichison 三十七尊 'The 37 deities' of the Diamond Realm Mandala (*Kongōkai mandara**). [S. II–8.]

Sankakudan 三角壇 'A triangular platform' used at an esoteric ritual for subduing enemies, etc. (*gōbukuhō**). A triangle is a symbol of fire and thus signifies the destruction of evil.

Sankaku no dan 三角の壇 See *sankakudan*. [Tai. 12.]

Sankashi 散華師 See *shichisō*.

Sanki 三歸 Also *sankie* 三歸依; 'the three refuges'; taking refuge in the Buddha, the Dharma, and the Sangha (Buddhist order). One takes the oath of the three refuges at the time of initiation.

〜**-e** --依 See *sanki*.

〜 **gokai** --五戒 'The three refuges and the five precepts'. At the time of initiation, one first takes the oath of the three refuges and then that of the five precepts. [S. II–8.]

Sanko 三鈷 A three-pronged *vajra*; an iron bar with three prongs on each end; see *kongōsho*.

Sankō tenshi 三光天子 'The three shining deities'; (1) Nittenshi 日天子, Sun Deity; 2) Gatsu-tenshi 月天子, Moon Deity; and (3) Myōjō-tenshi 明星天子, Morning-Star Deity. [Tai. 8.]

Sanmai 三昧 Sk. *samādhi*; also *sanmaji* 三摩地, *sanmadai* 三摩提, etc., and translated as *jō** 定, *shōju* 正受, *tōji* 等持, etc.; a mental state of concentration and focussing of thought on one object. The object of concentration can be a physical one, a metaphysical principle, or a transcendental existence. This exercise is usually practised repeatedly for a long period of time until the practitioner attains a concentration of thought in which he realizes some reality-principle or visualizes a transcendental object.

~-**dō** - -堂 'Meditation hall'; also *Hokke-dō* 法華堂. I. The Hokke-zanmai-in 法華三昧院 built on Mt. Hiei by Saichō*. II. Any Hokke-zanmai-in temple of the Tendai* sect, where the *Hokke-zanmai** was practised and lectures on the *Hoke-kyō** were given. III. A temple built near the ancestral grave-yard of a clan for the performance of the *Hokke-zanmai* rituals for the peace of the deceased ancestors. [O. V.]

~ **hottoku** - -發得 'Awakening or obtaining a Samādhi'; attainment of a specific Samādhi in which the practitioner realizes reality intuitively or visualizes some object of contemplation.

~-**sō** - -僧 A monk who lives in a hall called a Sanmai-dō*, Hokke-dō*, or Jōgyō-dō*, in order to practise the Hokke meditation or the *nenbutsu** meditation. [Tsu. 134.]

~ **sōzu** - -僧都 A *sōzu** of the Jōgyō-zanmai-dō 常行三昧堂 on Mt. Hiei. [O. III.]

Sanmaku 三惡 'The three evil (realms)'; see *sanmakudō*. [Hei. 3; S. I–6, Va–2, Vb–8.]

~-**dō** - -道 'The three evil realms'; hell, the realm of hungry spirits, and the realm of animals.

Sanmaya 三昧耶 (or 三摩耶) Also *samaya*; Sk. *samaya*. I. Time. II. Four meanings are given in esoteric Buddhism: (1) *byōdō* 平等 'equality', i.e. the intrinsic identity between the Buddha's physical, oral, and mental acts and those of living beings; (2) *honzei*

本誓 'the original vow' of the Buddha; (3) *joshō* 除障 'removing hindrances', i.e. the Buddha's act of removing evil passions from living beings; (4) *kyōkaku** 驚覺 'awakening' living beings from illusion or bodhisattvas from addiction to erroneous meditations.

~-gyō ---形 '*Samaya* forms'; refers to attributes held in the hands of divinities or their manual signs, because they represent the four meanings of *Samaya*. [S. II-4.]

~-kai ---戒 'The *Samaya* precepts'; the precepts in esoteric Buddhism to be received before the *denbō kanjō** (the Dharma-transmission *abhiṣeka* ceremony); cf. *kanjō* 灌頂. [Tai. 15.]

~-kaidan ---戒壇 'The platform for the ceremony of conferring the *Samaya* precepts.' [Tai. 15.]

Sanmitsu 三密 'The three mystic' practices: (1) *shinmitsu* 身密 'bodily mystic practice', forming the manual sign of a specific deity; (2) *kumitsu* 口密 'verbal mystic practice', reciting the spell of the deity; (3) *imitsu* 意密 'mental mystic practice', meditating on the deity. By these three mystic practices, one seeks to attain unity with the deity. [S. II-7, 8, 10.]

~ yuga --瑜伽 'The three mystic practices for achieving unity (with a divinity).' [Tai. 12, 18.]

Sanmon 山門 I. The gate of a temple; a temple. II. 'The Mountain School' of the Tendai* sect, i.e. the Enryakuji* on Mt. Hiei. It is opposed to *jimon** 寺門 'the Temple School', i.e. the Onjōji* 園城寺, Shiga Prefecture. The Tendai sect split into these two schools in 981, when monks of Enchin's* line left Mt. Hiei to live in the Onjōji. [S. I-7; Tsu. 226.]

~ no daishu --の大衆 'Monks of the Enryakuji' on Mt. Hiei. [Tai. 3.]

~ no kōken --の効験 'The efficacy (of a ritual performance by the monks) of the Enryakuji.' [Tai. 12.]

~ no zasu --の座主 'The head priest of the Enryakuji' on Mt. Hiei. [Tai. 8.]

~ shika-daihō --四箇大法 'The four great rituals of the Mountain School'; the four most important esoteric rituals performed in the Mountain School of Tendai: (1) *shijōkō-hō** 熾盛光法; (2) *shichibutsu yakushi no hō** 七佛藥師の法; (3) *Fugen enmei-hō**

普賢延命法; and (4) *anchin kokka-hō** 安鎮國家法.

Sanmonzeki 三門跡 'The three *monzeki** temples' of the Tendai* sect. I. The Shōren-in 青蓮院, the Myōhō-in 妙法院 and the Sanzen-in 三千院 are called *Eizan no sanmonzeki* 叡山の三門跡 'the three *monzeki* temples of Mt. Hiei' or *sanmon no sanmonzeki* 山門の三門跡 'the three *monzeki* temples of the Mountain School (*sanmon**)'; the abbot of one of them can also hold the post of chief abbot of the Enryakuji* 延暦寺. II. The Enman-in 圓滿院, the Shōgo-in 聖護院 and the Jissō-in 實相院 are called *Mii no sanmonzeki* 三井の三門跡 'the three *monzeki* temples of Mii' or *jimon no sanmonzeki* 寺門の三門跡 'the three *monzeki* temples of the Temple School (*jimon**)'. Mii 三井 is another name for the Onjōji* 園城寺, the head temple of the Temple School of Tendai. [Tai. 30.]

Sanmyaku-sanbodai 三藐三菩提 Sk. *samyak-sambodhi*, 'perfect enlightenment'. [Tai. 2.]

~ **no hotoke** -----の佛 'Perfectly enlightened buddha(s).' [Tai. 2.]

Sanmyō 三明 Sk. *tisro vidyāḥ*, 'three knowledges'; the three transcendental knowledges attained by a buddha, bodhisattva or arhat: (1) *shukumyōmyō* 宿命明, knowledge of the former lives of oneself and others; (2) *tengenmyō* 天眼明, ability to know the future destiny of oneself and others; (3) *rojinmyō* 漏盡明, ability to know all about the miseries of the present life and to remove their root-cause, i.e. evil passions. Cf. *rokutsū*. [S. III–1.]

~ **no kakuro** --の覺路 'The path leading to enlightenment in the three (transcendental) knowledges'; the path leading to buddhahood. [Tai. 21.]

Sanne 三衣 'The three robes' used by a Buddhist monk: (1) *sōgyari* 僧伽梨 (*saṃghāṭī*), a formal robe made of 9 to 25 pieces of cloth and worn when a monk goes about begging for alms or is invited to a royal palace; (2) *uttarasō* 欝多羅僧 (*uttara-āsaṅga*), a robe made of 7 pieces of cloth and worn at services, lectures, and ceremonies; and (3) *andae* 安陀會 (*antar-vāsa*), a robe which is the normal wear of a monk by day and night. [Tai. 11, 12.]

~**-bako** --箱 'A three-robe box.' [S. VIII–22.]

~ **ippatsu** --一鉢 'Three robes and an alms-bowl'; these were the only daily necessities a monk was allowed to possess in early Buddhism. [S. III–1.]

Sannetsu 三熱 'The three kinds of heat'; also *sangen* 三患 'the three torments'; the three kinds of torment which dragons are believed to undergo: (1) their skin and flesh are burnt by a hot wind and sand-storm; (2) an evil wind strips them of their robes and thus deprives them of any protection from the heat; and (3) they are attacked by *garuḍa* (*karura**). Cf. *ryū*. [Tai. 29.]

Sannō 山王 Refers to Sannō Gongen 山王権現, the guardian god of Mt. Hiei. Originally it was another name for the Hiyoshi (or Hie) 日吉 Shrine on Mt. Hiei where the Shinto god Ōnamuji 大己貴 was enshrined. Later, 21 shrines of this name were erected on the mountain for the worship of various Shinto gods who were believed to be incarnations of buddhas or bodhisattvas. [Hei. 2.]

~ **Daishi** --大師 I. 'Mountain-King Great Master'; usually, an honorary title for Enchin*, but here refers to Sannō Gongen; see *Sannō*. [Tai. 9.] II. According to the *Taiheikishō*, refers to Sannō Gongen and Saichō*. [Tai. 17.]

~ **Gongen** --権現 See *Sannō*.

Sannu 三有 See *san'u*.

San'ō 山王 See *Sannō*.

Sanpai 三拝 'Triple prostration' in worship; this Buddhist custom developed in China where bowing twice is customary. 'Three' indicates a threefold action by body, mouth and mind, and thus the deepest level of respect. [Tai. 4.]

Sanpan 生飯 See *sanban*.

Sanpō 三報 'The three rewards or retributions'; the three different periods in which good or bad karma matures and brings about its effect. They are: (1) *jungen-pō* 順現報 or *genpō** 現報, matures in the present life; (2) *junshō-hō* 順生報 or *shōhō** 生報, matures in the next life; and (3) *jungo-hō* 順後報 or *gohō** 後報, matures in a life after the next. Cf. *sanjigō*.

Sanpuku 三福 'The three meritorious acts': (1) *sefuku* 世福, worldly meritorious acts, such as devotion to one's parents, respectfully serving one's teachers, and performing the ten good acts (*jūzen**); (2) *kaifuku* 戒福, meritorious acts performed in observing precepts, such as the five precepts (*gokai**); and (3) *gyōfuku* 行福, meritorious acts performed in practising the Buddhist Way.

∼-bun --分 'The three meritorious portions'; refers to *sanpuku**. [S. VII–25, Xb–1.]

∼-den --田 See *sanfukuden*.

Sanraishi 三禮師 See *shichisō*.

Sanran 散亂 'Distraction'; lack of concentration.

∼ sodō no kokoro --騷動の心 'A mind which lacks concentration and is violently agitated.' [S. Va–12.]

Sanriki 三力 'The three powers.' I. In Shingon*, the three powers contributing to enlightenment: (1) *gakudoku-riki* 我功德力, the power of one's meritorious practices; (2) *nyorai-kaji-riki* 如來加持力, the tathagata's (*nyorai**) power endowed to the practitioner; and (3) *hokkai-riki* 法界力, the power of the Dharma-realm (*hokkai**), which refers to the enlightening activity of one's own buddha-nature. [S. Xb–3.] II. The three factors for curing with the Dharma-medicine the illness of the delusions of sentient beings: (1) *egen-riki* 慧眼力, the wisdom of having a good knowledge of the Dharma-medicine; (2) *hōgen-riki* 法眼力, the ability to diagnose illnesses correctly; and (3) *kedō-riki* 化導力, the ability to prescribe the right medicine.

Sanrin 三輪 'The three discs'; the three layers of different elements, which lie one on top of the other under the ground: (1) *konrin** 金輪 (*kāñcana-maṇḍala*), the gold layer under the soil, which supports the world; (2) *suirin** 水輪 (*jala-m.*), the water layer under the gold one; and (3) *fūrin* 風輪 (*vāyu-m.*), the wind layer under the water one.

Sanrō 參籠 'To confine oneself' in a shrine or temple to pray to a divinity.

Sanron 三論 Refers to *Sanronshū**. [K. 41.]

∼-shū --宗 The San-lun sect; 'the three-discourse sect'; a Mahayana sect founded in China based on the three discourses originally written by Indian masters: (1) Nāgārjuna's (Ryūju*) *Chū-ron* 中論, (2) his *Jūnimon-ron* 十二門論, and (3) Āryadeva's (Daiba) *Hyaku-ron* 百論. The doctrine was systematized by

Chi-tsang 吉藏 (Kichizō*). Based on the standpoint of total negation of all existing things, it claims that the ultimate truth or reality is revealed through negation. One of the six sects in the Nara period (*rokushū**). [S. IV–1.]

Sansai 三災 'Three calamities' which occur at the end of each cosmic change and at the end of the world; see *daisansai* and *shōsansai*. [Tai. 8.]

Sanseken 三世間 'The three categories of realm': (1) *shujō-seken* 衆生世間 'the realm of sentient beings', (2) *kokudo-seken* 國土世間 'the realm of non-sentient beings', and (3) *goon-seken* 五陰世間 (or *goun-seken* 五蘊世間) 'the realm of the five *skandhas*'; cf. *goon*.

Sanshin 三心 Also *sanjin*; the three thoughts or three aspects of faith mentioned in the *Kanmuryōju-kyō*, viz. (1) *shijōshin* 至誠心, sincere heart, (2) *jinshin* 深心, deep thought, and (3) *ekōhotsu-ganshin* 廻向發願心, aspiring to be born in Amida's* Pure Land by turning one's merit of practice toward it.

～ **nenbutsu no ki** --念佛の機 One who practises the *nenbutsu** with three thoughts; cf. *sanshin*. [S. II–5.]

Sanshin 三身 'The three bodies (of a buddha).' I. (1) *hosshin** 法身, Dharma-body; (2) *hōjin** 報身, reward- or enjoyment-body; and (3) *ōjin** 應身, accommodative body. II. (1) *jishōshin** 自性身, self-nature body, which corresponds to Dharma-body; (2) *juyūshin* 受用身, enjoyment-body, which corresponds to reward-body; and (3) *hengeshin* 變化身, transformed body, which corresponds to accommodative body. III. (1) *hosshin* 法身, Dharma-body; (2) *ōjin* 應身, accommodative body; and (3) *keshin** 化身, transformed body. In this classification, *hōjin* 報身 is included in *hosshin*, and *ōjin* 應身 in (I) is divided into *ōjin* and *keshin*. Cf. *nishin*, *shishin* and *jusshin*.

～ **busshō** --佛性 'The three potentialities of buddhahood': (1) *shōin busshō* 正因佛性, the buddha-nature or True Thusness (*shinnyo** 眞如) which is the proper cause of Dharma-body (*hosshin** 法身); (2) *ryōin busshō* 了因佛性, the transcendental wisdom which 'discerns' (*ryō* 了) reality and is the cause of reward-body (*hōjin** 報身); and (3) *en'in busshō* 緣因佛性, various meritorious acts which 'assist' (*en* 緣) in the development of buddha-nature and serve as the cause of accommodative body (*ōjin** 應身). Cf. *san'in busshō*.

~ **enman no kakuō** --圓滿の覺王 'The king of enlightenment who is completely provided with the three bodies.' [Hei. 2.]

~ **no myōka** --の妙果 'The wonderful fruition of attaining the three bodies of a buddha.' [S. II–7.]

Sanshin 三信☆ 'The three aspects of faith' mentioned in the Eighteenth Vow of Amida* Buddha. They are: (1) *shishin* 至心, a sincere mind; (2) *shingyō* 信樂, serene faith; and (3) *yokushō* 欲生, a desire to be born in the Pure Land. They are the three aspects of faith in Amida's salvation which, according to Shinran*, is Amida's heart transferred to the aspirant; cf. *hongan no mon*.

Sanshin 散心 'Distracted thought'; one's ordinary state of mind; opposite of *jōshin**, 'concentrated thought'. [IH.]

~ **shōmyō** --稱名 Reciting the *nenbutsu** with distracted thoughts, i.e. in one's ordinary state of mind. [IH.]

Sanshō 三生 'The three lives'; the past, present and future lives. [Tai. 36.]

Sanshō 三性 'The three modes of existence': (1) *hengeshoshūshō** 遍計所執性, the mode of existence produced from one's attachment; the imaginary existence from the Buddhist point of view, which includes all existences considered to be really existing because of our innate attachment; (2) *etakishō** 依他起性, the mode of existence originating from causes and conditions; (3) *enjō jisshō** 圓成實性, the mode of existence conforming to the ultimate reality. [S. III–1.]

Sanshō 三障 'The three hindrances.' I. (1) *bonnōshō* 煩惱障, evil passions, (2) *gōshō** 業障, evil karmas, and (3) *hōshō* 報障, the painful retributions of being reborn in hell, the realm of hungry spirits, etc. II. (1) *hi-bonnōshō* 皮煩惱障, 'skin' evil passions, i.e. evil passions arising from contact with external objects; (2) *niku-bonnōshō* 肉煩惱障, 'flesh' evil passions, i.e. wrong views; (3) *shin-bonnōshō* 心煩惱障, 'mind' evil passions, i.e. basic ignorance. [S. II–5, 7.]

Sanshu no shikan 三種の止觀 See *sanshu shikan*. [S. V–1.]

Sanshu no sokushin jōbutsu 三種の即身成佛 'The three kinds of *sokushin jōbutsu** (becoming a buddha with one's present body)':

(1) *rigu* 理具, 'intrinsic embodiment', namely, all living beings are in themselves buddhas; (2) *kaji** 加持, 'transference of power and response', namely, one attains unity with Buddha through the three mystic practices (*sanmitsu** 三密); (3) *kentoku* 顯得, 'manifest attainment', namely, one achieves the full realization of buddhahood. [S. I–3.]

Sanshu shikan 三種止觀 'The three kinds of *shikan** meditation' established in the Tendai* sect: (1) *zenji shikan* 漸次止觀, 'gradual *shikan*', the practice of meditation which gradually advances from a lower to a higher stage until reaching the highest meditation on the ultimate reality; (2) *fujō shikan* 不定止觀, 'indefinite *shikan*', the practice of meditation which does not necessarily follow the order of gradual advance from a lower to a higher stage; and (3) *endon shikan** 圓頓止觀, 'perfect and sudden *shikan*', the practice of meditation which directly aims at realizing the ultimate reality quickly.

Sansō 山僧 See *sanzō*.

Santai 三諦 Also pronounced *sandai*; 'the triple truth'; the Tendai* term to explain reality in three aspects; (1) *kūtai* 空諦, 'truth of voidness', i.e. all existences are void and non-substantial in essence; (2) *ketai* 假諦, 'truth of temporariness', i.e. all existences are temporary manifestations produced by causes and conditions; (3) *chūtai* 中諦, 'truth of the middle', i.e. the absolute reality of all existences cannot be explained in either negative or affirmative terms. [Hei. 2.]

∼ **shikan** - -止觀 'The *shikan** contemplation on the triple truth.' [Tai. 17.]

∼ **sokuze** - -卽是 Refers to *santai sokuze jissō* 三諦卽是實相: 'the triple truth is identical with reality-aspect'. The Tendai teaching that the triple truth (*santai**) regarding reality is inter-related and in perfect harmony with the ultimate reality-principle (*jissō**). [Hei. 2.]

Santō 三塔☆ 'The three towers or pagodas' on Mt. Hiei; refers to the three sections into which Mt. Hiei is divided, namely, Tōtō 東塔 (Eastern Pagoda), Saitō 西塔 (Western Pagoda), and Yokawa 橫川. [Hei. 1, 2; K. 578.]

∼ **junrei** - -巡禮 'Pilgrimage to the three pagodas', i.e. the Eastern Pagoda, Western Pagoda, and Yokawa, all on Mt. Hiei.

[Tsu. 238.]

Santoku 三德　Also *sandoku*. I. 'The three virtues' of the Buddha: (1) *ondoku* 恩德, the virtue of providing benefit to living beings; (2) *dantoku* 斷德, the virtue of destroying all passions; and (3) *chitoku* 智德, the virtue of illumining reality with absolute wisdom. II. 'The three virtues' of one who has attained Nirvana: (1) *hosshin* 法身, the eternal body of the law; (2) *hannya* 般若, absolute wisdom in knowing reality; and (3) *gedatsu* 解脫, absolute freedom and emancipation. [S. IV–1.]

San'u 三有　Also *sannu*; 'the three existences'; the three trans-migratory existences; the three realms (*sangai**). [S. I–9.]

Sanwaku 三惑　'The three delusions' into which all delusions and evil passions are classified in the Tendai* doctrine: (1) *kenji no waku* 見思の惑, 'delusions arising from (incorrect) views and thoughts'; (2) *jinja no waku* 塵沙の惑, 'delusions (which hinder knowledge of salvation methods and are as numerous as the number) of dust-motes or sand-grains (in the River Ganges)'; and (3) *mumyō no waku* 無明の惑, 'delusions which hinder knowledge (of the ultimate reality)'. The first type of delusion is to be dealt with by followers of Hinayana as well as Mahayana, but the last two are to be destroyed only by bodhisattvas because followers of Hinayana are not aware of them.

Sanze 三世　'The three periods'; i.e. the past, present, and future.

Sanzen 三千　Refers to *sanzen no shohō* 三千の諸法, '3,000 exis-tences'. The Tendai* sect conceives of the whole universe as having 3,000 modes of existence. Firstly, there are ten states of existence (*jikkai**), from hell up to the buddha realm; each of these contains all the ten realms as potential existences, thus making 100 realms (*hyakkai**). Each of these 100 realms has the ten suchness aspects (*jūnyoze**), and so there are in all 1,000 aspects of existence (*sennyo* 千如). Further, existences are dis-tinguished as being of three kinds (*sanseken**): (1) *shujō-seken* 衆生世間, sentient existences; (2) *kokudo-seken* 國土世間, land or environment; and (3) *goon-seken* 五陰世間 (or *goun-seken* 五蘊世間), the five constituent elements of living beings. As each aspect of existence has those three modes, there are altogether 3,000 modes of existence.

〜**-daisen-sekai** - -大千世界　Sk. *trisāhasra-mahāsāhasrāḥ loka-dhātavaḥ*, 'triple-thousand great one-thousand world'; trichilio-cosm. A thousand worlds make a small one-thousand world (*shōsen-sekai* 小千世界); a thousand of these make a medium one-thousand world (*chūsen-sekai* 中千世界); a thousand of these make a great one-thousand world (*daisen-sekai*). Because of this triple multiplication by a thousand, it is called 'triple-thousand great one-thousand worlds'. [K. 53.]

〜 **jikkai** - -十界　'3,000 (existences) in the ten realms'. [S. I-3.]

〜**-kai** - -界　Abbr. of *sanzen-daisen-sekai**. [K. 53.]

〜**-sekai** - -世界　'Three times a thousand worlds', i.e. $1,000 \times 1,000 \times 1,000$ worlds; also *sanzen-daisen-sekai* 三千大千世界 'three-thousand-great-thousand worlds'. Often used in the sense of the whole world or universe. [K. 113, 600.]

Sanzen 參禪　'Participation in meditation.' I. Practising Zen meditation under a master. II. Zen meditation itself. III. Engaging in a *kōan** practice.

Sanzenten 三禪天　'The Third Meditation Heaven'; one of the heavens in the realm of form (*shikikai**), where inhabitants enjoy great pleasure in both mind and body, arising from deep medi-tation.

Sanzō 三藏　'The three stores'; Skt. *tripiṭaka*, 'three baskets'. I. The three divisions of the Buddhist scriptures: (1) *kyō* 經 (*sūtra*), the Buddha's teachings; (2) *ritsu* 律 (*vinaya*), the precepts; and (3) *ron* 論 (*abhidharma*), commentaries on the Buddha's teachings. II. The Hinayana scriptures; see *sanzōkyō*. III. The Three-Vehicle teachings, i.e. (1) *shōmonzō* 聲聞藏, the teaching for shravakas (*shōmon**); (2) *engakuzō* 緣覺藏, the teaching for pratyekabuddhas (*engaku**); and (3) *bosatsuzō* 菩薩藏, the teach-ing for bodhisattvas (*bosatsu**); cf. *sanjō*. IV. One well-versed in all the three divisions of the Buddhist teachings; in this sense, see *sanzō hosshi*.

〜 **hosshi** - -法師　I. 'A *tripiṭaka* master'; a monk well-versed in all the three divisions of the Buddhist teaching; a title of respect for a monk with an extensive knowledge of Buddhism. II. Specifi-cally refers to Hsüan-chuang 玄奘 (Genjō*).

〜**-kyō** - -教　'The *tripiṭaka* teaching.' I. The teaching of Bud-

dhism with three divisions; the whole Buddhist teaching. II.
The Hinayana teaching; the first of the four teachings of the
Buddha classified in Tendai*; in this sense, also *zōkyō** 藏教; cf.
kehō no shikyō.

~ **no hōmon** --の法門 'The Buddhist teachings in three divisions.'
[S. III-3.]

Sanzō 山僧 I. A monk of a mountain temple; a practitioner who
lives in a mountain hut. II. A self-depreciatory term for a monk;
the same as *yasō* 野僧 'a country monk' or *sessō* 拙僧 'a stupid
monk'. III. A priest of the Enryakuji* on Mt. Hiei. It is opposed
to *jisō** 寺僧, a priest of the Onjōji*; cf. *sanmon*.

Sanzon 三尊 'The three revered ones'; often a buddha and his two
attendant bodhisattvas.

~ **raigō** --來迎 'The three revered ones coming to welcome';
said of Amida* and his two attendant bodhisattvas, namely
Kannon* and Seishi*, coming to welcome an aspirant at his
death. [Hei. 3.]

Sanzu 三途 I. 'The three paths (or realms)'; also written 三塗.
The three lowest states of existence: (1) the realm of fire (*kazu*
火途), i.e. hell, where fierce fire burns the sinners; (2) the realm
of blood (*ketsuzu* 血途), i.e. the realm of animals, where they
fight and kill each other; (3) the realm of the sword (*tōzu* 刀途),
i.e. the realm of hungry spirits (*gaki** 餓鬼), where they are
tormented with swords or sticks. [Ho. 35.] II. 'The three currents';
see *sanzu no kawa* below.

~ **no furusato** --の故郷 'One's accustomed dwelling-place in
the three (evil) realms.' [S. I-6.]

~ **no gōin** --の業因 'The acts which cause one to fall into the
three evil realms.' [S. III-8.]

~ **no kawa** --の川 Also *mitsuse-kawa* 三瀬川, *watari-kawa* わ
たり川 and *sōzuka* 葬頭河; the river which a dead man must
cross during the first week after death. It has three different
currents, slow, medium and fast; hence, *sanzu* 'three ways'. One
who has done good acts in his life-time crosses the slow current,
and one who has done evil acts has to cross the fast current.

~ **no kyūri** --の舊里 Also *sanzu no kuri*; the same as *sanzu no
furusato*.

~ **no taiga** --の大河 I. 'The great river of the three evil realms'; an analogy to show that the three evil realms engulf sentient beings. [Tai. 33.] II. 'The great river with three different currents.' [Tai. 29.]

~ **no tsuyu no soko** --の露の底 'The dewy bottom of the three evil realms.' [Tai. 4.]

Sarasōju 沙羅雙樹 See *sharasōju*.

Sasagemono 捧物 'An offering' to a buddha or other deity. [K. 69.]

Sato-hosshi 里法師 'A village priest'; a priest living among ordinary people. [S. VI–18.]

Satori 悟 'Enlightenment.' [S. I–1.]

Satta 薩埵 Sk. *sattva*, 'being'; used in the sense of a bodhisattva; see *bosatsu*.

Sawari 障 'Hindrance' in the pursuit of the Buddhist Way.

Sazen 作善 'Doing good'; meritorious deeds. [Tsu. 72.]

~ **shakku ruitoku** --積功累德 'Doing good and accumulating merit and virtue.' [Tai. 39.]

Sehō buppō 世法佛法 'The worldly law and the Buddhist law.' [S. III–1.]

Seiban 西蕃 'The western barbarian (countries)'; Central Asian countries west of China. [Tai. 24.]

Seigan 誓願 'A vow'; cf. *hongan*, *honzei* and *shiguzeigan*✩.

Seikai 制戒 'Prescribed rules of conduct'; precepts. [S. Xa–6.]

Seikaku 聖覺 A Jōdo* priest (1167–1235); one of the chief disciples of Hōnen*, who spread the Jōdo teaching extensively; the author of the *Yuishin-shō* 唯信鈔 (*A Tract on Faith Alone*), *Shijūhachigan-shaku* 四十八願釋 (*A Commentary on the Forty-eight Vows*), *Kurodani-genkū-shōnin-den* 黑谷源空上人傳 (*A Biography of Genkū Shōnin of Kurodani*), etc. [S. VI–15.]

Seimon 制門 'Prohibition.' [S. II–10.]

Seishi 勢至 Abbr. of *Daiseishi**. [K. 63, 71.]

Sejidokoro 世事所 The place or room where secular matters are dealt with. [IH.]

Sejizaiō 世自在王✩ Sk. Lokeśvararāja; n. of a buddha; see *Amida*.

Sejō 世上 The same as *seken** 世間; the secular world; secular matters. [S. IV–9.]

Sejō 世情 'Worldly emotion'; secular thought.

Seken 世間 'Secular world.'

~ **no kai** --の戒 'Worldly precepts'; precepts in the worldly sense which are not much different from moral codes; cf. *shusse no kai*. [S. IV–1.]

~**-sha** --者 'A man of the world'; a worldly man; the opposite of *shussesha** 出世者. [S. Va–3.]

~ **shusse** --出世 A contraction of *seken shusseken**.

~ **shusse no koto** --出世の事 'Worldly and supra-worldly matters.' [S. II–1.]

~ **shusseken** --出世間 'Worldly and supra-worldly.'

Sekkai 說戒 'Expounding the precepts'; the same as *fusatsu** 布薩. [S. Xb–3.]

Sekkyō 說經 'Exposition of a sutra'; sermon.

~**-shi** --師 A priest who expounds a sutra or a Buddhist teaching; a preacher.

Semuisha 施無畏者 'One who endows fearlessness'; one who saves living beings from suffering, thereby giving them peace and fearlessness. Another name for Kannon*. [S. II–4.]

~ **no daiji** ----の大士 'A great being (i.e. bodhisattva) who provides, i.e. inspires, fearlessness.' Refers to Kannon*. [Hei. 2.]

Senbō 懺法 I. A prescribed method of repenting one's evil acts. [K. 520.] II. Refers to *Hokke senbō**. [K. 57.]

Senbon no Shaka Nenbutsu 千本の釋迦念佛 The ceremony of reciting Shakamuni's* name in the Shaka Hall of the Daihōonji 大報恩寺, Senbon, Kyoto, which took place 9th–15th of the second month. [Tsu. 228.]

Senbon no tera 千本の寺 The Daihōonji 大報恩寺 at Senbon, Kyoto. [Tsu. 238.]

Senbutsu 千佛 '1,000 buddhas' who appear in the world during the present 'sustenance *kalpa*' (*jūkō**). Shakamuni* was the fourth buddha, and Miroku* will be the fifth. [Tai. 22.]

Sendai 闡提 Sk. *icchantika*; abbr. of *issendai**. [S. II–5.]

~ no higan --の悲願 'The compassionate vow of being like an *icchantika*'; the vow that one will not become a buddha until one saves all beings. [S. II–5.]

Sendaira 扇 (or 旃) 提羅 I. Sk. *caṇḍāla*; see *sendara*. II. Sk. *ṣaṇḍha*; one who has no distinctive sexual organ; a eunuch; abbreviated as *daira** 提羅.

Sendan 旃檀 Sk. *candana*; sandalwood.

Sendara 旃陀羅 Also 扇提羅, 旃荼羅 etc.; Sk. *caṇḍāla*; the lowest class of people in India; outcasts who made their living by hunting, slaughtering cattle, burying dead bodies, etc., and were considered to be on a level with animals.

Sendatsu 先達 I. A title of respect for a revered priest. II. (As *sendatsu no yamabushi*) The chief of a group of mountain Buddhists. [K. 28, 57.]

Senge 遷化 'The passing away' of a priest.

Sengō 先業 'Prior acts'; acts in the previous life. [S.I–7, IV–9, VI –10, 15, VII–9.]

Senjaku 染着 See *zenjaku*.

Senjaku-hongan-nenbutsu-shū 選擇本願念佛集   Pronounced *Senchaku-hongan-nenbutsu-shū* in the Jōdo* sect; '*Collection of Passages concerning the Nenbutsu of the Selected Original Vow*', 2 fasc., said to have been written by Hōnen* in 1198 at the request of Fujiwara Kanezane. The book justifies the *nenbutsu** as the most effective method of salvation, and its publication marked the independence of the Jōdo sect. [TT. 83, No. 2608.]

Senjaku-shū 選擇集   Abbr. of *Senjaku-hongan-nenbutsu-shū**. [S. II –8.]

Senjō 先生 'The previous life.'

Senju 千手 'Thousand-hand'; refers to Senju Kannon*. [Ma. 199.]

~-darani --陀羅尼 Abbr. of *Senju-sengen-kanzeon-bosatsu-kōdai-enman-muge-daihishin-darani* 千手千眼觀世音菩薩廣大圓滿無礙大悲心陀羅尼; also called *Daihi-darani* 大悲陀羅尼, or *Daihi-ju* (or *Daihi-shu*) 大悲呪; an 82-phrase dharani which expounds the merit of Senju Kannon*. It is extensively used in esoteric Buddhism and in the Zen* sect. The dharani appears in the *Senju-kyō**. [O. II.]

~ **Kannon** -- 觀音 'The thousand-hand Kannon'; Sk. Sahasra-bhuja-sahasra-netra (lit. 'one thousand arms and one thousand eyes'); the kind of Kannon having one thousand arms with an eye on the palm of each hand. Also Senju-sengen Kanjizai 千手千眼觀自在 'Kannon with a thousand arms and a thousand eyes', Senpi Kanzeon 千臂觀世音 'Kannon with a thousand arms', etc. 'A thousand' simply indicates 'countless' and, in fact, this type of Kannon usually has only forty arms. So many arms and eyes indicate his boundless saving activity. [Hei. 2.]

~-**kyō** -- 經 '*Senju* (*Kannon**) *Sutra*'; abbr. of *Senju-sengen-kanzeon-bosatsu-kōdai-enman-muge-daihishin-darani-kyō* 千手千眼觀世音菩薩廣大圓滿無礙大悲心陀羅尼經; 1 fasc., tr. by Bhagavad-dharma (Kabondatsuma 伽梵達摩) [TT. 20, No. 1060]. [Hei. 3; K. 300; Ma. 198.]

~ **no chikai** -- のちかひ 'The vow of Senju (Kannon).' [K. 266.]

~ **no jisha** -- の持者 'One who has (faith) in Senju (Kannon).' [S. VI–15.]

~ **no keshin** -- の化身 'An incarnation of Senju (Kannon).' [Tai. 24.]

~ **no nijūhachibu-shu** -- の廿八部衆 'The 28 gods attending Senju (Kannon).' [Hei. 2.]

Senju 專修 'An exclusive practice'; refers to *senju nenbutsu**. [Tai. 24.]

~ **nenbutsu** -- 念佛 'The exclusive practice of the *nenbutsu**'; refers to Hōnen's* *nenbutsu* teaching. [Tai. 24.]

~ **no tomogara** -- の輩 'Followers who exclusively practise (the *nenbutsu**).' [K. 66.]

Sennichi-kō 千日講 'A thousand-day lecture' on the *Hoke-kyō**; cf. *hyakunichi sennichi no kō*. [O. VI.]

Sennichi no goma 千日の護摩 'A *goma** (*homa*) rite lasting for 1,000 days.' [K. 44.]

Sennyo 千如 'One thousand suchness aspects (of existence)'; see *sanzen* 三千.

Senpuku 瞻富 (also 瞻蔔) Sk. *campaka*; an aromatic tree with fragrant yellow flowers.

~-**ke** -- 花 (also -- 華) '*Campaka* blossoms.' [S. II–10.]

Senryaku jinpi 淺略深祕 'A shallow and abridged (meaning) and a deep and secret (meaning)'; a twofold interpretation method employed in the Shingon* sect, according to which one and the same word is explained at two levels. [Tai. 18.]

Sen'yo Kokuō 仙輿國王 See *Sen'yo Ō*. [Tai. 36.]

Sen'yo Ō 仙豫(also 仙譽, 仙輿)王 King Ṛṣidatta (?); a king in ancient India who was a previous incarnation of the Buddha. He killed 500 brahmins who had abused Mahayana and after he was released from hell where he had undergone torment as retribution for this act, he awakened to a faith in Mahayana and attained birth in the land of a buddha.

Senze 先世 'The previous life or lives.'

~ **no gō** --の業 'Acts in the previous lives.' [S. VII–22.]

~ **no hōen** --の芳縁 'Good relationships in previous lives.' [Hei. 3.]

Senzu-darani 千手陀羅尼 See *Senju-darani*.

Seppō 說法 'Exposition of the Dharma'; sermon.

~ **rishō** --利生 'Preaching the Dharma and benefitting living beings.' [Tai. 15.]

~ **shue no jō** --衆會の場 'The place for sermons and assemblies.' [Tai. 22.]

Seryō 施料 'Donations' of provisions, etc., to monks or a temple. [Tai. 35.]

Sese no chigiri 世々の契 'A tie or bond in the past lives.' [K. 331.]

Seshin 世親 Vasubandhu; also translated as Tenjin 天親. Born in Gandhāra in the 4th century, he was at first a Hinayanist and wrote the *Abidatsuma-kusha-ron**; but was later converted to Mahayana and composed many other treatises, including *Yuishiki-sanjūju* 唯識三十頌 and *Jōdo-ron** 淨土論.

Seshu 施主 'One who makes donations'; Sk. *dāna-pati*; also *dannotsu** 檀越; one who bears the expenses of a Buddhist service, sermon, etc., or makes offerings to a priest; also the chief mourner at a funeral.

~**-dan** --段 'The section on the promoter (of a service)'; the section in an announcement or prayer read in a service, which explains the promoter's intention.   [S. VI–15.]

Sesō 施僧   'Donations to priests.'   [Tai. 20.]

Sessen 雪山   'The snowy mountains'; the Himalayas; also Daisessen* 大雪山.

Sesshō 殺生   'Taking life, killing living beings'; cf. *gokai*, *hassaikai* and *jikkai*.

Sesshu 攝 (or 接) 取   'To take in'; said of the protection and guidance given by a buddha or bodhisattva to lead one to salvation.

~ **no kōmyō** --の光明   '(Amida's*) light which envelops' those who practise the *nenbutsu**.   [S. I–10.]

Setsu 刹   I. Sk. *kṣetra*; world; country.   II. Sk. *yaṣṭi*; a staff or pole erected in front of a buddha hall as a sign of a temple; hence, a temple.   III. Abbr. of *setteiri** 刹帝利 (Sk. *kṣatriya*), a caste in India which consists of kings and warriors.

Setsuha 說破   Pronounced *seppa*; 'to refute and destroy (a heretical view, etc.)'.

Setsuissaiubu 說一切有部   See *Ubu*.

Setsuna 刹那   Sk. *kṣaṇa*; 'a moment, an instant'.

Setsuri 刹利   Abbr. of *setteiri** 刹帝利.   [Tai. 32.]

~**-shu** --種   'The Kshatriya caste'; the second highest of the four castes in India, which comprises kings and warriors.   [Tai. 35.]

Setteiri 刹帝利   Sk. *kṣatriya*; a caste in India which consists of kings and warriors.

Sezen 世善   'Worldly goodness'; the opposite of supra-worldly good which leads to enlightenment.   [S. IV–1.]

Sezoku 世俗   'Secular, worldly.'

~**-tai** --諦   Sk. *saṃvṛti-satya*; 'secular truth'; reality in the worldly sense; also *zokutai* 俗諦. One of the two kinds of truth or reality, the other being the ultimate reality (*daiichigitai**).

Shaaku shuzen 捨惡修善   'Abolishing evil acts and doing good ones.'   [Tai. 8.]

Shaba 娑婆   Sk. *sahā*, 'endurance'; translated as *nindo* 忍土, *kannindo* 堪忍土, etc., 'the land of endurance'. Refers to this world, where people must endure various afflictions and pain.

[S. II–4.]

~**-dō** --道 'The realm of Sahā'; this world of Sahā. [S. VI–8.]

~ **no eiga** --の榮花 'Prosperity in this world of Sahā.' [Hei. 1.]

~ **sekai** --世界 'Sahā world'; this world of ours. [Hei. 3.]

~ **sekai no honju** --世界の本主 'The original lord of the Sahā world'; here it refers to Kannon* Bodhisattva. [Hei. 2.]

Shabetsu 差別 'Distinction, discrimination.'

~ **no gimon** --の義門 The aspect of the teaching in which distinctive meanings are explained or discussed. [S. IV–1.]

Shae (koku) 舍衞(國) Sk. Śrāvastī; n. of a kingdom in central India. The Buddha often stayed at the Jetavana monastery (Gion shōja*) outside the capital. Its ruler, King Prasenajit (Hashinoku*), was his patron. [Tai. 13.]

Shaka 釋迦 Sk. Śākya; the Shaka clan; Shakamuni* Buddha.

~ **Bosatsu** --菩薩 'Shakamuni Bodhisattva'; Shakamuni in his previous incarnations as a bodhisattva. [S. Va–4.]

~ **Daishi** --大師 'The Great Master Shaka,' i.e. Shakamuni Buddha. [S. III–1.]

~**-muni** --牟尼 Sk. Śākyamuni, lit. 'sage of the Shaka clan'; the founder of Buddhism. Born to King Śuddhodana and Queen Māyā in Kapilavastu, Central India, he was called Siddhārtha and also Gautama. He married and had a son, but left his family to seek the way of salvation at 29 (or 19 according to another tradition). After 9 years' training, he attained enlightenment and was called Buddha ('the enlightened one'). He preached the Way (called Dharma) to many people and thus the Buddhist Order (Sangha) was formed. He died at the age of 80, but there are different traditions as to his dates: e.g. 565–486 B.C. according to J. Takakusu, 463–383 B.C. according to H. Nakamura. Theravada has a different tradition, according to which the Buddha's dates are 624–544 B.C.

~ **Nyorai** --如來 'Shaka Tathagata'; the Buddha Shakamuni.

~ **yuihō no deshi** --遺法の弟子 'The followers of the teaching left behind by Shakamuni Buddha.' [S. II–8.]

Shakara ryūō 娑竭羅龍王 'The dragon-king Sāgara.' [K. 4.]

Shakatsura ryūō 娑竭羅龍王 See *Shakara ryūō*.

Shakkō honge 迹高本下 'High in the state of incarnation and low in the original state'; magnificent in the incarnation aspect, while remaining obscure in the original body; cf. *honkō shakuge*. [Tai. 16.]

Shakkyō 釋教 'Shakamuni's* teaching'; Buddhism.

Shaku 釋 I. Abbr. of Shaka* 釋迦 (Śākya), affixed to the Buddhist name of a monk. II. Abbr. of Taishaku* 帝釋. III. Commenting on a scripture; a commentary on a scripture. IV. A man's exposition of the Buddhist teaching, as opposed to that of the Buddha or a bodhisattva.

Shakubuku 折(or 責)伏 'To break and suppress'; to denounce or defeat evil; to suppress devils and opponents of Buddhism, or to destroy heresies.

~ **shōju** --攝受 'To denounce or suppress (evil) and embrace (good).' [S. II–5.]

Shakugen jushin 釋眼儒心 'The eye of Buddhism and the heart of Confucianism'; one who interprets the Buddhist teaching with the Confucian spirit. [S. III–3.]

Shakujō 錫杖 A staff with metal rings attached to the top. [S. II–5.]

Shaku-makaen-ron 釋摩訶衍論 '*The Commentary on the Discussion on Mahayana*'; the commentary on the *Daijō-kishin-ron** ascribed to Nāgārjuna (Ryūju*); 10 fasc., tr. by Fa-t'i-mo-to 筏提摩多 (Batsudaimata) [TT. 32, No. 1668]. The traditional ascription of the work to Nāgārjuna has been doubted, and scholars are generally of the opinion that it was originally compiled in China in the seventh to eighth centuries. This is treated as an important work in Shingon*.

Shakumon 釋門 'Shakamuni's* gate.' I. Buddhism. II. A Buddhist priest. [Tai. 8.]

Shakuniku chūdai no sō 赤肉中臺之相 'The figures in the central section of the "red-flesh" mandala'; the nine deities in the central eight-petal section (*chūdai hachiyō-in**) of the Matrix-store Realm Mandala (*Taizōkai mandara**). [Tai. 39.]

Shakuron 釋論 Refers to *Shaku-makaen-ron**. [IH.]

Shakushi 釋子 'Shaka's son'; a follower of Shakamuni* Buddha; a Buddhist. [S. III-8.]

Shakushi 釋氏 'Shaka clan'; n. of the clan in India which produced Buddha Shakamuni*; hence, Shakamuni himself. [Tai. 1, 24.]

~ **no oshie** --の教 'Shakamuni's teaching'; Buddhism. [Tai. 1.]

Shakyō 寫經 'Copying of a sutra.'

Shami 沙彌 Sk. *śrāmaṇera*; a novice; see *goshu* and *shichishu*.

Shamini 沙彌尼 Sk. *śrāmaṇerikā*; a female novice; see *goshu* and *shichishu*. [S. VI-9.]

Shamon 沙門 Sk. *śramaṇa*. I. In India, generally, a religious mendicant who has renounced the world and seeks salvation; an ascetic; a monk. II. A Buddhist monk.

Shana 遮那 Also 舍那; abbr. of Birushana*; also, refers to *shanagō*. [Tai. 24.]

~-**gō** --業 'The practice centring around Birushana* (Vairocana)'; the esoteric practice performed on Mt. Hiei together with the *shikan** meditation; cf. *shana shikan*.

~ **shikan** --止觀 Refers to *shanagō** 遮那業 and *shikangō* 止觀業; the esoteric practice and the Tendai* practice; the two types of practice prescribed by Dengyō Daishi (Saichō*) for students on Mt. Hiei. Those who follow *shanagō* engage in chanting Shingon* spells and sutras, and those who follow *shikangō* study and chant the *Hoke-kyō**, *Konkōmyō-kyō**, *Ninnō-kyō**, etc., and also practise the four kinds of Samādhi (*shishu-zanmai**). [Tai. 24.]

Shanoku 舍迮 Also 車匿; Sk. Chaṇḍaka; the driver who accompanied the Buddha when the latter left his castle to seek the way of salvation; he later became a disciple of the Buddha. [S. III-1.]

Shararin 沙羅林 'A *śāla* forest'; see *sharasōju*. [S. Va-4.]

Sharasōju 沙羅雙樹 'The twin *śāla* trees' under which the Buddha passed away. [Hei. 1.]

Shari 舍利 Sk. *śarīra*; relics of the Buddha or a revered priest. [Ma. 146.]

~-**kō** --講 A ceremony dedicated to the Buddha's relics. [K.283.]

~-**rai no mon** --禮の文 'A statement of worship of the Buddha's relics', written by Amoghavajra (Fukū*). [S. II–1.]

Shari 捨離 'To abandon and leave'; abandoning objects to which one is attached, or unwholesome mental tendencies, evil passions, etc. [S. Xb–1.]

Sharihotsu 舍利弗 Sk. Śāriputra; also Sharishi 舍利子, Shinshi 身子, etc.; one of the ten great disciples of the Buddha, (*jūdai-deshi**) well known for his intelligence. Born as a brahmin's son, he first followed Sañjaya-velaṭṭhiputta (see *rokushi gedō*). He died before the Buddha himself. [Tai. 24.]

Shasō 社僧 A Buddhist priest attached to a Shinto shrine. [Tai. 6.]

Shasuiki 灑水器 'A watering pot'; a container of scented water which is sprayed on the platform in Shingon* ritual. [S. I–6.]

Shasui no in 灑水の印 'The manual sign for pouring water.'

Shiben 四辯 Abbr. of *shimugeben**. [S. III–1.]

Shibun mandara 支分曼荼羅 See *shibunshō mandara*. [S. IV–1.]

Shibu no deshi 四部の弟子 'The four kinds of (the Buddha's) disciples': monks, nuns, and lay men and women. See *shishu* 四衆. [Tsu. 106.]

Shibunshō mandara 支分生曼荼羅 'The mandala arising from parts (of the body)'; a kind of mandala based on the body of a deity, master or practitioner.

Shichi 四智 'The four wisdoms'; the Hossō* teaching distinguishes the four enlightenment-wisdoms corresponding to the eight consciousnesses (*hasshiki**): (1) *daienkyōchi** 大圓鏡智 (*ādarśa-jñāna*), 'great perfect mirror-wisdom', the wisdom corresponding to the eighth consciousness, which reflects all phenomenal things as they are, like a clear mirror; (2) *byōdōshōchi** 平等性智 (*samatā-j.*), 'wisdom of (awareness of) the sameness (of all things)', the wisdom corresponding to the seventh consciousness, which sees the ultimate sameness of things; (3) *myōkanzatchi** 妙觀察智 (*pratyavekṣaṇā-j.*), 'wisdom of wondrous observation', the wisdom corresponding to the sixth consciousness, which discerns the distinctive features of all phenomena; and (4) *jōshosachi** 成所作智 (*kṛtya-anuṣṭhāna-j.*), 'wisdom of accomplishing what is to be done (to benefit sentient beings)', the wisdom corresponding to the whole of the first five consciousnesses, which accomplishes metamorphoses. Cf. *gochi*.

Shichibun zentoku 七分全得 'Seven portions (of the merit) are wholly obtained.' It is explained in some sutras that if one performs meritorious acts for the sake of a deceased person, one receives seven portions of the merit and only one portion of it goes to the deceased person. [S. VII–11.]

Shichibutsu no tsūkai 七佛の通戒 'The precepts or admonition of the seven (past) buddhas'; the admonition in verse form which all the seven past buddhàs (*kako shichibutsu**) gave as a guide to the Buddhist way of life. [S. IV–1.]

Shichibutsu tsūkaige 七佛通戒偈 'The verse of admonishment of the seven Buddhas.' The verse reads: 'Commit no evil, Do all the good acts, And purify your thoughts; This is the teaching of all buddhas.'

Shichibutsu Yakushi 七佛藥師 I. Also *Yakushi shichibutsu*; Yakushi and six other buddhas who are his transformed bodies; the six buddhas are: Zenshōmyō-kichijōō 善稱名吉祥王, Hōgatsu-chigon-kōōn-jizaiō 寶月智嚴光音自在王, Konjiki-hōkō-myōgyō-jōju 金色寶光妙行成就, Muu-saishō-kichijō 無憂最勝吉祥, Hōkai-raion 法海雷音 and Hōkai-shōe-yuge-jinzū 法海勝慧遊戲神通. [Hei. 3.] II. Refers to *Shichibutsu yakushi no hō**. [Tai. 1.]

~ no hō ----の法 'The (Tendai*) service dedicated to the seven buddhas, with Yakushi* as the central one,' to pray for the stopping of calamities, easy birth, etc.; also called *shichibutsu no mishiho* 七佛の御修法; one of the four great rituals of the Mountain School of Tendai (*sanmon shikadaihō**). [Hei. 3.]

Shichidaiji 七大寺 'The seven great temples' of Nara, i.e Tōdai-ji* 東大寺, Kōfukuji* 興福寺, Gangōji☆ 元興寺, Daianji☆大安寺, Yakushiji* 藥師寺, Saidaiji☆西大寺, and Hōryūji 法隆寺. [O.V.]

Shichidan no mishiho 七壇御修法 'The seven-platform ritual'; see *Shichibutsu Yakushi no hō*.

Shichikakushi 七覺支 'The seven factors of wisdom'; also *shichi-kakubun* 七覺分, *shichibodaibun* 七菩提分, etc. The seven factors for cultivating superior wisdom: (1) *chakuhō* 擇法, distinguishing the true law from wrong ones; (2) *shōjin* 精進, making efforts to practise the true law; (3) *ki* 喜, rejoicing in the true law; (4) *kyōan* 輕安 or *jo* 除, eliminating sluggishness and attaining comfort and relaxation; (5) *nen* 念, being mindful so as to keep the equilibrium of concentration and insight; (6) *jō* 定, concentration; and (7) *gyōsha* 行捨, detaching one's thoughts from external objects, thereby securing serenity of mind. The above seven factors of wisdom are included in the 37 elements of enlightenment (*sanjū-shichi dōbon**).

Shichikōsō 七高僧 'The seven revered priests' in the line of transmission of the teaching of the Jōdoshin* sect of Pure Land Buddhism; also *shichiso* 七祖 'seven patriarchs or masters'. They are: (1) Nāgārjuna (Ryūju* 龍樹) (2nd or 3rd century); (2) Vasubandhu (Tenjin 天親 or Seshin* 世親) (4th century); (3) T'an-luan 曇鸞 (Donran*) (476–542); (4) Tao-ch'o 道綽 (Dōshaku*) (562–645); (5) Shan-tao 善導 (Zendō*) (613–681); (6) Genshin* 源信 (942–1017); and (7) Genkū 源空 (see Hōnen) (1133–1212). The first two are Indian, the next three Chinese, and the last two Japanese. Cf. *Jōdo goso*.

Shichiman 七慢 'The seven kinds of pride': (1) *man* 慢, the feeling of being superior towards those who are inferior; (2) *kaman* 過慢, the feeling of being superior towards those who are one's equals; (3) *mankaman* 慢過慢, the feeling of being superior towards those who are superior to oneself; (4) *gaman* 我慢, being proud of oneself and despising others; (5) *zōjōman* 増上慢, considering oneself to be more worthy or virtuous than one actually is; (6) *hiretsuman* 卑劣慢 or *higeman* 卑下慢, being humble but feeling pride at being so; and (7) *jaman* 邪慢, being proud thinking that one is virtuous although, in fact, one is a person of little virtue.

Shichinan 七難 'The seven troubles or disasters'; there are three versions. I. The *Ninnō-kyō** presents the following: (1) loss of brilliance of the sun and the moon; (2) loss of brilliance of constellations; (3) fire; (4) floods; (5) strong gales; (6) draughts; and (7) bandits. II. According to the *Yakushi-kyō**: (1) epidemics; (2) invasion by a foreign power; (3) civil war; (4) changes in constellations; (5) eclipses of the sun and moon; (6) unusual storms; and (7) storms out of season. III. According to the T'ien-t'ai (Tendai*) interpretation, the *Hoke-kyō** presents troubles or disasters arising from: (1) fire; (2) water; (3) *rākṣasas* (*rasetsu**); (4) the ruler; (5) demons; (6) torments with cangues and locks; and (7) bandits. [S. VI–15.]

Shichishōzai 七聖財 The seven holy virtues: (1) *shin* 信, belief in the Dharma; (2) *kai* 戒, precepts; (3) *mon* 聞, hearing the Dharma; (4) *zan* 慚, being ashamed of one's sin before oneself; (5) *gi* 愧, being ashamed of one's sin before others; (6) *sha* 捨, being indifferent and unattached; and (7) *e* 慧, wisdom.

Shichishu 七衆 'Seven groups (of Buddhists)'; the seven groups into which the disciples of the Buddha were divided: (1) *biku* 比丘 (*bhikṣu*), monks, (2) *bikuni* 比丘尼 (*bhikṣuṇī*), nuns, (2) *shikishamana* 式叉摩那 (*śikṣamāṇā*), female novices who receive pre-ordination training consisting particularly of the observance of the six precepts (*roppōkai**), (4) *shami* 沙彌 (*śrāmaṇera*), male novices, (5) *shamini* 沙彌尼 (*śrāmaṇerikā*), female novices, (6) *ubasoku* 優婆塞 (*upāsaka*), laymen who have received the five precepts (*gokai**), and (7) *ubai* 優婆夷 (*upāsikā*), laywomen who have received the five precepts. Cf. *shishu* 四衆. [S. IV-1.]

Shichishu no shōzai 七種の聖財 See *shichishōzai*. [S. III-3.]

Shichisō 七僧 'Seven priests' taking main parts in a big service: (1) a lecturer (*kōshi* 講師), (2) one who reads out the title of the sutra to be lectured on (*dokushi* 讀師), (3) one who reads out the statement describing the organizer's wishes, etc. (*juganshi* 呪願師), (4) one who worships the Buddha in the manner of triple pro-stration (*sanraishi* 三禮師), (5) one who leads the chanting of verses eulogizing the Buddha's virtue, etc. (*baishi* 唄師), (6) one who leads the scattering of flowers (*sankashi* 散華師), and (7) one who manages the proceedings and takes the statement and prayer-sheet to the one who reads them (*dōdatsu* 堂達).

Shidagonka 斯陀含果 Sk. *sakṛd-āgāmi-phala*; see *ichiraika*.

Shidai 四大 'The four great (elements)'; see *shidaishu*. [S. VIII-21.]

~-shu --種 'The four great seeds'; Sk. *catvāri mahābhūtāni*; popularly, *shidai* 四大; the four constituent elements of the material world: (1) *chidai* 地大, the earth element, which re-presents solidity and supports things; (2) *suidai* 水大, the water element, which moistens and contains things; (3) *kadai* 火大, the fire element, which represents heat and matures things; and (4) *fūdai* 風大, the wind element, which represents motion and causes things to grow. Cf. *rokudai*. [Ho. 23.]

Shidai 支提 Sk. *caitya*; a monument or *stūpa* (*sotoba**). [Tai. 12.]

Shidaitennō 四大天王 'The four great heavenly kings'; the same as Shitennō*. [S. VII–4.]

Shide no yamaji 死手の山路 'The mountain path leading to (the palace of Enma*) in the world of the dead.' A dead person takes this path before seeing Enma, who weighs his sins and merits and passes judgement upon him. [Ho. 30.]

Shido 四土 'The four lands' distinguished in the Tendai* sect: (1) *bonshō dōgodo** (or *bonjō dōgodo*) 凡聖同居土, the land where ordinary people and sages live together, e.g. this Sahā (*Shaba**) world; (2) *hōben uyodo** 方便有餘土, the land temporarily established for those who have destroyed major evil passions, thereby attaining emancipation from transmigration in the three realms (*sangai**), but who still have other minor delusions to be dealt with; (3) *jippō mushōgedo** 實報無障礙土, the land of non-hindrance as the true reward for the performance of meditation practice, the land provided for bodhisattvas of higher stages and reigned over by an enjoyment-body-for-others buddha (*tajuyū-shin**); and (4) *jōjakkōdo** 常寂光土, the land of eternal, tranquil light, the land of a Dharma-body buddha (*hosshin**) or a self-enjoyment-body buddha (*jijuyūshin**).

Shien 資緣 'An assisting condition'; refers to one's daily necessities and provisions because they assist one's performance of Buddhist practices. [IH.]

～ **muhonnin** -- 無煩人 'One who has no worries about the daily necessities.' [IH.]

～ **no kemō** -- の悕望 'Desire for daily necessities.' [IH.]

～ **shōryaku** -- 省略 'Reducing one's daily necessities and provisions.' [IH.]

Shigoku 至極 'Utmost'; the utmost state, ultimate principle, consummation.

Shihachisō 四八相 'Eight times four marks'; refers to the 32 marks of physical excellence of a buddha (*sanjūni-sō**). [K. 721.]

Shiharai 四波羅夷 See *shijūzai*.

Shihokkai 四法界 'The four Dharma-realms'; the four categories of existence established in the Kegon* sect. (1) *ji-hokkai* 事法界, the realm of phenomena, (2) *ri-hokkai* 理法界, the realm of the noumenal principle, i.e. the ultimate reality-principle which is the quintessence of all phenomenal existences, (3) *jirimuge-hokkai* 事理無礙法界, the mode of existence in which all phenomenal things are interfused with the noumenal principle, and (4) *jijimuge-hokkai* 事事無礙法界, the reality of existence known to enlightened persons, in which all phenomenal things are mutually unhindered and interfused.

Shihyakushi-byō 四百四病 'The 404 illnesses'; all sorts of illnesses. According to the *Daichido-ron**, one's body is made up of the four elements (*shidaishu**) and is liable to illnesses caused by the constituent elements; each element causes 101 illnesses. [S. IV–9.]

Shiigi 四威儀 'The four modes of acts'; walking, standing, sitting and lying (*gyōjūzaga**); they are meant to embrace all man's physical activities.

Shijji 悉地 See *shitchi*.

Shijōkō 熾盛光 I. 'Blazing light'; another name for *Konrin butchō* 金輪佛頂 (the Buddha's head manifesting a golden wheel), a deification of part of the Buddha's head. [Ma. 278.] II. Refers to *Shijōkōhō**. [Tai. 1.]

～-butchō-giki - - -佛頂儀軌 A popular title for the *Daishō-myōkichijō-bosatsu-setsujosai-kyōryōhōrin* 大聖妙吉祥菩薩說除災教令法輪, 1 fasc., tr. into Chinese by Hui-lin 慧琳 (Erin) in 796. This is the fundamental text for the *Shijōkō-hō** rite [TT. 19, No. 966].

～-hō - - -法 'Blazing light ritual'; also *daishijōkō-hō** 大熾盛光法; an esoteric ritual performed to prevent calamities and based on the *Shijōkō-butchō-giki** 熾盛光佛頂儀軌; one of the four great rituals of the Mountain School of Tendai* (*sanmon shika-daihō**). It was performed mainly for emperors or ex-emperors.

～ no midokyō - - -の御讀經 Refers to *Shijōkō-hō**.

Shijō no kokoro 至誠の心 Refers to *shijōshin* II. [S. VI–15.]

Shijōshin 至誠心 I. Sincere, true heart. II. One of the three thoughts required of the aspirant for the Pure Land mentioned in the *Kanmuryōju-kyō**; see *sanshin* 三心.

Shijū 四重 Refers to *shijūzai**. [Tai. 2.]

～ gogyaku - -五逆 See *shijūzai* and *gogyakuzai*. [Tsu. 111.]

～ no zainin - - - -の罪人 The sinners who have committed the four grave offences (*shijūzai**) and the five rebellious acts (*gogyakuzai**). [Tai. 2.]

~-kin --禁 See *shijūzai*.

~-zai --罪 'The four major sins'; also *shijūkin* 四重禁, 'the four major prohibitions'. Refers to *shiharai* 四波羅夷, 'the four *pārājika* offences', which are the gravest of all offences for monks: having sexual intercourse, stealing, killing a person, and telling a lie about his spiritual attainment. Cf. *shijū gogyaku*. [Tsu. 111.]

Shijū endan 四重圓壇 'The fourfold mandala'; the four divisions of the Matrix-store Realm Mandala (*Taizōkai mandara**); also *shijū mandara**. [S. I–1.]

Shijūhachi-gan 四十八願 'The forty-eight vows' which Amida* made when he was a bodhisattva named Hōzō*. [K. 36.]

Shijū-hosshin 四重法身 'The fourfold Dharma-body'; same as *shishu-hosshin**. [S. I–3.]

Shijūkujū Maniten 四十九重摩尼天 Also *Shijūkujū Maniden* 四十九重摩尼殿. 'The 49-storeyed Mani-jewelled Palace'; the palace miraculously created for Miroku* (Maitreya) by heavenly beings of the Tuṣita Heaven (Tosotsuten*). The palace is made of *maṇi*-jewels (*mani**). [K. 64.]

Shijū mandara 四重萬陀羅 See next entry. [S. I–1, 3.]

Shijū mandara 四重曼荼羅 'The fourfold mandala'; the four sections constituting the Matrix-store Realm Mandala (*Taizōkai mandara**); also *shijū endan**. [S. IV–1.]

Shijūnishō-gyō 四十二章經 '*The Forty-two Chapter Sutra*'; tr. by Kāśyapamātaṅga (Kashōmatō*) and Chu Fa-lan 竺法蘭 (Jiku Hōran*) in the 1st century A.D. [TT. 17, No. 784]; the first sutra ever rendered into Chinese. [Tai. 24.]

Shika 四花 'The four flowers'; refers to the Tendai* tradition which classifies the Buddha's life-time teaching into four; see *shikyō* 四教. [Tai. 24.]

Shika 四果 'The four fruits'; the four stages of sainthood in Hinayana: (1) *yoruka* 預流果 or *shudaonka* 須陀洹果 (Sk. *srota-āpatti-phala*), 'the fruit of entering the stream' of the sacred law to be attained by destroying various wrong views; (2) *ichiraika* 一來果 or *shidagonka* 斯陀含果 (*sakṛd-āgāmi-phala*), 'the fruit of returning once more' to be attained by destroying gross evil passions; one who has attained this stage is subject to rebirth only once more in the human and the heavenly realms before attaining the final emancipation; (3) *fugenka* 不還果 or *anagonka* 阿那含果 (*anāgāmi-phala*), 'the fruit of not returning' to be attained by destroying more of one's evil passions; one who has attained this stage is not subject to rebirth in the realm of desire (*yokkai**) any more; hence, 'not returning'; and (4) *arakanka* 阿羅漢果 (*arhat-phala*), 'the fruit of arhatship' to be attained by destroying all evil passions; cf. *arakan*. [K. 617.]

Shika daijō 四箇大乘 'The four Mahayana sects,' namely, Kegon*, Tendai*, Shingon* and Zen*. [S. IV–1.]

Shikai 四海 'The four seas'; in Buddhist cosmology, refers to the outer seas surrounding Mt. Sumeru (Shumisen*), in which there are four continents; cf. *naikai gekai*. The term is also used in the sense of the whole world. [Tai. 24.]

Shikaku 始覺 'Entering upon enlightenment', as opposed to *hongaku** 本覺. [S. I–9.]

~ **no bodai** --の菩提 'Enlightenment realized for the first time.' [S. Xb–2.]

~ **no nehan** --の涅槃 'Nirvana which one enters for the first time.' [S. I–9.]

Shikan 止觀 Sk. *śamatha* and *vipaśyanā*; 'tranquility and contemplation'; stopping evil thoughts and meditating on the truth. [S. I–3.] II. Refers to the *Makashikan**. [S. IV–1.]

~ **jōe no shuin** --定慧の修因 'The causal practices of tranquil and contemplative meditation and the cultivation of wisdom', which are causes of a higher state of existence in the next life. [S. Va–2.]

Shika no daiji 四箇の大寺 'The four great temples': Tōdaiji* 東大寺, Kōfukuji* 興福寺, Enryakuji* 延曆寺, and Onjōji* 園城寺. [Tai. 12, 18.]

Shiki 色 'Form'; Sk. *rūpa*; a general name for matter which consists of atoms and has a distinctive shape and colour; one of the five constituent elements of existences (*goun**); also the opposite of 'mind' (*shin* 心).

~-**hō** -報 'The reward or retribution in a physical form' of one's past karma. [S. Xb–1.]

∼-**kai** -界 'The realm of form'; see *sangai*.

∼-**kō chūdō** -香中道 '(Even) a (tiny) form and a (slight) scent are the Middle Way'; a contraction of *isshiki ikkō muhi chūdō** 一色一香無非中道. [S. Va–12.]

∼ **mushiki no ten** -無色の天 'Heavens of the realms of form and non-form'; cf. *sangai*.

∼-**shin** -心 'Matter and mind'; physical and mental elements.

∼-**shin** -身 'A material body'; physical form of a buddha. [S. I–3.]

∼-**sōkan** -相觀 Meditation or visualization of a buddha's body and land. [IH.]

∼ **soku ze kū** -卽是空 'Form is itself empty'; a phrase from the *Hannyashin-gyō**; that which exists in material form is devoid of substantiality; cf. *kū soku ze shiki*. [S. IV–1.]

∼-**ton** -貪 I. Greed which arises in the realm of form (*shikikai**). II. Greediness for pleasurable things having fine colours and forms. [IH.]

∼-**yoku** -欲 I. Sexual desire, lust. II. Attachment to pleasurable colours and forms; one of the five kinds of desires; cf. *goyoku*.

Shiki 識 'Consciousness'; Sk. *vijñāna*. I. The subjective mental faculty of one's existence, whose overall function is to cognize objects. Hinayana establishes six consciousnesses (*rokushiki**), and Mahayana, eight to ten; cf. *hasshiki*. II. Consciousness in general; one of the twelve causations (*jūni-innen**).

∼-**jō** -情 'Consciousness and feeling'; mind and heart.

∼-**muhenjo** -無邊處 'The Abode of Limitless Consciousness'; Sk. Vijñāna-ānantya-āyatana; the second of the four abodes in the realm of non-form (*mushikikai**), where inhabitants are only aware of the presence of consciousness; cf. *mushikikai*.

Shikishamana 式叉摩那 Sk. *śikṣamāṇā*; a female novice, aged between 18 and 20, who receives pre-ordination training consisting particularly of the observance of the six precepts (*roppōkai**); one of the seven groups of Buddhists (*shichishu**).

Shikishamani 式叉摩尼 Sk. *śikṣamāṇā*; see *shikishamana*. [S. VI –9.]

Shikō 四劫 'The four *kalpas*' or periods of cosmic change: (1) *jōkō* 成劫, the *kalpa* of creation; the period during which the whole world, from hell to the First Meditation Heaven (*shozenten** 初禪天), is formed and sentient beings gradually inhabit various states of existence; (2) *jūkō** 住劫, the *kalpa* of existence; the period during which the world continues to exist; in this period man's life-span decreases from 84,000 to 10 years at the rate of one year every 100 years; it then begins to increase by one year every 100 years until it reaches 84,000 years; in this period, buddhas appear in the world; (3) *ekō* 壞劫, the *kalpa* of destruction; the period during which the whole world, from hell to the First Meditation Heaven, is destroyed by great fires, etc. (cf. *sansai*); and (4) *kūgō* 空劫, the *kalpa* of annihilation. The duration of each period is 20 small *kalpas* (see *kō* 劫).

Shikūsho 四空處 'Four abodes of emptiness'; refers to the four abodes or heavens in the realm of non-form; see *mushikikai*.

Shikyō 四教 I. 'The four teachings' of the Buddha during his life. According to Tendai* doctrine, there are two kinds: (1) *kegi no shikyō** and (2) *kehō no shikyō**. [Hei. 2.] II. Refers to *kehō no shikyō**. [S. IV–1.]

Shikyō 始教 'Beginning doctrine'; i.e. the elementary teaching of Mahayana; refers to Hossō* and Sanron* teachings, one of the five teachings classified in Kegon*; see *gokyō*. [S. IV–1.]

Shima 四魔 'The four devils': (1) *bonnōma* 煩惱魔, evil passions which torment one's mind and body; (2) *onma* 陰魔, the five constituent elements of one's existence (*goun**) which produce various kinds of pain; (3) *shima* 死魔, death; and (4) *takejizaitenshima* 他化自在天子魔, the king of devils in the Paranirmitavaśavartin Heaven (Takejizaiten*) who tries to thwart one's attempts to do good. [S. II–5.]

Shima 死魔 'The devil of death'; one of the four devils (*shima**).

Shimagonjiki 紫磨金色 'Purplish gold colour'; cf. *shima ōgon*. [K. 37.]

Shiman 四曼 Abbr. of *shishu mandara**; 'the four mandalas'. [Tai. 18, 24.]

~ furi --不離 'The four mandalas are mutually inseparable.' [Tai. 18, 34.]

~ **sōsoku** --相卽 'Mutual identity of the four kinds of mandalas'; according to Kūkai*, the four kinds of mandalas (*shishu mandara**) interchange with each other without hindrance. Further, each existing thing contains all the four mandalas, and the four mandalas contained in a person and those of the cosmic buddha, Dainichi*, are identical with each other. [Tai. 39.]

Shiman 指鬘 'Finger-wreath'; another name for Ōkutsumara*.

Shima ōgon 紫磨黄金 'Purplish gold'; also *shikon* 紫金; the purplish gold said to be obtained from the river running through the mango forest in the Jambudvīpa continent (Enbudai*); the same as *enbudangon**. [Tai. 24.]

Shimeizan 四明山 Originally, n. of a mountain in China; used as another name for Mt. Hiei. [Tai. 12.]

Shimo hosshi 下法師 Also *chūgen hosshi* 中間法師; a lowly priest who does odd jobs in a temple. [Tsu. 218.]

Shimugeben 四無礙辯 'The four kinds of unhindered speech' of the buddha and bodhisattva: (1) *hō-muge* 法無礙, thorough knowledge and command of words and sentences explaining the Dharma; (2) *gi-muge* 義無礙, thorough knowledge of the meanings of the teachings; (3) *ji-muge* 辭無礙, absence of impediment in communicating in various dialects; (4) *gyōzetsu-muge* 樂說無礙, absence of impediment in preaching to people in accordance with their propensities. [S. III–1.]

Shimui 四無畏 See *shimushoi*.

Shimushoi 四無所畏 'The four forms of fearlessness'; Sk. *catvāri vaiśāradyāni*; the four kinds of fearlessness, or utter conviction, in preaching the Dharma. I. Those of a buddha are: (1) *shōtō-gaku-mui* 正等覺無畏, fearlessness in asserting that he has attained the perfect enlightenment (*shōtōgaku* or *shōgaku**); (2) *royōjin-mui* 漏永盡無畏, fearlessness in asserting that he has destroyed all defilements (*ro**); (3) *sesshōhō-mui* 說障法無畏, fearlessness in showing people those elements which hinder realization of the Dharma, i.e. evil passions; and (4) *setsushutsudō-mui* 說出道無畏, fearlessness in expounding the method of emancipation. II. Those of a bodhisattva are: (1) *nōji-mui* 能持無畏, fearlessness in expounding phrases and passages of the Dharma which he has heard from the teacher and keeps in his memory;

(2) *chikon-mui* 知根無畏, fearlessness in expounding appropriate teachings to people with a correct knowledge of their propensities; (3) *ketsugi-mui* 決疑無畏, fearlessness in countering an opponent's attack on the Buddhist teaching and clearing away his doubts; and (4) *tōhō-mui* 答報無畏, fearlessness in giving appropriate answers to questions that may be put to him.

Shinbon 心品   'Mental quality or grade.'   [S. Va–3.]

Shinbun Shingyō 神分心經   Also *jinbun Shingyō*; chanting the *Hannya-shin-gyō** at the beginning of a service to request the presence of good deities and drive away devils.   [O. VI.]

Shinchi 心地   See *shinji*.

Shindai 眞諦   Paramārtha (499–569); an Indian monk who went to China in 546 and translated 64 texts, including *Shō-daijō-ron* 攝大乘論 and *Daijō-kishin-ron** 大乘起信論. He is looked upon as the founder of the She-lun 攝論 (Shōron) sect.

Shindo 身土   'Body and land' of a buddha.   [S. I–3.]

Shindoku 眞讀   'The true reading'; refers to the chanting of the whole of the *Daihannya-kyō**; the opposite of *tendoku**.   [Tai. 23.]

~ **no Daihannya** -- の大般若   'The true reading (i.e. chanting the whole) of the *Daihannya-kyō**.'   [Tai. 23.]

Shinenjo 四念處   'The four stations or bases of mindfulness'; also *shinenjū* 四念住; the fourfold contemplation to be practised after one has completed the exercise of tranquilizing one's mind (*gojōshinkan**): (1) *shin-nenjo* 身念處, contemplating one's body as defiled; (2) *ju-nenjo* 受念處, contemplating one's feelings as painful: even though there are agreeable sensations, they are deceptive, and so there is no true pleasure in the world; (3) *shin-nenjo* 心念處, contemplating one's mind as constantly changing; and (4) *hō-nenjo* 法念處, contemplating things in general as devoid of fixed entities. The four stations or bases of mindfulness are included in the 37 elements of enlightenment (*sanjūshichi dōbon**).

Shinga 眞我   'One's true self.'   [S. Vb–11, VII–25.]

Shinge 信解   'Faith and understanding'; Sk. *adhimukti*; having both faith in and understanding of the Buddhist teaching.

Shinge no hō 心外の法   'Things outside the mind.'   [S. I–9.]

Shingo 心期 'State of mind'; receptivity, preparedness. [S. IV–1.]

Shingon 心言 'Thought and word.'

~ **michi taetari** --路たえたり 'Thought and words fail'; inconceivable and ineffable. [S. IV–1.]

Shingon 眞言 Sk. *mantra*. I. A syllable, word, or phrase which contains mystic truth. II. The Shingon sect; see *Shingon-shū*.

~ **darani** --陀羅尼 Sk. *mantra dhāraṇī*; mystic words and phrases, a spell. [Tsu. 222.]

~ **himitsu** --祕密 'The esoteric (teaching) of the Shingon sect.' [Tai. 12.]

~-**in** --院 Also Shuhō-in 修法院 and Mandara-dōjō 曼荼羅道場; the hall for esoteric practices at the imperial palace. Built in 835 at the suggestion of Kūkai* to perform the New Year seven-day ritual (*goshichinichi mishiho**). [Tai. 24.]

~ **no michi** --の道 'The Shingon Way'; the Shingon teaching. [Tai. 12.]

~-**shi** --師 'Master of spells'; a priest who chants esoteric spells and texts and recites prayers. [O. II.]

~ **shikan** --止觀 'The esoteric and *shikan** practice' performed on Mt. Hiei. [Tai. 24.]

~-**shū** --宗 The Shingon sect founded by Kūkai* at the beginning of the 9th century and based on the teaching he had brought from China; one of the 'eight and nine sects' (*hasshū kushū**) in Japan. The full name is Shingon-darani-shū 眞言陀羅尼宗 'the sect of true words and spells'; also Himitsu-shū 祕密宗 'the esoteric sect', Mandara-shū 曼荼羅宗 'the Mandara* sect', Yuga-shū 瑜伽宗 'the mystic unity sect' and Darani-shū 陀羅尼宗 'the spells sect'. It is also called Tōmitsu 東密 'the Tōji* esotericism' as opposed to the esoteric tradition practised on Mt. Hiei, which is called Taimitsu 台密 'the Tendai* esotericism'. The Shingon teaching is primarily based on two sutras:(1) the *Dainichi-kyō** 大日經 and (2) the *Kongōchō-kyō** 金剛頂經. According to tradition, Kongōsatta* (Vajrasattva) received esoteric teachings directly from Dainichi* (Mahāvairocana), the Cosmic Buddha, and deposited them in an iron tower in southern India. Later, Nāgārjuna (Ryūmyō*) opened the tower and transmitted the scriptures to the outside world, after which they were taken

to China and translated by Vajrabodhi (Kongōchi), Śubhākara-
simha (Zenmui*) and Amoghavajra (Fukū*) in the eighth
century. Kūkai received the esoteric teachings from Hui-kuo
惠果 (Keika) and systematized them. He opened Mt. Kōya in 816
as a centre for the practice of esoteric Buddhism, and later, in 823,
when he was given the Tōji*, he made it another centre for the
study and practice of the Shingon teaching. The Shingon practice
is characterized by elaborate rituals, the recitation of dharani
(*darani**) and contemplation on mandalas. Unity with a particular
buddha or deity and, consequently, enlightenment, are to be
attained through 'the three mystic practices' (*sanmitsu**).

Shingyō 心行 'Mental activity.' [S. Xa–10, Xb–1.]

~ **shometsu** - - 處滅 'Cessation of mental activity'; used to
describe the absolute reality which is beyond the reach of thought.
[S. Xb–3.]

Shingyō 心經 '*The Heart Sutra*'; refers to *Hannya-shin-gyō**. [K.
38; O. VI; S. I–3.]

Shingyō 信行 'Faith and practice.'

Shingyō 信敬 'Belief and respect.' [S. II–3.]

Shin'i 瞋恚 See *shinni*.

Shinigō 死業 'The karma which causes death'; some act in the
previous life which makes death inevitable. [Tai. 32.]

Shin'in 心印 'Mind-seal'; abbr. of *busshin'in** 佛心印 'seal of the
buddha-mind'; also *butsuin** 佛印 'buddha-seal'; *in* 印 is construed as *inka* 印可 or *inshō* 印證 'certification (of one's enlightenment)'. The term is used in Zen* and refers to the absolute mind-
essence transmitted from master to disciple. [Tai. 26.]

Shinji 心地 'Mind-ground'; the mind; mental state; mind is so
called, because it is the basis of all existences and also because it
is the base on which all practices are performed.

~-**kan-gyō** - - 觀經 '*Meditation on the Mind-base Sutra*'; abbr. of
Daijō-honshō-shinjikan-gyō 大乘本生心地觀經; 8 fasc., tr. by
Prajñā (Hannya 般若) [TT. 3, No. 159]. [S. I–6,II–10, III–2, VI–17,
18, Xa–2.]

~ **no shugyō** - - の修行 'Practice (to cultivate) the mind-ground';
a meditative practice. [S. IV–1.]

Shinjin 信心 I. Faith; belief in the buddha and Dharma or in the Three Treasures (*sanbō**). II. In Zen*, belief in the true nature of one's mind, i.e. the buddha-nature.

Shinjin 眞身 See *shinshin*.

Shinjo 心所 Abbr. of *shinshouhō* 心所有法 'elements possessed by the mind'; distinctive mental functions, as opposed to the overall cognitive function of one's consciousness, which is called *shinnō** 心王. Kusha* establishes 44 such elements, and Hossō* 51.

Shinju 神呪 'A mystic spell.' [S. I–3.]

Shinkū 眞空 'True void.' I. Refers to the Hinayana Nirvana, which is beyond all falsity (*shin* 眞) and above phenomenal forms (*kū* 空). II. Refers to the True Thusness (*shinnyo** 眞如), the reality-principle established in Mahayana, which is beyond delusory relative concepts. III. In Mahayana, the absolute void, as distinguished from the relative one which is simply a negation of existence; in this sense, *shinkū* is not separate from, but is identical with, *myōu** 妙有, the wondrous existence.

~ **jakumetsu** --寂滅 'The true void which is tranquil and extinct'; the absolute tranquillity and total extinction of the true void. [S. VI–16.]

~ **myōjaku** --冥寂 'True void is imperceptible and tranquil'; from the viewpoint of absolute reality, all existences are void (i.e. devoid of substance) and tranquil. [S. IV–1.]

Shinmei butsuda 神明佛陀 'Gods and buddhas.' [Hei. 2; Tai. 6.]

Shinnen 心念 'Thinking in the mind'; thought.

Shinni 瞋恚 'Anger, enmity.'

Shinnō 心王 'The mind-king'; the overall cognitive function of one's consciousness, as opposed to distinctive mental functions which belong to it and are called *shinjo** 心所. In Kusha*, only one mind-king is conceived, but Hossō* establishes eight, one for each of the eight consciousnesses (*hasshiki**). [S. VIII–23.]

Shinnyo 眞如 'The True Thusness'; the ultimate reality; as-it-is-ness.

~ **no ichiri** --の一理 'The one principle of the True Thusness.' [S. IV–1.]

~ **no myōri** -- の妙理 'The subtle principle of the True Thusness.'
[S. III–1.]

~ **no rigon** -- の離言 'Indescribability of the True Thusness.'
[S. IV–1.]

Shinran 親鸞 The founder of the Jōdoshin* sect (1173–1262).
Born of the Fujiwara clan at Hino 日野, southeast of Kyoto, he
was called Matsuwakamaro 松若麿. Bereft of his parents when
very young, he entered the priesthood at the age of nine under
Jien 慈圓 of the Shōren-in 青蓮院, Kyoto, and was named Hannen
範宴. Then he went to Mt. Hiei, where he practised the Tendai*
method of salvation until 29. Having found that 20 years of study
and practice were useless for attaining enlightenment, he left the
mountain to seek other ways. He attempted a 100-day confinement at the Rokkaku-dō* to pray to Prince Shōtoku (Shōtoku
Taishi*), who built the temple, for a revelation of the way he
should follow, and at dawn on the 95th day, he was given words
of inspiration. Encouraged by them and led by his friend,
Seikaku*, he went to see Hōnen*, who was at the time propagating
the *nenbutsu** teaching. He then became Hōnen's disciple and
changed his name to Shakkū 綽空 and, later, to Zenshin 善信.
Under the master's guidance he abandoned efforts to attain
salvation by his own power (*jiriki**) and entrusted himself whole-
heartedly to Amida* Buddha. When the *nenbutsu* teaching was
prohibited and Hōnen was exiled to Shikoku in 1207, he was
exiled to Kokubu 國府, Echigo Province (the present Niigata
Prefecture), where he married Eshin-ni 惠信尼. He was pardoned
in 1211 but, having heard of the death of Hōnen, he stayed on
and, in 1214, he left Echigo and went to Hitachi (Ibaragi Prefecture). While he propagated there the teaching of the *nenbutsu*
based on Amida's power (*tariki**), he wrote the foundation text
of the Jōdoshin sect, *Kyōgyōshinshō**. After staying in Hitachi
for about 20 years, he returned to Kyoto, where he continued his
literary activity until he died. His works include a large number
of hymns in Japanese (*wasan* 和讃). Emperor Meiji gave him the
posthumous name and title, Kenshin Daishi 見眞大師.

Shinren 心蓮 'Lotus of the mind'; the intrinsic nature of one's
mind, which is pure and undefiled, is compared to a lotus. [K.
500.]

Shinriki 信力 'Power of faith.' [K. 26.]

Shinse 信施 'Offerings or gifts from a devotee.' [Hei. 3; S. II–6.]

~ **muzan no tsumi** - -無慙の罪 'The sin of appropriating devotees' gifts to the temple or the Buddha without any feeling of shame or guilt.' [Hei. 3.]

Shinshi 身子 Sk. Śāriputra; see *Sharihotsu*. [Tai. 37.]

Shinshin 眞心 'The true mind'; the true mind-nature which is buddhahood; the same as *honshin**. [S. III–8, IV–1.]

Shinshin 眞身 'The true body' of a buddha. It refers to *hosshin** 法身 or *hōjin** 報身, as opposed to *ōjin** 應身. [S. II–4, 6.]

Shinshō 眞性 'The real nature' of existence; the intrinsic nature or essence of things. [S. II–9.]

Shinshū 眞宗 I. The true teaching of the Buddha. [Tai. 17.] II. Abbr. of Jōdoshin-shū*.

Shintai 眞諦 I. Sk. *paramārtha-satya*; the ultimate truth or reality. Cf. *daiichigitai*. II. Paramārtha (499–569); see *Shindai*.

~ **zokutai** - -俗諦 'The absolute and the relative reality'; the supra-worldly and the worldly; the Buddhist Way and secular affairs. [Tai. 20.]

Shinyoisoku 四如意足 'The four bases of transcendental knowledge'; also *shijinsoku* 四神足; the four qualities of the supernormal consciousness, which develops as it passes through the stages of concentration. They are: (1) *yoku-jinsoku* 欲神足, the transcendental knowledge based on the concentration of will; (2) *gon-jinsoku* 勤神足, the transcendental knowledge based on the concentration of effort; (3) *shin-jinsoku* 心神足, the transcendental knowledge based on the concentration of thought; and (4) *kan-jinsoku* 觀神足, the transcendental knowledge based on the concentration of investigation into the principle of reality. They are practised after the completion of the four right efforts (*shishōgon**). The four bases of transcendental knowledge are included in the 37 elements of enlightenment (*sanjūshichi dōbon**).

Shinza 陞座 See *shinzo*.

Shinzo 陞座 I. To take the chair in preaching the Dharma. [Tai. 26.] II. To take the chair in performing a memorial service for a dead person.

Shinzoku 眞俗 I. Refers to *shintai** 眞諦 (Sk. *paramārtha-satya*) and *zokutai** 俗諦 (Sk. *saṃvṛti-satya*); the absolute and the relative reality; the supra-worldly and the worldly; the Buddhist Way and secular affairs. [Tsu. 155.] II. Priests and laymen. [Tai.24.]

Shiō 四王 'The four kings'; refers to Shitennō* (the Four Guardian Kings). [Tai. 12.]

Shiōten 四王天 'The four-king heavens'; n. of the heavens reigned over by the Four Guardian Kings (*Shitennō**). [Tai. 8.]

Shippō 七寳 'The seven treasures.' There are several different versions; the one given in the *Amida-kyō** is: gold, silver, lapis lazuli, crystal, red pearls, diamond, and coral.

〜 **shōgon** --莊嚴 'Adornment with the seven treasures.' [Tai. 8.]

〜 **shōgon no sumika** --莊嚴のすみか 'A dwelling place adorned with the seven kinds of jewels.' [Hei. 2.]

〜**-tō** --塔 'A tower adorned with seven kinds of treasure.' [K. 51.]

Shira 尸羅 Sk. *śīla*; precept. [S. IV–1.]

Shiri jakumetsu 至理寂滅 'The ultimate principle being tranquil and extinct.' [S. III–8.]

Shiron-shū 四論宗 'The Ssu-lun sect; the four-discourse sect'; a Mahayana school of thought centring on the principle of the void (*kū** 空) and based on the four discourses originally written by Indian masters: (1) *Chū-ron* 中論, '*Discourse on the Middle*,' by Nāgārjuna (Ryūju*); (2) *Jūnimon-ron* 十二門論, '*Twelve-Gate Discourse*,' by Nāgārjuna; (3) *Hyaku-ron* 百論, '*One Hundred-Verse Discourse*,' by Āryadeva (Daiba); and (4) *Daichido-ron** 大智度論, '*Great Wisdom Discourse*,' by Nāgārjuna. This school did not develop as an independent sect but was absorbed by the San-lun (Sanron*) sect.

Shiryō 死靈 'The spirit of a dead person,' often a revengeful one. [Hei. 3.]

Shiryo funbetsu 思慮分別 'Contemplating and discerning.' [S. Xb –2.]

Shishi 師子 Sk. Siṃha; the 24th of the 28 patriarchs of the Zen* tradition in India; known as Shishi Sonja 師子尊者, Shishi Biku 師子比丘 and Shishibodai 師子菩提 (Sk. Siṃhabodhi). Having received the teaching from Kakurokuna 鶴勒那, he expounded it extensively in northwest India, but was killed by the king of Kashmir. He is also regarded as the 24th and last patriarch of the Tendai* tradition in India; cf. *konku sōjō.* [Tai. 24.]

Shishi 師資 'Master and disciple.'

Shishikoku 師子國 'The Land of Lions'; Sk. Siṃhala; the ancient name for Ceylon, now Sri Lanka; also Shishishū 師子州 'the Island of Lions'. [Tai. 32.]

Shishiku 師子吼 'A lion's roar'; often used to describe the Buddha's preaching of the Dharma. [Tai. 24.]

Shishin 四身 'The four bodies (of a buddha)'; there are several versions, of which the popular ones are as follows: I. (1) *hosshin** 法身, Dharma-body; (2) *hōjin** 報身, reward- or enjoyment-body; (3) *ōjin** 應身, accommodative body; and (4) *keshin** 化身, transformed body. II. (1) *jishōshin** 自性身, self-nature body, which corresponds to Dharma-body; (2) *jijuyūshin** 自受用身, self-enjoyment body, which partly corresponds to reward-body; (3) *tajuyūshin** 他受用身, the body for others' enjoyment, which also corresponds to reward-body; and (4) *hengeshin** 變化身, transformed body, which partly corresponds to accommodative and transformed bodies.

Shishingon no bosatsu 四親近の菩薩 'The four attendant bodhisattvas'; the four bodhisattvas in attendance on the four buddhas in the Diamond Realm Mandala (*Kongōkai mandara**). [S. II–8.]

Shishiō 師子王 'The king of lions'; the Buddha's steps are often compared to those of the king of lions. [Tai. 24.]

Shishō 四生 'The four modes of birth': (1) *taishō* 胎生, 'birth from the womb'; (2) *ranshō* 卵生, 'birth from an egg'; (3) *shisshō* 濕生, 'birth from moisture'; and (4) *keshō* 化生, 'metamorphosis'. [S. I–1, II–5, 8, III–1, 7; Tai. 23.]

~ **no eko** --の依怙 'The refuge for all living beings undergoing the four modes of birth.' [S. III–1.]

~ **no tenpen** --の轉變 'Undergoing various states of existence through the four modes of birth.' [S. I–9.]

Shishō 四聖 'The four holy ones.' I. The four kinds of sages: *shōmon** 聲聞 (*śrāvaka*), *engaku** 緣覺 (*pratyekabuddha*), *bosatsu** 菩薩 (*bodhisattva*) and *butsu** 佛 (*buddha*). II. The four great disciples of Kumārajīva (Kumarajū*): Tao-sheng 道生 (Dōshō),

Seng-chao 僧肇 (Sōjō), Tao-jung 道融 (Dōyū) and Seng-jui 僧叡 (Sōei). III. The four people especially mentioned as holy men for their parts in the construction and inauguration of the Tōdaiji*: Emperor Shōmu*, Rōben* 良辨, Baramon Sōjō* 婆羅門僧正 and Gyōgi* 行基; cf. *shishō dōshin no tera*. IV. In the Zen* sect, the four holy beings: Amida*, Kannon*, Daiseishi* and all the Daikaishu*.

∼ **dōshin no tera** --同心の寺 'The temple built by the joint effort of the four sages'; see *shishō* III. [S. Vb–10.]

Shishōbō 四攝法 'The four methods of winning (people) over'; also *shishōji* 四攝事 'the four matters (to be employed) in order to win (people) over'; Sk. *catur-saṃgraha-vastu*; the four methods which bodhisattvas employ in order to approach and save people. They are: (1) *fuse* 布施, giving the gift of the Dharma or something else people would like; (2) *aigo* 愛語, using kind words; (3) *rigyō* 利行, benefitting by kind conduct; and (4) *dōji* 同事, doing something together with the people.

Shishōgon 四正勤 'The four right efforts'; also *shiidan* 四意斷, *shishōdan* 四正斷, and *shishōshō* 四正勝; the fourfold endeavour to be made by the practitioner after the completion of the fourfold contemplation (*shinenjo**): (1) to strive to eliminate evils done; (2) to strive not to commit evils; (3) to strive to produce good; and (4) to strive to increase good done. The four right efforts are included in the 37 elements of enlightenment (*sanjūshichi dōbon**).

Shishōji 四攝事 'The four matters (to be employed) in order to win (people) over'; see *shishōbō*.

Shishōtai 四聖諦 'The fourfold noble truth'; part of the basic tenet of Buddhism: (1) *kutai* 苦諦, the truth of suffering, i.e. the reality that life is full of suffering; (2) *jittai* (or *juttai*) 集諦, the truth regarding the cause of suffering, i.e. the reality that the cause of suffering is evil passions; (3) *mettai* 滅諦, the truth regarding the extinction of suffering, i.e. the reality that Nirvana is the state where all sufferings are extinguished; and (4) *dōtai* 道諦, the truth regarding the path to Nirvana, i.e. the reality that the eightfold holy path (*hasshōdō**) leads to Nirvana.

Shishu 四修 The four practices in Pure Land Buddhism set forth in the *Ōjō-raisan**: (1) *kugyōshu* 恭敬修, 'the practice of worship (of Amida* and bodhisattvas)', (2) *muyoshu* 無餘修, 'the exclusive practice (of the *nenbutsu**)', (3) *mukenshu* 無間修, 'the uninterrupted practice (of the *nenbutsu*)', and (4) *jōjishu* 長時修, 'the sustained practice (of the *nenbutsu* throughout one's life)'. [IH.]

Shishu 四衆 'The four categories (of Buddhists)'; (1) *biku** 比丘, monk; (2) *bikuni** 比丘尼, nun; (3) *ubasoku** 優婆塞, layman; and (4) *ubai** 優婆夷, laywoman; cf. *shichishu*.

Shishu 四趣 'The four realms', i.e. hell and the three realms of hungry spirits, animals and fighting spirits. [Hei. 3.]

Shishū 四洲 'The four continents', which, according to Buddhist cosmology, lie in the ocean in the four cardinal directions from Mt. Sumeru (Shumisen*). They are: (1) Tōhotsubadai* 東弗婆提 (Pūrvavideha) to the east; (2) Nan'enbudai* 南閻浮提 (Jambudvīpa) to the south; (3) Saikudani* 西瞿陀尼 (Aparagodānīya) to the west; and (4) Hokkuru* 北俱盧 (Uttarakuru). The topography of each continent is different and the inhabitants likewise have distinct physical characteristics.

Shishu-hosshin 四種法身 'The four types of buddha-body' established in the Shingon* sect: (1) *jishō hosshin* 自性法身 'reality-essence-body', (2) *juyūshin* 受用身 'enjoyment-body', (3) *henge hosshin* 變化法身 'transformed body', and (4) *tōru hosshin* 等流法身 'homogeneous body'.

Shishu-mandara 四種曼荼羅 'The four Mandalas' distinguished in esoteric Buddhism: (1) *daimandara* 大曼荼羅 (*mahā-maṇḍala*), a buddha or bodhisattva's body, or a painting of his figure; (2) *sanmaya-mandara* 三摩耶曼荼羅 (*samaya-maṇḍala*), things held in the hands of a deity, such as an ensign, sword, wheel, jewel, or lotus flower; also a painting of such an object; (3) *hōmandara* 法曼荼羅 (*dharma-maṇḍala*), seed-letters (*shuji**), words and meanings of all sutras; and (4) *katsuma-mandara* 羯摩曼荼羅 (*karma-maṇḍala*), a posture and act-sign of a deity, or an image of him.

Shishu-sōmotsu 四種僧物 'The four kinds of monks' possessions': (1) *jōjū jōjū* 常住常住, properties or possessions of the monks of a temple which are in fixed places, such as halls, living quarters, ornaments; (2) *jippō jōjū* 十方常住, provisions, such as food, which can also be shared by monks from other places; (3) *genzen genzen* 現前現前, personal possessions of monks; and (4) *jippō* *genzen* 十方現前, personal possessions, such as those of deceased monks, which can be shared by monks from other places.

Shishu-zanmai 四種三昧 'The four kinds of Samādhi' established in the Tendai* sect: (1) *jōza-zanmai* 常坐三昧, constant sitting meditation for a period of 90 days; (2) *jōgyō-zanmai* 常行三昧, constant active meditation for a period of 90 days, in which the practitioner walks around a statue of Amida* Buddha while calling his name and remembering him; (3) *hangyō-hanza-zanmai* 半行半坐三昧, half-active and half-sitting meditation, in which the practitioner walks around a statue of the buddha while chanting a sutra and also meditates on reality while sitting in a cross-legged posture; and (4) *higyō-hiza-zanmai* 非行非坐三昧, meditation on reality in an unspecified posture for an unspecified period of time. [S. IV-1.]

Shiso 緇素 'The black(-robed) and the ordinary (people)'; priests and laymen. [Tai. 40.]

Shisō kakukan 思想覺觀 'Thought and contemplation.' [S. Vb-11.]

Shitai 四諦 'The four truths'; abbr. of *shishōtai**. [S. Xb-1.]

Shitchi 悉地 Also *shijji*; Sk. *siddhi*; translated as *jōju* 成就, 'perfection', *myōjōju* 妙成就, 'accomplishing well', etc. I. The final enlightenment attained by the three mystic practices (*sanmitsu**). II. The three mystic practices performed for attaining the final enlightenment. III. Various spiritual stages or supernatural powers attained by mystic practices. Cf. *musō no shitchi* and *usō no shitchi*. [S. II-8.]

Shitchin 七珍 See *shippō*.

~ **manbō** --萬寳 'Seven rare treasures, ten thousand treasures.' [Ho. 6.]

Shiten 四天 Refers to Shitennō*. [Tai. 16.]

~ **gōgyō no hō** --合行の法 See *Shitennō gōgyōhō*. [Tai. 16.]

Shitennō 四天王 'The Four Heavenly Kings'; the Four Guardian Gods; the guardians of the four directions: (1) Jikokuten 持國天 (Dhrtarāstra) in the east; (2) Zōjōten (or Zōchōten) 增長天 (Virūḍhaka) in the south; (3) Kōmokuten 廣目天 (Virūpākṣa) in the west; and (4) Tamonten 多聞天 (Vaiśravaṇa) in the north. They are the kings of the four heavenly realms around Mt.

Sumeru (Shumisen*). While serving Indra (Taishaku*), they protect Buddhism and its believers. [K. 35; S. Vb–7; Tai. 16, 29.]

~ **gōgyōhō** --- 合行法 'A ritual dedicated to all the Four Guardian Gods enshrined together (as the principal objects of worship)' with the object of stopping calamities and bringing about good fortune.

Shitoku 四德 'The four excellent qualities' of Nirvana (*nehan**): (1) *jō* 常, eternally abiding; (2) *raku* 樂, blissful; (3) *ga* 我, capable of manifesting oneself and doing anything at will; and (4) *jō* 淨, free of defilement. [Tai. 40.]

~ **no rakuhō** --の樂邦 'The land of bliss which has the four excellent qualities'; the realm of Nirvana. [Tai. 40.]

Shitsuri 蒺藜 A kind of useless tree (?). [S. VI–18.]

Shitsuu busshō 悉有佛性 'Universal possession of the buddha-nature'; the idea that all living beings have the buddha-nature comes from the *Nehan-gyō**. [Tai. 18.]

Shitta 悉達 Sk. Siddhārtha; also 悉多 and Shittatta 悉達多; the name of Shakamuni* before he renounced the world. The full name was Sarvārthasiddha or Sarvasiddhārtha 'one who has accomplished all aims'; he was so named because his parents' wishes were all fulfilled by his birth. [Tai. 33.]

~ **Taishi** --太子 'Prince Siddhārtha'; see *Shitta*. [Tai. 33.]

Shitta koji 質多居士 'The layman Citta'; a lay Buddhist at the time of the Buddha. [S. III–3.]

Shiu 四有 'The four stages of one's existence': (1) *shōu* 生有, the moment of birth; (2) *hon'u* 本有, the period of continued existence up to the time of death; (3) *shiu* 死有, the moment of death; and (4) *chūu* 中有, the intermediate state of existence between death and a new life.

Shiun 紫雲 'Purple cloud'; the cloud on which Amida* Buddha and/or sages come to the aspirant to take him to the Western Pure Land at the time of his death. [Ho. 30; K. 54.]

Shiyōbon 四要品 'The four important chapters' of the *Hoke-kyō**: 'Hōben-bon'* 方便品, 'Anrakugyō-hon'* 安樂行品, 'Juryō-bon'* 壽量品 and 'Fumon-bon'* 普門品. [Tai. 13.]

Shizenten 四禪天 'The four meditation heavens' in the realm of form (*shikikai**).

Shō 生 'Arising; coming into existence.'

~ **ni atarite fushō** -に當りて不生 'Things as they arise are non-arising'; the coming into existence of things is itself a non-coming into existence. [S. I–9.]

Shō 性 'Nature'; the nature of a thing or a person; see *sanshō*.

Shō 障 'Hindrance'; another term for *bonnō* 煩惱, 'evil passion', because one's evil passions hinder pursuance of the Buddhist Way.

Shoaku makusa 諸惡莫作 'Commit no evil'; the first line of the verse of admonishment of the seven past buddhas (*shichibutsu tsūkaige**). [K. 164; S. IV–1.]

Shōben 清辨 Sk. Bhāvaviveka; an Indian exponent of the doctrine of the void following the Mādhyamika (*Chūganha**) tradition of Nāgārjuna (Ryūju*) and Āryadeva (Daiba); flourished in the 6th century. [S. IV–1.]

Shōbō 正法 'The true Dharma.' I. The teaching of the Buddha, which conforms to the truth. II. Refers to *shōbōji**.

~-**genzō** --眼藏 'The treasury of the eye of the true Dharma'. I. The essence of Buddhism. [S. IV–1.] II. N. of a work by Dōgen*.

~-**ji** --時 'The period of the true Dharma'; one of the three periods after the Buddha's decease; see *shōzōmatsu*.

~-**nenjo-gyō** --念處經 '*Mindfulness of the Right Dharma Sutra*'; 70 fasc.; tr. by Prajñāruci (Hannyarushi 般若流支) between 538 and 543 [TT. 17, No. 721]. The sutra explains the causes and effects of the six transmigratory states (*rokudō**) and urges us to strive to escape from them. [S. VI–17.]

~-**rin** --輪 'The wheel of the true Dharma'; the true teaching of the Buddha, which is compared to a flying wheel (a kind of missile with which to attack enemies) because it destroys wrong views. [S. IV–1.]

~-**shū** --宗 'The school of the true Dharma'; Buddhism. [Tai. 24.]

Shōbō 正報 'The reward proper'; the principal reward which one receives in this life as the result of acts in previous lives, namely, one's own body and mind; the term is contrasted with *ehō** 依報.

Shobu no hannya 諸部の般若 'Various groups of *Hannya* (-*kyō*)'; five or eight kinds of *Hannya-kyō** are distinguished. The former is as follows: (1) *Makahannya-haramitta-kyō** 摩訶般若波羅蜜多經; (2) *Kongō-hannya** 金剛般若; (3) *Tennōmon-hannya* 天王問般若; (4) *Kōsan-hannya* 光讃般若 and (5) *Ninnō-hannya** 仁王般若. [S. IV–9.]

Shōchi 正智 'Right wisdom'; the wisdom of knowing reality; wisdom free of delusory discriminations. [S. IV–1.]

Shōchi gudon 小智愚鈍 '(Man of) small wisdom and stupidity.' [S. IV–1.]

Shochishō 所知障 'Hindrance to (the correct knowledge of) objects'; Sk. *jñeya-āvaraṇa*; a mental function of obscuring the correct knowledge of objects, which obstructs the realization of enlightenment; one of the two kinds of hindrance (*nishō**); cf. *bonnōshō*.

Shō daibodai 證大菩提 'To realize the Great Enlightenment.' [Hei. 3.]

Shōdan shitaku-mono 小壇支度物 A small mandala platform and other ritual utensils. [K. 52.]

Shōdō 聖道 I. 'The way of sages'; the Mahayana and Hinayana teachings to be practised by bodhisattvas and Hinayana sages, respectively. II. Refers to the eightfold holy way (*hasshōdō**). III. Refers to *shōdōmon**. IV. The holy way teachings, esp. those of Tendai* and Shingon*. [Tai. 24.]

~ **jōdo** ‑‑淨土 'Holy way and Pure Land '; refers to *shōdōmon** (the holy way) and *jōdomon** (the Pure Land way). [S. IV–1.]

~‑**mon** ‑‑門 'The holy way gate'; opposed to *jōdomon** 淨土門, 'the Pure Land way'. It embraces all the teachings, whether Mahayana or Hinayana, except the Pure Land teaching, whereby one attains enlightenment with one's own power in this world.

Shoen 所緣 I. The object of perception or conception. II. Relationship.

Shōen 勝緣 'A strong, superior condition' or external power. [S. I–3.]

Shōgaku 正覺 'The right, perfect enlightenment'; the buddha's enlightenment in which the ultimate reality is manifestly recognized. [S. IV–1.]

Shogan 所願 'That which one desires or aspires to'; desire; wish. [Tsu. 217.]

Shōge 障礙 'Hindrance, obstacle.'

Shōgi 勝義 'The superior principle'; abbr. of *shōgitai**. [S. Pref.]
~-**tai** --諦 See *daiichigitai*.

Shōgi 證義 'Affirming the principle'; one who judges at a ceremonial discussion-meeting (*rongi** 論議); an umpire. [Tai. 36.]

Shōgon 莊嚴 'Adornment, decoration, glorification'; glorious decorations or manifestations, as in the Pure Land.

~ **jōdo** --淨土 'Adorning the Pure Land'; said of a bodhisattva's establishment of a pure land adorned with glorious objects which are, in fact, embodiments of his meritorious acts. [S. IV –1.]

Shōgo no kokoro 惺悟の心 'Awakened mind'; a mind enlightened to reality. [S. III–8.]

Shogu 所具 'Contained (in), possessed (by).'

Shōgu 性具 'The inclusiveness (of all phenomenal things) in the intrinsic nature (of each individual being)'; also *taigu* 體具 and *rigu* 理具; an important term in the Tendai* sect. [S. I–3.]

Shōgu 聖供 'Sacred offering'; rice to be offered to sages or monks. [Tai. 17.]

Shōgun 勝軍 Sk. Jayasena; an Indian master of the Yogācāra school (*Yugagyōha**) around the 7th century, under whom Hsüan-chuang (Genjō*) studied for two years. [S. III–1.]

Shōgun Bishamon hō 勝軍毘沙門法 'A ritual dedicated (as a prayer) to Bishamon* (Vaiśravaṇa) for victory (in a war).'

Shōgun Bishamon no hō 勝軍毘沙門の法 See *shōgun Bishamon hō*. [Tai. 29.]

Shōgyō 所行 'That which is done'; an act.

Shōgyō 正行 'A right practice', as opposed to *zōgyō** 雜行 'miscellaneous practices'; a practice leading to birth in the Pure Land; five right practices are distinguished by Shan-tao (Zendō*); see *goshōgyō*.

Shōgyō 聖教 'A holy teaching'; Buddhist teaching; a Buddhist scripture.

Shogyō mujō 諸行無常 'All things are impermanent.' [Hei. 1.]

Shogyō-ōjō 諸行往生 'Birth (in Amida's* land) by various practices'; birth in the Pure Land by performing practices other than the *nenbutsu**; the term is contrasted to *nenbutsu-ōjō.** [S. I–10.]

Shōgyōryō 聖教量 'Knowledge obtained from the sacred scriptures'; Sk. *śabda*; one of the three means of the cognition of objects, the other two being *genryō** and *hiryō**.

Shohen 所變 'That into which someone or something has been transformed'; a transformation; an incarnation.

Shohō 諸法 'All (existing) things.'

~ **jissō** --實相 'All phenomenal things are themselves the ultimate reality'; the phrase comes from the *Hoke-kyō**. [S. Va–12.]

Shōhō 生報 'Maturity (of karma) in the next life'; also *junshō-hō* 順生報; one of the three types of karma distinguished according to the different times of their maturity (*sanpō**). [S. VII–5.]

Shohosshin 初發心 'The first awakening of aspiration (for Bodhi)'; cf. *bodaishin*. [S. II–9, Vb–10.]

Shoi 所爲 'That which is done'; an act.

Shōi 勝位 'A superior stage or rank (in Buddhist practices).' [Tai. 17.]

Shōi 攝意 'To contain one's thoughts' and fix them on one object. [S. Xb–3.]

Shoin 諸院 A collective term for *jōkō* 上皇 (an ex-emperor), *hōō** 法皇 and *nyoin** 女院. [K. 59.]

Shōin 勝因 'A dominant cause.' [K. 721.]

Shōin no gan 生因の願 'The vows setting forth the cause of birth (in Amida's* land)'; refers to the 18th, 19th and 20th vows of Amida Buddha, particularly the 18th; see *hongan no mon*. [S. I–10.]

Shōja 聖者 'A sage.'

Shōja 精舍 'A dwelling place for diligent (practitioners)'; a temple; *shō* is construed as *shōgyō* 精行 'a diligent practice'.

[Tai. 24.]

Shōja hissui 盛者必衰 Correctly, *jōsha hissui*; 'the prosperous inevitably decline.' [Hei. 1.]

Shōja hitsumetsu 生者必滅 'All living things must die.' [K. 470.]

Shoji 初地 'The first *bhūmi*'; the first stage of a bodhisattva, which is commonly known by the name of *kangiji* 歓喜地, 'stage of joy'. In the 52-stage scale, it is the 41st stage. [S. III–1.]

Shōji 生死 'Birth and death'; the cycle of birth and death. [Tsu. 41.]

~ **jidai** -- 事大 'The matter of birth and death (i.e. transmigration) is of great importance.' [S. Xb–3.]

~ **no bonbu** -- の凡夫 'Ordinary men subject to the cycles of birth and death.' [S. III–8.]

~ **no chūrin** -- の稠林 'The dense forest of birth and death'; an analogy to show that the world of transmigration is difficult to escape from as a forest or jungle; cf. *chūrin*. [S. IX–1.]

~ **no gō** -- の業 'An act contributing to cycles of birth and death.' [S. Va–10, VI–17.]

~ **no rōgoku** -- の牢獄 'The prison of birth and death'; the state of transmigration is compared to a prison. [S. IV–9.]

~ **no ruten** -- の流轉 'Drifting (i.e. transmigrating) in the realms of birth and death.' [S. Xb–2.]

~ **no sato** -- の郷 'The world of transmigration which is one's native place.' [S. Pref.]

~ **soku nehan** -- 卽涅槃 'Birth and death is itself Nirvana'; from the Mahayana viewpoint of non-duality, the sphere of transmigration is itself Nirvana. [S. V–1.]

mirai mugū no ~ **shutsuri** 未來無窮の--出離 'Emancipation from the endless cycles of birth and death in the future.' [Tai. 19.]

mushi no ~ 無始の-- 'Cycles of birth and death which have no beginning.' [S. I–9, Xb–2.]

Shōji 承仕 I. One who performs miscellaneous duties at the residence of an ex-emperor or regent. He is shaven-headed and wears a hunting dress without family crests. [K. 483.] II. Also *shōji hosshi** 承仕法師; a porter at a Buddhist hall in charge of decorations and ornaments; he can remain a layman and marry, or enter the priesthood.

~ **hosshi** --法師   See *shōji* II. [Tsu. 162.]

Shōji 勝士   'A superior man'; a man of outstanding merit and wisdom. [S. Xb–1.]

Shōjiki 正直   'Right and straight'; righteousness; the direct presentation of truth. [Tai. 12.]

~ **shahōben** --捨方便   'Directness (in expounding the truth) and the discarding of expedient means'; a phrase from the *Hoke-kyō**. [Tai. 12.]

Shōjin 生身   Also *shōshin*; 'a live body'; the body of a buddha or bodhisattva in human form, as opposed to *hosshin**, 'Dharma-body', which refers to the body of reality. [K. 331.]

~ **no hotoke** --の佛   'The live body of a buddha.' [K. 469.]

~ **no jōbutsu** --の成佛   'Becoming a buddha with one's present body.' [K. 584.]

~ **no Mida** --の彌陀   'The live Amida* (Buddha).' [K. 36.]

~ **no Miroku** --の彌勒   'The live Miroku* (Bodhisattva).' [Tai. 15.]

~ **no satta** --の薩埵   'A live (bodhi-)sattva.' [Tai. 26.]

Shōjin 精進   I. Diligence; one of the Six Pāramitās (*ropparamitsu**). II. Popularly, abstinence from eating fish and meat; see *saigatsu*.

Shōjō 小乘   'The lesser or smaller vehicle'; Sk. *hīnayāna*; a derogatory term applied by Mahayanists to various schools of Buddhism which aim at the salvation of one's own self; there were 20 Hinayana schools about 300 years after the Buddha's death; today the term Theravāda (school of elders) is popularly used for Hinayana.

~-**kai** --戒   'Hinayana precepts'; the general term for the precepts to be observed by monks, nuns, and other Buddhists. There are 250 precepts for a monk, and 500 for a nun. For other kinds of precepts, see *gokai*, *hassaikai*, and *jikkai*. The term is contrasted to *daijōkai** (Mahayana precepts). [Tai. 15.]

~ **retsukai** --劣戒   Pronounced ~*rekkai*; 'the inferior Hinayana precepts'; the Hinayana ones are considered inferior to the Mahayana precepts (*daijōkai**). [Tai. 15.]

Shōjōchi 清淨智 'Pure wisdom'; the undefiled wisdom of a buddha or bodhisattva. Same as *murochi** 無漏智. [K. 64.]

Shōjō Daibosatsu 證誠大菩薩 'The Great Bodhisattva Shōjō'; the *gongen** deity enshrined in the Shōjō Shrine 證誠殿 at Kumano; he is regarded as an incarnation of Amida* Buddha. He is called 'Shōjō' (lit. prove and testify) because Amida's law of salvation is praised and testified to by all the other buddhas. The term *shōjō* comes from the *Amida-kyō**. [Hei. 2.]

Shōjōgō 正定業 'The certainly assuring act'; the act which certainly assures birth in the Pure Land; the *nenbutsu** practice; the fourth of the five right practices (*goshōgyō**).

Shōjō hosshin 清淨法身 'The pure Dharma-body'; the reality-body which is pure and undefiled; cf. *hosshin*.

Shōjōju 正定聚 'Those who are rightly established.' I. Those who are certain to attain enlightenment; one of the three kinds of people distinguished according to the three different spiritual capacities; cf. *sanju*. II. In the Jōdoshin* sect, those who have attained absolute faith in Amida and are, consequently, assured of birth in the Pure Land and the attainment of buddhahood; cf. *futai* and *hitsujō*.

Shōjō no biku 清淨の比丘 'A pure monk'; a monk who strictly observes the precepts. [S. II–10.]

Shōjō no gō 正定之業 See *shōjōgō*. [S. Xa–1.]

Shōjō (no) shin 清淨(の)身 'The pure body'; refers to *shōjō hosshin**. [S. Xb–2.]

Shōjō seze 生々世々 Also *shōshō sese*; 'life after life'; in all lives in the past or future. [K. 6; Tai. 10.]

Shojū 所住 I. That on which thought dwells; an object of thought. II. The place where one dwells.

Shōju 正受 'Correctly receiving or perceiving'; correct perception of things; another name for *zenjō** 禪定, 'meditation'.

Shōju 聖衆 'A host of sages (of the Pure Land).' [K. 36, 63.]

~ raigō --來迎 'The welcome (of an aspirant to the Pure Land) by a host of sages.' [S. Xa–9.]

Shōju 攝受 'To embrace and receive'; said of the welcoming and salvation of living beings by a buddha or bodhisattva.

Shō-jū-i-metsu 生住異滅 'Coming into existence, staying, changing, and perishing.' These are the four changing aspects of phenomena (*shisō* 四相). [Tsu. 155.]

Shoka 初果 'The first fruit'; the first of the four stages of sainthood in Hinayana; same as *yoruka**; cf. *shika* 四果. [S. III–3.]

Shōkan 正觀 'The correct meditation or contemplation'; the prescribed method of meditation or contemplation; the opposite of *jakan** 邪觀.

Shōkan 相看 'Seeing each other.' I. In Zen*, going to see the master. II. Also in Zen, attaining the same spiritual state as the master.

Shōkannon 聖觀音 'The Holy Kannon'; Sk. Ārya-avalokiteś-vara; also 正觀音; the most usual of the six forms of Kannon (*rokkannon**). [Tai. 18.]

Shoke 所化 'One who is (to be) transformed (by receiving the teaching)'; a disciple. [Tsu. 238.]

Shōken 正見 'Right view'; the view which complies with the Buddhist teaching of causality; one of the items of practice in the eightfold holy path (*hasshōdō**).

Shōken 相見 The same as *shōkan** 相看.

Shōkensō 正見僧 'A monk having the right view.' [S. Xa–6, VI–17.]

Shōkō 小劫 'A small *kalpa*'; see *kō*.

Shōkō 少康 Ch. Shao-k'ang; one of the five Chinese Pure Land masters (*Jōdo goso** 浄土五祖); popularly known as 'Hou Shan-tao' 後善導 (Go-Zendō*), 'the later (incarnations of or successors to) Shan-tao (Zendō*)'. He first studied the Kegon* teaching, and was converted to Pure Land Buddhism when he read Shan-tao's passages on aspiration to the Pure Land at the White Horse Temple (Hakubaji* 白馬寺) in Lo-yang. He then propagated the Pure Land teaching extensively.

Shōkō 燒香 'To burn incense'; to offer incense.

Shokyō yuishin 諸境唯心 'All objects are nothing but the mind'; all things are transformations of one's mind. [S. III–1.]

Shōman 勝鬘 'A splendid garland'; Sk. *śrīmālā*. I. N. of a person; see *Shōman Bunin*. II. Refers to *Shōman-gyō**. [S. IV–1.]

~ **Bunin** --夫人 'Queen Śrīmālā'; a daughter of King Prasenajit (Hashinoku Ō 波斯匿王) of Rājagṛha (Ōshajō*) in central India and, later, the wife of the king of Ayodhyā (Ayuja 阿踰闍). Being a fervent believer in Buddhism, she is said to have expounded her faith in Mahayana in the *Shōman-gyō**.

~-**gyō** --經 Sk. *Śrīmālā-devī-siṃhanāda-sūtra*; 1 fasc., tr. by Guṇabhadra (Gunabatsudara 求那跋陀羅) in the period 394–468 [TT. 12, No. 353]. This sutra expounds the One-Vehicle (*ichijō**) teaching through the words of Queen Śrīmālā.

Shōmō 生盲 'One who is blind from birth.' [S. IV–1.]

Shōmoku kebutsu no Kanzeon 生木化佛の觀世音 '(A statue of) Kannon*, an incarnation of the buddha (Amida*, carved) from a live tree.' [Tai. 11.]

Shōmon 聲聞 'One who hears the voice'; a shravaka; Sk. *śrāvaka*; originally, a disciple of the Buddha; later, a follower of Hinayana who contemplates the principle of the fourfold noble truth (*shishōtai**) to attain Nirvana.

~-**kai** --戒 The rules of conduct for the followers of Hinayana. [S. III–5.]

Shōmu Tennō 聖武天皇 The 45th emperor (701–756); reigned 724–749. Being a great patron of Buddhism, in 728 he distributed copies of the *Konkōmyō-kyō** to various provinces to have it chanted in order to secure the peace of the state. In 741 he ordered the construction of a *kokubunji** in each province, and in 745 built the Tōdaiji* and its big statue of Birushana*. He personally attended the inaugural ceremony and vowed to the Buddha that he would dedicate himself to the Three Treasures (*sanbō**). After his abdication, he became a *nyūdō** and was called Shōman 勝滿.

Shōmyō 正命 'Right living'; one of the items of practice in the eightfold holy path (*hasshōdō**); living in accordance with the precepts and on alms alone; the opposite of *jamyō** 邪命.

Shōmyō 稱名 'Recitation of the name' of a buddha, esp. Amida*. [Tsu. 222.]

~ **nenbutsu** --念佛 'Recitation of the *nenbutsu**.'

Shōmyō 聲明 'The chanting' of Buddhist hymns. [Tsu. 227.]

Shōnen 正念 I. 'Right recollection'; mindfulness; one of the items of practice in the eightfold holy path (*hasshōdō**). II. Thinking of Amida* Buddha with a clear consciousness. III. Concentration on the *nenbutsu**.

~ **bunmyō** --分明 'The right thought or mindfulness being clear and manifest'; an unadulterated state of mindfulness. [S. VII–25.]

~ **genson** --現尊 'Right mindfulness which reveals sages (ready to welcome an aspirant).' [S. Xa–9.]

~ **ni jūsu** --に住す 'To dwell in the right thought'; to be mindful of Amida* Buddha. [K. 423.]

Shōnetsu daishōnetsu 焦熱大焦熱 'Scorching, great scorching'; the names of the sixth and seventh of the eight great hells (*hachi-daijigoku**). [Tai. 2.]

Shōnin 上人 'An eminent priest.'

~-**za** --座 'The seat for the highest priest.' [S. IV–1.]

Shōō 聖應 'The response of a sage' to living beings, by which he acts to save them. [S. II–9.]

Shōren jihi no manajiri 青蓮慈悲の眸 (for 眦) 'The compassionate eyes likened to blue lotus blossoms.' [Hei. 2.]

Shōrō 鐘樓 See *shurō*.

Shōrōbyōshi 生老病死 'Birth, old age, sickness, and death'; four pains; cf. *hakku*. [S. III–3.]

Shōryō 聖靈 'Holy spirit'; a term of respect for the spirit of a dead person. [K. 557.]

~-**e** --會 The ceremony held at the Tennōji 天王寺, Osaka, on the anniversary of Prince Shōtoku's* death, the 22nd of the second month. Apart from the Buddhist service, court dances and music were performed all day. [Tsu. 220.]

Shōryōshū 性靈集 A collection of Kūkai's* poems, petitions, prayers, etc., 10 fasc., compiled by Shinzei 眞濟, Kūkai's disciple.

Shosa 所作 'That which is done'; deed; act.

~ **no gō** --の業 'Acts which one has done.' [S. II–9.]

Shōsansai 小三災 'The three minor calamities' which occur at the time of some major cosmic changes: (1) *tōhyōsai* 刀兵災, people kill each other with sharp knives and swords; (2) *shitsuekisai*

疾疫災, prevalence of epidemics; and (3) *kikinsai* 飢饉災, famine; cf. *daisansai*.

Shōsetsu 正説 'A correct exposition' of the teaching.

Shosha 書寫 I. 'To copy (a sutra, etc.).' II. Refers to Mt. Shosha 書寫山.

~ **hosshi** --法師 'A priest who copies' the *Hoke-kyō**. See *goshu hosshi*.

~ **no shōnin** --の上人 'The master of Mt. Shosha'; refers to the master Shōkū 性空 (910–1007) of the Tendai* sect, the founder of the Enkyōji 圓教寺 of Mt. Shosha 書寫. [Tsu. 69.]

Shoshi 所司 'Administrators'; a general term for the three main posts in a temple, namely, *jōza** 上座, *jishu** 寺主, and *tsuina** 都維那. Also called *sangō* 三綱. [O. V.]

Shōshikki 捷疾鬼 'A swift devil'; refers to the two *rākṣasas* (*rasetsu**) who stole two of the Buddha's teeth after his cremation. [Tai. 8.]

Shoshin no bosatsu 初心の菩薩 'A beginner in the bodhisattva path.' [S. III–8.]

Shoshin no gyōja 初心の行者 'A beginner in Buddhist practices.' [S. III–8.]

Shōshin no dō 正眞の道 'The right and true Way.' [S. I–10.]

Shōsho 生所 'A state of existence one is born into.' [K. 458.]

Shōshō sese 生々世々 See *shōjō seze*.

Shōshū 小宗 'A small sect'; a lesser and inferior teaching; a Mahayana term for Hinayana. [S. Va–4.]

Shōso 生蘇 Curdled milk; one of the five tastes; see *gomi*.

Shōsō 性相 'Essential nature and characteristic.' I. The essential nature and phenomenal forms of existence. [S. Xb–2.] II. Refers to the teachings of Hossō* and Kusha*, which discuss the nature and characteristics of all conceivable existences more thoroughly than other schools; the term is traditionally read '*shōzō*'.

Shoson-betsugyō goma-hihō 諸尊別行護摩祕法 See *shoson-betsugyō gomahō*. [K. 52.]

Shoson-betsugyō gomahō 諸尊別行護摩法 'The ritual of offering fire (*goma**) to an individual deity'; cf. *shoson-gōgyō gomahō*.

Shoson-gōgyō gomahō 諸尊合行護摩法 'The ritual of offering fire (*goma**) to various deities at the same time'; cf. *shoson-betsugyō gomahō.*

Shōsui no uo 小水の魚 'A fish with little water.' The parable comes from the *Shutsuyō-kyō* 出曜經, which says, "When this day is past, one's life will perish, like a fish with little water. What pleasure is there to enjoy?" [Ho. 17.]

Shōta 勝他 'Winning against others.'

Shōtō 燒燈 'Burning lamps'; lighted candles and oil lamps. [Tai. 24.]

Shōtō inmo no toki 正當恁麼時 'At such a time' (a Chinese colloquial expression). [Tai. 4.]

Shotoku 所得 'That which has been acquired or perceived'; acquisition; possession. Cf. *mushotoku* and *ushotoku.* [S. III–1.]

Shōtoku 性德 'Essential qualities'; a Tendai* term. Good and evil qualities and the propensities towards delusion and enlightenment contained in the very nature of every existence, as opposed to *shutoku** 修德. [S. I–3.]

Shōtoku 證得 'To realize or attain' a higher level of spiritual development; attain enlightenment.

~ **no omoi** --の思 'A (false) idea that one has attained enlightenment.' [S. III–5.]

Shōtoku Taishi 聖德太子 Prince Shōtoku (574–621 or 622); the second son of Emperor Yōmei; also known as Jōgū Taishi 上宮太子, Yumedono Ōji 夢殿王子, Shōtoku Ō 聖德王, etc. He made an alliance with Minister Soga Umako 蘇我馬子 in eliminating the anti-Buddhist minister Mononobe Moriya 物部守屋, thus establishing Buddhism on a firm basis. He became the Prince Regent in 593, and assisted his aunt, Empress Suiko 推古. On his advice, an imperial decree supporting Buddhism was issued in 594. When a Korean monk, Eji 慧慈, came to Japan, the Prince studied under him, and later lectured on Mahayana sutras. He is reputed to have written commentaries on the *Hoke-kyō**, *Yuima-gyō** and *Shōman-gyō**. In 604, he promulgated the Seventeen-Article Constitution (*Jūshichijō kenpō* 十七條憲法). Apart from encouraging Buddhist studies by sending students to China, he founded many temples, including the Shitennōji 四天

王寺, Hōryūji 法隆寺 and Chūgūji 中宮寺. He is regarded as the father of Japanese Buddhism.

Shōyō 請用 'Inviting (a priest for a Buddhist service).' [S. VI–10, 13.]

Shōyoku chisoku 小欲知足 'Desiring little and knowing contentment.' [S. Va–3, VIII–23.]

Shōzai 聖財 'Sacred wealth'; the Buddhist teaching. [S. II–5.]

Shōzen 生善 'To produce good.'

Shozen bugyō 諸善奉行 'Respectfully practise various good acts'; correctly, *shuzen bugyō** 衆善奉行; the second line of the verse of admonishment of the seven past buddhas (*shichibutsu tsūkaige**). [S. VI–10.]

Shō-zenjūi-tenshi-shomon-gyō 聖善住意天子所問經 '*The Holy Sutra on the Questions Asked by Zenjūi, the Son of Heaven*'; 3 fasc., tr. by Vimuktisena (Bimokuchisen 毘目智仙) and Prajñāruci (Hannyarushi 般若流支) in the sixth century [TT. 12, No.341]; sometimes abbreviated as *Zenjū-tenshi-kyō**.

Shozenten 初禪天 'The First Meditation Heaven'; the lowest of the four meditation heavens in the realm of form (*shikikai**), where Brahma (Bonten***), the highest god in Hindu mythology, rules.

Shozen zōgyō 諸善雜行 'Various good acts and miscellaneous practices'; various meritorious practices other than the *nenbutsu**. [S. VI–10.]

Shōzō 性相 See *shōsō* II.

Shōzōmatsu 正像末 Refers to *shōbō** 正法 (the true Dharma), *zōbō** 像法 (the semblance Dharma), and *mappō** 末法 (the last Dharma), and signifies the three periods after the Buddha's decease: (1) In the period of the true Dharma, lasting 500 (some say 1,000) years, the Buddha's teaching is properly practised and enlightenment can be attained; (2) in the period of the semblance Dharma, lasting 1,000 (some say 500) years, the teaching is practised but enlightenment is no longer possible; (3) in the period of the last, decadent Dharma, lasting 10,000 years, only the teaching exists.

Shu 取 'Taking, grasping.' I. A mental function of grasping external objects; one of the twelve causations (*jūni-innen**). II.

A synonym of *ai** in the sense of egoistic desire. III. A general term for *bonnō** 煩惱, 'evil passions'.

Shubō 修法 Also pronounced *suhō* and *zuhō*; 'a method of practice'; refers to an esoteric ritual in which a practitioner makes an offering to a deity, recites spells, makes a manual sign and meditates on the deity as prescribed; same as *gyōbō** 行法, *hihō** 祕法 and *mippō** 密法.

Shubyō shitsujo no nyorai 衆病悉除の如來 'The Tathagata who removes all illnesses'; refers to Yakushi* Buddha. [Hei. 2.]

Shuda 首陀 Abbr. of *shudara**. [S. VIII–22.]

Shudaonka 須陀洹果 Sk. *srota-āpatti-phala*; see *yoruka*.

Shudara 首陀羅 Sk. *śūdra*; the lowest of the four castes in India; slaves; originally, Indian natives conquered by the Aryans.

Shudatsu 須達 Also Shudatta 須達多; Sk. Sudatta; a wealthy man of Śrāvastī (Shae*) and a patron of the Buddha; popularly called Gikkodoku* 給孤獨. He purchased a garden from Prince Jeta (Gita*) and there built a monastery, known as Gion shōja*, for the Buddha. [Tai. 24.]

Shugaku 修學 'The practice and study' of Buddhism.

~**-sha** --者 'One who practises and studies (Buddhism).' [Tai. 17.]

Shugen 修驗 'Practising mystical rites' deep in the mountains.

~**-dō** --道 A school of Buddhism which teaches ascetic practices in the mountains for attaining mystic powers; the mountain Buddhism. The founder was En-no-Ozunu* 役小角, and the followers are called *yamabushi** 山伏 or *shugenja* 修驗者.

~ **no gyōja** --の行者 'One who practises mystical rites'; a follower of *shugendō**; a *yamabushi**. [Tai. 32.]

Shūgi 宗義 'Doctrine, tenet.' [K. 61.]

Shugō 衆合 'Uniting'; Sk. *saṃghātā*; n. of one of the eight great hells (*hachidai-jigoku**), where sinners are crushed to death between two big iron mountains or in a big iron vessel. It is also the hell where many tortures 'unite' to torment sinners. [Tai. 27.]

Shūgyō 終教 See *jūkyō*.

Shugyō 執行 Also pronounced *shigyō*; the priest in charge of the clerical work in a temple. [Tai. 21.]

Shugyōza 修行者 Also *shugyōja* and *sugyōza*; 'a wandering ascetic'.

Shuhō 修法 See *shubō*.

Shuin 修因 'A practice performed as the cause (of a certain effect),' e.g. the *nenbutsu** practised as the cause of birth in Amida's* Pure Land. [K. 53.]

Shūin 習因 'A habitual cause'; the cause which brings about an effect of the same nature, e.g. a good act which brings about a good result; one of the six kinds of causes established in the Kusha* school; same as *dōrui-in* 同類因. [S. IV–1.]

Shūjaku 執著 'Attachment.'

~**-shin** --心 'The feeling of attachment.'

Shuji 種子 'A seed'; in Shingon*, refers to a seed-letter, Sk. *bīja*. A *shuji* is a Sanskrit letter which represents a deity or a specific thing, element or concept: e.g. *vaṃ* and *a* represent Dainichi*, and *hrīḥ* symbolizes Amida*. Cf. *shūji*.

Shūji 種子 Sk. *bīja*, 'seed'. I. As used in the Hossō* sect, the term refers to the energy or force that gives rise to each existence or act. Innumerable seeds are stored in the eighth consciousness of each individual, and when ripened, particular seeds produce their manifestations. The manifestations in turn leave their impressions in the eighth consciousness. Cf. *arayashiki*. [S. III–1.] II. In esoteric Buddhism, the Sanskrit syllable representing a particular deity; see *shuji*.

Shujō 拄杖 'A monk's stick.' [Tai. 39.]

Shujō 衆生 'Multitudinous beings'; a sentient being.

~**-kai** --界 'Realms of sentient beings'; the nine states of existence from hell up to the realm of bodhisattvas; all states of existence except the one of buddhas; cf. *jikkai*. [S. V–1.]

Shūjō 宗乗 'The teaching of a school or sect.' I. Specifically, the Zen* teaching or the essence of Zen. [S. Xb–3.] II. Later, the doctrine or tenet of a particular sect.

Shūka 習果 'A habitual effect'; the effect which is of the same nature as its cause, e.g. a good result brought about by a good act; one of the five effects established in the Kusha* school;

same as *tōruka* 等流果; cf. *shūin*. [S. IV–1.]

Shukke 出家 'Leaving the home'; one who has renounced home-life to become a monk or nun.

~ **no go-kudoku** --の御功徳 The merit produced by the re-nunciation of the world to become a monk or nun. [O. III.]

~ **tonsei** --遁世 'Leaving one's home or retreating from the world'; entering the priesthood or becoming a hermit. [Tai. 10.]

Shukō sekai 衆香世界 'The land of varied incense'; the land of a buddha named Kōshaku 香積, mentioned in the *Yuima-gyō**.

Shukubō 宿坊 'A lodging for monks.' [Tai. 2.]

Shukuen 宿縁 'Residual connections'; relationships from past lives.

Shukufuku 宿福 'Stored merit'; merit accumulated in some previous life. [Tai. 24.]

Shukugan 宿願 'Residual vow'; a vow made a long time ago, esp. in a past life. [K. 20; S. II–9.]

~**-riki** --力 'The power of a vow made in a past life.' [K. 36.]

Shukugō 宿業 'Residual karma'; good or bad acts done in one's past life or lives. [K. 430.]

Shukuhō 宿報 'Reward or retribution from (acts in) one's past life or lives.' [Tai. 27.]

~ **no kanka** --の感果 'The result or fruition brought about as reward or retribution for (acts in) one's past life or lives.' [Tai. 27.]

Shukuin 宿因 'Residual cause'; good or bad acts done in one's past life or lives which bring about good or bad effects in this one. [Tai. 27.]

Shukujū 宿習 'Residual habits'; habits or propensities cultivated in past lives; the influence of acts done in a former life. [S. I–7, VI–9; Tai. 4.]

Shukumyōchi 宿命智 'The ability to know the former lives of oneself and others'; one of the six transcendental faculties of a buddha, etc. See *rokutsū*. [S. III–1.]

Shukurō 宿老 'An elder' who has gone through long religious practice. [Tai. 17.]

Shukuse 宿世　Also *sukuse*.　I. The previous existences.　II. Relationships since previous existences.

～ **naki** --なき　'Without previous life'; having had no close relationship since a previous existence. Hence, not favoured by good luck.　[Ma. 95.]

Shukushu 宿種　'Stored seeds'; seeds stored in past lives; residual tendencies or habits from past lives.　[S. IV–1.]

Shukushū 宿執　'Residual attachments'; merit stored up from one's previous life or lives; a good or bad propensity acquired from previous lives; persistent pursuit.　[K. 116, 469, 480, 485, 491, 492; Tsu. 144.]

Shukushū 宿習　See *shukujū*.

Shukuzen 宿善　'Residual goodness'; good acts done in past lives.

～ **kaihotsu** --開發　'Development of the goodness stored in past lives'; often said of entering a new spiritual state owing to the maturing of some goodness stored from previous lives.　[S. Xa–10.]

Shumi 須彌　Sk. Sumeru; n. of a mountain; see *Shumisen*.

～**-sen** --山　Mt. Sumeru. In the Buddhist cosmology, the highest mountain, rising from the centre of the world. It has four sides, and is narrowest in the middle.

Shū no hōtō 宗の法燈　'The torch of Dharma within a sect'; the most important priest in a sect.　[Tsu. 60.]

Shura 修羅　Abbr. of *ashura**.

～**-dō** --道　'The realm of *asura* (*ashura**).'　[Tai. 31.]

～**-kutsu** --窟　'The cave of an *asura* (*ashura**)'; a cave where an *asura* king lives. It was believed in India that there were *asura* caves in deep mountains and valleys.　[Tai. 24.]

～ **no kenzoku** --の眷屬　'Subjects or dependants of *asura*.'　[Tai. 23.]

～ **no tōjō** --の闘諍　'The fighting of *asuras*' with Indra (Taishaku*); it is believed that *asuras* are constantly fighting with Indra.　[Tai. 15, 16.]

～ **no yakko** --の奴　'Servants of an *asura*.'　[Tai. 11.]

Shurihandoku 周利槃特　Sk. Cūḍapanthaka, Śuddhipanthaka, etc.; also 須利般特; the Buddha's disciple. He was dull and unable to memorize even one verse in four months. The Buddha gave him the job of cleaning monks' shoes, and this enabled him to attain salvation. [Ho. 36; S. II–1, Xb–3.]

Shurō 鐘樓   Also *shōrō*; 'a bell tower.' [Tai. 24.]

Shurri 出離   See *shutsuri*.

Shuryōgon 首楞嚴   Sk. *śūraṃgama*, 'heroic valour'; translated as *kensō* 健相, *kengyō* 健行, and *issaijikyō* 一切事竟; n. of a *samādhi* (*sanmai**).

〜-**gyō** - - -經   '*The Heroic Valour Sutra*'; 10 fasc., tr. by Pramiti (Hanramitti 般剌蜜帝) of the T'ang Dynasty [TT. 19, No. 945]. The full title is *Daibutchō-nyorai-mitsuin-shushō-ryōgi-shobosatsu-mangyō-shuryōgon-gyō* 大佛頂如來密因修證了義諸菩薩萬行首楞嚴經. [Tai. 26.]

〜-**jō** - - -定   Sk. *śūraṃgama-samādhi*, 'heroic valour *samādhi*'; a *samādhi* (*sanmai**) attained by bodhisattvas of higher stages in which they can clearly observe people's thoughts, distinguish their spiritual capacities, and know their destinies; this *samādhi* can protect its practitioners from evil passions and devils. [S. IV–1.]

Shūshin 執心   'Attachment, tenacity'; also used in the sense of firm belief.

Shushō 修正   'The ritual (*shuhō* 修法) in the 1st month (*shōgatsu* 正月)'; a service held at temples throughout the country at the beginning of the year to pray for the peace of the state. [Tai. 24.]

Shuso 首座   I. The senior monk at a Zen* temple who sits next to *jūji* 住持, the head priest; also *zentō* 禪頭, *shushu* 首衆, *jōza* 上座, *zagen* or *zogen* 座元, *rissō* 立僧 and *daiichiza* 第一座. II. The superintendent at a Zen temple during the period of the three-month retreat (*ango**).

Shūsoku shōdō no gyōnin 執則障道の行人   'The practitioner who is attached to rules (of conduct, i.e. precepts) and thus impedes his own enlightenment.' [S. IV–1.]

Shusse 出世   I. Supraworldly. II. Renouncing the world to practise Buddhism. III. A buddha or bodhisattva's appearance in the world to save its people. IV. Promotion of a Zen* monk to the headship of a temple, etc. V. A noble who dwells on Mt. Hiei and possesses an *in** 院 title. VI. One who has an *in** title and performs duties at a *jibutsudō**; he is a noble's true or adopted son. [Tai. 21.]

~ **gedatsu no dō** --解脱の道 'The supraworldly path leading to emancipation'; the Buddhist Way. [S. Xb–3.]

~ **no bodai** --の菩提 'Supraworldly enlightenment'; enlightenment which is beyond all worldly things. [S. II–7.]

~ **no dōnin** --の道人 'A practitioner of the Buddhist Way who has renounced the world.' [S. Va–3.]

~ **no hōzai** --の法財 'The provisions of the Dharma for one who has renounced the world', i.e. sutras, the objects of worship, etc. [IH.]

~ **no kai** --の戒 'Supraworldly precepts'; precepts to be observed for supraworldly purposes, e.g. the performance of a bodhisattva's duties; cf. *seken no kai*. [S. IV–1.]

~-**sha** --者 'A man who has renounced the world'; a man who seeks the Buddhist Way; the opposite of *sekensha** 世間者. [S. Va–3.]

Shutara 修多羅 Sk. *sūtra*; also *sotara* 蘇多羅, *sotaran* 素怛纜, etc.; translated as *kyō** 經, *kaikyō** 契經, etc.; the Buddha's teachings recorded in writings; one of the three divisions of scriptures (*sanzō**); also one of the nine and the twelve kinds of scriptures (*kubu-kyō** and *jūnibu-kyō**). The term is also used as a general term for all the twelve kinds of scriptures or for the eleven of them excluding *ubadaisha** 優婆提舍 (*upadeśa*).

~-**zō** ---藏 See *sotaranzō*.

Shuto 衆徒 A general term for priests. [K. 431.]

Shutoku 修德 'Acquired qualities'; a Tendai* term. Meritorious qualities developed by practice, as opposed to *shōtoku** 性德. [S. I–3.]

Shutsujin 出塵 'Escape from dust'; escape from the secular world.

~ **no to** --の徒 'One who has escaped the world'; one who has abandoned the world to seek the Buddhist Way. [Tai. 8.]

Shutsuri 出離 Also *shurri* and *shutchi*; 'departing' the world of transmigration; deliverance; emancipation.

~ **gedatsu** --解脱 'Deliverance and emancipation.' [S. Va–2, 3, Xa–2.]

~ **no michi** --の道 'The path leading to emancipation.' [S. Xa–7.]

~ **no sen'yō** --の詮要 'The key to deliverance.' [IH.]

~ **no yōdō** --の要道 'The essential path leading to deliverance.' [IH.]

~ **shōji** --生死 'Deliverance from the cycles of birth and death.' [K. 57; S. I–6.]

Shuyu 須臾 A very short period of time; a moment.

~ **tenpen** --轉變 'Changing every moment'; constant transience. [Tai. 10.]

Shuza 首座 See *shuso*.

Shuzen 修善 'Doing good acts.'

Shuzen bugyō 衆善奉行 'Respectfully practise various good acts'; the second line of the verse of admonishment of the seven past buddhas (*shichibutsu tsūkaige**). [S. IV–1.]

So 酥 Curd, butter; see *gomi*. [Tai. 35.]

Sōan 送行 I. In Zen*, to see off a monk who sets out on a walking tour (*angya** 行脚). II. Also, used in the sense of setting out on a walking tour.

Sōbō 僧坊 'The resident priest's quarters.'

Sōbō 僧法 'The rules of priesthood'; rules of conduct or practices prescribed for priests. [Tai. 24.]

Sōbō 僧寶 I. 'The treasure of Sangha'; the Buddhist order, as one of the three treasures (*sanbō**); also monks in general. [S. III–5.] II. 'A monk to be respected as a treasure.' [S. VI–17.]

Sōdō 僧堂 'A hall for monks'; a hall in a Zen* temple where monks live and practise meditation. [Tai. 24.]

Sōgai 繪蓋 'A silken canopy'; see *tengai*.

Sogō 麤強 'Coarse and strong.'

~ **no bonnō** --の煩惱 'Coarse and strong evil passions', as opposed to fine and less noticeable passions. [S. Xb–3.]

Sōgō 相好 Refers to *sanjūni-sō** 三十二相 (32 major physical characteristics) and *hachijūshu-kō** 八十種好 (80 minor marks of physical excellence), which are attributed to a buddha.

Sōgō 僧綱 Higher ranks of priests in charge of superintending monks and nuns and maintaining the rules (*gō*) of the Buddhist order; also *sōkan* 僧官 'priestly officers.' There were three main

ranks, each with sub-divisions: (1) *sōjō* 僧正 (archbishop)—
daisōjō 大僧正 (great archbishop), *sōjō*, and *gonsōjō* 權僧正
(archbishop of the lower rank); (2) *sōzu* 僧都 (bishop)—*daisōzu*
大僧都 (great bishop), *gondaisōzu* 權大僧都 (great bishop of the
lower rank), *shōsōzu* 小僧都 (minor bishop), and *gonshōsōzu*
權小僧都 (minor bishop of the lower rank); (3) *risshi* 律師 (superintendent)—*dairisshi* 大律師 (great superintendent), *chūrisshi*
中律師 (superintendent of the middle rank), and *gonrisshi* 權律師
(superintendent of the lower rank). Cf. *sōi*. [K. 23; M. 133; O V.]

Sogon 麤言 I. 'Rough (unrefined) words.' II. Refers to the
Hinayana teaching.

Sōgya 僧伽 Sk. *saṃgha*; also 僧佉, etc.; translated as *shu* 衆
'multitude' and *wagōshu* 和合衆 'those who have gathered
together'; a company of monks; Buddhist order; one of the
Three Treasures (*sanbō**).

~ **no ku** -- の句 'Sangha's phrases'; special phrases used in
prayers to conjure up deities. [Hei. 3.]

~**-ran** -- 藍 Sk. *saṃgha-ārāma*, 'resting-place for a company (of
monks)'; a Buddhist monastery or a temple; popularly abbreviated as *garan*.

~**-ri** -- 梨 Sk. *saṃghāṭī*; one of the three robes of a monk; see
sanne.

Sōgyō 僧形 'The form of a monk.' [Tai. 18.]

Sōi 僧位 'Priestly ranks'; ranks or titles of respect for monks of
outstanding virtue. There were three: (1) *hōin* 法印 or *hōin-
daikashō-i* 法印大和尚位 'the rank of the Dharma-seal great
master'; (2) *hōgen* 法眼 or *hōgen-kashō-i* 法眼和尚位 'the rank of
the Dharma-eye master'; and (3) *hokkyō** 法橋 or *hokkyō-shōnin-
i** 法橋上人位 'the rank of the master of the Dharma-bridge'.
They correspond respectively to *sōjō*, *sōzu* and *risshi*; cf. *sōgō*.

Sōji 精進 See *shōjin*.

Sōji 總持 'Having all'; a translation of the Sk. *dhāraṇi* (*darani**)
because a dharani (a spell or mystic formula) contains boundless
meanings. [Tai. 12.]

~ **no hōken** -- の法驗 'The efficacy of (repeating) a dharani.'
[Tai. 12.]

Sōjō 宗乘 See *shūjō*.

Sōjō 相承 'Transmitting.'

Sōjō 僧正 The first grade in the Buddhist hierarchy; an archbishop; see *sōgō*. [Tsu. 45.]

Sōjō no ninjin 爪上の人身 'The human existence which is rarely attained'; among all living beings, the number of those who are born into human existence is compared to the speck of earth that can rest on the tip of a finger nail. [S. I–6.]

Sōkan 僧官 'Priestly officers'; see *sōgō*.

Sōkan-gyō 雙卷經 'The two-fascicle sutra'; refers to the *Muryōju-kyō**. [S. I–10.]

Soku 觸 'Contact, touch.' I. The mental function that brings the consciousness into contact with external objects. II. A tactile object; one of the six objects of perception and sensation (*rokkyō** or *rokujin**). III. Contact with external objects; one of the twelve causations (*jūni-innen**).

Sokusai 息災 'Stopping calamities.'

~ **annon** --安穩 'Stopping calamities and securing peace.' [S. I–1.]

~**-hō** --法 'The rite for stopping calamities'; one of the five rituals in esoteric Buddhism (*goshuhō**).

Sokushin jōbutsu 即身成佛 'Becoming a buddha with one's present body'; the essential doctrine of the Shingon* sect. This idea is interpreted in three ways: (1) *rigu* 理具, intrinsic embodiment, i.e. all sentient beings are originally buddhas; (2) *kaji* 加持, endowment of power and response, i.e. one attains unity with the buddha by the endowment of power by the buddha and one's responsive practice; (3) *kentoku* 顯得, manifest realization, i.e. the complete and manifest realization of buddhahood. [K. 54; S. I–3.]

Sokushin ni 即身に 'With this body; immediately with one's present body.' [Tai. 15.]

Sokushin zedō 即心是道 'The mind is itself the Way'; the Buddhist Way lies in one's mind and its activities. [S. Vb–7.]

Sokushō mujō daibodai 速證無上大菩提 'To realize quickly the highest great enlightenment.' [Tai. 13.]

Sōmoku jōbutsu 草木成佛 'Grass and trees attain buddhahood';

because of the universal presence of buddha-nature, insentient things as well as sentient beings attain buddhahood. Also *hijō jōbutsu**. [S. III–4.]

Sōmon 桑門 Sk. *śramaṇa*; also *shamon** 沙門; a Buddhist monk. [Ho. 37; Tai. 12, 30.]

Sōmon 總門 'The main gate' of a temple; also *daimon* 大門. [Tai. 24.]

Sōmotsu 僧物 'Things belonging to priests'; for the two kinds of *sōmotsu*, see *nishu-sōmotsu*. [Tai. 35.]

Sonjō-darani 尊勝陀羅尼 See *Sonshō-darani*.

Sonjōō 尊星王 'The August Star Ruler'; refers to Myōken* 妙見. [Tai. 36.]

~ no hō ---の法 'The ritual dedicated to the August Star Ruler.' This esoteric ritual, traditionally performed at the Onjōji* 園城寺, is dedicated to Myōken*, the deification of the Great Bear (*hokuto shichisei* 北斗七星), as a prayer for longevity and the elimination of calamities. [Tai. 36.]

Sonshō-butchō 尊勝佛頂 'The most august (sage manifested from the) Buddha's head'; the most revered of all deities produced from the Buddha's head. Being capable of removing all evil passions and troubles, he is also called Joshō-butchō 除障佛頂 'the remover of hindrances (who is manifested) from the Buddha's head.'

Sonshō-darani 尊勝陀羅尼 Short title for the *Butchō-sonshō-darani* 佛頂尊勝陀羅尼. A dharani of 87 phrases which reveals the merit and inner realization of 'the most august sage manifested out of the Buddha's head' (Sonshō-butchō* 尊勝佛頂) [TT. 19, pp. 383–4, etc.]. This dharani has been widely used for the purpose of preventing natural disasters and securing longevity. Also used to ward off devils. [K. 69; O. III.]

Sonshōhō 尊勝法 'The ritual dedicated to Sonshō-butchō*' to pray for the elimination of calamities and sins and an increase of merit; also called *sonshōku**. The ritual includes reciting of the *Sonshō-darani**.

Sonshōku 尊勝供 'The ritual dedicated to Sonshō-butchō*'; see *sonshōhō*. [Tai. 23.]

Sonshōō 尊星王 See *sonjōō*.

Sonshōō no mishiho 尊勝王の御修法   The esoteric ritual of praying for the cessation of calamities and the eradication of sin, based on the *Sonshō-darani**. [Ma. 278.]

Sonshuku 尊宿   'A venerable elder'; a title of respect for a priest of outstanding virtue. [Tai. 12.]

Sōō 相應   'To comply with, agree with.'

Sōrin 雙林   Refers to *sharasōju** *no hayashi*; the forest with the twin *śāla* trees under which the Buddha passed away. [Tai. 8.]

~-ju --樹   The same as *sōrin* above. [Tai. 18]

Sōrin 叢林   'A forest.'   I. Living together by many monks.   II. A Zen* temple.

Sosai 麤細   'Rough and minute; coarse and fine.'   [S. III–1.]

Soshitsujihō 蘇悉地法   The ritual practice expounded in the *Soshitsuji-kyō**; one of the three secret practices (*sanbu-daihō**).

Soshitsujikara-kyō 蘇悉地羯羅經   '*Sutra on the Act of Perfection*'; Sk. *Susiddhikara-sūtra*; 3 fasc., tr. by Śubhākarasiṃha (Zenmui*) in 724 [TT. 18, No. 893]; one of the three mystic sutras of esoteric Buddhism, the other two being *Dainichi-kyō** and *Kongōchō-kyō**.

Soshitsuji-kyō 蘇悉地經   Refers to *Soshitsujikara-kyō**. [Hei. 2.]

Sōsoku 相卽   'Mutually identical.'   [S. Va–5, 6, Vb–10.]

Sōtai 僧體   'A priest's body'; the appearance of a priest.

Sotaranzō 素多覽藏   Sk. *sūtra-piṭaka*, 'collection of sutras'; also *shutarazō* 修多羅藏, *kyōzō** 經藏, etc. One of the three or five divisions of the Buddhist scriptures; contains the Buddha's teachings. Cf. *gozō* and *sanzō*. [S. II–8.]

Sotoba 卒(also 率)都婆   Sk. *stūpa*.   I. A tomb mound or a personal shrine; a pagoda. [Tsu. 201.]   II. A tall wooden tablet with a sacred name or spell written in Chinese or Shittan script and the Buddhist name of the dead person in Chinese; it is set up on the mound or by the grave; the top of the tablet is in the tiered shape of a *stūpa*. See *tō*☆. [Tsu. 30.]

Sōyakuhō 增益法   Also *zōyakuhō*; 'the ritual for increasing (merit)'; one of the five kinds of rituals established in esoteric Buddhism (*goshuhō**). It aims at increasing merit and securing prosperity.

Sōza 僧座   'Seat for a priest.'   [O. VI.]

Sōzu 僧都 The second grade in the Buddhist hierarchy, below *sōjō** 僧正 (archbishop) and above *risshi** 律師 (superintendent); a bishop. There are four ranks: *daisōzu* 大僧都, *gon-daisōzu* 權大僧都, *shōsōzu* 小僧都, and *gon-shōsōzu* 權小僧都; see *sōgō*.

Sue no yo 末の世 See *masse*. [Tsu. 23.]

Sugyōza 修行者 See *shugyōza*.

Suigatsu 水月 'The moon reflected in the water'; an analogy to show the unsubstantiality of existence. [S. III–1.]

Suijaku 垂迹 (or 跡) 'To drop traces'; manifesting an incarnate form; incarnation; the transformed body of a certain buddha or bodhisattva; cf. *honji suijaku*.

~ **geyū no hikari** --外融之光 The guiding light of an incarnated divinity; *geyū* literally means 'fusing with the outside'. [Tai. 9.]

~ **no higan** ----の悲願 'The compassionate vow to manifest oneself' in the world of suffering in order to save people. [Tai. 3.]

~ **no hōben** --の方便 'The expedient means for manifesting an incarnation.' [Tai. 12.]

~ **no tsuki** --の月 The month when Sannō Gongen* manifested his incarnation in Japan, i.e. the 4th month. [Hei. 2.]

~ **wakō** --和光 'Manifesting an incarnation by concealing the original majestic body'; cf. *wakō no suijaku*. [Tai. 5.]

~ **wakō no migiri** --和光の砌り The state of incarnation in which a deity manifests himself in a less awesome form as a man. [Tai. 2.]

Suikan 水觀 'Water contemplation'; refers to *suisōkan** 水想觀, one of the 16 contemplations (*jūrokkan**). [S. VI–10.]

Suikyo 吹嘘 In Zen*, 'to commend' a monk for a post of distinction. [Tai. 26.]

Suirin 水輪 'The water (layer in the form of a) disc'; the middle of the three layers (*sanrin**) under the ground. [Tai. 19.]

Suishō no in 水生の印 'Water-producing mudra'; a manual sign which has the magical effect of producing water at will. [K. 596.]

Suisōkan 水想觀 'Contemplation on water'; one of the 16 contemplations centring on Amida* and his land presented in the *Kanmuryōju-kyō*.* This is a preliminary contemplation leading to one on the earth of the land; see *jūrokkan*. [Tai. 37.]

Sukuse 宿世　See *shukuse*.

Sumizome 墨染　'Dyed in black ink'; refers to *sumizome no koromo* below. [Tai. 20.]

~ **no ikō** --の衣袴　'Black robe and trousers' worn by a priest. [K. 488.]

~ **no koromo** --の衣　'A black robe' worn by a priest.

Susume hosshi すすめ法師　'A priest who urges' people to build temples, etc. [K. 494.]

T

Tabonkai 他犯戒　'The precept of not committing adultery.' [Tai. 25.]

Tachi 多智　'Much knowledge' of the Buddhist teaching.

Tachikawa-ryū 立川流　'The Tachikawa school' of the Shingon* sect; an immoral and heretical teaching based on a mixture of esoteric Buddhism and the *yin-yang* (*on'yō* or *onmyō* 陰陽) philosophy. Ninkan 仁寛, a 12th-century Shingon monk, is popularly regarded as its founder. While he was in exile at Izu on charges of involvement with the civil war of the Hōgen era (1156), an *on'yō* master from Tachikawa in Musashi Province studied esoteric Buddhism under him and developed a doctrine identifying sexual union with the unity of the noumenal principle and transcendental wisdom.

Tagara-kō 多伽羅香　Sk. *tagara*; n. of the incense obtained from the *tagara* tree. [S. VI–8.]

Tahōtō 多寶塔　A tower for the Buddha Tahō (Sk. Prabhūtaratna). A tower, often one-storeyed, modelled after the tower mentioned in the *Hoke-kyō**. [K. 6.]

Tai 胎　Refers to *Taizōkai mandara**. [S. I–1.]

Taibon gejō no sotoba 退梵(=凡)下乗の卒都婆 The two stone towers said to have been erected on the path to Vulture Peak (Ryōjusen*) by King Bimbisāra (Binbashara*). He dismounted from his carriage (*gejō*, 'dismount') at the first tower and walked on; when he came to the second tower, he left his retainers there (*taibon*, 'dismiss ordinary men') and proceeded to the Buddha's congregation on Vulture Peak. [Hei. 2.]

Taige 體解 'Understanding with the body'; thorough understanding. [S. III–1.]

Taigen Myōō 大元帥明王 See *Taigensui Myōō*.

Taigen no hō 大(or 太)元の法 Refers to *Taigensui mishiho**. [Hei. 3; Tai. 24.]

Taigen no mishiho 大元帥の御修法 See *Taigensui mishiho*.

Taigensui mishiho 大(or 太)元帥御修法 Also pronounced '*Taigen no mishiho*'; the ritual performed at the imperial palace from the 8th to the 14th of the 1st month for the purpose of praying for the long life of the emperor and the peace of the state. The principal deity worshipped is Taigensui Myōō*.

Taigensui Myōō 大元帥明王 Commonly pronounced 'Taigen Myōō'. Sk. Āṭavaka; a *yakṣa* (*yasha**) general who protects the state and people.

Taihōzō 對法藏 Sk. *abhidharma-piṭaka*, 'collection of discourses'; also *abidatsumazō* 阿毘達磨藏 and *ronzō* 論藏. One of the three or five divisions of the Buddhist scriptures, which contains discourses explaining the Buddha's teaching. Cf. *gozō* and *sanzō*. [S. II–8.]

Taiji 對治 'To administer an antidote'; to remove or destroy (hindrances). [S. IV–9.]

Taiju kinna 大樹緊那 'The *kinnara* king named Great Tree', who is said to live on the Kōsuisen*; see *kinnara*. [Tai. 39.]

Taikon ryōbu 胎金兩部 'The two (mandalas), Matrix(-store Realm) (*Taizōkai**) and Diamond (Realm) (*Kongōkai**)'; see *ryōbu mandara*. [S. I–1.]

Tairei 台嶺 '(T'ien-)t'ai mountain.' Mt. Hiei was so called after T'ien-t'ai-shan 天台山 in China where the Tendai* sect was founded. [K. 52.]

Taishaku 帝釋 Sk. *śakra devendra*; popularly known as Indra; the lord god of the Trāyastriṃśa Heaven (Tōriten*); originally a Hindu god but in Buddhism considered as a god who protects Buddhism and its followers. [Hei. 2.]

Taishakugū 帝尺宮 Properly, 帝釋宮; 'Taishaku's palace'; Indra's palace in the Trāyastriṃśa* Heaven (Tōriten*), called Kiken 喜見 'Joyful Sight'. [Tai. 10.]

Taishō 體性 'Substance and nature'; the essential nature of things.

~ **jakumetsu** --寂滅 'The substance or the essential nature of all existences is tranquil and non-existent.' [S. IV–1.]

Taiten 退轉 'To retrogress, fall back'; cf. *futai*.

Taiyū 體用 'Substance and function'; the essential body and the derivative function. [S. II–8, III–1.]

~ **funi** --不二 'Non-duality of the essence and its activity'; the absence of distinction between the ultimate reality or buddha-nature and its activity. [S. Xb–3.]

~ **muge** --無礙 Unobstructedness between the essence and its activity. [S. II–4.]

Taizō 胎藏 Abbr. of *taizōkai**.

~**-kai** --界 Sk. *garbha-dhātu*, 'matrix-store realm'.

~**-kai mandara** --界曼茶羅 'The Matrix-store Realm Mandala'; Sk. *garbha-dhātu maṇḍala*; one of the two main mandalas used in esoteric Buddhism, the other being *Kongōkai mandara**. There are more than 200 deities depicted in it, in 13 divisions. See *ryōbu mandara*.

~ **no gyōbō** --の行法 A ritual devoted to the deities of the Matrix-store Realm Mandala. [S. II–8.]

~ **no hyakuhachijū-son no shuji** --の百八十尊の種子 The Sanskrit syllables representing the 180 deities of the Matrix-store Realm Mandala. [S. II–8.]

~ **no kuson** --の九尊 'The nine divinities of the Matrix-store Realm Mandala'; (1) Dainichi* 大日 (Sk. Mahāvairocana), (2) Hōdō 寶幢 (Ratnaketu), (3) Kaifuke 開敷華 (Saṃkusumitarāja), (4) Muryōju* 無量壽 (Amitāyus), (5) Tenkuraion 天鼓雷音 (Divyadundubhimeghanirghoṣa), (6) Fugen* 普賢 (Samantabhadra), (7) Monju* 文殊 (Mañjuśrī), (8) Kannon* 觀音 (Avalokiteśvara), and (9) Miroku* 彌勒 (Maitreya). The first five are buddhas, and the rest bodhisattvas. [S. I-1.]

Tajuyūshin 他受用身 'Enjoyment-body-for-other'; one of the four buddha bodies (*shishin**), which partly corresponds to the enjoyment or reward body (*hōjin**). This buddha body is manifested in order to make others partake of and enjoy the bliss of the truth he himself has attained; cf. *jijuyūshin*.

Takejizaiten 他化自在天 'The Paranirmitavaśavartin Heaven'; the sixth heaven in the realm of desire (*yokkai**), where there are heavenly beings who cause hindrances to the followers of Buddhism.

~-shima -----子魔 'The king of devils in the Paranirmitavaśavartin Heaven'; he seeks to thwart one's attempts to do good; one of the four devils (*shima**).

Takuryō 度量 'Measuring'; mental calculation; discrimination. [S. III-1.]

Tamaraba-kō 多摩羅跋香 Sk. *tamāla-pattra*; n. of the incense obtained from *tamāla* leaves. [S. VI-8.]

Tamon 多聞 'Much hearing.' I. Having heard much and remembered much about the Buddhist teaching; hence, learned. II. Refers to Tamonten*. [Tai. 29.]

~ daiichi --第一 'The first and foremost in hearing the sermons'; an epithet for Ānanda (Anan*).

~-ten --天 'Much-hearing heaven'; Sk. Vaiśravaṇa; also Bishamon 毘沙門; one of the four guardians, who protects the northern part of the world. He is known by this name because he protects Buddhism and likes to hear sermons; see *shitennō*.

~-tennō --天王 'The heavenly king Vaiśravaṇa ('much-hearing')'; see *Tamonten*. [Tai. 24.]

Tandai 探題 '(One who) decides the subject (of discussion)' at a discussion meeting held at the *Yuima-e** or *Hokke-e* 法華會; also *daisha* 題者. He not only sets the question for discussion but also supervises at the discussion meeting; he is appointed by the emperor. [S. Va-2.]

Tanden 單傳 'Simple transmission'; transmitting singly; transmission of Zen* from mind to mind without having recourse to written words. [S. Vb–10.]

Tanen 多念 'Many thoughts'; refers to many recitations of the *nenbutsu**; cf. *ichinen*. [K. 66.]

Tanji 彈指☆ Also *danshi*. I. Snapping of fingers at a Buddhist service. II. A unit of time; 20 thought-moments (*nen** 念) are equal to one twinkling of an eye (*shun* 瞬); 20 twinklings of an eye are equal to one *tanji*.

Tanjō 端正 'Upright, respectable, proper.'

Tankū 單空 'One-sided (view of) emptiness'; a one-sided view of understanding the doctrine of emptiness in negative terms only; same as *henkū**.

Tannen 湛然 Ch. Chan-jan (711–82); a Chinese T'ien-t'ai (Tendai*) monk; popularly known as Ching-hsi 荊溪 (Keikei) because he came from Ching-hsi Province; also called Miao-le Ta-shih 妙樂大師 (Myōraku Daishi) because he lived in the Miao-le-ssu 妙樂寺. In his early years he received the Tendai* practice and doctrine, and later dedicated himself to the revival of the Tendai teaching. He compiled many works and is regarded as the fifth patriarch of the T'ien-t'ai sect.

Tannen no shinji 湛然の心地 'The tranquil mental state.' [S. Xb–3.]

Tanza 端坐 'Sitting upright.'

Tariki 他力 'The other-power'; refers to the power of a buddha or a bodhisattva, especially Amida* Buddha, as opposed to the practitioner's own power (*jiriki**). [S. II–8.]

~ **hongan** --本願 '(Amida's) original vow (to save sentient beings) by other-power'; 'other-power' refers to Amida's* power, as opposed to the aspirant's own (*jiriki**); cf. *hongan*. [S. Xa–1.]

~ **no gōen** --の強縁 'The dominant condition (for birth in the Pure Land)', namely other-power; Amida's* power which causes one to be born in his land. [IH.]

Tashō 他生 I. That which has been produced by an external cause. II. The same as *tase* 他世, a future life; the after-life.

Tashō 多生 'Many lives' in transmigration. [S. I–6.]

~ **kōgō** --曠劫 'Many lives through innumerable *kalpas* (*kō**)'; existing for a very long time while repeating many cycles of birth and death. [Hei. 1.]

~ **no en** --の縁 'Close relationships in many lives in the past.'
[Tai. 1.]

~ **no jūku** --の重苦 'Great pains (one has to suffer) for many
lives.' [S. VII–7.]

Tatchū 塔頭 I. The graveyard of a noble priest. II. A small hall
in the premises of a Zen* temple, where a retired head priest
lives. [S. Xb–3.]

Tazetsugyo 多舌魚 'The fish called "many tongues".' According
to the *Kōkigyō-kyō** 興起行經, in one of the Buddha's previous
lives he went to a pond near his village and hit on the head two
fish which had been caught by a villager. One of the fish was
called '*fu*' 𩹄 and the other '*tazetsu*', and they were previous
incarnations of King Virūdhaka (Ruri Ō*) and his wicked brahmin
friend. The latter instigated the king to attack and massacre
the Śākya (Shaka*) clan. [Tai. 35.]

Teihatsu 剃髮 'Shaving one's head'; becoming a monk.

~ **zen'e no sugata** --染衣の姿 'One's appearance with a shaven
head and dyed robe'; the appearance of a monk. [Tai. 27.]

Tekkutsu jigoku 鐵崛地獄 See the next entry. [Tai. 35.]

Tekkutsu jigoku 鐵窟地獄 'The iron-cave hell'; n. of a hell mentioned in the *Kanbutsu-zanmai-kyō** 觀佛三昧經. It is an iron
mountain full of red-hot iron balls. On the side of the mountain
there are hundreds of swords and knives planted in the ground.
Sinners born there feel as if they are in a large iron cave full of
molten copper and iron. Their bodies are torn by the swords and
knives, and as they run about to escape from the mountainside,
they hit their heads against the iron balls. These also pierce their
bodies from head to toe. They die instantly, but the next
moment they revive and their torment begins again.

Tekkutsu kusho 鐵窟苦所 'The place of afflictions with iron caves';
refers to the iron-cave hell (*tekkutsu jigoku** 鐵窟地獄) mentioned
in the *Kanbutsu-zanmai-kyō**. [Tai. 26.]

Ten 天 I. A heavenly realm; one of the six or ten states of existence
(*rokudō** and *jikkai**); there are various heavens in the three
realms (*sangai**). II. Inhabitants of a heaven. III. A supernatural being possessed of some transcendent power; a demi-god

or a spirit. IV. A title of respect for a Hinayana or Mahayana sage who has destroyed his own evil passions. V. Used to describe a man of distinguished virtue, as in *tenge* 天華 'a heavenly flower.'

Tencha 奠茶 'To offer tea'; offering tea to a deceased person at the funeral. [Tai. 33, 40.]

~ **butsuji** --佛事 'A Buddhist ceremony of offering tea' to a deceased person; this is part of the funeral service in the Zen* sect.

Tendai 天台 I. Refers to *Tendai-shū**. II. Refers to *Tendai Daishi**.

~ **Daishi** --大師 'The Great Master Tendai'; refers to Chigi*. [S. IV–1.]

~**-shū** --宗 'The Tendai (Ch. T'ien-t'ai) sect'; a Mahayana sect founded in China by Chih-i 智顗 (Chigi*) (538–597) based on the *Hoke-kyō** and the philosophical views of Nāgārjuna (Ryūju*). It classifies the Buddha's teachings according to five periods (*gojikyō**). Based on the doctrine of 'ten suchness-aspects' (*jūnyoze**) presented in the *Hoke-kyō*, this sect sees the whole universe in each existence (see *ichinen sanzen, santai* and *sanzen jikkai*). The Tendai teaching was first brought to Japan by Chien-chen 鑑眞 (Ganjin*) in the middle of the eighth century, but was not widely accepted then. In 805, Saichō* 最澄 brought back from China the Tendai tradition and made the temple he had built on Mt. Hiei, the Enryakuji*, a centre for the study and practice of Tendai. However, what he had transmitted from China was not exclusively Tendai, but also included Zen*, esoteric teachings and Mahayana precepts. There is therefore some esoteric tendency in the doctrine he advocated. This tendency became marked in the doctrines of his successors, such as Ennin* 圓仁 and Enchin* 圓珍. The Tendai sect flourished under the patronage of the imperial family and nobles. At the time of Ryōgen* 良源, the sect was divided into two schools, *sanmon** 山門 'Mountain School' and *jimon** 寺門 'Temple School', and later, in the 15th century, it saw the rise of a third school, Shinzei (or Shinsei) 眞盛.

~ **zasu** --座主 'The head priest of (the Enryakuji* of) the Tendai sect.' [K. 578; O. V; Tai. 9.]

Tendō 天堂 'A heavenly palace.' [S. Xa–4.]

Tendō 天童 'Heavenly boy'; an incarnation of a deity who serves and protects a follower of Buddhism; cf. *gohō tendō*. [O. VI.]

Tendō 顛倒 'Perverted, wrong-headed.' [S. I–1.]

~ **no oroka naru kokoro** --の愚なる心 'Perverted and stupid mind.' [S. Va–5.]

~ **no sō** --の想 'A perverted view'; a delusory thought. [Tsu. 242.]

Tendoku 轉讀 I. Chanting a sutra. II. A ritual chanting of a sutra in which few lines of each chapter are read and the rest omitted; cf. *shindoku*.

Ten'e 轉依 See *tenne*.

Tengai 天蓋 'A heavenly cover or umbrella'; also *bangai* 幡蓋, *sōgai** 繪蓋, etc.; an ornamental canopy or umbrella suspended above the head of a buddha statue, or used as a shade for a priest in a procession. [Tai. 24.]

Tengoku 諂曲 'Flattery and deviousness; deceitfulness.' [K. 40; O. VI.]

Tengu 天狗 A kind of flying devil, with wings and beak.

~**-dō** --道 'The path of *tengu**'; the realm or state of existence of *tengu*. [Tai. 25, 27.]

Tengū 天宮 'A heavenly palace'; a palace of heavenly beings. [Tai. 24.]

Tenjiku 天竺 A corrupted transcription of *Sindhu*, an ancient name for India.

Tenjin 天親 Vasubandhu. See *Seshin*. [S. III–1.]

Tenjin 點心 I. In a Zen* temple, a small quantity of food taken before lunch. II. Sometimes, in a Zen temple, lunch itself. III. Any snack taken between meals. IV. Tea and cakes.

Tenjin chigi 天神地祇 'Heavenly gods and earth deities.' [S. VII–4.]

Tenjō 天上 'The heavenly realm.'

~ **no fuku** --の福 'Happiness in heaven.' [S. IV–1.]

~ **no gosui** --の五衰 See *tennin no gosui*. [Tai. 3.]

Tenma 天魔 'A heavenly devil'; also *tenshima* 天子魔; the king of the Paranirmitavaśavartin Heaven (Takejizaiten*) is so called because he causes hindrances to those who follow the Buddhist

Way. Cf. *shima* and *takejizaitenshima*. [S. III–5.]

~ **hajun** -- 波旬 'The king of devils, Pāpīyas'; see *Hajun*. [Tai. 24.]

~ **no shōge** -- の障礙 'Hindrance caused by heavenly devils.' [Tai. 12.]

Tenne 轉依 'Reversing the basis (of one's existence)'; Sk. *āśraya-parāvṛtti*; reversing one's existence-base, which results in relinquishing one's evil passions and delusions and attaining Nirvana and enlightenment. According to the Hossō* teaching, one's existence-base (*e* 依 or *shoe* 所依, *āśraya*) is one's eighth consciousness (*arayashiki**, *ālaya-vijñāna*), which stores seeds of evil passions (*bonnōshō**) and those of hindrance to correct knowledge (*shochishō**). Reversing one's existence-base means relinquishing these defiled seeds and attaining undefiled wisdom (i.e. enlightenment) and Nirvana, which is the state in which evil passions are extinguished.

Tennin 天人 'A heavenly being.'

~ **no gosui** -- の五衰 The five marks of decrepitude of heavenly beings before they die. According to the *Nehan-gyō**, they are: (1) clothes become dirty; (2) flowers in the headdress wither; (3) the whole body emits foul smells; (4) there is sweating under the arms; and (5) there is a disinclination to take proper seats and postures. [Hei. 2.]

Tenpōrin 轉法輪 'Turning the wheel of the Dharma'; preaching the Dharma, or Buddhist law.

~ **no sō** --- の相 'The aspect of turning the wheel of the Dharma'; one of the eight major events in the Buddha's life (*hassō**); the Buddha's preaching of the law after enlightenment. [Tai. 8.]

Tenrinjōō 轉輪聖王 'Wheel-turning Noble King'; Sk. cakravartin. The ideal king conceived in India who rules the world with the wheel (Sk. *cakra*) which he spontaneously obtains at the time of enthronement. There are four kinds of kings, according to the different qualities of the wheel. One with a gold wheel (*konrin-ō* 金輪王) rules all the four continents of the world (*shishū**); one with a silver wheel (*ginrin-ō* 銀輪王) rules three continents; one with a copper wheel (*dōrin-ō* 銅輪王) rules two; and one with an iron wheel (*tetsurin-ō* 鐵輪王) rules one. Besides the wheel, which crushes the enemy, the king is possessed of six other treasures, namely, elephants, horses, gems, ladies, attendants, and generals. [O. V.]

Tenrinnō 轉輪王　Refers to *Tenrinjōō**. [S. VI–17.]

~ **butchō** --- 佛頂　'Wheel-King Buddha's head'; see *Kinrin butchō*.

Tenryū hachibu 天龍八部　'The eight kinds of (gods and demi-gods who protect Buddhism, such as) heavenly beings and dragons'; see *hachibushu*. [Tai. 24, 25.]

Ten ryū yasha 天龍夜叉　'Devas (heavenly beings), dragons and *yakṣa* (*yasha**, a kind of demi-god).'

Tenshi 天子　'Heaven's child; the son of a god.' I. A god of a lower rank. II. The son of a god. III. A king or an emperor. IV. The king of the Paranirmitavaśavartin Heaven (Takejizaiten*); cf. *tenma*.

~ **honmyō no dōjō** -- 本命の道場　'A hall of the emperor's birth-star'; a hall where the emperor's birth-star is enshrined and prayers are offered to it for the long life of the emperor and the peace of the state. The first temple of this kind built in Japan was Sōji-in 總持院 on Mt. Hiei, which Emperor Montoku built in 851. Here the term refers to Enryakuji*, the main temple on Mt. Hiei. *Honmyō* refers to *honmyōsei**. [Tai. 24.]

Tenshin 點心　See *tenjin*.

Tenshu 天衆　'Heavenly beings.' [K. 36.]

Tentei 天帝　'The heavenly lord'; refers to Indra (Taishaku*). [Tai. 7, 10.]

Tentō 奠湯　'To offer hot water'; offering hot water, with honey or sugar in it, to a deceased person at his funeral. [Tai. 33, 40.]

~ **butsuji** -- 佛事　'A Buddhist ceremony of offering hot water', with honey or sugar in it, to a deceased person; this is part of the funeral service in the Zen* sect.

Tenzu 轉ず　I. To arise, evolve. II. To cause something to arise. III. To revolve, turn. IV. To turn round, reverse. V. To change, transform.

Tera-hosshi 寺法師　'A monk of the Temple (School)'; a monk of the Onjōji*, as opposed to *yama-hōshi**, a monk of Mt. Hiei. [K. 52; S. Va–7; Tai. 15; Tsu. 86.]

Tera mōde 寺詣 'Visit to a temple.' [Ma. 155.]

Tetsujō 鐵城 'An iron castle' in hell, where sinners are tortured. [Tai. 20.]

Tettō 鐵湯 'Molten iron' in hell, with which sinners are burned; cf. *mōka tettō*. [Tai. 10.]

Tōba 塔婆 Sk. *stūpa*; a tower built for a deceased person. Also *sotoba**. [K. 6.]

Tōdaiji 東大寺 The head temple of the Kegon* sect in Nara; historically known by such names as Sō-kokubunji 總國分寺 'headquarters of all *kokubunji**', Daikegonji 大華嚴寺 'great Kegon temple' and Konkōmyō Shitennō gokoku no tera 金光明四天王護國之寺 'the state-protecting temple through the power of the Four Guardian Gods (Shitennō*) in the spirit of the *Konkōmyō-kyō**'; the name Tōdaiji came to be used in contrast to the Saidaiji 西大寺. It was built in 745 by the wishes of Emperor Shōmu*, but three other people are especially mentioned for their parts in the construction and inauguration of the temple: (1) Rōben* 良辨 as the founder (*kaiki* 開基); (2) Gyōgi* 行基 as the chief promoter (*kanjin** 勸進); and (3) Baramon Sōjō* 婆羅門僧正 who led the inaugural service (cf. *shishō dōshin no tera*). A large statue of Birushana* Buddha, made of gold and copper, was erected in 746. The temple was burned to the ground in 1180 by Taira Shigehira 平重衡. After being rebuilt, it was again destroyed by fire during the civil war in 1567. The present building was erected in 1692 by Kōkei 公慶.

Tōgaku 等覺 'Equal enlightenment.' I. 'Enlightenment of (non-differentiation and absolute) equality', i.e. the Buddha's enlightenment. II. 'Enlightenment equal (to the Buddha's)', i.e. enlightenment of the bodhisattvas of the highest stage. cf. *gojūni-i*☆.

Tōhotsubadai 東弗婆提 Sk. Pūrvavideha; also Tōshōshinshū* 東勝身洲; one of the four continents (*shishū**); it lies to the east of Mt. Sumeru (Shumisen*) and is crescent-shaped. Its inhabitants' life-span is 250 years, and they have superior physical qualities.

Tōji 東寺 The temple in Kyoto originally built by Emperor Kanmu in 796 after the capital had been moved to Kyoto in 794. It flourished as a guardian temple of the new capital. Later, in

823, it was given to Kūkai* by Emperor Saga as a centre of Shingon* practice. It was then called Konkōmyō-shitennō-kyōō-gokokuji Himitsu-denpō-in 金光明四天王教王護國寺祕密傳法院, or simply, Kyōō-gokokuji 教王護國寺. Supported by the nobility and other classes, it has enjoyed great prosperity and is now the head temple of the Tōji school of the Shingon sect. The beautiful five-storey pagoda dominating the area was reconstructed by Tokugawa Iemitsu 德川家光 (1604–51). [Tai. 24.]

～ **no kanjō** --の灌頂 'The *kanjō** ceremony at the Tōji.' [Tai. 24.]

Tōjō 鬪諍 'Dispute, strife, quarrel.'

～ **kengo** --堅固 'Steadfast engagement in (doctrinal) disputes'; the characteristic feature of Buddhism in the fifth 500-year period after the Buddha's death; see *go-gohyakusai*. [Tai. 31.]

Tojun 杜順 Ch. Tu-shun (557–640); the first patriarch of the Chinese Hua-yen (Kegon*) sect. He entered the priesthood at 18, practised meditation under Seng-chen 僧珍 (Sōchin), and later retired to Mt. Chung-nan 終南山 (Shūnanzan), where he wrote the *Gokyō-shikan* 五教止觀, *Hokkai-kanmon* 法界觀門, etc. Said to have performed miracles, he won the patronage of Emperor T'ai-tsung 太宗 (Taisō), who gave him the title Ti-hsin Tsun-che 帝心尊者 (Teishin Sonja). His disciple Chih-yen 智儼 (Chigon) succeeded to the Dharma and further developed the Hua-yen doctrine. [S. Xb–2.]

Tōkatsu jigoku 等活地獄 'Equally reviving hell'; one of the eight great hells (*hachidai-jigoku**); Sk. *saṃjīva*. In this hell sinners are beaten with iron bars or slashed with sharp knives. When they die, a cool breeze, or a voice from the sky or a guardian demon crying, "Come back to life!", restores them, but they then suffer the same tortures as before. It is said that those who have killed living beings during their lives must suffer in this hell. [Tai. 35.]

Toki 齋 I. Abstention from eating after noon. II. A meal taken before noon. [Tsu. 60.] III. A meal served at a Buddhist service.

Tokiryō 時料 See 齋料. [S. Xa–8.]

Tokiryō 齋料 'Food costs.' [K. 423.]

Tokka 得果 'Acquiring the fruit'; attaining spiritual fruition. [S. IV–1.]

Tokko 獨鈷 See *dokko*.

Toko 獨鈷 See *dokko*.

Tokuchi no zenji 得智の禪師 'A Buddhist master of outstanding wisdom.' [Tai. 4.]

Tokudatsu 得脱 'To attain deliverance' from the world of transmigration. [K. 692.]

Tokudō 得道 'Attaining the Way'; attainment of enlightenment.

~ **tokka** --得果 'Attaining the Way and the fruit,' i.e. the Buddhist Way or ideal and a higher spiritual state. [S. II-10.]

Tokugyō 德行 'Virtuous conduct, meritorious act.'

Tokugyū zenshin 犢牛前身 'Previous incarnations of calves'; Kuei-shan 潙山 (Isan) (771–853), a Chinese Zen* monk, said one day that he would be reborn as a female buffalo 100 years after his death. It followed from this that his disciples at the time were earlier incarnations of the calves which the buffalo would bear. The term came to be used derogatively for Zen monks. [Tai. 24.]

Tokuhon 德本 'The root of virtue'; meritorious acts. [S. I-10.]

Tokuyaku 得益 'Acquiring benefit.'

Tokuyū 德用 'Function, activity.' [S. I-3.]

Tōmandara 東曼陀羅 'The Eastern Mandala'; refers to *Taizōkai mandara**; one of the two most important mandalas used in esoteric Buddhism; hung on the eastern side of a hall. Cf. *sai-mandara*. [Hei. 3.]

Ton'ai 貪愛 'Greed, covetousness.' [IH.]

Tonbō 頓法 'An abrupt method'; a method of practice whereby one's wishes are quickly fulfilled. [Tai. 26.]

Tondai 頓大 Abbr. of *tongyō** 頓教, 'abrupt teaching' or 'the teaching of sudden enlightenment', and *daijō** 大乘, 'Mahayana'; the combined reference is to the *Kegon-gyō**.

~ **sanshichinichi** --三七日 'The sudden Mahayana (teaching expounded) for three weeks'; it is believed that the *Kegon-gyō** was preached during the period of three weeks immediately following the Buddha's enlightenment. [Tai. 18.]

Tongo 頓悟 'Sudden enlightenment.' [S. II-8.]

~ **tonshu** --頓修 'Sudden enlightenment and sudden practice';

attaining enlightenment very quickly and accomplishing all meritorious practices very quickly, too; cf. *tongo zenshu*. [S. III –8.]

~ **zenshu** --漸修 'Sudden enlightenment and gradual practice'; attaining enlightenment very quickly but spending a long time accomplishing meritorious practices; cf. *tongo tonshu*. [S. III–8.]

Tongyō 頓教 'The abrupt teaching'; the opposite of *zengyō** 漸教 'the gradual teaching'; a higher teaching expounded directly without explaining intermediate teachings of lower levels; also, a teaching which enables one to attain enlightenment very quickly; cf. *gokyō* and *kegi no shikyō*.

Ton'in 貪淫 'Attachment and lust.' [S. Xb–1.]

Tonjinchi no sandoku 貪瞋癡の三毒 'The three poisons of greed, hatred and stupidity'; they are the three major evil passions. [Tai. 23.]

Tonsei 遁世 Also *tonzei*; 'retreating from the world'; renouncing the world in order to live in seclusion and practise Buddhism. After the Kamakura period (1192–1333), however, entering the priesthood became a fashion, and there were many who renounced the world in a purely formal way simply because they were attracted to living in seclusion. Cf. *tonseisha*.

~ **hijiri** --聖 'A recluse sage'; a Buddhist recluse. [S. I–3.]

~**-mon** --門 'The gate of renunciation of the world'; retirement from the world for the purpose of concentrating on Buddhist practices; also used in the sense of *tonseisha**. [S. II–6, III–8, IV–6.]

~**-mono** --者 See *tonseisha*.

~ **no shōnin** --の上人 'A revered priest who has renounced the world.' [S. I–3.]

~ **nyūdō** --入道 'A *nyūdō** who has renounced the world.' [S. IV–9.]

~**-sha** --者 I. 'One who has renounced the world'; generally, a Buddhist recluse. II. A kind of Buddhist recluse, esp. after the Kamakura period (1192–1333), who, although ordained, left ecclesiastical society and lived alone. III. A person after the Kamakura period, often belonging to the Ji sect (Jishū*), who acted as aide and adviser in artistic matters in the residences of feudal lords. [Tai. 36, 37, 39.]

Tonshō 頓證 'Sudden enlightenment.' [S. III–1.]

Ton'yoku 貪欲 'Greed, lust'; attachment to pleasurable things.

Tōrai 當來 'The future.'

~ **chigu no en** --値遇の緣 'The relationship which will enable one to meet (a buddha) in the future.' [Tai. 22.]

Tōri 忉利 Refers to *Tōriten**. [Tai. 18.]

~**-ten** --天 Sk. Trāyastriṃśa; also Sanjūsanten* 三十三天 'the heaven of the thirty-three (gods)'. One of the heavens in the realm of desire (*yokkai** 欲界), it is located on the top of Mt. Sumeru (Shumisen*). At each of its corners there is a peak, where eight gods dwell, and in the palace lives the lord of the heaven, Śakra (also, Indra; Taishaku* 帝釋). [K. 681.]

Tōru 等流 'The same stream.' I. Homogeneity of a certain cause and its effect. II. Becoming one with something. [S. I–3.]

~ **hosshin** --法身 'Homogeneous forms of the Dharma-body'; transformations of the buddha into the same forms as human or heavenly beings, animals, etc., manifested in order to save living beings; cf. *shishu hosshin*. [S. I–3.]

~ **no shin** --の身 'A homogeneous body'; refers to *tōru hosshin**. [S. I–3.]

Tōsabutsu no ki 當作佛の記 'The prediction that one will become a buddha.' [S. III–1.]

Tōshō 當生 A contraction of *tōrai no shōsho* 當來の生處 'the place of rebirth in the future'; a future state of existence. [S. VI –10.]

Tōshōshinshū 東勝身洲 'The eastern continent (whose inhabitants have) superior physiques'; one of the four continents (*shishū**); also Tōhotsubadai*.

Tosō 斗藪 Also 抖擻; 'throwing away (everything)'; a translation of Sk. *dhūta* (*zuda**). Originally, the rules of frugal living for Buddhist mendicants, but in Japan often used in the sense of wandering about the country begging for alms and teaching the Dharma. [Tai. 35, 39.]

~ **no hijiri** --の聖 'A wandering sage who performs the *dhūta* (*zuda**) practices.' [Tai. 35.]

Tosotsu 兜(or 都)率 Refers to *Tosotsuten**.

~ **naiin** --內院 See ~ *no naiin* below. [K. 484.]

~ **no jōshō** --の上生 'Rebirth in the Tuṣita Heaven.' [S. II–8.]

~ **no naiin** --の內院 'The inner palace of the Tuṣita Heaven,' where Miroku* (Maitreya) lives. The heavenly inhabitants live in outer palaces (*gein* 外院). [S. II–8, VI–10; Tai. 8.]

~**-ten** --天 'The Tuṣita Heaven'; the fourth of the six heavens in the realm of desire, in which the future Buddha dwells. [S. I–1.]

~ **tengū** --天宮 'The palace of the Tuṣita Heaven'; the same as *Tosotsu no naiin**. [Tai. 24.]

Tōtai 當體 'A thing itself; a thing as it is.'

Tōzan kenju 刀山劍樹 The mountain covered with swords and knives sticking out of the ground, and trees with leaves of knife-blades; part of hell where sinners suffer great torments. [Tai. 7.]

Tōzuōkyō 當途王經 'The king of sutras currently circulating in the world'; another name for the *Kannon-gyō** or 'Fumon-bon*' (Chapter on the Universal Gate) of the *Hoke-kyō**. [Tai. 13.]

Tsū 通 'Going through'; non-obstruction in the exercise of physical and mental power; supernatural power; transcendental ability. [Tsu. 8.]

Tsūgan 通願 'The common vow'; the vow common to all bodhi-sattvas; opposed to *betsugan**. [S. III–1.]

Tsuifuku 追福 Doing meritorious acts to increase the merit of a deceased person; cf. *tsuizen*. [Tsu. 222.]

Tsuifun 追賁 'Adorning (the merit of a dead person)'; also *tsuigon* 追嚴; performing a Buddhist service for the repose of a dead person, esp. an emperor. [Tai. 20.]

Tsuikyō no sazen 追孝の作善 'Doing good deeds out of filial piety (towards a dead parent).' [Tai. 20.]

Tsuina 都維那 Also *ina* 維那; Sk. *karma-dāna*; a priest in charge of the clerical work in a temple.

Tsuizen 追善 Strictly, 追薦; doing meritorious acts, such as holding a memorial service, to increase the merit of a deceased person; see also *tsuifuku*. [Tsu. 222.]

~ **no on-butsuji** --の御佛事 'A Buddhist service for increasing the merit of a deceased person.' [Tai. 24.]

Tsujidō 辻堂 'A Buddhist hall by the road-side.' [Tai. 5.]

Tsūkai 通誡 'A universal admonition'; an admonition given by all masters or buddhas; cf. *shichibutsu tsūkai ge.* [S. Xb–1.]

Tsukuri-botoke つくり佛 'A coloured statue of a buddha.' [Ma. 84.]

Tsūsō 通相 'A common feature or characteristic', as contrasted with *bessō** 別相 'a special feature or characteristic'.

U

U 有 'Being, existence.' I. Existence, as opposed to non-existence (*mu* 無 or *kū* 空). II. One of the twelve causations (*jūni-innen**); the state of being in which various karma are created. III. A specific state of existence produced by one's karma; cf. *san'u, shiu, nijūgo-u* and·*nijūku-u.*

Ubadaisha 優婆提舍 Sk. *upadeśa*, 'a discourse'; a kind of Buddhist scripture which consists of discussions of doctrine, often in question and answer form; one of the nine and the twelve kinds of scriptures (*kubu-kyō** and *jūnibu-kyō**).

Ubai 優婆夷 Sk. *upāsikā*; a lay woman; cf. *shichishu* and *shishu.*

Ubari 優婆梨 Also Upari 優波離; Sk. Upāli; n. of one of the ten great disciples of the Buddha (*jūdai-deshi**); being the most conversant with the precepts laid down by the Buddha, at the first conference held after the Buddha's death he recited them, together with the circumstances in which they were first provided, etc. [S. IV–1.]

Ubasoku 優婆塞 Sk. *upāsaka*; a layman cf. *shichishu* and *shishu.*

Ubu 有部 'Existence School'; abbr. of Setsuissai-ubu 說一切有部; Sk. Sarvāstivāda; one of the Hinayana schools, developed some

200 years after the Buddha's death, this school holds the view that all things really exist. [S. IV–1.]

Ubutsu mubutsu 有佛無佛 'Regardless of whether the Buddha is in the world or not.' [S. Xb–2.]

Uchi kōgyō no shōnin 有智高行の上人 'A revered priest of outstanding wisdom and noble conduct.' [Tai. 8.]

Uchi kōtoku 有智高德 '(Person of) wisdom and noble virtue.'

Uchi-rongi 內論議 'The discussion at the imperial palace'; *uchi* 內 refers to Daidairi 大內裏, the imperial palace. The discussion on a Buddhist text which takes place on the last day of the Gosai-e* lecture-meeting, namely the 14th of the 1st month. It dates back to 813 during the reign of Emperor Saga, when statues of Dainichi*, Kannon* and Kokūzō* were enshrined and monks discussed the doctrine of the *Konkōmyō-kyō*. [Tai. 24.]

Uchōten 有頂天 'The Highest Heaven'; Sk. Akaniṣṭha. I. Another name for Shikikukyōten 色究竟天, the fourth and uppermost heaven in the realm of form (*shikikai*). II. Another name for Hisōhihisōten* 非想非非想天, the fourth and uppermost heaven in the realm of non-form (*mushikikai*). [Tai. 19.]

Udai 有待 See *utai*.

Udana 優陀那 Sk. *udāna*; an exposition of the Dharma by the Buddha without awaiting questions or requests from his disciples; hence, translated as *jisetsu* 自說 'expounding of (the Buddha's) own accord'; one of the nine and the twelve kinds of scriptures (*kubu-kyō* and *jūnibu-kyō*).

Udennō 優轉王 'King Udayana'; also 優塡王; the king of Kauśāmbī and a patron of Buddhism. Tradition has it that when the Buddha went up to the Trāyastriṃśa Heaven (Tōriten*) and did not come back for a long time, the king was very worried and finally became ill. His ministers therefore had a statue of the Buddha made from a piece of sandal-wood, whereupon the king was cured of the illness. A copy of this statue was later transmitted to China and then to Japan. It is now in the Shōryōji 清凉寺 in Saga, Kyoto. [S. IV–2.]

Udon 優曇 Sk. *uḍumbara*; a flower said to bloom only once in 3,000 years. Used metaphorically to describe the rare appearance of a buddha in the world. [S. I–6.]

~-ge --華(or 花) An *uḍumbara* blossom. [S. III–7; Ta.; Tai. 20.]

Uen 有縁☆ 'Related (closely from the past).' [S. I–3.]

~ no gyō --の行 'The practice or method of salvation with which one is especially linked' or familiar, owing to some past relationship with it. [S. IV–1.]

~ no hō --の法 'The teaching with which one is especially linked' or familiar, owing to some past relationship with it. [S. IV–1.]

~ no ichigyō --の一行   See *uen no gyō*.

~ no ki --の機 'The person with whom (a specific teaching) is especially linked' owing to some past relationship and to whom it is most applicable. [S. IV–1.]

~ no shujō --の衆生 Sentient beings related to a buddha or bodhisattva in the past and, hence, ready to accept his teaching in this life. [Hei. 2.]

Uennichi 有縁日 See *ennichi*.

Ugen 有験 'Possessed of supernatural power.'

~ no hito --の人 'A man of supernatural power.' [K. 50.]

~ no kōsō --の高僧 'Revered priests who have supernatural powers.' [Tai. 33.]

~ no kōsō kisō --の高僧貴僧 'Revered and noble priests who have supernatural powers.' [Hei. 3.]

~ no mono --の者 'A man of supernatural power.' [S. Xb–1.]

~ no sō --の僧 'A priest with supernatural power.' [K. 482.]

Ugi 有義 'Having meaning'; meaningful, purposeful; opposite of *mugi**. [S. III–8.]

Ui 有爲 'Active, created'; Sk. *saṃskṛta*; phenomena; the phenomenal world; the world of transience; the opposite of *mui** 無爲.

~ no hō --の法 'Phenomenal things'; things in the phenomenal world. [S. Va–5.]

~ no komō tenpen no seken --の虚妄轉變の世間 'The conditioned world which is vain and constantly changing.' [S. Xa–4.]

~ no sakai --の境 'The realm of activity or phenomena.' [Tai. 33.]

~ **tenpen no yo no narai** --轉變の世の習 'The way of the world that all things must change.' [Tai. 36.]

Ujidera 氏寺 'A clan-temple'; the temple to which a clan belongs, e.g. the Kōfukuji* 興福寺 for the Fujiwara clan and the Enryaku-ji* 延暦寺 for the Taira clan. [O. III, VI.]

Ujō 有情 'A sentient being.' [Tsu. 128.]

Ukiyo 浮世 'This ephemeral world.' [Tai. 11.]

Ukyō 右脇 'The right side'; lying on the right side (at the time of death). [K. 64.]

Umon 有門 'The gate (i. e. teaching) of existence'; the teaching that claims the existence of something. [S. IV–1.]

Unen 有念 'Having thought'; discriminating thought, as opposed to *munen** 無念. [S. II–1.]

Unshin kuyō 運心供養 'Offering mental effort'; recitation of a spell, a manual sign, etc., performed as an offering to a deity; also *rikuyō* 理供養 'offering non-phenomenal things' and *naikuyō* 內供養 'offering internal things'. Cf. *genkuyō*.

Upari 優波離 See *Ubari*.

Urabon 盂蘭盆 Sk. *ullambana*, a corrupted form of *avalambana*, which literally means 'hanging down'; translated as *tōken* 倒懸 'hanging upside down'. A service performed for a dead person to save him from such tortures as being suspended upside down. Later, more generally a service for the repose of a dead person. According to the *Urabon-gyō**, the first such service was held by Maudgalyāyana (Mokuren*), a disciple of the Buddha, who wanted to save his mother from the suffering in the realm of hungry spirits (*gaki**). In Japan, the *urabon* festival has been held annually since 657. It was held from the 13th to the 15th of the 7th month during the Edo period (1603–1867). Today, it takes place either on the 15th July or the 15th August. Popularly, this festival is called *bon*'e 盆會 or, simply, *bon* 盆 or *o-bon* お盆. [Tai. 24.]

~**-gyō** ---經 '*The Ullambana Sutra*'; translated into Chinese by Dharmarakṣa (Hōgo 法護) at sometime between 266 and 313 [TT. 16, No. 685]. The sutra relates that Maudgalyāyana (Mokuren*) saved his dead mother from torment in the realm of hungry spirits (*gaki**) by making offerings to a company of monks on

the 15th of the 7th month. This was the origin of the *urabon**
(or simply *bon* 盆) festival.

Uro 有漏 'Having outflows'; Sk. *sāsrava*; defilement in the sense
of an oral and mental defiling element which causes obstruction
to enlightenment; impurity; the opposite of *muro**. [S. IV–1.]

〜 **no kahō** --の果報 'Reward of the nature of defilement': e.g.
the state of a heavenly being, attained as the result of some good
acts, which is still 'defiled' with evil passions and moral and
mental imperfections. [S. IV–1.]

Ushiki 有職 Refers to *ushiki no sankō* 有職の三綱, the three
ranks next to the *sōgō** in the hierarchy of priests, namely, *ikō**
已講, *naigu** 內宮, and *ajari** 阿闍梨. [O. V.]

Ushin 有心 'Having thought'; thoughtful.

Ushitsu 烏瑟 Abbr. for *ushitsunisha**. [Tai. 26.]

〜**-nisha** --膩沙 Sk. *uṣṇīṣa*; also *utsunisha* 欝尼沙, *ushitsu* 烏瑟,
etc.; translated as *butchō** 佛頂 'the crown of a buddha's head'
and *nikkei** 肉髻 'fleshy protuberance'; the protuberance on
the head of a buddha; one of the 32 physical characteristics of a
buddha.

Ushō mushō 有性無性 '(Those) having the (buddha-)nature and
(those) having no (buddha-)nature'; all living beings whether they
have the buddha-nature or not. [Tai. 24.]

Ushotoku 有所得 I. 'Possessing something.' [S. VI–17.] II. Perceiving and recognizing something as existing. III. Taking up
something or other and being attached to it.

〜 **no seppō** --の説法 'Preaching the Dharma with a feeling of
attachment.' [S. Xa–6.]

Ushū 有宗 'Existence sect'; refers to the *Hossō** sect, which
recognizes the existence of a conscious substance underneath
phenomena; the opposite of *kūshū**. [S. IV–1.]

Usō 有相 'Having a form or shape'; a perceptible or conceivable
form. [S. II–7.]

〜 **no chigyō** --の知行 'Activity of intellect concerned only with
perceptible objects.' [S. VII–20.]

〜 **no fuku** --の福 'Merit that is possessed of characteristics';
meritorious acts done with the mind attached to external forms.

[S. VI–17.]

~ no gi --の義 The principle that all existing things have definable and perceptible characteristics; the view of the Hossō* teaching; cf. *musō*. [Tai. 24.]

~ no gyōtoku --の行德 'The merit accruing from practices having perceptible forms' which are superficial and inferior to practices having no perceptible forms (*musō** 無相). [S. VII–20.]

~ no hōben --の方便 'An expedient means which takes a phenomenal form.' [S. Vb–9.]

~ no shitchi --の悉地 'A mystic spiritual attainment having a perceptible form,' such as the supernatural power of ascending into the sky; opposed to *musō no shitchi**. See also *shitchi*. [S. II –7.]

~ no yuga jōju --の瑜伽成就 The achievement of meditation in which one sees non-sensory objects. [S. II–8.]

Ususama 烏蒭沙摩 Sk. Ucchuṣma; n. of a *myōō** capable of removing defilements. [Tai. 1.]

Utai 有待 Also *udai*; 'that which relies (on many things for its existence)'; the human existence. [Tai. 39.]

~ no mi --の身 'The body which relies (on many things for its existence)'; the human existence sustained by many things, such as food and clothes. [Tai. 26.]

~-shin --身 See *utai no mi*.

Uten'ō 優轉王 See *Udennō*.

Uttan'otsu 欝單越 Sk. Uttarakuru; see *Hokkuru*.

Uttarasō 欝多羅僧 Sk. *uttara-āsaṅga*; one of the three robes of a monk; see *sanne*.

Uzue 卯杖 'U-sticks'; a bundle of two or three pieces of peach or other wood, cut to a length of 5 feet 3 inches, tied round with strings of five colours, and covered at the top with white paper. In the Heian period (794–1192) it was the custom for the six sections of the imperial guard (*Rikuefu* 六衞府) to offer *u*-sticks to the imperial family on the 1st *u* day of the 1st month; they were believed to be effective in driving devils away. (*U* 'hare' is one of the twelve zodiac signs.) [Ma. 151.]

~ no hosshi --の法師 A priest who performs the ceremony of

presenting the *uzue* at the imperial palace on the 1st *u* day of the 1st month. [Ma. 151.]

W

Wagara 和伽羅 Sk. *vyākaraṇa* 'prediction'; translated as *juki** 授記; a kind of scripture which contains prophecies by the Buddha regarding his disciples' attainment of buddhahood; one of the nine and the twelve kinds of scriptures (*kubu-kyō** and *jūnibu-kyō**).

Wajō 和尚 See *oshō*.

Wakō 和光 'Obscuring the light'; concealing the original majestic body; refers to *wakō dōjin**. [S. Pref., I–1, 2, 3, 6.]

~ **dōjin** -- 同塵 'Obscuring the light and mixing with the dust'; said of a buddha or bodhisattva's altruism in saving suffering beings by transforming himself into a less conspicuous form. [S. I–3, 4.]

~ **no chiri ni majiwaru** -- の塵に交る See *wakō dōjin*. [Tai. 17.]

~ **no gogan** -- の御願 'The vow to appear as an incarnation.' [Tai. 17.]

~ **no gohōben** -- の御方便 'The (skilful) means (of salvation) in appearing as an incarnation.' [S. I–9.]

~ **no gohoi** -- の御本意 'The intention of appearing as an incarnation.' [S. I–7.]

~ **no hōben** -- の方便 See *wakō no gohōben*. [S. I–6.]

~ **no honji** -- の本地 'The original body of an incarnation.' [S. I–8.]

~ **no shinjo** -- の神助 'The divine help of an incarnation.' [Tai. 17.]

~ **no suijaku** -- の垂跡 'Manifesting an incarnation'; cf. *suijaku* *wakō.* [S. I–3.]

Waku 惑 'Delusion'; the state of being ignorant and confused as to the real nature of an object; a general name for evil passions.

Waniguchi 鰐口 See *konku* 金鼓.

Y

Yaku 益 'Benefit.'

Yakuō 藥王 'Medicine King'; n. of a bodhisattva who is able to cure various illnesses.

Yakushi 藥師 'Medicine Master'; n. of a popular buddha whose full name is Yakushi-rurikō* 'Emerald Light of the Master of Medicine'; Sk. Bhaiṣajya-guru-vaiḍūrya-prabha. He is the buddha of the Land of Emerald (Rurikō) in the east. When he was a bodhisattva, he made 12 vows, which included a vow to cure diseases. [K. 266.]

∼ **Butsu** --佛 'The Medicine-Master Buddha.' [Ma. 199.]

∼-**ji** --寺 One of the three main temples of the Hossō* sect in Nara; one of the seven and the fifteen great temples of Nara (*shichidaiji** and *jūgodaiji**). The origin of the temple dates back to 680, when Emperor Tenmu had a big service performed to pray for the recovery of his wife from illness. As the prayer was answered, he had a gold and copper statue of Yakushi* made and constructed a temple in which to house it. The temple was completed in 698 after his death, and later, in 718, it was moved to its present site. It thrived as a centre for the study of the Hossō and Sanron* teachings, and also became well-known for the *Saishō-e**. The temple was burned down in 973 and several times later. In the late 19th century, after the Meiji Restoration, the temple belonged to the Shingon* sect, but soon it became independent. The only original building surviving is the three-storey pagoda, Tōtō 東塔.

~-ji no saishō-e - -寺の最勝會 The *Saishō-e** ceremony at the Yakushiji.

~-ji saishō-e - -寺最勝會 See *Saishō-e*. [Tai. 24.]

~-kyō - -經 'Medicine-Master Sutra'. Abbr. of *Yakushi-rurikō-nyorai-hongan-kudoku-kyō* 藥師瑠璃光如來本願功德經 (Sk. *Bhagavān-bhaiṣajya-guru-vaiḍūrya-prabhāsa-pūrvapraṇidhāna-viśeṣa-vistara*), tr. by Hsüan-chuang 玄奘 (Genjō*) [TT. 14, No. 450]. [O. II.]

~ no hi - -の日 'The days (*ennichi**) for Yakushi Buddha', i.e. the eighth and twelfth of the month. [Hei. 2.]

~ no hō - -の法 See *Shichibutsu Yakushi no hō*. [Tai. 8.]

~ no jūni-jinshō - -の十二神將 Also ...-*shinshō*; 'the 12 heavenly generals attending Yakushi'; see *jūni-jinshō*. [Tai. 33.]

~ no jūni-jinshō no hō - -の十二神將の法 'The ritual dedicated to the 12 heavenly generals attending Yakushi.' [Tai. 33.]

~ no jūni no seigan - -の十二の誓願 'The 12 vows of Yakushi'; the 12 vows made by Yakushi when he was a bodhisattva: (1) to attain effulgence of his physical light and enable other beings to attain the same; (2) to guide and enlighten sentient beings; (3) to fulfil their wishes; (4) to establish them in Mahayana; (5) to enable them to perform undefiled good acts and to abide by the three groups of pure precepts (*sanjujōkai**); (6) to cure beings of their physical imperfections; (7) to give them peace of mind and comfort and enable them to proceed towards enlightenment with ease; (8) to change all women into men (so that they can attain buddhahood); (9) to remove heretical views and establish beings in the right view; (10) to save all beings from the dangers of torture and harm by evil rulers, bandits, etc.; (11) to assuage their hunger and thirst; and (12) to clothe the poor and destitute. [K. 266.]

~-rurikō Butsu - -瑠璃光佛 'The Buddha Emerald Light of the Master of Medicine'; Sk. Bhaiṣajya-guru-vaiḍūrya-prabha; the full name of Yakushi. [Tai. 18.]

Yama 山 'Mountain'; refers particularly to Mt. Hiei.

Yama-bōshi 山法師 See *yama-hōshi*.

Yamabushi 山伏 'Mountain sleeper'; a follower of mountain

Buddhism (*shugendō**); so called because he lives in the mountains while engaged in ascetic practices.

Yamabushi 山臥 See *yamabushi* above. [Tai. 2.]

Yama-gomori 山ごもり 'Mountain confinement'; performing austere practices on Mt. Hiei without leaving the mountain for a long period, e.g. 12 years. [Ma. 67.]

Yama-hōshi 山法師 'Mountain-monk'; a monk of the Enryakuji*, Mt. Hiei; also *yama-bōshi*. Cf. *tera-hosshi*. [K. 431.]

Yasha 夜叉 Also 藥叉 and 夜乞叉; Sk. *yakṣa*. I. Popularly, a kind of demon of fearsome appearance who harms and even eats men. II. A type of demi-god; one of the eight kinds of supernatural beings who protect Buddhism (*hachibushu**). The *yakṣa* come under the command of the god Bishamon* and protect the northern part of the world.

Yashudara 耶輸陀羅 Sk. Yaśodharā 'having fame'; translated as Myōmon 名聞 'fame', etc.; the Buddha's wife and the mother of Rāhula (Ragora*). After the Buddha's enlightenment, she renounced the world and joined the Buddhist order together with 500 court ladies.

Yōbō 要法 'The essential teaching.'

Yōdō 要道 'The important path or teaching.'

Yōgō 永劫 'An eternal *kalpa*'; an incalculably long period of time; see *kō*.

Yogyō yogō 餘行餘業 'Other practices and acts'; practices other than the *nenbutsu**. [S. VI–10.]

Yogyō yozen 餘行餘善 'Other practices and good (acts)'; meritorious practices other than the *nenbutsu**. [S. VI–10.]

Yoi no sō 夜居僧 See *gojisō*.

Yōka 永嘉 Ch. Yung-chia; the popular name for Hsüan-chüeh 玄覺 (Genkaku*). [S. Va–5.]

Yōkan 永觀 Popularly, Eikan (1032–1111); a son of Minamoto Kunitsune 源國經, a doctor of literature. At 11, he was ordained at the Zenrinji, 禪林寺, Kyoto, and studied esoteric teachings under Jinkan 深觀. Later, he studied Sanron* teachings at the Tōdaiji* under Yūkei 有慶, and also Hossō* and Kegon* teachings under other masters. At 30, he retired to Mt. Kōmyō 光明 in

Yamato Province and devoted himself for 10 years to the Pure Land practices centring on Amida* Buddha. Then, at his friends' request, he came back to the Zenrinji, where he taught both Sanron and Pure Land teachings. In 1085, he was appointed as a lecturer at the *Yuima-e**, and in 1100, as the head priest (*bettō**) of the Tōdaiji*. His works include *Ōjō-jūin* 往生十因, *Mida-yōki* 彌陀要記 and *Ōjō-kōshiki* 往生講式.

Yōkan 用觀 'Applying meditative practices.' [S. III-8.]

Yokkai 欲界 'The realm of desire'; Sk. *kāma-dhātu*; the lowest of the three realms of transmigration (*sangai**). It comprises hell, the states of existence of hungry spirits (*gaki**), animals, fighting spirits (*ashura**), and human beings, and some heavens. Beings of this realm are characterized by strong sexual desires, etc. For the heavens belonging to this realm, see *rokuten*. [Tai. 23.]

~ no rokuten --の六天 'The sixth heaven in the realm of desire', namely, Takejizaiten*; cf. *rokuten*. [Tai. 23.]

Yōkō 影向 'An incarnation' of a buddha or a deity. [O. VI.]

Yokumō 欲網 'A net of desire'; an analogy to show that one's false desires capture one's mind. [S. VII-2.]

Yokuten 欲天 'A heaven in the realm of desire (*yokkai**).' [S. II-8.]

Yōmon 要文 'An important passage (of a sutra, etc.).'

Yonen 餘念 'Other thoughts'; thoughts other than the *nenbutsu** in particular.

Yo no sue 世の末 'End of the world'; refers to *masse**. [K. 70; Tsu. 119.]

Yōraku 瓔珞 Sk. *keyūra*, *muktāhāra* and *hāra*; originally, in India, a string of precious stones and metal pieces worn on the head, across the chest, or around the neck. In Buddhism, pictures and statues of buddhas and bodhisattvas often show them wearing *yōraku*. It is also a temple ornament consisting of a string of beads and metal plates shaped like flowers, hung near statues of buddhas and bodhisattvas. In a buddha land, many *yōraku* hang from the branches of jewelled trees. [Tai. 24.]

Yorimashi よりまし(神子) A boy or a girl used as a medium in an esoteric rite to exorcise an evil spirit from a sick person, etc. [Hei.

3.]

Yoruka 預流果　Sk. *srota-āpatti-phala*, 'the fruit of entering the stream' of the sacred law, attained by destroying various wrong views; also *shudaonka* 須陀洹果; the first of the four stages of sainthood in Hinayana; cf. *shika*.

Yōsai 榮西　See *Eisai*.

Yoshimizu no kashō 吉水の和尚　'The master at Yoshimizu'; a common appellation for Jien* (1155–1225) of the Tendai* sect, also known as *Yoshimizu no sōjō* 吉水の僧正. [Tsu. 67.]

Yoshimizu no sōjō 吉水の僧正　See *Yoshimizu no kashō*.

Yoshū 餘執　'Lingering attachment.'

Yuga 瑜(or 踰)伽　Sk. *yoga*, 'connection, concentration'. I. Concentration of one's thoughts, mental abstraction, meditation; a practice performed in order to attain unity or harmony with a reality-principle or a divinity. II. In esoteric Buddhism, the union of a practitioner with a divinity attained by mystic practices. III. Refers to Yogācāra (*Yugagyōha**).

~-gyōha --行派　'The Yogācāra school.' One of the two major Mahayana schools in India, the other being *Chūganha** 中觀派. This school, founded by Maitreya (Miroku*) and developed by Asaṅga (Mujaku*) and Vasubandhu (Seshin*), emphasizes meditation on conceivable objects which represent the reality-principle.

~ jōjō no ri --上乘之理　'The principle of the highest teaching concerning *yoga*'; here, the term refers to the Shingon* teaching of the mystic practice through which a practitioner becomes one with the cosmic buddha, Dainichi*; cf. *sanmitsu yuga*. [Tai. 39.]

~-ron --論　Abbr. of *Yugashiji-ron**. [S. Va–4.]

~ sanmitsu --三密　'Meditation and the Three Mystic Practices'; see *sanmitsu*. [Tai. 1.]

~-shiji-ron --師地論　'*The Discourse on the Stages of Concentration Practices*'; Sk. *Yogācāra-bhūmi*; 100 fasc., tr. by Hsüan-chuang 玄奘 (Genjō*) [TT. 30, No. 1579]; the author is said to be Maitreya (Miroku*) but, according to Tibetan tradition, it was Asaṅga (Mujaku*). This is one of the basic texts of the Yogācāra School (*Yugagyōha**), which explains spiritual states and practices to be performed in the 17 stages leading to buddhahood. [S. Va–4.]

~ **yuishiki** --唯識 'The consciousness-only (doctrine) of the Yogācāra (school)'; the school of Buddhism which emphasizes meditative practice for becoming one with ultimate reality and theoretically expounds the basic, universal consciousness from which all existences manifest themselves. [S. I–7.]

Yugyō-hijiri 遊行聖 'A wandering sage'; see *hijiri* IV.

Yuihō 遺法 'The teaching bequeathed' by the Buddha. Cf. *Shaka yuihō no deshi.*

Yuiju ichinin 唯受一人 'Only one person receives (the oral teaching).' [Tai. 17.]

Yuikai 遺戒 Usually, 遺誡: 'one's dying instructions.' [S. Xb–3.]

Yuikyō 唯境 'Sole (existence of) external objects'; a view that objects exist but the mind does not. [S. IV–1.]

~ **mushiki** --無識 'Sole (existence of) external objects and absence of consciousness.' [S. IV–1.]

Yuikyō 遺教 I. 'The teaching bequeathed' by the Buddha. II. Refers to the *Yuikyō-gyō**. [S. IV–9.]

~**-gyō** --經 *'The Last Teaching (of the Buddha) Sutra'*; abbr. of *Butsu-suihatsunehan-ryakusetsu-kyōkai-gyō* 佛垂般涅槃略說教誡經, 1 fasc., tr. by Kumārajīva (Kumarajū*) [TT. 12, No. 389]. [S. III–3, Va–2, 11.]

Yuima 維摩 Sk. Vimalakīrti ('spotless fame'); also Jōmyō 淨名, etc. A rich man in Vaiśālī, India, renowned for his profound understanding of Mahayana. According to the *Yuima-gyō**, he lived in a small room of ten feet square (*hōjō**). When he became ill, the Buddha sent to his place his disciples, headed by Monju*, to whom he revealed the profound Mahayana teaching.

~**-e** --會 'Yuima lecture-meeting'; the annual lecture on the *Yuima-gyō** at the Kōfukuji*, Nara, held for a week beginning on the 16th of the 10th month. [O. V.]

~**-gyō** --經 Sk. *Vimalakīrti-nirdeśa-sūtra*. Three Chinese translations are extant, of which Kumārajīva's (Kumarajū*) *Yuima-kitsu-shosetsu-gyō* 維摩詰所說經, 3 fasc., has been most generally used [TT. 14, No. 475]. The sutra expounds the profound principle of Mahayana and refutes Hinayana through the mouth of the layman bodhisattva Yuima*. [O. V.]

~-gyō kuyō --經供養 A service held to mark the completion of a new copy of the *Yuima-gyō**. [O. V.]

~-kitsu-shosetsu-kyō --詰所說經 See *Yuima-gyō*.

~ no ejō --の會場 'The hall where the *Yuima-e** takes place.' [Tai. 39.]

Yuina ゆいな(維那) See *tsuina*. [S. VI–12.]

Yuishiki 唯識 Sk. *vijñapti-mātratā*; the 'consciousness-only' doctrine, which explains all phenomena as manifestations of one's consciousnesses, of which the eighth, called *Ālaya* (*Araya** 阿賴耶), is the basic one; cf. *Yuga yuishiki*. [S. I–7.]

~ mukyō --無境 'Sole (existence of) consciousness and absence of external objects.' [S. IV–1.]

~-ron --論 Refers to the *Jōyuishiki-ron**. [S. I–9.]

~-shō --性 'The real nature or quintessence of the consciousness-only.' [S. III–1.]

Yuishin 唯心 'Mind-only'; the Mahayana principle that mind is the ultimate existence and all phenomena are its manifestations or transformations. [S. Xb–2.]

Yujun 由旬 Sk. *yojana*; the distance covered by the royal army in a day; said to be equivalent to 40 (or 30) Chinese *li* 里.

Yumyō shōjin 勇猛精進 'Making a heroic effort', as in Buddhist practices. [S. II–5.]

Yūzū 融通 'Fusing and penetrating.' [K. 53.]

~-nenbutsu --念佛 '(The mutual) fusing and penetrating of (merit from) the *nenbutsu**'; see *Yūzū-nenbutsu-shū*. [K. 53.]

~-nenbutsu-shū --念佛宗 'The Yūzū-nenbutsu sect'; one of the 13 sects (*jūsan-shū**), founded by Ryōnin* 良忍 in 1117 and based on the verse of inspiration he received from Amida*, namely, "One man (permeates) all other men; all other men, one man. One practice (penetrates) all other practices; all other practices, one practice." This sect uses the *Kegon-gyō** and the *Hoke-kyō** as its principal canons and the three Pure Land sutras (*Jōdo sanbukyō**) as the secondary ones. It teaches that one's merit from the *nenbutsu** permeates others and that of others permeates oneself; that the merit of the *nenbutsu* and other practices penetrate and merge with each other; and that thus birth in Amida's Pure Land is attainable by all beings. Followers perform daily practice of the *nenbutsu*, especially of reciting it ten times every morning facing west. The sect flourished for some time after Ryōnin. When it declined, the seventh patriarch, Hōmyō 法明, and later the 46th, Yūkan 融觀, revived it.

Z

Za 座 'A gathering, meeting.' [O. VI.]

Zaiaku no chi 罪惡の地 'The land of sins and evils'; evil realms, such as hell and the realm of hungry spirits. [K. 72.]

Zaibuku 摧伏 'To crush and suppress (devils, etc.).' [Tai. 29.]

Zaifuku 罪福☆ 'Sin and merit'; evil acts and meritorious deeds. [S. Xb–1.]

Zaigō 罪業 'Sinful karma'; an evil, sinful act; a karmic evil.

Zaihō 罪報 'Retribution of one's sin.'

~ **no shujō** --の衆生 'Sentient beings (suffering) the retribution of their sins.' [K. 72.]

Zaike 在家 'Staying at home'; a layman, as opposed to a monk.

~ **hosshi** --法師 A priest who has shaved his head but has a home, i.e. wife and children; a type of a lay priest. [S. IV–7.]

~**-nin** --人 'A layman.' [S. VI–18.]

Zaise 在世 'Existing in the world'; when the Buddha was living in the world.

Zaishō 罪障 'A sin or evil act which hinders one' from attaining a blissful state or from following the Buddhist Way; karmic hindrances (*gōshō** 業障).

Zaiten no shinnyo 在纏の眞如 'True Thusness in the state of bondage'; the ultimate reality concealed by delusions and evil passions. [S. IV–1.]

Zange 懺悔 See *sange*.

Zangi sange 慚愧懺悔 'To be ashamed of one's sins and repent of them.' [S. II–3.]

Zaō Gongen 藏王權現 'The Incarnate Zaō'; also Kongō-zaō 金剛藏王 and Zaō Bosatsu 藏王菩薩. The bodhisattva in fierce form in whom En-no-Ozunu* 役小角 perceived after a thousand-day confinement on Mt. Kinpu 金峰山, Yamato. His original bodies are Shaka*, Senju Kannon*, and Miroku*. [S. I–3.]

Zasu 座主 'Master of the (highest) seat'; the head priest of a temple, esp. of the Enryakuji* on Mt. Hiei.

Zazen 坐禪 'Sitting meditation'; meditation with one's legs crossed.

~ **kanbō** --觀法 'Meditation with one's legs crossed, in which one contemplates an object or a reality-principle.' [S. Xb–3.]

Zehi 是非 'Right and wrong.'

~ **henshū** --偏執 'A biased view, thinking that one thing is right and another wrong.' [S. IV–1.]

~ **hōbō** --謗法 Also ~ *bōhō*; 'abusing the Dharma (by arguing about) right and wrong teachings.' [S. IV–1.]

~ **jōron** --靜論 'Argument as to which is right and which is wrong.' [S. IV–1.]

Zen 禪 I. Meditation. II. The Zen sect; see *Zenshū*.

Zenbō 禪法 'The Zen* teaching.' [Tai. 24.]

Zenbutsu 前佛 'The former buddha.' [Tai. 39.]

Zenchishiki 善知識 See *zenjishiki*.

Zendō 善導 Ch. Shan-tao (613–681); the third of the five Pure Land masters (*Jōdo goso**) and the fifth of the seven patriarchs in the tradition of the Jōdoshin* sect (*shichikōsō**). He entered the priesthood when young, and especially practised meditation on Amida* and his Pure Land. When he heard of Tao-ch'o 道綽 (Dōshaku*), Shan-tao went to see him and received from him the Pure Land teaching. The rest of his life was dedicated to the practice and dissemination of this teaching. He is said to have copied the *Amida-kyō** more than 100,000 times and made more than 300 paintings of the Pure Land. Besides chanting sutras and reciting the *nenbutsu** constantly, he successfully performed meditation in which he visualized Amida and his land. He wrote five works in nine fascicles, including commentaries on different sections of the *Kanmuryōju-kyō**. He was popularly known as 'the Master fo the Kuang-ming-ssu' 光明寺和尚 (*Kōmyōji no kashō*), 'the Great Master of Chung-nan' 終南大師 (*Shūnan Daishi*), etc. Shan-tao's Pure Land tradition was inherited by Hōnen*, who founded the Jōdo* sect in the 12th century. [IH.; S. I–10, III–1, IV–1, VII–25, Xb–1.]

Zen'e 染衣 'Dyeing one's robe'; becoming a monk, wearing a robe of a dark colour. [S. III–1, 8.]

Zen'en 善縁 'A good condition'; circumstances favourable for a desired objective.

Zen'etsu 禪悅 'Joy of practising meditation.' [S. IV–1.]

Zengō 前業 'Previous karma'; acts in one's past life or lives.

Zengō 善業 'A good karma or deed.'

Zengon 善根 Sk. *kuśala-mūla*; 'root of goodness'; a meritorious, good act. 'Root' because of the firmness of good acts, and because they produce good fruit. [Tsu. 175.]

Zengo saidan 前後際斷 'The severing of the past and the future'; transcending the sequence of time. [S. IV–1.]

Zengyō 善巧 Sk. (*upāya-*)*kauśalya*; 'skilful (means)', said of a buddha or bodhisattva's method of saving suffering beings. [S. I–3.]

~**-hōben** --方便 Sk. *upāya-kauśalya*, 'skilful means'; skilful means of salvation. [S. III–1.]

Zengyō 漸教 'The gradual teaching.' I. The teaching preached for a gradual advancement from a lower level to a higher one; the opposite of *tongyō** 頓教. II. One of the four methods of preaching by the Buddha (*shikyō**) established in the Tendai* sect; exposition of the teaching from a shallow to a deeper level. III. In the Kegon* sect, the elementary and final doctrines of Mahayana are called *zengyō* because they provide methods of gradual advancement towards enlightenment; cf. *gokyō**.

Zen'in 善因 'A good cause'; a meritorious act.

Zen'in 禪院 A temple where meditation is practised; a Zen* temple. [S. III–4.]

Zenjaku 染着(or 著) 'Imbued attachment'; attachment; the same as *shūjaku** 執着 (or 著).

~ **no kokoro** --のこころ 'Mind of attachment'; clinging. [O. V.]

Zenji 禪師 'Meditation master'. I. A Buddhist master who practises meditation. II. The title by which a Zen* master or monk is referred to by the people. III. The title given by an emperor to a monk of outstanding virtue.

Zenji 漸次 'Gradual advancement'; stages of gradual advancement. [S. Va–2.]

Zenjishiki 善知識 Also *zenchishiki*; 'good knowledge'; Sk. *kalyāṇa-mitra*, 'a good or virtuous friend'; a good friend or teacher who leads one to the Buddhist Way. [S. I–10; Tai. 20.]

Zenjō 禪定 I. Sk. *dhyāna*; meditation, concentration. II. Abbr. of *zenjōmon**.

~ **bikuni** --比丘尼 'A meditation nun'; a woman who has shaved her head and entered the Buddhist Way. [S. VI–1.]

~**-mon** --門 'The path of meditation'; a layman who has shaved his head and entered the Buddhist Way; abbreviated as *zenjō* or *zenmon**.

~ **taikō** --太閤 A regent who has entered the priesthood. Cf. *zenkō**.

Zenjō 染淨 'Defiled and pure'; tainted with evil passions and free of them.

~ **koyū no enzetsu** --虚融の演說 'Expounding the teaching that defilement and purity are void and fused together'; expounding various Mahayana teachings which present the doctrine of voidness and non-duality. [Tai. 18.]

Zenjū-tenshi-kyō 善住天子經 Refers to *Shō-zenjūi-tenshi-shomon-gyō**. [S. II–10.]

Zenkiku 禪鞠 A ball made of hair, which is used by Zen* monks to keep them awake. It is placed on the head of a monk when he gets sleepy, so that it will wake him up if it falls off. [S. II–1.]

Zenkō 禪閤 Abbr. of *zenjō taikō**. [K. 289.]

Zenkyō 禪教 'Meditation and the teachings'; the Zen* school which concentrates on meditation and is not based on written scriptures, and other schools which are based on written scriptures. [S. III–8, IV–1.]

Zenma 染汚 'Defiled'; defiled by evil passions.

Zenmon 禪門 I. The path of meditation. II. The teaching and practice of Zen*. III. A layman who has shaved his head and entered the Buddhist Way (to be distinguished from one who has become a lay practitioner of Zen meditation). In this sense, also called *zenjō* or *zenjōmon**. [Tsu. 160.]

Zenmonshu 前門主 'The former chief abbot.'

Zenmui 善無畏 Sk. Śubhākarasiṃha (637–735); also Jōshishi 淨師子; said to have been a prince in central India. He acceded to the throne at 13 but, after a while, abdicated and went to Nālanda, where he learned esoteric Buddhism in particular. He went to Chang-an 長安 (Chōan) in 716 taking with him Sanskrit scriptures. Under the patronage of Emperor Hsüan-tsung 玄宗 (Gensō), he produced translations of basic esoteric texts, including *Dainichi-kyō** 大日經 and *Soshitsujikara-kyō** 蘇悉地羯羅經, thereby laying the foundation of Chinese esoteric Buddhism. His disciple I-hsing 一行 (Ichigyō*) helped with the translation. [S. Xb–3.]

Zenni 禪尼 'A meditation nun'; a woman who has shaved her head and entered the Buddhist Way. [Tsu. 184.]

Zennyo ryūō 善女龍王 'The dragon king Zennyo' said to inhabit the pond called Munetsuchi* in the northern part of the Himalayas. [Tai. 12.]

Zenpō 禪法 See *zenbō*.

Zenpō biku 善法比丘 'The monk Good Dharma.' [S. III–3.]

Zenpōdō 善法堂 'The Good-Dharma Hall'; n. of the hall in the heaven of Indra (Taishaku*). It is located in the southwest of the palace, and is used as a meeting place to discuss matters concerning heavenly and human beings. [Tai. 23.]

Zenrai biku 善來比丘 'Welcome, o monk'; originally, the Buddha's utterance to welcome a person to his order. It was believed that the Buddha's divine power enabled a person, through this utterance, to receive the precepts for a monk and enter the priesthood instantaneously. [Tai. 35.]

Zenrin no jūin 禪林の十因 The *Ōjō-jūin** 往生十因, 1 fasc., by
Yōkan* 永觀 of the Zenrinji 禪林寺, Kyoto. The work explains
by giving ten reasons (*jūin*) that the *nenbutsu** is sufficient cause
for birth in Amida's* Pure Land. [Tsu. 49.]

Zenritsu 禪律 I. The Zen* sect and the Ritsu* sect. II. The rules
of conduct in the Zen sect. III. An official in charge of various
matters concerning Zen temples.

Zenryo 禪侶 I. A monk who practises meditation. II. A general
term for a monk. III. A group of monks who perform a specific
service in alternating shifts day and night, as in the Hokkedō*
法華堂 and Jōgyōdō* 常行堂 on Mt. Hiei.

Zenshi Bosatsu 善思菩薩 Aniruddha Bodhisattva, one of the ten
great disciples of the Buddha; commonly, Anaritsu 阿那律. See
jūdai-deshi. [S. III–3.]

Zenshitsu 禪室 I. A room or hall for Zen* practice. II. Another
name for *hōjō** 方丈, the head priest's room. III. The head
priest himself.

Zensho 善處 'A good place'; a good realm; refers particularly to
the worlds of human and heavenly beings; the same as *zenshu**.
[S. Va–2.]

Zenshō 前生 'Previous life.'

Zenshu 善趣 'Good realms'; blissful states of existence; refers to
the realms of human and heavenly beings, because one can be
reborn there by performing morally good acts.

Zenshū 禪宗 'The Ch'an (Zen) sect'; the school of Buddhism
based primarily on the practice of meditation, from which the
name *zen** 禪 (*dhyāna* in Skt. and *jhāna* in Pali, meaning 'meditation') derives. According to tradition, Shakamuni* transmitted
the secret of the Buddhist Dharma to his disciple, Mahākāśyapa
(Makakashō*), when the Buddha lifted a bouquet of flowers and
the latter responded to this by smiling (see *nenge mishō*). The
transmission of the teaching of this school is known as *kyōge
betsuden* 敎外別傳, 'special transmission outside the written
scriptures', and also as *ishin denshin* 以心傳心, 'mind-to-mind
transmission'. The 28th Indian patriarch, Bodhidharma (Bodaidaruma*), went to China, in 520 according to tradition, and

became the first Chinese patriarch. The Ch'an sect flourised, especially after the sixth patriarch, Hui-neng 慧能 (Enō*); the lineage of the transmission split into five houses (*goke* 五家). Various forms of Zen tradition were brought to Japan at different periods: Rinzai 臨濟 by Eisai* 榮西 in 1191, Yōgi 楊岐 (Yōgi) school of Rinzai by Shunjō 俊芿 in 1211, Sōtō 曹洞 by Dōgen* in 1227 and Ōbaku 黃檗 by Yin-yüan 隱元 (Ingen) in 1654.

Zensō 禪僧 'A Zen* monk.'

Zenzei 善逝 'Well-gone'; Sk. *sugata*; one of the ten epithets for the Buddha (*jūgō**); the term is construed as 'one who has gone to the state of emancipation'. [Tai. 15.]

Zessō gongo 舌相言語 'Words spoken with the (Buddha's broad) tongue'; words of the Buddha's eloquence. [S. II–8.]

Zō-agon-gyō 雜阿含經 '*Miscellaneous Āgama Sutras*'; Sk. *Samyukta-āgama-sūtra*; one of the four collections of sutras in the Āgama (*agon**) division belonging to Hinayana; 50 fasc., tr. by Guṇabhadra (Gunabatsudara 求那跋陀羅) in the fifth century [TT. 2, No. 99]. Those sutras not belonging to the three other collections are compiled in this one; see *Agon-gyō*.

Zōban 繪幡(or 旛) 'A silken banner.'

Zōbō 像法 I. 'Semblance Dharma'; imitative teaching. II. Refers to *zōbōji**.

~-ji --時 'The period of the semblance Dharma'. One of the three periods after the Buddha's decease. See *shōzōmatsu*.

~-ketsugi-kyō --決疑經 '*The Sutra Resolving Doubts Concerning the Period of Semblance Dharma*'; 1 fasc. [TT. 85, No. 2870]. [S. IV–1.]

Zōgai 繪蓋 See *sōgai*.

Zōgyō 雜行 'Miscellaneous practices'; practices other than the five Pure Land practices centring on the *nenbutsu** (*goshōgyō** 五正行); this distinction was made by Shan-tao (Zendō*). [S. I–10.]

Zōitsu-agon-gyō 增一阿含經 '*Increasing-by-One Āgama Sutras*'; Sk. *Ekottara-āgama-sūtra*; one of the four collections of sutras in the Āgama (*agon**) division belonging to Hinayana; 51 fasc., tr. by Gautama-saṃghadeva (Kudon-sōgyadaiba 瞿曇僧伽提婆)

in 397 [TT. 2, No. 125]. This collection has 52 chapters, containing 451 sutras in all. Subjects expounded are numbered from one to eleven, and the sutras grouped according to their contents. See *Agon-gyō*.

Zōjō 増上 'Increasing, powerful, dominant, strengthened.'

~**-en** --縁 Sk. *adhipati-pratyaya*; 'a dominant by-cause'; a condition or by-cause which assists the coming into existence of a thing. [S. I–3.]

~**-man** --慢 See under *shichiman*.

~ **no shōen** --の勝縁 'A powerful and superior conditioning cause or circumstance.' [S. II–9.]

Zōkō 増劫 'Increasing *kalpa*'; a period of cosmic change during which man's life-span increases from 10 to 80,000 years at the rate of one every 100 years. After man's life-span reaches 80,000, it begins to decrease; cf. *genkō*.

Zokugyō 俗形 'A layman's form.'

Zokujin 俗塵 'Worldly dust'; secularity, worldliness. [K. 500.]

Zokutai 俗諦 'The conventional truth'; Sk. *samvṛti-satya*; the relative and worldly reality, as distinguished from *shintai** 眞諦; cf. *shinzoku*. [S. Va–6.]

Zokutai 俗體 'A layman's form'; a lay appearance. [Tai. 18.]

Zōkyō 藏教 'Piṭaka teaching'; *zō (piṭaka)* refers to *sanzō** 三藏, the three divisions of the Buddhist teachings; the first of the four teachings of the Buddha classified in Tendai*; cf. *kehō no shikyō* and *sanzōkyō*.

Zōsakuma 造作魔 'A (house, etc.) building devil'; one who is very eager to build a house, etc. [Tai. 18.]

Zōshu 藏主 See *zōsu*.

Zōsu 藏主 Also *chizō* 知藏; the superintendent of a library in a Zen* temple; also used for a senior monk next in rank to the head monk. [Tai. 16.]

Zōyaku 増益 'Increasing merit,' etc.

~**-hō** --法 See *sōyakuhō*.

Zōzen 雜善 'Miscellaneous good acts', i.e. other than the *nenbutsu** practice; cf. *zōgyō*. [K. 63.]

Zōzen sekai 雜染世界 'The world of various defilements'; refers to this world of Sahā (*shaba**). [S. IV–1.]

Zu 頌 See *ju*.

Zuda 頭陀 Sk. *dhūta*; translated as *tosō** 抖擻, *kijo* 棄除, etc.; the rules of frugal living for Buddhist mendicants; see *jūni-zuda*. [S. III–1.]

~-gyō --行 '*Dhūta* practice'; refers particularly to begging for food, which is one of the 12 ascetic practices (*jūni-zuda**). [O. II.]

Zuhō 修法 See *shubō*.

Zuhoku-mensai 頭北面西 'Head to the north and face to the west'; the posture in which the Buddha passed away. Hence, Buddhists often take this posture when they die. [K. 51, 63.]

Zuien 隨緣 'Following conditions'; in accordance with conditions, the state of things, or the nature of sentient beings.

Zuigu-darani 隨求陀羅尼 'Wish-fulfilling spell'; the dharani which appears in the *Zuigu-kyō**; it is Zuigu Bodhisattva's dharani, which is effective for realizing one's wish.

Zuigu-kyō 隨求經 An abbr. of *Fuhenkōmyō-shōjōshijō-nyoihōin-shinmunōshō-daimyōō-daizuigu-darani-kyō* 普遍光明清淨熾盛如意寶印心無能勝大明王大隨求陀羅尼經, 2 fasc., tr. into Chinese by Amoghavajra (Fukū*) [TT. 20, No. 1153]. The sutra expounds the *Zuigu-darani**. [Ma. 198.]

Zuiichi 隨一 'One of many.' (In Buddhist texts, the term is not used in the ordinary sense of 'the best of all' or 'first and foremost'.)

Zuiki 隨喜 'The joy which follows' the act of hearing or seeing something good.

Zuirui 隨類 'In conformity with the forms (and propensities of living beings).' [S. I–3.]

~ no shin --の身 'A physical form in conformity with the types (of living beings to be saved).' [S. III–1.]

Zuisō 瑞相 'An auspicious sign; a good omen.' [K. 36.]

Zukō 頭光 'Nimbus, halo.' [K. 63.]

Zukyō 誦經 See *jukyō*.

Zushi 厨子 A small shrine or sanctuary for a buddha or sage.

APPENDIXES

I. CHINESE-JAPANESE WORD INDEX

The Chinese characters for the main entries and their variants are arranged below according to the total number of strokes and followed by the Japanese readings under which the entries are listed.

1 STROKE

2 STROKES

七七の忌日　nanuka nanuka no
七大寺　shichidaiji　⌊kinichi
七分全得　shichibun zentoku
七佛の通戒　shichibutsu no tsū-
　　kai　　　　　　　　⌈kaige
七佛通戒偈　shichibutsu　tsū-
七佛藥師　shichibutsu yakushi
七珍　shitchin
七高僧　shichikōsō
七衆　shichishū
七聖財　shichishōzai
七僧　shichisō
七慢　shichiman
七種の聖財　shichishu no shōzai
七壇御修法　shichidan no mi-
七難　shichinan　　　　⌊shiho
七寶　shippō
七覺支　shichikakushi
九分經　kubunkyō
九界　kukai
九品　kuhon
九條の袈裟　kujō no kesa
九部經　kubukyō
九會曼荼羅　kue mandara
九輪　kurin
了知　ryōchi
了義　ryōgi
二力　niriki
二十八部衆　nijūhachi-bushu
二十九有　nijūku-u
二十五の圓通　nijūgo no enzū
二十五有　nijūgo-u

二十五菩薩　nijūgo-bosatsu
二王　niō
二世　nise
二身　nishin　⌈gen no daidōshi
二佛中間の大導師　nibutsu chū-
二佛性　nibusshō
二河白道　niga byakudō
二取の相　nishu no sō
二乘　nijō
二障　nishō
二際　nisai
二種僧物　nishu sōmotsu
二諦　nitai
二禪天　nizenten
二轉の果　niten no ka
人工　ninku
人天　ninden
人中天上　ninchū tenjō
人身　ninjin
人我　ninga
人法　ninbō
人師　ninshi
入　nyū
入定　nyūjō
入室　nisshitsu
入重玄門　nyūjū genmon
入滅　nyūmetsu
入道　nyūdō
入觀　nyūkan
八十種好　hachijūshu-kō
八大地獄　hachidai-jigoku
八大龍王　hachidai-ryūō

八正道　hasshōdō
八功德水　hakkudokusui
八字文殊　hachiji monju
八戒　hakkai
八災　hassai
八宗　hasshū
八音　hatton
八風　happū
八苦　hakku
八相　hassō
八部衆　hachibushu
八寒八熱　hachikan hachinetsu
八寒地獄　hachikan-jigoku
八葉　hachiyō 　　　　　　 ⌈mon
八萬の法門　hachiman no hō-
八萬四千の光　hachiman-shisen
　　no hikari 　⌈sen no hōmon
八萬四千の法門　hachiman-shi-
八聖道　hasshōdō
八種梵音聲　hasshu-bon'onjō
八種清淨音　hasshu-shōjōon
八熱地獄　hachinetsu-jigoku
八幡大菩薩　hachiman daibo-
八講　hakkō 　　　　　　 ⌊satsu
八齋戒　hassaikai
八識　hasshiki
八難　hachinan
刀山劍樹　tōzan kenju
十一面の化身　jūichimen no ke-
　　shin 　　　　　　 ⌈kannon
十一面の觀音　jūichimen no
十二の願王　jūni no gannō
十二の觀　jūni no kan
十二入　jūni-nyū
十二分經　jūnibun-kyō

十二因緣　jūni-innen
十二神將　jūni-jinshō
十二處　jūni-sho
十二部經　jūnibu-kyō
十二頭陀　jūni-zuda
十二禪衆　jūni-zenshu
十八空　jūhachi-kū
十八道　jūhachi-dō
十八賢　jūhachi-ken
十八變　jūhachi-hen
十力　jūriki
十大弟子　jūdai-deshi
十三宗　jūsan-shū
十方　jippō
十五大寺　jūgo-daiji
十不善業　jūfuzengō
十六大國　jūroku-daikoku
十六善神　jūroku-zenjin
十六觀　jūrokkan
十如是　jūnyoze
十地　jūji
十身　jusshin
十戒　jikkai
十念　jūnen
十利　jissetsu
十界　jikkai
十重　jūjū
十乘の床　jūjō no yuka
十乘觀法　jūjō-kanbō
十惡　jūaku
十善　jūzen
十萬億土　jūman(n)okudo
十號　jūgō
十種の勝利　jusshu no shōri
十種供養　jusshu-kuyō

十輪經　jūrin-gyō
十齋日　jūsainichi
十禪　jūzen

十禪師　jūzenji
十羅刹　jūrasetsu

3 STROKES

丈六　jōroku
三力　sanriki
三十七尊　sanjūshichi-son
三十七道品　sanjūshichi-dōhon
三十二相　sanjūni-sō
三十三天　sanjūsanten
三千　sanzen
三大阿僧祇劫　sandai-asōgikō
三大僧祇　sandai-sōgi
三心　sanshin
三世　sanze
三世間　sanseken
三生　sanshō
三光天子　sankō tenshi
三因佛性　san'in-busshō
三有　san'u
三衣　sanne
三災　sansai
三角壇　sankakudan
三身　sanshin
三受　sanju
三性　sanshō
三明　sanmyō
三毒　sandoku
三法印　sanbōin
三門跡　sanmonzeki
三阿僧祇劫　san'asōgikō
三信　sanshin
三品成就　sanbon jōju

三品悉地　sanbon shitchi
三拜　sanpai
三昧　sanmai
三昧耶　sanmaya
三界　sangai
三乘　sanjō
三時の行法　sanji no gyōhō
三時業　sanjigō
三般若　sanhannya
三國の佛法　sangoku no buppō
三國相傳　sangoku sōden
三國傳來　sangoku denrai
三密　sanmitsu
三途　sanzu
三部大法　sanbu-daihō
三報　sanpō
三尊　sanzon
三惑　sanwaku
三惡　san'aku
三智　sanchi
三塔　santō
三會　san'e
三業　sangō
三道　sandō
三鈷　sanko
三福　sanpuku
三福田　sanfukuden
三種止觀　sanshu-shikan
三綱　sangō

大元帥明王　taigensui myōō
大元帥御修法　taigensui mishiho
大方便佛報恩經　daihōben-bu-
　tsu-hōon-gyō　「kyō
大方等大集經　daihōdō-daishū-
大方廣十輪經　daihōkō-jūrin-
大日　dainichi　∟gyō
大叫喚　daikyōkan
大自在天　daijizaiten
大自在王菩薩　daijizaiō bosatsu
大衣　daie
大佛頂如來…　daibutchō nyo-
大佛頂呪　daibutchō-ju ∟rai...
大佛頂陀羅尼　daibutchō-darani
大劫　daikō
大我　daiga
大事　daiji
大刹　daisetsu
大定　daijō
大念佛　dainenbutsu
大法祕法　daihō hihō
大品經　daibon-gyō
大威德　daiitoku
大乘　daijō
大峰數度の先達　omine sūdo no
大師　daishi　∟sendatsu
大海衆　daikaishu
大涅槃經　dainehan-gyō
大神通　daijinzū
大般若　daihannya
大般涅槃經　daihatsu-nehan-gyō
大梵　daibon
大梵天　daibonten
大梵王　daibonnō
大雪山　daisessen

大悲　daihi
大智　daichi
大菩薩　daibosatsu
大衆　daishu
大集經　daishū-kyō
大黑天　daikokuten
大勢至　daiseishi
大勢忿怒　daisei funnu
大圓鏡智　daienkyōchi
大塔　daitō
大會　daie
大聖　daishō
大僧正　daisōjō
大慈　daiji
大德　daitoku
大論　dairon
大樹緊那　taiju kinna
大熾盛光　daishijōkō
大檀那　daidanna
大藏會　daizō-e
大藏經　daizōkyō
大願力　daiganriki
大權　daigon
女院　nyōin
小三災　shōsansai
小水の魚　shōsui no uo
小劫　shōkō
小宗　shōshū
小法師　kobōshi
小乘　shōjō
小康　shōkō
小欲知足　shōyoku chisoku
小智愚鈍　shōchi gudon
小壇支度物　shōdan shitaku-
尸羅　shira　∟mono

山	yama	山門	sanmon
山ごもり	yama-gomori	山僧	sanzō
山王	sannō	工夫	kufū
山伏	yamabushi	己心の佛性	koshin no busshō
山法師	yama-hōshi	己界	kokai
山臥	yamabushi	巳講	ikō

4 STROKES

不了の妄念	furyō no mōnen	中天	chūten
不了義	furyōgi	中有	chūu
不二一體	funi ittai	中劫	chūkō
不生	fushō	中阿含經	chū-agon-gyō
不立文字	furyū monji	中堂	chūdō
不妄語戒	fumōgo-kai	中陰	chūin
不邪婬戒	fujain-kai	中尊	chūzon
不定の人間	fujō no ningen	中間	chūgen
不知足	fuchisoku	中道	chūdō
不空	fukū	中臺八葉院	chūdai hachiyō-in
不空成就	fukūjōju	中壇	chūdan
不空羂索…	fukūkensaku...	中機	chūki
不退	futai	中觀派	chūganha
不偸盗戒	fuchūtō-kai	互具	gogu
不動	fudō	五力	goriki
不殺生戒	fusesshō-kai	五大	godai
不淨觀	fujōkan	五大明王	godai-myōō
不飲酒戒	fuonju-kai	五大尊	godaison
不輕	fugyō	五大虚空藏	godai kokūzō
不增不減經	fuzō-fugen-gyō	五山	gozan
不請の友	fushō no tomo	五五百歳	go-gohyakusai
不請の阿彌陀佛	fushō no a-	五分法身	gobun hosshin
不還果	fugenka ⌊mida butsu	五日八講	gonichi hakkō
不斷如法經	fudan nyohōkyō	五正行	goshōgyō
不斷經	fudankyō	五字文殊呪	goji monju-ju
不覺	fukaku	五字呪	goji-ju

五字陀羅尼　goji darani
五百門論　gohyaku-monron
五百羅漢　gohyaku rakan
五色　goshiki
五佛　gobutsu
五戒　gokai
五見　goken
五卷の日　gokan no hi
五味　gomi
五念行　gonengyō
五念門　gonenmon
五性各別　goshō kakubetsu
五品　gohon
五相成身觀　gosō jōshinkan
五相瑜伽　gosō yuga
五重唯識觀　gojū yuishikikan
五家　goke
五時　goji
五根　gokon
五衰　gosui
五逆　gogyaku
五停心觀　gojōshinkan
五教　gokyō
五條袈裟　gojō-gesa
五欲　goyoku
五瓶　gobyō
五部大乘經　gobu daijōkyō
五陰　goon
五智　gochi
五衆　goshu
五葉　goyō
五鈷　goko
五塵　gojin
五種行　goshugyō
五種法　goshuhō

五種法師　goshu-hosshi
五種說法　goshu-seppō
五箇五百歲　goko-gohyakusai
五蓋　gogai
五輪　gorin
五壇法　godanhō
五濁　gojoku
五藏　gozō
五蘊　goun
五體　gotai
仁王　niō
仁王般若　ninnō-hannya
仁王會　ninnō-e
仁王經　ninnō-kyō
仁王講　ninnō-kō
仁王護國…　ninnō-gokoku-…
今世　konse
今生　konjō
今師相承　konshi sōjō
內外八海　naige hachikai
內我　naiga
內供　naigu
內典　naiten
內空　naikū
內海外海　naikai gekai
內院　naiin
內陣　naijin
內論議　uchi-rongi
內證　naishō
內鑑冷然　naikan reinen
公案　kōan
公請　kōshō
六の街　mutsu no chimata
六入　rokunyū　　　　　「shu
六八の願主　rohukachi no gan-

六大　rokudai
六天　rokuten
六字の名號　rokuji no myōgō
六字加輪　rokuji-karin
六字河臨法　rokuji-karinhō
六字訶臨　rokuji-karin
六角堂　rokkakudō
六宗　rokushū
六法戒　roppōkai
六波羅密　ropparamitsu
六卽　rokusoku
六度　rokudo
六相　rokusō
六師外道　rokushi gedō
六時　rokuji
六根　rokkon
六畜　rokuchiku
六神通　rokujinzū
六欲　rokuyoku
六通　rokutsū
六道　rokudō
六塵　rokujin
六境　rokkyō
六趣　rokushu
六蔽　rokuhei
六齋日　rokusainichi
六識　rokushiki
六譬般若　rokuhi hannya
六觀音　rokkannon
分別　funbetsu
分身　bunshin
分段　bundan
化す　kesu
化人　kenin
化主　keshu

化生　keshō
化佛　kebutsu
化身　keshin
化法の四敎　kehō no shikyō
化俗結緣　kezoku kechien
化菩薩　kebosatsu
化儀　kegi
化樂天　kerakuten
化緣　keen
化導利生　kedō rishō
化屬　kezoku
反化　henge
天　ten
天の羽衣　ama no hagoromo
天人　tennin
天台　tendai
天狗　tengu
天竺　tenjiku
天帝　tentei
天宮　tengū
天神地祇　tenjin chigi
天堂　tendō
天衆　tenshu
天童　tendō
天蓋　tengai
天親　tenjin
天龍八部　tenryū hachibu
天龍夜叉　ten ryū yasha
天魔　tenma
太元の法　taigen no hō
太元帥　taigensui
孔雀明王　kujaku myōō
孔雀經　kujaku-kyō
幻化　genke
引接　injō

引導　indō
引攝　injō
心を修む　kokoro o osamu
心王　shinnō
心外の法　shinge no hō
心印　shin'in
心地　shinji
心行　shingyō
心言　shingon
心念　shinnen
心所　shinjo
心品　shinbon
心期　shingo
心經　shingyō
心蓮　shinren
支分(生)曼荼羅　shibun(shō)
支提　shidai　⌊mandara
文字の法師　monji no hosshi
文殊　monju
文證　monshō
斗藪　tosō
方丈　hōjō
方便　hōben
方袍　hōhō
方廣　hōkō
日本國現報善惡靈異記　nihon-
　koku-genpō-zenmaku-ryōiki
日光　nikkō
日蓮　nichiren

月光　gakkō
月忌　gakki
月輪觀　gatsurin-kan (gachirin-
止觀　shikan　　　　　⌊kan)
比丘　biku
比丘尼　bikuni
比丘僧　bikusō
比量　hiryō
氏寺　ujidera
水月　suigatsu
水の印　mizu no in
水生の印　suishō no in
水想觀　suisōkan
水輪　suirin
水觀　suikan
火の印　hi no in
火印　kain
火宅　kataku
火車　kasha
火界の呪　kakai no ju
火界眞言　kakai shingon
爪上の人身　sōjō no ninjin
父母師長の恩田　bumo shichō
　no onden
牛羊の眼　goyō no manako
牛頭　gozu
犬防ぎ　inufusegi
王三昧　ō zanmai
王舍城　ōshajō

5 STROKES

世の末　yo no sue
世上　sejō
世々の契　sese no chigiri

世自在王　sejizaiō
世事所　sejidokoro
世法佛法　sehō buppō

世俗　sezoku
世情　sejō
世善　sezen
世間　seken
世親　seshin
他力　tariki
他化自在天　takejizaiten
他犯戒　tabonkai
他生　tashō
他受用身　tajuyūshin
付法藏　fuhōzō
付法灌頂　fuhō kanjō
付屬　fuzoku
仙豫王　sen'yo ō
仙興國王　sen'yo kokuō
代受苦　daijuku
令法久住　ryōhō kujū
以心傳心　ishin denshin
出世　shusse
出家　shukke
出塵　shutsujin
出離　shutsuri
功　kō; ku
功能　kunō
功德天　kudokuten
加行　kegyō
加供　kagu
加持　kaji
加被　kabi
加備　kabi
加護　kago
北俱盧　hokkuru
北嶺　hokurei
半跏坐　hankaza
卯杖　uzue

古德　kotoku
叫喚　kyōkan
台嶺　tairei
右脇　ukyō
四八相　shihachisō 「niten
四十九重摩尼天　shijūkujū ma-
四十二章經　shijūni-shōgyō
四十八願　shijūhachi-gan
四土　shido
四大　shidai
四大天王　shidai tennō
四大種　shidaishu
四天　shiten
四天王　shitennō
四王　shiō
四王天　shiōten
四正勤　shishōgon
四生　shishō
四如意足　shinyoisoku
四有　shiu
四百四病　shihyakushi-byō
四劫　shikō
四身　shishin
四念處　shinenjo
四明山　shimeizan
四果　shika
四法界　shihokkai
四波羅夷　shiharai
四空處　shikūsho
四花　shika
四威儀　shiigi
四洲　shishū
四要品　shiyōbon
四重　shijū
四重法身　shijū hosshin

四重曼荼羅　shijū mandara
四重圓壇　shijū endan
四重萬陀羅　shijū mandara
四修　shishu
四海　shikai
四教　shikyō
四曼　shiman
四部の弟子　shibu no deshi
四智　shichi
四無所畏　shimushoi
四無畏　shimui
四無礙辯　shimugeben
四衆　shishu
四聖　shishō
四聖諦　shishōtai
四種三昧　shishu-zanmai
四種法身　shishu-hosshin
四種曼荼羅　shishu-mandara
四箇の大寺　shika no daiji
四箇大乘　shika daijō
四德　shitoku
四論宗　shironshū
四趣　shishu
四親近の菩薩　shishingon no
四諦　shitai　⌊bosatsu
四禪天　shizenten
四攝法　shishōbō
四攝事　shishōji
四辯　shiben
四魔　shima
外用　geyū
外供養　gekuyō
外典　geten
外法成就の人　gehō jōju no hito
外空　gekū

外相　gesō
外陣　gejin
外道　gedō
外境　gekyō
外護　gego
央掘摩羅　ōkutsumara
尼陀那　nidana
尼師壇　nishidan
尼堂　amadō
尼連禪河　nirenzenga
市の聖　ichi-no-hijiri
市上人　ichi-no-shōnin
布字觀　fujikan
布施　fuse
布薩　fusatsu
平生　heizei
平等　byōdō
弘法　kōbō
弘通　guzū
弘誓　guzei
必定　hitsujō
忉利　tōri
本不生　honpushō
本心　honshin
本生　honshō
本地　honji
本寺本山　honji honzan
本有　hon'u
本性　honshō
本事　honji
本來無事　honrai buji
本命星　honmyōsei
本師　honshi
本高迹下　honkō shakuge
本堂　hondō

本尊　honzon
本誓　honzei
本質　honzetsu
本願　hongan
本覺　hongaku
末の世　sue no yo
末世　masse
末代　matsudai
末寺　matsuji
末法　mappō
末學　matsugaku
未來永劫　mirai yōgō
未曾有法　mizou-hō
正行　shōgyō
正見　shōken
正受　shōju
正命　shōmyō
正定之業　shōjō no gō
正定業　shōjōgō
正定聚　shōjōju
正念　shōnen
正法　shōbō
正直　shōjiki
正眞の道　shōshin no dō
正報　shōbō
正智　shōchi
正當恁麼時　shōtō inmo no toki
正說　shōsetsu
正像末　shōzōmatsu
正覺　shōgaku
正觀　shōkan
永劫　yōgō
永嘉　yōka
永觀　yōkan
犯戒　bonkai

犯制の行儀　bonsei no gyōgi
玄奘　genjō
玄義　gengi
玄覺　genkaku
甘露　kanro
生　shō
生々世々　shōjō sese
生木化佛の觀世音　shōmoku
　　　kebutsu no kanzeon
生因の願　shōin no gan
生死　shōji
生老病死　shōrōbyōshi
生住異滅　shō-jū-i-metsu
生身　shōjin
生所　shōsho
生盲　shōmō
生者必滅　shōja hitsumetsu
生善　shōzen
生報　shōhō
生飯　sanban
生蘇　shōso
用觀　yōkan
由旬　yujun
白衣　byakue
白馬寺　hakubaji
白傘蓋佛頂呪　byakusangai-
白蓮　byakuren 　└butchō-ju
白蓮社　byakurensha
白鷺池　hakurochi
目連　mokuren
石の鉢　ishi no hachi
示現　jigen
立川流　tachikawa-ryū
立像　ryūzō
立願　ryūgan

6 STROKES

任運　nin'un
伊帝目多　iteimokuta
先世　senze
先生　senjō
先業　sengō
先達　sendatsu
光明眞言　kōmyō shingon
光明遍照　kōmyō henjō
再往　saiō
劣機　rekki
印　in
印可　inka
印信　injin
印契　ingei
印相　inzō
合掌　gasshō
吉水の和尚　yoshimizu no kashō
吉水の僧正　yoshimizu no sōjō
吉祥　kichijō
吉藏　kichizō
同行　dōgyō
同事　dōji
同居　dōgo
同法　dōhō
同體無緣の慈悲　dōtai muen no
　　　　　　　　　　　　　　　⌐jihi
名目　myōmoku
名色　myōshiki
名利　myōri
名見　myōken
名號　myōgō
名聞　myōmon
吒祇尼天　daginiten

回向　ekō
因行　ingyō
因位　inni
因果　inga
因緣　innen
在世　zaise
在家　zaike
在纏の眞如　zaiten no shinnyo
地力相應　jiriki sōō
地上戒　jijōkai
地祇　chigi
地獄　jigoku
地藏　jizō
地觀　jikan
多生　tashō
多舌魚　tazetsugyo
多伽羅香　tagara-kō
多念　tanen
多智　tachi
多聞　tamon
多摩羅跋香　tamaraba-kō
多寶塔　tahōtō
好堅樹　kōkenju
如　nyo
如如　nyonyo
如來　nyorai
如法　nyohō
如意　nyoi
如意寶珠　nyoihōshu
如實の行　nyojitsu no gyō
如說の(修)行　nyosetsu no (shu-)
妄分別　mōfunbetsu　　⌐gyō

妄心　mōjin
妄念　mōnen
妄執　mōshū
妄情　mōjō
妄想　mōzō
妄業　mōgō
妄境　mōkyō
妄語　mōgo
妄縁　mōen
字輪觀　jirinkan
安心　anjin
安立諦　anryūtai
安居　ango
安陀會　andae
安樂行品　anrakugyō-hon
安樂集　anraku-shū
安慧　anne
安養　annyō
安鎭國家法　anchin kokka-hō
寺主　jishu
寺法師　tera-hosshi
寺物　jimotsu
寺門　jimon
寺詣　tera mōde
寺僧　jisō
年忌　nenki
式叉摩尼　shikishamani
式叉摩那　shikishamana
曲彔　kyokuroku
有　u
有心　ushin
有佛無佛　ubutsu mubutsu
有宗　ushū
有念　unen
有性無性　ushō mushō

有所得　ushotoku
有門　umon
有待　utai
有相　usō
有情　ujō
有部　ubu
有頂天　uchōten　　　　「shōnin
有智高行の上人　uchi kōgyō no
有智高德　uchi kōtoku
有爲　ui
有義　ugi
有漏　uro
有縁　uen
有職　ushiki
有驗　ugen
死手の山路　shide no yamaji
死業　shinigō
死魔　shima
死靈　shiryō
求那拔摩　gunabatsuma
求聞持法　gumonjihō
牟尼　muni　　　　　　「gyō
百日の加行　hyakunichi no ke-
百日千日の講　hyakunichi sen-
　　nichi no kō
百日講　hyakunichi-kō
百王鎭護の伽藍　hyakuō chingo
　　no garan
百行律儀　hyakugyō ritsugi
百界　hyakkai
百喩經　hyakuyu-kyō
百僧　hyakusō
百福莊嚴　hyakubuku shōgon
竹林精舍　chikurin shōja
老少不定　rōshō fujō

耳根　nikon

肉髻　nikkei

自力　jiriki

自心本不生　jishin honpushō

自他　jita

自在の妙藥　jizai no myōyaku

自行の要法　jigyō no yōbō

自利　jiri

自受用身　jijuyūshin

自受法樂　jiju hōraku

自性　jishō

自法愛樂　jihō aigyō

自施　jise

自恣　jishi

自淨其意　jijō goi

自善根　jizengon

自然　jinen

自業自得　jigō jitoku

自解佛乘　jige butsujō

自慳　jiken

自說　jisetsu

自證　jishō

至理寂滅　shiri jakumetsu

至極　shigoku

至誠の心　shijō no kokoro

至誠心　shijōshin

舌相言語　zessō gongo

色　shiki

色心　shikishin

色身　shikishin

色界　shikikai

色相觀　shikisōkan

色香中道　shikikō chūdō

色欲　shikiyoku

色貪　shikiton

色報　shikihō

色無色の天　shiki mushiki no ten

血脈　ketsumyaku (kechimya-

行　gyō　⌊ku)

行人　gyōnin

行住坐臥　gyōjūzaga

行佛性　gyōbusshō

行法　gyōbō

行門　gyōmon

行相　gyōsō

行者　gyōja

行基　gyōgi (gyōki)

行淫　gyōin

行脚　angya

行盜　gyōtō

行業　gyōgō

行解　gyōge

行道　gyōdō

行儀　gyōgi

行德　gyōtoku

衣鉢　ehatsu

西天　saiten

西方淨土　saihō jōdo

西牛貨洲　saigokeshū

西來之宗旨　sairai no shūshi

西曼陀羅　saimandara

西蕃　saiban

西瞿陀尼　saikudani

西瞿耶尼　saikuyani

辻堂　tsujidō

7 STROKES

伴僧　bansō
伽陀　kada
伽耶城　gaya-jō
伽陵頻(伽)　karyōbin(ga)
伽樓羅炎　karuraen
伽藍　garan
伽羅陀山　kyaradasen
住劫　jūkō
住持　jūji
住着　jūjaku
住僧　jūsō
佉羅陀山　kyaradasen
何阿彌陀佛　nani-amidabutsu
佛　butsu; hotoke
佛子　busshi
佛心印　busshin'in
佛生日　busshōbi
佛印　butsuin
佛名　butsumyō
佛肉　butsuniku
佛弟子　butsudeshi
佛見　bukken
佛事　butsuji
佛供　butsugu
佛性　busshō
佛所　bussho
佛果　bukka
佛法　buppō
佛物　butsumotsu
佛知見　butchiken
佛舍　bussha
佛舍利　busshari

佛陀　butsuda
佛陀伽耶　buddagaya
佛勅　butchoku
佛前佛後の導師　butsuzen bu-
佛界　bukkai　⌊tsugo no dōshi
佛乘　butsujō
佛家　bukke
佛師　busshi
佛祖　busso
佛神領　busshin-ryō
佛眼　butsugen
佛頂　butchō
佛意　butsui
佛會　butsu-e
佛殿　butsuden
佛經　bukkyō
佛道　butsudō
佛境　bukkyō
佛種　busshu
佛閣　bukkaku
佛德　buttoku
佛壇　butsudan
佛藏經　butsuzō-kyō
作善　sazen
作業　sagō
初心　shoshin
初地　shoji
初果　shoka
初發心　shohosshin
初禪天　shozenten
別相　bessō
別時　betsuji

別教　bekkyō
別當　bettō
別解脫戒　betsugedatsukai
別離の苦患　betsuri no kugen
別願　betsugan
利他　rita
利生　rishō
利物　rimotsu
利門　rimon
利根　rikon
利益　riyaku
利養　riyō
助業　jogō
助觀の功　jokan no kō
劫　kō
劫火　kōka
劫末　kōmatsu
劫盡　kōjin
卵塔　rantō
含識　ganshiki
吹噓　suikyo
告文　gōmon
坊　bō
坊主　bōzu
坊官　bōkan
坐禪　zazen
妙用　myōyū
妙行　myōgyō
妙見　myōken
妙典　myōden
妙定　myōjō
妙法　myōhō
妙音天　myōonten
妙音樂天　myōongakuten
妙莊嚴王　myōshōgon ō

妙雲如來　myōun nyorai
妙解　myōge
妙樂　myōraku
妙體　myōtai
妙觀察智　myōkanzatchi
孝養　kyōyō
巡禮　junrei
希有　keu
希望　kemō
延若達多　ennyadatta
延壽堂　enjudō
延曆寺　enryakuji
形像　gyōzō
役小角　en-no-ozunu
役行者　en-no-gyōja
役優婆塞　en-no-ubasoku
忌日　kinichi
忍辱　ninniku
快樂　keraku
成劫　jōkō
成所作智　jōshosachi
成唯識論　jōyuishiki-ron
成熟　jōjuku
我功德力　gakudokuriki
我相　gasō
我執　gashū
我慢　gaman
戒　kai
扶律顯常　furitsu kenjō
折伏　shakubuku
杜順　tojun
決了　ketsuryō
決定の業　ketsujō no gō
決定往生　ketsujō ōjō
沈香　jinkō

沒滋味　motsujimi

沙門　shamon

沙彌　shami

沙彌尼　shamini

沙羅林　shararin

沙羅雙樹　sharasōju

災障　saishō

究竟　kukyō

良忍　ryōnin

良源　ryōgen

見佛　kenbutsu

見性成佛　kenshō jōbutsu

見性悟道　kenshō godō

見解　kenge

見道　kendō

見境　kenkyō

見聞覺知　kenmon kakuchi

言語道斷　gongo dōdan

言說　gonzetsu

赤肉中臺之相　shakuniku chū-⌐dai no sō

身土　shindo   ⌐dai no sō

身子　shinshi

車匿　shanoku

那智千日の行者　nachi sennichi ⌐no gyōja

那羅延　naraen   ⌐no gyōja

邪見　jaken

邪命　jamyō

邪定聚　jajōju

邪執　jashū

邪淫　jain

邪慢　jaman

邪觀　jakan

里法師　sato-hosshi

8 STROKES

事　ji

事事無礙法界　jijimuge hokkai

事法供養　jihō kuyō

事法界　ji-hokkai

事相　jisō

事理　jiri

事觀　jikan

來世　raise

來迎　raigō

例事　reiji

侍法師　samurai-bōshi

供　ku

供米　kumai

供佛　kubutsu

供具　kugu

供奉　gubu

供奉僧　kubusō

供物　kumotsu

供花　kuge

供料　kuryō

供僧　kusō

供養　kuyō

依他　eta

依正　eshō

依身　eshin

依報　ehō

依詮　esen

兒　chigo

兩舌　ryōzetsu

兩金剛　ryōkongō

両界　ryōkai
両部　ryōbu
両業　ryōgō
具足　gusoku
制戒　seikai
制門　seimon
刹　setsu
刹利　setsuri
刹那　setsuna
刹帝利　setteiri
効験　kōken
卒都婆　sotoba
卷數　kanju
取　shu
受　ju
受戒　jukai
受法灌頂　juhō kanjō
受持　juji
受樂　juraku
周利槃特　shurihandoku
呪咀　juso
咒願　jugan
和光　wakō
和伽羅　wagara
和尙　kashō; oshō
吒祇尼天　daginiten
垂迹　suijaku
夜叉　yasha
夜居僧　yoi no sō
奇特　kidoku
奇瑞　kizui　　　　　　　　「no soko
奈利八萬の底　nairi hachiman
奈良法師　nara hōshi
奈落　naraku
奈落伽　naraka

奉行　bugyō
始敎　shikyō
始覺　shikaku
季(の)御讀經　ki (no) midokyō
孤起頌　kokiju
宗の法燈　shū no hōtō
宗乘　shūjō
宗義　shūgi
官僧　kansō
定　jō
定力　jōriki
定心　jōshin
定光　jōkō
定印　jōin
定性　jōshō
定相　jōsō
定善業　jōzengō
定業　jōgō
定慧　jōe
居士　koji
彼我　higa
彼岸　higan
往生　ōjō
念　nen
念佛　nenbutsu
念念　nennen
念珠　nenju
念誦　nenju
念慮　nenryo
忿怒　funnu
性　shō
性具　shōgu
性相　shōzō
性德　shōtoku
性靈集　shōryōshū

房主　bōzu
所化　shoke
所司　shoshi
所行　shogyō
所住　shojū
所作　shosa
所具　shogu
所知障　shochishō
所得　shotoku
所爲　shoi
所緣　shoen
所願　shogan
所變　shohen
承仕　shōji
承當　jōtō
拄杖　shujō
拈香　nenkō
拈華微笑　nenge mishō
拈華瞬目　nenge shunmoku
拔苦　bakku
拔提河　batsudaiga
放生　hōjō
放逸　hōitsu
明　myō
明王　myōō
明呪　myōshu
易往易行の道　iō igyō no michi
易往無人　iō munin
東大寺　tōdaiji
東弗婆提　tōhotsubadai
東寺　tōji
東曼陀羅　tō-mandara
東勝身洲　tōshōshinshū
林下　ringe
果位　kai

果佛　kabutsu
果報　kahō
果德　katoku
欣求　gongu
毒鼓　dokku
法　hō
法力　hōriki
法文　hōmon
法王　hōō
法句經　hokku-kyō
法用　hōyū
法印大和尚位　hōin-daikashō-i
法名　hōmyō
法衣　hōe
法住法位の理　hōjū hōi no ko-
法利　hōri　　　　　⌊towari
法身　hosshin
法事讚　hōji-san
法味　hōmi
法命　hōmyō
法性　hosshō
法花　hokke
法門　hōmon
法威　hōi
法施　hōse
法流　hōryū
法界　hokkai
法皇　hōō
法相　hossō
法音　hōon
法師　hosshi
法師子　hosshishi
法席　hōseki
法務　hōmu
法執　hosshū

法堂　hattō
法宿大菩薩　hōshuku daibosatsu
法理　hōri
法眷　hakken
法眼　hōgen
法喜　hōki
法無礙　hōmuge
法然　hōnen
法華　hokke
法華經　hoke-kyō
法愛　hōai
法會　hōe
法滅　hōmetsu
法滅盡經　hōmetsujin-kyō
法照　hosshō
法義　hōgi
法慳悋　hōkenrin
法慳恪　hōkenrin
法爾　hōni
法樂　hōraku
法談　hōdan
法論　hōron
法器　hōki
法橋　hokkyō
法機　hōki
法燈　hōtō
法親王　hōshinnō
法藏　hōzō
法驗　hōken
法體　hottai
波旬　hajun
波斯匿王　hashinoku ō
波逸提　haitsudai
波羅夷　harai
波羅奈國　harana-koku

波羅密　haramitsu
波羅蜜　haramitsu
泥佛　deibutsu
泥梨　nairi
炎魔　enma
物忌　monoimi
盂蘭盆　urabon
直指人心　jikishi ninshin
知見　chiken
知足　chisoku
知足天　chisokuten
知識　chishiki
社僧　shasō
空　kū
空也　kūya
空劫　kūgō
空宗　kūshū
空門　kūmon
空海　kūkai
空寂　kūjaku
空無邊處　kūmuhenjo
空華　kūge
空觀　kūgan
竺法蘭　jiku hōran
舍利　shari
舍利弗　sharihotsu
舍遮　shanoku
舍衞　shae
花藏　kezō
花嚴　kegon
表白　hyōbyaku
迎接　gōshō
迎講　mukae-kō
迎攝　kōshō
金　kin; kon

金口 konku
金光明經 konkōmyō-kyo
金光明最勝王經 konkōmyō-sai-
金言 kingen ⌊shōō-kyō
金剛 kongō
金翅鳥 konjichō
金皷 konku
金輪 kinrin
金輪佛頂 kinrin butchō
金錍論 konbei-ron
長老 chōrō
長夜 jōya
長阿含經 jō-agon-gyō
長者 chōja
長時修 jōjishu
長講 jōgō
門主 monshu
門徒 monto
阿字 aji
阿伽 aka
阿含 agon
阿私仙 ashi sen
阿私陀仙 ashida sen
阿那含果 anagonka
阿防羅刹 abō rasetsu
阿放羅刹 ahō rasetsu
阿波陀那 ahadana
阿育大王 aiku daiō
阿育王 aiku ō ⌈kusha-ron
阿毘達磨俱舍論 abidatsuma-
阿毘達磨藏 abidatsumazō

阿修羅 ashura
阿浮達磨 abudatsuma
阿傍羅刹 abō rasetsu
阿逸多 aitta
阿僧祇 asōgi
阿閦 ashuku
阿鼻 abi
阿練若 arennya
阿耨多羅三藐三菩提 anoku-
tara-sanmyaku-sanbodai
阿耨達池 anokudatchi
阿賴耶 araya
阿輸伽王 ashuka ō
阿彌陀 amida
阿闍世 ajase
阿闍梨 ajari
阿羅漢 arakan
阿難 anan
阿蘭若 arannya
陀羅尼 darani ⌈manajiri
青蓮慈悲の眸 shōren jihi no
非人法師 hinin hōshi
非安立諦 hianryūtai
非法 hihō
非時 hiji
非情成佛 hijō jōbutsu
非想天 hisōten
非想非非想天 hisōhihisōten
非想非非想處 hisōhihisōjo
非業 higō
非學生 higakushō

9 STROKES

係念 kenen

俗形 zokugyō

俗塵　zokujin
俗諦　zokutai
俗體　zokutai
信力　shinriki
信心　shinjin
信行　shingyō
信施　shinse
信敬　shingyō
信解　shinge
剃髮　teihatsu
前生　zenshō
前佛　zenbutsu
前門主　zenmonshu
前後際斷　zengo saidan
前業　zengō
勅願寺　chokuganji
勅願所　chokuganjo
勇猛精進　yumyō shōjin
南山大師　nanzan daishi
南州　nanshū
南京の法師　nankyō no hōshi
南浮　nanbu
南無　namu
南都　nanto
南閻浮提　nan'enbudai
南嶽　nangaku
南瞻部州　nansenbushū
即心是道　sokushin zedō
即身に　sokushin ni
即身成佛　sokushin jōbutsu
品品　honbon
契印　geiin
契經　kaikyō
威將軍　i shōgun
威儀　igi

帝尺宮　taishaku-gū
帝釋　taishaku
度　do
度生　doshō
度量　takuryō
廻す　esu
廻心　eshin
廻向　ekō
律　ritsu
律戒の門　ritsukai (rikkai) no ⌊mon
律宗　risshū
律師　risshi
律院　ritsuin
律僧　rissō
律儀　ritsugi
律藏　ritsuzō
後七日　goshichinichi
後の世　nochi no yo
後世　gose
後生　goshō
後身　goshin
後善導　go-zendō
後報　gohō
思想覺觀　shisō kakukan
思慮分別　shiryo funbetsu
怨敵調伏の法　onteki jōbuku ⌊no hō
怨靈　onryō
恆沙　gōja
恆河沙　gōgasha
恆順衆生　gōjun shujō
持佛堂　jibutsudō
持戒　jikai
持律　jiritsu
持者　jisha
持經　jikyō

韋天將軍　iten shōgun
韋陀　ida
韋陀天　idaten
韋提希　idaike
韋馱天　idaten
飛瀧大薩埵　hiryū daisatta
飛瀧權現　hiryū gongen
首陀　shuda
首陀羅　shudara
首座　shuso

首楞嚴　shuryōgon
香　kō
香山　kōsen
香花　koge
香染　kōzome
香華院　kōge-in
香象　kōzō
香盤　kōban
香醉山　kōsuisen

10 STROKES

乘　jō
乘戒　jōkai
乘急　jōkyū
修正　shushō
修因　shuin
修多羅　shutara
修行者　shugyōza
修法　shubō
修善　shuzen
修德　shutoku
修學　shugaku
修羅　shura
修驗　shugen
俱生神　kushōjin
俱舍　kusha
俱胝　kutei
值遇　chigū
冥　myō
冥土　meido
冥目　myōmoku
冥加　myōga
冥伽　myōga

冥助　myōjo
冥見　myōken
冥官　myōkan
冥界　myōkai
冥途　meido
冥衆　myōshu
冥道　myōdō
冥應　myōō
冥譴　myōken
冥護　myōgo
冥鑒　myōkan
冥顯　myōken
准陀　junda
唄　bai
唄師　baishi
唄匿　bainoku
夏　ge
夏中　gechū
夏安居　ge-ango
娑婆　shaba
娑竭羅龍王　shakara ryūō ⌈myō
宮の御佛名　miya no gobutsu-

宮中御齋會　kyūchū gosai-e
宮毘羅大將　kubira daishō
宮殿樓閣　kūden rōkaku
宴坐　enza
差別　shabetsu
師子　shishi
師資　shishi
座　za
座主　zasu
庫裡　kuri
庫裏　kuri
恩田　onden
恩所　onjo
恩愛　onnai
恩德　ondoku
恭敬　kugyō
息災　sokusai
悟　satori
悟道　godō
扇提羅　sendaira
旃陀羅　sendara
旃提羅　sendaira
旃檀　sendan
時　ji
時宗　jishū
時料　tokiryō
時衆　jishu
時節　jisetsu
書寫　shosha
根性　konjō
桑門　sōmon
浮世　ukiyo
浮香世界　fukō sekai
涅槃　nehan
烏瑟　ushitsu

烏蒭沙摩　ususama
特留此經…　dokuru shikyō…
特尊　dokuson
畜生道　chikushōdō
益　yaku
眞心　shinshin
眞如　shinnyo
眞我　shinga
眞言　shingon
眞身　shinshin
眞宗　shinshū
眞性　shinshō
眞空　shinkū
眞俗　shinzoku
眞諦　shintai
眞讀　shindoku
破戒　hakai
祕法　hihō
祕密主　himitsushu
祕密咒　himitsuju
祕密灌頂　himitsukanjō
祕藏　hizō
神力　jinriki
神子　yorimashi
神分心經　shinbun shingyō
神咒　shinju
神明佛陀　shinmei butsuda
神宮寺　jingūji
神通　jinzū
神境通　jinkyōtsū
神變　jinpen
純陀　junda
素多覽藏　sotaranzō
索　saku
耆婆　giba

能取所取　nōshu shoshu
能念所念　nōnen shonen
能所　nōjo
能緣所緣　nōen shoen
般舟讚　hanju-san
般若　hannya
般特　handoku
荊溪　keikei
草木成佛　sōmoku jōbutsu
記　ki
記別　kibetsu
起信　kishin
起請　kishō
起龕　kigan
迷悟　meigo
迷情　meijō
迹高本下　shakkō honge
追孝の作善　tsuikyō no sazen
追善　tsuizen
追貫　tsuifun
追福　tsuifuku「gejō no sotoba
退梵(= 凡)下乘の卒都婆　taibon

退轉　taiten
送行　sōan
逆修　gyakushu
逆罪　gyakuzai
逆緣　gyakuen
陞座　shinzo
院　in
院家　inge
院號　ingō
除災與樂　josai yoraku
馬鳴　memyō
馬頭　mezu
馬頭觀音　batō kannon
高座　kōza
高祖大師　kōso daishi
高野聖　kōya hijiri
高野大師　kōya daishi
高貴德菩薩　kōkitoku bosatsu
高聲念佛　kōshō nenbutsu
鬼畜　kichiku
鬼道　kidō

11 STROKES

乾闥婆　kendatsuba
假名字　kemyōji
假色　keshiki
假法　kehō
假相　kesō
假諦　ketai
偏小十二季　henshō jūninen
偏空　henkū
偏執　henshū
健行　kengyō

健相　kensō
偸盜　chūtō
兜率　tosotsu
動靜一致　dōjō itchi
勘發　kanbotsu
參禪　sanzen
參籠　sanrō
唯心　yuishin
唯受一人　yuiju ichinin
唯境　yuikyō

唯識　yuishiki
問佛決疑經　monbutsu-ketsugi- └kyō
問者　monja
啓白　keibyaku
國分尼寺　kokubunniji
國分寺　kokubunji
國家護持の棟梁　kokka goji no
國鎮　kokuchin └tōryō
執心　shūshin
執行　shugyō
執則障道の行人　shūsoku shōdō └no gyōnin
執著　shūjaku
堂　dō
堂舍　dōsha
堂童子　dōdōji
堂衆　dōshu
堂達　dōdatsu
堂僧　dōsō
堅牢地祇　kenrō jigi
堅牢地神　kenrō jijin
堅誓師子　kensei shishi
婆羅門　baramon
婬事對治　inji taiji
婬著　injaku
宿世　shukuse
宿因　shukuin
宿老　shukurō
宿坊　shukubō
宿命智　shukumyōchi
宿執　shukushū
宿習　shukujū
宿善　shukuzen
宿報　shukuhō
宿業　shukugō
宿福　shukufuku

宿種　shukushu
宿緣　shukuen
宿願　shukugan
寂光　jakkō
寂然　jakunen
寂滅　jakumetsu
寂照　jakushō
寂道樹　jakudōju
寂靜涅槃　jakujō nehan
寄進　kishin
密印　mitsuin
密行　mitsugyō
密宗　misshū
密法　mippō
密迹金剛　misshaku kongō
密教　mikkyō
密號　mitsugō
密嚴　mitsugon
專修　senju
常不輕　jōfugyō
常在靈山　jōzai ryōzen
常行三昧　jōgyō-zanmai
常行堂　jōgyōdō
常住　jōjū
常寂光土　jōjakkōdo
常樂會　jōraku-e
常燈　jōtō
常隨佛學の願　jōzui-butsugaku └no gan
庵室　anshitsu
得果　tokka
得益　tokuyaku
得脫　tokudatsu
得智の禪師　tokuchi no zenji
得道　tokudō ┌mishuhō
御七日御修法　goshichinichi

御八講　gohakkō
御牙　onkiba
御佛名　onbutsumyō
御坊　gobō
御物忌　onmonoimi
御祈の師　oinori no shi
御修法　mishiho
御堂　midō
御誦經　mizukyō
御影堂　mieidō
御嶽　mitake
御齋會　gosai-e
御願所　goganjo
御讀經　midokyō
御靈會　goryō-e
悉地　shitchi
悉有佛性　shitsuu busshō
悉達　shitta
情　jō
情念　jōnen
情量　jōryō
情識　jōshiki
捧物　sasagemono
捨惡修善　shaaku shuzen
捨離　shari
捷疾鬼　shōshikki
授記　juki
探題　tandai
接取　sesshu
教文　kyōmon
教主　kyōshu
教行　kyōgyō
教判　kyōhan
教法　kyōbō
教門　kyōmon

教相　kyōsō
教起　kyōki
教院　kyōin
教授師　kyōjushi
教權理實　kyōgon rijitsu
救世　kuse
晚出家　banshukke
曼陀羅華　mandarake
曼荼　manda
梵土　bondo
梵天　bonten
梵王　bonnō
梵行　bongyō
梵砌　bonzei
梵音　bonnon
梵唄　bonbai
梵席　bonseki
梵僧　bonsō
梵網　bonmō
欲天　yokuten
欲界　yokkai
欲網　yokumō
殺生　sesshō
淨土　jōdo
淨名　jōmyō
淨行　jōgyō
淨妙の國　jōmyō no kuni
淨妙國土　jōmyō kokudo
淨戒　jōkai
淨利　jōsetsu
淨法界　jōhokkai
淨眼　jōgen
淨業　jōgō
淨飯王　jōbon ō
淨瑠璃世界　jōruri sekai

淨瑠璃醫王の主　jōruri iō no shu
淨頗梨　jōhari
淨藏　jōzō
淫心　inshin
深信　jinshin
淳陀　junda
清水まうで　kiyomizu mōde
清淨の比丘　shōjō no biku
清淨(の)身　shōjō (no) shin
清淨法身　shōjō hosshin
清淨智　shōjōchi
清辨　shōben
淺略深祕　senryaku jinpi
猛火鐵湯　mōka tettō
率都婆　sotoba
現化　genke
現世　genze
現生　genshō
現供養　genkuyō
現前に　genzen ni
現益　genyaku
現報　genpō
現量　genryō
現當　gentō
現證　genshō
理　ri
理佛性　ribusshō
理具の成佛　rigu no jōbutsu
理性　rishō
理法界　ri-hokkai
理卽　risoku
理智　richi
理觀　rikan
畢波羅窟　hipparakutsu
異見　iken

異香　ikyō
第一義　daiichigi
第二果　dainika
第三果　daisanka
第六天　dairokuten
第四果　daishika
第四兜率天　daishi tosotsuten
紫雲　shiun
紫磨金色　shimagonjiki
紫磨黄金　shima ōgon
終教　jūkyō
習因　shūin
習果　shūka
茶吉尼天　dakiniten
茶毗　dabi
莊嚴　shōgon
虚(or 虗)說　kosetsu
袈裟　kesa
貧士　hinshi
貪欲　ton'yoku
貪淫　ton'in
貪愛　ton'ai
貪瞋癡の三毒　tonjinchi no san-
貫主　kansu　　　　　⌊doku
貫首　kanshu
貫頂　kanchō
責伏　shakubuku
軟語　nango
通　tsū
通相　tsūsō
通誡　tsūkai
通願　tsūgan
速證無上大菩提　sokushō mujō
造作魔　zōsakuma　⌊daibodai
連枝　renshi

陰入　onnyū
陰德　intoku
陰魔　onma
雪山　sessen
頂上王　chōshō ō

頂生王　chōshō ō
頂禮　chōrai
鳥窠　chōka
鳥鼠比丘　chōso biku
鹿野苑　rokuya-on

12 STROKES

勝士　shōji
勝他　shōta
勝因　shōin
勝位　shōi
勝軍　shōgun
勝義　shōgi
勝緣　shōen
勝鬘　shōman
割愛　katsuai
報　hō; mukui
報土　hōdo
報身　hōjin
報命　hōmyō
報恩經　hōon-gyō
奠茶　tencha
奠湯　tentō
厨子　zushi
善女龍王　zennyo ryūō
善巧　zengyō
善因　zen'in
善住天子經　zenjū-tenshi-kyō
善來比丘　zenrai biku
善法比丘　zenpō biku
善法堂　zenpōdō
善知識　zenjishiki
善思菩薩　zenshi bosatsu
善根　zengon

善處　zensho
善逝　zenzei
善無畏　zenmui
善業　zengō
善緣　zen'en
善趣　zenshu
善導　zendō
喝食　kasshiki
單空　tankū
單傳　tanden
富樓那　furuna
尊星王　sonjōō
尊宿　sonshuku
尊勝王　sonshōō
尊勝供　sonshōku
尊勝法　sonshōhō
尊勝佛頂　sonshō-butchō
尊勝陀羅尼　sonshō-darani
悲田　hiden
悲門　himon
悲智の方便　hichi no hōben
悲華經　hike-kyō
悲增　hizō
悲願　higan
惑　waku
惠心僧都　eshin sōzu
惡知識　aku chishiki

無爲　mui

無量光　muryōkō

無量劫　muryōkō

無量壽　muryōju

無間　muken

無想天　musōten

無意　mui

無愧　mugi

無義　mugi

無著　mujaku

無道心　mudōshin

無慚無愧　muzan mugi

無漏　muro

無盡　mujin

無際智　musaichi

無熱池　munetsuchi

無窮　mugū

無緣　muen

無靜念　mujōnen

無餘修　muyoshu

無縫塔　muhōtō

無礙　muge

無邊世界　muhen sekai

焦熱大焦熱　shōnetsu daishō-

琰魔　enma　⌐netsu

發心　hosshin

發菩提心　hotsubodaishin

發露懺悔　hotsuro sange

盛者必衰　shōja hissui

筆受　hitsuju

等活地獄　tōkatsu jigoku

等流　tōru

等覺　tōgaku

結界　kekkai

結衆　kesshū

結集　ketsujū

結緣　ketsuen

結願　ketsugan

給孤獨　gikkodoku

着す　jaku su

菩提　bodai

菩薩　bosatsu

華藏世界　kezō sekai

華嚴　kegon

衆生　shujō

衆合　shugō

衆香世界　shukō sekai

衆徒　shuto　⌐jo no nyorai

衆病悉除の如來　shubyō shitsu-

衆善奉行　shuzen bugyō

補陀落山　fudarakusen

補處の菩薩　fusho no bosatsu

補墮落能化の主　fudaraku nōke

訶利帝　karitei　　　⌐no shu

貴僧　kisō

超佛越祖　chōbutsu osso

都率　tosotsu

都維那　tsuina

酥　so

開山　kaisan

開白の日　kaibyaku no hi

開眼　kaigen

開結二經　kaiketsu nikyō

開會　kaie

開曉　kaikyō

開顯　kaiken

雁塔　gantō

順生　junshō

順次　junji

順後業　jungogō

順逆　jungyaku
順現(業)　jungen(gō)
順縁　jun'en
須臾　shuyu
須陀洹果　shudaonka
須達　shudatsu
須彌　shumi
黑衣の身　kokue no mi

虛妄　komō
虛言　kyogon
虛空藏　kokūzō
虛受信施の罪　koju shinse no
虛假　koke　　　　　　└tsumi
虛說　kosetsu
黑闇天　kokuanten

13 STROKES

傳法　denbō
傳授　denju
傳教大師　dengyō daishi
勢至　seishi
勤行　gongyō
勤修　gonshu
園城寺　onjōji
圓仁　ennin
圓成　enjō
圓宗　enshū
圓珍　enchin
圓座　enza
圓教　engyō
圓通　entsū
圓頂　enchō
圓頓　endon
圓融　en'yū
圓覺　engaku
塔婆　tōba
塔頭　tatchū
奧院　oku no in
微塵數　mijinju
意巧　igyō
意樂　igyō

愚癡　guchi
愛　ai
愛別離苦　aibetsuriku
愛見　aiken
愛念　ainen
愛染明王　aizen myōō
愛染寶塔　aizen hōtō
愛恚　aii
愛善寶塔　aizen hōtō
愛著　aijaku
愛樂　aigyō
感果　kanka
感得　kantoku
感應　kannō
敬田　kyōden
敬愛の祕法　kyōai no hihō
敬愛法　keiaihō
暗證の禪師　anshō no zenji
暗證之朋黨　anshō no hōtō
會(す)　e(su)
會中　echū
會者定離　eshajōri
會座　eza
會離　eri

萬緣	man'en	道念	dōnen
萬機	manki	道服	dōbuku
落謝	rakusha	道林	dōrin
著す	jaku su	道果	dōka
著心	jakushin	道俗	dōzoku
著相	jakusō	道品	dōbon
著處	jakusho	道宣	dōsen
解了	geryō	道者	dōsha
解行	gegyō	道場	dōjō
解信	geshin	道業	dōgō
解脱	gedatsu	道種智	dōshuchi
解義	gegi	道綽	dōshaku
資緣	shien	達磨	daruma
資糧	shiryō	違順	ijun
遁世	tonsei	違緣	ien
遊行聖	yugyō-hijiri	鈴の印	rei no in
運心供養	unshin kuyō	鉤召法	kōchōhō
遐代	kadai	隔生則忘	kyakushō sokumō
遍小十二幸	henshō jūninen	頌	ju
遍計	henge	預流果	yoruka
過去七佛	kako shichibutsu	頓大	tondai
過去帳	kakochō	頓法	tonbō
道	dō	頓悟	tongo
道人	dōnin	頓教	tongyō
道元	dōgen	頓證	tonshō
道心	dōshin	鳩摩羅什	kumarajū
道行	dōgyō	鳩摩羅炎	kumaraen

14 STROKES

像法	zōbō	僧形	sōgyō
僧正	sōjō	僧官	sōkan
僧伽	sōgya	僧法	sōbō
僧位	sōi	僧物	sōmotsu
僧坊	sōbō	僧座	sōza

僧堂　sōdō

僧都　sōzu

僧綱　sōgō

僧寶　sōbō

僧體　sōtai

厭苦　enku

厭離　onri

嘉祥　kajō

塵　jin

塵勞　jinrō

塵塵　jinjin

塵境　jinkyō

境界　kyōgai

境緣　kyōen

壽命經　jumyō-kyō

壽量品　juryō-bon

夢幻虛假　mugen koke

夢想　musō

實有　jitsuu

實我實法の妄情　jitsuga jippō

實法　jippō　⌊no mōjō

實相　jissō

實教　jikkyō　⌈miyako

實報寂光の都　jippō jakkō no

實報無障礙土　jippō mushōge-

實智　jitchi　⌊do

實際　jissai

實證　jisshō

對治　taiji

對法藏　taihōzō

慈心三昧　jishin-zanmai

慈氏尊　jishison

慈救呪　jikushu

慈救眞言　jiku-shingon

慈善根　jizengon

慈尊　jison

慈悲　jihi

慈童　jidō

慈慧大師　jie daishi

慈覺　jikaku

慚愧懺悔　zangi sange

慳　ken

慳貪　kendon

摧伏　zaibuku

榮西　eisai

漏　ro

演若達多　ennyadatta

漸次　zenji

漸敎　zengyō

薰習　kunjū

獄卒(or 率)　gokusotsu

瑠璃　ruri

疑難　ginan

盡十方無礙光　jinjippō-mugekō

盡未來際　jinmiraizai

福力　fukuriki

福分　fukubun

福田　fukuden

福舍　fukusha

福智　fukuchi

福業　fukugō

種子　shuji; shūji

稱名　shōmyō

端正　tanjō

端坐　tanza

精舍　shōja

精進　shōjin

維摩　yuima

綱位　kōi

綺語　kigo

緇素 shiso
緊那羅 kinnara
聞法 monbō
聞思修 monshishu
疾蔾 shitsuri
蒀別 kibetsu
蓋 gai
誓願 seigan
誑言 ōgon
語錄 goroku
誠文 jōmon
誠諦 jōtai

誦經 jukyō
說一切有部 setsuissaiubu
說戒 sekkai
說法 seppō
說破 setsuha
說經 sekkyō
賓頭盧 binzuru
輕業 kyōgō
障 sawari; shō
障礙 shōge
領解 ryōge

15 STROKES

儀軌 giki
億劫 okkō
劍印 ken'in
增一阿含經 zōitsu-agon-gyō
增上の勝緣 zōjō no shōen
增上慢 zōjō-man
增上緣 zōjō-en
增劫 zōkō
增益 zōyaku
增益法 sōyakuhō
墨染 sumizome
寫經 shakyō
幢幡 dōban
廣大金剛法界宮 kōdai kongō
彈指 tanji ⌐hōkaigū
影向 yōkō
德本 tokuhon
德用 tokuyū
德行 tokugyō
慧文 emon

慧光法燈 ekō hōtō
慧命 emyō
慧思 eshi
慧能 enō
慧遠 eon
摩尼 mani
摩利支天 marishiten
摩耶 maya
摩訶陀 makada
摩訶止觀 makashikan
摩訶衍論 makaen-ron
摩訶般若波羅蜜經 makahan-
　　nya-haramitsu-kyō
摩訶迦葉 makakashō
摩訶迦羅天 makakaraten
摩訶薩 makasatsu
摩睺羅迦 magoraga
摩竭陀 makada
摩竭魚 makatsugyo
摩羯陀 makada

摩羯魚　makatsugyo
摩醯伊濕伐羅　makeishubara
摩醯首羅　makeishura
摩醯脩羅王　makeishura ō
摩騰　matō
撫物　nademono
撥無　hatsumu
數珠　juzu
樂欲　gyōyoku
樂說無礙　gyōzetsu muge
樓至佛　rushi butsu
樓閣　rōkaku
澆季　gyōki
澆薄　gyōhaku
熟蘇　jukuso
瞋恚　shinni
稽古　keiko
緣　en
緣ず　enzu
緣日　ennichi
緣因　en'in
緣起　engi
緣務　enmu
緣覺　engaku
練行　rengyō
練若　rennya
羯磨師　katsumashi

蓮の身　hachisu no mi
蓮の臺　hachisu no utena
蓮華　renge
蓮華藏世界　rengezō sekai
蓮臺　rendai
誹謗　hibō
調伏　jōbuku
調達　chōdatsu
諂曲　tengoku
談義　dangi
請用　shōyō
論談　rondan
論藏　ronzō
論議　rongi
賢劫　gengō
賢首　genju
賢愚經　gengu-gyō
賢愚因緣經　gengu-innen-gyō
賢聖　kenshō
質多居士　shitta koji
輪王　rinnō
輪廻　rinne
輪藏　rinzō
輪寶　rinbō
輪觀　rinkan
遮那　shana
遷化　senge

16 STROKES

儒童　judō
器界　kikai
壇　dan
學生　gakushō
學匠　gakushō

學侶　gakuryo
學律の者　gakuritsu no mono
學解　gakuge
導師　dōshi　　　「oshie
憶持不忘の教　okuji fumō no

懈怠　kedai

曇鸞　donran

機　ki

機法　kihō

機根　kikon

機情　kijō

機感　kikan

歷緣對境　ryakuen taikyō

濁世　jokuse

濁惡世　jokuakuse

燃燈　nentō

熾盛光　shijōkō

燒香　shōkō

燒燈　shōtō

獨古　dokko

獨股　dokko

獨尊　dokuson

獨鈷　dokko

獨覺仙（人）　dokkaku sen(nin)

盧舍那佛　rushana butsu

磬　kei

興起行經　kōkigyō-kyō

興福寺　kōfukuji

興禪護國論　kōzen-gokoku-ron

融通　yūzū

親鸞　shinran

諸行往生　shogyō-ōjō

諸行無常　shogyō mujō

諸法　shohō

諸院　shoin

諸部の般若　shobu no hannya

諸善奉行　shozen bugyō

諸善雜行　shozen zōgyō

諸尊合行護摩法　shoson gōgyō gomahō

諸尊別行護摩（祕）法　shoson betsugyō goma(hi)hō

諸惡莫作　shoaku makusa

諸境唯心　shokyō yuishin

踰伽上乘之理　yuga jōjō no ri

辨才天　benzaiten

遺戒　yuikai

遺法　yuihō

遺敎　yuikyō

選擇本願念佛集　senjaku-hon-gan-nenbutsu-shū

選擇集　senjaku-shū

醍醐　daigo

醍醐寺　daigoji

錠光　jōkō

錫杖　shakujō

閼伽　aka

閻王　en'ō

閻浮　enbu

閻摩　enma

隨一　zuiichi

隨求陀羅尼　zuigu-darani

隨求經　zuigu-kyō

隨喜　zuiki

隨緣　zuien

隨類　zuirui

頭北面西　zuhoku-mensai

頭光　zukō

頭陀　zuda

頻伽羅　bingara

頻婆娑羅　binbashara

餓鬼　gaki

餘行餘善　yogyō yozen

餘行餘業　yogyō yogō

餘念　yonen

餘執　yoshū

龍　ryū

龍女　ryūnyo

龍王　ryūō

龍宮　ryūgū

龍神　ryūjin

龍猛　ryūmyō

龍華下生三會の曉　ryūge geshō san'e no akatsuki

龍華會　ryūge-e

龍樹　ryūju

龜茲國　kijikoku

17 STROKES

優波離　upari

優陀那　udana

優婆夷　ubai

優婆梨　ubari

優婆提舍　ubadaisha

優婆塞　ubasoku

優曇　udon

優轉王　udennō

彌陀　mida

彌勒　miroku

應化　ōke

應用　ōyū

應作　ōsa

應身　ōjin

應供　ōgu

應現　ōgen

戲論　keron

檀　dan

檀那　danna

檀波羅蜜　dan-haramitsu

檀度　danto

檀施　danse

檀徒　danto

檀特山　dandokusen

檀越　dannotsu

濟度　saido

癈詮　haisen

禪　zen

禪尼　zenni

禪定　zenjō

禪林の十因　zenrin no jūin

禪法　zenbō

禪門　zenmon

禪侶　zenryo

禪室　zenshitsu

禪律　zenritsu

禪師　zenji

禪悅　zen'etsu

禪院　zen'in

禪教　zenkyō

禪僧　zensō

禪閣　zenkō

禪鞠　zenkiku

縵衣　man'e

總門　sōmon

總持　sōji

聲明　shōmyō

聲聞　shōmon

臨終　rinjū

薄地　hakuji

薄伽梵　bagabon

螺髮　rahotsu

螺髻 rakei	闍多伽 jataka
謗法 hōbō	闍梨 jari
講 kō	隱形の印 ongyō no in
講行 kōgyō	隱形の呪 ongyō no ju
講師 kōshi	點心 tenshin
講問 kōmon	齋 sai; toki
講莚 kōen	齋月 saigatsu
講經 kōgyō	齋日 sainichi
講讀師 kōtokuji	齋戒 saikai
還來穢國 genrai ekoku	齋料 tokiryō
還俗 genzoku	齋燈 saitō
闍王 ja ō	

18 STROKES

叢林 sōrin	藏主 zōsu
斷惑 danwaku	藏敎 zōkyō
歸伏 kibuku	轉ず tenzu
歸依 kie	轉依 tenne
瞻富 senpuku	轉法輪 tenpōrin
瞻葡 senpuku	轉輪王 tenrinnō
瞿曇 kudon	轉讀 tendoku
禮盤 raiban	醫王 iō
禮讚 raisan	薩埵 satta
穢土 edo	鎖龕 sagan
穢國 ekoku	鎮守 chinju
繪蓋 zōgai	鎮護國家 chingo kokka
繪幡 zōban	雙卷經 sōkan-gyō
繪旛 zōban	雙林 sōrin
擧似 koji	雜行 zōgyō
舊業 kugō	雜阿含經 zō-agon-gyō
薰修 kunshū	雜染世界 zōzen sekai
薰習 kunjū	雜善 zōzen
藏王權現 zaō gongen	題名僧 daimyōsō

19 STROKES

壞劫　ekō
壞見の者　eken no mono
廬山の慧遠　rozan no eon
懷感　ekan
曠劫　kōgō
犢牛前身　tokugyū zenshin
癡愛　chiai
繩床　jōshō
繫念　kenen
繫緣法界一念法界　keen-hōkai
　　　　　　　　　　Ｌichinen-hōkai
羅什　rajū
羅刹　rasetsu
羅漢　rakan
羅睺羅　ragora
羂索　kensaku
藕絲　gūshi
藥王　yakuō
藥師　yakushi

證大菩提　shō daibodai
證得　shōtoku
證義　shōgi
證誠大菩提　shōjō daibodai
識　shiki
識情　shikijō
識無邊處　shikimuhenjo
辭無礙　jimuge
邊見　henken
邊邪　henja
難行苦行　nangyō kugyō
難解難入の門　nange　nannyū
願　gan　　　　　　　　Ｌno mon
願力　ganriki
願文　ganmon
願生西方　ganshō saihō
願書　ganjo
顛倒　tendō

20 STROKES

勸進　kanjin
勸請　kanjō
勸請神　kanshōjin
勸學會　kangaku-e
寶土　hōdo
寶生　hōshō
寶海　hōkai
寶珠　hōju
寶珠法　hōshuhō
寶堂莊嚴　hōdō shōgon
寶號　hōgō

寶蓋　hōgai
寶篋印陀羅尼　hōkyōin-darani
寶藏　hōzō
懺法　senbō
懺悔　sange
爐壇　rodan
蘇悉地法　soshitsujihō
蘇悉地經　soshitsuji-kyō
蘇悉地羯羅經　soshitsujikara-
覺了　kakuryō　　　　　　Ｌkyō
覺者　kakusha

覺悟の蓮花　kakugo no renge

覺道　kakudō

觸　soku

譬喩　hiyu

釋　shaku

釋子　shakushi

釋氏　shakushi

釋門　shakumon

釋迦　shaka

釋教　shakkyō

釋眼儒心　shakugen jushin

釋摩訶衍論　shaku-makaen-ron

釋論　shakuron

鐘樓　shurō

闡提　sendai

鬪諍　tōjō

鰐口　waniguchi

21 STROKES

攝取　sesshu

攝受　shōju

攝意　shōi

櫻會　sakura-e

灌佛　kanbutsu

灌頂　kanjō

蘭若　rannya

護身　goshin

護法　gohō

護法香の火　gohōkō no hi

護法童子　gohōdōji

護持僧　gojisō

護國三部經　gokoku sanbukyō

辯才天　benzaiten

鐵崛地獄　tekkutsu jigoku

鐵湯　tettō

鐵窟苦所　tekkutsu kusho

鐵城　tetsujō

魔　ma

魔女　manyo

魔王　maō

魔民　mamin

魔往生　maōjō

魔界　makai

魔業　magō

魔道　madō

魔障　mashō

魔網　mamō

魔緣　maen

鶴林　kakurin

22 STROKES

權化　gonke

權者　gonja

權教　gonkyō

權現　gongen

權智　gonchi

權實　gonjitsu

灑水の印　shasui no in

灑水器　shasuiki

籠僧　komorisō

聽聞　chōmon

覽字　ranji
讀師　dokushi

讀經　dokyō
龕　gan

23 STROKES

變化　henge
變成男子　henjō nanshi
變成就　henjōju
顯宗　kenjū
顯密　kenmitsu
顯教　kengyō
顯道無二　kendō muni
顯德の成佛　kentoku no jōbutsu

驗　gen
驚覺　kyōkaku
體用　taiyū
體性　taishō
體解　taige
鷲峰　juhō
鷲嶺　juryō

24 STROKES

靈山　ryōzen
靈性　reishō
靈知　reichi
靈異記　ryōiki
靈智　reichi

靈龜　reiki
靈驗　reigen
靈鑑　reikan
靈鷲山　ryōjusen

25 STROKES

觀心　kanjin
觀世音　kanzeon
觀自在王　kanjizaiō
觀行　kangyō
觀佛三昧經　kanbutsu-zanmai-
觀念　kannen　　　　　└kyō
觀法　kanbō

觀音　kannon
觀智　kanchi
觀無量壽經　kanmuryōju-kyō
觀照　kanshō
觀經　kangyō
觀解　kange

26 STROKES

欝多羅僧　uttarasō

欝單越　uttan'otsu

讃佛　sanbutsu

27 STROKES

鑽仰　sangō

33 STROKES

矗言　sogon　　　　　矗細　sosai
矗強　sogō

	陣 *jin*		偈 *ge*
	眞 *shin*		祇, 耆 *gi*
CH'EN	沈, 塵 *jin*		其, 期 *go*
	瞋 *jin, shin*		啓 *kei*
CHENG	靜 *jō*		奇, 起, 綺, 器 *ki*
	正 *jō, shō*		乞 *kotsu*
	證 *shō*		七 *nana, nanuka,*
CH'ENG	澄 *chō*		*shichi*
	成, 城, 乘, 盛,		齊 *sai*
	誠 *jō*		砌 *zei*
	承 *jō, shō*	CHIA	迦, 跏, 嘉 *ka*
	稱 *shō*		加 *ka, ke*
CHI	計 *ge, ke*		家, 假, 袈 *ke*
	基, 給 *gi, ki*	CHIANG	降 *gō*
	極 *goku*		講 *kō*
	忌 *imi, ki*		將 *shō*
	寂 *jaku*	CHIAO	澆 *gyō*
	集 *jū, shū*		角 *kaku*
	稽, 髻, 繫 *kei*		脚 *kyaku*
	季, 記, 寄, 誋,		叫, 敎 *kyō*
	機 *ki*		焦 *shō*
	吉 *kichi, yoshi*	CH'IAO	巧 *gyō*
	己 *ko*		雀 *jaku*
	急 *kyū*		橋 *kyō*
	濟, 際 *sai*	CHIEH	街 *chimata*
	迹 *shaku*		界 *gai, kai*
	疾, 葵 *shitsu*		解 *ge*
	卽 *soku*		劫 *gō, kō*
	跡 *zeki*		竭, 羯 *ka, katsu*
CH'I	契 *chigiri, gei,*		戒, 階 *kai*
	kai		結 *ketsu*

	濁 *joku*		床 *yuka*
CHʻO	綽 *shaku*	**CHUI**	追 *tsui*
CHOU	舟, 咒 *ju*	**CHʻUI**	槌 *chi*
	呪 *ju, shu*		吹, 垂 *sui*
	周 *shu, shū*	**CHUN**	准 *jun*
	州, 洲 *shū*	**CHʻUN**	純, 淳 *jun*
CHʻOU	稠 *chū*	**CHUNG**	中 *chū*
CHU	竹 *chiku*		重 *jū*
	註 *chū*		終 *jū, shu*
	著 *jaku*		衆, 鐘 *shu*
	竺 *jiku*		種 *shu, su*
	助 *jo*	**CHÜ**	居 *go, ko*
	住 *jū*		具 *gu*
	諸 *sho*		聚 *ju*
	拄, 珠 *shu*		鞠 *kiku*
	主 *shu, zu*		舉 *ko*
CHʻU	畜 *chiku*		俱 *ku*
	除 *jo*		咀 *so*
	初, 杵, 處 *sho*	**CHʻÜ**	曲 *goku, gyoku,*
	閦 *shuku*		*kyoku*
	出 *shutsu*		去 *ko*
	觸 *soku*		瞿 *ku*
	蒭 *su*		佉 *kya*
	厨 *zu*		取, 趣 *shu*
CHUAN	專 *sen*	**CHÜAN**	卷 *kan*
	轉 *ten*		眷, 羂 *ken*
CHʻUAN	傳 *den*	**CHʻÜAN**	權 *gon*
	川 *kawa*		犬 *inu*
CHUANG	奘 *jō*		勸 *kan*
	莊 *shō*		詮 *sen*
CHʻUANG	幢 *dō*		全 *zen*

	溪, 醯 *kei*		心	*jin, kokoro,*
	喜 *ki*			*shin*
	細 *sai*		信	*shin*
	西 *sai, sei*	HSING	行	*an, gyō*
	席 *seki*		形	*gyō*
	錫 *shaku*		興	*kō*
	悉 *shitsu*		星	*sei*
	息 *soku*		性, 惺	*shō*
HSIA	下 *a, ge, shimo*	HSIU	修	*osa(mu),*
	夏 *ge*			*shi, shu*
	遐 *ka*		脩	*shu*
HSIANG	降 *gō*	HSIUNG	匈	*gai*
	祥 *jō*	HSÜ	虛	*ko*
	向, 香 *kō*		噓	*kyo*
	相, 想 *sō*		須	*shu*
	象, 像 *zō*	HSÜAN	玄	*gen*
HSIAO	小 *ko, shō*		宣, 選	*sen*
	効 *kō*	HSÜEH	學	*gaku*
	孝 *kō, kyō*		血	*ketsu*
	曉 *kyō*		雪	*setsu*
	笑 *shō*	HSÜN	旬, 巡	*jun*
HSIEH	邪 *ja*		熏, 薰	*kun*
	懈 *ke*	HU	互, 護, 翩	*go*
	血 *ketsu*	HUA	化	*ge, ke*
	脇 *kyō*		花	*hana, ke*
	寫, 謝 *sha*		華	*ke*
HSIEN	現 *gen*		話	*wa*
	賢 *gen, ken*	HUAI	懷, 壞	*e*
	顯 *ken*	HUAN	幻, 患, 還	*gen*
	仙, 先, 僊 *sen*		喚, 緩	*kan*
HSIN	欣 *gon*	HUANG	皇	*ō*

HUI	廻, 惠, 會, 慧 *e*		JIH	日 *hi, ni, nichi,*
	悔 *ge*			*nit-/nis-*
	恚 *i* (*ni*)		JO	若 *nya*
HUN	昏 *kon*		JOU	柔 *jū, nyū*
HUNG	紅 *gu*			肉 *niku*
	弘 *gu, kō*		JU	儒 *ju*
HUO	火 *hi, ka, ko*			辱 *niku*
	活 *katsu*			如 *nyo*
	貨 *ke*			入 *nyū*
	惑 *waku*		JUAN	軟 *nan*
I (YI)	依 *e*		JUI	叡 *ei*
	衣 *e, koromo*			瑞 *zui*
	役 *en*		JUNG	榮 *ei*
	義, 儀, 疑, 顗,			融 *yū*
	議 *gi*		KAI	蓋 *gai*
	已, 以, 伊, 夷,		K'AI	開 *kai*
	易, 異, 意, 醫		KAN	甘, 乾, 感 *kan*
	i		K'AN	龕 *gan*
	一 *ichi*			看, 勘 *kan*
	逸 *itsu*		KANG	剛 *gō*
	詣 *mōde*			綱 *gō, ki*
	億, 憶 *oku*		K'ANG	康 *kō*
	益 *yaku*		KAO	告 *gō*
	遺 *yui*			高 *kō*
JAN	然, 燃 *nen*		KEI	給 *gik-*
	染 *sen, zen*		K'E	可, 窠 *ka*
JE	熱 *netsu*		KEN	根 *kon*
JEN	恁 *in*		KO	各, 閣 *kaku*
	人 *jin, nin*			割, 渴 *katsu*
	仁 *ni, nin*			箇 *ko*
	任, 忍 *nin*			隔 *kyaku*

KOU	狗 *gu*		勒 *roku*
	鉤 *kō*	LENG	冷 *rei*
	垢 *ku*		楞 *ryō*
K'OU	口 *ku*	LI	禮 *rai, rei*
KU	古, 股, 孤, 鈷		例 *rei*
	ko		利, 梨, 理, 裡,
	鼓 *ku*		裏, 蓻, 離 *ri*
K'U	苦, 庫 *ku*		力 *riki*
K'UAI	快 *ke*		歷, 曆 *ryaku*
KUAN	官, 貫, 灌, 觀		立 *ryū, tachi*
	kan		里 *sato*
KUANG	光, 廣 *kō*	LIANG	良 *ra, rō, ryō*
K'UANG	曠 *kō*		兩, 梁, 量 *ryō*
	誑 *ō*	LIAO	了, 料 *ryō*
KUI	鬼, 歸, 貴, 龜 *ki*	LIEH	劣 *retsu*
K'UI	愧 *gi*	LIEN	蓮 *hachisu, ren*
KUNG	供 *gu, ku*		連, 練 *ren*
	宮 *gū, ku, kyū,*	LIN	林, 恡, 悋, 臨
	miya		*rin*
	公 *kō*	LING	鈴, 嶺 *rei*
	功 *kō, ku*		靈 *rei, ryō*
	工, 恭 *ku*		令, 領 *ryō*
K'UNG	孔 *ku*	LIU	六 *roku*
	空 *kū*		流, 琉, 留, 瑠
KUO	果, 過 *ka*		*ru*
	國 *koku*	LO	羅, 螺 *ra*
LAI	來, 賴 *rai*		落 *ra, raku*
LAN	嵐, 藍, 蘭, 覽	LOU	漏 *ro*
	ran		樓 *rō*
LAO	老, 牢, 勞 *rō*	LU	露, 廬, 爐, 鷺
LE	樂 *gyō, raku*		*ro*

		/has-/hat-	PIEH	別	betsu
PAI	唄	bai	PIEN	便, 辨, 辯	ben
	白	byaku, haku		遍, 邊, 變	hen
	拜	hai, pai	P'IEN	偏	hen
	百	hyaku	PIN	賓	bin
PAN	伴	ban	P'IN	頻	bin
	半, 般, 斑	han		品	bon, hon
P'AN	盤	ban		貧	hin
	槃	han	PING	病	byō
PANG	謗	bō, hō	P'ING	平	byō, hei
PAO	薄	ba, haku		瓶	byō
	寶	hō	PO	薄	ba, haku
	報	hō, mukui		波	ha
P'AO	袍	hō		鉢	hachi, hatsu
PEI	被, 備	bi		撥	hatsu
	悲	hi		搏	tan
	北	hoku	P'O	婆	ba
PEN	本	bon, hon, pon		破, 頗	ha
	賁	fun	PU	布, 補	fu
P'EN	盆	bon		不	fu, pu
P'ENG	朋	hō	P'U	菩	bo
	捧	sasage		普	fu
PI	鼻	bi		葡	puku
	比	bi, hi	SA	薩	satsu
	蔽	hei		灑	sha
	彼, 祕	hi	SAI	塞	soku
	必, 畢, 筆	hitsu	SAN	三	mi, san, zan
P'I	毘, 毗	bi		散, 傘	san
	譬	hi	SANG	桑	sō
	錍	bei	SE	色	shiki
PIAO	表	hyō		瑟	shitsu

	瞬 *shun*	T'AN	談, 壇, 檀 *dan*	
SHUO	說 *setsu*		曇 *don*	
SO	所 *dokoro, sho*		探 *tan*	
	鎖 *sa*		貪 *ton*	
	索 *saku*	TANG	當, 黨 *tō*	
	娑 *sha*	T'ANG	堂 *dō*	
SOU	藪 *sō*		湯 *tō*	
SSU	似 *ji*	TAO	倒, 道, 導 *dō*	
	寺 *ji, tera*		刀, 忉, 盜, 禱	
	四, 司, 思, 斯,		*tō*	
	絲 *shi*	TE	德 *doku, toku*	
	死 *shi, shini*		得 *toku*	
SU	宿 *shuku*	T'E	特 *doku*	
	素, 酥, 蘇 *so*	TENG	等, 燈 *tō*	
	速 *soku*	T'ENG	騰 *tō*	
	俗 *zoku*	TI	地 *chi, ji*	
SUI	歲 *sai*		第 *dai*	
	隨 *zui*		弟 *de*	
SUNG	頌 *ju*		諦 *tai*	
	誦 *ju, zu*		帝 *tai, tei*	
	送 *sō*	T'I	提, 醍, 題 *dai*	
TA	大 *dai, ō, tai*		體 *tai*	
	達 *da(tsu)*		剃 *tei*	
T'A	闥 *datsu*	TIAO	調 *chō, jō*	
	他 *ta*	T'IAO	條 *jō*	
	塔 *ta(tsu), tō*	T'IEH	鐵 *tetsu*	
TAI	代, 怠 *dai*	TIEN	殿 *den*	
	待 *tai*		典, 奠, 點, 顚	
T'AI	太, 台, 臺, 胎		*ten*	
	tai	T'IEN	天 *ama, ten*	
TAN	單, 彈 *tan*		田 *den*	

T'UNG	同, 童 *dō*	YAO	藥 *yaku*
	通 *tsū, zū*		要 *yō*
TZU	字, 自, 茲, 滋 *ji*	YEH	業 *gō*
	子, 恣, 紫, 資,		葉 *shō*
	緇 *shi*		也, 夜, 耶, 野 *ya*
T'ZU	慈, 辭 *ji*	YEN	炎, 延, 宴, 莚,
	此 *shi*		琰, 演, 閻 *en*
WAI	外 *ge*		厭 *en, on*
WAN	晚 *ban*		雁 *gan*
	萬 *ban, man*		眼, 驗 *gen*
WANG	妄, 忘, 望 *mō*		言, 嚴 *gon*
	王, 往 *ō*	YIN	引, 印, 因, 婬,
WEI	穢, 衞 *e*		淫 *in*
	位, 威, 畏, 韋,		陰 *in, on*
	爲, 違 *i*		音, 飲, 隱 *on*
	未, 味, 微 *mi*	YING	影 *ei, yō*
	唯, 維 *yui*		迎 *gō, kō,*
WEN	文, 問, 聞 *mon*		*mukae*
WO	臥 *bushi, ga*		應 *ō*
	我 *ga*		櫻 *sakura*
WU	無 *bu, mu*		瓔 *yō*
	五 *go, itsutsu*	YU	友 *tomo*
	悟 *go, satori*		右, 有, 優 *u*
	汚 *ma*		由, 遊 *yu*
	物 *mono, motsu*	YUNG	永 *ei, yō*
	務 *mu*		用 *yō, yū*
	烏 *u*		勇 *yu*
YA	牙 *kiba*	YÜ	語 *go*
YANG	仰 *gō*		御 *go, mi, on*
	央 *ō*		獄 *goku*
	羊, 養 *yō*		愚 *gu*

III. JAPANESE INDEX

(excluding main entries)

I

K

M

IV. CHINESE INDEX

V. SANSKRIT AND PALI INDEX

C

D

SUPPLEMENT

This Supplement represents part of the work which has been done since the first edition was published in 1984. The author wishes to express his gratitude to the Bukkyō Bunka Kenkyūsho, Ryukoku University, for affording him the research grant for the period 1985–87, which made it possible to work with Professor P.G. O'Neill as before. It is through the kindness of the publisher, Nagata Bunshōdō, that a supplement has been added to the third edition.

The author's sincere thanks are due to Profesor O'Neill for his continued assistance in major stages of publication and to Prof. Hoyu Ishida of Shiga Prefectural Junior College, Prof. Zuiyo Sasaki of Ikenobo Junior College and his wife, Mrs. Zuie Sasaki, for their kind help with the proof-reading.

The author wishes to take this opportunity to make an appeal to scholars of Buddhism and Japanology. Since his wish is to compile a more complete dictionary adequate to the needs of students of Asian studies as well as general users, he would be grateful to receive any lists of Buddhist terms and names with explanations and references which such scholars may have available. These will be given full consideration with a view to incorporating them fully or in part into a new edition with, of course, due acknowledgement.

H. Inagaki

Takatsuki, February, 1988

EXPLANATORY NOTES

This Supplement contains about 450 additional entry-words and phrases, including Buddhist terms used widely in modern Japan. The Japanese classics from which most of the entry-words originate can be classed into four categories: (1) *Nihon-ryōiki*, (2) Pure Land Buddhist texts, (3) Zeami's essays on *Nō* and (4) *Nō* texts.

(1) *Nihon-ryōiki* 日本靈異記 (abbreviated as R.) is the popular name for *Nihonkoku-genpō-zenmaku-ryōiki* 日本國現報善惡靈異記 ('*Miraculous stories told in Japan concerning the retributions for good and evil acts in the present life*'), 3 fasc., compiled by Kyōkai 景戒, a monk of the Yakushiji, who is believed to have flourished in the early 9th century. The text in NKT. Vol. 70 has been used. Volumes and sections are indicated by Roman and Arabic figures, respectively.

(2) The Pure Land Buddhist texts employed as source references are as follows: a) *Anjin-ketsujōshō* 安心決定抄 ('*Tract on the firm establishment of faith*') (=AK.), by an unknown author; b) *Jōdo wasan* 淨土和讃 ('*Hymns on the Pure Land*') (=JW.) by Shinran 親鸞 (1173–1262); and c) part of *Tannishō* 歎異抄 ('*Notes lamenting differences*') (=TAN.) attributed to Yuien 唯圓, Shinran's disciple. Numerals following JW. are hymn numbers and those following TAN. indicate chapters. The texts used are the *Shinshū shōgyō zensho* editions, Kyoto, Vols. 2 and 3. For readily available texts of the *Jōdo wasan* and *Tannishō* containing both the Japanese originals and English translations, *Ryukoku Translation Series* (Ryukoku University, Kyoto), Vols. 2 and 4, are recommended.

(3) Zeami 世阿彌 (1363–1443), the greatest figure in the

history of *Nō*, recorded his teachings in a number of essays; Buddhist terms found in the following are listed: *Fūshikaden* 風姿花傳 (=FK.), *Sarugaku dangi* 申樂談儀 (=SG.) and *Shūgyoku tokka* 拾玉得花 (=ST.). These works are contained in NKT. Vol. 65.

(4) The *Nō* texts from which entry-words have been taken are as follows: *Arashiyama* 嵐山 (=ARA.), *Atsumori* 敦盛 (=ATSU.), *Bashō* 芭蕉 (=BA.), *Tōboku* 東北 (=BOKU.), *Chikubushima* 竹生島 (=CHIKU.), *Eguchi* 江口 (=EGU.), *Izutsu* 井筒 (=IZU.), *Kamo* 賀茂 (=KAMO), *Kiyotsune* 清經 (=KIYO.), *Nonomiya* 野宮 (=NONO.), *Sanemori* 實盛 (=SANE.), *Tadanori* 忠度 (=TADA.), *Takasago* 高砂 (=TAKA.), *Tamura* 田村 (=MURA.), *Teike* 定家 (=TEI.), *Tōbōsaku* 東方朔 (=TO.), *Tomonaga* 朝長 (=TOMO.), *Uneme* 采女 (=UNE.), *Yashima* 八島 (=YASHI.), *Yōrō* 養老 (=YO.) and *Yorimasa* 賴政 (=YORI.). The texts in NKT. Vols. 40 and 41 and *Nihon koten bungaku zenshū*, Shōgakukan, Vols. 33 and 34 have been used.

A

Aimō no gō 愛網の業 'The karma of being caught in the net of love and attachment'; karmic bondage caused by attachment. [R. III–38.]

Aishū 愛執 'Love and attachment'; attachment.

Aizen Daimyōjin 愛染大明神 Refers to Aizen Myōō*. [Yashi.]

Akuma 惡魔 'A devil'; Sk. *māra*; see *ma*. [Ara.]

Akunin 惡人 'An evil person.'

~ **jōbutsu** --成佛 'Evil persons becoming buddhas.' [Tan. 3.]

Ango-e 安居會 'A lecture-meeting during the *ango** period. [R. III–19.]

Anjin-ketsujōshō 安心決定抄 *'Tract on the Firm Establishment of Faith'*; the author is unknown but is presumed to have been someone closely related to the Seizan* sect. Rennyo found this to be a highly inspirational book and compared it to a gold mine. [AK.]

Anraku 安樂 'Peace and bliss'; n. of Amida's* land; Sk. Sukhāvatī. [JW. 17.]

Anrakukoku 安樂國 'The Land of Peace and Bliss'; another name for Amida's* Pure Land. [Sane.]

Anraku sekai 安樂世界 'The World of Peace and Bliss'; Amida's* Pure Land. [Mura.]

Anryū 安立 'Securely establishing.' I. Placing someone securely, as in the Buddhist path. II. Provisional establishment, as of a reality-principle. III. Peace of mind, security. [FK.]

Ariwara-dera 在原寺 A temple in Nara constructed by Ariwara Narihira 在原業平 (825–880), one of the 'six poetic geniuses' (*rokkasen* 六歌仙). [Izu.]

B

Bagaba 婆伽婆 Sk. *bhagavat*; see *bagabon*. [JW. 33.]

Baku 縛 'Binding'; spellbinding; see *jubaku*. [R. I–15.]

Bansoku 幡足 Perhaps 'stripes attached to a banner.' [R. II–Pre.]

Batsunanda 跋難陀 Sk. Upananda; one of the eight great dragon kings; see *hachidai-ryūō*. [JW. 103.]

Bensō 辨宗 N. of a monk of Daianji*. [R. III–3.]

Betchi no gugan 別異の弘願 'The very special great vow'; Amida's* vows distinguish themselves from those of other buddhas in that they promise salvation for ordinary beings filled with evil passions; in this sense, the term specifically refers to his 18th vow. The term comes from the *Gengi-bun**. Cf. *hongan* and *hongan no mon*. [AK.]

[Betsuji 別時]

~ **no shōmyō** --の稱名 'The *nenbutsu** practice performed for a fixed period of time.' [Sane.]

Binaya-kyō 鼻奈耶經 Refers to *Binaya* 鼻奈耶 [TT. 24, No. 1464]. [R. II–5.]

Binpatsu 鬢髮 'Beard and hair.'

~ **o teijo** --を剃除 'To shave one's beard and hair (to become a monk)'; to take the tonsure.

Bōfu hakurei 亡婦魄靈 'The soul of a deceased woman.' [Izu.]

Bongu 凡愚 'An ordinary, ignorant person.'

Bongyō 凡形 'Appearance of an ordinary person.' [R. III–30.]

Bonji 凡地 A short form for *bonbu no jii* 凡夫の地位 'the stage of an ordinary person' as opposed to that of an enlightened sage. [JW. 93.]

Bosatsu-yōraku-hongō-kyō 菩薩瓔珞本業經 '*Sutra on the Bodhi-*

sattvas' Original Acts which are their Ornaments'; 2 fasc.; tr. by Chu Fo-nien 竺佛念 [TT. 24, No. 1485]. This sutra explains, among other things, the 42 stages of a bodhisattva, based on which T'ien-tai (Tendai*) developed the theory of 52 stages (*gojūni-i**).

Bōshin 亡心 'A departed soul'; a ghost. [Yashi.]

Buji 無事 1. Having nothing to do; having nothing demanding to do before attaining enlightenment. 2. Without hindrance; free of obstruction. [Kiyo.]

[Butsu 佛**]**

~ **nehan no hi** - 涅槃の日 'The memorial day of the Buddha's passing into Nirvana'; the 15th of the second month; cf. *nehan-e*. [R. III–30.]

Butsu-e 佛慧 Pronounced '*butte*'; 'the Buddha's wisdom.' [JW. 50.]

Butsugan no tai ni kaeru 佛願の體にかえる 'Return to the essence of (Amida) Buddha's vow'; Amida's* vow is the very essence or substance of the faith and practice for one's birth in the Pure Land. When one has attained the absolute faith, it does not stay in one's heart but returns to Amida's vow from which it originated. [AK.]

Butsuriki 佛力 'A buddha's power.' [FK.]

Butsujin sanbō 佛神三寶 'Buddhas, gods and the three treasures (buddha, dharma and sangha)'; cf. *sanbō*.

~ **mo sutehate tamō** ---- も捨て果て給ふ 'Buddhas, gods and the three treasures have forsaken me.' [Kiyo.]

Button 佛恩 'The Buddha's benevolence; one's indebtedness to the Buddha.' [JW. 50.]

Byakudō 白堂 'Announcing the wishes of a devotee to the inner sanctuary.' [R. III–3.]

Byōdō daie 平等大慧 'The great wisdom which works without discrimination'; the buddha's unbiased wisdom. [Yori.]

Byōdōgaku 平等覺 'Equal enlightenment'; one who has been enlightened to ultimate equality and sameness of all existences; refers to Amida*. [JW. 5.]

Byōdōriki 平等力 'Equal power; equalizing power'; refers to Amida*, for he makes those born in his land attain the equal qualities in mind and body. [JW. 22.]

Byōdōshin 平等心 'Mind of equality; non-discriminative mind';
one who has attained enlightenment is above discrimination and
looks upon all living beings with compassion in a spirit of complete equality. [JW. 92.]

C

Chiekōbutsu 智慧光佛 'Buddha of Wisdom Light'; one of Amida's*
12 names; cf. *jūnikōbutsu*. [JW. 11.]

Chiji no sō 知寺の僧 'A priest supervising all the temple business.'
[R. II–32.]

Chikai no ami 誓ひの網 'The net of the vow'; Amida's* vow of
salvation. [Sane.]

Chikan 智鑒 'Mirror of wisdom'; metaphorically, superior wisdom.
[R. I–22.]

Chikō 智光 I. Jñānaprabha; an Indian master who dwelt at
Nālanda. One of the chief disciples of Śīlabhadra (Kaigen 戒賢),
and well-known for his extensive knowledge of Buddhism and
non-Buddhist teachings. When Hsüan-chuang (Genjō*) visited
Nālanda, he studied with Jñānaprabha, and after returning home
to China, he corresponded with him to ask him questions about
the Buddhist doctrine.
II. A Sanron* master of the 8th century; he learned the Sanron
teaching from Chizō 智藏 of the Gangōji* Temple, and was
celebrated as one of his two leading disciples, the other being
Raikō 禮光 (also 頼光). After Raikō's death, Chikō had a dream
that Raikō had been reborn in Amida's* Pure Land. Thereupon,
he had an artist paint a picture of the Pure Land he had seen,
built a hall in the premises of the Gangōji and placed the picture
in it. This painting came to be known as the 'Chikō mandala'.
[R. II–7.]

Chikō mandara 智光曼陀羅 'Chikō mandala'; the Pure Land mandala painted on the basis of Chikō's* dream. Amida* and his two attendant bodhisattvas are at the centre, with various adornments around them.

Chimoku gyōsoku 智目行足 'The eye of wisdom and the legs of practice'; the cultivation of wisdom and the performance of meritorious practices are compared to the eye and legs, for together they lead to enlightenment.   [AK.]

Chinzei 鎮西 The Chinzei school; one of the schools of the Jōdo* sect founded by Benchō 辨長. After receiving the Pure Land teaching from his master, Hōnen*, Benchō returned to his native place in Kyushu in 1204 and built the Zendōji 善導寺 there. While he extensively propagated the *nenbutsu** teaching in Kyushu, his chief disciple Ryōchū 良忠 engaged in spreading the teaching in the Kanto area and also in Kyoto. This school developed into six subschools, of which the Shirahata-ryū 白籏流 has thrived most and is now considered to be the orthodox school of the Jōdo sect. The general head temple (*sōhonzan* 總本山) of the Shirahata-ryū is the Chion-in 知恩院; the Zōjōji 増上寺 in Tokyo is one of the major head temples (*daihonzan* 大本山). The number of temples belonging to this school is now more than 7,000.

Chokumei 勅命 'The emperor's order'; refers to Amida's* call summoning people to take refuge in him.

Chōnichigakkō 超日月光 'Light outshining sun and moon'; one of Amida's* 12 names; cf. *jūnikōbutsu*. [JW. 14.]

Chōsai yōkō 兆載永劫 'An incalculable number of kalpas'; *chō* and *sai* are large numbers said to be equal to a million and to 1 followed by 44 zeros, respectively. The term refers to the length of time during which Amida* performed his bodhisattva practices for the sake of all living beings. [AK.]

Chūyō 中夭 'Dying young; untimely death.' [JW. 99.]

D

Daian'i 大安慰 'The great consoler'; refers to Amida*; he is so called because one finds in him an inexhaustible source of consolation. [JW. 10.]

Daianji 大安寺 A Shingon* temple in Yamato Province (present-day Nara Prefecture); one of the seven great temples (*shichidaiji**) in Nara. Originally built by Prince Shōtoku*, it was moved to a new site near the Kudara River by Emperor Jomei 舒明 and renamed Kudara-daiji 百済大寺. It was moved again by Emperor Tenmu 天武 and the name was changed to Daikan-daiji 大官大寺. When the capital was moved to Nara in 710, the temple was also moved there. It was remodelled in 729 and renamed as Daianji. As the temple is located in the south of the new capital, it was popularly called Nandaiji 南大寺. In 829 Kūkai* was appointed head priest (*bettō**). Only a small hall has survived natural calamities until today. [R. II–24, 28.]

Daiba 提婆 See Daibadatta. [FK.]

Daibyakugosha 大白牛車 'A cart drawn by a great white bullock'; as it appears in the parable of a burning house in the *Hoke-kyō**, it represents the supreme One-Vehicle teaching (*ichijō**). See *kataku-yu*. [R. III–38.]

Daihōdō-kyō 大方等経 Abbr. of *daihōdō-daishū-kyō* 大方等大集経; see *Daishū-kyō*. [R. I–20.]

Daijakujō 大寂定 'The great tranquility samādhi,' I. Originally, refers to Nirvana in which all passions are calmed and all mental functions cease. II. The name of the samādhi (*sanmai**) which the Buddha entered before preaching the *Muryōju-kyō**. [JW. 53.]

Daijōbu 大丈夫 'A great man'; a bodhisattva who is devoted to cultivating virtue, compassion and wisdom.

Daijōbu-ron 大丈夫論 '*The Discourse on the Great Man*'; written by Daibara 提婆羅 (Deva); tr. by Tao-t'ai 道泰; 2 fasc. [TT. 30, No. 1577]. This work praises the virtue of charity and explains how it should be practised. Cf. *Jōbu-ron*.

Daimyōjin 大明神 'A great illuminating divine being'; a general term of respect for a god, demi-god or spirit that is believed to have especially strong power. [Une.]

Daiōgu 大應供 'A great arhat'; an epithet for Amida*; cf. *ōgu*. [JW. 8.]

Daishinkai 大心海 'The great mind-ocean'; refers to the magnanimous, all-embracing mind of Amida*; hence, Amida himself. [JW. 18.]

Daishinriki 大心力 'Great mind-power'; refers to Amida's* great spiritual power which has fulfilled his vow; used as an epithet for him. [JW. 27.]

Daishutaraku 大修多羅供 Also pronounced *daisutaraku*; 'fund for an unusually large group of monks to study and discuss a particular sutra (e.g., *Daihannya-kyō*)' at *Daianji**, Nara; cf. *jōshutaraku* and *shutarabun*. [R. II–28.]

Dan 檀 I. Sk. *dāna*; 'donation; charity.' II. Refers to *sendan** 'sandalwood'; cf. *danzō*.

Dannotsu 檀越 Sk. *dānapati*; translated as *seshu* 施主, *danshu* 檀主; a donor; also used in addressing the second person. [R. II–32.]

Danshu 檀主 'A donor'; see *dannotsu*. [R. I–10, II–36.]

Danzō 檀像 'A sandalwood statue.' [R. II–39.]

Datta 達多 Short for *Daibadatta**. [JW. 78.]

Dentōjūi 傳燈住位 'The rank of dwelling in the transmission of the lamp'; the third of the six ranks of priests established in 798. See *rokui*. [R. III–38.]

Dō 幢 Sk. *dhvaja*, *ketu* or *patākā*; Japanese reading *hataboko*; a kind of banner tied to the top of a pole or hung on a pillar. Originally used in India as an ensign of a king when leading an army, it was adopted into Buddhism as an ensign of a buddha or a bodhisattva on the analogy of leading an army to defeat devils. Also often used as a decoration in a temple.

Dōji 童子 'A boy'. I. Sk. *kumāra*; a boy over 8 who serves monks from a desire to become a monk himself. II. Refers to a bodhisattva, since he is considered as a son of a buddha.

Dōjō 道場 'A hall' where the Buddha is worshipped and the Buddhist Way is practised; also a simple temple building or a temple at an early stage of development.

Dōkō 道光 'Enlightenment-brilliance'; the radiance emanating from Buddha's enlightenment; cf. *dō* III. [JW. 9.]

Dōkyō 道鏡 A monk of the Hossō* sect, whose lay name was Yuge 弓削. He studied the Hossō teaching under Gien*, and then entered Kazuragi-san 葛木山 to practise esoteric Buddhism. In 761 he successfully prayed for the recovery from illness of the ex-emperor Kōken 孝謙, after which he won imperial patronage. In 764 he was given the title of *Daijin-zenji* 大臣禪師 'Minister Zenji,' and in the following year, *Dajōdaijin-zenji* 太政大臣禪師 'Prime Minister Zenji,' and again in 766 the title of *Hōō** 法王 'Dharma-king.' He thus held the highest political and religious power. When he sought to claim the throne, a loyal subject, Wake no Kiyomaro 和氣淸麿, intervened and stopped him. Later, in 770, he was banished to Shimotsuke Province (now Tochigi Prefecture) and died there in 772. [R. III–38.]

Donmukatsu 曇無竭 Ch. T'an-wu-chieh; a monk of the Liu-Sung dynasty. Having heard of Fa-hsien's 法顯 (Hokken*) pilgrimage to India, he himself set out together with 25 monks to visit sacred places there in 420. After returning home, he translated sutras, including the *Kanzeon-bosatsu- juki-kyō**.

Dōshō 道照 Also 道昭; a native of Kawachi Province (now part of Osaka Prefecture); his family name was Funamuraji 船連. He first studied Buddhism at the Gangōji* Temple, and went to T'ang China in 653, where he learned the Hossō* teaching from Hsüan-chuang (Genjō*) and also Zen from Hui-man (Eman 慧滿). After he returned home in 660, he built a hall in the compound of the Gangōji Temple and propagated the Hossō teaching. This is the first transmission of the Hossō doctrine; this and its second transmission from China have been traditionally called *Nanjiden* 南寺傳 (Southern-Temple tradition) as distinguished from the third and the fourth ones which have been called *Hokujiden* 北寺傳

(Northern-Temple, i.e. Kōfukuji*, tradition). He was appointed *daisōzu** in 698 and died later in the same year at the age of 72. [R. I–22, 28.]

E

E 會 Same as *hōe** 法會.

Eka 依果 A contraction of *ehō** *no ka* 依報の果 'the fruition or result (of one's karma) manifested as the dependent reward'; refers to the glorious adornments of Amida's* land. [JW. 45.]

Ekō-hotsuganshin 廻向發願心 'Aspiring to be born in the Pure Land by transferring one's merit of practice towards it'; one of the three thoughts or aspects of faith mentioned in the *Kanmuryōju-kyō**; see *sanshin* 三心. [Sane.]

Ekoku 穢國 'A defiled land'; specifically refers to this world, known in Buddhism as Sahā (*Shaba** 娑婆). [JW. 17.]

Endonkai 圓頓戒 'The precepts for perfect and sudden (enlightenment)'; also *daijō endonkai* 大乘圓頓戒; the Mahayana precepts to be observed by bodhisattvas; transmitted to Japan by Saichō*. They include the ten major precepts (*jūjūkai** 十重戒) and the forty-eight minor ones (*shijūhachi kyōkai** 四十八輕戒) of the *Bonmō-kyō**. Unlike the Hinayana precepts (*shōjōkai** 小乘戒), which only benefit the practitioner and whose substance (*kaitai* 戒體) perishes at the time of death, these Mahayana precepts are primarily for the benefit of other beings and their substance continues to be active indefinitely.

Enra 閻羅 'Yama'; see *Enma*. [R. II–7.]

Enzū 圓通 'Perfect penetration'; refers to the ultimate principle, True Thusness (*shinnyo**), for it penetrates everything and nothing exists without it. [JW. 111.]

Eshō 惠勝 I. A monk of Engōji 延興寺. [R. I–20.] II. A monk of Daianji*, Nara. [R. III–24.]

F

Fudankōbutsu 不斷光佛 'Buddha of Unceasing Light'; one of Amida's* 12 names; he is so called because his light illumines the world unceasingly; cf. *jūnikōbutsu*. [JW. 12.]

Fujō 不定 'Indeterminate.'

∼ **no shushō** --の種性 'The indeterminate nature'; the class of people whose destiny is not determined. See *sanjō fujōshō* under *goshō kakubetsu*; see also *shushō*. [R. III–38.]

Fujōhō 不定法 'Impermanent law'; the law or teaching which is subject to change. [ST.]

Fukashigison 不可思議尊 'The inconceivable sage'; an epithet for Amida*; he is so called because his accomplishments for the sake of sentient beings are beyond our comprehension. [JW. 37.]

Fukasuisha 不果遂者 '(If ...) is not fulfilled'; the phrase, which is part of the text of the 20th vow of Amida*, means that he vowed not to become a buddha unless salvation of *nenbutsu** practitioners is fulfilled; cf. *kasui no gan*. [JW. 64.]

Fukuden'e 福田衣 'Merit-field robe'; another name for *kesa** 袈裟; the Buddhist robe is so called because one who wears it or sees and pays respect to it gains great merit, and also because the pattern of the robe is like paddies and fields. [R. III–17.]

Fundarike 芬陀利華 Sk. *puṇḍarīka*, 'a white lotus'; used in the *Kanmuryōju-kyō** as a word of high praise for practitioners of the nenbutsu*; cf. *goshu kayo* and *myōkōnin*.

Fukuin 福因 'Meritorious cause'; merit-accruing acts which are the cause of a better life in the future. [R. II–28.]

Fushō 鳧鐘 'A bell made by (a Chinese named) Fushi 鳧子'; used as a gong to accompany the *nenbutsu** recitation. [Atsu.]

Fushu shōgaku 不取正覺 '(I) will not attain perfect enlightenment'; see *nyaku-fushōja*.

Futai 不退 'Not falling back'; Sk. *avinivartanīya, avaivartika*; unyielding, steadfast; proceeding to the highest enlightenment without falling back to a lower spiritual stage. I. Generally, in Mahayana, this corresponds to the 41st stage in the 52-stage scale, at which the bodhisattvas attain undefiled wisdom or insight and are assured of attaining buddhahood. II. In the Jōdoshin* sect, this is said of the moment of awakening to the pure faith, at which aspirants become assured of attaining birth in the Pure Land and of realizing enlightenment.

G

Gakkō 月光 'Moonlight'; Sk. Candraprabha. I. One of King Bimbisāra's (Binbashara*) ministers. [JW. 76, 78.] II. One of the two attendant bodhisattvas of Yakushi* Buddha, the other being Nikkō*. [Tai. 3, 9, 18.]

Gakutō 學頭 'A superintendent of a sect or school'; one of the three main posts in their administrative structure, lower than *bettō** and *sangō**; one in charge of financial affairs. [R. II–28.]

Gangōji 元興寺 One of the seven big temples in Nara (*nanto no shichidaiji**); when first built by Soga no Umako 蘇我馬子 in 569, it was called Hōkōji 法興寺, also Asuka-dera 飛鳥寺 and Asuka-no-ōdera 飛鳥大寺. Later the name of the temple was changed to Gangōji. First, the Korean monks Eji 慧慈 and Esō 慧聰 were invited to live there. In 579 a copper image of the Buddha, 16 feet high, was made and enshrined in the temple by the order of Prince Shōtoku*. In 598 Ekan 慧灌 of Korea established his residence at this temple, and propagated the teaching of Sanran*. When the capital was moved to Nara (710), the main part of the temple was also moved there (716) and was called Shingangōji 新元興寺. Later, Chikō* 智光 and Raikō 禮光 came to dwell there and further propagated the Sanron teaching. In addition, Dōshō 道昭, Chitsū 智通 and Chitatsu 智達 dwelt at this temple and promulgated the Hossō* teaching; the school of the Hossō sect transmitted there was called *Nanji-den** 南寺傳 (Southern-Temple tradition), as contrasted to the school of the Hossō sect which thrived at the Kōfukuji* Temple, Nara, called *Hokuji-den** 北寺傳 (Northern-Temple tradition).

Gangyō enman 願行圓滿 'Consummation of the vow and practice'; the same as *gangyō jōju**. [AK.]

Gangyō jōju 願行成就 'Accomplishing the vow and practice'; said of Amida's* fulfilment of the vow and practice necessary for the aspirant's birth in the Pure Land. The phrase '*namu amida butsu*' is construed as containing in it both the vow (*namu*) and the practice (*amida butsu*). For this reason, it is said that those who believe in the phrase and recite it can attain birth in the Pure Land. Cf. *myōgō* and *rokujishaku*. [AK.]

Ganriki 願力 'Vow-power'; the power produced when a bodhisattva makes a vow; once generated, it continues to work to fulfil the vow. [JW. 27.]

Ganshu 願主 'One who has made a special vow.'

Gayajō 迦耶城 'Gayā Castle'; used by Shinran* in the *Jōdo wasan* to refer to the castle or town where Shakamuni* was born, namely, Kapilavastu (Kabirajō*). [JW. 88.]

Gengibun 玄義分 '*On the Essential Meaning*'; the first part of the four-section commentary on the *Kanmuryōju-kyō** by Shan-tao (Zendō*) of T'ang China; [TT. 37, No. 1753]; this part explains the essentials of the sutra it comments on and of the Pure Land teaching: e.g. the meaning of '*namu amida butsu*' and the nature of the Pure Land; cf. *shijō no so*.

Genka 現過 A contraction of *genzai* 現在 and *kako* 過去, 'present and past.'

Gesho 外書 'Outer books'; non-Buddhist scriptures; same as *geten**. [R. Pre.]

Geten 外典 'Outer books'; non-Buddhist scriptures; same as *gesho**. [R. Pre.]

Giba 耆婆 Sk. Jīvaka; a physician who cured the Buddha and

King Bimbisāra (Binbashara*) of their illnesses and later led Ajātasatru (Ajase*) to Buddhism. [JW. 76, 77, 78.]

Gion-e 祇園會 'Gion festival'; originally a ceremony held for the Heavenly King Gozu 牛頭 (Ox-Head) at Gion Shrine, Kyoto; also *Gion goryōe* 祇園御靈會 and *Tennō-sai* 天王祭, and popularly called *Gion-matsuri* 祇園祭. The origin of this festival dates back to the reign of Emperor En'yū 圓融, when a *goryō-e** (soul-appeasing ceremony) was held to stop epidemics. The ceremony became popular during the Tokugawa period (1603–1868). From the beginning of the Meiji era (1868–1911), the ceremony became a totally Shinto one.

Godaisan 五台山 'Mt. Wu-t'ai'; a high mountain with five peaks situated in the district of Wu-t'ai 五台, Shan-si 山西. Tradition has it that the Indian monks Kāśyapamātaṅga (Kashōmatō*) and Chu Fa-lan (Jiku Hōran*) came to dwell on this mountain. Later many monks dwelt there to study and practise the Way; the number of temple buildings in the mountain once reached a hundred. It is also reputed that this is the sacred abode of the Bodhisattva Monju* (文殊). Since, in the *Kegon-gyō**, he is said to dwell on the mountain called Shōryō 清涼, this mountain is also called Mt. Ch'ing-liang 清涼山 (Shōryōzan). [R. I–5.]

Gogen 五眼 'Five eyes'; Sk. *pañca-cakṣus*. The five kinds of eyes are distinguished for five types of beings: (1) *nikugen* 肉眼, *māṃsa-cakṣus*, 'flesh-eye'; ordinary human eyes which perceive colours, forms, etc.; (2) *tengen* 天眼, *divya-c.*, 'heavenly eye'; the supernatural ability possessed by heavenly beings to see things far and near without obstruction; (3) *egen* 慧眼, *prajñā-c.*, 'wisdom-eye'; the ability of Hinayana sages to perceive the principle of voidness; (4) *hōgen** 法眼, *dharma-c.*, 'dharma-eye'; bodhisattvas' ability to discern teaching methods for guiding people; and (5) *butsugen** 佛眼, *buddha-c.*, 'buddha-eye'; the buddha's eye possessing all the four capacities mentioned above. According to the *Daichido-ron**, the last three eyes correspond to the triple truth (*santai** 三諦), namely: the wisdom-eye realizes the truth of voidness (*kūtai* 空諦); the dharma-eye discerns provisional methods of teaching (*ketai* 假諦); and the buddha-eye recognizes the truth of the mean (*chūtai* 中諦). These three eyes again correspond to the triple wisdom (*sanchi** 三智).

Gohyaku-jinden-gō 五百塵点劫 '500 dust-speck kalpas'; an analogy given in the *Hoke-kyō** to describe innumerable kalpas of time. If one were to grind to pieces 500 thousand trichiliocosms (*sanzendaisen-sekai**), multiplied by 10,000 koṭis (*kutei**) of nayutas (*nayuta**) of asaṃkhyas (*asōgi**), and then drop one piece after passing through 500 nayutas of asaṃkhyas of worlds, and another after passing through the same number of worlds until all the pieces are exhausted, and if one were then to grind up all the worlds one has covered, the number of pieces thus obtained is the number of kalpas here referred to. [AK.]

Gōja jinju 恆沙塵數 '(As numerous as) the sand-grains of the River Ganges or specks of dust.' [AK.; JW. 108.]

Gojūni-i 五十二位 'The 52 stages'; the 52-stage division of a bodhisattva's career. This theory, unknown in India, was established by T'ien-tai (Tendai*) based on the *Yōraku-kyō**. The 52 stages are as follows (in ascending order): (1) *jusshin* 十信 'ten beliefs' (1st–10th), (2) *jūjū* 十住 'ten dwellings' (11th–20th), (3) *jūgyō* 十行 'ten practices' (21st–30th), (4) *jūekō* 十廻向 'ten merit-transferences' (31st to 40th), (5) *jūji** 十地 'ten stages or *bhūmis*' (41st–50th), (6) *tōgaku** 等覺 'equal enlightenment' (51st), (7) *myōgaku** 妙覺 'wondrous enlightenment' (52nd). The 52nd stage is the stage of a buddha. The idea of *jūji** 'ten stages' presumably developed first in India, with other stages being added later. The 30 stages comprising *jūjū*, *jūgyō* and *jūekō* are summarily called *sangen** 三賢.

Gojū tenden no kuriki 五十展轉の功力 'The merit-power (of the *Hoke-kyō** which remains strong) after it has been expounded from person to person until the teaching reaches the fiftieth person'; this comes from the *Hoke-kyō*, 'Zuiki kudoku-hon' 隨喜功德品 'Chapter on Rejoicing in the Merit,' TT. 9, 46. [Yori.]

Gokamon 五果門 'The five effect-gates'; the five kinds of merit one attains after birth in the Pure Land as the effect of the five practice-gates of mindfulness (*gonenmon** 五念門). They are: (1) *gonmon* 近門, approaching enlightenment; (2) *daieshumon* 大會衆門, joining the multitude of Mahayana sages; (3) *takumon*, 宅門 entering the buddhas' residence; (4) *okumon* 屋門 entering the inner building, i.e., the heart of enlightenment; and (5) *onrinyugejimon* 薗林遊戲地門, saving other living beings who are in the condition of birth and death.　See *gonengyō* and *gonenmon.*

Gōke 業繋　'Karma-bondage, karmic bond'; the state in which one is bound by a particular kind of constriction due to one's evil acts done in the past; in a broad sense, refers to the state in which one repeats a cycle of birth and death bound to the effects of evil karma one has done.　[JW. 7.]

Gokō chōsai 五劫兆載　'Five kalpas and incalculable kalpas'; when Amida* was a bodhisattva, he contemplated for five kalpas before he made the forty-eight vows, and then he performed a bodhisattva's practices for incalculable kalpas before he fulfilled them. Cf. *chōsai yōkō.*　[AK.]

Gonjitsu shinke 權實眞假　'Provisional, real, true and temporary'; in the Jōdoshin* sect, the true and real teaching refers to the law of salvation based on the 18th vow of Amida*, and the provisional and temporary teachings refer to the methods of salvation in conformity with the 19th and 20th vows.　[JW. 71.]

Gonke 權假　'Provisional and temporary (teachings)'; see *gonjitsu shinke.*　[JW. 72.]

Goshin 五辛　'Five kinds of acrid food'; the five pungent roots forbidden to monks.　There are several versions of the five but they invariably include garlic, leeks and some kinds of onions.　[R. I–4.]

Goshu 五趣　'The five destinations'; see *godō* 五道.

Goshu kayo 五種嘉譽　'The five kinds of praise and glorification'; the five words of high praise Shan-tao (Zendō*) used for practitioners of the nenbutsu* in his *Sanzengi**: (1) *kōnin* 好人, an excellent person; (2) *jōjōnin* 上上人, a superior person; (3) *myōkōnin** 妙好人, a wondrous, excellent person; (4) *keunin* 希有人, a rare person; and (5) *saishōnin* 最勝人, a most excellent person.　They are given as synonyms of *fundarike*, 'a white lotus,' the word of praise for one who practises the *nenbutsu** which appears in the *Kanmuryōjukyō**.

Gugan 弘願　'A great and universal vow.'　I. In the Jōdoshin* sect and the Seizan* school, refers to the 18th vow of Amida*.　II. In the Chinzei* school, refers to his 18th, 19th, 20th and 35th vows.　Cf. *guzei.*

Gusokukai 具足戒　'Fully possessed precepts'; Sk. *upasampadā*;

also *gon'enkai* 近圓戒 and *shingukai* 進具戒. The precepts which monks and nuns receive before entering the priesthood. In the tradition transmitted to China and Japan, the number of these precepts is 250 for a monk and 348 for a nun. [R. III–38.]

Guzei 弘誓 'A great and universal vow.' I. Bodhisattvas' vows in general; cf. *shiguzeigan*. II. Amida's* vows, especially the 18th. Cf. *gugan*.

[Gyakuen 逆緣]

~ **nagara** --ながら Often used in *Nō* texts in the sense of 'through a passing relationship' and, hence, 'in passing'. [Tada.; Nono.]

~ **no onriyaku** --の御利益 'Benefit to be obtained from a casual encounter.' [Boku.]

Gyōja 行者 I. Sk. *ācārin*; one who practises the Buddhist Way. II. An attendant novice at a Zen monastery; in this case, pronounced *anja*. III. An ascetic practitioner, such as a *yamabushi**.

Gyōu 行雨 Also Ugyō* 雨行; Sk. Varṣakāra; one of King Bimbisāra's (Binbashara*) ministers. [JW. 78.]

H

Hachi 鈸 Cymbals; used in religious services; also *dōhachi* 銅鈸, *dōban* 銅盤.

Hachijū-kegon 八十花嚴 '*The Eighty-Fascicle Kegon Sutra*'; one of the Chinese versions of the *Kegon-gyō** translated by Śikṣānanda (Jisshananda 實叉難陀); see *Kegon-gyō* (2). [R. III–19.]

Hana-matsuri 花まつり 'Flower festival'; the popular name for the Buddha's birthday celebration, which falls on April 8th and is traditionally called *busshō-e* 佛生會, *tanjō-e* 誕生會, *kanbutsu-e* 灌佛會 and *Shakuson gōtan-e* 釋尊降誕會. The first *hana-matsuri* celebration was held in Hibiya Park, Tokyo, in 1917 by a joint group of Buddhists, headed by Andō Ryōgan

安藤嶺丸 and Watanabe Kaikyoku 渡邊海旭. This, however, was preceded by a birthday celebration for the Buddha held in Berlin in 1901 by a group of 18 Japanese scholars who were studying there at that time, such as Sonoda Shūe 薗田宗恵, Haga Yaichi 芳賀彌一, Anezaki Masaharu 姉崎正治, Minobe Tatsukichi 美濃部達吉, Matsumoto Bunzaburō 松本文三郎, Ikeyama Eikichi 池山榮吉 and Chikazumi Jōkan 近角常觀. They called this celebration 'Blumenfest,' 'flower-festival', which is the origin of the Hana-matsuri. The term is also used for the Shinto ceremonies held in December and January in parts of Aichi Prefecture.

Hana mo tae naru nori no michi 花も妙なる法の道 'The wondrously flowered path of the Dharma'; refers to the teaching of *Hoke-kyō**. [Boku.]

Hannya-kenki 般若驗記 '*Record of Miraculous Stories Concerning the Prajñāpāramitā Sūtra*'; the full title is *Kongō-hannya-kyō-jikkenki* 金剛般若經集驗記, 3 fasc., compiled by Meng Hsien-chung (Mō Kenchū 孟獻忠) in 718; Zoku. I–2, 乙, 22. [R. Pre.]

Hari 頗梨 Sk. *sphaṭika*; translated as 水精 (lit. 'water-essence'), i.e. 'crystal'; one of the seven treasures (*shippō**). There are two kinds: *kaju** 火珠 'fire-gem' and *suiju* 水珠 'water-gem.' It is said that the palace of the sun is made of fire-gem, and that of the moon is made of water-gem.

Henji 邊地 'The border land'; a term for the transformed land (*kedo**) of Amida* Buddha where aspirants who believe in their own power and hence lack pure faith, will be born. [JW. 67; Tan. 11.]

[Henjō nanshi 變成男子]

~ no gan --の願 'The vow to transform women into men'; refers to Amida's* 35th vow, which promises that those women who, having heard his name, entertain pure faith, awaken the Bodhi-mind and seek to abandon female forms, will not be born again as women. [JW. 60.]

Hijō 非情 'An insentient being'; opposite of *ujō** 有情, 'a sentient being'. [Taka.]

Hikkyōe 畢竟依 'The ultimate resort'; refers to Amida*. [JW. 7.]

Hiyu-hon 譬喩品 'Chapter on Parables'; the third of the 28 chapters of the *Hoke-kyō**, which tells the famous parable of a burning house (*kataku-yu**). [Boku.]

Hōban 寶幡 'A jewelled banner'; a banner made of brocade or other fine material and adorned with precious metals and gems. [R. II–16.]

Hōdō 法幢 'Dharma-ensign'; cf. *dō*.

Hōgi 法儀 'Buddhist ritual'; prescribed manner; priestly form.

Hōji 法事 I. That which is done for the sake of the Dharma; Buddhist duties in general. II. Buddhist services. III. Memorial services for the repose of the deceased.

Hōki 法喜 'Joy of the Dharma'; joy produced from hearing, contemplating or studying the Dharma. [JW. 10.]

Hokkaishin 法界身 'Dharma-realm body'; also *hokkaijin*. I. Buddha's Dharma-body (*hosshin** 法身), for it pervades the entire universe and is responsive to sentient beings in it. Thus one buddha-body can manifest innumerable bodies; in this case *hokkai* means universe. II. Buddha-body in general, for it is produced out of the mind of a sentient being; in this case, *hokkai* is construed as mind-element.

Hokke-e 法華會 'A Hokke lecture-meeting'; a series of lectures on the *Hoke-kyō**. Prince Shōtoku* was the first to give such lectures in 606. When Rōben* gave lectures at Tōdaiji* in 746, the Hokke lecture-meeting became an annual event by imperial order and lasted until 1680. A similar lecture-meeting held at Enshūji 圓宗寺, Kyoto, enjoyed great popularity as one of the three annual lecture-meetings in Kyoto (*hokkyō san'e* 北京三會). At Enryakuji*, a Hokke lecture-meeting, called Shimotsuki-e 霜月會 (November lecture-meeting), was held in memory of the founder, Saichō*. Another Hokke lecture-meeting used to be held at Takao 高雄, Kyoto. Cf. *Hokke hakkō*.

Hokke jikyō 法華持經 'To hold the *Hoke-kyō**.'
~ **no mi** --の身 'One who always keeps and recites the *Hoke-kyō*.' [Ba.]

Hokken 法顯 Ch. Fa-hsien; a monk of the Eastern Chin (東晉) dynasty. Having heard that the Chinese *vinaya* texts (*ritsu**) were incomplete, he left Chang-an 長安 together with a dozen or more monks in 399 and took six years to reach India overland. He visited Buddhist sites, studied Sanskrit and returned to China by sea in 414 with many scriptures. He translated the *Makasōgi-ritsu* 摩訶僧祇律 with Buddhabhadra (Kakuken 覺賢) and also produced translations, including *Daihatsu-naiongyō* 大般泥洹經. He died at the age of 82 (or 86). His record of travel, known as the *Hokkenden* 法顯傳, is a source of valuable information.

Hōkōkyō 方廣經 'A Mahayana sutra.' [R. I–8.]

Hokujiden 北寺傳 'The Northern-Temple tradition'; refers to the third and fourth transmissions of the Hossō* teaching from China; cf. *nanjiden*.

Hōmetsu hyakusai no ki 法滅百歳の機 'Those who will be born during the 100-year period after the Dharma becomes extinct'; even those people will be saved by Amida*. [AK.]

Hōō 法皇 I. 'Dharma-emperor'; refers to a buddha. II. Abbr. of *dajō hōō* 太上法皇 'Chancellor Dharma-Emperor'; a title accorded an emperor who, after his abdication, had his head shaved to enter the priesthood. The first such *hōō* was the Emperor Uda 宇多 (reigned 887–897). III. The title given to Dōkyō*.

Hōshin sangi 法臣參議 'Dharma-minister chancellor'; a special government post held by high-ranking priests at the time when Dōkyō* was in power. Actually it consists of two titles, *hōshin* 法臣 'Dharma minister' and *hōsangi* 法參議 'Dharma chancellor.' [R. III–38.]

Hosshin 法身 II. Refers to the aspect of Amida's* body which can be conceived and perceived as having a definitive form; this corresponds to *hōben hosshin* 方便法身, 'the Dharma-body of expediency', which is one of the two Dharma-bodies distinguished by T'an-luan (Donran*); cf. *nishin*. [JW. 3.]

Hotoke 佛 'Buddha'; etymologically, said to derive from 浮圖家 (*futoke*; *futo* is an ancient transcription of Sk. *buddha*) or from *hotoorike* 'fever,' because when Buddhism was first transmitted to Japan people suffered from a fever. It is also said that when Mononobe Moriya 物部守屋, the leader of the anti-Buddhist faction* at that time, destroyed the altar and seized the statue of Amida which had been sent to the port of Osaka from India through China and Korea, he found that the statue was hot and feverish; so he claimed that the statue was suffering from a fever and threw it into a nearby pond.

I

Ichijin hokkai 一塵法界 'The Dharma-realm in a speck of dust'; to the eye of an enlightened sage, a speck of dust contains the entire universe. [Ba.]

Ichiju no kage 一樹の蔭 '(In the) shadow of one tree'; when one happens to be with somebody under the same tree, it is due to a long past relationship with him; cf. *nise no chigiri*. [Tomo.]

[Ichinen 一念**]**

~ **dairi mujō** --大利無上 'The unsurpassed great benefit of even one thought (of joy in Amida's* salvation).' [JW. 30.]

~ **kyōki** --慶喜 'One thought of joy'; the joy awakened in one's heart upon hearing Amida's name and realizing, through it, his saving power. [JW. 26.]

~ **Mida Butsu** --彌陀佛 'Thinking of Amida Buddha once' or 'saying Amida's name once.' [Sane.]

~ **sokumetsu muryōzai** --卽滅無量罪 'If one thinks of Amida* Buddha once (or says his name once), the immeasurable sins one has committed are immediately cancelled'; a phrase quoted in Genshin's* *Busshin-hōyō* 佛心法要. [Sane.]

~ **zuiki no shinjin** --隨喜の信心 'Faith or belief accompanied by (even) one joyful thought'; *ichinen zuiki* comes from the *Hoke-kyō**, 'Hosshi-bon' 法師品 'Chapter on Dharma-preacher.' [Ba.]

Igyō 易行 'An easy practice'; the practice of Pure Land Buddhism centring on recitation of the *nenbutsu** is easy as compared with other Buddhist practices; hence, Pure Land teaching is called *igyōdō* 易行道 'path of easy practice,' or *igyō no ichimon* 易行の

一門 'gate of easy practice.' [Tan. Pre.]

Igyō 異形 'A strange form'; a miraculous phenomenon.

Iken 威験 'A miraculous effect.' [R. III–4.]

Ikiryō 生霊 'The spirit of a live person'; often a revengeful one; cf. *shiniryō*. [FK.]

Ikontō 已今當 'Past, present and future.' [JW. 29.]

Insū 因數 'A cause-number'; an incomplete number, e.g. 7 and 8, as opposed to *kasū** 果數. [R. III–38.]

Inten suru 印点する 'To mark with a magical sign.' [R. III–8.]

Iō ni munin 易往而無人 '(The Pure Land) is easy to go to, but very few actually go there'; a phrase from the *Muryōju-kyō**; see *iō munin*.

Iriai 入相 'Sunset'; the striking of a gong at sunset. [Mura.]

Isshiji 一子地 'One-child stage'; one who has attained enlightenment looks upon all living beings as if each were his only child. [JW. 92.]

Isshūki 一周忌 'The first anniversary of the death of a person'; cf. *nenki*.

Ittai funjin 一體分身 'One body divided into different forms'; incarnations of the originally one body. [Ara.]

Itsutsu no onjō いつつの音聲 'Five musical scales'; the five musical scales in China, viz. *kung* 宮 (*kyū*), *shang* 商 (*shō*), *chiao* 角 (*kaku*), *cheng* 徴 (*chi*) and *yü* 羽 (*u*). [JW. 41.]

J

Jido 自度 I. 'Saving oneself'; said of Hinayana believers' concern about their own salvation rather than the salvation of others. II. 'Self-ordination'; becoming a monk or a nun without proper authorization; same as *shido** 私度.

Jinjin 神人 'A person with divine power.' [R. III–Pre.]

Jiririta enman 自利利他圓滿 'Perfect accomplishment of one's own benefit and the benefit of others'; said of Amida's* enlightenment by which both his own benefit and the benefit of others are perfectly accomplished. [JW. 37.]

[Jissō 實相]

∼ **muro no taikai** - -無漏の大海 'The great ocean of ultimate reality and absolute purity.' [Egu.]

∼ **no hanazakari** - -の花盛り 'The flowers of reality are in full bloom.' [Ara.]

Jobungi 序分義 '*On the Introductory Part*'; the second part of the four-section commentary on the *Kanmuryōju-kyō** by Shan-tao (Zendō*) of T'ang China; [TT. 37, No. 1753]; cf. *shijō no so*.

Jōhō 定法 'Constant law'; the permanent and constant law of teaching. [ST.]

Jōjitsu-ron 成實論 '*The Discourse on Establishing Truth*'; Sk. *Satya-siddhi*; a discourse on the analysis of all existence and on the practice leading to liberation. The text was written by Harivarman (Karibatsuma) and translated into Chinese by Kumārajīva (Kumarajū*); 16 or 20 fasc. [TT. 32, No. 1619]. [R. II–32.]

∼ **shūbun** - - -宗分 'Fund for the study of the *Jōjitsu-ron*'; the fund for a group of monks to study the *Jōjitsu-ron* at Daianji*, Nara. [R. II–32.]

Jōjitsushū 成實宗 'Jōjitsu school'; the school of Buddhism based on the *Jōjitsu-ron**; one of the thirteen sects in China and one of the six sects in Japan. This sect, or rather school, centres round the theory of voidness of both persons and things—a theory which is more advanced than ordinary Hinayana teachings. Through meditation on these two kinds of voidness one attains liberation from the bondage of evil passions. The process of liberation is divided into 27 stages. This school flourished in China for some time after the translation of the *Jōjitsu-ron* by Kumārajīva (Kumarajū*), but declined by the early T'ang dynasty. This school of thought was transmitted to Japan together with the Sanron* school, and was studied as an auxiliary subject of the Sanron teaching.

Jōraku 常樂 'Eternity and bliss'; the first two of the four distinguished qualities of Nirvana; see *nehan no shitoku*.

Jōsan 定散 'Concentration and distraction'; meditative and non-meditative; the state of mind which is deeply concentrated on a specific object (*jō* 定 or *sanmai* 三昧) and the ordinary state of mind which is not; also the acts done in such states of mind.

~ **jiriki no shōmyō** --自力の稱名 'The self-power practice of the *nenbutsu** with meditative or non-meditative state of mind.' [JW. 66.]

~ **shoki** --諸機 'Persons with the propensity of practising meditative good (*jōzen* 定善) and those with the propensity of practising non-meditative good (*sanzen* 散善).' [JW. 62, 81.]

Jōshutaraku 常修多羅供 Also pronounced *jōsutaraku*; 'fund for an ordinary group of monks to study a particular sutra (e.g., *Daihannya-kyō**)' at Daianji*, Nara; cf. *daishutaraku* and *shutara-bun*. [R. II–28.]

Jō-tōshōgaku 成等正覺 =*Tōshōgaku o jōzu* 'to realize equal, perfect enlightenment'; see *tōshōgaku*. [Boku.]

Jōzengi 定善義 '*On the Meditative Good*'; the third part of the four-section commentary on the *Kanmuryōju-kyō** by Shan-tao (Zendō*) of T'ang China; [TT. 37, No. 1753]. This part explains important concepts and terms which appear in the section 'Meditative Good' (*jōzen** 定善), i.e. the first 13 of the 16 contemplations (*jūrokkan** 十六觀); cf. *shijō no so*.

Ju 呪 'A spell'; also pronounced *shu*; Sk. *dhāraṇī* or *mantra*; a mystic phrase, often comprised of incomprehensible Sanskrit syllables and believed to possess some supernatural power; cf. *darani*.

Jubaku 呪縛 'To bind by means of a spell'; to cast a spell on someone so that he cannot move. [R. I–15, III–33.]

Jugo 呪護 'To protect with a spell.' [R. I–31.]

Juhō 呪法 'A dharani ritual'; an esoteric ritual based on the chanting of a dharani.

Juji 誦持 'To recite and retain (in the mind)'; constantly reciting a sacred name, etc.

Jūnikōbutsu 十二光佛 'Twelve-Light Buddhas.' According to the *Muryōju-kyō** [TT. 12, p. 270a–b], Amida* has 12 other names which describe different aspects of his light; they are as follows: (1) Muryōkōbutsu 無量光佛 'Buddha of Immeasurable Light', (2) Muhenkōbutsu 無邊光佛 'Buddha of Boundless Light', (3) Mugekōbutsu 無碍光佛 'Buddha of Unhindered Light', (4) Mutaikōbutsu 無對光佛 'Buddha of Incomparable Light', (5) Ennōkōbutsu 炎王光佛 (also Kōennōbutsu* 光炎王佛) 'Buddha of Majestically Flaming Light', (6) Shōjōkōbutsu 清淨光佛 'Buddha of Pure Light', (7) Kangikōbutsu 歡喜光佛 'Buddha of Joyful Light', (8) Chiekōbutsu 智慧光佛 'Buddha of Wisdom Light', (9) Fudankōbutsu* 不斷光佛 'Buddha of Unceasing Light', (10) Nanjikōbutsu 難思光佛 'Buddha of Inconceivable Light', (11) Mushōkōbutsu 無稱光佛 'Buddha of Ineffable Light' and (12) Chōnichigakkōbutsu 超日月光佛 'Buddha of Light Outshining Sun and Moon'.

Jūshichijō kenpō 十七條憲法 'The Seventeen-Article Constitution'; an edict published by Shōtoku Taishi* in 604. Comprising 17 clauses, it is not a code of laws but a series of ethical maxims compiled in the spirit of Buddhism, Shinto and Confucianism.

K

Kaibyaku 開白 'An opening statement'; a statement made to a buddha before the start of a service or lecture-meeting.

Kaimyō 戒明 A monk of the Kegon* sect. Born in Sanuki (present-day Kagawa Prefecture), he learned the Kegor doctrine from Kyōshun 慶俊 of Daianji*. During the Hōki 寶龜 era (770–780) he went to T'ang China by imperial order; after returning home, he dwelt at Daianji. [R. III–19.]

Kairō 戒臘 'Years which have passed since receiving the precepts'; also *hōrō* 法臘 (Dharma-age), *gerō* 夏臘 (summer-retreat age) and *zarō* 坐臘 (sitting age). [SG.]

Kaishu 戒珠 'Gem of the precepts'; metaphorically, perfect observance of the precepts. [R. I–22, III–30.]

Kakugo 覺悟 'Enlightenment'; understanding; comprehension. [Tan. Pre.]

Kamyō 果名 'Fruition-name'; the name acquired in the stage of fruition, i.e. the stage of buddhahood. Refers to '*myōgō**,' Amida's* name. [AK.]

Kangyō 觀經 '*The Meditation Sutra*'; abbr. of *Kanmuryōju-kyō**. [JW. 62.]

Kanjō 勸請 'Requesting the presence of a person or deity'; summoning up a Buddhist or Shinto deity; asking someone to come. Cf. *daishi kanjō no kishō*.

Kanka 感果 'A result effected.' [AK.]

Kannon-juki-kyō 觀音授記經 Abbr. of the *Kanzeon-bosatsu juki-kyō**.

Kannon senbō 觀音懺法 'The rite dedicated to Kannon* for anulling one's sins'; the rite performed to pray for the welfare of a person, etc., or for the well-being of a deceased person. [Tomo.]

Kanroku 觀勒 A monk from Paekche who came to Japan in 607 bringing books on the calendar, astronomy, geography and the Taoist arts. He dwelt at the Gangōji* Temple. Later, in 624, he was given the title of *sōjō**. [R. I–5.]

Kanzeon-bosatsu-juki-kyō 觀世音菩薩授記經 '*The Sutra of the Prediction Made to Kannon Bodhisattva*'; also, *Kanzeon-bosatsu Tokudaiseishi-bosatsu juki-kyō* 觀世音菩薩得大勢至菩薩授記經 '*The Sutra of the Prediction Made to Kannon Bodhisattva and Seishi Bodhisattva*'; 1 fasc., tr. by T'an-wu-chieh 曇無竭 (Donmukatsu*) [TT. 12, No. 371]. In this sutra the Buddha first expounded the illusion-like samādhi (*nyogen-zanmai* 如幻三昧) to the assembly headed by the Bodhisattva Flower-Virtue Treasure-house (Ketokuzō 華德藏). He then emitted light, which illumined Amida's* land. When the two great bodhisattvas of that land,

Kannon* and Seishi*, came to visit the Buddha's assembly, he gave them a prediction of their attainment of buddhahood, saying that after Amida's passing into Nirvana, Kannon would become his successor as lord of the Pure Land. Abbr. *Kannon juki-kyō**.

Karudai 迦留陀夷 Sk. Kālodayin; a disciple of the Buddha; formerly the Buddha's retainer when he was a prince. He often broke the precepts but finally attained Nirvana. Said to have become the teacher of Queen Mallikā (Mari 末利, 摩利), wife of King Prasenajit (Hashinoku Ō*); he also converted 999 families into Buddhism in Śrāvastī (Shae*). [R. II–5.]

Kasū 果數 'An effect-number'; a full or complete number, i.e. 10 or a multiple thereof; opposed to *insū** 因數. [R. III–38.]

Kasui no gan 果遂の願 'The vow to accomplish (salvation)'; refers to the 20th vow of Amida*, which promises the salvation of those who recite the *nenbutsu**; cf. *fukasuisha*. [JW. 65.]

Kataku-yu 火宅喩 'The parable of a burning house'; one of the seven parables in the *Hoke-kyō**. The parable goes as follows: A man of great wealth has a big house with only one gate. A fire suddenly breaks out and quickly spreads to the entire house. His children, unaware of the fire, are playing inside the house. The man calls to them, saying, "I have wonderful gifts for you: carts drawn by a goat, a deer and an ox. Why don't you come out of the house quickly." Hearing this, the children come safely out of the house. The man then gives each of them a splendid cart drawn by a big white bullock. The three carts refer to the teachings for shravakas (*shōmon**), pratyekabuddhas (*engaku**) and bodhisattvas (*bosatsu**), and the bullock represents the supreme One-Vehicle teaching (*ichijō**) of the *Hoke-kyō*.

Ke 化 I. Refers to *kyōke* 教化; transforming people by teaching; teaching people and transforming their evil into good. II. Magical transformation or creation. III. Refers to *senge* 遷化; lit. 'moving (the centre of teaching activity) to another place'; a respectful term for the death of a virtuous priest.

Kedo 化土 'Transformed land.' I. A land temporarily manifested by a buddha for bodhisattvas at lower stages, practitioners of Hinayana or ordinary people; while dwelling there, they hear the Dharma from a transformed buddha and practise the Way to attain higher spiritual stages. II. A transformed realm within the Pure Land of Amida* Buddha provided for those who lack pure faith and, hence, are unable to be born in the land of full enlightenment. In Pure Land Buddhism, it is called by such names as *henji**, *kemangai**, *gijō* 疑城 and *taigu* 胎宮.

Kega Jigoku 灰河地獄 'Hell of the river of ashes'; one of the 16 subsidiary hells, where sinners are driven into a river of hot ashes. [R. II–10.]

Kegen 化現 'Apparitional manifestation'; an incarnation.

Kegon-gyō-tangenki 華嚴經探玄記 '*The Record of Exploring the Deep Meanings of the Garland Sutra*'; a commentary on the 60-fasc. text of the *Kegon-gyō** by Fa-ts'ang (Hōzō* 法藏); 20 fasc. [TT. 35, No. 1736].

Keka 悔過 'Repentance'; repenting of sins knowingly or unknowingly committed in the past.

Kemangai 懈慢界 'The realm of sloth and pride'; a land in the west where those who aspire to be born in the Pure Land stay because of the pleasures they can enjoy, but who are therefore unable to proceed to the Pure Land. Used in the Jōdoshin* sect as a term for the transformed land (*kedo**) of Amida* Buddha.

Kemon 假門 'A temporary gate, i.e. teaching'; in the Jōdoshin* sect, refers to the provisional method of salvation as promised in the 19th vow. [JW. 61.]

Kemyō 假名 'An assumed name, a provisional name.'

~ **no shami** --の沙彌 'A novice only in name.' [R. I–27.]

Kenju 劍樹 'A sword-tree'; n. of one of the 16 small hells; leaves of the trees of this hell are knife-blades; when sinners enter there, a strong wind blows over the trees, causing the blades to fall upon them and cut their bodies. [SG.]

Kenrō jijin 堅牢地神 'The goddess of the solid earth'; Sk. Dṛidhā pṛithivī-devatā, meaning 'Dṛidhā (solid), the earth-goddess'.

Keō 化翁 'One incarnated as an old man.' [R. I–6.]

Kentoku 驗德 'Efficacy, virtue, benefit.' [R. I–5.]

Keshu 化主 'The lord who transforms (people by teaching).' I.

The lord teacher; refers to a buddha. II. A Buddhist teacher.

Kien 機緣 I. An opportunity for saving people; in this case, *ki* means one who receives the Dharma. II. An opportunity; in this case, *ki* means *jiki* 時機.

Kihō ittai 機法一體 'Oneness of the receiver and the Dharma'; those to be saved and Amida* himself are one. Amida has attained the goal indicated by the phrase '*namu amida butsu*,' in which '*namu*' (taking refuge) indicates the aspirant's believing heart and hence the aspirant himself. *Hō* here means one who embodies the law of salvation; hence, Amida. [AK.]

Kijin 鬼神 'Demon-spirit.' I. A spirit, often possessed of supernatural power and believed to cause harm to people. II. Refers to *yasha** I.

Kikyō 歸敬 'To take refuge and respect.'

Kōdai-e 廣大會 'Great assembly'; used as an epithet for Amida*, since the first assembly of his Dharma exposition after his attainment of enlightenment was attended by innumerable sages. [JW. 16.]

Kōdō 講堂 'A lecture-hall'; a hall where Buddhist teachings are explained and sermons given.

Kōennōbutsu 光炎王佛 'The King of Light-flame Buddha'; one of Amida's* 12 names; also *Ennōkōbutsu** 'Buddha of Majestically Flaming Light'; he is so called because his light is the most brilliant of all buddhas'; cf. *jūnikōbutsu*. [JW. 8.]

Kōgen 光顏 'Shining countenance.' [JW. 53.]

Kōgyō 光曉 'Light-dawn'; Amida's* light of wisdom which dispels the darkness of ignorance and thus puts an end to the long night of illusion. [JW. 4.]

Kōkōshōgon 香光莊嚴 'Adornment with fragrant light'; said of a *nenbutsu** follower who is adorned with Amida's* virtue and glory and hence exudes a good 'scent' around him. [JW. 116.]

Komu shishin mugoku tai 虛無之身無極體 'Bodies of emptiness, bodies of limitlessness'; said of the bodies of those born in Amida's* land; the phrase originally comes from the *San-amidabutsu-ge* 讚阿彌陀佛偈 by T'an-luan (Donran*). [JW. 22.]

[Kōmyō henjō 光明遍照]

~ **jippō sekai nenbutsu shujō sesshu fusha** ----十方世界念佛衆生攝
取不捨 'Amida's* light shines over the worlds of the ten directions embracing all who practise the *nenbutsu** and not forsaking
them'; a well-known phrase which appears in the *Kanmuryōju-
kyō**. [Tada.]

Kongōshin 金剛心 'Diamond mind.' I. The firm resolution of a
bodhisattva which is as indestructible as a diamond. II. The
mind of the bodhisattva of the highest stage just before attaining
buddhahood; this is a state of deep concentration in which he
destroys his basic ignorance. III. In the Jōdoshin* sect, the faith
endowed by Amida*.

Konshu ubasoku 金鷲優婆塞 'The Golden Eagle Upāsaka'; refers
to the eminent monk Rōben*. [R. II–21.]

Kontai ryōbu 金胎兩部 'The two (mandala) sections of the Kon-
gōgai and Taizōkai'; see *ryōbu mandara*. [Ara.]

Konzen 金山 'A gold mountain; a gold mountain-range'; specifically refers to the sevenfold gold mountain-ranges surrounding
Mt. Sumeru (*Shumisen**); often used to describe a buddha's
physical glory. [JW. 43.]

Kōrin 光輪 'Light-wheel'; Amida's* light is compared to a wheel
because (1) its activity in benefiting beings is perfect; (2) its
activity continues on and on like a wheel; and (3) it destroys evil
passions and hindrances like the cakravartin's (*tenrinjōō**) wheel.
[JW. 3.]

Koromo no tama 衣の珠 'A gem (hidden) in the clothes'; refers to a
metaphor in the *Hoke-kyō**, 'Gohyaku deshi juki-hon' 五百弟子授
記品 'Chapter on Giving Predictions to 500 Disciples.' When a
poor man got drunk at his friend's house, the friend sewed a
gem into his clothes. Without knowing this, the man wandered
about poverty-stricken. When he happened to meet the friend
again, he was told of the gem and so he was able to escape
poverty. The metaphor shows that one has a hidden spiritual
treasure—buddha-nature—and one can become enlightened as
soon as one is told of this fact. [Ba.]

Kōse 興世 'To arise, i.e. appear, in the world'; said of a buddha's
appearance in the world. [JW. 54.]

Koshin no Mida no kuni 己心の彌陀の國　'Amida's* land which is in one's own mind.' [Sane.]

Kōzui 香水　'Scented water'; water invested with magical power by an esoteric ritual; see *kaji kōzui*. [R. I–8.]

Kudoku 功德　'Quality; virtue, merit'; Sk. *guṇa*. I. Excellent quality of a physical existence, e.g. *hakkudokusui**. II. Excellent moral or spiritual quality or energy inherent in the ultimate reality or buddhahood, or cultivated by performing good acts; merit can be stored and directed towards a specific end or person.

Kuon jitsujō 久遠實成　'Actual attainment (of buddhahood) since time immemorial.' I. Said of Shakamuni*, who, according to the *Hoke-kyō**, has been a buddha since time immemorial. II. According to Shinran*, Amida* is an eternal buddha, although the Pure Land sutras refer to him as a buddha 10 kalpa (*kō**) old. [JW. 88.]

Kushō Nyorai 九生如來　'The Nine-birth Tathagata.' I. Refers to Dainichi* because of his position in the Matrix-store Realm Mandala (*Taizōkai mandara**), where he is surrounded by four buddhas and four bodhisattvas. II. Refers to Amida*, probably because of his association with the nine grades of aspirants (*kuhon**). [Chiku.]

Kyōgyō 經行　Also *kinhin*; a walking exercise in a certain area or going to and coming back from a certain place. This exercise is often taken between meditation sessions to stretch one's legs and refresh one's mind.

Kyōji 脇士　Also 脇侍, 夾侍; a bodhisattva, arhat, etc., who attends a buddha on his left or right; he assists the buddha in his act of saving sentient beings. The following pairs of bodhisattvas are well-known: Kannon* and Seishi* for Amida*, Monju* and Fugen* for Shakamuni*, and Nikkō* and Gakkō* for Yakushi*.

Kyōkai 景戒　A monk of the Yakushiji* and the author of the *Nihonkoku-genpō-zenmaku-ryōiki**, who is believed to have flourished in the early 9th century.

Kyōshi 經師　'Sutra master.' I. A priest in charge of chanting sutras. II. In Zen, one who is attached to letters and words and seeks only to know their meanings. III. Pronounced *kyōji*; one who mounts copied sutras and paintings; paperer, mounter. IV. One who copies sutras.

M

Mangyō 萬行 'Ten thousand practices'; the various meritorious practices for the attainment of birth in the Pure Land. In the Jōdoshin* sect, they are based on the aspirant's self-power and are considered inferior and inefficacious as compared with the *nenbutsu**. [JW. 63.]

Mōki no fuboku 盲龜の浮木 'Driftwood for a blind tortoise'; a metaphor to show the difficulty of being born as a human being and of meeting the Buddhist teaching. A tortoise, which is thought to have only one eye in its stomach, rises to the surface of the water only very occasionally; in order for it to see the sun, it must cling to a piece of driftwood with a hole in it. [Sane.]

Monjushiri 文殊師利 Sk. Mañjuśrī; n. of the bodhisattva popularly known as Monju* 文殊. [R. I–6.]

Mugekōbutsu 無碍光佛 'The Buddha of Unhindered Light'; one of the 12 names of Amida*; see *jūnikōbutsu*. [JW. 87.]

Mugenin 無碍人 'An unhindered person'; refers to a buddha, since he has attained unhindered wisdom. [JW. 48.]

Muku Sekai 無垢世界 'The World Undefiled'; n. of the world mentioned in the *Hoke-kyō**, 'Daibadatta-bon' 提婆達多品 'Chapter on Devadatta,' where an eight-year-old dragon girl became a buddha; cf. *ryūnyo*. [Une.]

Muryōjubutsu 無量壽佛 'The Buddha of Immeasurable Life'; another name for Amida*. [Sane.; Tō.]

Mushōbutsu 無稱佛 'The ineffable Buddha'; refers to Amida*; he is so called because his merit and virtue cannot be fully praised even by the eloquence of Shakamuni* Buddha. [JW. 28.]

Mushōkōbutsu 無稱光佛 'Buddha of Ineffable Light'; one of Amida's* 12 names; cf. *jūnikōbutsu*. [JW. 14.]

Musō shinnyo 無相眞如 'Formless True Thusness'; the True Thusness, or the ultimate reality, is formless and characterless. [Ba.]

Mutōdō 無等等 'One equal to the unequalled'; a peerless one; refers to Amida*. [JW. 15.]

Myōgaku 妙覺 'Wondrous enlightenment'; the supreme enlightenment; the enlightenment of a buddha. Cf. *gojūni-i.*

Myōkan 冥感 'Unseen perception'; said of unseen divinities' being moved and impressed by some extraordinary acts of a man. [Boku.]

Myōkon 命根 'Life-root; life-organ'; Sk. *jīvita-indriya*; an element or force which sustains one's body for a life-time; one's life. [ST.; R. II–22.]

Myōkōnin 妙好人 'A wondrous, excellent person'; a devout follower of the Jōdoshin* sect who lives a life of total dedication to Amida* Buddha and whose acts and sayings, though they often run counter to common sense, reveal the depth of faith and true humanity. Those known as *myōkōnin* have been often found to have little education but a surprisingly deep understanding of the teaching.   The term originally comes from the *Sanzengi** 散善義. In commenting on the word *fundarike* 分陀利華 which was used in the *Kanmuryōju-kyō** to praise practitioners of the *nenbutsu**, the author Shan-tao (Zendō*) gives five other words of high praise, one of which is *myōkōnin*. Cf. *fundarike* and *goshu kayo.*

Myōtai funi 名體不二 'Oneness of the name and the substance'; Amida's* name and Amida himself are not separate.   [AK.]

Myōtoku Bosatsu 妙德菩薩 'Excellent Virtue Bodhisattva'; 'myōtoku' is a translation of Sk. Mañjuśrī, 'Monju'* 文殊. [R. I–5.]

N

Naikyō 内經 'Inner sutras'; Buddhist sutras; same as *naiten**. [R. Pre., III-Pre.]

[Namu 南無]

~ **kimyō** --歸命 'I take refuge in'; '*kimyō*' is the translation of '*namu*;' a repetitive use of the two words together expresses a strong feeling of devotion or adoration. [Yashi.]

~ **to ippa sunawachi kore kimyō** --と言っぱすなはちこれ歸命 '*Namu* means to take refuge in'; reference is made here to Shantao's (Zendō*) explanation of the sacred phrase, *namu amida butsu**; see *rokujishaku*. [Sane.]

Nanda 難陀 Sk. Nanda. I. Buddha Shakamuni's* brother-in-law, whose mother was Mahāprajāpatī; he was also called Sundarananda, or 歡喜 in Chinese translation, because he had a wife called Sundarī before he became a monk. He was renowned as the first and foremost among the Buddha's disciples for the control of his sense-organs. II. One of the ten great masters of the Yogācāra school (*yugagyōha**) in India in about the sixth century; see *yuishiki jūdaironji*. III. One of the eight great dragon kings; see *hachidai-ryūō*. [JW. 103.]

Nanjiden 南寺傳 'The Southern-Temple tradition'; refers to the first and second transmissions of the Hossō* teaching from China; see *Dōshō* and *hokujiden*.

Nanjikōbutsu 難思光佛 'Buddha of Inconceivable Light'; one of Amida's* 12 names; he is so called because the working of his light is beyond human conception; cf. *jūnikōbutsu*. [JW. 13.]

[Nehan 涅槃]

~ **no shitoku** --の四德 'The four qualities of Nirvana'; *jō* 常 'eternity,' *raku* 樂 'bliss,' *ga* 我 'true selfhood possessing unrestricted power' and *jō* 淨 'purity.'

Nenhi Kannonriki 念彼觀音力 Pronounced *nenpi kannonriki*; 'the power of concentrating on Kannon*.'

~ **tōjin dandan** -----刀刃段段 'By the power of concentrating on Kannon, the sword (which is about to kill a person) becomes broken into pieces'; a well-known phrase from the *Hoke-kyō**. [SG.]

Nenki 年忌 'The anniversary of a death'; the popular anniversaries observed in Japan are: the 1st, 3rd, 7th, 13th, 17th, 23rd, 27th, 33rd, 37th, and 50th. Originally in Buddhism, memorial services

for a deceased person did not go beyond the period of the intermediate state (*chūin**), i.e. 49 days after death. The custom of
holding services every 7th day during the *chūin* period came from
China. The 100th-day service and the first and third anniversary
services are of distinctly Chinese origin, formulated under the
influence of Confucianism. The 7th and later anniversaries
developed in Japan. The 7th anniversary came from an analogy
of the Chinese Buddhist custom of holding 7th-day services 7
times after the death of a person. The 13th anniversary came
from the zodiac, i.e., after completing a cycle of 12, one returns to
the first in the 13th year. The numbers 17, 23, 27, ect., are
obtained by adding 10 or a multiple of it to 3 and 7. The 25th
anniversary, which is sometimes observed, comes from the fact
that the same sign of the zodiac returns on the 25th year. As
practised, the 3rd anniversary, 7th anniversary, etc., are actually
held in the second calendar year, sixth calendar year, etc., after
the year of death.

Nenshō no zō 捻攝の像　'A clay image'; cf. *shōzō*. [R. III–17.]

Nichi 二智　'The two wisdoms'; the twofold wisdom of enlightened
sages. I. *jitchi** 實智, 'reality-wisdom' or the wisdom of knowing
the ultimate reality, and *gonchi** 權智, 'expediency-wisdom' or
the wisdom of discerning the methods of expedient means of
salvation; [JW. 47.] II. *konponchi* 根本智, 'basic wisdom' or the
wisdom of realizing emptiness of self and things, and *gotokuchi*
後得智, 'acquired wisdom' or the wisdom of discerning correctly
all things; III. *issaichi* 一切智, 'all-knowing wisdom' or the
wisdom of knowing all existing things, and *issaishuchi* 一切種智,
'wisdom of all seeds' or the wisdom of knowing all the causes of
existences of sentient beings and all teachings of buddhas. Cf.
sanchi.

Nichimani 日摩尼　'A fire-gem'; see *nisshōmani*.

～ shu ---手　One of the hands of Senju Kannon* which holds a
fire-gem. [R. III–12.]

Nise no chigiri 二世の契り　'The relationship which binds one person to another in their present and future lives'; the man and
wife relationship is believed to be one extending over these two
periods; cf. *sanze no onchigū*. [Tomo.]

Nishushō 二種性 'The two natures or spiritual potentialities'; according to the *Yuishiki-ron**, they are: (1) *honshōjūshushō* 本性住種姓 'originally inherent nature'; the undefiled nature inherent in the individual; and (2) *shūshojōshushō* 習所成種姓 'acquired nature'; the good nature acquired through hearing the undefiled teaching of the Way. Cf. *shushō*.

Nishu zange 二種懺悔 Also pronounced *nishu sange*; 'the two kinds of repentance': (1) *jisen* 事懺, 'repentance in phenomenal appearance,' to repent of one's sins before the statue of a buddha or in the presence of a buddha visualized in meditation; and (2) *risen* 理懺, 'repentance in the noumenal principle,' to repent of one's sins by realizing the principle of the non-arising of all existences. The former corresponds to the first two of the three kinds of repentance (*sanshu kehō**) and the latter to the last one.

Nisshōmani 日精摩尼 'A sun-essence mani-gem'; also *nichimani** 日摩尼 and *kaju* 火珠; a fire-gem or flaming gem. It is said that if a blind man touches the gem, he gains his sight.

Nori 法 Sk. *dharma*; the Buddhist law or teaching. Cf. hō.

~ no chikara -の力 'The power of the Buddhist Dharma.' [Chiku.]

Nyaku-fushōja 若不生者 'If (others) are not born...'; a phrase in the concluding part of the 18th vow of Amida*; coupled with the following phrase *fushu shōgaku* 不取正覺, 'I will not attain perfect enlightenment,' this part shows Amida's strong resolution to save beings; cf. *hongan no mon*. [JW. 26.]

[Nyohō 如法]

~ shōjō ni --清淨に Cleansing one's body and purifying one's mind according to a prescribed method (before copying a sutra). [R. III–10.]

O

Odori nenbutsu 踊念佛 'Dancing *nenbutsu**'; dancing while reciting the *nenbutsu* or chanting hymns; also *nenbutsu odori*; the practice originated and spread by followers of the Ji sect (Jishū*). [Sane.]

Ōgen 應現 'Responsive appearance'; a buddha or bodhisattva's manifestation of incarnated bodies in accordance with the needs of living beings.

Onbyō 怨病 'Illness caused by someone's desire for revenge.' [R. III–34.]

Onpō 怨報 'Revengeful retribution.' [R. II–5.]

Onshin no hijiri 隱身の聖 'A sage whose original body is hidden from (an ordinary person's sight).' [R. II–29.]

Onshin no shōnin 隱身の聖人 'An invisible holy man'; an unseen god who protects Buddhism; one whose original body is hidden from the sight of ordinary people. [R. II–1.]

R

Ra 羅 Abbr. of Ragora*. [R. III–24.]

[Ri 理**]**

~ **no hosshinbutsu** -の法身佛 'The Dharma-body buddha, an embodiment of the noumenal principle'; the Dharma-body is itself the ultimate reality-principle; see *hosshin*. [R. II–23.]

Rikisha hōshi 力者法師 'A palanquin-bearing monk'; a monk engaged in heavy work at a temple, often of low moral standards and fond of fighting; such monk-servants on Mt. Hiei and elsewhere often started riots in the streets and were popularly known as *sōhei* 僧兵 (monk-soldiers).

Rokkan-shō 六巻抄 '*The Six-Fascicle Tract*'; a popular name for the *Shibunritsu-gyōji-shō**. [R. III–24.]

Rokui 六位 'The six ranks (of priesthood)' established in 798. They are: (1) *mui* 無位 'no rank'; (2) *dentōnyūi* 傳燈入位 'rank of

entering the transmission of the lamp'; (3) *dentōjūi** 傳
'rank of dwelling in the transmission of the lamp'; (4) *den*
傳燈滿位 'rank of completing the transmission of the lan   (5)
dentōhosshii 傳燈法師位 'rank of master in the transmi: ion of
the lamp'; and (6) *daihosshii* 大法師位 'rank of great master.'

Rokuji 六時 'The six periods' of the day: (1) *jinjō* 晨朝, 6 to 10
a.m., (2) *nitchū* 日中, 10 a.m. to 2 p.m., (3) *nichibotsu* 日没, 2 to
6 p.m., (4) *shoya* 初夜, 6 to 10 p.m., (5) *chūya* 中夜, 10 p.m. to
2 a.m., (6) *goya* 後夜, 2 to 6 a.m.

Rokuji-shaku 六字釋 'Explanation of the six-character phrase'
used of Amida* Buddha; the sacred phrase, *namu amidabutsu*,
literally means 'adoration to Amida Buddha' or 'I take refuge in
Amida Buddha.' Its soteriological meaning, according to
Shan-tao (Zendō*), is as follows: (1) *namu* 南無 means *kimyō* 歸命
'to take refuge in'; it also has the significance of *hotsugan-ekō*
發願廻向 'to have aspirations for birth in the Pure Land and transfer the merit one cultivates to this end'; (2) *amidabutsu* 阿彌陀佛
signifies *gogyō* 其行 'its practice,' namely, the practice to be performed to fulfil the aspiration of birth.

Rokushushō 六種性 'The six natures or states of spiritual progress'
distinguished in the *Bosatsu-yōrakuhongō-kyō**. They are: (1)
shūshushō 習種性 'the state of practising'; the state in which one
practises the meditation of voidness; this state corresponds to the
stages of ten dwellings (see *gojūni-i*); (2) *shōshushō* 性種性 'the
state of comprehending the nature of existences'; the state in which
one teaches other beings while fully conversant with the nature of
existences; this state corresponds to the stages of ten practices;
(3) *dōshushō* 道種性 'the state of contemplating the Middle Way';
the state in which one becomes conversant with all the Buddhist
teachings by contemplating the principle of the Middle Way
(*chūdō**); this state corresponds to the stages of ten merit-transferences; (4) *shōshushō* 聖種性 'the state of holiness'; the state in
which one realizes sacred wisdom; this state corresponds to the
stages of ten *bhūmi*; (5) *tōgakushō* 等覺性 'the state of equal or
proximate enlightenment'; the state next to the highest enlightenment; this state corresponds to the 51st stage; and (6) *myōgakushō*
妙覺性 'the state of wondrous enlightenment'; the state of the
highest enlightenment. The first five are sometimes treated

separately and called *goshushō* 五種性. Cf. *shushō*.

Rusui chōja 流水長者 'A wealthy man called "Pouring Water".' According to the *Konkōmyō-kyō**, a man saved the lives of many thousands of fish by pouring water into a pond which was nearly dried up. Later, the fish, having been reborn in heaven, repaid him by giving him 4,000 gems. [R. II–5.]

Ryōbu Shintō 兩部神道 'Twofold Shintō'; a kind of Shintō transmitted within the tradition of Buddhist esotericism; the full name is *Ryōbu shūgō Shintō* 兩部習合神道, 'Twofold syncretic Shinto'; based on the doctrine of *honji suijaku**, this school teaches that the Inner and Outer Grand Shrines of Ise are incarnations of the two forms of Dainichi*, i.e. Dainichi in each of the two realms of mandala, Taizōkai* and Kongōkai*.

Ryōge 領解 'Understanding'; construed as '*ryōju geryō*' 領受解了, 'receiving' the teaching and 'understanding' its import or implications. Used in Shin* Buddhism in the sense of '*shinjin*' 信心 (faith) or '*anjin*' 安心 (settled mind). [AK.]

S

Saga no dainenbutsu 嵯峨の大念佛 The big *nenbutsu** ceremony held at Shōryōji 清凉寺, Saga, Kyoto, for ten days from the 5th to the 15th of the 3rd month; this was first begun by Engaku 圓覺 in 1279. [FK.]

Saidaiji 西大寺 The head temple of the Shingon-ritsu* 眞言律 sect and one of the seven great temples of Nara (*shichidaiji**). Also called Takano-dera 高野寺 and Shiō-in 四王院. First built in 765 by Emperor Shōtoku 稱德 (also known as Takano 高野), the temple was destroyed by fire several times. Eison 叡尊 rebuilt it in 1236, after which the temple became a centre for the Ritsu* sect. It once enjoyed great prosperity, having more than 300 buildings and halls, but suffered a severe damage during a civil war in 1502. The present buildings date from the Tokugawa period (1603–1868).

Saie 齋會 'A Buddhist service in which a meal is offered to priests.' [R. III–8.]

Saigoya 最後夜 Same as *goya** 後夜; the last watch of the night, i.e. 2 to 6 a.m. [R. III–28.]

Saigyō 西行 A monk and a poet in the late Heian period, who lived 1118–1190; one of the greatest poets in the anthology *Shinkokinshū* 新古今集. His layman's name was Satō Norikiyo 佐藤義清, and his Buddhist name, En'i 圓位. He was a warrior attending the ex-emperor Toba 鳥羽, but at 23, after the sudden death of a friend, he renounced his family and the secular world to become a wandering monk. [Egu.]

Sanbon no zange 三品の懺悔 Also pronounced *sanbon no sange*; 'the three grades of repentance': (1) *jōbon no zange* 上品の懺悔, 'the upper grade of repentance', to repent of one's sins by shedding blood from his eyes and his whole body; (2) *chūbon no zange* 中品の懺悔, 'the middle grade of repentance', to repent of one's sins by shedding blood from his eyes and perspiration from his whole body; (3) *gebon no zange* 下品の懺悔, 'the lower grade of repentance', to repent of one's sins by shedding tears.

Sandai'e 三大會 'The three lecture-meetings'; the three annual lecture-meetings held under imperial sponsorship; also *sandai-choku'e* 三大勅會 (three big lecture-meetings held by imperial order) and *san'e* 三會 (three lecture-meetings). First held in Nara, similar lecture-meetings were later held in Kyoto, too. I. *Nankyō no sandai'e* 南京の三大會 (the three big lecture-meetings in the Southern Capital): the *Yuima-e** at Kōfukuji*, the *Saishō-e** at Yakushiji*, and the *Gosai-e** at the Daigokuden 大極殿 of the Imperial Palace. II. *Hokkyō no sandai'e* 北京の三大會 (the three big lecture-meetings in the Northern Capital); also called *Tendai no san'e* 天台の三會: the *Hokke-e** and the *Saishō-e* at Enshūji 圓宗寺 and the *Daijō-e* 大乘會 at Hosshōji 法勝寺.

San'e 三會 I. 'The three lecture-meetings'; see *sandai'e*. [O.V.] II. 'The three assemblies' at which the future buddha Miroku* (Maitreya) will preach the Dharma; cf. *Ryūge-e*. [Tai. 22, 39.]

[Sangai 三界**]**

~ muan -- 無安 'There is no peace in the three realms.' [Boku.]

ganri ni chiriatte ~ suboku 眼裏に塵あって--窄く 'If you have the dust (of delusion) in your eyes, even the three realms are felt to be too small'; part of the passage from the *Musō Kokushi* goroku 夢窓國師語録, which is followed by *shintō buji ni shite isshō hiroshi* 心頭無事にして一床寛し 'If your mind is without hindrance, a small floor is felt to be spacious.' [Kiyo.]

Sange 懺悔 'San' stands for *sanma* or *senma* 懺摩, Sk. *kṣama*, meaning 'to ask pardon for something'; repenting of one's sins or transgressions before the buddha or other people. Cf. *nishu-sange*, *sanbon no sange* and *sanshu-kehō*.

Sangen 三賢 'Three (stages of) sagacity'; the three classes of 10 stages of bodhisattvas. They comprise 'ten dwellings' (*jūjū* 十住), 'ten practices' (*jūgyō* 十行) and 'ten merit-transferences' (*jūekō* 十廻向). They correspond to the 11th to the 40th stages in the 52-stage division of a bodhisattva's career; cf. *gojūni-i*. [R. III–32.]

Sanjūsan Kannon 三十三觀音 'Thirty-three Kannons'; 33 types of Kannon* conceived and developed in Japan probably during the Tokugawa period (1603–1868) after the 33 incarnations of Kannon mentioned in the *Hoke-kyō**. Mostly based on popular beliefs in China and Japan, they have no authentic scriptural references, but have become popular themes in drawings and paintings. They are as follows: 1. Yōryū* 楊柳 'Willow', 2. Ryūzu 龍頭 'Dragon Head', 3. Jikyō 持經 'Sutra-holding', 4. Enkō 圓光 'Circular Light', 5. Yuge 遊戲 'Playing', 6. Byakue 白衣 'White Robe', 7. Renga 蓮臥 'Lotus-lying', 9. Takimi 瀧見 'Waterfall-observing', 9. Seyaku 施藥 'Medicine-giving', or Seraku 施樂 'Pleasure-giving', 10. Gyoran 魚籃 'Fish Basket', 11. Tokuō 德王 'King of Virtue', 12. Suigatsu 水月 'Water-Moon', 13. Ichiyō 一葉 'One Leaf', 14. Shōkyō 青頸 'Blue Neck', 15. Itoku 威德 'Majestic Virtue', 16. Enmei 延命 'Life-prolonging', 17. Shubō 衆寶 'Various Gems', 18. Iwado 岩戸 'Rock Door', 19. Nōjō 能靜 'Tranquilizing Well', 20. Anoku 阿耨 'Ana(vatapta)?', 21. Amadai 阿摩提 'Abhetrī', 22. Yōe 葉衣 'Leaf-Robe', 23. Ruri 瑠璃 'Lapis-lazuli', 24. Tara 多羅 'Tārā', 25. Kōri 蛤蜊 'Clam', 26. Rokuji 六時 'Six Periods or Times', 27. Fuhi 普悲 'Universal

Compassion', 28. Merōfu 馬郎夫 'Merō's Wife', 29. Gasshō 合掌 'Joining of the Palms Together', 30. Ichinyo 一如 'Oneness', 31. Funi 不二 'Non-dual', 32. Jiren 持蓮 'Lotus-holding', and 33. Shasui 洒水 'Water-sprinkling'.

Sanjūsan-shin 三十三身 'The 33 bodies (of Kannon*)'; according to the *Hoke-kyō**, Kannon is capable of manifesting 33 different forms in order to save sentient beings. [Mura.]

Sansha 三車 'The three carts'; the carts drawn by a goat, a deer and an ox mentioned in the parable of a burning house in the *Hoke-kyō**; they refer to the teachings for shravakas (*shōmon**), pratyekabuddhas (*engaku**) and bodhisattvas (*bosatsu**); see *kataku-yu*.

Sanshin 三心 'The three thoughts or aspects of faith.' I. The three aspects of faith mentioned in the 18th vow of Amida*: (1) *shishin* 至心, 'sincere mind'; (2) *shingyō* 信樂, 'joyful faith'; and (3) *yokushō* 欲生, 'desire to be born' in the Pure Land; according to Shinran*, they represent the pure faith, which is not contaminated by the aspirant's self-power (*jiriki**), and is itself Amida's heart transferred to him. II. The three aspects of faith mentioned in the *Kanmuryōju-kyō**: (1) *shijōshin* 至誠心, 'sincere heart'; (2) *jinshin* 深心, 'deep mind'; and (3) *ekōhotsuganshin* 廻向發願心, 'aspiring (to be born in the Pure Land) by turning one's merit of practice toward it.' In this sense, the term is also pronounced *sanjin*. III. The three minds mentioned in the *Daijō-kishin-ron**: (1) *jikishin* 直心, 'sincere and pure mind'; (2) *jinshin* 深心, 'deep mind'; and (3) *daihishin* 大悲心, 'great compassion.'

Sanshin 三信 'Three faiths.' I. The three aspects of pure faith in Shin* Buddhism; see *sanshin* 三心 I. II. The three aspects of pure faith mentioned in T'an-luan's (Donran*) *Ōjō-ronchū**: (1) *junshin* 淳心, 'sincere mind'; (2) *isshin* 一心, 'single-mindedness'; and (3) *sōzokushin* 相續心, 'continuous faith.'

Sanshō kasui 三生果遂 'Accomplishment (of salvation) in three lives'; an important term in the Jōdo* sect which is related to the 20th vow of Amida*. The Chinzei* school interprets the 'three lives' in two ways: i) in the immediately preceding life, one heard the sacred name of Amida and aspired to be born in the

Pure Land; in the present life, he attains the three aspects of pure faith (*sanshin**); and in the next life, he will be born in the Pure Land; ii) in the present life, one hears the sacred name, and in the next, he will attain pure faith; finally, in the life after next, he will be born in the Pure Land. The Seizan* school also speaks of salvation in the third life. Cf. *fukasuisha* and *kasui no gan*.

Sanshu kehō 三種悔法 'The three methods of repenting of one's sins': (1) *sahōsen* 作法懺, to confess one's sins before the statue of a buddha according to a prescribed method; (2) *shusōsen* 取相懺, to visualize in meditation that one confesses his sins before a buddha and that the buddha comes to him and strokes his head; (3) *mushōsen* 無生懺, to destroy one's sins by meditating on the principle of the non-arising of all existences, including the sins themselves. Cf. *nishu zange*.

Santō 三塔 'The three towers or pagodas'; refers to the three centres on Mt. Hiei; also San'in 三院 (three temples). They are: (1) Tōtō 東塔 (Eastern Pagoda), also known as Shikan-in 止觀院 (Tranquility-contemplation Temple); (2) Saitō 西塔 (Western Pagoda), also Hōdō-in 寶幢院 (Treasure-banner Temple); and (3) Yokawa* 横川, also Shuryōgon-in 首楞嚴院 or Ryōgon-in 楞嚴院 (Śūraṃgama Temple).

[Sanze 三世]

~ no onchigu --の御値遇 'An encounter with somebody which is made possible by a past relationship and will bind them together long into the future'; a lord and retainer relationship is believed to be one extending over these three periods. [Tomo.]

Sanzen-gi 散善義 '*On the Meaning of Non-meditative Good*,' 1 fasc.; the last part of the four-section commentary of the *Kanmuryōjukyō** by Shan-tao (Zendō*) of T'ang China [TT. 37, No. 1753]; in this part the author explains important concepts and terms which appear in the section 'Non-meditative Good' (*sanzen** 散善), i.e. the last three of the sixteen contemplations (*jūrokkan** 十六觀; it is in this part that the famous parable of 'two rivers and a white path' (*niga byakudō** 二河白道) appears; cf. *shijō no so*.

Seizan 西山 The Seizan school; one of the schools of the Jōdo* sect founded by Shōkū*, a disciple of Hōnen* for 23 years. After Hōnen's death, he dwelt at the Sangoji 三鈷寺 (also Kitao Ōjō-in

北尾往生院) in Nishiyama 西山, Yamashiro 山城 Province (Kyoto), and propagated the Pure Land teaching. His teaching was continued by four leading disciples: Jōon 淨音, Enkū 圓空, Shōnyū 證入 and Dōkan 道觀.

Sejizaiō 世自在王 'World-Sovereign King'; Sk. Lokeśvararāja; n. of the buddha under whose guidance Amida* made vows to become a buddha; also *Sennyōō** and *Nyōō* 饒王.

Sen 仙 Sk. *ṛṣi*. I. A sage in ancient India. II. A hermit or a religious mendicant in general, esp. a non-Buddhist sage of eminent virtue, who is believed to possess some supernatural powers. III. Refers to the Buddha; used in such a word as *daisen* 大仙, 'great immortal sage.' IV. Refers to *sennin* 仙人, a Taoist hermit or immortal sage.

Senpuku 薝蔔 Sk. *campaka*; also 占婆, 瞻婆, 旃波迦, etc. A kind of magnolia tree which bears fragrant, yellow blossoms. [R. III–32.]

Senyōō 世饒王 'World-Benefiting King'; Sk. Lokeśvararāja; n. of the buddha under whose guidance Amida* made vows to become a buddha; more popularly, *Sejizaiō**. [JW. 56.]

[Sesshu 攝取]

~ **fusha** --不捨 'Take in and not forsake'; said of Amida's* all-embracing salvation. [Tan. 1.]

Setsu 節 Also pronounced *sechi*; refers to *sechie* 節會; originally, ceremonies held on days marking seasonal changes; later, those and other days when Buddhists observe the precepts and abstain from doing evil. See *sainichi*.

Shari 舍利 I. Sk. *śarīra*; relics of the Buddha or a revered priest. [Ma. 146; R. II–31.] II. Sk. *śārī*; n. of Śāriputra's (Sharihotsu*) mother; the full name is Rūpaśārī.

~ **Bosatsu** --菩薩 A nickname given to a nun who is well-versed in Buddhism. [R. III–19.]

Shibunritsu 四分律 'The Four-part Vinaya'; also called *Don-mutoku-ritsu* 曇無德律 (Dharmagupta Vinaya); 60 fasc.; tr. by Buddhayaśa (Buddhayasha 佛陀耶舍). Of the four parts of the text, the first contains the prescribed rules of conduct for monks, and the second those for nuns. [TT. 22, No. 1428]

Shibunritsu-gyōji-shō 四分律行事鈔 '*On the Prescribed Acts of the Four-part Vinaya*'; the full title is *Shibunritsu-sanhan-hoketsu-gyōji-shō* 四分律刪繁補闕行事鈔, popularly called *Gyōji-shō* 行事鈔 and *Rokkan-shō** 六巻鈔; written by Tao-hsüan 道宣 (Dōsen*). One of the basic texts of the Nan-shan 南山 school of the Ritsu* sect, this work presents essential points of the doctrine of *Shibunritsu** 四分律. This work exists in 3-, 6-, and 12-fascicle texts. [TT. 40, No. 1804]

Shichishichinichi 七七日 'Seven times seven days'; 49 days; the period of the intermediate state between death and a new life; see *chūin*. [R. II–39.]

Shido 私度 'Self-ordination'; becoming a monk or a nun without proper authorization; same as *jido** 自度 II.

Shiguzeigan 四弘誓願 In the Sōtō* sect, pronounced *shikuseigan*. 'The four great vows.' I. The four great vows which all bodhi-sattvas make at the outset of their spiritual careers. According to the *Shikan-taii* 止観大意, they are: (1) *shujō muhen seigando* 衆生無邊誓願度 'I vow to save boundless numbers of sentient beings'; (2) *bonnō mushu sengandan* 煩悩無數誓願斷 'I vow to extinguish innumerable evil passions'; (3) *hōmon mujin sengangaku* 法門無盡誓願學 'I vow to study all the inexhaustible Buddhist teachings'; and (4) *butsudō mujō seiganjō* 佛道無上誓願成 'I vow to attain the supreme Buddha Way.' II. According to the *Ōjōyōshū**, they are: (1) and (2) as above; (3) *hōmon mujin seiganchi* 法門無盡誓願知 'I vow to know all the inexhaustible Buddhist teachings'; and (4) *mujō bodai seiganshō* 無上菩提誓願證 'I vow to realize the supreme enlightenment.'

Shiji 四事 'Four things'; the four kinds of things to be offered to a buddha or monk: 1. living quarters. 2. clothing, 3. food and drink, and 4. scattering flowers and burning incense; also, 1. clothing, 2. food and drink, 3. scattering flowers, and 4. burning incense.

Shijō no so 四帖の疏 '*The Four-section Commentary*'; a popular name for *Kanmuryōjubutsu-kyō-so* 觀無量壽佛經疏, 4 fasc., by Shan-tao (Zendō*) [TT. 37, No. 1753]; the four sections corre-sponding to the four parts of the *Kanmuryōju-kyō** of which this is a commentary are as follows: (1) *Gengibun** 玄義分, '*On the Essential Meaning*', (2) *Jobungi** 序分義, '*On the Introductory Part*', (3) *Jōzengi** 定善義, '*On the Meditative Good*' and (4) *Sanzengi** 散善義, '*On the Non-meditative Good*.'

Shijūhachi kyōkai 四十八輕戒 'The forty-eight minor precepts' provided for bodhisattvas in the *Bonmō-kyō**; they include abstaining from drinking intoxicating liquor, eating meat, eating the five acrid foods and despising beginners.

Shikikō 四季講 'Four-season lectures'; the lecture-meeting held four times a year before the statue of Miroku* (Maitreya) at Jōshinbō 定心房 on Mt. Hiei.

Shiniryō 死靈 'The spirit of a dead person'; often a revengeful one; cf. *ikiryō*. [FK.]

Shinjitsu hōdo 眞實報土 'The true land of recompense'; refers to Amida's* land which has come into existence as the result or reward (*hō* 報) of his vows and practice and into which those who have the pure faith, i.e. followers of the 18th vow, will be born. The term is contrasted to *hōben kedo* 方便化土, 'transformed land of expediency', or simply *kedo* 'transformed land', which Amida provides in the 19th and the 20th vows for those who still cling to their self-power. [JW. 58.]

Shinmon 眞門 'The true gate.' In the Jōdoshin* sect, refers to the teaching of salvation in accord with the 20th vow of Amida*. [JW. 64.]

Shinnyo 眞如 'The True Thusness'; Sk. *tathatā, bhūtatathatā*; the ultimate reality; the universal and eternally abiding true substance of all that exists. The term is construed as 'true and not delusory' (*shin* 眞) and 'unchanging and unalterable' (*nyo* 如). Exclusively used in Mahayana, the term has many synonyms, such as *nyo** 如, *hosshō** 法性, *hokkai** 法界, *jissai** 實際, *jissō** 實相, and *ichinyo** 一如. In Hossō*, the True Thusness is considered as the noumenal reality-principle underlying the phenomenal existence. According to the *Daijō-kishin-ron**, the True Thusness has two aspects; it is in itself above all changes, unproduced and unperishing, but manifests itself as phenomenal existence.

~ **no mon** --の門 'The gate of True Thusness'; the teaching which leads one to the realization of ultimate reality; refers to

Amida's* law of salvation based on the 18th vow. [JW. 66.]

~ zuien -- 隨緣 'Following conditions, the True Thusness (manifests itself as phenomena)'; in its dynamic aspect, the True Thusness assumes various phenomenal forms. [Egu.]

Shinsen 神仙 'A divine hermit.' I. A Taoist sage; a hermit who seeks the Taoist way of longevity. II. A hermit in general. III. A divinity. IV. Buddha Shakamuni*.

Shinshō 心性 'Mind-nature'; the essential nature of mind. In Mahayana, one's mind-nature is the Buddha-nature. [ST.]

Shion 四恩 'The four obligations'; the four groups of persons or objects to which one is most indebted. According to the *Shinjikan-gyō**, they are: (1) one's parents, (2) other sentient beings, (3) one's king, and (4) the three treasures (*sanbō**). [R. I–35, II–6.]

Shiraki no nenbutsu 白木の念佛 'The plain-wood *nenbutsu*'; the *nenbutsu** untainted by the practitioner's self-power or calculation; the type of *nenbutsu* practice promulgated by Shōkū*, the founder of the Seizan* school.

Shirikikuta 尸利掬多 Sk. Śrīgupta; according to the *Daishōgonronkyō* 大莊嚴論經, a person who once tried to poison the Buddha. His attempt was foiled by the Buddha's supernatural power, and he then repented of his evil.

Shitennōji 四天王寺 The oldest temple in Japan, situated in south Osaka; popularly called Tennōji 天王寺; formerly a special head temple of the Tendai* sect but now the head temple of the Wa sect (Washū 和宗). The origin dates back to the time of Shōtoku Taishi*. When he fought Mononobe Moriya 物部守屋, he vowed that if he won, he would build a temple; after his victory, the prince built this temple in 587. It was called by such names as Gokoku daiji 護國大寺, Naniwa no daiji 難波の大寺, Horie no tera 堀江の寺 and Kyōden-in 敬田院. Destroyed by fire several times, most recently in an air-raid during World War II, the temple has now been restored to its original scale and magnificence.

Shitsunen no shōnen 失念の稱念 'Recitation of (Amida's³) name without mindfulness'; said of the *nenbutsu** recitation of the lowest grade of the lower class who are, at their death, too tormented by the retribution of their evil acts done during their lifetime to concentrate their thoughts on Amida and recite his name, even when they are taught to do so by a Buddhist teacher. Even such *nenbutsu* recitation is said to be effective in enabling them to attain birth in the Pure Land. Cf. *gebon geshō*. [AK.]

Shoe 初會 'The first assembly.' I. The assembly at which a buddha preaches the Dharma for the first time after attaining enlightenment. [JW. 16.] II. The first session of a series of expositions of the Dharma by a buddha.

[Shōgaku 正覺] [Chiku.]

~ **no ichinen** --の一念 'The moment of one's perfect enlightenment'; the moment when Amida* attained enlightenment and became a buddha. This moment implies the once-and-for-all consummation of perfect enlightenment in which the salvation of all living beings has also been accomplished. [AK.]

Shōjinnyo-mon-kyō 精進女問經 Refers to the *Muku-shōjin-nyo-mon-kyō* 無垢精進女問經, '*The Sutra on Questions from a Lady named Undefiled Devotion*', which is also called *Muku-ubai-mon-kyō* 無垢優婆夷問經, '*The Sutra on Questions from a Laywoman named Undefiled*.' [TT. 14, No. 578]. [R. I–13.]

Shōjō gonen 證誠護念 'Testifying and protecting'; said of the testimony of many buddhas to the truth of Amida's* law of salvation and their protection of those who follow it. The reference is to the *Amida-kyō**. [JW. 84, 85.]

Shōko 鉦鼓 A metal musical instrument used for beating time in the recitation of the *nenbutsu**; also used in court music. [SG.]

Shokoku ikken no sō 諸國一見の僧 'A monk who wanders about in various provinces (to visit temples, etc.)'; a wandering monk. [Yori.; Izu.; Egu.; Une.]

Shōkū 證空 One of Hōnen's* leading disciples and the founder of the Seizan* school of the Jōdo* sect; 1177–1247. Born as the eldest son of Minamoto Chikasue 源親季, governor of Kaga Province (present Ishikawa Prefecture), other names of his were Gedatsu-bō 解脱房 and, later, Zenne-bō 善慧房. He became Hōnen's disciple at the age of 14 and learned the Pure Land teaching from him for 23 years. He further received from Hōnen the bodhisattva precepts (*endonkai**), and also learned the

Tendai* teaching from Ganren 願蓮 and the esoteric doctrines from Jien 慈圓 and Kōen 公圓. When Hōnen completed the *Senjaku-shū**, Shōkū lectured on it to Fujiwara Kanezane 藤原兼實, who had requested Hōnen to write the work. After Hōnen's death, he lived in the Kitao Ōjō-in 北尾往生院 (also Sangoji 三鈷寺), Nishiyama, for 12 years, lecturing on Shan-tao's (Zendō*) works. His lectures were later compiled into *Kangyō-yōgishō* 觀經要義鈔, 41 fasc. Later, with imperial sanction, he built the Kangishin-in 歡喜心院, and he also frequently visited the imperial court to expound the Pure Land teaching and to impart the bodhisattva precepts. He died on the 26th of the 11th month, 1247, at the age of 70. In 1796 he was given a posthumous title, Kanchi Kokushi 鑑智國師. His doctrine is reputed to have been philosophical, but he actually promulgated 'the plain-wood *nenbutsu*' (*shiraki no nenbutsu** 白木の念佛), which is the *nenbutsu** practice untainted by the practitioner's self-power or calculation. He had many disciples, of whom the following are the chief ones: Jōon 淨音, Enkū 圓空, Shōnyū 證入 and Dōkan 道觀.

Shokyōyōshū 諸經要集 '*A Collection of Important Passages from Various Sutras*'; 20 fasc., compiled by Tao-shih 道世 (Dōse) of the T'ang dynasty. Passages from various scriptures are arranged under 185 headings in 30 sections. [R. III–38.]

Shōnin 聖人 'A holy man.' I. A title of respect for a buddha or a bodhisattva. II. That for a sage who has attained insight into reality. III. Sometimes used for *shōnin** 上人 with an additional weight of respect.

Shōren no manajiri 靑蓮の眸 'Blue lotus-blossom eyes'; said of the eyes of a buddha or a bodhisattva. [Ara.]

Shōryōzan 淸涼山 'Mt. Ch'ing-liang'; another name for Mt. Wu-t'ai 五台山 (Godaisan*).

Shou 諸有 'Various states of existence' in the realm of samsara. [JW. 72.]

Shoya 初夜 I. The first watch of the night, about 8 in the evening. II. One of the six periods of the day (*rokuji**), from 6 to 10 p.m.

Shozen 諸善 'Various good acts'; the various merit-accruing acts for the attainment of birth in the Pure Land. In the Jōdoshin*

sect, said of the acts to be practised by the followers of the 19th vow of Amida*; the same as *shuzen* 衆善. [JW. 62.]

Shujō 衆生 'Many births'; Sk. *sattva, bahujana*; living beings, sentient beings; also *ujō* 有情. Etymologically, *shujō* is construed as: (1) multitudes of men (衆人) come into existence (生); (2) many (衆多) elements temporarily unite to produce (生) life; or (3) living beings undergo many (衆多) births (生) and deaths.

Shūribun 修理分 Also pronounced *suribun*; 'fund for repairing a temple.' [R. II–42.]

Shushō 種性 'Nature, potentiality'; the spiritual potentialities of living beings are classified into different groups; see *goshō kakubetsu, nishushō* and *rokushushō*.

～ **naki shujō** -- なき衆生 'Those sentient beings who have no potentiality for spiritual progress or enlightenment; see *mushō ujō* under *goshō kakubetsu*. [R. III–38.]

Shutarabun 修多羅分 Also pronounced *sutarabun*; 'fund for students of sutras'; cf. *shutarashū*. [R. III–3.]

Daianji no ～ 大安寺の---- The special fund for the monks who chanted and studied the *Daihannya-kyō** at Daianji*. [R. II–24.]

Shutarashū 修多羅宗 Also 修多羅衆; 'a sutra school'; a group of monks studying a particular sutra or group of sutras, e.g. the *Daihannya-kyō**, at a big temple in Nara. Founded in the Nara period (710–794), such study groups developed and became institutionalized. Other study groups of this kind include Kusha* and Hossō* sects. In this case, *shū* 宗 does not mean 'a sect' but implies 'an institutionalized study group.'

Shutsuyō-kyō 出曜經 '*The Allegory Sutra*'; a sutra composed of didactic verses and expository stories; 30 fasc., also 20 fasc.; tr. by Chou Fo-nien 竺佛念 (Jikubutsunen) [TT. 4, No. 212]. *Shutsuyō* is a translation of the Sk. *avadāna* (*ahadana** 阿波陀那). [R. II–30.]

[Sōgō 相好]

～ **shōgon** -- 莊嚴 'Glorious appearance of majestic features' of a buddha or deity. [Kamo.; JW. 43, 44.]

Soman 蘇曼 Sk. Somanā; the youngest daughter of Sudatta

(Shudatsu*), a wealthy man of Śrāvastī (Shae*). Intelligent and beautiful, she attended the Buddha. One day a prince of Takṣaśilā saw her, and prevailed upon King Prasenajit (Hashinoku*) to give Somanā to him. She bore ten eggs, which produced ten children. Later they became the Buddha's disciples. [R. III–19.]

Sonja 尊者 'A venerable one'; one worthy of respect for his noble virtue; a title of respect for an *arhat* (*arakan**). [JW. 51.]

Sutebito 捨人 A contraction of *yosutebito* 世捨人 'one who has renounced the world.' [Egu.]

T

Taamidabutsu 他阿彌陀佛 I. Another name of Shinkyō 眞教, the second patriarch of the Ji sect (Jishū*). II. A popular name for the chief priest of the head temple of the Ji sect.

Taihō 太方 'The great direction'; the Buddhist Way. [R. III–12.]

Tamu-no-mine 多武峰 Also pronounced *Tō-no-mine*, *Ta(f)u-no-mine*, *Tan-no-mine*, etc.; n. of a mountain in the Yamato Province (in present-day Sakurai City, Nara Prefecture). On top of the mountain there is a mausoleum to Fujiwara Kamatari, originally built by his son, Jōe 定慧, and called Gokoku-in Myōrakuji 護國院妙樂寺. The mausoleum flourished as a temple under the jurisdiction of the Enryakuji*. After the Meiji Restoration in 1868 it was deprived of its Buddhist character and turned into a Shinto shrine. [SG.]

Tanji 彈指 Also *danshi*. I. Snapping of the fingers, esp. at a Buddhist service, to show one's joy, warning, approval, repentance, regret, etc. II. A unit of time; 20 thought-moments (*nen** 念) are equal to one twinkling of an eye (*shun* 瞬); 20 of these are equal to one *tanji*.

Tannishō 歎異抄 '*Notes Lamenting Differences*'; a Shinshu* text of probably the late 13th century; the author is unknown but is generally believed to be Yuien 唯圓, a direct disciple o Shinran*. The text is commonly divided into two parts: th first is a collection of Shinran's words in ten sections, and the second is the author's criticisms of eight heretical views which were current in his day. Because of abundant quotations of Shinran's words, which are both highly inspirational and thought-provoking, this work is widely read by the Japanese. [Tan.]

[**Tariki** 他力]

~ **no sanshin** --の三信 'The threefold faith of the other-power'; the three aspects of faith, mentioned in the 18th vow of Amida*. They are: *shishin* 至心 (sincere mind), *shingyō* 信樂 (serene and joyful faith) and *yokushō* 欲生 (desire for birth). Cf. *sanshin* 三心 and 三信. [AK.]

~ **no shin** --の信 'Faith of the other-power'; the faith endowed or awakened by the power of Amida*. In the Jōdoshin* sect, it is the whole-hearted trust in his salvation which is free of one's selfish desires or calculations; refers to faith in the 18th vow. [JW. 67.]

Tashō 他生 I. 'Arising from or produced by other things'; the opposite of *jishō* 自生 'produced by itself.' II. 'The other life'; the previous or the following life.

~ **no tane no en** --の種の緣 '(By) the cause of some relationship in a past life.' [Yori.]

Tenjō no hōdō 天上の寶堂 'The jewelled hall in heaven'; refers to the inner palace of the Tuṣita Heaven (Tosotsuten*) where Miroku* (Maitreya) is said to be living. [R. III–Pre.]

Tenjō tenge yuiga dokuson 天上天下唯我獨尊 'Above heaven and below heaven, I alone am the honoured one'; in all the world I am the one to be honoured. This is the remark the Buddha is said to have uttered upon his birth after taking seven steps.

Tenshishu 天祀主 'A priest who worships god'; a Brahmanic priest who performs sacrifices. [R. II–5.]

Tetsugan 鐵丸 'An iron ball.' I. Red-hot iron balls which sinners are forced to swallow in hell. II. N. of one of the 16 small hells; here sinners are forced to pick up red-hot iron balls, which burn their limbs. [SG.; R. I–30, II–9.]

Tō 塔 'A tomb mound, tower'; a corruption of Sk. *stūpa* or Pali *thūpa*; also transcribed as 塔婆, 兜婆, 偸婆 as well as 卒都婆 (*sotoba**). A tomb mound or a tower containing the relics of a holy sage, or one for marking out a sacred area, constructed to accumulate merit or to show one's gratitude to the Buddha, etc. According to the *Jō-agon-gyō**, the Buddha recommended the construction of towers for four kinds of persons: buddhas, pratyekabuddhas (*engaku**), shravakas (*shōmon**), and cakravartins (*tenrinjōō*). As for the number of stories constituting the tower, the *Tangen-ki** quotes *Jūniinnen-gyō* 十二因縁經 (now lost) as stipulating the following: (1) eight or more stories for a tower dedicated to a buddha, (2) seven for a bodhisattva, (3) six for a pratyekabuddha, (4) five for an arhat (*arakan**), (5) four for an anāgāmin (*anagonka**) sage, (6) three for a sakṛdāgāmin (*shidagonka**) sage, (7) two for a srota-āpanna (*shudaonka**) sage, and (8) one story for a cakravartin king.

Tokudo 得度 I. To attain emancipation from cycles of birth-and-death. II. To be ordained into the priesthood. [R. II–21.]

Tokugō 得業 'One who has done a particular work or duty'; a rank of scholarship in the priesthood: (1) In Nara, the title given to one who has served as a respondent at the three major lecture-meetings, i.e. the *Yuima-e** and *Hokke-e** held at Kōfukuji* and the *Saishō-e** at Yakushiji*. (2) On Mt. Hiei, the title given to one who has attended the *Shikikō** 四季講 (four-season lectures) and *Sankō* 三講 (three lectures).

Tokuhon 德本 'Root of virtue'; refers to Amida's* sacred name, for it comprises all the virtue of good acts; the same as *zenpon**. [JW. 65.]

Tōruka 等流果 'A homogeneous effect'; Sk. *niṣyanda-phala*; an effect which is in nature similar to, or the same as, the cause, e.g. a good effect produced from a good cause; one of the five kinds of effect (*goka* 五果). [R. III–38.]

Tōshōgaku 等正覺 'Equal, perfect enlightenment'; Sk. *samyak-sambodhi*; also *tōgaku** 等覺 and *shōhenchi* 正遍知; refers to the Buddha's enlightenment which realizes the all-equal and undifferentiated nature of all existence. The term also means 'equal to perfect enlightenment', i.e. enlightenment of the bodhisattvas of the highest stage, which is almost equal to the Buddha's.   [Boku.]

Tsukimono 憑物   'A haunting spirit.'   [FK.]

U

Uen 有縁   II. 'Those who have a karmic relationship with someone.'
[Tan. 5; JW. 19.]

Ugyō 雨行   Also Gyōu*; Sk. Varṣakāra; one of King Bimbisāra's
(Binbashara*) ministers.   [JW. 80.]

Umu 有無   'Being and non-being, existence and non-existence.'
I. The two aspects of things: (1) phenomenal appearances through
causal relationships and (2) absence of ultimate essence or substance.   II. Refers to *uhō* 有法, things which have definable
substances of their own, and *muhō* 無法 imaginary things which
have no substance of their own.   III. The view that living beings
continue to exist eternally while undergoing births and deaths and
the view that they become totally extinct at the time of death;
generally, an existence view and a nihilistic view.

Utsutsu no inga 現の因果   'The causal relationship from the present
life'; a good or bad result originating from some good or evil
act done in the present life.   [Atsu.]

W

Warawa 童子   'A temple boy'; a boy who does various odd duties
at the temple; cf. *dōji*.   [R. I–3.]

Y

Yōgō 影向 'Appearing like a shadow'; a deity's manifestation of his body in front of a believer. [Kamo.; Ara.; Une.]

Yokawa 横川 One of the three centres on Mt. Hiei; also called Hokutō 北塔 (Northern Pagoda) and Shuryōgon-in 首楞嚴院 or Ryōgon-in 楞嚴院 (Śuraṃgama Temple). This centre was first opened by Ennin* in 829. Cf. *santō.*

Yomi 黄泉 Also 夜見; in Japanese mythology, a dark nether world to which the souls of the dead are destined to go.

Yōryū Kannon Bosatsu 楊柳觀音菩薩 'Willow Kannon Bodhisattva'; one of the 33 types of Kannon*; so called because he complies with the wishes of people just as the long drooping branches of a willow bend to the wind. Identified with Yakuō Kannon 藥王觀音, a bodhisattva produced from the "willow" hand, one of the 40 hands of Senju Kannon*. He holds a willow branch in the right hand and raises the left hand in the mudra sign of endowing fearlessness. Cf. *sanjūsan Kannon.* [Yo.]

Yōsō 羊僧 'A sheep-monk'; a stupid monk; a word by which a monk refers to himself. [R. III–Pre.]

Yugyō no nagare 遊行の流れ 'Followers of Yugyō Shōnin*'; followers of the Ji sect (Jishū*). [Sane.]

Yugyō Shōnin 遊行上人 'A wandering sage.' I. Any Buddhist monk of high virtue who wanders about the country. II. Refers to Ippen*, the founder of the Ji sect (Jishū*). III. A title of respect for the chief priest of the Shōjōkōji (清浄光寺, popularly called Yugyōji 遊行寺), Fujisawa, the head temple of the Ji sect. [Sane.]

Yuichi saaku no ki 唯知作惡の機 'People who only know of doing evil'; people who do nothing but evil. [AK.]

Yuishiki jūdaironji 唯識十大論師　'The ten great discourse-masters of the Consciousness-Only doctrine'; the ten great Indian masters renowned for their commentaries on the *Thirty Verses on Consciousness-Only* (*Yuishiki-sanjūju**) of Vasubandhu (Seshin*). They are: (1) Guṇamati (Tokue 德慧), c. 420–500; (2) Sthiramati (Anne 安慧), c. 470–550; (3) Nanda (Nanda 難陀), c. 450–530; (4) Dharmapāla (Gohō 護法), c. 530–561; (5) Bandhuśrī (Shinshō 親勝), (6) Citrabhāna (火辯), (7) Śuddhacandra (Jōgatsu 淨月), (8) Viśeṣamitra (Shōu 勝友), (9) Jinaputra (Shōshi 勝子), and (10) Jñānacandra (Chigatsu 智月).

Yuishiki-sanjūju 唯識三十頌　'*Thirty Verses on Consciousness-Only*'; Sk. *Vijñaptimātratā-siddhi-triṃśikā*, a work by Vasubandhu (Seshin*) which laid the foundation of the Consciousness-Only school which is known in Japan as the Hossō* sect. Cf. *Jōyuishiki-ron* and *Yuishiki jūdaironji*.

Z

Zaifuku 罪福　'Sin and merit.'　I. Evil acts and meritorious deeds. II. The law of causality whereby an evil act brings about suffering, and a good one happiness.

Zangi 慙愧　Also 慚愧　'To be ashamed of one's sins and repent of them.'　*Zan* and *gi* are interpreted as 'to feel ashamed before heaven' and 'to be ashamed before the world' respectively, and also 'to feel ashamed in oneself' and 'to feel ashamed in front of others.'　[AK.]

~ hotsuro -- 發露　'To repent of and confess one's offences.' [R. II–7.]

Zenju 善珠　A monk of the Hossō* sect.　When young, he studied the Hossō teaching from Genbō 元昉, and then learned other teachings extensively.　Later, he founded Akishino-dera 秋篠寺 in Nara Prefecture and dwelt there.　He was invited by Saichō* to officiate at the dedication ceremony of the Konponchūdō 根本中堂 on Mt. Hiei.　In 797 he lectured on the *Hannya-kyō**

at the imperial court and successfully prayed for the recovery from illness of the prince. For this distinguished act, he was appointed *sōjō**, but died in the same year at the age of 75. He left commentaries on Hossō works. [R. III–35, 39.]

Zenkōnin 染香人 'An incense-scented person'; one who has the smell of incense around him because he handles much of it; used to describe a *nenbutsu** follower who has the 'scent' of Amida's* virtue. [JW. 116.]

Zenpon 善本 'Root of good'; refers to Amida's* sacred name, for it comprises all the merits of good acts; the same as *tokuhon**. [JW. 65.]

Zensha 繕寫 'To repair and copy'; to make a clean, correct copy of a sutra, etc. [R. III–8, 10, 22.]

Zenshūji 善種子 'A good seed (Sk. *bīja*)'; a stock of good energy stored in one's consciousness. When ripened, it manifests itself as a good act or works to create a pleasant state of existence in the future. See *shūji*. [R. III–38.]

Zōbara Bindara jigoku 曾婆羅頻陀羅地獄 Names of two different hells mentioned in the *Muryōjubutsu-myōgō-riyaku-daiji-innen-gyō* 無量壽佛名號利益大事因緣經, a sutra of dubious origin. [JW. 95.]

Zōbō-ketsugi-kyō 像法決疑經 '*The Sutra on Resolving Doubts Regarding the Semblance Dharma*'; 1 fasc. [TT. 85, No. 2870]. [R. III–32.]

Zuien shinnyo 隨緣眞如 'True Thusness following conditions'; following conditions, ultimate reality manifests itself as phenomena; cf. *shinnyo*. [Egu.]

Zuifū 瑞風 'Propitious wind'; the chanting of a sutra. [Tomo.]

Zuiōke 瑞應華 Sk. *uḍumbara*; also *udonge** 優曇華 and *reizuike* 靈瑞華; a mythical flower said to bloom only once in 3,000 years. Used metophorically to describe the rare appearance of a buddha in the world.

Zumen ni raisu 頭面に禮す 'To worship with one's head to the ground'; to worship by prostrating oneself. [JW. 49.]

著者紹介　神戸外国語大学英米学科卒業後、龍谷大学文学研究
科修士課程並びに博士課程真宗学専攻を修了。
1966年より68年まで British Council（英国文化振
興会）の留学生としてロンドン大学博士課程在学、
1968年に Ph. D. 取得。1969年より12年間、同大学
School of Oriental and African Studies の佛教
学講師。1981年帰国、現在龍谷大学教授。

主　著 : *Index to the Larger Sukhāvatīvyūha Sūtra: a
Tibetan Glossary with Sanskrit and Chinese
Equivalents*（蔵梵漢「大無量寿経」索引）1978年
永田文昌堂刊。増版　*A Tri-lingual Glossary of
the Sukhāvatīvyūha Sūtras*（梵蔵漢「大無量寿
経」・「阿弥陀経」比較語彙索引）1984年。　*The
Anantamukhanirhāra-dhāraṇī Sūtra and Jñāna-
garbha's Commentary*（出生無辺門陀羅尼経とジュ
ニァーナガルバの広釈）1987年永田文昌堂刊。

翻 訳 書 : 空海著「即身成佛義」、善導著「観念法門」、親鸞著
「教行信証」（部分訳・共著）その他多くの翻訳・論
文がある。